# BEHAVIOR MANAGEMENT

## APPLICATIONS FOR TEACHERS

### Fourth Edition

**Thomas J. Zirpoli**
*McDaniel College*

PEARSON
Merrill
Prentice Hall

Upper Saddle River, New Jersey
Columbus, Ohio

**Library of Congress Cataloging-in-Publication Data**

Zirpoli, Thomas J.
  Behavior management : applications for teachers / Thomas J. Zirpoli.—4th ed.
    p. cm.
  Includes bibliographical references and indexes.
  ISBN 0-13-110667-8
  1. Behavior modification—United States. 2. Children—United States—Conduct of life. 3.
Behavioral assessment of children—United States. 4. Classroom management—United
States. I. Title.

LB1060.2.Z57 2005
371.15'3—dc22                                                                    2003065120

**Vice President and Executive Publisher:** Jeffery W. Johnston
**Acquisitions Editor:** Allyson P. Sharp
**Editorial Assistant:** Kathleen S. Burk
**Production Editor:** Sheryl Glicker Langner
**Design Coordinator:** Diane C. Lorenzo
**Photo Coordinator:** Kathy Kirtland
**Cover Designer:** Ali Mohrman
**Cover art:** This drawing was done by Nick Baum when he was 5 years old. Diagnosed with ADHD
and with Bipolar 1, Nick has progressed through the educational system with the support of
families, teachers, psychologists, and psychiatrists. He is living as a happy, healthy, 12-year-old in
the fifth grade. He wants to be an inventor and create things that will help the world.
**Production Manager:** Laura Messerly
**Director of Marketing:** Ann Castel Davis
**Marketing Manager:** Autumn Purdy
**Marketing Coordinator:** Tyra Poole

This book was set in Palatino by Carlisle Communications Ltd. It was printed and bound by R. R.
Donnelley & Sons Company. The cover was printed by Coral Graphics.

**Photo Credits:** Anne Vega/Merrill, pp. 2, 172, 226, 291, 420, 485; Bachrach Photographers, p. 20;
National Library of Medicine, p. 26; George Dodson/PH College, p. 40; Anthony Magnacca/Merrill,
pp. 51, 69, 80, 101, 129, 150, 188, 200, 211, 268, 339, 382, 402, 451, 470; Scott Cunningham/Merrill,
pp. 124, 156; Todd Yarrington/Merrill, pp. 176, 238; Shirley Zeiberg/PH College, p. 328; Karen
Mancinelli/Pearson Learning, pp. 357, 442; Stan Wakefield/PH College, p. 378; David Coley, p. 428;
Chris Rupp, p. 435; Julie Peters/Merrill, p. 480.

Pearson Education Ltd.
Pearson Education Singapore Pte. Ltd.
Pearson Education Canada, Ltd.
Pearson Education—Japan

Pearson Education Australia Pty. Limited
Pearson Education North Asia Ltd.
Pearson Educación de Mexico, S.A. de C.V.
Pearson Education Malaysia Pte. Ltd.

PEARSON
Merrill
Prentice Hall

10 9 8 7 6 5 4 3
ISBN: 0-13-110667-8

*To Susan, Christopher, and Julia*

# PREFACE

This text acknowledges the comments and suggestions of many reviewers and users on how we might update and improve the third edition. The text continues to provide readers with both technical and functional understanding of applied behavior analysis, as well as a discussion of the everyday applications of behavior management in classrooms and other educational settings. We try to communicate this information in language that is understandable to professionals and paraprofessionals. As with the third edition, readers will observe several major differences with this text compared to other behavior management or applied behavior management texts. These differences are based on specific values regarding the management of behavior and the recognition of current trends in society.

Chapter 5 has been added in order to take a more detailed look at the relationship between student behavior and classroom curriculum through curriculum-based assessment. The topic of functional behavioral assessment has also been expanded and is now covered in greater detail in a new Chapter 6. Chapter 3, which included functional behavioral assessment in the previous edition, now focuses exclusively on data collection procedures and related issues.

Cognitive behavior management, a significant topic in the behavior management literature, has been largely ignored in current behavior management texts. In view of this, Chapter 8 includes information that will help fill that void for readers who would like to gain an understanding of behavior management beyond the traditional methods of applied behavior analysis.

With constant changes in the law and many court rulings regarding discipline in schools, Chapter 11 provides the very latest information for educators regarding the legal issues of behavior management in the schools.

This text also recognizes the growing preschool field and the expansion of day care and other services provided for infants, toddlers, and preschoolers. Although the basic principles of behavior management apply for all children, preschool teachers and day-care workers must understand that infants and young children have unique characteristics that demand special consideration. The growing number of early childhood programs require that we address this population directly, and so we acknowledge the special issues of early childhood behavior in Chapter 12.

Adolescent issues are also a significant and growing concern to many educators. The number of adolescents referred to out-of-home treatment facilities is at an all-time high. Clearly, this population requires special attention in the field of behavior management, and we address these special issues directly in a new Chapter 13.

A person's behavior is influenced by his or her ethnic background, gender, culture, and a variety of other individual variables. In a much improved and updated Chapter 14, we urge all educators to learn about, and become sensitive to, individual differences and how these characteristics may influence a child's behavior within the classroom. The danger of stereotyping is always possible while writing about multicultural issues. We have tried to avoid this trap, recognizing the uniqueness of all individuals, while at the same time acknowledging the influence of traditions and customs of those who share a common ethnic and cultural background.

Finally, we recognize that the best and most effective behavior management strategy is the teaching and reinforcement of appropriate behaviors. This belief is integrated throughout the text.

This text includes the basic mechanics of applied behavior analysis. In many areas, however, the text breaks from the traditional applied behavior analysis texts and includes current topics and issues in behavior management, as well as special populations (e.g., diversity, early childhood, and adolescent issues). We hope our readers will find these additional chapters useful and informative. We also hope that our readers will share their thoughts with us on how this fourth edition may be improved. We welcome and look forward to your comments. Please email the author at *tzirpoli@mcdaniel.edu* with your comments and suggestions.

## AUDIENCE

This text is designed for use in both undergraduate and graduate behavior management, classroom management, or applied behavior management courses. The text is appropriate for the preservice and in-service training of regular and special educators; preschool, elementary, and secondary educators; educational administrators; counselors; psychologists; and social workers.

## ACKNOWLEDGMENTS

First, thank you to the individuals who made significant and important contributions to this project: Joel Macht of Hilton Head, South Carolina, who contributed Chapters 5 and 6; Mitchell Yell, Todd Busch, and Erik Drasgow, all from the University of South Carolina, who contributed Chapter 8; Kristine Melloy, University of St. Thomas, the primary contributor for Chapters 2 and 10; Mitchell Yell, who provided Chapter 11; Susan Bishop Zirpoli for her help with Chapter 12; Stephanie D. Madsen, McDaniel College, who contributed Chapter 13; and Julia L. Orza, McDaniel College, who contributed Chapter 14.

Second, thank you to the folks at McDaniel College and Target Community & Educational Services, Inc. who support my scholarship. Special thanks to Joel Macht for his considerable assistance and encouragement of my writing.

Third, thank you to the reviewers of the manuscript for their timely and helpful reviews: Jim Burns, The College of St. Rose; Dan Fennerty, Central Washington University; and Philip Swicegood, Sam Houston State University.

Finally, I appreciate the advice, assistance, and support from all the helpful professionals at Merrill/Prentice Hall, especially Allyson Sharp, my editor, and Sheryl Langner, my production editor. Thank you also to my copy editor, Mariellen Hanrahan.

Thomas J. Zirpoli
*McDaniel College*

# EDUCATOR LEARNING CENTER: AN INVALUABLE ONLINE RESOURCE

Merrill Education and the Association for Supervision and Curriculum Development (ASCD) invite you to take advantage of a new online resource, one that provides access to the top research and proven strategies associated with ASCD and Merrill—the Educator Learning Center. At **www.EducatorLearningCenter.com** you will find resources that will enhance your students' understanding of course topics and of current educational issues, in addition to being invaluable for further research.

## HOW THE EDUCATOR LEARNING CENTER WILL HELP YOUR STUDENTS BECOME BETTER TEACHERS

With the combined resources of Merrill Education and ASCD, you and your students will find a wealth of tools and materials to better prepare them for the classroom.

### Research

- More than 600 articles from the ASCD journal *Educational Leadership* discuss everyday issues faced by practicing teachers.
- A direct link on the site to Research Navigator™ gives students access to many of the leading education journals, as well as extensive content detailing the research process.
- Excerpts from Merrill Education texts give your students insights on important topics of instructional methods, diverse populations, assessment, classroom management, technology, and refining classroom practice.

### Classroom Practice

- Hundreds of lesson plans and teaching strategies are categorized by content area and age range.
- Case studies and classroom video footage provide virtual field experience for student reflection.
- Computer simulations and other electronic tools keep your students abreast of today's classrooms and current technologies.

## LOOK INTO THE VALUE OF EDUCATOR LEARNING CENTER YOURSELF

A four-month subscription to Educator Learning Center is $25 but is **FREE** when used in conjunction with this text. To obtain free passcodes for your students, simply contact your Merrill/Prentice Hall sales representative, and your representative will give you a special ISBN to give your bookstore when ordering your textbooks. To preview the value of this website to you and your students, please go to **www.EducatorLearningCenter.com** and click on "Demo."

# DISCOVER THE COMPANION WEBSITE ACCOMPANYING THIS BOOK

## THE PRENTICE HALL COMPANION WEBSITE: A VIRTUAL LEARNING ENVIRONMENT

Technology is a constantly growing and changing aspect of our field that is creating a need for content and resources. To address this emerging need, Prentice Hall has developed an online learning environment for students and professors alike—Companion Websites—to support our textbooks.

In creating a Companion Website, our goal is to build on and enhance what the textbook already offers. For this reason, the content for each user-friendly website is organized by topic and provides the professor and student with a variety of meaningful resources. Common features of a Companion Website include:

### For the Professor—

Every Companion Website integrates **Syllabus Manager**™, an online syllabus creation and management utility.

- **Syllabus Manager**™ provides you, the instructor, with an easy, step-by-step process to create and revise syllabi, with direct links into Companion Website and other online content without having to learn HTML.
- Students may logon to your syllabus during any study session. All they need to know is the web address for the Companion Website and the password you've assigned to your syllabus.
- After you have created a syllabus using **Syllabus Manager**™, students may enter the syllabus for their course section from any point in the Companion Website.
- Clicking on a date, the student is shown the list of activities for the assignment. The activities for each assignment are linked directly to actual content, saving time for students.
- Adding assignments consists of clicking on the desired due date, then filling in the details of the assignment—name of the assignment, instructions, and whether or not it is a one-time or repeating assignment.
- In addition, links to other activities can be created easily. If the activity is online, a URL can be entered in the space provided, and it will be linked automatically in the final syllabus.
- Your completed syllabus is hosted on our servers, allowing convenient updates from any computer on the Internet. Changes you make to your syllabus are immediately available to your students at their next logon.

## For the Student—

- **Overview** and **General Information**—General information about the topic and how it will be covered in the website.
- **Web Links**—A variety of websites related to topic areas.
- **Content Methods and Strategies**—Resources that help to put theories into practice in the special education classroom.
- **Reflective Questions and Case-Based Activities**—Put concepts into action, participate in activities, examine strategies, and more.
- **National and State Laws**—An online guide to how federal and state laws affect your special education classroom.
- **Behavior Management**—An online guide to help you manage behaviors in the special education classroom.
- **Message Board**—Virtual bulletin board to post and respond to questions and comments from a national audience.

To take advantage of these and other resources, please visit the *Behavior Management: Applications for Teachers,* Fourth Edition, Companion Website at

**www.prenhall.com/zirpoli**

# BRIEF CONTENTS

# Contents

PART

I

# UNDERSTANDING AND ASSESSING BEHAVIOR

# FOUNDATIONS FOR UNDERSTANDING AND MANAGING BEHAVIOR

*Thomas J. Zirpoli*

*Why do people behave the way they do? It was probably first a practical question: How could a person anticipate and hence prepare for what another person would do? Later it would become practical in another sense: How would another person be induced to behave in a given way? Eventually it became a matter of understanding and explaining behavior. It could always be reduced to a question about causes.*

—SKINNER *(1974, p. 10)*

nderstanding why individuals behave the way they do and how behavior may be taught, changed, or modified is the primary concern of this text. In this chapter the basic concepts, assumptions, misconceptions, and historical foundations of the study of behavior and behavior management are addressed.

*Behaviorists,* those who study behavior and behavior management strategies, do not employ a single technique to teach, change, or modify behavior (thus the term *behavior modification*). *Behavior modification,* and more recently, *applied behavior analysis,* are terms used to describe a variety of behavior management techniques that have a solid foundation in the research literature. As Kazdin (1989) notes, these techniques have been successfully applied across a wide range of populations, settings, and situations to both clinical (e.g., abusive behaviors, depression, sexual deviance) and nonclinical behavior problems (e.g., academic performance, noncompliance, tantrums). Behaviorists use these techniques to:

- observe, measure, and evaluate current observable behavioral patterns;
- identify environmental antecedents and consequences associated with specific target behaviors;
- establish new behavioral objectives; and
- advance the learning of new behavior or modify current behavior via the manipulation of identified antecedents and consequences (Kazdin, 1989; Rimm & Masters, 1974).

When behaviorists talk about behavior and the management of behavior, they employ their own language and terminology. Understanding these basic concepts of behavior, outlined in the next section of this chapter, is critical to understanding the foundations of behavior management techniques.

# BASIC CONCEPTS OF BEHAVIOR AND BEHAVIOR MANAGEMENT

## Behavior

The term *behavior* is defined broadly by many who study behavior and behavior management. Behavior may refer to both *covert* responses (such as feelings and emotions) and *overt* responses (such as tantrums and aggression) (Rimm & Masters, 1974). Behaviorists are largely concerned with overt responses or behaviors that are observable and measurable. These are the behaviors that teachers and parents are able to observe and target for change. Baer, Wolf, and Risley (1968) state that something must be observable and quantifiable to qualify as a behavior.

A behavior is considered *observable* when it can be seen and *measurable* when it can be counted in terms of frequency and/or duration. These two criteria must be met in order to make the direct observation of behavior meaningful and reliable.

Behaviors may be in the form of unconditioned reflexes (eye blinks) or purposeful intent (giving someone a kiss). Some behaviors are conditioned or learned (avoiding a hot stove), and some are simply the result of modeling (a young girl acting like her older sister). Behaviors may be as simple as body movements (touching) or very complex, involving the integration of many behaviors (telling a story). Our everyday lives are filled with many examples of behaviors that can be observed, measured, studied, and modified in some way. Whether they are the unconditioned responses of internal emotions or the result of environmental conditions, behaviors provide the focal point of any behavior management plan.

## Antecedents

*Antecedents* are thought of as stimuli that occur prior to behaviors. (Definition and a discussion of stimuli are outlined in the following sections.) While stimuli refer to specific events or prompts before a target behavior, antecedents refer to the broader picture of influences that exist within the environment before a target behavior. In a classroom setting, antecedents are abundant and include the classroom curriculum (see Chapter 5 on the relationship between classroom curriculum and student behavior).

The relationship between behavior and consequences seems to receive a disproportionate amount of attention in the field of behavior management. While consequences focus on what happens after the occurrence of a target behavior, the study of antecedents provides us with the opportunity to modify a behavior before it occurs. Clearly, certain environmental conditions are likely to elicit behaviors in individuals that may be avoided or prevented by means of simple environmental modifications. By making these changes, the antecedents to certain behaviors are removed, and the likelihood of seeing certain behaviors is decreased or eliminated. For example, placing children within an environment containing few rules and little supervision is likely to promote the occurrence of many inappropriate behaviors.

When monitoring the antecedents to a target behavior, a long list of interrelated stimuli may be observed. For example, in Vignette 1.1, antecedents related to the behavior of Jill's running out of the classroom may include the onset of the reading lesson, the behavior of another child in her reading group, her general seating arrangement, or a combination of all these factors. Bandura (1977) writes about the important role antecedents play in the formation of behavior and behavioral expectations:

> *Without anticipatory capacities people would be forced to act blindly in ways that might prove to be unproductive, if not hazardous. Information about the probable effects of*

**VIGNETTE 1.1**

●

*Example of Classroom Antecedents and Consequences*
*Related to Running-Away Behavior*

Jennifer, an elementary school teacher, had a student, Jill, in her first-grade class who frequently ran out of the classroom and onto the playground. Unfortunately, Jennifer's classroom, located on the first floor, had a direct-access door to the playground. Although Jennifer
tried to keep the door locked, Jill had learned how to unlock the door and run onto the playground before anyone could stop her. Jennifer noticed that this behavior usually occurred
shortly after the children were directed into their reading groups. Although Jill was progressing well with her reading, Jennifer also noticed that Jill did not get along well with the
other members of her group.

   Jennifer could not leave her students unsupervised. Thus, while monitoring Jill from the
classroom window, she would call her principal, report that Jill had run onto the playground
(again), and ask the principal to bring Jill back to the classroom. At this point the principal
would go to the playground, bring Jill back into the school's main office, and talk to Jill about
the dangers of running away from her classroom. The principal was a gentle man and was
greatly admired by all the students in the school. After talking with Jill for about 5 minutes,
the principal would provide her with a drink of juice and return her to Jennifer's classroom.
Upon returning to the classroom, Jennifer would thank the principal and direct Jill to rejoin
her reading group.

---

*specific actions or events is conveyed by environmental stimuli. One can be informed of*
*what to expect by the distinctive features of places, persons, or things, or by social signals*
*in the language, gestures, and actions of others. (p. 58)*

## Consequences

The relationship between behaviors and consequences represents the heart of behavior management strategies. *Consequences* are events or changes in the environment following a target behavior. For example, in Vignette 1.1, what were the
consequences of Jill's running-away behavior? Who provided these consequences?
In your opinion, were these consequences primarily reinforcing or punishing? Do
you think Jill will want to run away again?

   Cooper, Heron, and Heward (1987) outline two forms of consequences. In the
first form, a consequence is represented by the *addition* of a new stimulus to the environment. For example, a child's asking for a snack in an appropriate polite manner (target behavior) may be followed by attention from the teacher and a snack
(new stimulus). In Vignette 1.1, Jill was presented with the principal's attention
and a drink of juice (reinforcing consequences) after running away from her classroom (target behavior or behavior targeted for change).

   In the second form, a consequence is represented by the *removal* of a stimulus
already present within the environment. For example, when a child is behaving in

an inappropriate manner, a teacher may decide to ignore the child (remove attention) until the maladaptive behavior is terminated.

A consequence may also be represented by a *change* in current environmental stimuli following a target behavior. While attention to a behavior may be added or terminated as outlined earlier, the level of attention may be modified or changed as a consequence of a child's behavior. For example, a teacher's changing facial expression while listening to a child tell a story represents an ever-changing consequence for the child's ongoing behavior. In summary, a consequence may be represented by the addition, removal, or change in environmental stimuli following a target behavior.

In addition to the form a consequence may take, a second and very important element of consequences is the effect of the consequence on the preceding target behavior. The question of "effect" refers to how the consequence influences or changes the target behavior. For example, the probability of the target behavior occurring again may be increased or decreased, or the actual rate of occurrence may increase or decrease as a result of the consequence. Other possible behavioral changes may include an increase or decrease in duration and intensity. All of these behavioral changes are related to the consequence(s) that followed the behavior. Thus, a reciprocal relationship between behavior and consequence is established. Each has an influence on the other, and each can be manipulated in an effort to modify the other. A more complete review of consequences is provided in Chapters 7 and 9.

## Stimuli

As described earlier, *stimuli* are events or activities within the environment that are capable of forming a relationship with behavior as either an antecedent or a consequence. For example, turning the lights on and off in a classroom may be an antecedent stimulus for the children to look at the teacher and pay attention. A pat on the back by a teacher is a stimulus that could be provided as a consequence following a child's outstanding performance. In this case, the stimulus (a pat on the back) is in the form of a reinforcer. A stimulus may become a *discriminative stimulus* (SD; also discussed in Chapter 7) for a specific behavior when it is repeatedly associated with that behavior. In the previous example, turning the lights on and off may become an SD for looking at the teacher and paying attention (behavior). A bell in school may serve as a stimulus for children to change classes. Although the sound of a bell does not naturally elicit children to change classes, it may became a conditioned or learned stimulus after it is consistently used to signal children to change classes. The end of a specific morning TV program may become a stimulus for a child to leave home for school. When the relationship between the SD and behavior is firmly established, then the behavior is considered to be under stimulus control.

We must make a distinction between an SD and an S-delta. While an SD is an antecedent that serves as an appropriate cue for a behavior and results in reinforcement, an *S-delta* is an antecedent that does not serve as the appropriate cue for a behavior and thus does not result in reinforcement. For example, if a teacher claps her hands in an effort to get the children's attention and the children continue to play (and the teacher's behavior is not reinforced), the stimulus (clapping hands) in this case would not be considered an S$_D$ but an S-delta.

*Stimulus generalization* refers to the performance of a behavior following a stimulus (prompt or cue) not presented during the initial stimulus-response training. For example, if the teacher merely reached for the light switch and the children responded as they were taught to respond (looking and paying attention) to the lights being turned on and off, we would say that stimulus generalization had occurred from one stimulus (turning the lights on and off) to another stimulus (reaching for the light switch).

## Responses

A *response* is a behavior that is observable and measurable. Individuals are constantly responding as they move around and complete daily tasks. Many of these behaviors or responses are under stimulus control: for example, getting up in the morning in response to the alarm clock, following a schedule throughout the day, responding to others in a manner consistent with a previous history of knowing that person, and so on. Many behaviors are in response to new stimuli that are added to the environment, such as a new student walking into the classroom or a sudden change in the schedule. Many behaviors are in response to internal feelings, such as being hungry and getting something to eat or feeling tired and taking a nap.

*Response generalization* refers to changes in behaviors other than the behavior that was targeted for change or modification. In keeping with our previous example, if the teacher turned the lights on and off and the children *also* put their hands on their desk and sat up straight, these additional behaviors exhibited by the children represent a response generalization from the target behaviors (looking at the teacher and paying attention).

## Reinforcement

The relationships formed between stimuli and responses provide the foundation for behavior management. *Reinforcement,* discussed in greater detail in Chapter 7, is a type of stimulus that serves as a consequence for a response/behavior. However, by definition, a stimulus may not be considered a reinforcer unless it affects the preceding behavior in one of the ways outlined in the following list. Used appropriately, reinforcement has several potential effects on the response it follows. For example:

- Reinforcement may *maintain* the current rate, duration, or intensity of a response.
- Reinforcement may increase the *probability* that a new response will occur again.

- Reinforcement may *increase* the future rate, duration, or intensity of a response.
- Reinforcement may *strengthen* a response that is weak and inconsistent.

Because of these properties, behaviorists believe that reinforcement provides the key to understanding the etiology and management of behavior. Reinforcement is a powerful tool used to teach new behaviors and change current behaviors; it is the foundation of Skinner's operant conditioning (discussed later in this chapter). It is the treatment of choice for today's contemporary application of behavior modification and, specifically, applied behavior analysis.

An important property of reinforcement that teachers must understand is that the effects of reinforcement do not differentiate between appropriate and inappropriate behaviors. Reinforcement is under the control of the user who may, even unknowingly, apply it following any behavior, appropriate or inappropriate. Reinforcement may be, and frequently is, used to maintain or increase inappropriate as well as appropriate behaviors. The most common example of this is the child who has temper tantrums that are reinforced when teachers give in to the child's demands. A primary objective of this text is to provide a greater understanding of how reinforcement may be used to increase appropriate behaviors and how the removal of reinforcement may be used to decrease inappropriate behaviors.

## Punishment

*Punishment* (discussed in greater detail in Chapter 9), like reinforcement, is also a type of stimulus that may serve as a consequence for behavior. By definition, a stimulus may be classified as a punisher only if the preceding response/behavior changes in one of the following ways:

- The probability of a new behavior occurring again is decreased.
- The future rate, duration, and/or intensity of a current behavior is decreased or eliminated.
- Other dimensions of the behavior are weakened.

Like reinforcement, punishment does not differentiate between appropriate and inappropriate behaviors. Unknowingly, teachers may punish appropriate behaviors, as well as behaviors perceived to be inappropriate. For example, when we become angry at young children for asking too many questions, we may be punishing age-appropriate behavior. Moreover, punishment procedures tend to have many undesirable side effects (discussed in Chapter 9). In this text, we hope to encourage teachers to concentrate on methods of reinforcement to manage behavior.

## Prompts and Cues

Although some consider *cues* to involve verbal guidance and *prompts* to involve physical guidance, in this text we use the terms synonymously and use the term *prompt* to describe both terms. Prompts are antecedent stimuli that supplement discriminative stimuli in order to produce a specific target behavior. Donnellan, LaVigna, Negri-Shoultz, and Fassbender (1988) define a prompt as "the assistance provided to the learner after the presentation of the instructional stimulus, but before the response. This procedure is used to assure a correct response" (p. 53). For example, a teacher may supplement ringing a bell (an $S_D$ for starting an activity) with the verbal prompt "Children, what are you supposed to do when you hear the bell?"

The use of prompts to supplement a discriminative stimulus is usually a temporary instructional aid and should be systematically phased out as soon as possible. In the previous example, the teacher does not want to use the additional verbal prompt for the whole school year. The goal is for the students to respond to the $S_D$ without additional prompts. This is accomplished when the teacher slowly phases out the use of prompts and reinforces students for responding to the $S_D$. Several different types of prompts are briefly described and discussed in the following sections.

## Natural Prompts

A *natural prompt* is an environmental stimulus that naturally occurs prior to target behaviors. Natural prompts are always preferable, whereas unnatural or artificial prompts should be replaced with natural prompts whenever possible. For example, in the Classroom Application 1.1, the start of morning announcements becomes a natural prompt for the students to sit down, be quiet, and listen to the announcements. Susan can teach her students to exhibit this target behavior (sit down, be quiet and listen to the classroom announcements) without telling them (a verbal prompt) each and every day. Initially, a verbal prompt will be necessary ("The announcements are starting so you must sit down, be quiet, and listen to the announcements"). When the target behavior is reinforced ("Thank you for sitting down, being quiet, and listening to the announcements!") as the artificial verbal prompt is phased out over time, the natural prompt (the start of the announcements) will soon serve as the $S_D$ for the target behavior.

Figure 1.1 provides a list of target behaviors and the natural prompts frequently associated with each. The less dependent children are on artificial prompts, especially verbal prompts, and the more they are reinforced for responding appropriately to natural prompts, the easier behavior management becomes for teachers.

## Verbal Prompts

Verbal prompts are the most common type of prompt used with children and include the following (Cuvo & Davis, 1980):

- Giving directions or instructions regarding a whole target behavior. This may serve as the $S_D$ for the expected appropriate behaviors ("Class, it's time for lunch").

**FIGURE 1.1.** Target behaviors and natural prompts

| Target Behaviors | Natural Environmental Prompts |
|---|---|
| Getting up in the morning | Alarm clock |
| Going to school on time | Clock or watch |
| Being quiet and listening | Teacher or someone else beginning to talk |
| Changing classes | School bell |
| | Classroom clock |
| Being loud and playful | Entering the gym or playground |
| Raising your hand | When you need help |
| | When you have a question |
| | When you know the answer to a teacher's question |

- Specific prompts concerning expected behaviors within a task ("Line up by the door" or "Go to the bathroom and wash your hands"). These provide additional verbal prompts (instructional prompts) for the specific behaviors included within the whole target behavior—going to lunch.
- Asking questions ("What should you do now?").

In the following example, a verbal direction serves as the SD for a student's behavior:

- *Behavior:* Going to the lunchroom for lunch.
- *Discriminative Stimulus (SD):* A specific time, such as 12 noon, or a verbal SD such as "Class, it is time for lunch."
- *Additional instructional verbal prompts:*
  1. "Line up by the door."
  2. "Walk to the bathroom and wash your hands."
  3. "Walk to the cafeteria."

Initially, a teacher may have to use the SD and additional instructional verbal prompts when teaching the child what is expected when the SD is given. Over time, the teacher should phase out the use of the additional verbal prompts and allow each step in the sequence of going to the cafeteria for lunch to act as the natural prompt for the next behavior. Thus, *lining up by the door at 12 noon* serves as a natural prompt for *walking to the bathroom to wash hands,* and so on.

When gestural, modeling, and physical prompts are necessary, teachers are encouraged to pair these prompts with verbal prompts. As the more intrusive prompts are relinquished, the verbal prompt serves as the SD for the appropriate behavior. Over time, even the verbal prompt may be phased out as still more natural prompts (environmental conditions, time of day, etc.) serve as the SD for the appropriate behavior.

The effectiveness of verbal prompts alone, and verbal prompts used in combination with other prompts, has been studied with a variety of populations. For example, Hodges (2001) investigated the effect of instructors' use of verbal prompts on high-risk college students' participation in tutoring and supplemental instruction. Houghton (1993) combined verbal prompts with visual prompts to decrease littering with high school students. And Coyne and Hoskins (1997) used verbal prompts and reinforcement to increase the eating independence levels of elderly nursing home patients with dementia.

## Gestural Prompts

A *gestural prompt* refers to a simple gesture, usually a pointing prompt, that visually directs an individual in a particular direction. For example, in addition to the verbal prompt "Line up by the door," a teacher may also point in the direction of the door. In this case, the gestural prompt (pointing) is paired with the verbal prompt ("Line up by the door"). Over time, the gestural and verbal prompts should be phased out, and the students should receive reinforcement for completing the target behavior following the S𝐷 "Class, it's time for lunch."

## Modeling Prompts

*Modeling prompts* "consist of demonstrating part or all of the desired behavior to the student who imitates or repeats the action immediately" (Snell & Zirpoli, 1987, p. 126). As with gestural prompts, modeling should be paired with an appropriate verbal prompt or verbal S𝐷 that the child will be expected to respond to after the modeling prompt is phased out. For example, when instructing a group of students on expected behavior during story time, the teacher may model where the children should sit, how they should sit quietly with their hands to themselves without disturbing others, how they should look at the teacher or the pictures in the storybook, and so on. Then, following the verbal S𝐷 "Children, it is time to read a story," the teacher may ask the children to imitate or practice this behavior while a story is being read to them. Appropriate behaviors are then reinforced ("John, I like the way you are listening!"). Sometimes the teacher may ask another student to model a particular behavior for the other students. Regardless of who is providing the model, Bandura (1971) recommends that:

- the children's attention should be gained prior to the presentation of the model,
- the children readily imitate the model, and
- the modeled behavior be kept short and simple, especially for young children.

Kazdin (1989, p. 21) states that the imitation of a model by an observer is more likely when:

- the model (child) is similar to the observer,

## Classroom Application 1.1

## Setting Up Natural Prompts in the Classroom Routine

Susan, a sixth-grade teacher, does not want to spend each morning instructing her home-room students how to walk into her classroom, get their materials ready for their first class, sit down and listen to the morning announcements, wait for the bell, and, after the bell rings, leave her room in an orderly fashion for their first class. While verbal cues and prompts would work, she knows that she would end up having to yell over all the noise. Besides, she wants her students to follow the natural prompts of the homeroom routine without her daily guidance and verbal directions.

On the first day of school, Susan provides a verbal and visual overview of the homeroom routine. After the students walk into her room, she instructs them to look at the homeroom routine she outlined on the board as follows:

- Walk into the classroom and directly to your desk.
- Prepare your materials for your first class.
- Be seated and wait for the morning announcements.
- Listen to the announcements (no talking at this time).
- Remain in your seat and wait for the first bell to ring.
- When the first bell rings, walk to the door and directly to your first class.

Susan reviews the routine by reading each line and asking the students if they have any questions. For the first week of classes, Susan keeps the outline on the board and asks the students to "Remember the routine we talked about on the first day." She verbally reinforces the students when they follow the routine and corrects them when they do not. After the first week, Susan no longer needs to verbally prompt the students. Instead, she can focus on individual students who are slow to learn the routine and need individual guidance, reinforcement, and consequences as they learn the natural prompts of the homeroom classroom.

- the model is more prestigious than the observer,
- the model is higher in status and expertise than the observer, and
- several models perform the same behavior.

### *Physical Prompts*

A *physical prompt* consists of physically guiding a child in the performance of a target behavior. Obviously, physical prompts are the most intrusive prompt form and are recommended only as a last resort. Physical prompts should be phased out as soon as possible since they are very unnatural and, when used to modify a student's behavior, may promote hostility and defensiveness.

Understanding the basic concepts of behavior, the antecedents of behavior, the different types of consequences for behavior, and the different types of prompts to teach new behaviors provides behaviorists with a foundation of terminology to communicate with each other and practitioners about behavior management. Beyond the basic concepts of behavior management, there are also some basic assumptions about behavior that guide a behaviorist's thinking about behavior. These assumptions about behavior and how behavior is changed provide a foundation for understanding why a person behaves the way he or she does and how the person's behavior may be modified.

For example, it is important to note that effective practices in behavior management place a primary emphasis on overt behaviors and current influences (antecedents and consequences) within the environment that are observed to be related to those behaviors. In other words, while most behaviorists do not deny the possible relationship between a student's challenging behaviors and real psychological, physiological, or other emotional disturbances, they are more interested in assessing a person's overt behaviors within a specific environment than a person's mind. They are aware that a classroom teacher can be taught to modify classroom antecedents and consequences more easily than the thoughts within a student's mind, if at all. And while most behaviorists do not disregard the influences of heredity, nor are they insensitive to a child's developmental stage when evaluating a behavior problem, they understand that behavior is learned and that students must be taught appropriate social skills if they are to be successful adults in a social world. A more complete outline of the basic assumptions of behavior and behavior management appears in the following section.

## BASIC ASSUMPTIONS OF BEHAVIOR AND BEHAVIOR MANAGEMENT

While most behaviorists believe that at least some of the following assumptions have exceptions, these assumptions do represent the philosophical foundations of behaviorism:

- Most behaviors are learned.
- Most behaviors are stimulus-specific.
- Most behaviors can be taught, changed, or modified.
- Behavior change goals should be specific and clearly defined.
- Behavior change programs should be individualized.
- Behavior change programs should focus on the here and now.
- Behavior change programs should focus on the child's environment.

## Most Behaviors Are Learned

Behaviorists believe that the majority of behaviors observed in children are learned. That is, children tend to exhibit behaviors that are reinforced and avoid behaviors that have not been previously reinforced or have been punished. Behaviorists believe that there is no difference between appropriate and inappropriate behaviors—both are learned in the same manner. The goal of behavior management is to provide learning experiences for individuals that promote appropriate, prosocial behaviors.

## Most Behaviors Are Stimulus-Specific

Behaviorists believe that individuals behave differently within different environments. That is, the behavior a child shows within a particular situation indicates only how the child typically behaves in that specific situation. This is because each environment contains its own set of antecedents (e.g., people, tasks, expectations) and consequences (reinforcers and punishers) for behavior. In addition, individuals have different histories of reinforcement and punishment within different environments. For example, a child may have learned that within one environment (the home), tantrums are reinforced. In another environment (the school), however, tantrums are not reinforced. As a result, the child's rate of tantrums is likely to be different in the home (frequent tantrum behaviors) compared to the school (little or no tantrum behaviors).

## Most Behaviors Can Be Taught, Changed, or Modified

Because most behaviors are learned, teachers can teach new behaviors and change or modify current behaviors. Behaviorists are quick to point to the many research studies that document the efficacy of behavioral techniques and the lack of evidence supporting the traditional psychoanalytic approach. Since the behavioral approach is effective in teaching new behaviors and modifying current behaviors, it serves as a functional approach for teachers in everyday situations.

## Behavior Change Goals Should Be Specific and Clearly Defined

Effective behavior management strategies are based on planned and systematic approaches. Behavior change goals are stated in specific terms, and they are clearly observable and measurable. Behaviorists talk about reducing *specific* behaviors such as "talking when the teacher is talking," "hitting others," and "getting out of seat." The strategies used in the behavioral approach are also very specific and must be applied systematically. Objectives, methods, reinforcement strategies, intervention strategies, and so on, are outlined in writing so that the program may be implemented consistently by all teachers who have contact with the student.

## Behavior Change Programs Should Be Individualized

Behaviorists believe that individuals function differently within different environments in which there are different antecedents and consequences. Each of us has developed many different associations among many different behaviors, antecedents, and consequences. Also, individuals respond differently to different types of environmental stimuli and responses. For example, what one child finds reinforcing, another may find punishing. Thus, behavior change programs must be individualized for each child and the child's environment. The idea of using a single behavior management strategy for all children within a school or even a classroom is not congruent with the basic assumptions of behaviorism and effective behavior management.

## Behavior Change Programs Should Focus on the Here and Now

Unlike the psychoanalytic approach, in which a considerable amount of time and effort is invested by delving into an individual's past experiences, the behaviorist is not very concerned with past events. Instead, the behaviorist concentrates on current events within an individual's environment in order to identify the influences on the person's current behavior. The behaviorist looks at what is going on in the classroom environment and sees little benefit from identifying and discussing underlying causes of childhood fears, anxieties, relationships with others, and so on; these approaches have no role in changing current behaviors. Again, the behaviorist points to the lack of evidence supporting the usefulness of identifying and discussing historical events when attempting to modify current behaviors within the classroom.

## Behavior Change Programs Should Focus on the Child's Environment

While the psychoanalytic approach concentrates primarily on the individual and looks for an explanation of problem behaviors within the individual, the behaviorist concentrates on the individual's environment and looks for an explanation of problem behaviors within that environment. Behaviorists are interested in environmental, situational, and social determinants of behavior. While the psychoanalytic approach views inappropriate behavior mainly as the result of a flawed personality and other internal attributes, the behavioral approach considers antecedents and consequences as the most significant factors related to appropriate and inappropriate behavior. It is not necessary for the child to have "insight" as to why he or she is behaving in a certain way for that behavior to be changed.

In addition to the basic concepts and assumptions of behavior and behavior management, behaviorists have had to defend themselves against many misconceptions about their field and the application of their research to the typical classroom teacher. In this next section, the myths and misconceptions about behavior and behavior management will be discussed in light of the basic concepts and assumptions of behavior just discussed.

## MYTHS AND MISCONCEPTIONS ABOUT BEHAVIOR AND BEHAVIOR MANAGEMENT

Many myths and misconceptions are associated with behavior management and have led to public and professional hostility toward behavioral principles and behavior modification in general (Gelfand & Hartmann, 1984; Kazdin, 1975, 1978). These misconceptions have developed over the long history of behavior management as the term *behavior modification* and the techniques associated with the term have been abused and misused. The association of behavior modification with nonbehavioral methods such as drug therapy, electroconvulsive therapy, psychosurgery, and sterilization provides an example of common errors made among the uninformed. According to Kazdin (1978):

> It cannot be overemphasized that these techniques are not a part of behavior modification. They are not derived from psychological research nor do they depend upon reversible alterations of social and environmental conditions to change behavior. (p. 341)

Although many of these medical interventions do change or modify behavior and thus may be confused with behavior modification, "clear differences exist between medical and behavioral interventions" (Kazdin, 1978, p. 341). Unfortunately, these differences are not understood by many individuals who are misinformed about both the medical and behavioral techniques.

The perception of punishment as the primary strategy of behaviorists has also led to negative reactions, even among professionals, when behavior modification strategies are suggested to manage behavior. Alberto and Troutman (1995) go so far as to discourage teachers from using the term *behavior modification* when communicating with others about behavior management techniques:

> We simply suggest that teachers avoid using the term with uninformed or misinformed people. In many cases, other professionals, including administrative staff and fellow teachers, may be as confused as parents and school board members.  .  .  . It may be as necessary to educate these fellow professionals as it is to teach children. (p. 43)

Some suggest replacing the terminology used in behavior modification with more humanizing language (Saunders & Reppucci, 1978; Wilson & Evans, 1978). Kazdin and Cole (1981) found that individuals labeled identical intervention procedures as less acceptable when they were described in behavioral terms (reinforcement, punishment, contingencies) compared to humanistic terms (personal growth and development).

Why has behavior modification developed such a poor image in the minds of so many? First, as previously stated, there has been a gross misuse of the term *behavior modification*. The term is frequently associated with unpopular techniques that have nothing to do with the behavioral approach. Yet, these techniques continue to be discussed under the heading of behavior modification in the mass media, books, and other sources.

Second, a long history exists of documented abuses of many behavior management techniques, especially with individuals who were unable to protect themselves from these abuses. As mentioned earlier, many behavior modification strategies were first applied to people living within institutional settings. Most of these individuals were children and individuals with various mental, emotional, and physical disabilities. In addition, behavioral techniques have been employed by inadequately trained professionals and paraprofessionals who, at best, had a surface understanding of the variety of techniques applicable within the behavioral approach.

In an interview with Coleman (1987), B. F. Skinner talked about the decline of behaviorism and blamed the decline on the association between behaviorism and punishment. Skinner was an opponent of punishing methods such as spanking and other aversive techniques used to control behavior. On numerous occasions before his death in 1990, Skinner encouraged caregivers to use positive behavior management approaches and to avoid the use of aversive interventions. Changing the negative image of many effective behavior management techniques will require a significant amount of education for professionals and the general public. An attempt to outline additional behavior management concerns and a brief discussion of each are provided next.

## Myth: Changing Another Person's Behavior Is Coercive

The idea that many behavior management strategies are coercive because they are used to change another person's behavior is an interesting position. For some, trying to change another person's behavior is a violation of that person's freedom and other rights. For example, in Vignette 1.2, Randy's teacher does not believe that it is coercive to mandate that he wear a coat before going outside. To her, teaching Randy to wear a coat in the winter is both educational and a health-related concern.

To further address this issue, we must first consider what our responsibilities are regarding the children placed in our care. Do teachers have a responsibility to prepare students for their place within society, to teach them the social skills necessary to survive in the world, and to teach behaviors that will allow them to interact effectively and communicate with others within the home, school, workplace, and general community? Most teachers (and parents) would respond yes. In our opinion, then, the question is not whether it is coercive to change a child's behavior; we do this daily in our homes and schools. Rather, the significant questions are as follows: *Who* decides whether a child's behavior should be changed? *What* behaviors should be changed? *Which* techniques should be used? (Gelfand & Hartmann, 1984). These three questions raise several ethical issues that deserve considerably more discussion than the scope of this introductory chapter can supply. However, these issues will be addressed in Chapter 9.

## VIGNETTE 1.2

●

*Using Natural Consequences to Teach Compliance*

Jill is a kindergarten teacher who teaches a group of 5- and 6-year-olds within an inclusive program. Included in her group of 16 students are 3 students with a variety of disabilities. One of these students, Randy, has several labels including learning disabled and ADHD. Noncompliance is his primary challenging behavior.

One winter day, Jill asked her students to put on their coats as she prepared them for a visit to the playground. "I don't want to put on my coat," yelled Randy. "You don't have to put on your coat, Randy," responded his teacher. "But only children who have their coats on may go outside to play." "Mary (the teacher's aide) will stay inside with the children who don't want to put on their coats and go outside to play." Jill then gathered up the children who had put on their coats and took them to the playground. Randy immediately had a temper tantrum and started to yell and scream. Both Jill and Mary ignored Randy's behavior.

When Randy's mother came to pick him up from school, Jill told her what happened. "We can never get Randy to wear a coat," said his mother. "So we just let Randy decide if he needs to wear one or not." "Not in this classroom," Jill responded. "Our rule is that all the children must wear a coat before going outside in the cold. Those who don't follow the rule will stay inside."

The next day when Jill announced that it was time to go outside and everyone should put on their coats, Randy quickly put on his coat and joined his classmates on the playground. From that point on, Randy was seldom noncompliant within the preschool setting. But his mom continued to complain about his inappropriate behavior at home.

## Myth: The Use of Reinforcement to Change Behavior Is a Form of Bribery

Some teachers believe that reinforcing children for appropriate behavior is simply a form of "bribery" used to get children to behave appropriately. In a worst-case situation, the children may even turn the tables and try to bribe the teacher (e.g., "I'll behave if you give me a cookie"). Kazdin (1975) states that people who confuse reinforcement with bribery do not understand the definition and intent of each. He describes the difference between bribery and reinforcement this way:

> *Bribery refers to the illicit use of rewards, gifts, or favors to pervert judgment or corrupt the conduct of someone. With bribery, reward is used for the purpose of changing behavior, but the behavior is corrupt, illegal, or immoral in some way. With reinforcement, as typically employed, events are delivered for behaviors which are generally agreed upon to benefit the client, society, or both. (p. 50)*

Clearly, there are significant differences between bribery and giving children attention for appropriate behaviors. Moreover, if children do not get our attention following appropriate behavior, they will try to get our attention by acting inappropriately. In Vignette 1.2, Randy's behavior was met with both punishing and reinforcing consequences. When he was noncompliant, he was not allowed to go outside with the other children and, thus, his behavior was punished. When he did wear his coat, he was allowed to go outside and, thus, his behavior was reinforced. Many teachers use consequences in this manner every day, but will state that they do not believe in using reinforcement or other principles of behavior management.

## Myth: Children Will Learn to Behave Appropriately Only for Reinforcement

The fear that using reinforcement will lead to manipulation by children is generally unsupported (Kazdin, 1975). Manipulative behavior, however, can be promoted in children. For example, if a teacher provides a reinforcer to a student for terminating disruptive behavior, the child is likely (a) to be disruptive more frequently and (b) to demand a reinforcer before terminating future disruptive behavior. However, if the teacher provides reinforcement to the same child following a specific period of time during which disruptive behavior is not observed, the child is less likely to engage in disruptive behavior. In the first case, the child learned that *disruptive behavior* was reinforced. In the second case, the child learned that the *absence of disruptive behavior* was reinforced.

## Myth: Children Should "Work" for Intrinsic Reinforcers

Although "doing the right thing" for its intrinsic value is certainly an admirable situation, extrinsic reinforcers are a part of everyday life. People who say that extrinsic reinforcement is inappropriate appear to have higher expectations for children than adults. How many adults would continue going to work without an occasional paycheck? How many adults appreciate a pat on the back for a job well done? How many adults work harder at activities they find reinforcing? The behaviorist applies these simple principles to the management of behavior. As previously stated, extrinsic reinforcers are a part of everyday life, and teachers should learn how to use these natural reinforcers to teach new skills and promote appropriate behaviors. As children grow older and become more mature, we hope that they will learn the value of intrinsic reinforcement.

## Myth: All Children Should Be Treated in the Same Way

The issue here is whether one child should be singled out for a behavior program in which the child will receive a special reinforcer for learning a new behavior. For example, if John, 1 of 25 children in a classroom, frequently gets out of his seat, is it "fair" to reinforce him for staying in his seat? What about the other children who already stay in their seats and do not need a special program? These questions focus on the issue of fairness; teachers do not want their students to think that one child is receiving special attention. In fact, research shows that caregivers *do* interact differently with individual children (Bell & Harper, 1977; Zirpoli, 1990). All children have individual needs that call for individual attention. Some children need more individual attention than others. The idea of treating everyone the same is incongruent with effective educational practice.

Regarding our previous example, John's teacher has a professional responsibility to identify John's needs and to use the best method for him and his behavior. If reinforcement of in-seat behavior will increase John's in-seat behavior, then John has the right to receive the most effective intervention. Although the other children who already have appropriate in-seat behavior do not need a systematic reinforcement program, good educational practice tells us that they should also receive attention for their appropriate behavior in order to maintain that behavior. The level of attention for in-seat behavior may vary because John's needs are different from his classmates'. However, the other children are unlikely to have a problem with this difference; children are very sensitive to other children who have special needs. Research has shown that children recognize and accept these differences, frequently better than adults (Casey-Black & Knoblock, 1989; Melloy, 1990).

Now that we have outlined the basic concepts, assumptions and misconceptions about behavior and behavior management, it is possible to review the foundations of current thinking about behavior, behavior analysis, and behavior management. As we have noted, many of the myths about behaviorists and behavior modification are founded on a long and sometimes-not-so-honored employment and abuse of behavioral techniques. The focus on punishment, instead of reinforcement, as the primary consequence to change behavior is one example of how these myths developed. Understanding the history and foundation of what we refer to today as applied behavior analysis will help the reader understand current use of the principles discussed in this text.

## HISTORY AND FOUNDATIONS OF CURRENT BEHAVIOR ANALYSIS AND MANAGEMENT

Morris (1985) identifies *classical conditioning, operant conditioning,* and *social learning* as the "general theoretical positions . . . that form the basis of contemporary behavior modification approaches" (p. 4). These, in addition to *behavior therapy* and *applied behavior analysis,* make up the primary "streams" of behavior management and will be discussed here.

### Classical Conditioning

*Classical conditioning* (also called *Pavlovian conditioning*) refers to the relationship between stimuli and reflex responses. *Stimulus* refers to any "condition, event, or change in the physical world" (Cooper, Heron, & Heward, 1987, p. 18). Stimuli include light, noise, touch, temperature, the taste of food, smells, textures, and so on, that evoke/elicit responses or respondent behavior.

Stimuli may be unconditioned or conditioned. An *unconditioned stimulus* (UCS) is naturally stimulating or unlearned. Examples include food and sex. A person does not have to learn that food and sex are reinforcing. A *conditioned stimulus* (CS) is one that has been learned or conditioned. For example, a child may learn to fear anyone wearing white clothing after spending months in a hospital that included painful treatments by medical personnel dressed in white. Meeting a certain person may serve as a conditioned stimulus for happiness or fear, depending on previous experiences with that person.

*Respondent behaviors* are usually not controlled by the individual and are frequently referred to as involuntary, reflex behaviors or unconditioned responses. An unconditioned stimulus usually produces an unconditioned response. For example, a bright light (unconditioned stimulus) focused on a person's eyes will probably produce unconditioned responses such as closing the eyelids, covering the eyes, and turning away. These respondent behaviors are not learned; they occur automatically as a result of the stimulus (light).

Ivan P. Pavlov (1849–1936), a Russian physiologist and 1904 Nobel Prize winner, is commonly referred to as the father of classical conditioning. During his research on animal digestion, Pavlov studied how different foods placed in the digestive system elicited unconditioned reflexes such as the production of gastric secretions and saliva. More significantly, Pavlov discovered that these responses could be stimulated when certain stimuli associated with the presentation of food were also present in the environment. For example, Pavlov observed that his dogs began to produce saliva when his assistant merely opened the cage door at meal time.

Ivan Petrovich Pavlov
(1849–1936)

In 1927 Pavlov conducted his now famous study demonstrating that he could condition a dog to produce saliva (an unconditioned response) following the ringing of a bell. In his study, Pavlov paired the presentation of food (an unconditioned stimulus) with the ringing of a bell (a neutral stimulus to the dog). Over time, Pavlov found that merely ringing the bell, even in the absence of food, caused the dog to salivate. The ringing of the bell had become a learned or *conditioned stimulus* producing a learned or *conditioned response* (salivation). Pavlov went on to discover that the bell could lose its ability to elicit the production of saliva if it were repeatedly rung without the presentation of food. The dog learned that the bell was no longer associated with food and thus no longer acted as a conditioned stimulus for salivation. A model of Pavlov's classical conditioning of a salivation response in his dog is provided in Figure 1.2.

Pavlovian conditioning has expanded significantly since the days of Pavlov. Rescorla (1988) describes the modern understanding of classical conditioning as much more complex than the simple but inadequate explanation provided earlier:

> *Pavlovian conditioning is not a stupid process by which the organism willy-nilly forms associations between any two stimuli that happen to co-occur. Rather, the organism is better seen as an information seeker using logical and perceptual relations among events, along with its own preconceptions, to form a sophisticated representation of its world.* (p. 154)

Rescorla and others have expanded the traditional understanding of classical conditioning. Balsam and Tomie (1985) note that learning must be understood beyond the identification of conditioned and unconditioned stimuli. The properties of the stimuli and the context in which these stimuli are presented not only become part of the stimulus (called a *stimulus package*) but play a role in the type of response forms that follow. A conditioned stimulus presented in one environment may elicit a different response in a second environment. For example, how a child responds to another child's provocation within the classroom environment may be very different from how the child would respond to the same stimulus within the child's neighborhood. Indeed, behavior is far more complex than a simple understanding

**FIGURE 1.2.** Model of Pavlov's classical conditioning by the pairing of food and a bell to elicit a conditioned salivation response in a dog

***Before classical conditioning***

| | |
|---|---|
| Food presented (Unconditioned Stimulus) | Salivation (Unconditioned Response) |

***During classical conditioning***

| | |
|---|---|
| Food + bell presented (Unconditioned + Conditioned Stimulus) | Salivation (Unconditioned Response) |

***After classical conditioning***

| | |
|---|---|
| Bell only presented (Conditioned Stimulus) | Salivation (Conditioned Response) |

of the pairing of stimuli and associated responses; many other variables are involved. Pavlov, however, must be credited with providing the foundation for classical conditioning, which "continues to be an intellectually active area, full of new discoveries and information relevant to other areas of psychology" (Rescorla, 1988, p. 151). Classical conditioning provides the basis for many current behavior therapy techniques, described later in this chapter.

As stated by Kazdin (1989), Pavlov was also noted for his precise scientific methods:

> Pavlov used precise methods that permitted careful observation and quantification of what he was studying. For example, in some of his studies, drops of saliva were counted to measure the conditioned reflex. His meticulous laboratory notes and his rigorous methods helped greatly to advance a scientific approach toward the study of behavior. (p. 9)

Another animal psychologist who made significant contributions toward the understanding of human behavior and the advancement of the scientific method for psychological research was John B. Watson (1878–1958). Influenced by the work of Pavlov, Watson led the way in the study of behavior on the American front. He pushed for major changes in traditional psychological thinking. He called himself a *behaviorist* (Watson, 1919) and advocated a different psychological approach to understanding behavior, which he referred to as *behaviorism* (Watson, 1925). Learning, according to Watson, could explain most behaviors.

Like Pavlov, Watson conducted experiments using the principles of classical conditioning. In a famous study with an 11-month-old baby named Albert, Watson and Rayner (1920) paired a startling loud noise with the touching of a white rat. While Albert was playing with the rat, the noise was sounded each time he touched the rat. After only seven pairings, Albert, who was startled by the loud noise (unconditioned stimulus), was conditioned also to fear the white rat (a previously neutral stimulus). Even without the loud noise, Albert would cry when he was presented with the white rat. The rat had become a conditioned stimulus that elicited the conditioned response of fear.

Watson urged the psychological establishment to study overt behavior (behavior that is observable) rather than mental phenomena that could not be directly observed (e.g., emotions, feelings, thoughts, instinct). In his *Psychology from the Standpoint of a Behaviorist,* Watson criticized psychologists for their use of subjective and unproven interventions and the lack of a scientific methodology as modeled by Pavlov. Although Watson (1924), by his own admission, went "beyond my facts" (p. 104) and extended his research findings on conditioning and learning to explain all behavior, he nevertheless set the stage for a new psychology.

## Operant Conditioning

An *operant* is a behavior or response that is controlled or at least influenced by events within the environment (Skinner, 1974). For example, as a result of environmental influences, a child may learn to say please when asking for assistance.

Students learning to talk quietly when visiting their school library is also an example of operant behavior. It is important to differentiate operant behavior from the previously described respondent behaviors, such as blinking in response to a bright light, which are involuntary or reflexive.

*Operant conditioning* refers to the relationship between overt events in the environment and changes in specific target behaviors. These events are classified as either antecedents or consequences. *Antecedents* are events in the environment that precede a target behavior or operant. For example, when John hits Mike after Mike takes a toy from John, the antecedent for hitting is the action of Mike taking a toy away from John. An observant teacher could easily identify the antecedent to John hitting Mike. However, the relationship between an antecedent and a behavior may not be so obvious or direct. For example, when a child comes to school hungry and attends poorly to the teacher, hunger is an indirect antecedent to the poor attention. Unless a teacher were told that the child was hungry, he or she may not be able to identify hunger as the antecedent to the child's poor behavior in the classroom (See functional behavioral assessment in Chapter 6).

A *consequence* refers to events in the environment that occur *after* a target behavior or response. For example, when a teacher pays attention to a child for disruptive classroom behavior (i.e., talking out, making noise), the attention serves as a consequence for the disruptive behavior. This relationship is explained by Donnellan et al. (1988): "A consequence is defined as an environmental stimulus or event that contingently follows the occurrence of a particular response and, as a result of that contingent relationship, strengthens or weakens the future occurrence of that response" (p. 20).

In operant conditioning, the consequence is identified as a *reinforcer* if the preceding behavior increases or is maintained at a current rate, duration, or intensity. The consequence is identified as a *punisher* if the preceding behavior decreases in rate, duration, or intensity. This relationship among antecedents, behaviors, and consequences serves as the foundation for operant conditioning as well as for most applications employed in applied behavior analysis. According to behaviorists, when this relationship is understood, the manipulation of antecedents and consequences may be used to teach new skills and modify current behaviors.

Operant conditioning also has its roots in animal research. Edward L. Thorndike (1874–1949) was one of the first researchers to apply basic operant conditioning principles and study the relationship between animal behavior (responses) and environmental conditions, especially the relationship between behavior and consequences. In his *law of effect*, Thorndike (1905) talked about the relationship between acts that produced "satisfaction" and the likelihood of those acts (behavior) to recur (p. 203). In his *law of exercise*, Thorndike (1911) also outlined how behaviors became associated with specific situations. The study of these associations between responses and consequences and between responses and situations is sometimes referred to as *associationism*. Thorndike's work provided a solid foundation for future research on positive reinforcement (*law of effect*) and stimulus control (*law of exercise*).

Thorndike (1911) demonstrated that the provision of reinforcement as a consequence increased the rate of learning. In his famous cat experiments, Thorndike used food to reinforce cats when they learned how to remove a barrier and escape from a box. After repeated trials, he noted the time it took the cat to escape from the box to get to the food decreased.

Thorndike's research on reinforcement influenced the work of B. F. Skinner (1904–1990), whose name has become synonymous with operant conditioning and behavior modification. Skinner (1938) also conducted many of his early studies using laboratory animals such as rats and pigeons. He expanded on Thorndike's research on the relationships between various consequences and behavior. Skinner also helped clarify the differences between operant conditioning and Pavlov's classical conditioning (Kazdin, 1989): "The consequences which shape and maintain the behavior called an operant . . . have become part of the history of the organism. To alter a probability is not to elicit a response, as in a reflex" (Skinner, 1974, pp. 57–58).

Skinner (1974) described the concept of operant conditioning and the relationship between behavior and consequences as "simple enough":

> When a bit of behavior has the kind of consequence called reinforcing, it is more likely to occur again. A positive reinforcer strengthens any behavior that produces it: a glass of water is positively reinforcing when we are thirsty, and if we draw and drink a glass of water, we are more likely to do so again on similar occasions. (p. 51)

Skinner is also noted for expanding his laboratory research to the promotion of operant conditioning as a method for improving societal conditions. His book *Walden Two* (1948) outlines how these principles could be used to develop a utopian society. His next book, *Science and Human Behavior* (1953), promotes the application of operant conditioning in education, government, law, and religion.

Skinner (1953) stated that behaviorists needed to be more concerned with the *description* of behavior, and the antecedents and consequences related to behavior, rather than the explanation of behavior. Also, Skinner emphasized the importance of the current situation regarding a specific behavior rather than the long-term history of the behavior problem. For example, Skinner was more interested in teaching a child to sit in his seat within a classroom environment (by reinforcing the child for sitting) than trying to explain or understand *why* the child frequently ran around the classroom.

Skinner did not totally reject the philosophy of cognitive psychology or, as he called it, "the world within the skin" (1974, p. 24). He did, however, seem to grow wary of the minimal progress made in understanding behavior under the traditional principles of cognitive psychology: "Behaviorism, on the other hand, has moved forward" (1974, p. 36). Operant conditioning clearly emphasizes the study of observable, overt behaviors that can be measured and studied by methods of direct observation (see Chapters 2, 3, 4, and 6).

Tawney and Gast (1984) list Skinner's contributions as follows:

- Discovery of operant conditioning
- Demonstration of how reinforcement contingencies can change the rate of behaviors

B. F. Skinner
(1904–1990)

- Promotion of the use of valid and reliable methods of behavioral observation and research of single organisms
- Establishment of strategies for the experimental analysis of behavior
- Promotion of the study of observable behavior (p. 14)

The work of Pavlov, Skinner, Thorndike, and Watson represented a major shift from the work of Sigmund Freud (1856–1939) and others who promoted a more traditional psychoanalytic approach. While the behavioral approach focuses on overt behaviors and environmental events related to those behaviors, the psychoanalytic approach focuses on psychological forces such as drives, impulses, needs, motives, conflicts, and personality traits existing within the individual. Whereas the behavioral approach views inappropriate behavior as conditioned or learned, the psychoanalytic approach views inappropriate behavior primarily as the result of some maladaptive psychological process or some underlying defect in personality. In other words, the source of the child's inappropriate behavior exists within the child.

Dissatisfaction with the psychoanalytic approach has revolved around several issues. First, assessment procedures commonly used in the psychoanalytic approach remove the child from the situation in which inappropriate behaviors occur. The psychiatrist or psychologist preparing the assessment may never observe the child within the environment where the problem behaviors occur. Direct observations are usually limited to behaviors observed within the professional's office. Problem behaviors exhibited within the child's everyday life situations and environments may not even occur within the confines of the professional's office. For example, Brown (1990) found that regardless of their behavior outside the clinic, 85% of children behaved appropriately in the clinic. Frequently, the professional's understanding of the inappropriate behavior is limited to a qualitative description of the behavior provided by the child's teachers and/or parents.

Second, the identification of underlying psychological causes of behavior yields little information that can be used in the development of an intervention plan. For example, if a psychologist identifies a specific personality trait as the cause of inappropriate behavior exhibited within the classroom, this information does not help the child's teacher establish a program to decrease the occurrence of the inappropriate behavior within the classroom. In fact, there is usually limited communication between therapists and teachers.

Third, the generalization of therapy or treatment (e.g., psychotherapy or psychoanalysis) effects to functional environments such as the home or classroom has been disappointing. Rimm and Masters (1974) state that psychoanalysis and related schools of therapy have failed to provide hard data to support their effectiveness. Kazdin (1988, 1989) found that while more than 200 forms of psychotherapy have been identified for children and adolescents, the effectiveness of many of these treatments lacks significant empirical support, and they remain virtually unknown. Table 1.1 provides an outline of differences between the psychoanalytic and behavioral approaches.

**TABLE 1.1 • Psychoanalytic Versus Behavioral Approach**

| Variable | Psychoanalytic Approach | Behavioral Approach |
|---|---|---|
| Behavioral focus | Covert behaviors such as drives, impulses, and motives | Overt behaviors such as walking and talking |
| View of inappropriate behavior | Maladaptive psychological process or underlying defect in personality | Conditioned or learned |
| Assessment approach | Conducted by psychiatrist or psychologist outside the environment where behavior occurs; limited direct observations | Direct observation of child's behavior within natural environments |
| Concern for environmental influences | Low | High |
| Concern for psychological influences | High | Low |
| Empirical support | Low | High |
| Direct application for teachers and parents | Low | High |

## Social Learning Theory

Bandura (1977) states that "behavior, other personal factors, and environmental factors all operate as interlocking determinants of each other":

> Personal and environmental factors do not function as independent determinants, rather they determine each other. Nor can "persons" be considered causes independent of their behavior. It is largely through their actions that people produce the environmental conditions that affect their behavior in a reciprocal fashion. (p. 9)

Bandura (1977) refers to this integrated approach as a process of *reciprocal determinism*. According to Bandura, the world and a person's behavior cause each other (Boeree, 1998).

Bandura also stresses the importance of modeling on the acquisition of behavior. According to Bandura (1977), an individual observes a behavior, cognitively retains the information observed, and performs the modeled behavior. These three steps were labeled attention, retention, and reproduction (Boeree, 1998). This performance is then regulated by reinforcement and motivational processes (e.g., the integration of environmental and cognitive influences on behavior). For example, Bandura (1969) found that young children imitated aggressive behavior viewed during a film. Bandura (1977) warns about the influential source of social learning provided by the developing mass media, especially television and films: "The mass media play an influential role in shaping behavior and social attitudes. With increasing use of symbolic modeling, parents, teachers, and other traditional role models may occupy less prominent roles in social learning" (p. 39).

Kazdin (1989) states that the development of social learning theory was an attempt to integrate the "aspects of different learning paradigms and to take cognitive processes into account" (pp. 21–22).

The student of social learning theory strives to understand how behavior is influenced by classical and operant conditioning principles, along with the influences of the child's social and cognitive development. Human behavior, according to social learning theory, is much too complex to understand without this integrated approach.

In a text titled *Self-Efficacy: The Exercise of Control,* Bandura (1997) published a scholarly review of his own research on social learning theory, as well as the work of his students and colleagues.

## Behavior Therapy

Behavior therapy may be considered an extension or a practical application of classical conditioning. While some believe that behavior modification and behavior therapy are synonymous and share the same principles and methods (e.g., Kanfer & Phillips, 1970), others disagree. Rimm and Masters (1974) state that while behavior modification and behavior therapy share many of the same principles, behavior modification stresses operant conditioning and behavior therapy stresses classical conditioning. Also, behavior therapy and classical conditioning have been used primarily with covert behaviors and mental illness such as anxiety and neuroses, while behavior modification and operant conditioning have been used primarily with overt behaviors that are observable and measurable, such as aggression and tantrums. Tawney and Gast (1984) state that behavior therapy "refers primarily to clinical treatment of so-called behavior disorders" (p. 10).

In 1963 H. J. Eysenck founded the first professional journal to focus on behavior therapy. Titled *Behavior Research and Therapy*, it was followed by other journals such as *Behavior Therapy* (founded by C. M. Franks in 1970) and *Behavior Therapy and Experimental Psychiatry* (founded by Joseph Wolpe in 1970).

Several treatment strategies are frequently associated with behavior therapy, including systematic desensitization, flooding, aversion therapy, covert conditioning, modeling, and biofeedback (Kazdin, 1978). A brief description of each of these follows.

### *Systematic Desensitization*

Joseph Wolpe, a South African medical doctor, used a form of classical conditioning to reduce anxiety in cats. Building on Pavlov's research, Wolpe (1958) demonstrated that the strength of anxiety-producing stimuli could be reduced when paired with non-anxiety-producing stimuli. First, Wolpe exposed cats to only a small amount of the anxiety-producing stimuli. He then exposed the cats to positive stimuli such as food. Eating food and engaging in other positive behaviors in the presence of small amounts of the anxiety-producing stimuli reduced the anxiety response. Over time, Wolpe slowly increased the amount of anxiety-producing stimuli paired with the competing positive stimuli (eating food) until the anxiety response was eliminated.

Wolpe later extended his work and developed an anxiety reduction treatment for humans called *systematic desensitization*. According to Wolpe (1958), systematic desensitization is an example of *counterconditioning* or the substitution of an inappropriate emotional response with an appropriate response. The majority of Wolpe's desensitization research focused on the substitution of anxiety. Rimm and Masters (1974) state that "Wolpe assumes that individuals learn to experience anxiety in the presence of certain stimuli through a process of classical, or Pavlovian, conditioning" (p. 76).

Using the same fundamental principles with humans, Wolpe paired relaxation with gradually increasing amounts of anxiety-producing stimuli. He taught his subjects how to become relaxed through relaxation exercises. The subjects were then encouraged to pair an imagined representation of the anxiety-producing stimuli with their relaxation skills. Wolpe systematically increased the anxiety-producing stimuli as his subjects became better able to relax in the presence of smaller amounts of the stimuli. Over time, the human subjects were able to overcome the anxiety response in the presence of the original anxiety-producing stimuli.

Today, systematic desensitization is used to reduce a variety of behaviors, including childhood phobias (King, Heyne, Gullone, & Molloy, 2001), speech anxiety (Ayres & Hopf, 2000), claustrophobia (Bernstein, 1999), and high school students' math anxiety (Zyl & Lohr, 1994).

### Flooding

Like desensitization, flooding is used to treat anxiety. Unlike desensitization, in which the anxiety-producing stimulus is presented in a hierarchical fashion, *flooding* involves the repeated presentation of the anxiety-producing stimulus at full strength until the stimulus no longer produces anxiety. In effect, the stimulus loses its ability to elicit anxiety. This technique has been effective in reducing or eliminating anxiety associated with specific social situations, test taking, specific animals (spiders and snakes), and others (Kazdin, 1978). This technique is not recommended for children.

### Aversion Therapy

*Aversion therapy* involves pairing an aversive stimulus (feeling pain, being sick, losing a job) with another stimulus (alcohol, cigarettes, drugs) in order to discourage the behavior associated with the second stimulus (drinking, smoking, taking drugs). Aversion therapy employs both classical conditioning (the pairing of an aversive stimulus with another stimulus) and operant conditioning (the use of an aversive stimulus as a consequence for a target behavior). Aversion therapy has been effective in treating alcohol abuse, cigarette smoking, overeating, and "sexual attraction toward socially censured stimuli" (Kazdin, 1978, p. 220).

However, the use of aversives to change a person's behavior, especially in operant conditioning, has been seriously questioned on both ethical and efficacy grounds. The use of aversion therapy has been discouraged by many professional organizations, current texts, and individual therapists (LaVigna & Donnellan, 1986; Meyer & Evans, 1989). We agree with this contemporary assessment of aversion therapy and hope this text will promote the use of nonaversive methods of behavior change as the intervention of first choice.

### Covert Conditioning

*Covert conditioning,* developed by Joseph R. Cautela (1972), is a covert (imagined) form of classical and operant conditioning. Those who practice covert conditioning believe that overt behavior can be changed when an individual imagines target behaviors paired with reinforcing or punishing consequences—depending on the desired outcome. For example, an individual may imagine drinking and getting sick, or the individual may imagine avoiding a drink and receiving reinforcement from others for demonstrating self-control. This procedure is used primarily with older adolescents and adults. Many questions have been raised regarding the efficacy of covert conditioning. The primary question involves the generalization of covert behavior changes to overt behavior changes. The efficacy of covert conditioning has not been clearly determined.

## Modeling

*Modeling* refers to the observation and learning of new behaviors from others. Within a therapeutic application, modeling may involve a child who is afraid of dogs watching other children play with dogs. This type of modeling application has been successfully used to "treat" other fears (e.g., snakes, heights, water) (Bandura, 1971). The classic example of modeling as a behavior therapy technique was reported by Jones (1924), who helped a young boy overcome his fear of rabbits and other furry objects. The young boy, Peter, and three other boys were placed in a room with a rabbit. After watching the other three boys play with the rabbit, Peter's anxiety about touching the rabbit was decreased, and he was soon touching the rabbit.

## Biofeedback

*Biofeedback* involves providing an individual with immediate information (visual and/or auditory) about a physiological process (e.g., heart rate, pulse rate, blood pressure, skin temperature) and the use of operant conditioning (reinforcement and/or punishment) to modify the physiological process. The goal of biofeedback is to teach individuals how to control or manipulate involuntary physiological processes.

Biofeedback has been used with adults to treat a variety of conditions to include panic disorder (Meuret, Wilhelm & Roth, 2001), poor health (Russoniello & Estes, 2001), sexual dysfunction (Araoz, 2001), and incontinence (Folkerts, 2001). With children, biofeedback has been used in the treatment of headaches and seizures (Womack, Smith, & Chen, 1988), incontinence (Duckro, Purcell, Gregory, & Schultz, 1985; Killam, Jeffries, & Varni, 1985), constipation and encopresis (Lampe, Steffen, & Banez, 2001), pain (Allen & Shriver, 1998), anxiety (Wenck & Leu, 1996), and poor academic performance (Robbins, 2000).

There is evidence that relaxation training and frequent rest breaks are equally effective in reducing anxiety and chronic pain (Cummings & Trabin, 1980). According to Cummings and Trabin (1980), the effectiveness of biofeedback is largely related to individuals' attitudes, which "affect their diligence in carrying out the practice regimen" involved in biofeedback therapy (p. 145). Middaugh (1990) adds that the most important variable regarding the efficacy of biofeedback is the selection of the right technique for the right individual.

Other questions regarding biofeedback are concerns about the generalization of clinical effects to functional environments where the stimuli for anxiety and other problems originate. In other words, are the physiological changes achieved during a biofeedback session generalized to the individual's functional environments?

## Applied Behavior Analysis

The term *applied behavior analysis* refers to the direct application of behavior change principles in nonlaboratory, everyday situations and settings. Horner

(1991) describes applied behavior analysis as "the application of behavioral principles to produce socially significant changes in behavior" (p. 607). Kazdin (1989) defines applied behavior analysis as an "extension of operant conditioning principles and methods of studying human behavior to clinical and socially important human behaviors" (p. 23). For example, using behavioral principles to improve classroom performance (on-task behaviors, number of math problems completed, use of manners, etc.) would be considered an applied use of behavior modification. The use of behavioral principles and techniques in applied settings began in the late 1950s and early 1960s (Kauffman, 1989). Early research using behavior modification strategies with people in applied settings employed persons living in institutional settings. This research included people with disability labels such as severely mentally retarded, psychotic, autistic, and emotionally disturbed. As time passed, and as the successful use of behavior change strategies became documented in the professional literature, the same techniques were also used with people who had mild disabilities and with populations who were nondisabled.

In the first issue of the *Journal of Applied Behavior Analysis* (founded by Montrose Wolf in 1968), Baer et al. (1968) outlined several basic elements of applied behavior analysis that are still applicable today. These elements included the following basic understandings or beliefs:

- While both applied and basic research ask "what controls the behavior under study," applied research looks beyond variables that are convenient for study or important to theory (p. 91).
- Behaviors should be observed and studied within their natural environments (the real world) rather than in the laboratory.
- Applied research is "eminently pragmatic;" it is interested in physical behaviors, not what an individual can be made to say or feel (p. 93).
- The real-world application of applied behavior analysis may not allow the same precise measurement possible in the laboratory, but "reliable quantification of behavior can be achieved, even in thoroughly difficult settings" (p. 93).
- Behaviors and techniques used to modify behavior should be "completely identified and described" so that a "trained reader could replicate that procedure well enough to produce the same results, given only a reading of the description" (p. 95).
- Procedures of applied behavior analysis "strive for relevance to principle" rather than "a collection of tricks" to change behaviors (p. 96, referring to the principles of behavior modification of the time).
- A behavioral technique should be judged as having an application for society (applied) when it produces a behavior change that is "large enough" to have "practical value" (p. 96).

- The generality or durability of behavioral change over time is an important concern that should "be programmed, rather than expected or lamented" (p. 97).

In a second review of the important elements of applied behavior analyses, Baer et al. (1987) restate that applied behavior analysis ought to be *applied, behavioral, analytic, technological, conceptual, effective,* and capable of appropriate *generalized outcomes* (p. 313). These qualities are consistent with the dimensions of applied behavioral analysis outlined previously and listed by the same authors some 20 years earlier (Baer et al., 1968). According to the authors, these dimensions "remain functional" (p. 314).

Table 1.2 provides an overview of the general theoretical streams of behavior management that have been outlined in this chapter. Table 1.3 presents an overview of historical researchers discussed in this chapter and their important contributions to the understanding of behavior.

## SUMMARY

Behavior management strategies include a variety of techniques used to increase appropriate behaviors, decrease inappropriate behaviors, and teach new behaviors. These active intervention approaches involve the observation, measurement, and evaluation of target behaviors and the identification of environmental antecedents and consequences that maintain target behaviors.

The basic concepts of behavior management include behavior, antecedents, consequences, stimuli, responses, reinforcement, punishment, and prompts and cues. Prompts may be natural, verbal, gestural, modeling, or physical. Behaviorists

**TABLE 1.2 • General Theoretical Streams of Behavior Management and Related Researchers**

| Theoretical Stream | Focus of Behavioral Research | Researchers |
|---|---|---|
| Classical conditioning | Relationship between stimuli and reflex responses (conditioned and unconditioned) | Pavlov, Watson |
| Operant conditioning | Relationship between overt events in the environment (antecedents and consequences) and changes in behavior | Thorndike, Skinner |
| Social learning or cognition theory | Relationship among behavior and child's social and cognitive development; integrates classical and operant learning principles | Bandura |
| Behavior therapy | Practical applications of classical conditioning used primarily with covert behaviors and mental illness | Eysenck, Wolpe, Cautela |
| Applied behavior analysis | Practical applications of operant conditioning in nonlaboratory, everyday situations and settings | Baer, Wolf, Risley, Kazdin |

**TABLE 1.3 • Historical Figures in Behavioral Research and Important Contributions**

| Researcher | Important Contributions |
| --- | --- |
| I. Pavlov (1849–1936) | A Russian physiologist and Nobel Prize winner. Considered to be the father of classical conditioning. Conducted research on animal digestion and unconditional reflexes. Conditioned a dog to produce saliva in response to a bell by pairing bell with presentation of food. Promoted the use of precise scientific methods. |
| J. B. Watson (1878–1958) | Called himself a "behaviorist." Wrote *Psychology from the Standpoint of a Behaviorist* in 1919 and *Behaviorism* in 1925. Noted for his research in classical conditioning of fear responses. Urged the psychological establishment to study overt behavior rather than mental phenomena. |
| E. L. Thorndike (1874–1949) | Applied operant conditioning to the study of animal behavior. His *law of effect* (1905) and *law of exercise* (1911) outlined his research on reinforcement and stimulus control. |
| B. F. Skinner (1904–1990) | Considered to be the father of operant conditioning. Noted for his study of rat and pigeon behavior in the "Skinner Box." Expanded on Thorndike's research on the relationship between behavior and consequences. His books *Walden Two* (1948) and *Science and Human Behavior* (1953) promoted the use of operant conditioning as a method of improving social conditions. Emphasized the study of observable, overt behaviors that could be measured. |
| J. Wolpe (1915–1997) | A South African medical doctor noted for his classical conditioning and behavior therapy research. Developed an anxiety reduction treatment called *systematic desensitization.* |
| A. Bandura (1925–) | Noted for his research on social learning theory and the use of modeling to teach behavior. Promoted an integrated approach in which personal and environmental factors operate as interlocking determinants of each other. Warned of the social influence of the mass media. |

believe that most behaviors are learned, behaviors are stimulus-specific, and behaviors can be taught and modified. Behavioral interventions focus on individualized programming, interventions for the here and now, and goals that are specific and clearly defined.

The primary differences between the behavioral and psychoanalytic approaches include the focus on overt rather than covert behaviors, a different understanding of inappropriate behavior, a different approach to assessment, and a different understanding of the importance of environmental and psychological influences on behavior. The behavioral approach provides teachers and parents with direct applications for classroom and home settings.

Many myths and misconceptions exist concerning behavior management techniques. These have developed over a long history of abusive interventions with a focus on punishment. The perception of punishment as the primary strategy of behavior management has led to negative reactions, even among professionals. Others believe that changing another person's behavior is coercive, the use of reinforcement is a form of bribery, and children should work for intrinsic, not extrinsic, reinforcers. Current behavioral interventions, however, stress the reinforcement of appropriate behavior and focus less on the modification of inappropriate behavior directly.

Classical conditioning refers to the relationship between various environmental stimuli and reflex responses. Classical conditioning was initially promoted by Pavlov, who demonstrated that he could condition a response (salivation) in a dog at the sound of a bell (conditioned stimulus). Today, our understanding of learning has expanded beyond the simple relationship of conditioned and unconditioned stimuli. However, the work of Pavlov, Watson (1919), and others has provided a firm foundation for many current intervention strategies.

Operant conditioning describes the relationship between environmental events and behavior. Antecedent events occur prior to the target behavior. Consequent events occur after a target behavior. A consequent event is considered a reinforcer if the preceding behavior increases or is maintained. A consequent event is defined as a punisher if the preceding behavior decreases in rate, duration, or intensity. Operant conditioning has its roots in the animal research conducted by Thorndike (1905, 1911) and Skinner (1938, 1953). Thorndike demonstrated the relationship between reinforcement and rates of learning. Skinner, whose name is synonymous with operant conditioning and behavior modification, helped clarify the differences between operant conditioning and classical conditioning. He encouraged researchers to study observable behavior and promoted the use of valid and reliable scientific methods of behavioral research.

Behavior therapy is considered a modern, practical application of classical conditioning involving several treatment strategies. These strategies include systematic desensitization, flooding, aversion therapy, covert conditioning, modeling, and biofeedback. Wolpe (1958) used systematic desensitization as an anxiety-reducing procedure.

Social learning theory expands the behavioral model and stresses the interdependence and integration of internal variables (thoughts and feelings) with environmental factors. The role of modeling, for example, was researched by Bandura (1977) as a significant learning tool.

Applied behavior analysis expanded laboratory principles of operant conditioning to everyday situations and settings. Baer et al. (1968, 1987) state that applied behavior analysis ought to be applied, behavioral, analytic, technological, conceptual, effective, and capable of generalized outcomes.

## DISCUSSION QUESTIONS

1. Discuss the basic concepts of behavior and behavior management.
2. List and give examples of the different types of prompts and cues that may be used as antecedent stimuli to teach new behaviors.
3. What is behaviorism? Discuss the basic assumptions of behavior and behavior management.

4. Discuss the relationship among antecedents, behavior, and consequences in operant conditioning. Give examples of this relationship as observed in everyday experiences.
5. What are the differences between classical and operant conditioning? Provide examples of each as observed in everyday situations.
6. Describe the primary differences between the psychoanalytic and behavioral approaches to understanding behavior.
7. Discuss and give examples of how some of the treatment strategies in behavior therapy are related to classical conditioning.
8. Discuss the treatment strategies frequently associated with behavior therapy. Could any of the treatment strategies be applied to the classroom setting and, if so, how?

## REFERENCES

Alberto, P. A., & Troutman, A. C. (1995). *Applied behavior analyses for teachers.* Upper Saddle River, NJ: Merrill/Prentice Hall.

Allen, K. D., & Shriver, M. D. (1998). Role of parent mediated pain management strategies in biofeedback treatment of childhood migraine. *Behavior Therapy, 29*(3), 477–491.

Araoz, D. Sexual hypnotherapy for couples and family counselors. *Family Journal, 9*(1), 75–82.

Ayres, J., & Hopf, T. (2000). Are reductions in CA an experimental artifact? *Communication Quarterly, 48*(1), 19–27.

Baer, D. M., Wolf, M. M., & Risley, T. R. (1968). Some current dimensions of applied behavior analysis. *Journal of Applied Behavior Analysis, 1,* 91–97.

Baer, D. M., Wolf, M. M., & Risley, T. R. (1987). Some still-current dimensions of applied behavior analysis. *Journal of Applied Behavior Analysis, 20,* 313–327.

Balsam, P. D., & Tomie, A. (1985). *Context and learning.* Hillsdale, NJ: Erlbaum.

Bandura, A. (1969). *Principles of behavior modification.* New York: Holt, Rinehart, & Winston.

Bandura, A. (1971). Psychotherapy based upon modeling principles. In A. E. Bergin & S. L. Garfield (Eds.), *Handbook of psychotherapy and behavior change: An empirical analysis* (pp. 653–708). New York: Wiley.

Bandura, A. (1977). *Social learning theory.* Upper Saddle River, NJ: Prentice Hall.

Bandura, A. (1997). *Self-efficacy: The exercise of control.* New York: Freeman Publishing.

Bell, R. Q., & Harper, L. V. (1977). *Child effects on adults.* Hillsdale, NJ: Erlbaum.

Bernstein, S. (1999). A time-saving technique for the treatment of simple phobia. *American Journal of Psychotherapy, 53*(4), 501–513.

Boeree, G. C. (1998). Albert Bandura. cgboeree@ark.ship.edu

Brown, I. D. (1990, April). *Attention deficit-hyperactivity disorder and self-control training.* Paper presented at the 68th Annual Convention of the Council for Exceptional Children, Toronto.

Casey-Black, J., & Knoblock, P. (1989). Integrating students with challenging behaviors. In R. Gaylord-Ross (Ed.), *Integration strategies for students with handicaps* (pp. 129–148). Baltimore: Brookes.

Cautela, J. R. (1972). Rationale and procedures for covert conditioning. In R. D. Rubin, H. Fensterheim, J. D. Henderson, & L. P. Ullmann (Eds.), *Advances in behavior therapy* (Vol. 4). New York: Academic Press.

Coleman, D. (1987, August 16). B. F. Skinner. *New York Times.*

Cooper, J. O., Heron, T. E., & Heward, W. L. (1987). *Applied behavior analysis.* Upper Saddle River, NJ: Merrill/Prentice Hall.

Coyne, M. L., & Hoskins, L. (1997). Improving eating behaviors in dementia using behavioral strategies. *Clinical Nursing Research, 6*(3), 275–291.

Cummings, C., & Trabin, T. E. (1980). Locus of control and patients' attitudes towards biofeedback, relaxation training and group therapy. *American Journal of Clinical Biofeedback, 3,* 144–147.

Cuvo, A. J., & Davis, P. K. (1980). Teaching community living skills to mentally retarded persons: An examination of discriminative stimuli. *Gedrag, 8,* 14–33.

Donnellan, A. M., LaVigna, G. W., Negri-Shoultz, N. N., & Fassbender, L. L. (1988). *Progress without punishment: Effective approaches for learners with behavior problems.* New York: Teachers College Press.

Duckro, P. N., Purcell, M., Gregory, J., & Schultz, K. (1985). Biofeedback for the treatment of anal incontinence in a child with ureterosigmoidostomy. *Biofeedback and Self-Regulation, 10,* 325–334.

Folkerts, D. (2001). Nonsurgical options for treating incontinence. *Nursing Home Long Term Care Management, 50*(5), 40–42.

Gelfand, D. M., & Hartmann, D. P. (1984). *Child behavior analysis and therapy.* New York: Pergamon.

Hodges, R. (2001). Encouraging high-risk student participation in tutoring and supplemental instruction. *Journal of Developmental Education, 24*(3), 2–8.

Horner, R. H. (1991). The future of applied behavior analysis for people with severe disabilities. In L. H. Meyer, C. A. Peck, & L. Brown (Eds.), *Critical issues in the lives of people with severe disabilities* (pp. 607–612). Baltimore: Brookes.

Houghton, S. (1993). Using verbal and visual prompts to control littering in high schools. *Educational Studies, 19*(4), 247–255.

Jones, M. C. (1924). A laboratory study of fear: The case of Peter. *Pedagogical Seminary and Journal of Genetic Psychology, 3,* 308–315.

Kanfer, F. H., & Phillips, J. S. (1970). *Learning foundations of behavior therapy.* New York: Wiley.

Kauffman, J. M. (1989). *Characteristics of behavior disorders of children and youth.* Upper Saddle River, NJ: Merrill/Prentice Hall.

Kazdin, A. E. (1975). *Behavior modification in applied settings.* Homewood, IL: Dorsey.

Kazdin, A. E. (1978). *History of behavior modification.* Baltimore: University Park Press.

Kazdin, A. E. (1988). *Child psychotherapy: Developing and identifying effective treatments.* Elmsford, NY: Pergamon.

Kazdin, A. E. (1989). *Behavior modification in applied settings.* Pacific Grove, CA: Brooks/Cole.

Kazdin, A. E., & Cole, P. M. (1981). Attitudes and labeling biases toward behavior modification: The effects of labels, content, and jargon. *Behavior Therapy, 12,* 56–68.

Killam, P. E., Jeffries, J. S., & Varni, J. W. (1985). Urodynamic biofeedback treatment of urinary incontinence in children with myelomeningocele. *Biofeedback and Self-Regulation, 10,* 161–172.

King, N. J., Heyne, D., Gullone, E., & Molloy, G. N. (2001). Usefulness of emotive imagery in the treatment of childhood phobias. *Counselling Psychology Quarterly, 14*(2), 95–102.

Lampe, J. B., Steffen, R. M., & Banez, G. A. (2001). Empirically supported treatments in pediatric psychology: Constipation and encopresis. *Clinical Pediatrics, 40*(8), 471–473.

LaVigna, G. W., & Donnellan, A. M. (1986). *Alternatives to punishment: Solving behavior problems with non-aversive strategies.* New York: Irvington.

Melloy, K. J. (1990). *Attitudes and behavior of non-disabled elementary-aged children toward their peers with disabilities in integrated settings: An examination of the effects of treatment on quality of attitude, social status and critical social skills.* Unpublished doctoral dissertation, University of Iowa, Ames.

Meuret, A. E., Wilhelm, F. H., & Roth, W. T. (2001). Respiratory biofeedback: Assisted therapy in panic disorder. *Behavior Modification, 25*(4), 584–606.

Meyer, L. H., & Evans, I. M. (1989). *Nonaversive intervention for behavior problems: A manual for home and community.* Baltimore: Brookes.

Middaugh, S. (1990). On clinical efficacy: Why biofeedback does—and does not—work. *Biofeedback and Self-Regulation, 15,* 191–208.

Morris, R. J. (1985). *Behavior modification with exceptional children.* Glenview, IL: Scott, Foresman.

Rescorla, R. A. (1988). Pavlovian conditioning: It's not what you think it is. *American Psychologist, 43,* 151–160.

Rimm, D. C., & Masters, J. C. (1974). *Behavior therapy: Techniques and empirical findings.* New York: Academic Press.

Robbins, J. (2000, September 26). Some see hope in biofeedback for attention disorder. *New York Times,* 150(51523), p. F7.

Russoniello, C. V., & Estes, C. A. (2001). Biofeedback: Helping people control their health. *Parks and Recreation, 36*(12), 24–30.

Saunders, J. T., & Reppucci, N. D. (1978). The social identity of behavior modification. In M. Hersen, R. Eisler, & P. Miller (Eds.), *Progress in behavior modification* (Vol. 6). New York: Academic Press.

Skinner, B. F. (1938). *The behavior of organisms: An experimental analysis.* New York: Appleton-Century.

Skinner, B. F. (1948). *Walden two.* New York: Macmillan.

Skinner, B. F. (1953). *Science and human behavior.* New York: Macmillan.

Skinner, B. F. (1974). *About behaviorism.* New York: Knopf.

Snell, M. E., & Zirpoli, T. J. (1987). Intervention strategies. In M. E. Snell (Ed.), *Systematic instruction of persons with handicaps* (pp. 110–149). Upper Saddle River, NJ: Merrill/Prentice Hall.

Tawney, J. W., & Gast, D. L. (1984). *Single subject research in special education.* Upper Saddle River, NJ: Merrill/Prentice Hall.

Thorndike, E. L. (1905). *The elements of psychology.* New York: Seiler.

Thorndike, E. L. (1911). *Animal intelligence: Experimental studies.* New York: Macmillan.

Watson, J. B. (1919). *Psychology from the standpoint of a behaviorist.* Philadelphia: Lippincott.

Watson, J. B. (1924). *Psychology from the standpoint of a behaviorist* (2nd. ed.). Philadelphia: Lippincott.

Watson, J. B. (1925). *Behaviorism.* New York: Norton.

Watson, J. B., & Rayner, R. (1920). Conditioned emotional reactions. *Journal of Experimental Psychology, 3,* 1–4.

Wenck, L. S., & Leu, P. W. (1996). Anxiety in children: Treatment with biofeedback training. *Journal of Clinical Psychology, 52*(4), 469–474.

Wicks-Nelson, R., & Israel, A. C. (1991). *Behavior disorders of childhood.* Upper Saddle River, NJ: Prentice Hall.

Wilson, G. T., & Evans, I. M. (1978). The therapist-client relationship in behavior therapy. In A. S. Gurman & A. M. Razin (Eds.), *The therapist's contribution to effective psychotherapy: An empirical approach.* New York: Pergamon.

Wolpe, J. (1958). *Psychotherapy by reciprocal inhibition.* Stanford, CA: Stanford University Press.

Womack, W. M., Smith, M. S., & Chen, A. C. N. (1988). Behavioral management of childhood headache: A pilot study and case history report. *Pain, 2,* 279–283.

Zirpoli, T. J. (1990). Physical abuse: Are children with disabilities at greater risk? *Intervention in School and Clinic, 26,* 6–11.

Zyl, T. V., & Lohr, J. W. (1994). An audiotaped program for reduction of high school students' math anxiety. *School Science & Mathematics, 94*(6), 310–314.

# chapter 2

# FORMAL BEHAVIORAL ASSESSMENT

*Kristine J. Melloy and Thomas J. Zirpoli*

*But I am also clear that in lecture halls, seminar rooms, field settings, labs, and even electronic classrooms—the places where most people receive most of their formal education—teachers possess the power to create conditions that can help students learn a great deal—or keep them from learning much at all. Teaching is the intentional act of creating those conditions, and good teaching requires that we understand the inner sources of both the intent and the act.*

—PALMER (1998, P. 6)

Typically when we think of behavior management, problematic behavior of children in school and other settings comes to mind. It is important for teachers and others who care for children to realize that behavior management has as much to do with promoting appropriate behavior as it does with helping children change inappropriate behavior. It is also important to realize that teachers have a lot to do with how children behave in school. It is our job to listen to what students say and watch what they do. Our students tell us, by their behavior, exactly what their strengths are and what they need; the mystery and challenge for us is to figure it all out so that we can create classrooms that are conducive to maximum opportunities for teaching and learning.

This chapter is the first of five chapters dedicated to assisting educators in completing and understanding behavioral assessment in order to (a) identify student strengths and needs related to their behavior, (b) identify environmental antecedents and consequences maintaining student behavior, (c) evaluate the relationship between classroom variables (including curriculum) and student behavior, (d) plan educational interventions directed at helping students maintain and/or change their social and academic related behaviors, (e) document baseline and intervention data via single subject design, and (f) evaluate the effectiveness of interventions.

In this chapter we will discuss common features of behavioral assessment. Then, we will focus on the indirect assessment strategies and techniques that are utilized in the first three steps of a seven-step model for behavioral assessment. Steps 4 through 7 will be discussed in other chapters.

Finally, for steps 1 through 3 we will offer an illustration of the methods applied in the case of a student named Rick. The scope of this text does not allow for an in-depth description of how to administer most of these methods. References are provided, however, to find out more specifics for each of the methods described.

## COMMON FEATURES OF BEHAVIORAL ASSESSMENT

Mash and Terdal (1997) suggested a "prototype" view of behavioral assessment. According to their *behavioral assessment prototype,* several common features exist with regard to strategies and procedures used, regardless of the child's age and behavioral characteristics. For example, although the actual data from a behavioral assessment completed for a child who demonstrates withdrawn and anxious behavior characteristics may look very different from a child who exhibits aggressive behavior, several features would be common to both *assessment protocols* (Mash & Terdal, 1997):

- Assessment should be based on "conceptualizations of personality and abnormal behavior that give greater relative emphasis to a child's thoughts, feelings, and behaviors as they occur in specific situations rather than to global underlying traits or dispositions" (Mash & Terdal, 1997, p. 10). Interest is on behaviors viewed as direct samples of the child's behavioral characteristics rather than as signs of underlying causes.

- Assessment should focus on the individual child and family rather than comparisons to a norm group. This is also true when describing and understanding the characteristics of the child and family, the context in which these characteristics are expressed, and the functional relationships between situations, behaviors, thoughts, and emotions.

- Assessment is primarily interested in discovering situational influences on behavior rather than historical experiences, except in cases where an earlier event (e.g., physical or sexual abuse) may help understand current behavior. In behavioral assessment it is important to describe the behavior and the situations in which behaviors occur (e.g., home, school, community environments).

- Behaviors may change as the result of the context in which they occur. As antecedent and consequent stimuli change, the behavioral response may change also or remain stable given the situation. For example, a group of students who consistently follow the classroom rules when their regular teacher is present may become disruptive and noncompliant when a substitute teacher visits their classroom for the day.

- The primary purpose of assessment is to obtain information that will assist in developing effective intervention strategies. Assessment data should aid in identifying and defining target behaviors and ideas for intervention, and conducting ongoing evaluation of the intervention effects. Completing assessment for any other reason is viewed as unethical and a waste of valuable time.

- During assessment a multimethod approach is employed whereby no one assessment instrument, strategy, or technique is thought to be better than another. A variety of instruments, strategies, and informants are utilized to provide information on the student and his or her family, the contexts in which behaviors occur, and the functional relationship of the student's behavior and the situation.

- Decisions about specific assessment strategies are based on empirical data available on child and family characteristics, as well as the literature on specific behavior disorders. Behavioral assessment relies on data obtained through interviews, checklists and rating scales, and behavioral observations. All of these strategies are supported in the research literature on behavioral assessment. They are considered to be reliable and valid methods for obtaining data that is useful in making decisions about students and their behavior.

# ASSESSMENT FOR INTERVENTION PLANNING: A SEVEN-STEP MODEL

With these common features in mind, the first three steps of a seven-step model for behavioral assessment will be described in detail. The seven steps are outlined in Figure 2.1. After each step is discussed, suggestions for data collection strategies that complement that step will be provided. In addition, examples will be provided to demonstrate application of the behavioral assessment model in school settings.

## Step 1: Decide If a Problem Exists

Teachers and others decide if a problem exists when they notice that a student or students demonstrate behaviors that potentially cause problems for themselves or others. This step is commonly referred to as "screening" for behavior problems as defined in IDEA 1997 (cited in Turnbull, Turnbull, Shank, & Leal, 1999; Yell, 1998). Given, however, that all children have potential for benefiting from behavior management, it is suggested that behavioral assessment, and in particular step 1 of the process, be used in a broader sense to help teachers in their work with students.

Characteristics of some common behavior problems are described in Chapter 10 of this text. Briefly, however, behavior problems usually are described by teachers in behavior categories or response classes including on/off task, aggressiveness, disruptiveness, noncompliance, depression, and withdrawn behavior. Peers and others may describe behavior problems using terms such as "he's mean," "she is a bully," "he is shy," or "she doesn't do her work." It is important to note that in step 1, teachers also notice students who do not demonstrate problem behavior.

| Step 1 | Decide if a problem exists. |
|--------|------------------------------|
| Step 2 | Determine if intervention is warranted. |
| Step 3 | Determine if medical and/or psychological reasons exist that contribute to the problem behavior. |
| Step 4 | Perform a functional assessment. |
| Step 5 | Determine if the problem is the result of a skill or performance deficit. |
| Step 6 | Develop behavior management intervention. |
| Step 7 | Conduct ongoing evaluation. |

**FIGURE 2.1.** Behavioral assessment 7-step model

This is crucial when determining the social validity of target behaviors for intervention. In other words, if the majority of the children engage in the behavior (even if it is an aggravating behavior), is it justifiable to expect change in the behavior for one or a few children?

Typically, teachers and others will be able to determine if a problem exists by collecting behavioral assessment data using the following strategies and methods: (a) checklists and rating scales; (b) teacher rankings; (c) sociometric techniques; (d) interviews with parents, target students, and others who know the child; and (e) behavioral observations: anecdotal reports. Checklists, rating scales, teacher rankings, sociometric techniques, and interview methods are described in this chapter. Anecdotal reporting as a form of naturalistic behavioral observation will be described in Chapters 3, 5, and 6. Charting behavioral observations using single subject designs will be described in Chapter 4.

Teachers and parents are often the most knowledgeable when it comes to considering children's behavior. Use of assessment methods that are designed to identify problems early in their development will potentially prevent the problem from getting worse. Early intervention often ameliorates the problem and places students at risk for long-term problems with their behavior in a much more favorable place. When most people hear the term "early intervention," they usually think that it refers to a student's age. However, many behavior problems can develop at any age, so we encourage teachers to also think of early intervention as "early in the problem."

Early identification of children who experience *externalizing* (e.g., aggressive, acting out, oppositional) and/or *internalizing* (e.g., social withdrawal, anxiousness, fears) *behavior problems* is important. The literature stated that these children were at risk for developing ongoing problems into adulthood (Elksnin & Elksnin, 1998; Goleman, 1990; Hops, Finch, & McConnell, 1985; Kazdin & Frame, 1983). Children who demonstrated externalizing behavior problems were more likely to drop out of school, become delinquent, and/or need mental health services. Academic underachievement and peer rejection have been some problems reported in children who demonstrated internalizing behavior problems. Screening of all children in elementary school is necessary for identifying special needs in terms of *behavioral deficits* or *excesses*. Early identification and intervention is likely to result in positive educational and social outcomes for most children.

Due to the nature of step 1, the data collection procedures are brief and usually administered to large groups of students or individuals in the quickest manner possible. For example, some measures are administered in a few minutes to individual students who have been brought into a school or other community-based setting during *child find* as part of a screening process. The term *child find* refers to the mandate in IDEA 97 to locate and identify all children with disabilities (See Chapter 11 for a full discussion on legal issues). Those children who perform poorly on screening measures designed to assess behavioral disorders may be considered "at risk" for future problems in behavior or demonstrate characteristics of specific behavior disorders. Several screening procedures are available for determining if a problem exists (Kauffman, 1997; Kerr & Nelson, 1998).

# Data Collection Methods for Step 1

## Rating Scales and Teacher Ranking

These types of assessment instruments are usually norm-referenced measures. Rating scales require that the person completing the instrument know the child well enough to make qualitative judgments about his or her behavior. Typically, the person is given a list of behaviors and asked to rate the child using a Likert-type scale to indicate the degree to which the child engages in the behavior or does not engage in the behavior (Mash & Terdal, 1997). A Likert scale (Likert, 1932) is an evaluative scale. Persons are asked to respond to each item in terms of a varied-point scale defined by labels such as "agree strongly," "agree," "undecided," "disagree," and "disagree strongly" (Melloy, 1990). Rating scales are designed to be completed in about 10 to 15 minutes for an individual child. They are usually scored and interpreted by a person other than the one completing the instrument (e.g., school psychologist).

Teacher rankings require that the teacher rank order the students in his or her class based on criteria established by the test author (Melloy, Davis, Wehby, Murry, & Leiber, 1998). Rank ordering activities should not take more than about 10 minutes per class. This information is then used to decide if further assessment is needed for the children who have been rank ordered.

*Multimethod screening instruments.* The *Systematic Screening for Behavior Disorders* (SSBD) (Walker & Severson, 1999) and the *Early Screening Project* (ESP) (Walker, Severson, & Feil, 1995) are two examples of multimethod assessment procedures that can be used to collect data for step 1. The SSBD and the ESP include teacher rating and teacher ranking instruments. To date, these are the only comprehensive screening systems that have been developed and researched adequately to be used in screening for behavior problems and emotional/behavioral disorders. The SSBD and the ESP utilize multiple assessment methods to identify elementary-aged children in grades 1 through 5 and preschool children ages 3 to 5 years old who demonstrate behavioral problems. The SSBD and the ESP have the potential to assist teachers in systematically and objectively identifying children who demonstrate externalized and/or internalized behavior problems. In the past, children with behavior problems were typically referred by their teachers based mainly on subjective decisions. Also, there has been a tendency to refer children who demonstrated externalized behavior problems (e.g., disruptive, aggressive, noncompliant, out of seat) and less often children who showed internalized behavior problems (e.g., excessive shyness, severe withdrawal, poor peer interactions) (Walker, Severson, Stiller, Williams, Haring, Shinn, & Todis, 1988).

"The SSBD is a three-stage, multiple gating screening system designed for the standardized screening and identification of students in grades 1 to 5 who may be at risk for their externalizing or internalizing behavior disorders" (Walker & Severson, 1999, p. 33). During the first stage of screening, teachers are asked to rank order every child in their class based on behavioral criteria for externalized and internalized behavior problems or disorders. Children who are ranked at the top of the list are further assessed by a teacher rating of behavior in stage 2 of the assessment process.

Finally, in stage 3, children who meet criteria for behavior disorders in stage 2 are observed in classroom and playground settings to determine if their academic and social behavior deviates significantly from the behavior of their peers. Children identified in each stage may warrant further assessment, pre-referral interventions, and/or referral to a *child study team.* Cheney and Barringer (1994) reported the effective use of the SSBD to assist in identifying students who could be successful in inclusive school settings. The ESP is also a multiple gating system, which includes procedures that are very similar to the SSBD.

Research on the reliability and validity of the SSBD and ESP indicated that these screening processes showed promise for screening all preschool and elementary-age children for purposes of identifying those at risk of developing or maintaining behavior problems and/or disorders (Walker & Severson, 1992 & 1995; Walker, Severson, & Feil, 1995).

### Self-ratings

A number of *self-rating instruments,* or *self-reports,* are available to assist in collecting data to determine if a problem exists. Students complete self-ratings, which typically include questions about behaviors and how the child feels he or she matches the description. The following are examples of questions from a self-rating on social skills: "Is it easy for me to listen to someone who is talking to me?" and "Do I tell others without getting mad or yelling when they have caused a problem for me?" (McGinnis & Goldstein, 1997, p. 294). Self-ratings have been designed to measure a variety of constructs including social skills, locus of control, level of self-control, aggression, anxiety, and depression (Bellack & Hersen, 1998; Martin, 1988; Mash & Terdal, 1997).

### Sociometric Techniques

Sociometric measures are most useful to assess individuals in social settings such as classrooms to determine which children appear to be popular, rejected, neglected, isolated, or accepted by the other children (Kauffman, 1997; Melloy et al., 1998). These techniques provide general information on acceptance, desirability, and social status of children. Peer nomination and peer rating strategies are useful in determining friendship (or lack of friendship) among peers (Mash & Terdal, 1997). Sociometric techniques have been most widely used to screen children who may benefit from social skills training in order to improve acceptance among peers (Sugai & Lewis, 1996). With regard to their usefulness in helping to determine if a problem behavior exists, sociometric techniques assist the teacher in identifying children who may be perceived as having behavior problems related to peer relationships. The most popular sociometric techniques are *peer nomination* and *peer rating* (McConnell & Odom, 1987). *Peer evaluation* techniques are similar to sociometric techniques and will also be discussed.

**Peer nomination.** The peer nomination method has become the most commonly applied sociometric assessment (McConnell & Odom, 1986). It was developed by

Moreno (1934) and requires children to select one or more classmates with whom they would or would not like to engage in an activity (e.g., play with, hang out with, work with). Generally, social status scores are derived by adding the numbers of choices a child receives. Scores derived from such measures indicate levels of popularity or acceptance and are designed to identify "stars" in a class (those frequently nominated on positive criteria), the "isolates" (those not nominated frequently on positive criteria), and the "rejectees" (those frequently nominated on negative criteria) (Ollendick & Hersen, 1984, p. 127).

Peery (1979) used the two dimensions of social impact and social preference to describe social status. His classification categories included:

- Popular   High social impact, positive social preference
- Rejected   High social impact, negative social preference
- Isolate   Low social impact, negative social preference
- Amiable   Low social impact, positive social preference

Coie, Dodge, and Coppotelli (1982) described a "controversial" category in addition to Peery's (1979) classifications. According to Coie and his colleagues, "controversial" students were identified by their peers as children who "exhibited a high measure of social impact and high frequencies of both positive and negative nominations" (1982, p. 557). McConnell and Odom (1986) pointed out that inclusion of negative criteria in sociometric assessment is a controversial aspect. They remarked, however, that the efficiency of peer nomination assessments decreased markedly when negative nominations were not used (McConnell & Odom, 1986). Also, inclusion of negative nominations allows for identification of rejected children in a class—often prime candidates for social skills training and teaching replacement behaviors. Mrs. Lake, described in Classroom Application 2.1, wanted to screen children who might benefit from social skills training. A sociogram from one of the third-grade classes in Mrs. Lake's school is depicted in Figure 2.2.

*Peer rating.* The peer rating method of sociometric assessment involves the use of a Likert-type rating scale. Children are asked to rate each class member along a continuum of attraction-rejection (McConnell & Odom, 1986; Sugai & Lewis, 1996).

Typically, raters are given a class roster and asked to rate each classmate according to how much they like or dislike to play with or work with the child. Individual scores for peer ratings are generally calculated as the sum of numerical ratings provided by all other members of the group (McConnell & Odom, 1986). For example, a peer rating scale was administered to measure social status in a study conducted with 350 elementary-age children (Melloy, 1990). The format of the peer rating instrument included a roster of each classroom and a four-point Likert-type scale following each child's name. Points on the continuum indicated "like to play with a lot," "just kind of like to play with," "do not like to play with," and "I don't know this person." Ratings were assigned a weighted value (i.e., like to . . . a lot = 3; just kind of . . . play with = 2; does not . . . play with = 1; and don't know . . . person = 0). The sum of the ratings was calculated and

**FIGURE 2.2.** Sociogram resulting from a peer nomination process administered in a third-grade class

| Child's Name | Percentage of classmates who indicated a positive choice for question: | | |
|---|---|---|---|
| | 1 | 2 | 3 |
| Connor | 45 | 30 | 0 |
| Elizabeth | 0 | 5 | 2* |
| Ryan | 90 | 95 | 0 |
| Trevor | 79 | 87 | 0 |
| Ellie | 50 | 45 | 0 |
| Nancy | 39 | 56 | 0 |
| Heather | 76 | 67 | 0 |
| Jacob | 67 | 85 | 0 |
| Eric | 98 | 96 | 0 |
| George | 10 | 11 | 1** |
| Jennifer | 0 | 0 | 50* |
| Timothy | 1 | 3 | 5* |
| Sheryl | 0 | 15 | 30* |

*Indicates children who were "rejected"
**Indicates children who were "neglected"/"isolated"

yielded an overall social status score. Scores were ranked to reveal the relative social standing of each child in the class as suggested by McConnell and Odom (1986). An example of the peer rating instrument is presented in Figure 2.3.

Peer ratings tend to result in higher reliability and stability coefficients when compared to peer nominations (McConnell & Odom, 1986). The major advantages for using the peer rating technique compared to peer nomination include: (a) every child in the class is rated, (b) higher test-retest reliability results over time, and (c) this technique is more sensitive to subtle changes in social status depending on criteria used (McConnell & Odom, 1986). A disadvantage of the peer rating method is that children, especially younger ones, may tend to rate most classmates in the middle of the scale or to give everyone in the class the same rating (McConnell & Odom, 1986).

According to Foster, Inderbitzen, and Nangle (1993), peer ratings do not distinguish children who are rejected, neglected, or controversial. They argued that this impacted intervention decisions. Foster et al. (1993) reported that peer nominations may be more useful for differentiating types of acceptance among children's peers. According to Landau (cited in Mash & Terdal, 1997, p. 352) "peer ratings of children's social behavior typically provide the best predictions of sociometric status and social behavior observations." Sociometric techniques were effective in screening individuals in need of social skills training to improve social competence (Sheridan, 1997).

## Classroom Application 2.1

## Using a Peer Nomination Sociometric Technique

Mrs. Lake, the principal of an elementary school, met with the curriculum committee to discuss the need for social skills training for some of the children in grades 1 through 3. The committee decided that they would screen candidates for training using a peer nomination sociometric technique. Parents of the children were informed of this decision and were given the option for their child not to participate. Teachers in the first, second, and third grades were given a list of three questions to ask of the children in their classes. The questions were:

- Who is someone in this class that you like to work with on a math problem?
- Who is someone in this class that you like to play with at recess?
- Who is someone in this class that you do not like to work with?

Once the peer nomination had been administered in each classroom, the teachers completed a sociogram and were able to obtain preliminary information about children in the class who were popular, rejected, neglected/isolated, and amiable (using Peery [1979] definitions). Children who were identified as being neglected or isolated in each classroom were considered at risk for needing training in social skills. According to Sheridan (1997), children who received few or no positive nominations would be considered as "neglected," and those receiving no positive nominations would be "rejected." Students considered to be "controversial" received nominations in each category. Further assessment was completed on these children before decisions were made about intervention.

*Peer evaluation.* The peer evaluation method is often referred to as a measure of social status, although it differs from sociometric measures. Peer evaluation techniques require children to judge their peers' behavior, whereas sociometric methods require children to make judgments about the number and identity of their friends (Mash & Terdal, 1997). Peer assessment procedures are often combined with sociometric measures to provide information about a child's relationships with peers (McConnell & Odom, 1986). They have been used to examine variables that contribute to or affect sociometric status (McConnell & Odom, 1986). In a peer evaluation children are asked to nominate or rate classmates according to a variety of behavioral criteria. Generally, children are given descriptions of children and the child "guesses" who in the class best fits the description. The number of nominations for positive and negative measures are computed to yield a qualitative score (i.e., positive or negative).

| | Peer Rating | | | |
|---|---|---|---|---|

Name _____ Grade _____ Date _____

Listen as each name on this list is read. Circle the number next to each child's name that matches the description of how much you would like to play with him or her.

| | Rating | | | |
|---|---|---|---|---|
| Student names | I like to play with this person a lot. | I just kind of like to play with this person. | I don't like to play with this person. | I don't know this person. |
| Ashley | 1 | 2 | 3 | 4 |
| Carissa | 1 | 2 | 3 | 4 |
| Kelli | 1 | 2 | 3 | 4 |
| Matthew | 1 | 2 | 3 | 4 |
| Jaclyn | 1 | 2 | 3 | 4 |
| Allison | 1 | 2 | 3 | 4 |
| Tyler | 1 | 2 | 3 | 4 |
| Zachary | 1 | 2 | 3 | 4 |
| Alex | 1 | 2 | 3 | 4 |
| Kacie | 1 | 2 | 3 | 4 |
| Clift | 1 | 2 | 3 | 4 |
| Clint | 1 | 2 | 3 | 4 |
| Colen | 1 | 2 | 3 | 4 |
| Mackenzie | 1 | 2 | 3 | 4 |
| Theresa | 1 | 2 | 3 | 4 |

**FIGURE 2.3.** Peer rating questionnaire

*Source:* From *Attitudes and Behavior of Non-Disabled Elementary-Aged Children toward Their Peers with Disabilities in Integrated Settings: An Examination of the Effects of Treatment on Quality of Attitude, Social Status and Critical Social Skills,* by K. J. Melloy, 1990, doctoral dissertation, University of Iowa, Iowa City. Reprinted by permission.

Coie et al. (1982) used peer evaluation to measure types of behavior that contributed to the social status of children in regular classrooms. They found that behaviors that seemed to correlate with social preference were cooperativeness, supportiveness, and physical attractiveness. Social preference was negatively related to disruptiveness and aggression.

Another peer evaluation technique that has been used to measure social competence is the *behavioral template approach* (Bem & Fender, 1978; Hoier & Cone, 1987; Melloy, 1990; Strain, Odom, & McConnell, 1984). This procedure requires children identified as rejected through sociometric techniques to identify *hopeful playmates* (i.e., the rejected child nominates a peer with whom he or she would like to play but doesn't play with). These hopeful playmates are asked through formal peer evaluation to identify the types of behavior that they like about children with whom they

Students complete a peer rating as part of a behavioral assessment to identify students/peers at risk for behavior problems.

did play. Hoier and Cone (1987) developed a behavioral template using formal peer assessments consisting of 50 behavioral descriptions that the hopeful playmate sorted into "like my friend" and "not like my friend" categories. The behaviors identified in the behavioral template were compared to the behaviors observed in rejected children. Hoier and Cone suggested that discrepancies between the behavioral template and the target child's actual behavior could be used for social skills interventions. Through several studies, they concluded that this procedure could assess the social validity of the template behaviors. A Q-sort was used across 50 behavioral descriptors. Each child sorted the 50 items into two piles labeled "like my friend" and "not like my friend." This sorting process was repeated until descriptors evolved that described 10 behaviors that were very much like the friend the child had in mind. A behavioral template was generated through these interviews. These descriptors were identified as *critical social skills* needed for positive peer interactions. Discrepancies between this behavioral template and the target child's observed behavior were suggested as goals for social skills intervention (Melloy, 1990; Strain et al., 1984). The following list provides examples of the behavioral descriptors identified by Hoier and Cone (1987).

1. Tells me I did well
2. Smiles at me, laughs
3. Gives me things without being asked
4. Shares
5. Gives me hugs, kisses, pats on the back
6. Says nice things about me
7. Says things about the way I feel

8. Tells me how he/she feels
9. Agrees with me
10. Goes along with my ideas, complies
11. Gives me reason when he/she doesn't do what I say
12. Looks at me when I am talking
13. Starts games for me
14. Talks first before I do
15. Talks a lot when we are together
16. Explains games or stories to me
17. Asks for help
18. Encourages me, tells me to keep trying
19. Looks at me when she/he is talking
20. Stays close to me when we play/hang out
21. Tells jokes
22. When I decide to do something she/he goes along
23. Includes me in what he/she is doing
24. Invites me over
25. Asks questions
26. Teases
27. Tells on others, tattles
28. Blames others
29. Takes things without asking
30. Hurts or threatens to hurt others

The behavioral template approach was used in a study conducted by Melloy (1990) to determine critical social skills in four elementary schools with children who were identified as being rejected by their peers. Following identification of deficits in these critical skills among the children, intervention in the form of teaching replacement behaviors and supporting use of these behaviors took place. Intervention resulted in the rejected children becoming more competent in demonstrating critical social skills and a slight increase in interactions with their more popular peers. The procedure used to generate behavioral templates follows:

1. Interview children who are rejected by peers to identify hopeful playmates (child with whom they would like to be friends but are not).
2. Interview the hopeful playmate to determine behaviors he or she likes in friends.
3. Interview/template generation:
   a. Ask hopeful playmate to think about his or her best friends.
   b. Have the child sort the 50 behavior descriptors (Hoier & Cone, 1987) into two piles: "Like my friend" and "Not like my friend."

Child's name _____ Date_____

Grade _____ Teacher _____ School _____

Name of child who identified this child as a hopeful playmate

_____ (complete only after interview with

hopeful playmate).

Record the number of the behavior descriptor under the
categories listed below as the child sorts the descriptor cards:

| Like my friend | Not like my friend |
|---|---|
| Very much like my friend | Somewhat like my friend |

Trial 1

Trial 2

Trial 3

Final 10 behavioral descriptions:

Rank order of final 10:

1.   2.   3.   4.   5.   6.   7.   8.   9.   10.

**FIGURE 2.4.** Example of a behavior template worksheet

*Source:* From *Attitudes and Behavior of Non-Disabled Elementary-Aged Children toward Their Peers with Disabilities in Integrated Settings: An Examination of the Effects of Treatment on Quality of Attitude, Social Status and Critical Social Skills,* by K. J. Melloy, 1990, doctoral dissertation, University of Iowa, Iowa City. Reprinted by permission.

(Record the number of these behaviors on the template worksheet from Figure 2.4.)

   c. Have the child sort the items in the "like my friend" category into two piles: "very much like my friend" and "somewhat like my friend." (Record the number of responses on worksheet.)

   d. Repeat the previous step until only 10 descriptors remain in the "very much like my friend" category. (Record.)

   e. Have the child rank order the final 10 items from the "most important for your friend to do" to "least important for your friend to do."

4. The rank-ordered behaviors provide possible targets for social skills intervention.

5. Observe target children to determine deficits in skills or performance of the behavior compared to those behaviors identified in the behavior template.

6. Deficit behaviors become targets for social skills intervention.

Figure 2.4 shows a worksheet that can be used while interviewing hopeful playmates to record responses to the interviewer. An example of a completed worksheet is provided in Figure 2.5.

**FIGURE 2.5.** Example of a completed behavior template worksheet

*Source:* From *Attitudes and Behavior of Non-Disabled Elementary-Aged Children toward Their Peers with Disabilities in Integrated Settings: An Examination of the Effects of Treatment on Quality of Attitude, Social Status and Critical Social Skills,* by K. J. Melloy, 1990, doctoral dissertation, University of Iowa, Iowa City. Reprinted by permission.

---

**Behavior Template Worksheet**

Child's name <u>Joshua</u>    Date <u>9/24/03</u>

Grade 5 Teacher <u>Mr. Rogers</u> School <u>Goodhue Elementary</u>

Name of child who identified this child as a hopeful playmate <u>William</u> (complete only after interview with hopeful playmate).

Record the number of the behavior descriptor under the categories listed below as the child sorts the descriptor cards:

| **Like my friend** | **Not like my friend** |
|---|---|
| 33,5,38,48,2,16,13,10,22, 17,17,25,19,32,21,37,24,8, 11,20,9,23,12,15,4,18,1,6 | 26,50,39,46,49,42,40, 30,47,44,35,29,7,27,28, 31,3,43,45,41,36,34 |

**Very much like my friend**          **Somewhat like my friend**

**Trial 1**

6,1,18,4,15,23,8,24,21,          5,33,12,9,20,11,32,37,
13,2,25,22,17,10                 38,48,16,19

**Trial 2**

10,18,1,8,21,24,2,17,25,22       13,6,23,15,4

**Trial 3**

(ten descriptors in Trial 2)

**Final 10 behavioral descriptions:**

10,8,1,21,24,2,17,25,22,18

**Rank order of final 10:**

**1.** 24  **2.** 25  **3.** 17  **4.** 2  **5.** 8  **6.** 18  **7.** 1  **8.** 21  **9.** 10  **10.** 22

---

## Interviews with Parents, Target Students, and Others Who Know the Child

Interview data for step 1 is usually collected less formally than interview data for the other steps of behavioral assessment. For example, step 1 interviews may consist of teacher-to-teacher discussion of a student or students suspected of having problem behavior. Also, teachers generally take the opportunity to discuss student behavior with parents during phone calls and during parent teacher conferences. It is a good idea for teachers to document this information and to use it in the data collection process for step 1.

Step 1 of the behavioral assessment model allows teachers and others to determine if a problem exists related to student behavior. Behavior checklists, questionnaires, rating scales, teacher ranking, sociometric techniques, informal interviews, and behavioral observation anecdotal reports are assessment strategies that have been found helpful in collecting step 1 behavioral assessment data. Figure 2.6 depicts an example of the results of completed assessment strategies for step 1 for a fifth-grade child named Rick.

The results of the completed step 1 assessment strategies for Rick indicated that he did in fact demonstrate problem behavior. His teacher and others decided that they should continue the assessment process with "Step 2: Determine If Intervention Is Warranted" to determine if his problem behavior was serious enough to require the development of an individual behavior management plan. A description of step 2 in the behavioral assessment model follows.

## Step 2: Determine If Intervention Is Warranted

Once teachers and others have completed step 1 of the behavioral assessment model, they have a "rough sketch" of children and the manner in which their behavior is perceived by themselves and significant others. Through screening, some children may be identified as needing further assessment of their behavior problems. In step 2 of the behavioral assessment model the objective is to pinpoint behavior problems and to provide information about whether or not behavioral

Name of Student: <u>Rick</u>    Age of student: <u>11</u>    Grade Level: <u>5</u>

Date: <u>9/10/03</u>    Name of person managing    Relation to student: <u>Behavior</u>
    assessment: <u>M. Corn</u>    <u>Consultant</u>

| Assessment Strategy | Name of Person(s) Involved in Assessment | Summary of Results |
|---|---|---|
| SSBD Teacher Ranking | P. Nordness (teacher) | Rank ordered with the top three students for internalized behavior problems. |
| SSBD Teacher Rating | P. Nordness (teacher) | Significantly below the normative criteria for internalized behavior problems. |
| SSBD Academic and Playground Observations | M. Corn (Behavior Specialist) | Student observed to be on task during reading and math class; student observed to isolate himself during recess. |
| Sociometric Peer Nomination | P. Nordness | Student nominated by only 1 out of 25 students in the class as someone they would like to play with or work with. |

**FIGURE 2.6.** An example of completed assessment strategies for behavioral assessment step 1: Decide if a problem exists

intervention is warranted. This section will cover procedures that have been suggested for evaluating problem behaviors to determine if they warrant intervention.

Step 2 of the assessment process allows teachers and others to make finer discriminations of problem behavior and to obtain clues to effective intervention. Methods for collecting behavioral assessment data for step 2 include strategies for determining social validation of problem behaviors, behavioral observations in natural settings, and ranking of target behaviors. Assessment instruments and techniques for socially validating target behaviors and ranking target behaviors are provided in this chapter. Chapter 3 offers excellent suggestions for obtaining data through behavioral observation methods of target students and their peers using event and interval recording that will assist in the decision about whether or not intervention is warranted.

Behavioral assessment beyond step 1 incorporates multiple assessment methods that rely on several informants concerning the nature of the children's difficulties across multiple situations. Informants provide information about the target child through responses to checklists and rating scales, and participate in direct observation sessions with the target child. Typically these instruments are administered by a teacher or other "case manager." Once the information has been gathered, it is scored and interpreted by the person who administered the assessment strategy. For step 2 of the behavioral assessment model informants may include parents, teachers, other educators, and peers. The data from these sources should provide information to teachers and others to determine if behavior management intervention is needed for prevention of more serious problems, and/or intervention for current problems. The data from step 2 should also reveal student behavior strengths.

Social validation of target behaviors is accomplished by interpreting the results of checklists and rating scales across persons and settings (Sugai & Lewis, 1996) and by observing peers in the same setting as the target student(s). Several examples of the strategies that are appropriate for step 2 data collection methods are described.

## Data Collection Methods for Step 2

### Checklists and Ratings by Others

Teachers and others are often asked to provide an overall perception of a child's behavior via behavioral checklists or ratings. Behavioral ratings by others are administered as part of the total assessment process that takes place during step 2 of the behavioral assessment process. The reader should note that the rating scales used in step 2 are usually more comprehensive than those used in step 1. Step 2 checklists and rating scales are designed to get to the specific behavior(s) of concern whereas the instruments used in step 1 are more global or general in nature. Ratings by others are scales that are completed by teachers, parents, and peers that yield useful information for identifying target behaviors that may be correlates of important social outcomes such as peer acceptance and rejection (Gresham, 1986). Foster and her colleagues (1993) reported that ratings by teachers have limitations. They suggested that rating scale information could at best provide global information about a child's social competence. This suggests that although these instruments are useful, they should be used in combination with other methods for seeking information about the child. Several of these scales have received recognition in the literature as being useful for this purpose.

Behavioral checklists and rating scales of the type described in this section require the teacher or parent to read a behavioral descriptor and then make a judgment about the presence or absence of the behavior in the child. Behavior checklists and rating scales typically use a *Likert-type* rating scale to judge the degree to which the behavior is perceived to be a problem (Mash & Terdal, 1997). These measures provide information on how a child's behavior compares to peers'.

Checklists and ratings by others are available for preschool-age through adolescent-age children. A number of behavior rating scales are available. Included in this chapter are examples of widely used, reliable, and valid instruments for assessing a variety of behavior problems. Instruments of this type are easily administered to a variety of persons across settings, thus providing information to determine social validation for intervening with a student's behavior. Checklists and rating scales that have been particularly helpful in collecting assessment information for step 2 are described briefly. The reader is encouraged to refer to the individual test manuals for specifics about administration of the instruments and other pertinent information.

*Skillstreaming checklists.* Behavior checklists for teachers, parents, and students are available with the *Skillstreaming* social skills curricula (McGinnis & Goldstein, 1990, 1997). These checklists provide a source of information across persons and settings with regard to social skills deficits demonstrated by students. They are designed to be completed in 10 to 15 minutes. Behavior checklists in the preschool, elementary, and adolescent versions of the curricula allow respondents to decide if the target student engages in the social skill on a scale from "almost never" to "almost always." Using the *Skillstreaming* checklists, social skills such as listening, ignoring distractions, staying out of fights, and expressing one's feelings are measured based on an individual's perception of the frequency with which the student performs each of the skills (Goldstein & McGinnis, 1997).

*Social Skills Rating System.* Gresham and Elliott (1990) designed the *Social Skills Rating System* (SSRS). The instrument measures frequency of occurrence of the social skills and the perceived importance of the skill (Walker, Calvin, & Ramsey, 1995). The SSRS is a teacher rating scale. The results from the SSRT reveal social sills deficits in internalizing and externalizing behaviors (Gresham, Lane, MacMillan, & Bocian, 1999).

*Walker-McConnell Scale of Social Competence and School Adjustment.* Walker and McConnell (1988, 1993) developed a teacher rating scale of social competence and school adjustment. Designed for use in identification of social skills deficits among children in kindergarten through 12th grade, the *Walker-McConnell Scale of Social Competence and School Adjustment* (W-M) (Walker & McConnell, 1988, 1993) consists of positively worded descriptions of social skills that were designed to sample the two primary adjustment domains within school settings: adaptive behavior and social competence. These descriptions are distributed across three subscales—two measure interpersonal social skills with adults or peers, and one measures adaptive behavior required for success in the classroom. The descriptions are rated by the teacher on a 5-point Likert scale ranging from "never occurs" to "frequently occurs." The instrument yields three factor scores (subscale 1:16 items, teacher-preferred social behavior; subscale 2:17 items, peer-preferred social behavior; subscale 3:10 items, school adjustment behavior) and a composite score of social competence. Representative samples from the three scales of the elementary version of the W-M are presented here:

*Scale 1: Teacher-Preferred Behavior*

1. Shows sympathy for others.
2. Accepts constructive criticism from peers without becoming angry.
3. Cooperates with peers in group activities or situations.

*Scale 2: Peer-Preferred Behavior*

1. Spends recess and free time interacting with peers.
2. Interacts with a number of different peers.
3. Invites peers to play or share activities.

*Scale 3: School Adjustment Behavior*

1. Uses free time appropriately.
2. Does seatwork assignments as directed.
3. Answers or attempts to answer a question when called on by the teacher.

***Behavioral and Emotional Rating Scale.*** The *Behavioral and Emotional Rating Scale* (BERS) (Epstein & Sharma, 1998) is a strength-based assessment instrument. Based on the premise that all children have strengths (Epstein & Rudolph, 1999), the BERS serves to help teachers and others identify a child's strengths by rating him or her on 52 items that are designed to assess five behavior areas. The behavior areas include interpersonal strength, family involvement, intrapersonal strength, school functioning, and affective strengths (Epstein & Rudolph, 1999). Teachers and other adults complete the rating scale by rating the child on a 4-point scale that indicates the behavior is "not at all like the child" to "very much like the child." When interventions are designed to take into account children's strengths, their needs are addressed more effectively (Epstein & Rudolph, 1999). The BERS can be used for children and adolescents.

***Behavior Assessment System for Children.*** The *Behavior Assessment System for Children* (BASC) (Reynolds & Kamphaus, 1992) is another rating scale available to provide information on several dimensions of student behavior, including externalizing and internalizing behavior, school problems, atypicality, and a behavioral symptoms index. Forms are available for teachers and parents to complete on children ages 4 to 18. The BASC also includes a self-report instrument for children ages 8 to 18. Teachers are asked to complete the BASC by responding to 109 to 148 test items (depending on the age of the child) on a scale indicating that the behavior "never" occurs to "almost always" occurs. Parents respond in a similar manner to behavior descriptions.

The BASC has been used in a number of studies in which normative data on children's behavior in school settings was useful for pinpointing behavior problems and justifying interventions for behavior change (Blair, Umbreit, & Bos, 1999). The BASC is unique compared to other rating scales because it is designed to measure positive behaviors as well as problem behaviors.

The W-M, SSRS, and BERS rating scales, and the *Skillstreaming* checklists provide information about behavioral strengths and deficits that students may present in the school setting. The BASC is most appropriate when more in-depth information is needed about a particular student and his or her behavior problems when a behavior disorder is suspected. Decisions about which checklists and rating scales to use in step 2 will depend on the information needed to help determine if intervention is warranted. Since all of these instruments can be administered across persons and settings, the resulting information will be helpful in deciding social validity.

### Ranking Target Behaviors

Once target behaviors have been identified based on information from step 1 and step 2 (i.e., completed behavior checklists and rating scales), these behaviors can be ranked according to a series of questions (Wolery, Bailey, & Sugai, 1988). Responses to these questions will assist teachers and others in determining if intervention is warranted. Often, teachers become stumped when more than one target behavior has been identified for one or more students being considered for behavior management plans. To eliminate the guessing game that accompanies these quandaries, teachers should ask priority questions and gain consensus of persons who have frequent contact with the target student. It is not unusual for teachers to experience a scenario similar to the one depicted in Classroom Application 2.2. The teachers in the example are perplexed about which behavior to target for intervention. See if you can help them out.

Answering "yes" to questions 1 through 3 indicates that the target behavior is in need of immediate intervention development since there is potential of injury or loss of learning. If question 4 is answered "yes," the behavior will probably go away as the child gets older or if other antecedents and consequences change. Any behavior that will go away on its own or with relatively simple interventions doesn't need more complicated behavior management–based intervention. If the behavior is observed to occur as often as that of the peers', then it probably wouldn't be valid to intervene with the behavior unless the answer to questions 1 through 3 were "yes." In that case, a whole-class behavior management intervention may be appropriate. If the answer to question 6 is "yes," indicating that the behavior is due to a skill deficit in some other area, then perhaps the target behavior needs to be changed. Changing the target behavior would necessitate applying the ranking

## Classroom Application 2.2

# Prioritizing Target Behaviors

Desmond is an eighth grader at Sunny View Middle School. Desmond's school records indicate that he is capable of doing 8th-grade work and in fact has skills in math that are more typical of a 10th-grade student. His teachers are perplexed about Desmond's behavior in school. He often looks like he is on task during independent work time but seldom hands in any of his completed assignments. Desmond rarely raises his hand in response to teacher questions, and has little to say to his peers when they work in cooperative groups. Lately, Desmond has been observed to demonstrate disruptive behavior during class lectures and discussions when he gets out of his seat, roams around the classroom, and at times leaves the classroom to wander in the halls. Desmond's teachers are concerned about his seemingly problematic behavior as it is resulting in poor grades and complaints from his peers. They have put their heads together and completed the assessment instruments suggested by the behavior specialist, but still don't know which behavior to work on first.

Perhaps you can assist Desmond's teachers by answering the following questions, which will allow you to prioritize target behaviors.

1. Does the behavior cause injury to the student or others?
2. Does the behavior interfere with the student's or others' learning?
3. Does the behavior present a safety risk to the student or to others?
4. Is the behavior age-appropriate or likely to be transient?
5. Does the behavior occur at frequencies similar to that of peers' behavior?
6. Is the behavior due to skill deficits in other areas?
7. Does the behavior cause others to avoid interacting with the student? (Wolery et al., 1988)

questions to the new target behavior. Also, it is important to consider how changing one behavior affects the other behaviors. For example, if Desmond were taught to change his disruptive behavior to more appropriate classroom behavior through social skills training, would he then complete more of his work and hand it in? If in fact staying in his seat resulted from being taught replacement behaviors for roaming behavior, then the need to intervene with handing in assignment behavior may not be necessary. Finally, a "yes" for question 7 may indicate a precursor to more serious problems related to adult and peer relationships. Therefore, ameliorating the problem behavior now may result in preventing future problems.

A teacher's first impulse may be to count up the number of yes's and no's for each target behavior under question, and then declare that the behavior with the most yes's is the most salient and therefore the one needing intervention first.

However, in order to make prudent decisions about intervention priorities and whether a target behavior is worth development of an intervention, the teacher and others concerned should carefully consider the meaning of each question as it relates to the target behaviors and the impact of the behavior on the target student and others.

To obtain the information they need to decide if intervention is needed and worthwhile, teachers should (a) complete from one to three checklists and/or rating scales for each of the target students under consideration for intervention; (b) conduct three to five 15-minute naturalistic observations of the target student and his or her peers in a school setting in which the target behavior is demonstrated; and (c) rank the target behaviors in terms of their severity and amenity to intervention. Figure 2.7 provides an example of the results of the assessment strategies completed for Rick in step 2 of the behavioral assessment process.

After examining the assessment information, Rick's teachers decided to use the ranking questions to determine which of two target behaviors—disruptive behavior and handing in assignments—would justify intervention. Figure 2.8 provides an example of a grid format that the teachers employed to help them in their efforts.

The results shown in Figure 2.8 should help to clarify for the teachers that intervention would be justified for both target behaviors. Even though it seemed that neither target behavior would cause injury, both are interfering with the target student's learning. The disruptive behavior was noted to interfere with the learning of others, and to pose a safety risk to the target student and others.

Neither of the behaviors seem to be age appropriate and they are not likely to go away without intervention. In fact, the teachers indicated in their discussion about Rick that they had tried some simple interventions that had worked in the past with other students. These interventions were not effective in helping Rick reduce his inappropriate behavior and increase appropriate behavior.

Observation and other assessment information indicated that Rick engaged in disruptive behavior more frequently than his peers and that this behavior was starting to cause problems in his relationships with adults and peers. In addition, compared to his peers, Rick was observed to hand in assignments less frequently, which was affecting his grades.

It was not clear to the teachers if Rick's inappropriate behavior was related to skills deficits in other areas. However, the teachers noted that Rick's behavior has changed significantly compared to his behavior in the first quarter, and they have decided to continue the assessment process to find out more about him. We will continue with Rick's case in the following section.

Teachers and others interested in assessment for the purpose of finding out more about students should complete step 3 in the behavior assessment model to determine if medical reasons are contributing to the problem behavior. Step 3 and data collection methods associated with it are discussed next.

Name of Student: <u>Rick</u>  Age of student: <u>11</u>  Grade Level: <u>5</u>

Date: <u>9/30/03</u>  Name of person managing  Relation to student: <u>Behavior Specialist</u>
 assessment: <u>M. Corn</u>

| Assessment Strategy | Name of Person(s) Involved in Assessment | Summary of Results |
|---|---|---|
| Checklist: W-M Scale of Social Competence and School Adjustment | P. Nordness (Language Arts Teacher) T. Vandercook (Math and Science Teacher) | Rick's scores on the W-M indicated that he had significantly different factor scores from the norm group for the *Teacher Preferred Behavior* and *School Adjustment* dimensions. His scores on the *Peer Preferred Behavior* dimension were within normal range when compared to the norm group. These scores were consistent across two teachers. |
| Rating Scale: BASC | P. Nordness, T. Vandercook (teachers); Mrs. Rimerez (Rick's mother) | Scores on the BASC were in the normal range across externalizing and internalizing dimensions. These scores were consistent across all three informants. |
| Naturalistic Observation: Target student and peers; classroom settings; interval recording, paper-and-pencil measure of target behaviors. Permanent product recording for the target behavior of "handing in assignments." | M. Corn (Behavior Specialist) | Observations of Rick and his peers revealed that he and his peers engaged in the target behaviors described as on/off task; participative or disruptive; and get teacher attention appropriately/not appropriately in each of the three 15-minute observations. Rick was observed to be on task at the same rate as his peers during independent-work time. However, during lecture and discussion periods, Rick was observed to be engaged in disruptive behavior at a much higher rate than his peers. This behavior resulted in peers' distraction and loss of academically engaged time for all students. A review of the teachers' assignment record books indicated that Rick handed in fewer assignments per week than his peers. His grades—in the "C" range—during the second and third quarter, were considerably lower than his grades—in the "A" range—first quarter. |

**FIGURE 2.7.** An example of completed assessment strategies for behavioral assessment step 2: Determine if intervention is warranted

Target Behaviors (undesired behaviors):

1. "Disruptive" is defined as getting out of seat, roaming around the room without permission and/or talking to peers while roaming.

2. "Not handing in assignments" is defined as failure to provide the teacher with a completed assignment by the due date.

|  | Question 1 | Question 2 | Question 3 | Question 4 | Question 5 | Question 6 | Question 7 |
|---|---|---|---|---|---|---|---|
| Disruptive Behavior | no | yes | yes | no | no | ? | yes |
| Assignment Behavior | no | yes | no | no | no | ? | no |

**FIGURE 2.8.** Example of ranking target behaviors for Rick

## Step 3: Determine If Medical and/or Psychological Reasons Exist That Contribute to the Problem Behavior

Before intervention ideas are explored, mental health and medical personnel may need to examine the student to determine if he or she has any medical problems that may be causing the behavior problems. For example, mental health professionals may assist in identifying clinical depression. This assessment information may also be helpful in determining if the child is eligible for special education or other helpful related services.

To rule out treatable diseases and allergies, it is necessary to include a physical examination by a physician as part of the assessment of behavioral problems. Often, parents will first report behavior problems to a physician during routine physical examinations. It is important for physicians to collaborate with behavioral experts before making recommendations about behavior intervention. Physicians can then refer parents to appropriate professionals for adequate assessment and subsequent recommendations for intervention.

Several pediatric clinics have moved toward offering on-site comprehensive services, including behavioral assessment, as a service to families. Medical and other personnel concerned about the care of children have found it necessary and meaningful to collaborate with educators to ensure that the most effective educational programming for children with behavior and/or medical problems is provided (P. Blasco, personal communication, 1994). We know of at least one school where the medical personnel are full-time employees of the school district and are housed in one of the school sites. Others are listed as part-time staff members. These mental health and medical professionals provide valuable input in collaborative efforts aimed at assessment and development of effective behavior support systems for students (Melloy & Townsend, 1999).

## Data Collection Methods for Step 3

In school settings, medical data for behavioral assessment is usually contributed by the school nurse. Brief medical screenings are routine in most schools throughout the United States. For example, each school year students in elementary schools are screened for vision and hearing problems. If screening information indicates a problem, it is usually suggested that the child be seen in a clinical setting for a more thorough examination and assessment. Medical problems such as those associated with vision may contribute to behavioral problems. A child who experiences vision or hearing problems may not be able to access educational information as easily as his or her peers and in frustration, act out in, or withdraw from, the classroom setting.

In addition to in-school medical screenings, all children are required by law to receive a physical examination and necessary inoculations *before* being admitted to a public elementary school. Like in-school screenings, these routine examinations sometimes reveal medical problems that may contribute to behavior problems in a school setting (e.g., ear infections, migraine headaches, stomachaches). Whereas many medical problems dissipate with treatment, chronic illnesses, such as migraine headaches, will contribute to changes in behavior and at times will result in ongoing behavior problems. Medical personnel may decide that medical intervention such as medication may be appropriate. Teachers should not suggest this type of intervention, but when medical conditions impact a student's education, then collaboration among medical personnel and the student's teachers is certainly appropriate.

Parents should share with educators medical information that may contribute to understanding their child's behavior problems. Often, however, parents do not share their child's medical information unless they are certain the medical condition will impact their child's education. When medical information is available and pertinent, it should be considered helpful in the behavioral assessment process. If this information is not relevant or not available, the behavior assessment process can be continued.

In addition to school nurses and physicians, school psychologists, clinical psychologists, psychiatrists, and other mental health professionals can also contribute information that may be relevant to school-related behavior problems. Mental health professionals collect data using rating scales; behavioral interviews with parents, target children, and teachers and others who know the child; behavioral observations in natural and clinical settings; psychometric assessment; and laboratory measures. We briefly describe several of these data collection methods in the following paragraphs.

### *Rating Scales*

Rating scales were described earlier in this chapter. In this section we have provided examples of three rating scales that are typically administered in clinical and school settings. These instruments in particular have been used to assist in the clinical diagnosis of specific behavior and mental health disorders demonstrated by children (Sterba & Dowd, 1998) and in determining eligibility for special education services.

***Scale for Assessing Emotional Disturbance.*** The *Scale for Assessing Emotional Disturbance* (SAED) (Epstein & Cullinan, 1998) is a 52-item teacher rating scale designed to measure behaviors in students ages 5 to 18 that are associated with the IDEA 97 definition of Emotional Disturbance. Teachers and other professionals complete this rating scale by rating each item on a 4-point scale (i.e., "not a problem," "mild problem," "considerable problem," and "severe problem"). The SAED may be helpful to teachers and others in their efforts to differentiate children who demonstrate behavior problems from those who may demonstrate behaviors characteristic of emotional disturbance and behavior disorders.

***Child Behavior Checklist.*** The *Child Behavior Checklist* (CBCL) (Achenbach, 1991a) is a behavior rating instrument designed to be completed by parents and parent surrogates of children ages 4 to 18. The 113-item rating scale requires about 20 to 30 minutes to administer. Parents are asked to rate their child's behavior on a Likert-type scale using the descriptors "not true," "sometimes true," "very true," or "often true" about their child. The results of the rating scale assist in determining the presence of externalizing or internalizing behavior problems. *Scaled scores* are provided for the following: (a) withdrawn, (b) somatic complaints, (c) anxious/depressed, (d) social problems, (e) thought problems, (f) attention problems, (g) delinquent behavior, and (h) aggressive behavior. The instrument also yields a social competence rating based on parents' answers to several questions about their child's involvement in social activities. Comparisons of parents' perceptions can be made when both parents are available to complete the rating on a child. Children who score in the top 3% to 5% for age and sex on standardized behavior rating scales of major behavior symptoms may be candidates for further assessment of behavior problems. Sample items from the CBCL are provided in Figure 2.9.

***Teacher's Report Form.*** The *Teacher Report Form* (TRF) (Achenbach, 1991b) is one of the most popular rating scales of its type. A 113-item rating scale that takes about 20 to 30 minutes for teachers to complete, it has scales available for boys and girls ages 6 to 16. The TRF asks teachers to judge each behavioral descriptor as "not true," "somewhat or sometimes true," or "very true or often true" about a student in their class. The completed behavior ratings indicate externalizing or internalizing behavior problems by providing scaled scores for (a) withdrawn, (b) somatic complaints, (c) anxious/depressed, (d) social problems, (e) thought problems, (f) attention problems, (g) delinquent behavior, and (h) aggressive behavior. A score is also obtained for school performance and adaptive functioning based on the teacher's responses to items related to academic subjects. Sample items from the TRF are provided in Figure 2.10.

**FIGURE 2.9.** Sample items from a rating scale for parents

*Source:* From *Child Behavior Checklist for Ages 4–18* (pp. 3–4) by T.M. Achenbach, 1991a. Burlington: University of Vermont. Reprinted by permission.

Below is a list of items that describe children and youth. For each item that describes your child **now or within the past 6 months,** please circle the **2** if the item is **very true or often true** of your child. Circle the **1** if the item is **somewhat or sometimes true** of your child. If the item is **not true** of your child, circle the **0.** Please answer all items as well as you can, even if some do not seem to apply to your child.

| | | | |
|---|---|---|---|
| 1. Acts too young for his/her age | 0 | 1 | 2 |
| 2. Disobedient at school | 0 | 1 | 2 |
| 3. Shy or timid | 0 | 1 | 2 |
| 4. Threatens people | 0 | 1 | 2 |
| 5. Steals at home | 0 | 1 | 2 |
| 6. Withdrawn, doesn't get involved with others | 0 | 1 | 2 |
| 7. Not liked by other children | 0 | 1 | 2 |
| 8. Sudden changes in mood or feelings | 0 | 1 | 2 |
| 9. Secretive, keeps things to self | 0 | 1 | 2 |
| 10. Sleeps more than most children during day and/or night | 0 | 1 | 2 |

**FIGURE 2.10.** Sample items from a rating by others scale for teachers

*Source:* From *Teacher's Report Form* (pp. 3–4) by T.M. Achenbach, 1991b. Burlington: University of Vermont. Reprinted by permission.

Below is a list of items that describe pupils. For each item that describes the pupil **now or within the past 2 months,** please circle the **2** if the item is **very true or often true** of the pupil. Circle **1** if the item is **somewhat or sometimes true** of the pupil. If the item is **not true** of the pupil, circle the **0.** Please answer all items as well as you can, even if some do not seem to apply to this pupil.

| | | | |
|---|---|---|---|
| 1. Argues a lot | 0 | 1 | 2 |
| 2. Destroys property belonging to others | 0 | 1 | 2 |
| 3. Doesn't get along with other pupils | 0 | 1 | 2 |
| 4. Easily jealous | 0 | 1 | 2 |
| 5. Fears going to school | 0 | 1 | 2 |
| 6. Has difficulty learning | 0 | 1 | 2 |
| 7. Talks out of turn | 0 | 1 | 2 |
| 8. Threatens people | 0 | 1 | 2 |
| 9. Overly anxious to please. | 0 | 1 | 2 |
| 10. Withdrawn, doesn't get involved with others. | 0 | 1 | 2 |

### Naturalistic Behavioral Observations

Chapters 3–6 provide an in-depth description of behavioral assessment using naturalistic observations. Note that accurate decisions about children's behavior should not be made without collecting data through naturalistic observations (Alberto & Troutman, 1999). Although it is common for the evaluation for specific behavior problems—such as ADHD, conduct disorders, and depression—to take place in a clinical setting, it is imperative that the person conducting the assessment visit the child's school or home to observe behavior in those settings. Brief descriptions of several behavioral observation systems that have been used by mental health and other medical professionals to assess specific behavior problems are provided in the following section.

***Daily School Behavior Report Card.*** Barkley and Murphy (1998) described a *Daily School Behavior Report Card* that was designed to assist in teacher observations of children's ADHD-related behavior. Teachers are asked to rate children's behavior daily in two school settings: the classroom and recess. Examples of the behaviors to be rated include class participation, follows classroom rules, does not tease others, and gets along well with other children. The report cards are intended to be sent home on a daily basis to provide consistent school-to-home communication. Over time, the report cards provide a progress report that can also be shared with medical personnel in monitoring recommended intervention effects.

***Kazdin's Behavioral Codes.*** Kazdin (1988) described behavioral codes to use in direct observation of children to determine whether they demonstrated overt behaviors affiliated with depression. Kazdin broke the codes into three categories: (a) social activity (e.g., talking, playing a game); (b) solitary behavior (e.g., playing a game alone, grooming); and (c) affect-related expressions (e.g., smiling, arguing). These and other behavioral codes were used to observe children in clinical, home, and school settings. Typically, children high in depression "engaged in significantly less social behavior and evinced less affect-related expression than did children low in depression" (Kazdin, 1988, p. 178). An example of the use of Kazdin's Behavioral Code is described in Classroom Application 2.3.

***Behavioral Avoidance Tests.*** These observational systems have been used to "assess children's motor reactions to fear- and anxiety-producing stimuli, which include blood, darkness, medical procedures, school events, strangers, and water" (Mash & Terdal, 1997, p. 242). Mash and Terdal (1997) described the procedures generally employed for assessment of fears and anxieties using these instruments. According to these authors, the child is placed in a setting that includes the feared stimulus. The child is asked to perform a series of graduated tasks that call for approaching the feared stimulus. An observer records the motor responses (e.g., grimacing, stiffness, crying) the child demonstrates during the observation period. The number of graduated tasks the child is able to accomplish toward the stimulus helps to determine the level of fear and anxiety the child experiences when expected to perform in the presence of the feared stimulus.

## Classroom Application 2.3

## Using a Behavioral Code

Melissa, a 9-year-old, third-grade student, was referred to a behavior management clinic for assessment of behavior characteristic of depression and suicidal verbalizations. She was observed in the clinic setting by a psychiatrist named Dr. Antonians using the Kazdin Behavioral Code. Dr. Antonians requested Melissa to interact as she normally would with her mother and father during three 15-minute observation sessions. These behavioral observations were conducted in the clinic setting in a room with a one-way window. Melissa and her parents were seated in the room while Dr. Antonians positioned himself in the room on the other side of the window so that he could observe Melissa's behavior in an unobtrusive manner.

Dr. Antonians used the same coding system to observe Melissa's behavior in the school setting when he visited Melissa's school on two separate occasions prior to Melissa's visit to the clinic. Dr. Antonians conducted six 15-minute observations at the school. Three observations were made of Melissa's interaction behavior on the playground, and three observations of her behavior were made while Melissa ate lunch with her peers. For each of the observations, Dr. Antonians positioned himself close enough to Melissa so that he could see and hear Melissa interacting with her peers. Since Melissa did not know Dr. Antonians at this point, Dr. Antonians explained to the play/lunch groups that he was there simply to watch children play and eat.

### Psychometric Assessment

During parent and teacher interviews, the interviewer needs to obtain information about the child's academic achievement and effects of behavior problems on that achievement. When learning disabilities are suspected, additional information is necessary regarding intellectual functioning through psychometric assessment of *global intelligence* and *academic achievement.* A number of authors provide descriptions of assessment instruments and procedures that can be used to assess these constructs (e.g., Lerner, 1997; Turnbull et al., 1999). These instruments will not be described in this text. This information, however, will assist in making accurate intervention decisions about the child's learning problems that may be associated with behavior problems.

### Laboratory Measures

Laboratory measures are available to use in the assessment of children who demonstrate behavior problems (frequently used to identify "ADHD characteristics"). Teachers and others should be cautioned, however, in using these measures as indicators of the presence of behavior problems. Just as information

Once behavioral assessment data have been gathered, a professional scores and completes an interpretation of each measure before a team meeting on a child and his or her behavior.

from the other assessment procedures previously described would never be used in isolation, a laboratory measure provides only part of the information needed to determine a child's specific behavior problems and ideas for intervention. Basing intervention decisions on the information gained solely from any one measure would indeed be a mistake on the part of professionals and others.

Figure 2.11 depicts an example of a format that can be used to summarize medical information that may be helpful in determining the existence of medical or psychological reasons that contribute to problem behavior. Figure 2.12 is meant to contribute to the readers' understanding of step 3 by offering a completed medical summary form for Rick.

The results of step 3 for Rick indicated that there did not appear to be any medical or psychological reasons that contributed to his behavior problems. Rick's teachers decided to complete a functional assessment of Rick's behavior as described in Chapters 5 and 6, to review how classroom variables may be affecting his behavior and to continue to collect data on antecedents and consequences maintaining Rick's behavior (see Chapters 3 and 4).

Name of Student: Date:
Name and title of person completing review form:
Person(s) interviewed for information and relationship to student:
Source of records reviewed:

1. Identify known physical and/or mental health conditions.
   - Medical diagnosis:
     Physical health:
     Mental health:
     Does the diagnosis have known behavior features?   yes   no
     If yes, describe the features that the student demonstrates in the current setting:
   - Review of vision and hearing tests:

|  | Date of last exam, source | Nature of any problems | Accommodations required |
|---|---|---|---|
| Vision |  |  |  |
| Hearing |  |  |  |

2. Complete medication summary.

| Medication/ Dosage | Anticipated benefit | Behavior and other side effects | Source of information |
|---|---|---|---|
|  |  |  |  |

   - Note recent change in medication:
   - Potential effect of the medication on behavior:
   - Examination of time the medication is taken and result on behavior:
3. Describe sleep cycle and diet.
   - Current sleep pattern:
   - Food allergies or restrictions:
   - Need for diet/sleep changes:
4. Describe any unusual responses or sensitivity to environmental stimuli.
   - Tactile:
   - Auditory:
   - Visual:
   - Movement:
   - Vibration:
   - Smell or taste:
5. List periodic precipitating factors.
   - Note any periodically occurring events that have led to an increase in problem behavior:
6. Does this student have an identified disability?
   - Special Education (IDEA 97):
   - DSM IV Diagnosis:
   - Does the disability have known behavior features?   yes   no   NA
     If "yes," describe the behavior features the student demonstrates in this setting:

**FIGURE 2.11.** Example of a medical review format for completing behavioral assessment model step 3

*Source:* Adapted from N. Kurtzman (1997). *Best practices in functional assessment.* Stillwater, MN: Stillwater Public Schools. Reprinted by permission.

**Medical and Psychological Assessment Review Form**

Name of Student: Rick     Date: October 1, 2003

Name and title of person completing review form: M. Corn, Behavior Specialist

Person(s) interviewed for information and relationship to student: P. Nordness (teacher); J. Rimerez (Rick's mother); B. Bladderson (school nurse)

Source of records reviewed: school cumulative file

1. Identify known physical and/or mental health conditions.
   - Medical diagnosis:

     Physical health: migraine headache

     Mental health: no known conditions

     Does the diagnosis have known behavior features?  (yes)  no
   - If yes, describe the features that the student demonstrates in the current setting:
     When Rick gets a migraine headache, it comes on suddenly with an aura that lasts for about 30 minutes. During the aura, Rick has vision difficulties and may become disoriented. Once the headache begins, Rick may cry due to pain: he will be irritable and will want to lie down.
   - Review of vision and hearing tests:

|  | Date of last exam, source | Nature of any problems | Accommodations required |
|---|---|---|---|
| Vision | 9/15/00; school screening | none evident | none |
| Hearing | 9/30/00; school screening | none evident | none |

2. Complete medication summary.

| Medication/ Dosage | Anticipated benefit | Behavior and other side effects | Source of information |
|---|---|---|---|
| Motrin, Jr.- 200 mg at onset of headache | Pain will dissipate | Child will want to sleep | J. Rimerez |

   - Note recent change in medication: none
   - Potential effect of medication on behavior: Rick will not be able to continue schoolwork. Rick will want to lie down when he gets a headache. If he can't lie down and sleep, he will become irritable.
   - Examination of time the medication is taken and result on behavior: Medication at best will relieve some of the pain. Rick will need to sleep for 8 to 10 hours before the headache subsides.

**FIGURE 2.12.** Example of a completed medical review format for Rick

*Source:* Adapted from N. Kurtzman, (1997). *Best practices in functional assessment.* Stillwater, MN: Stillwater Public Schools. Reprinted by permission.

3. Describe sleep cycle and diet.
   - **Current sleep pattern:** Rick sleeps 8 hours per night.
   - **Food allergies or restrictions:** Rick cannot eat chocolate, cheese, MSG.
   - **Need for diet/sleep changes:** none except when he gets a headache.
4. Describe any unusual responses or sensitivity to environmental stimuli.
   - **Tactile:** none
   - **Auditory:** When Rick gets a headache, he is very sensitive to any sound.
   - **Visual:** Overall, Rick is sensitive to light. He requires wearing of sunglasses when he goes outside, even on cloudy days. When Rick gets a headache, he is very sensitive to any light.
   - **Movement:** Rick experiences increased pain when he moves while he has a headache.
   - **Vibration:** none
   - **Smell or taste:** While Rick has a headache, he has an increased sensitivity to smells and may become nauseated. He usually does not want to eat when he has a headache.
5. List Periodic precipitating factors.
   - **Note any periodically occurring events that have led to an increase in problem behavior:** none that seem medically or psychologically related
6. Does this student have an identified disability? no
   - **Special Education (IDEA 97):** no
   - **DSM IV Diagnosis:** no
   - **Does the disability have known behavior features?**   yes   no   (NA)
   - **If "yes," describe the behavior features the student demonstrates in this setting:** NA

**FIGURE 2.12.**  *Continued*

## SUMMARY

The purpose of behavioral assessment is to identify student strengths and needs related to their behavior, plan educational interventions designed to assist students in changing or maintaining social and academic behavior, evaluate the effectiveness of interventions, and determine eligibility for special education services. In this chapter we described steps 1 through 3 of a seven-step model for conducting behavioral assessment. An outline of the model is presented here, summarizing each of the first three steps for behavioral assessment and suggestions for data collection methods to gather information about students.

*Step 1: Decide if a problem exists.*

Purpose: Screening for behavior problems.

*Data Collection Methods:*
- Checklists and ratings by others (SSBD, ESP)
- Teacher ranking (SSBD, ESP)

- Self-rating (Skillstreaming)
- Sociometric techniques (peer rating, peer nomination, peer evaluation)
- Interviews with teachers, parents, others (informal: phone calls, conferences)
- Behavioral observations (SSBD, ESP)

### Step 2: Determine if intervention is warranted.

Purpose: Social validation of target behaviors and ranking of problem behaviors.

### Data Collection Methods:

- Checklists and ratings by others (Skillstreaming checklists, SSRS, W-M, BASC)
- Naturalistic observations (target student and peers)
- Ranking target behavior questions

### Step 3: Determine if medical and/or psychological reasons exist that contribute to the problem behavior.

Purpose: Identify physical and mental health conditions that may affect behavior.

### Data Collection Methods:

- Checklists and ratings by others (SAED, CBCL, TRF)
- Clinical and naturalistic behavior observations (Daily School Behavior Report Card, Kazdin's Behavioral Codes, BAT)
- Psychometric assessment (intelligence tests, tests of academic achievement)
- Laboratory measures (GDS)

Form: *Medical Review Form*

Table 2.1 provides a matrix that depicts the types of assessment instruments recommended for steps 1 through 3 of the Behavioral Assessment Model. Table 2.2 outlines the names and purposes of each indirect assessment instrument described in this chapter.

Teachers and other educational professionals will find opportunities to maximize teaching and learning when they develop effective behavior support plans based on assessment data. The information provided in this chapter is meant to assist teachers and others in gaining knowledge about indirect behavioral assessment methods. Chapters 3 and 4 provide information about direct behavioral assessment strategies. The information in these chapters combined with the information in the chapters about intervention (i.e., Chapters 7, 8, 9, and 10) and specific behavior

**TABLE 2.1 • Steps 1–3 of the Behavioral Assessment Model: Strategies for Assessment**

| Behavior Assessment Model Step: | Assessment Strategy | | | |
| --- | --- | --- | --- | --- |
| | Checklist/ Rating Scale | Self- Rating | Observation | Interview |
| 1. Does problem exist? | X | X | X | X |
| 2. Intervention? | X | | X | |
| 3. Medical/ Psychological reasons? | X | | X | X |

influences (Chapters 12, 13, and 14) will contribute to this knowledge base and help teachers and others to build effective interventions designed to teach and support acceptable behavior that is demonstrated by students.

## DISCUSSION QUESTIONS

1. What is behavioral assessment? List and explain the common features of behavioral assessment.
2. Choose one of the assessment instruments or techniques described in this chapter. Obtain the instrument and study the guide for administration, scoring, and interpretation. Practice the administration of this instrument.
3. Compare the definitions of disruptive behavior given in the examples about Desmond, described in the section on step 2, and Rick. Even though these behaviors are called "disruptive behavior," how do they differ in the way that each of the students demonstrates the behavior in the school setting?

## REFERENCES

Achenbach, T. M. (1991a). *Child behavior checklist for ages 4–18.* Burlington, VT: Department of Psychiatry, University of Vermont.

Achenbach, T. M. (1991b). *Teacher report form.* Burlington, VT: Center for Children, Youth & Families, University of Vermont.

Alberto, P. A., & Troutman, A. C. (1999). *Applied behavior analysis for teachers* (5th ed.). Upper Saddle River, NJ: Merrill/Prentice Hall.

Barkley, R. A., & Murphy, K. R. (1998). *Attention-deficit hyperactivity disorder: A clinical workbook* (2nd ed.). New York: The Guilford Press.

Bellack, A. S., & Hersen, M. (1998). *Behavioral assessment: A practical handbook* (4th ed.). Boston: Allyn & Bacon.

**TABLE 2.2 • Description of Indirect Assessment Instruments**

| Name of Instrument | Acronym | Instrument Type and Usage |
|---|---|---|
| Systematic Screening for Behavior Disorders (Walker & Severson, 1999) | SSBD | Multi-assessment instrument (teacher rating, ranking; observation); used to screen for behavior problems and disorders (grades 1–5) |
| Early Screening Project (Walker et al., 1995) | ESP | Multi-assessment instrument (teacher rating, ranking; observation); used to screen for behavior problems and disorders (ages 3–5) |
| Skillstreaming checklists Goldstein & McGinnis, 1997; McGinnis & Goldstein, 1990; 1997) | | Teacher, parent rating checklist of student social skills; student self-rating checklist of social skills |
| Social Skills Rating System (Gresham & Elliott, 1990) | SSRS | Teacher rating of individual student's social skills |
| Walker-McConnell Scale of Social Competence and School Adjustment (Walker & McConnell, 1988, 1993) | W-M | Teacher rating of elementary students' and adolescents' level of social competence. |
| Behavior Assessment System for Children (Reynolds & Kamphaus, 1992) | BASC | Teacher rating, parent rating, and self-rating of student behavior |
| Behavioral and Emotional Rating Scale: A Strength-based Approach to Assessment (Epstein & Sharma, 1998) | | Teacher rating of student behavior strengths |
| Scale for Assessing Emotional Disturbance (Epstein & Cullinan, 1998) | SAED | Teacher rating of student behavior |
| Child Behavior Checklist (Achenbach, 1991) | CBCL | Parents' rating of their child's behavior |
| Teacher Report Form (Achenbach, 1991) | TRF | Teacher rating of children's behavior |
| School Archival Records Search (Walker et al., 1991) | SARS | Paper-and-pencil recording instrument for summarizing existing school records |
| Reinforcement Survey for Children and Adolescents (no author) | | Self-report instrument on reinforcing people, places, things, and activities |
| Reinforcement Inventory (no author) | | Forced-choice self-report instrument on reinforcing consequences |

Bem, D. J., & Fender, D. C. (1978). Predicting more of the people more of the time: Assessing the personality of situations. *Psychological Review, 85,* 485–501.

Blair, K., Umbreit, J., & Bos, C. (1999). Using functional assessment and children's preferences to improve the behavior of young children with behavioral disorders. *Behavioral Disorders, 24,* 151–166.

Cheney, D., & Barringer, C. (1994, November). *Project destiny: Creating the context for the social/ emotional development of middle school students using an interagency staff development model.* Paper presented at the 18th Annual TECBD National Conference on Severe Behavior Disorders, Tempe, AZ.

Coie, J. D., Dodge, K. A., & Coppotelli, H. (1982). Dimensions and types of social status: A cross-age perspective. *Developmental Psychology, 18,* 557–570.

Elksnin, L. K., & Elksnin, N. (1998). Teaching social skills to students with learning and behavior problems. *Intervention in School and Clinic, 33,* 131–140.

Epstein, M. H., & Cullinan, D. (1998). *Scale for assessing emotional disturbance.* Austin, TX: Pro-Ed.

Epstein, M. H., & Rudolph, S. (1999). Strength based assessment. In *The Behavior Home Page, www.state.ky.us/agencies/behave/homepage.html*

Epstein, M. H., & Sharma, J. M. (1998). *Behavioral and emotional rating scale: A strength-based approach to assessment.* Austin, TX: Pro-Ed.

Foster, S. L., Inderbitzen, H., & Nangle, D. W. (1993). Assessing acceptance and social skills with peers in childhood: Current issues. *Behavioral Modification, 17*(13), 255–286.

Goldstein, A. P., & McGinnis, E. (1997). *Skillstreaming the adolescent: New strategies for teaching prosocial skills* (Rev. ed.). Champaign, IL: Research Press.

Goleman, D. (1990, October). Child's skills at play crucial to success, new studies find. *New York Times,* pp. B1, B6.

Gresham, F. M. (1986). Conceptual issues in the assessment of social competence in children. In P. Strain, M. Guralnick, & H. Walker (Eds.), *Children's social behavior: Development, assessment, and modification* (pp. 143–179). New York: Academic Press.

Gresham, F., & Elliott, S. N. (1990). *Social skills rating system.* Circle Pines, MN: American Guidance Service, Inc.

Gresham, F. M., Lane, K. L., MacMillan, D. L., & Bocian, K. M. (1999). Social and academic profiles of externalizing and internalizing groups: Risk factors for emotional and behavioral disorders. *Behavioral Disorders, 24,* 231–245.

Hoier, T. S., & Cone, J. D. (1987). Target selection of social skills for children: The template-matching procedure. *Behavior Modification, 11,* 137–163.

Hops, H., Finch, M., & McConnell, S. R. (1985). Social skills deficits. In P. H. Bornstein & A. E. Kazdin (Eds.), *Handbook of clinical behavior therapy with children* (pp. 543–598). Homewood, IL: Dorsey Press.

Kauffman, J. M. (1997). *Characteristics of behavior disorders of children and youth* (6th ed.). Upper Saddle River, NJ: Merrill/Prentice Hall.

Kazdin, A. E. (1988). Childhood depression. In E. J. Mash & L. G. Terdal (Eds.), *Behavioral assessment of childhood disorders* (2nd ed., pp. 157–195). New York: Guilford Press.

Kazdin, A., & Frame, C. (1983). Aggressive behavior and conduct disorder. In M. Richards & T. Kratochwill (Eds.), *The practice of child therapy* (pp. 167–192). Elmsford, NY: Pergamon Press.

Kerr, M. M., & Nelson, C. M. (1998). *Strategies for managing behavior problems in the classroom* (3rd ed.). Upper Saddle River, NJ: Merrill/Prentice Hall.

Kurtzman, N. (1997). *Best practices in functional assessment.* Stillwater, MN: Stillwater Public Schools.

Lerner, J. (1997). *Learning disabilities: Theories, diagnosis, and teaching strategies* (7th ed.). Boston: Houghton Mifflin Co.

Likert, R. (1932). A technique for the measurement of attitudes. *Archives of Psychology,* No. 140.

Martin, R. P. (1988). *Assessment of personality and behavior problems.* New York: Guilford Press.

Mash, E. J., & Terdal, L. G. (1997). *Behavioral assessment of childhood disorders* (3rd ed.). New York: Guilford Press.

McConnell, S. R., & Odom, S. L. (1986). Sociometrics: Peer referenced measures and the assessment of social competence. In P. S. Strain, M. J. Guralnick, & H. M. Walker (Eds.), *Children's social behavior, development, assessment, and modification* (pp. 215–284). New York: Academic Press.

McConnell, S. R., & Odom, S. L. (1987). Sociometric measures. In *Dictionary of behavioral assessment techniques* (pp. 432–434). Elmsburg, NY: Pergamon Press.

McGinnis, E., & Goldstein, A. P. (1990). *Skillstreaming in early childhood: Teaching prosocial skills to the preschool and kindergarten child.* Champaign, IL: Research Press.

McGinnis, E., & Goldstein, A. P. (1997). *Skillstreaming the elementary school child: New strategies and perspectives for teaching prosocial skills* (Rev. ed) Champaign, IL: Research Press.

Melloy, K. J. (1990). *Attitudes and behavior of non-disabled elementary-aged children toward their peers with disabilities in integrated settings: An examination of the effects of treatment on quality of attitude, social status and critical social skills.* Unpublished doctoral dissertation, University of Iowa.

Melloy, K. J., Davis, C. A., Wehby, J. H., Murry, F. R., & Leiber, J. (1998). *Developing social competence in children and youth with challenging behavior.* Reston, VA: CCBD Mini Library Series: Successful Interventions for the 21st Century.

Moreno, J. L. (1934). *Who shall survive? A new approach to the problem of human interrelations.* Washington, DC: Nervous and Mental Disease Publishing Co.

Ollendick, T. H., & Hersen, M. (Eds.). (1984). *Child behavioral assessment: Principles and procedures.* New York: Pergamon Press.

Palmer, P. (1998). *The courage to teach: Exploring the inner landscape of a teacher's life.* San Francisco, CA: Jossey-Bass Publishers.

Peery, J. C. (1979). Popular, amiable, isolated, rejected: A reconceptualization of sociometric status in preschool children. *Child Development, 50,* 1231–1234.

Reynolds, C. R., & Kamphaus, R. W. (1992). *Behavior Assessment System for Children.* Circle Pines, MN: American Guidance Service, Inc.

Sheridan, S. M. (1997). *The tough kid social skills book.* Longmount, CA: Sopris West.

Sterba, M., & Dowd, T. (1998). *Treating youth with DSM-IV disorders: The role of social skill instruction.* Boys Town, NE: Boys Town Press.

Strain, P. S., Odom, S. L., & McConnell, S. (1984). Promoting social reciprocity of exceptional children: Identification, target behavior selection, and intervention. *Remedial and Special Education, 5,* 21–28.

Sugai, G., & Lewis, T. (1996). Preferred and promising practices for social skills instruction. *Focus on Exceptional Children, 29,* 1–16.

Turnbull, A., Turnbull, R., Shank, M., & Leal, D. (1999). *Exceptional lives: Special education in today's schools* (2nd ed.). Upper Saddle River, NJ: Merrill/Prentice Hall.

Walker, H. M., Block-Pedego, A., Todis, B., & Severson, H. H. (1991). *School Archival Records Search.* Longmont, CO: Sopris West.

Walker, H. M., Calvin, G. & Ramsey, E. (1995). *Antisocial behavior in school settings, strategies and best practices.* Albany, NY: Brooks/Cole.

Walker, H. M., & McConnell, S. R. (1988). *Walker-McConnell scale of social competence and school adjustment.* Austin, TX: Pro-Ed.

Walker, H. M., & McConnell, S. R. (1993). *Walker-McConnell scale of social competence and school adjustment* (rev. ed.). Austin, TX: Pro-Ed.

Walker, H. M., & Severson, H. H. (1999). *Systematic Screening for Behavior Disorders (SSBD): A multiple gating procedure* (2nd ed.). Longmont, CO: Sopris West.

Walker, H. M., & Severson, H. H. (1995). *Early Screening Project (ESP): A proven child find success.* Longmont, CO: Sopris West.

Walker, H. M., Severson, H. H., & Feil, E. G. (1995). *Early Screening Project (ESP).* Longmont, CO: Sopris West.

Walker, H. M., Severson, H. H., Stiller, B., Williams, G., Haring, N., Shinn, M., & Todis, B., (1988). Systematic screening of pupils in the elementary age range at risk for behavior disorders: Developement and trial testing of a multiple gating model. *Remedial and Special Education, 9*(3), 8–14.

Wolery, M., Bailey, D. B., & Sugai, G. M. (1988). *Effective teaching: Principles and procedures of applied behavior analysis with exceptional students.* Boston: Allyn & Bacon.

Yell, M. L. (1998). *The law and special education.* Upper Saddle River, NJ: Merrill/Prentice Hall.

# chapter 3

# DATA COLLECTION TECHNIQUES

*Thomas J. Zirpoli*

*There is a need for intervention and measurement methods that are practical and which allow for the documentation of empirically and socially valid outcomes. The teacher's interest is . . . in gathering information that can be used in ongoing decision making and problem solving. Teachers require measurement systems that are useful in formative program evaluation; competent instructional decision making is ongoing and does not occur only upon completing of a program. Teachers also need evidence that the outcomes associated with their efforts are meaningful for the students themselves.*

—MEYER AND JANNEY (*1989, P. 269*)

The primary goal of this chapter is to provide teachers with an understanding of the importance of direct behavioral observation, the measurement of behavior, and the documentation of these observations and measurements. In addition, by the end of this chapter, teachers will have the technical skills to complete these important tasks.

## TARGET BEHAVIORS

A *target behavior* is the behavior targeted for observation, measurement, and assessment and/or modification. The target behavior is identified by teachers as the behavior needing to be learned, increased, or decreased. Frequently, teachers are faced with several students who may have many challenging behaviors and training needs. In such situations, teachers are encouraged to prioritize behaviors according to their severity and need for remediation. Several questions have been recommended to assist in identifying and prioritizing target behaviors that need to be modified or eliminated (Barlow & Hersen, 1984; Kazdin, 1982):

- Is the behavior dangerous to the student or to others in the student's environment?
- Is the behavior interfering with the student's academic performance or placement?
- Is the behavior interfering with the student's social integration or causing the student to be socially isolated from peers?
- Is the behavior interfering with effective parental interactions (e.g., bonding or communication)?
- Is a change in the target behavior likely to produce positive outcomes for the student in the areas of academic performance and social acceptance?

Once target behaviors are identified, they must be clearly defined so that they can be objectively observed and measured. This, perhaps, is the most critical step in assuring accurate, reliable observations and measurements of target behaviors.

## Defining Target Behaviors

Target behaviors must be defined precisely so that there will be a minimum amount of variation from one observer to the next in the interpretation of the behavior. Precisely defined behaviors are stated in terms that are observable and measurable. *Observable* means that you can see the behavior occur. *Measurable* means that you can quantify the frequency, duration, or other dimensions of the behavior (dimensions of behavior are discussed later in this chapter). For example, increasing John's "appropriate" behavior and/or decreasing John's "inappropriate" behavior are not target behaviors that are stated in observable and measurable terms; the behaviors are not directly observable since the observer does not have a precise behavior to observe. A target behavior defined as "increasing John's attendance in English class" is precise and may be easily observed and measured. Few individuals would have trouble understanding what to count when measuring the frequency of John's English class attendance. The following lists provide additional examples of observable and nonobservable target behaviors:

*Examples of Observable Target Behaviors*

Chris will *complete his assignments* during math class.

Adam will *use his fork* to pick up food during mealtime.

Julia will *talk to other children* on the playground.

John will *ask for a break* when he is angry.

Tommy will *complete all school assignments* before going home.

Jeremy will *share his toys* with other children during free play.

Jill will *practice the piano* 1 hour per day.

Jason will *say "Thank you"* when given gifts for his birthday.

Mike will *say "Excuse me"* before interrupting others at home.

Justen will *look both ways* before crossing the street.

Melissa will *wait for her turn* during group work at school.

*Examples of Nonobservable Target Behaviors*

Chris will *be a good boy* during math class.

Adam will *be polite* during mealtime.

Julia will *be cooperative* on the playground.

John will *think* before he acts when he is angry.

Tommy will *remember* to do his schoolwork.

Jeremy will *be nice* to the other children during free play.

Jill will *apply herself* during piano practice.

Jason will *understand* the importance of saying "Thank you."

Mike will *demonstrate appropriate manners* with others.

Justen will *be careful* when crossing the street.

Melissa will *get along* with others during group work.

Notice that in most cases, the target behavior is presented in positive terms. Teachers should try to state target behaviors in terms of how children should behave instead of how they should not behave. This will help teachers focus on positive student behaviors instead of unacceptable or disruptive behaviors.

Hawkins and Dobes (1977) state that definitions of target behaviors should be *objective, clear,* and *complete.* A target behavior is *objective* when the observer can see the behavior or when the behavior is overt. Covert feelings or states are not objective. For example, "hitting other children" is overt and can be observed and measured. "Feeling angry" at other children is a state that is difficult to define, observe, and accurately measure. A target behavior is *clearly* defined when the definition is "unambiguous, easily understood, and readily paraphrased" (Barlow & Hersen, 1984, p. 111). For example, stating that a student "will behave" during group activities is not a clearly defined target behavior. Stating that the student "will stay seated" or "will keep her hands on the desk" is clear and unambiguous. A *complete* definition "includes the boundaries of the behavior, so that an observer can discriminate it from other, related behaviors" (Barlow & Hersen, 1984, p. 111). In the previous example, the target behavior "will behave" does not discriminate one behavior (e.g., "staying in seat") from other behaviors that could also be the intended behavior to be observed under the definition of "will behave" (e.g., "keeping hands on desk"). After a target behavior is identified and defined, teachers must establish a behavioral objective.

## Establishing Behavioral Objectives

A *behavioral objective* describes an anticipated behavior, new or modified from current behavior, subsequent to the completed behavior change program. As demonstrated in the first of the following examples, a behavioral objective includes several basic elements: the desired *terminal behavior* (in-seat behavior), the *conditions* under which the behavior is to occur (during each 45-minute math class), a level of performance or *behavioral criteria* (45 consecutive minutes), and a specified number of *consecutive observations* (three math classes) during which the behavioral criteria must be exhibited. The terminal behavior is what the student's behavior will look like after the behavior change program is completed. If the target behavior is the behavior you wish to teach or modify, the terminal behavior defines the student's behavior when the behavioral objective has been achieved. For example, a student may have a problem staying in his seat during math class. "Staying in seat" or "getting out of seat" is the target behavior. "Staying in seat for the entire 45-minute math class" may be the terminal behavior you wish to observe at the end of your behavior change program. An appropriate behavioral objective may be stated as follows:

John will stay in his seat during each 45-minute math class, unless he has permission from the teacher to leave his seat, for three consecutive math classes.

Behavioral criteria may be stated in many ways depending on the behavior and environmental expectations. In the preceding example, the behavioral objective for John's in-seat behavior was stated in terms of *what* behavior will be exhibited (staying in his seat), *when* the behavior will be exhibited (during each 45-minute math class), and for *how many* (three consecutive) math classes the behavior must be exhibited. Criteria may also be stated in the form of a percentage when a certain percentage of correct or appropriate responses is desired. For example:

John will comply with teacher requests with a 90% compliance rate over four consecutive days, or

John will complete 80% of his class assignments for five consecutive school days.

During the behavior change program, a student's behavior may be evaluated on the basis of the behavioral criteria outlined in the behavioral objective. The criteria outlined in behavioral objectives should reflect realistic expectations based on current performance (determined by a review of baseline data), academic necessity, and social norms.

Before teachers can develop behavioral objectives, baseline observations and data collection must be completed (as described later in this chapter). Baseline observations not only provide information about current performance levels from which behavioral objectives are developed, but they also help determine whether the target behavior is as problematic as perceived. With this information, teachers can establish objectives that are challenging yet realistic. Table 3.1 provides a review of these terms and their definitions.

**TABLE 3.1 • Definitions for Writing Behavioral Objectives and Examples**

| *Term* | *Definition* | *Example* |
|---|---|---|
| Target behavior | The behavior you want to teach or modify. When teaching a new behavior, the target and terminal behavior may be the same. | Temper tantrums at the grocery store or asking "please" when making a request |
| Terminal behavior | The desired behavior | The absence of temper tantrums |
| Behavioral criteria | A desired performance level of the terminal behavior. When the child reaches this performance level, the program is complete. | Zero tantrums for five consecutive shopping trips to the grocery store |
| Behavioral objective | A statement including the terminal behavior and the behavioral criteria | John will have zero tantrums for five consecutive shopping trips to the grocery store. |

# Naturalistic Observation

The purpose of naturalistic observations is to observe and record behavioral patterns across natural settings and situations, to measure the dimensions of specific target behaviors, and to identify the variables associated with specific target behaviors. All of this information will be useful to help us understand the function of a particular target behavior. In addition, observational data provide information on the effectiveness of behavior interventions and necessary modifications to ongoing programming (Cartwright & Cartwright, 1984; Cooper, 1981).

Green (1990) recommends that observers record occurrences of the target behavior under different conditions and pay particular attention to:

- the time of day;
- factors in the physical environment such as space, noise, temperature, light, materials, etc.;
- behaviors of others before and after occurrences of the problem behavior (see next section on ABC analysis);
- task demands;
- the student's communication skills; and
- conditions under which the disruptive behavior *does not* occur.

These factors will help teachers understand when a target behavior occurs and under what conditions. In addition, a functional analysis must include the systematic presentation of different antecedents and consequences to verify the purpose of the target behavior. This procedure is outlined in the next section on ABC analysis.

# Anecdotal Observation: The ABC Analysis

A good start to identify or confirm the purpose of a target behavior is by observing and recording the antecedents and consequences (defined earlier in Chapter 1) of the behavior. This can best be done through an ABC analysis:

A = Antecedent
B = Behavior
C = Consequence

Sometimes referred to as an *anecdotal observation,* an *ABC analysis* was first described by Bijou, Peterson, and Ault (1968). During an anecdotal observation, the observer records everything noticed about an individual's behavior. For example, if an anecdotal observation was completed for Jason during a 15-minute free-time period, the observer would record Jason's behaviors, whom he played with, what he played with, and what he said. The product of this anecdotal observation would probably include a narrative describing Jason's behavior during the 15-minute observation period. From this information, specific target behaviors may be identified for modification. It is important to note that ABC recording presents an

*ABC presents an objective description of actual behavior not interpretat.*

*objective* description of actual behavior, not interpretations of that behavior. For example, "Jason hit Mike," not "Jason was angry."

In addition to behavioral observation and data collection, an anecdotal record includes an analysis of antecedent and consequent events occurring within the observed environment. As Lennox and Miltenberger (1989) state, understanding behavior is incomplete without understanding the "events surrounding the target behavior and, subsequently, [determining] the extent to which specific events may be related to the occurrence of the behavior" (p. 306). The focus of an ABC analysis is on "external events that appear to influence the behavior" (Snell & Grigg, 1987, p. 78).

To complete an ABC analysis or anecdotal record of the antecedents, behaviors, and consequences within a student's environment, practitioners should prepare an observation form that will facilitate record keeping during the observation period. This form may be a simple sheet of paper divided into three sections: antecedent events, observed behaviors, and consequent events. An example of an anecdotal observation form, suitable for an ABC analysis, is provided in Figure 3.1.

An ABC analysis provides teachers with the following information:

- A descriptive record of a student's behavior during a specific observational period. The observational period could coincide with activities or settings in which the person's behavior has been especially problematic.

*[handwritten margin note: Was Michael part of students in circle?]*

---

Child's name: <u>Michael</u>                  Observer: <u>Ms. Garris</u>
Environment: <u>Playground</u>                 Date: <u>11/5/03</u>
Observation start time: <u>12:30 pm</u>         Stop: <u>12:45 pm</u>

| Antecedent Events | Observed Behavior | Consequent Events |
|---|---|---|
| 12:36: Students running around in a circle | Michael pushed Tim from behind. | Tim turned around and yelled at Michael to "Stop!" |
| 12:42: Students standing in a circle and talking | Michael told Tim, "You're a nerd," and hit him on the head. | Tim said nothing and did nothing. Michael laughed. |
| 12:45: Bell rings for kids to return to classroom. Kids begin to run toward building. | Michael hit Tim on the back as the two were running toward the building. | Tim continued to run toward the building. Did not give Michael a response. Michael laughed. |

**FIGURE 3.1.** Example record form for an ABC analysis

- A descriptive record of the student's environment, the significant people in the student's environment and their interactions with the student, and the activities occurring within the student's environment.
- Information about antecedent events occurring before the student's behavior. This information will help teachers identify events that may set the stage for specific behaviors. For example, what are the adult or peer behaviors (requests, demands, proximity) that occur prior to the student's behavior?
- Information about consequent events occurring after the student's behavior. This information will help teachers identify events that may maintain, reinforce, or punish specific behavior. For example, what comments do others make following the student's behavior, or how do other students respond after the student's behavior?

The preceding information will help teachers identify disruptive behaviors, events that are maintaining the disruptive behavior, alternative social skills that need to be learned, and environmental conditions that need modification to meet the needs of the student.

## Assessment Interviews

In addition to a structured observation as described in the ABC analysis, Umbreit and Blair (1997, p. 77) developed an assessment interview. They used the assessment interview to identify "the conditions under which a target behavior is likely and unlikely to occur" from the perspective of teachers, parents, or other significant others who spend a significant amount of time with the student and have the opportunity to observe patterns related to the target behavior. These interviews with significant others can help identify:

- when and how often the behavior occurs,
- how long the behavior has been occurring,
- the behavior reduction procedures the staff has previously used,
- whether other behaviors signal or occur along with the target behavior, and
- whether the target behavior's occurrence is related to skill deficits, allergies, medication, hunger or thirst, or other discomfort.

## DIMENSIONS OF BEHAVIOR

After a target behavior has been identified and defined and behavioral criteria have been established, two additional questions remain (Tawney & Gast, 1984, p. 112): What are the dimensions or "characteristics" of the student's behavior that should be observed and measured, and how will the dimensions of the target behavior be measured? This section addresses the first question by defining and discussing the five primary dimensions of behavior: *frequency, duration, rate, latency,* and *intensity.*

## Frequency

*Frequency* or *number* refers to a simple count of the number of times a behavior occurs during a specific time period. If one frequency count is to be compared with a second, the observation period must be constant across both. For example, if you observe Chris having 5 tantrums on day 1 and 10 tantrums on day 2, the duration of the observation periods across the two days must be the same for the two frequency counts to be directly comparable. In other words, you cannot assume that Chris had more tantrums on the 2nd day since the increase may be due to a longer observation period. Because teachers do not always have a constant observation period from day to day, frequency counts alone are not recommended.

When a constant observation period can be established, frequency counts are best used when the target behavior has clear starting and stopping points (Foster, Bell-Dolan, & Burge, 1988). For example, counting the number of times one student *hits* another student is easily done. However, counting the number of times a student *talks* to another student may be more complicated since clear starting and stopping points between *talks* may be blurred.

Kazdin (1989) recommends that frequency only be used when each occurrence of the target behavior "takes a relatively constant amount of time each time it is performed" (p. 58). Using our previous example, each *hit* probably takes the same time to perform, while each *talk* may not. A student could talk for 1 second to one student ("Hi!") or have a 5-minute conversation with a second student. A simple frequency count (two) would not discriminate the two *talking* behaviors as different. For behaviors that may vary in duration, teachers are encouraged to measure frequency and duration.

Another caution regarding the use of frequency counts alone is knowing the number of response opportunities. For example, if a teacher reports that a student completed five assignments during math class, this information is incomplete without knowing the total number of assignments requested. Knowing that the student completed 5 of 5 or 5 of 10 assignments communicates a more complete picture of the student's performance than the frequency count alone. A second example involves the measurement of compliance. If a teacher reports a frequency count of eight compliances during a school day, without reporting the total number of opportunities to be compliant, the information is incomplete and not very useful. A frequency count of 8 compliances of 10 opportunities represents a different level of performance than 8 compliances of 20 requests.

## Duration

Duration data are recommended when teachers are concerned about how long a behavior continues once started or the amount of time consumed when a behavior is performed. Duration is a necessary dimension to measure when teachers want to increase or decrease the amount of time a student performs a behavior or participates in an activity. In addition to how often some behaviors occur, the duration of behaviors such as crying, throwing temper tantrums, listening, or working on a task is a significant dimension that should be measured. For example, if a student has a 60-minute temper tantrum one day and a 5-minute tantrum the next, information that the student had one tantrum each day (frequency) does not provide a complete picture of the student's behavior. In this example, the duration of tantrum behavior has significantly decreased from the 1st to the 2nd day. This change in behavior would not have been noted if the duration of the behavior was not measured.

There are two types of duration: *total duration* (Tawney & Gast, 1984) and *response duration* (Kazdin, 1989). Total duration refers to the total amount of time a student performs a target behavior during an observation period. For example, if a student had two tantrums during a 1-hour observation period and each tantrum lasted 5 minutes, the total duration was 10 minutes. Teachers would be interested in measuring total duration if they were trying to increase or decrease the total amount of time a student was engaged in an activity or behavior within a specific time period or activity. For example, a teacher may wish to increase a student's total time on task in a reading class. Total duration may be used to estimate the percentage of total observation time in which a student is engaged in a behavior (Kazdin, 1989). For example, if a student worked on task for a total duration of 30 minutes during a 45-minute class period, it may be stated that the student was on task for 66.6% of the class period.

$$(30/45 = 0.666 \times 100 = 66.6\%)$$

A response duration refers to the amount of time a student performs each individual target behavior. In the earlier example, the response duration for the first and second tantrum was 5 minutes. Teachers would be interested in measuring response duration if they were trying to increase or decrease the amount of time a student exhibits a specific behavior. Referring back to our temper tantrum example, it is helpful to know the duration of each individual tantrum, not total duration, when trying to decrease tantrum behavior. In addition, the use of response duration allows teachers to estimate a median response duration per behavior occurrence.

## Rate

*Rate* refers to the frequency of a target behavior divided by the number of minutes or hours of observation time. This will yield a rate-per-minute or rate-per-hour measurement:

*frequency of behavior/observation time = rate*

For example, if John is noncompliant 10 times during a 5-hour observation period, John's hourly rate of noncompliance is 2. This was calculated by dividing the frequency (10) of noncompliance by the number (5) of observation hours (10/5 = 2).

*frequency of noncompliance/total observation hours = rate per hour of noncompliance*

Rate is often stated in terms of minutes. For example, if a teacher observes Julia kicking her desk six times during a 30-minute social studies class, then Julia's

*[handwritten margin note: Total duration = total amount of time kid performs a target behavior during an observation period.]*

kicking rate per minute is 0.20. This was calculated by dividing the frequency (6) of kicking by the number (30) of observation minutes (6/30 = 0.20).

frequency of kicking/total observation minutes = rate per minute

Rates are useful when the observation periods are not constant and vary in duration. The measurement of the rate allows teachers to compare the frequency of behavior across observation periods even if the duration of the observation period varies from day to day. For example, if Julia kicks her desk 12 times during another 1-hour observation period, her minute rate of kicking is 0.20 (12/60 = .20). The minute rate (0.20) from the first observation period may be compared with the rate (0.20) from the second observation period since the difference in the duration of the observation period was accounted for during the rate calculation. In this case, a summary of Julia's performance for the two days may conclude that the rate of her kicking was constant (0.20 per minute). On the other hand, if the teacher reported frequency alone (6 kicks on day 1 and 12 kicks on day 2), an observer might incorrectly conclude that Julia's kicking behavior doubled on the 2nd day.

Teachers are recommended to use rate when reporting the number of times a behavior occurred unless the observation periods are constant. However, given the busy schedules of classrooms and homes, observation periods are unlikely to be constant, and teachers should plan on using rates when reporting behavioral data.

## Latency

*Latency* refers to the amount of time it takes for a student to begin a behavior once he or she has received a direction or an instruction to complete a task or modify a behavior. Latency is most useful when teachers are concerned about students' compliance or behaviors related to following directions. For example, when a teacher asks a student to help pick up toys after a free-time activity, latency is recorded by keeping track of the number of minutes or seconds between the initial request and the point when the student actually starts to pick up the toys. When teachers are working with children who tend to be noncompliant, the objective is to reduce the latency period to an acceptable level (5 to 10 seconds). This goal is accomplished by reinforcing children when they show improvement in decreasing their latency period and when they respond appropriately within an acceptable period of time.

Sometimes teachers want to increase latency periods. A common example is the student who responds incorrectly to a teacher's directions because he or she begins an activity before the teacher provides all the instructions. Children who are too quick to answer a teacher's question, without allowing some time to think about the question, may commit many errors because of short latencies. When this is a problem, teachers may want to require a certain latency period (thinking time) before children are allowed to volunteer an answer.

## Intensity or Magnitude

*Intensity* refers to the force or strength of a behavior. Intensity of behavior is a useful measurement with behaviors such as acts of aggression, temper tantrums, verbal responses, or other noises and body movements. For example, since the variability in crying behavior is considerable, teachers working with a student who cries when he or she is brought to day care each morning may be interested in measuring intensity, in addition to the frequency and duration of crying. A student who cries for 5 minutes once each morning may seem, with just frequency and duration measures, to be making poor progress adjusting to day care. However, the intensity measurement may record a significant change in the student's crying behavior from "loud screaming" to "mild whining."

Intensity measures are either estimates based on a predetermined qualitative scale or, for a more objective measure, an automated apparatus used to measure a behavior's intensity. For example, Greene, Bailey, and Barber (1981) have used an automated apparatus to measure noise levels during a program to decrease disruptive behavior on school buses. In most cases, however, teachers do not have access to such automatic equipment; moreover, qualitative estimates of intensity will probably serve the needs of most teachers and parents. When an objective method of measuring the intensity of a target behavior is not possible, the following are some example scales that may be used, depending on the behavior:

- very strong, strong, weak, very weak;
- mild, moderate, severe, very severe;
- very loud, loud, quiet, very quiet;
- very fast, fast, slow, very slow.

We must stress, however, that these "ratings" provide subjective measurements of behavior. When these are used, precise criteria should be established per rating, and independent observers should complete reliability checks.

# MEASUREMENT OF BEHAVIOR

It is important that we demonstrate to teachers that behavioral observation, measurement, and documentation may be completed without significant sacrifices of teacher time from the typical classroom routine. Unfortunately, many teachers consider data collection as too demanding (Fisher & Lindsey-Walters, 1987), and many teachers use intuition rather than classroom data when making instructional decisions (Grigg, Snell, & Loyd, 1989). In addition, teachers tend to discount their classroom data as invalid (Grigg et al., 1989) and unreliable (Fisher & Lindsey-Walters, 1987).

Wacker (1989) provides two primary reasons why teachers should measure behavior: to document what occurred and to identify the variables responsible for the occurrence. "Measurement, in short, provides us with guidance regarding what we should do next" (p. 254). In addition, a systematic process of behavioral measurement can:

- help teachers identify learning and behavior problems;
- provide information concerning program effectiveness;
- identify the need for program modifications; and
- facilitate communication with parents, administrators, other teachers, and support personnel.

Tawney and Gast (1984, p. 84) provide several guidelines for measuring and evaluating behavior:

- Define the target behavior in measurable and observable terms.
- Collect sufficient data to provide the information necessary to make programming decisions. It is not necessary to collect data constantly on all behaviors.
- Become familiar with data collection alternatives so intelligent decisions can be made regarding the most effective measurement method per student and behavior.
- Select a data collection method that is practical. In other words, choose a method that can be consistently and reliably used within the constraints of the environment. A simple data collection system is more likely to be used than a demanding one.
- Integrate data collection into the daily routine. Again, data collection should not take an extraordinary effort on the part of teachers.
- Review and evaluate the data regularly, and use the data to make programming decisions.

The primary purpose of data collection is to provide teachers with objective information with which to make informed programming decisions. It is disturbing to observe teachers collect data only to fulfill an organizational requirement, place the data in a file, and never use the data for program evaluation.

Several types of data collection methods or observational recording systems are used to monitor behavior. An understanding of these different methods will allow teachers to select the simplest and most informative data collection procedure. A description of the primary types of behavioral observation and measurement methods is outlined in the next sections.

## Frequency Recording/Event Recording

When observing for an individual target behavior, an easy method of measuring the target behavior is simply to count the behavior every time it occurs during a specific time period. This method of data collection is called *frequency recording* or *event recording*. The result of a frequency recording is a frequency count or rate of occurrence per observation period. For example, a teacher may use event recording to count how many times a student hits other students during a 30-minute recess. Koorland, Monda, and Vail (1988) make the following recommendations concerning event recording:

- Event recording should be used only when the target behavior is "discrete, uniform in duration, brief, and repeatable" (p. 59).
- The observation periods per day may be fixed or variable. Thus, teachers may decide to count a target behavior once per day, twice per day, or whatever schedule is convenient with the teacher's schedule.
- The duration of each observation period may vary. When the observation period is constant, a frequency count may be reported per observation. When the observation periods vary, however, the rate of the behavior must be determined by dividing each number of occurrences per observation period with the number of minutes per observation period.

Figure 3.2 illustrates an event recording data form used to count hitting behavior. Data collected include the number of times hitting was observed, the length of the observation periods in minutes, and the rate of hitting per minute. Note that the observation periods vary in length, and the rate per minute is calculated for each observation so that the data are comparable. The rate of the target behavior, per minute, may also be charted on a graph as demonstrated in Figure 3.2.

## Duration Recording

Recording the duration of a behavior is important when teachers are concerned with the amount of time a student engages in a target behavior. Teachers may record duration along with frequency by making a note of the time the target behavior begins and ends. A duration can then be calculated. For example, if a student begins to tantrum at 10:15 and ends at 10:25, the duration of the tantrum is 10 minutes.

Duration may be recorded in two ways. First, teachers may be interested in the *average duration* of a behavior over a specific period of time. For example, if a student had three tantrums during one class period lasting 10, 5, and 3 minutes each, the average duration is 6 minutes.

$$10 + 5 + 3 = 18/3 = 6$$

Second, teachers may also be interested in the *total duration* of the target behavior. Using our same example, the total duration of tantrum behavior is 18 minutes.

## Interval Recording

*Interval recording* refers to the division of a specific observation period into equal intervals of smaller time periods or intervals. The observer then indicates whether the target behavior occurred (+) or did not occur (−) during each interval. Note

**FIGURE 3.2.** Example of event recording data form and graph of recorded new data

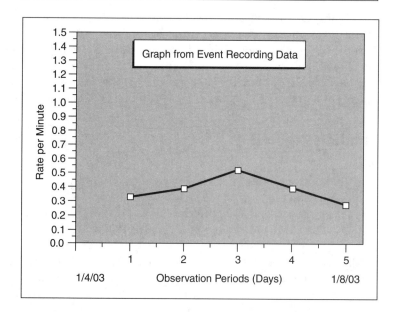

Student's name: _Mike_       Observer: _Ms. Garris_

Environment: _Playground_       Date: _1/4/03–1/8/03_

Target behavior: _Hitting others_

| Day/Time | Observation Period | Frequency of Behavior | Rate per Minute |
|---|---|---|---|
| 1/4/03 | 30 minutes | 10 | 0.33 per min. |
| 1/5/03 | 20 minutes | 08 | 0.40 per min. |
| 1/6/03 | 15 minutes | 08 | 0.53 per min. |
| 1/7/03 | 30 minutes | 12 | 0.40 per min. |
| 1/8/03 | 20 minutes | 06 | 0.30 per min. |

that the frequency of the target behavior during each interval is *not* recorded, which is a limitation of interval recording. A second drawback is that the size of the intervals will partly determine the recorded rate (percentage of intervals) of the target behavior. If the intervals are too long, a summary of the intervals may always indicate a target behavior rate of 100%, regardless of real decreases in the target behavior. For example, although a student's frequency of hitting may have decreased from 10 to 5 per interval, the observer would indicate only a "+" to indicate that the target behavior (hitting) occurred during that particular interval. As a result, the observer may then report that hitting was still occurring during 100% of the intervals. Although this statement would be correct, the decrease in the ac-

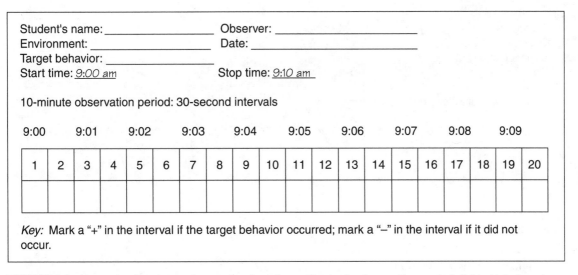

Student's name: _____   Observer: _____
Environment: _____   Date: _____
Target behavior: _____
Start time: _9:00 am_   Stop time: _9:10 am_

10-minute observation period: 30-second intervals

9:00   9:01   9:02   9:03   9:04   9:05   9:06   9:07   9:08   9:09

| 1 | 2 | 3 | 4 | 5 | 6 | 7 | 8 | 9 | 10 | 11 | 12 | 13 | 14 | 15 | 16 | 17 | 18 | 19 | 20 |
|---|---|---|---|---|---|---|---|---|----|----|----|----|----|----|----|----|----|----|----|
|   |   |   |   |   |   |   |   |   |    |    |    |    |    |    |    |    |    |    |    |

*Key:* Mark a "+" in the interval if the target behavior occurred; mark a "–" in the interval if it did not occur.

**FIGURE 3.3.** Example of an interval recording form for a 10-minute observation period divided into twenty 30-second intervals

tual frequency of hitting may not be documented. On the other hand, intervals that are too short may result in the recording of artificially low rates of behavior. (Note later in Figure 3.3, for example, how the resulting percentages may be manipulated by changing the duration of the intervals.)

The size of each interval within the total observation period may range from 5 to 30 seconds. Trudel and Cote (1996) used six-second intervals to observe and record the behavior of ice hockey coaches during games. Because they were observing 16 different categories of coach behaviors and 8 categories describing to whom their behavior was directed, Trudel and Cote decided to use a six-second interval to "decrease the possibility of occurrence of too many behaviors within a given interval" (p. 50).

Kazdin (1989) recommends 10- to 15-second intervals; Cooper, Heron, and Heward (1987) suggest 6- to 15-second intervals; and Alberto and Troutman (1995) state that the intervals should not be longer than 30 seconds. Repp, Nieminen, Olinger, and Brusca (1988) have found that shorter intervals produced more accurate data than longer intervals. The total observation period for interval recording may range from 10 to 60 minutes, depending on the teacher's schedule.

An example of an interval recording form is provided in Figure 3.3.

A 10-minute observation period is divided into 30-second intervals. Since there are twenty 30-second intervals during a 10-minute observation period, the 10-minute observation period is divided into 20 intervals. Thus, the total number of intervals depends on the total observation time and the length of the intervals.

Once the length of the total observation period and the size of the intervals have been decided, the next step is to observe the student and indicate whether the target behavior occurred during each interval. It does not make a difference how

Student's name: _Chris_          Observer: _Ms. Hawkins_
Environment: _Science_          Date: _3/2/03_
Target behavior: _On Task_
Start time: _9:00 am_          Stop time: _9:10 am_

10-minute observation period: 30-second intervals

| 9:00 | | 9:01 | | 9:02 | | 9:03 | | 9:04 | | 9:05 | | 9:06 | | 9:07 | | 9:08 | | 9:09 | |
|---|---|---|---|---|---|---|---|---|---|---|---|---|---|---|---|---|---|---|---|
| 1 | 2 | 3 | 4 | 5 | 6 | 7 | 8 | 9 | 10 | 11 | 12 | 13 | 14 | 15 | 16 | 17 | 18 | 19 | 20 |
| − | + | + | + | − | + | + | − | + | + | + | − | − | + | + | + | + | − | + | + |

*Key:* + = The behavior occurred during the interval.
     − = The behavior did not occur during the interval.

**Summary of Interval Recording Observation**
Total number of intervals                              20
Intervals target behavior occurred                    14
Percentage of intervals behavior occurred             70%
Intervals target behavior did not occur                6
Percentage of intervals behavior did not occur        30%

**FIGURE 3.4.** Sample data for an interval recording form for a 10-minute observation period divided into twenty 30-second intervals

many times the target behavior occurred during each interval. During the observation period, a "+" is recorded if the behavior occurred at any time during each interval and a "−" if it did not (see Figure 3.4). At the end of the interval, teachers may calculate the percentage of intervals in which the target behavior occurred and did not occur. This is calculated by dividing the number of intervals with a "+" by the total number of intervals. In our hypothetical data provided in Figure 3.4, the target behavior was observed in 14 of the 20 intervals. By dividing 14 by 20, we find that the target behavior occurred during 70% of the total intervals.

The two primary methods of interval recording are *partial-interval recording* and *whole-interval recording*. Partial-interval recording requires the observer to record whether the behavior occurred at any time during the interval. The frequency or duration of the behavior within the interval is not monitored. Whole-interval recording, however, requires the observer to record the occurrence of the behavior only if the behavior was present throughout the entire interval. Thus, the duration of the behavior is monitored. The decision to use partial- or whole-interval recording depends primarily on the observed behavior. The partial-interval approach is preferred for behaviors that are short in duration (hitting and touching), while the whole-interval approach is appropriate for behaviors that occur for an extended

Students' names: <u>Mellisa, Jill & Julia</u>
Target behavior: <u>Talking</u>
Environment: _____ Date: _____
Start time: _____ Stop time: _____

5-minute observation period: 30-second intervals

| Name | | 1 | | 2 | | 3 | | 4 | | 5 |
|------|---|---|---|---|---|---|---|---|---|---|
| Mellisa | | | | | | | | | | |
| Jill | | | | | | | | | | |
| Julia | | | | | | | | | | |

*Key:* Next to the appropriate child's name, mark a "+" in the interval if the target behavior was observed; mark a "−" in the interval if the target behavior did not occur.

**FIGURE 3.5.** Interval recording form for a 5-minute observation period divided into ten 30-second intervals for three students

duration (off-task and talking). Repp et al. (1988) noted that, in comparison with continuous measurement, partial-interval recording tends to overestimate the continuous measures, while whole-interval recording underestimates.

Teachers may use interval recording to monitor the behavior of several students or behaviors at the same time. However, teachers should not try to monitor more than three children or behaviors during a single observation period. Figure 3.5 shows a sample recording form used to monitor talking behavior among three children during a 3-minute observation period divided into ten 30-second intervals. A similar form could also be used to observe three different behaviors for one student.

## Time Sampling

*Time sampling,* sometimes referred to as *momentary time sampling,* refers to another common method of behavior measurement. Like interval recording, time sampling requires the observer to divide the total observation period into smaller time intervals. However, unlike interval recording in which the observer records whether the behavior occurred at *any* time during the interval, time sampling requires the observer to record whether the behavior was observed at the *end* of the interval. For example, if an observer was monitoring Julia's on task behavior, the observer would look at Julia at the end of each interval and record a "+" if she was on task at that *moment* or a "−" if she was not on task. Time sampling is most appropriately used when monitoring behaviors that have some duration. For example on-task/off-task, in-seat/out-of-seat, and talking are examples of behaviors that may be monitored with time sampling.

The total length of observation for time sampling may be significantly longer than interval recording since the observer is actually required to look at the student only at the end of each interval. In addition, while the intervals in interval recording are usually seconds long, the intervals in time sampling are usually minutes long. For example, a 60-minute observation period may be divided into twelve 5-minute intervals. Like interval recording, the observer records the percentage of intervals for which the target behavior was recorded (number of "+" notes divided by the total number of intervals). A recording form for such an observation is provided in Figure 3.6.

Two concerns arise with regard to time sampling. First, as the length of the intervals increases, the amount of observed or sampled behavior decreases. As the amount of observed behavior decreases, the collected data are less likely to be consistent with the actual occurrence of the target behavior. Thus, it is recommended that interval periods for time sampling not exceed 5 minutes. Second, if the student knows that a teacher is monitoring his or her behavior and that the teacher is looking at the student only at the end of a specific time interval, the student may modify his or her behavior so that the target behavior is not observed at the end of the interval. If this is a problem or a potential concern, teachers have three options: (a) keep the interval length a secret, (b) use interval recording instead of time sampling, or (c) vary the length of the interval. While varying the length of the intervals, teachers maintain an average interval period (e.g., 5 minutes), while the actual intervals may range, for example, from 2 to 8 minutes.

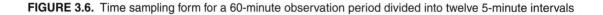

Student's name: _____     Observer: _____
Environment: _____     Date: _____
Target behavior: _____
Start time: _9:00 am_     Stop time: _9:10 am_

60-minute observation period: 5-minute intervals

9:00                    9:15                    9:30                    9:45                    10:00

| 1 | 2 | 3 | 4 | 5 | 6 | 7 | 8 | 9 | 10 | 11 | 12 |
|---|---|---|---|---|---|---|---|---|----|----|----|
|   |   |   |   |   |   |   |   |   |    |    |    |

*Key:* Mark a "+" in the interval if the target behavior was observed at the end of the observation period; mark a "−" in the interval if the target behavior was not observed.

**FIGURE 3.6.** Time sampling form for a 60-minute observation period divided into twelve 5-minute intervals

Murphy and Harrop (1994) completed a comparison of momentary time sampling (MTS) and partial-interval recording (PIR) using 60 college students' observations of two 10-minute videotaped sequences. They found that MTS yielded less error into observers' recordings than PIR and that observers showed some preference for MTS.

As with interval recording, time sampling allows observers to calculate the percentage of total intervals the behavior was observed and not observed. For example, if the behavior was observed at the end of 6 of 12 intervals, we would report that the behavior was observed during 50% of the total intervals.

## ACCURACY OF BEHAVIORAL OBSERVATION AND MEASURES

Repp et al. (1988, p. 29) outline several factors that may "potentially affect the accuracy of data collected during direct observations": reactivity; observer drift; the recording procedure; location of the observation; observer expectancy; and characteristics of subjects, observers, and settings. Personal values and biases are additional sources of observer error. Each of these is described in the following sections.

### Reactivity

*Reactivity* refers to changes in a student's behavior as a result of being observed. For example, when children know that a teacher is counting how often they get out of their seats, the children may increase or decrease the target behavior in response to this knowledge. The exact effect on a student's behavior depends on the student, the behavior, the observer, and many other situational variables. Since the observer cannot be sure whether his or her presence will have an impact on the student's behavior, sometimes unobtrusive observations (i.e., when the student is unaware that his or her behavior is being observed) are preferable. For example, unobtrusive observations are recommended when baseline data, discussed later in this chapter, are collected.

### Observer Drift

*Observer drift* refers to a gradual shift by the observer of his or her understanding of the target behavior being observed and measured. For example, a teacher counting the frequency of a student getting out of his or her seat may have a different definition of the target behavior at the end of the observational period than the original definition used at the beginning of the observational period. In this case, differences observed and recorded in the student's behavior from one day to the next may have more to do with observer drift than actual changes in the student's behavior.

To control for observer drift, the target behavior should be defined in very specific terms that will remain clear throughout the duration of a program. Moreover, teachers should define the topography of the target behavior prior to any observation. Thus, when out-of-seat behavior is being observed, teachers should define what "out-of-seat" means—what is counted and what is not counted as an out-of-seat behavior. For example, a good description of out-of-seat behavior may state "Paul will be considered to be 'out of seat' when his buttocks are at least 12 inches from his chair." This clearly defines out-of-seat behavior such that teachers know when to count the target behavior as occurring. Observer drift is more common when target behaviors are vaguely defined.

## The Recording Procedure

The *recording procedure* refers to the procedure selected to measure the dimensions of a behavior (e.g., frequency, duration). The primary methods of measuring behavior include event recording, interval recording, and time sampling. As we have discussed, some procedures produce a more accurate picture of the behavior than others depending on the dimensions of the behavior to be measured.

## Location of the Observation

At the beginning of this chapter, we discussed the importance of direct observation within natural settings. That is, if a student is exhibiting an unacceptable behavior within a classroom setting, it is important that the student's behavior be observed and measured within the classroom. Direct observations in natural settings provide a more accurate picture of the student's typical behavior within functional environments. Observations within natural environments also allow the observer to monitor teacher behavior, peer behavior, and other environmental influences related to the unacceptable behavior. These same considerations hold true for unacceptable behavior exhibited in other environments.

## Observer Expectancy

*Observer expectancy* refers to the expectations teachers have about the children they observe. For example, when a teacher hears "things" from other teachers about a student's behavior, the teacher develops certain expectations about the student's behavior. These expectations may bias a teacher's observation of the student.

Teachers' expectations may also affect how children behave. Observer expectations are less likely to influence observational data when target behaviors are clearly defined. Also, the periodic use of independent observers for reliability checks will help monitor these influences on teacher observations.

Direct observation is a necessary and significant element of behavioral assessment.

## Characteristics of Subjects, Observers, and Settings

*Characteristics of subjects, observers, and settings* refer to variables such as gender differences, the complexity of the behavior being observed, and familiarity with the setting and children being observed (Repp et al., 1988). Results of studies suggest that gender differences may affect the way observers score children's behaviors. In fact, the gender of both the student and the observer may influence the data collected during direct observation (Repp et al., 1988; Yarrow & Waxler, 1979). Using both male and female observers to observe and measure children's behaviors is an excellent solution to gender influences. However, given the overwhelming proportion of female teachers in our schools, this may not be practical within school environments.

Regarding the setting, research has shown that "familiarity with the setting may make observation easier and thereby increase observer accuracy" (Repp et al., 1988, p. 32). This is certainly a positive finding for classroom teachers and parents who are interested in observing and measuring behaviors within their own school or home setting.

## Personal Values and Bias

*Personal values* refer to social, cultural, or religious values that affect a teacher's perception of children's behavior. For example, different personal values regarding behavior will affect a teacher's definition of "appropriate" and "inappropriate" behavior. Observer *bias* refers to beliefs or emotional feelings about individual children. For example, among teachers, teachers may report different observations than parents who were asked to observe for the same behavior. Whether a teacher likes a student, how the student looks, and the culture and gender of the student are other variables that may bias the teacher's perceptions and observations (Bell & Harper, 1977; Grossman, 1995; Repp et al., 1988; Zirpoli & Bell, 1987).

Many variables may provide a threat to the accuracy of data collected during direct observation. However, these threats are easily overcome. First, teachers should become aware of the potential threats given their specific situation and available resources. Second, as previously stated, the target behavior must be stated in observable and measurable terms. This is the most important variable regarding the accurate measurement of behavior. A clear, concise definition of the target behavior will help eliminate misunderstandings of exactly what behaviors are and are not included in the target behavior. Third, teachers may want to practice using their data collection method and correct any "bugs" before a full-scale implementation. Fourth, reliability data should be completed periodically to check for the reliability of data across teachers. Checking reliability is discussed later. Repp et al. (1988, p. 33) outline five additional recommendations to improve the accuracy of data collected during direct observations:

- *Train observers well regarding the definition and measurement of the target behavior.* This point is especially important for teachers within educational environments where many teachers may be involved in collecting data.
- *Use an adaptation period for both teachers and children.* This approach is necessary only when the teacher is a stranger to the student and reactivity becomes a potential problem. It is not an issue for parents or teachers who are collecting data within their own classrooms.
- *Observe unobtrusively.* Try to integrate data collection into the teaching routine.
- *Use permanent products* (e.g., videotapes, audiocassettes, etc.). This is not always possible or practical when teaching or caring for children in the home. However, at times a teacher may need to document a student's behavior on film in order to show others and receive suggestions and other assistance.
- *Observe frequently and systematically.* Obviously, a longer period of observation is likely to document a more accurate "picture" of a student's typical behavior than a shorter period. However, a systematic approach to data collection need not take a significant amount of a teacher's time.

## Data Collection Aids

Teachers do not have to purchase sophisticated and expensive recording devices when collecting data. For example, teachers may use a simple wrist counter or golf counter to record frequency during event recording. Also, teachers may use a wristwatch with a second hand or a stopwatch to monitor duration. Descriptions of other less technical, homemade aids or techniques follow.

## Pocket Counting

*Pocket counting* is the transfer of pennies or other small objects from one pocket to another each time a target behavior is observed. At the end of the observation period, the teacher simply counts the number of pennies in the receiving pocket to measure the frequency of the target behavior. The frequency count can then be recorded on the appropriate data collection form.

## The Empty Jar

Teachers may drop pennies or other small objects into a jar each time a target behavior occurs. At the end of the observation period, the teacher simply counts the number of objects in the jar to measure the frequency of the target behavior. We observed one teacher drop paper strips into jars placed on the students' desks each time appropriate behavior was observed. At the end of the day the student with the most paper strips was provided with a special reinforcer. The paper strips also provided the teacher with a frequency count of appropriate behaviors exhibited per student or small groups of students.

## Masking Tape on the Wrist

Another teacher told us about placing masking tape on her wrist. A few select names and target behaviors were written on the tape, and the teacher recorded slash marks next to the appropriate behavior. At the end of class the teacher counted the slash marks, which served as a frequency count per target behavior. Of course, a clipboard with a data collection form would serve the same purpose. Teachers could tape a watch or stopwatch to the clipboard in order to measure both frequency and duration. However, some teachers may consider a clipboard obtrusive and difficult to carry while teaching or completing other teacher responsibilities.

These recording tools ease the task of data collection in addition to facilitating accuracy and reliability. Teachers should use their imagination and creativity when planning data collection methods and procedures. The most effective methods achieve the following aims:

- To make data collection easier than if no tools were used
- Not to interfere with teaching or other teacher duties
- To be simple to use
- To ensure accurate monitoring of the target behavior

## RELIABILITY OF OBSERVATIONS

When measuring a target behavior, *reliability* refers primarily to the accuracy of data collected across observers. This kind of reliability is most commonly called *interrater reliability;* other terms include *interobserver reliability* and *interobserver agreement.* For example, when observing a student's out-of-seat behavior, two observers are said to have perfect (100%) interrater reliability when both observe and record the student getting out of the seat the same number of times. However, if one teacher observes 5 occurrences of the behavior while a second teacher observes 10, the interrater reliability between the two observers is only 50% ($5/10 = 0.5 \times 100 = 50\%$).

Reliability measures provide independent confirmation that the data collected by one observer are accurate. Kazdin (1989) cites three primary reasons why reliability is important. First, the assessment of an individual's behavior should be a function of the individual's true behavior, not a function of inconsistent data collection. If teachers are going to use direct observation to evaluate the effectiveness of an intervention program, the data collected must be reliable. Second, monitoring reliability identifies and minimizes the possible biases of individual observers. Having a second observer periodically monitor the same target behavior provides a check and balance on the first observer's observation and recorded data. Lastly, reliability provides evidence regarding how well the target behavior is defined. High reliability scores reflect a well-defined target behavior. Low reliability scores may reflect a target behavior that is not clearly identified and defined, which may result in an inconsistent application of the intervention plan. Inconsistency is the primary deficiency of many behavior management programs.

Teachers will obtain satisfactory reliability measures when target behaviors are clearly defined and all observers are adequately trained. Observer training should include an overview of the program, the topography of the target behavior(s) to be observed, and the measurement techniques to be employed during observation.

Reliability measures greater than 70% to 80% are usually considered adequate. Of course, the closer the reliability is to 100%, the better. When reliability is lower than 70%, serious questions should be raised regarding the accuracy of the collected data. Behavior change programming decisions are difficult to make with inconsistent or deficient data. The method used to calculate reliability depends to a large extent on the dimension of behavior measured or the type of data collection procedure used.

### Reliability of Frequency Counts

If a frequency count or event recording procedure is employed, interrater reliability may be calculated by dividing the lower frequency by the higher frequency. Referring back to the previous example, one observer recorded 5 out-of-seat behaviors; the second observer, 10. The lower frequency (5) is then divided by the higher frequency (10), which equals 0.5. This quotient (0.5) is then multiplied by 100, and an interrater reliability of 50% is calculated as demonstrated here:

$5 = frequency\ recorded\ by\ first\ observer$
$10 = frequency\ recorded\ by\ second\ observer$
$reliability = 5/10 = 0.5 \times 100 = 50\%$

## Reliability of Duration and Latency Measures

A similar procedure is used to calculate interrater reliability when two observers are measuring the duration or latency of a target behavior. These measures involve a measurement of time instead of frequency. To find the reliability between the two time periods, the shorter duration/latency observed is divided by the longer duration/latency observed. For example, if one observer records that a student was on task for 10 minutes and a second observer records that the same student was on task for 15 minutes, their interrater reliability would equal 66.6%, or 67%, as demonstrated here:

$10\ minutes = duration\ observed\ by\ first\ observer$
$15\ minutes = duration\ observed\ by\ second\ observer$
$Reliability = 10/15 = 0.666 \times 100 = approximately\ 67\%$

## Reliability for Interval Recording and Time Sampling

To calculate interrater reliability for interval and time sampling procedures, a slightly more complex method is required. As previously outlined, both interval recording and time sampling involve dividing an observation period into smaller intervals of time. Two concerns arise regarding the reliability of data collected using these two procedures. First, observers want to know whether the *number* of intervals that the target behavior was recorded across the two observers is reliable. We will call this *frequency reliability*, which is calculated in the same manner as event recording reliability. Thus, if one teacher observes the behavior in 7 intervals and the second teacher observes the behavior in 12 intervals, their frequency reliability is calculated as follows:

$$7/12 = 0.58 \times 100 = 58\%$$

The second reliability concern during interval recording or time sampling may be referred to as *agreement reliability*. This measure is more important than frequency reliability because it communicates a more accurate picture of the interrater reliability between two observers. In looking at Figure 3.7, note that both teachers recorded that the student was on task 5 of the 10 intervals. Thus, their frequency reliability is 100% ($5/5 = 1 \times 100 = 100\%$). Also note, however, that both observers *agree* on when the student was on task (interval 7) and when the student was not on task (interval 3) only in 2 of the 10 intervals. That is, during interval 7

**Interval**

*Observer 1*

| 1 | 2 | 3 | 4 | 5 | 6 | 7 | 8 | 9 | 10 |
|---|---|---|---|---|---|---|---|---|---|
| + | + | − | + | − | − | + | − | + | − |

*Observer 2*

| 1 | 2 | 3 | 4 | 5 | 6 | 7 | 8 | 9 | 10 |
|---|---|---|---|---|---|---|---|---|---|
| − | − | − | − | + | + | + | + | − | + |

*Agreement between observers 1 and 2*

| 1 | 2 | 3 | 4 | 5 | 6 | 7 | 8 | 9 | 10 |
|---|---|---|---|---|---|---|---|---|---|
| No | No | Yes | No | No | No | Yes | No | No | No |

*Key:* + = on-task behavior observed during interval
       − = on-task behavior not observed during interval

*Summary*
   Agreements = 2
   Total intervals = 10
   2/10 = 0.20 × 100 = 20% agreement

   Frequency reliability = 100%
   Agreement reliability = 20%

**FIGURE 3.7.** Interrater reliability (frequency and agreement) of two interval recording observations of on-task behavior

both observers marked a "+," indicating that they observed the student to be on-task, and during interval 3 both observers marked a "−," indicating that they did not observe on task behavior. Interestingly, although they both recorded that the student was on task 5 of the 10 intervals and received a 100% frequency reliability, the observers hardly agree at all!

To calculate the agreement reliability for interval recording and time sampling, the following formula is recommended:

*agreements/total intervals* $\times$ *100 = % of agreement*

Measuring interrater reliability during every observation period is not necessary. In fact, most teachers and parents will not be interested in collecting reliability data unless requested. If reliability data are required, a weekly reliability check (1/5 or 20% of observation periods) is usually adequate. That is, for every 5 days of data collection, there should be 1 day when an independent observation is recorded and compared with the teacher's data. For long-term interventions, every other week should be satisfactory.

# RECORDING OBSERVATIONS

Having discussed how to observe and measure behaviors, we will now review some recording methods that will simplify the observation process and facilitate the collection of reliable measurements. Methods used to record behavioral observations include permanent product recording, various data collection forms, and coding systems. In addition, several data collection aids are available for teachers to use that may increase the accuracy of data collected.

## Permanent Product Recording

*Permanent products* are materials that are produced as a result of behavior. Teachers may then measure and evaluate the product of the behavior. For example, when a teacher gives students a paper-and-pencil math test, the test becomes a permanent product of the students' math performance. The teacher may then use the test to measure and evaluate the students' math performance. Researchers have used permanent product recording to measure a variety of academic skills (Stern, Fowler, & Kohler, 1988), independent living skills (Williams & Cuvo, 1986), and safety skills (Sowers-Hoag, Thyer, & Bailey, 1987). Other examples of permanent products include completed puzzles, artwork, writing projects, building projects, and so on. Usually, the student's performance or behavior is not measured during the completion of the product (e.g., taking the test, writing the paper). Rather, the product is measured and evaluated after it is completed.

Children can be taught how to observe and record data regarding their own behavior. The results of this self-monitoring may also produce permanent products, generated by the children, that teachers may use to evaluate behavior. Self-monitoring is frequently used as part of a self-management strategy to improve classroom behavior of students (e.g., Shapiro, DuPaul, & Bradley-Klug, 1998).

When an audio or video recorder is used during direct observation of children's behavior, the completed tape provides teachers with the ultimate permanent product of behavior. The recorded behavior can then be observed immediately or stored for future observation of specific target behaviors, which can be measured and remeasured at the teacher's convenience.

## Data Collection Forms

A *data collection form* is a prepared sheet of paper used to record raw data collected during behavioral observations. Sometimes referred to as *raw data sheets*, these forms are prepared to assist the observer in recording data effectively and accurately. Many examples of data collection forms are provided throughout this chapter. Note that the forms are very simple in design. Teachers are encouraged to design their own data collection forms according to their individual needs.

Figure 3.8 provides an additional sample form that teachers may use for event recording and/or duration measurement. Data collection forms should include, at a minimum, the student's name, the target behavior, the environment or situation in which the student is being observed, the name of the observer, and dates of observation. Data collection forms may also include space for observer comments.

Student's name: _____    Observer : _____
Environment: _____    Dates: from _____ to _____
Target behavior: _____
Recording code: _____

| Date/Time | Frequency of Behavior | Start Time | Stop Time | Total Frequency | Total Duration |
|---|---|---|---|---|---|
| | | | | | |
| | | | | | |
| | | | | | |
| | | | | | |
| | | | | | |
| | | | | | |
| | | | | | |

Observation comments:

**FIGURE 3.8.** Sample data collection form for event and/or duration recording

## Coding Systems

*Coding systems* refer to a list of codes added to a data collection form that assists teachers in efficiently recording observed behaviors. Coding systems are especially useful when many target behaviors are being observed at the same time. Under a coding system, each target behavior is given a code. Readers are encouraged to keep the coding system as simple as possible. During the observation period, the observer simply records the code corresponding to the target behavior(s) observed. Coding systems can be used when teachers are making anecdotal observations or during interval recordings. When used during interval recordings, the observer records within each interval the code of any target behavior observed during the interval. Figure 3.9 provides an example of an interval recording form using a

---

Student's name: _Jeremy, Jason, Justin_____
Target behavior: _See coding system_____

Coding System: T = talking appropriately to other children
            C = working on the computer
            D = on task at desk
            G = playing a game with others
            A = playing alone

Environment: _Classroom free time_____          Date: _____
Start time: _____          Stop time: _____

5-minute observation period: 30-second intervals

| Name | | 1 | | 2 | | 3 | | 4 | | 5 |
|------|---|---|---|---|---|---|---|---|---|---|
| Jeremy | | | | | | | | | | |
| Jason | | | | | | | | | | |
| Justin | | | | | | | | | | |

*Note:* Next to the appropriate student's name, record the appropriate code or codes within each interval indicating which target behaviors were observed during each 30-second interval. Record a "–" if none of the target behaviors was observed.

---

**FIGURE 3.9.** Sample interval recording form using a coding system (5-minute observation period divided into ten 30-second intervals)

coding system. Teachers can calculate the percentage of intervals each target behavior was observed by counting the number of intervals each code was recorded and dividing by the total number of intervals.

Another option includes having the codes prerecorded within each interval. The observer can then simply circle the appropriate code corresponding to the behavior(s) observed within each interval.

## DISPLAYING OBSERVATIONAL DATA

Once observational data have been recorded on data collection forms, displaying the raw data on a graph provides teachers with a picture of the data. Ideally, graphs should be updated regularly as new raw data are collected. Graphs give teachers important information on behavioral trends and intervention comparisons over time that are usually difficult to decipher by looking at a list of numbers recorded on raw data sheets. Moreover, graphs provide teachers with an effective mode of communication when reporting a student's progress to other teachers. For example, during parent-teacher meetings, a simple graph reflecting a student's behavior from the beginning of the school year provides an effective way for teachers to display student progress. By using a simple graph, teachers can determine whether a student's performance is increasing, decreasing, or remaining stable. Kerr and Nelson (1989) outline three primary reasons for using graphs:

- To summarize data in a convenient manner for daily decision making
- To communicate program effects
- To provide feedback to teachers involved with the program (p. 91)

Graphs also provide feedback to children about their performance or progress toward a goal. Children can look at a graph and visually inspect their own progress. Moreover, many children find a graphic display of their progress especially reinforcing. The graph may become part of the treatment program as the student is visually reinforced by the accelerating trends noted on the graph. Also, children can be taught to chart their own performance data on their own graphs. The graphs can be displayed on a bulletin board at school or the refrigerator at home so the student can monitor his or her progress. Make it fun!

### Line Graphs

A line graph is the most common graph used to chart a student's performance over time. The line graph, as shown in Figure 3.10, consists of a *horizontal axis* and a *vertical axis*. The horizontal axis is frequently referred to as the *abscissa* or *x-axis*. The x-axis is used to indicate the passage of time and intervention changes or phases over the duration of the intervention program. Note in Figure 3.10 that the x-axis is marked in equal intervals of time, which may represent program sessions, days, weeks, and so on. The x-axis should be clearly labeled, as is the one in

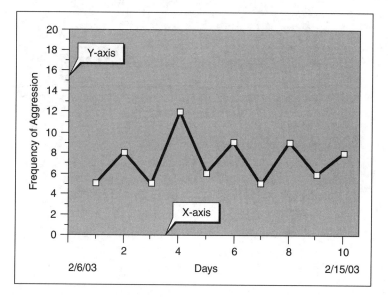

**FIGURE 3.10.** Example of a line graph of frequency aggression over 10 days of observation

Figure 3.10. In this example, the x-axis indicates the days on which aggression was observed and counted. Recording the dates of these observations under the x-axis is a good idea.

The vertical axis is frequently referred to as the *ordinate* or *y-axis*. The y-axis is always drawn on the left side of the x-axis and is used to indicate the values of a behavioral dimension (e.g., frequency, rate, duration, etc.) Thus, the y-axis may represent the frequency, rate, duration, latency, or percentage measurements of behavior. In our example, the y-axis represents the frequency of aggressive behavior. Like the x-axis, the y-axis is clearly labeled to indicate what dimension of behavior is being charted and marked at equal intervals starting at zero at the point where the x- and y-axes intersect. As you move up the y-axis, the values of frequency, rate, and so on, increase. As you move from left to right on the x-axis, time progresses.

Each data point on the graph indicates an intersection point between a value from the y-axis and a point in time from the x-axis. For example, in Figure 3.10, the first data point indicates that the student was aggressive five times on the 1st day, eight times on the 2nd day, five times on the 3rd day, and so on. When data points are charted on a graph, they may show one of four patterns or trends: accelerating, decelerating, stable, or variable. All of these data trends will be reviewed, along with examples, in our later discussion on baseline and intervention measures.

## Cumulative Graphs

As illustrated in Figure 3.11, teachers may display the same data charted in Figure 3.10 on a cumulative graph. In a cumulative graph, the frequency of aggression for each day is added to the previous day's data.

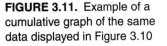

**FIGURE 3.11.** Example of a cumulative graph of the same data displayed in Figure 3.10

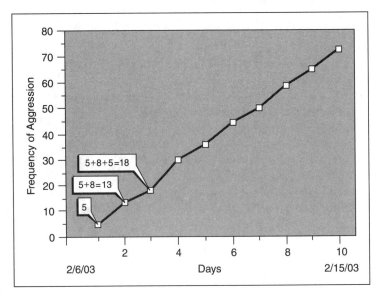

In our example, the student was aggressive five times on the 1st day and eight times on the 2nd day. In a typical line graph, each data point would be charted independently. In a cumulative graph, however, the first data point reflects the five aggressive acts observed on the 1st day, and the second data point reflects an additional eight aggressive acts observed on the 2nd day. Thus, the second data point represents 13 aggressive acts observed over the first 2 days of observation. Each additional data point indicates the number of behaviors observed that day *plus* the number of behaviors observed in all previous days of the program.

Cumulative graphs are used when the total number of behaviors observed is required from day to day. For example, a teacher's supervision may require a daily report on the total number of target behaviors observed from a specific start date or during a specific time period. Cumulative graphs are also useful when recording skill acquisition over a specific time period. For example, a reading teacher may need to keep a cumulative record of the number of new words learned by an individual student.

As demonstrated in Figure 3.11, the cumulative graph may give the impression that the frequency of the target behavior (aggression) is increasing rapidly. A graph like this might give the wrong impression to teachers who do not understand the nature of a cumulative graph. Thus, in most cases, teachers are encouraged to use a noncumulative line graph to chart behaviors.

## Bar Graphs

Another way to display raw data is with a *bar graph* or *histogram*. Like the line graph, the bar graph also has an x- and y-axis. However, instead of data points to indicate the frequency, rate, and duration of the target behavior, the bar graph uses

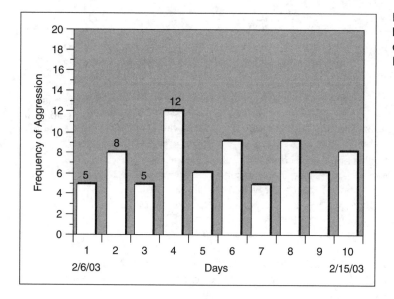

**FIGURE 3.12.** Example of a bar graph using the same raw data given in the line graph of Figure 3.10

vertical bars. Each vertical bar represents one observation period. The height of the bar corresponds with a value on the y-axis. Figure 3.12 displays the same raw data used in the line graph shown in Figure 3.10. Since five aggressive acts were observed on the 1st day of observation, the first bar in Figure 3.12 is drawn to the value of 5 on the y-axis. Since eight aggressive acts were observed on the 2nd day, the second bar is drawn to the value of 8 on the y-axis. The corresponding frequency count of the first four bars of our example is recorded on top of each bar.

Bar graphs present an excellent opportunity for teachers to get students involved in monitoring their own behavior. While teachers can place a mark where the top of a bar should stop, children can draw in the space from zero to the line. Also, teachers can draw "empty" bars and have young children fill or color in the bars. Again, this feedback will provide children with information about their own behavior and reinforcement for increasing or decreasing behaviors.

## Baseline and Intervention Measures

*Baseline data* refer to the measurement of a target behavior prior to the implementation of any intervention plan intended to modify the behavior. For example, in Vignette 3.1, Mike's teacher is frustrated because he frequently reports to school without his homework completed. At the same time, she clearly does not have a handle on how severe the problem is because she has no measurement of the behavior. For Mike, a baseline measurement of his target behavior (completing homework) may include a count of the number of days during an observation period (4 to 5 days) that his homework was completed. During this baseline observation period, his teacher simply observes and measures the rate of homework completion. The teacher may also choose to measure the amount of homework completed.

**VIGNETTE 3.1**

●

*Drawing a "Before and After" Picture of the Behavior*

Mike was a fifth grader and, according to his teacher, had trouble completing homework assignments.

"He never does his homework!" his teacher yelled in frustration to the school counselor.

"What do you mean by never?" the counselor responded. "To me," the counselor continued, "never means that he has not completed a homework assignment all year. Is that what you mean to say?"

"Oh, well he does his homework sometimes," the teacher said.

"How often is sometimes?" asked the counselor.

"I don't know. Maybe once or twice per week," said the teacher.

"Well," said the counselor, "we need to draw a better picture of his behavior than that. Let me show you how to complete a baseline measurement."

---

For example, if Mike had four homework assignments due on Monday and completed two, his teacher would record that Mike completed 50% of his Monday homework.

Baseline data are essential for developing realistic behavioral objectives. In our example, Mike's teacher would find it difficult to establish realistic objectives and goals for Mike without baseline data indicating his current performance levels. Baseline data provide a benchmark from which Mike's teacher can outline future performance objectives. Without baseline data, the teacher may establish objectives that are not challenging or are unrealistic, given Mike's current performance.

Teachers should follow several steps when they want to obtain a baseline measure on a target behavior. These steps outline the important relationship between collecting baseline data and the establishment of behavioral objectives. Each of these steps is discussed in this chapter.

- Identify the target behavior.
- Define the target behavior in measurable and observable terms.
- Observe the target behavior.
- Collect data on the target behavior.
- Review the data.
- Establish behavioral objectives based on current performance measures as outlined in the baseline data.

Baseline data serve many purposes. Referring back to our example, Mike's teacher may use the baseline data on Mike's homework for the following purposes:

- To document Mike's current homework completion performance. Thus, she can communicate much more effectively with the school counselor, Mike's parents, and others about his homework.
- To help decide whether Mike's homework completion performance needs to be modified.

- To provide objective data to Mike's parents and other significant teachers about his homework completion performance in order to justify the initiation of a homework completion program.
- To serve as comparative data for future intervention program data. Once she starts her program with Mike, she will have baseline data to compare with her intervention or program data.

An important question about baseline data involves the number of observation periods necessary for a reliable baseline measurement. That is, how many observations of the target behavior are appropriate before the intervention plan can be introduced? The general rule is that teachers should collect data points until the baseline data are stable (typically four to five). As previously stated, a *data point* refers to a point on a graph representing a single observation period. Thus, if Mike's teacher observed and measured his homework completion for 5 days, she would have five baseline data points. When these data points are transferred to a graph, a "picture" of Mike's homework completion performance can be reviewed. Figure 3.13 provides a hypothetical example of Mike's homework completion baseline data and a graph of the same data collected during the 5 days of baseline observation. Note that in this example the y-axis indicates the *percentage* of homework completed each day.

As previously stated, baseline data should be collected for 4 to 5 days or until the data are stable. Data are *stable* when they do not appear to have either an upward or downward trend and the data points do not vary significantly from each other. An *accelerating* trend refers to a pattern of data points that is increasing in value across time, from left to right along the x-axis. A *decelerating* trend refers to a pattern of data points that is decreasing across time. If the baseline data points show an accelerating or decelerating trend, teachers may want to extend the baseline collection period beyond the normal four to five observations until a more stable measurement is obtained.

For example, if the baseline data show an accelerating trend, Mike's teacher may want to take a wait-and-see attitude since an accelerating trend indicates that Mike's homework completion performance is improving without intervention. Mike may have discovered that his teacher is keeping track of his homework, and, as a result, an improvement in his homework completion is observed. If the trend continues, Mike's teacher may consider the act of monitoring Mike's homework performance an effective intervention. If the baseline data trend is decelerating, Mike's teacher may not want to wait for additional evidence that an intervention program is necessary since, in this case, a decelerating trend indicates that Mike's homework completion performance is decreasing. For inappropriate behavior (e.g., aggression), however, a decelerating trend would be welcomed, and teachers may want to take a wait-and-see attitude before starting an intervention plan.

A *variable* trend refers to a pattern of data points that varies from day to day and does not show a definite accelerating or decelerating trend. According to Tawney and Gast (1984), a "minimum of three separate, and preferably consecutive,

**FIGURE 3.13.** Mike's hypothetical baseline raw data and graph for homework completion performance

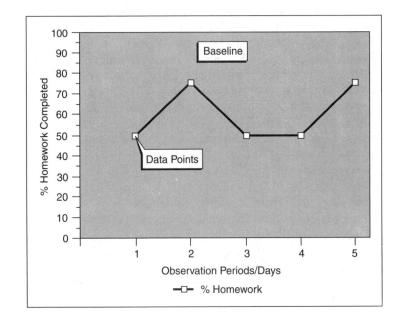

| Student's name: | Mike |
| Target behavior: | Homework Completion |

| Observation Period | Percentage of Homework Completed |
| --- | --- |
| Monday | 50% |
| Tuesday | 75% |
| Wednesday | 50% |
| Thursday | 50% |
| Friday | 75% |

observation periods are required to determine the level of stability and trend of data" (p. 160). Figure 3.14 shows some hypothetical data with accelerating, decelerating, stable, and variable trends.

Once baseline data have been collected and teachers have decided that an intervention program is necessary, data collection should continue through the intervention phase of the program. While baseline refers to the data collected *prior* to the introduction of an intervention, *intervention data* refer to the measurement of a target behavior *during* the intervention phase or phases of a behavior change program. Using the previous example, suppose that Mike's teacher decides to initiate a homework completion program that includes giving Mike a verbal prompt before he leaves school each day (such as "Mike, don't forget to do your home-

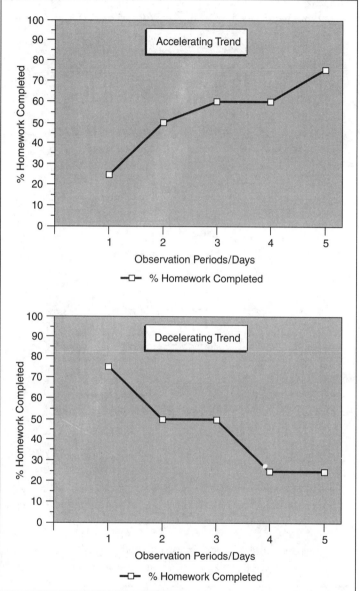

**FIGURE 3.14.** Examples of data showing accelerating, decelerating, stable, and variable trends

work!"), plus extra attention when he completes more than 75% of his homework assignments. Intervention data would include a measurement of Mike's homework completion performance starting on the 1st day of the homework completion program and every day after until the program's behavioral criteria has been reached.

**FIGURE 3.14.** Continued

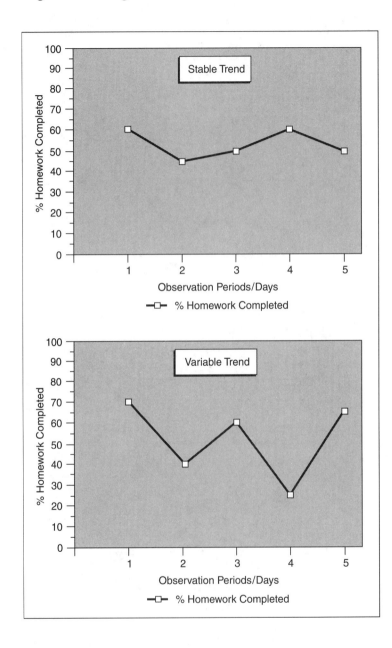

Intervention data are separated from baseline data by simply drawing a line down the graph between the two data types. Note in Figure 3.15 that the word *Baseline* is inserted on the left side of the graph. In this same manner, the word *Intervention* or *Treatment* should be inserted on the right side of the graph where the data points representing intervention data are graphed. For example, say that Mike's teacher decides to introduce the homework completion program (outlined

**FIGURE 3.15.** Mike's hypothetical intervention data and graph for homework completion performance

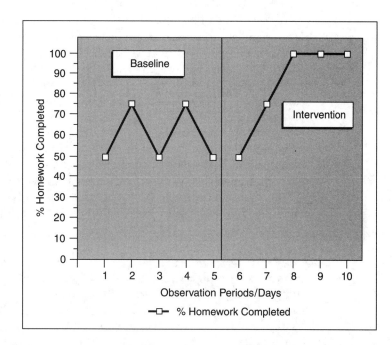

Student's name:      Mike
Target behavior:      Homework Completion

| Observation Period | Percentage of Homework Completed |
| --- | --- |
| Monday | 50% |
| Tuesday | 75% |
| Wednesday | 100% |
| Thursday | 100% |
| Friday | 100% |

earlier) for five consecutive school days. If the results look encouraging, Mike's teacher may decide to continue the intervention program. During the 5 days of intervention, Mike's teacher continued to observe and measure Mike's homework completion performance in the same manner that the baseline data were collected. Figure 3.15 outlines Mike's hypothetical intervention data and a graph of the five data points collected by Mike's teacher during the 5 days of intervention. These intervention data are added to the baseline data previously recorded on the graph. Note the line between the baseline data and the intervention data. Mike's teacher may now compare the intervention data with the baseline data and decide whether Mike's homework completion performance has improved since the implementation of the homework completion program.

Like baseline data, intervention data charted on a graph may also indicate an accelerating, decelerating, stable, or variable trend. For example, after showing a variable trend during baseline, Mike's intervention data showed an accelerating trend as his homework completion increased from 50% on the 1st day of intervention to 75% on the 2nd day and 100% on the 3rd, 4th, and 5th days. In this case, since we want Mike's homework completion to increase, an accelerating trend on the intervention side of the graph means that Mike's homework completion is rising and teachers should continue the current program. If, however, the intervention data showed a decelerating, stable, or variable trend, teachers should review and modify Mike's behavior change program.

If modifications are made to the intervention plan, a second line should be drawn down the graph, similar to the line separating baseline from the first intervention plan, that separates the first and second intervention plan. The second plan may be a simple program modification or a totally new intervention. Regardless, each "new" intervention or phase of the program should be separated from each other and labeled accordingly. Teachers may then review the data collected and charted across interventions and compare the effectiveness of each. Examples of multi-intervention programs charted on a single graph are provided later in our discussion of single-subject designs.

Again, the purpose of data collection and graphing is to provide feedback about current programming so that teachers may distinguish effective from ineffective interventions. By comparing the intervention data with the baseline data, and by looking at the data trends within each intervention plan, teachers should be able to make decisions regarding the effectiveness of their interventions and make modifications accordingly. Also, the graph provides teachers with an effective manner of communicating intervention results to others.

## SUMMARY

The purposes of direct observation are to record behavioral patterns across natural settings and situations, to measure the dimensions of specific target behaviors, and to identify the variables associated with these target behaviors. Data from direct observations allow teachers to monitor and evaluate the effectiveness of behavior change programs. Before a target behavior can be observed, however, it must be identified and defined in observable and measurable terms.

After an initial baseline observation to determine current performance levels of the target behavior, teachers can establish behavioral objectives, which include the desired terminal behavior and performance criteria. Once these are established, teachers must identify the dimensions of the behavior to be measured and determine how the dimensions will be measured. The five primary dimensions of behavior are frequency, duration, rate, latency, and intensity. Frequency refers to a simple count of the number of times a behavior occurs. Duration describes the time period for which a behavior continues once started. Rate refers to the frequency of a target behavior divided by the amount of observation time. Latency refers to the amount of time it takes for a student to begin a behavior once directions are provided. Lastly, intensity describes the force or strength of a behavior.

Measurement of behavior may include anecdotal observations, or an ABC analysis. Anecdotal observations provide teachers with a descriptive record of a behavior and related antecedents and consequences. Other measurement methods include event recording, interval recording, and time sampling.

The accuracy of behavioral observations is influenced by reactivity; observer drift; the recording procedure; the location of the observation; observer expectancy; characteristics of subjects, observers, and settings; and personal values and biases. Recommendations to reduce error in direct observations include having precise definitions of target behaviors, training observers, using adaptation periods for both observer and children, conducting unobtrusive observations, using permanent product recording, and observing frequently and systematically.

Interrater reliability refers to the accuracy of data collected across observers. Teachers will obtain satisfactory reliability measures when target behaviors are clearly defined and when all observers are adequately trained. Reliability measures may be calculated for frequency, duration, and latency measures, as well as for event, interval, and time sampling recording.

Teachers may record their observations using permanent product recording, a variety of data collection forms, and coding systems. Data collection aids include wrist counters, watches, and other homemade devices and techniques. These tools ease the task of data collection and facilitate accuracy and reliability.

Teachers are encouraged to display collected data on graphs in order to summarize data in a convenient manner, communicate program effects, and provide feedback to teachers and the student. The line graph is the most common graph, but cumulative and bar graphs are also used to display data. Graphs are used to chart both baseline and intervention data. While baseline data refer to the data collected prior to the introduction of an intervention, intervention data refer to the measurement of a target behavior during the behavior change program. A visual analysis of differences between baseline and intervention data and of the trends of the data gives teachers information regarding the effect of the intervention.

With the techniques learned in this chapter and Chapter 4, teachers are encouraged to investigate the purpose of student classroom behavior through both functional and curriculum-based assessments, as outlined in Chapters 5 and 6. We firmly believe that through a comprehensive, functional and curriculum-based assessment, teachers will be able to better assess why their students behave the way they do and become better classroom managers.

## DISCUSSION QUESTIONS

1. Discuss the importance of stating target behaviors in observable and measurable terms. Give examples of behaviors stated in observable and nonobservable ways.
2. Describe the four elements of well-stated behavioral objectives, using examples from behaviors observed in both classroom and home settings.

3. What are the dimensions of behavior? Provide examples of each as used in a classroom situation.

4. Discuss the various methods of data collection and the types of behavior and situations in which each may be used.

5. What variables may influence the accuracy of behavioral observations? What may be done to control for these influences?

6. Discuss the advantages of graphing data for teachers, parents, and students. How may this information be used during teacher-parent conferences?

7. How may students be encouraged to participate in their own data collection?

## REFERENCES

Alberto, P. A., & Troutman, A. C. (1995). *Applied behavior analysis for teachers.* Upper Saddle River, NJ: Merrill/Prentice Hall.

Barlow, D. H., & Hersen, M. (1984). *Single case experimental designs: Strategies for studying behavior change.* New York: Pergamon.

Bell, R. Q., & Harper, L. V. (1977). *Child effects on adults.* Hillsdale, NJ: Erlbaum.

Bijou, S. W., Peterson, R. F., & Ault, M. H. (1968). A method to integrate descriptive and experimental field studies at the level of data and empirical concepts. *Journal of Applied Behavior Analysis, 1,* 175–191.

Cartwright, C. A., & Cartwright, G. P. (1984). *Developing observation skills.* New York: McGraw Hill.

Cooper, J. O. (1981). *Measuring behavior.* Upper Saddle River, NJ: Merrill/Prentice Hall.

Cooper, J. O., Heron, T. E., & Heward, W. L. (1987). *Applied behavior analysis.* Upper Saddle River, NJ: Merrill/Prentice Hall.

Fisher, M., & Lindsey-Walters, S. (1987, October). *A survey report of various types of data collection procedures used by teachers and their strengths and weaknesses.* Paper presented at the annual conference of the Association for Persons with Severe Handicaps, Chicago.

Foster, S. L., Bell-Dolan, D. J., & Burge, D. A. (1988). Behavioral observation. In A. S. Bellack & M. Hersen (Eds.), *Behavioral assessment: A practical handbook* (pp. 79–103). New York: Pergamon.

Green, G. (1990). Least restrictive use of reductive procedures: Guidelines and competencies. In A. C. Repp & N. N. Singh (Eds.), *Perspectives on the use of nonaversive and aversive interventions for persons with developmental disabilities,* (pp. 479–493). Sycamore, IL: Sycamore.

Greene, B. F., Bailey, J. S., & Barber, F. (1981). An analysis and reduction of disruptive behavior on school buses. *Journal of Applied Behavior Analysis, 14,* 177–192.

Grigg, N. C., Snell, M. E., & Loyd, B. (1989). Visual analysis of student evaluation data: A qualitative analysis of teacher decision-making. *Journal of the Association for Persons with Severe Handicaps, 14,* 23–32.

Grossman, H. (1995). *Special education in a diverse society.* Boston: Allyn & Bacon.

Hawkins, R. P., & Dobes, R. W. (1977). Behavioral definitions in applied behavior analysis: Explicit or implicit. In B. C. Etzel, J. M. LeBlanc, & D. M. Baer (Eds.), *New directions in behavioral research: Theory, methods, and applications* (pp. 167–188). Hillsdale, NJ: Erlbaum.

Kazdin, A. E. (1982). *Single-case research designs: Methods for clinical and applied settings.* New York: Oxford University Press.

Kazdin, A. E. (1989). *Behavior modification in applied settings.* Pacific Grove, CA: Brooks/Cole.

Kerr, M. M., & Nelson, M. C. (1989). *Strategies for managing behavior in the classroom.* Upper Saddle River, NJ: Merrill/Prentice Hall.

Koorland, M. A., Monda, L. E., & Vail, C. O. (1988). Recording behavior with ease. *Teaching Exceptional Children, 21,* 59–61.

Lennox, D. B., & Miltenberger, R. G. (1989). Conducting a functional assessment of problem behavior in applied settings. *Journal of the Association for Persons with Severe Handicaps, 14,* 304–311.

Meyer, L., & Janney, R. (1989). User-friendly measures of meaningful outcomes: Evaluating behavioral interventions. *Journal of the Association for Persons with Severe Handicaps, 4,* 263–270.

Murphy, M., & Harrop, A. (l994). Observer error in the use of momentary time sampling and partial interval recording. *British Journal of Psychology, 85*(2), 169–180.

Repp, A. C., Nieminen, G. S., Olinger, E., & Brusca, R. (1988). Direct observation: Factors affecting the accuracy of observers. *Exceptional Children, 55,* 29–36.

Shapiro, E. S., DuPaul, G. J., & Bradley-Klug, K. (1998). Self-management as a strategy to improve the classroom behavior of adolescents with ADHD. *Journal of Learning Disabilities, 31*(6), 545–556.

Snell, M. E., & Grigg, N. C. (1987). Instructional assessment and curriculum development. In M. E. Snell (Ed.), *Systematic instruction of persons with severe handicaps.* Upper Saddle River, NJ: Merrill/Prentice Hall.

Sowers-Hoag, K., Thyer, B., & Bailey, J. (1987). Promoting automobile safety belt use by young children. *Journal of Applied Behavior Analysis, 21,* 103–109.

Stern, G., Fowler, S., & Kohler, F. (1988). A comparison of two intervention roles: Peer monitor and point earner. *Journal of Applied Behavior Analysis, 21,* 103–109.

Tawney, J. W., & Gast, D. L. (1984). *Single subject research in special education.* Upper Saddle River, NJ: Merrill/Prentice Hall.

Trudel, P., & Cote, J. (1996). Systematic observation of youth ice hockey coaches during games. *Journal of Sport Behavior, 19*(1), 50–66.

Umbreit, J., & Blair, K. S. (l997). Using structural analysis to facilitate treatment of aggression and noncompliance in a young child at risk for behavioral disorders. *Behavior Disorders, 22*(2), 75–86.

Wacker, D. P. (1989). Introduction to special feature on measurement issues in supported education: Why measure anything? *Journal of the Association for Persons with Severe Handicaps, 14,* 254.

Williams, G., & Cuvo, A. (1986). Training apartment upkeep skills to rehabilitation clients. *Journal of Applied Behavior Analysis, 19,* 39–41.

Yarrow, M. R., & Waxler, C. Z. (1979). Observing interactions: A confrontation with methodology. In R. B. Cairns (Ed.), *The analysis of social interactions: Methods, issues, and illustrations.* Hillsdale, NJ: Erlbaum.

Zirpoli, T. J., & Bell, R. Q. (1987). Unresponsiveness in children with severe disabilities: Potential effects on parent-child interactions. *The Exceptional Child, 34,* 31–40.

# SINGLE-SUBJECT DESIGNS

## Thomas J. Zirpoli

*The use of single-subject designs has increased steadily since about the mid-sixties, paralleling the increased application of behavior modification techniques. Whereas previously single-subject research was generally equated with a descriptive, case-study approach, it now became associated with a more controlled, experimental approach.*

—L. R. Gay *(1996, p. 374–375)*

**M**ost teachers do not use elaborate single-subject designs to demonstrate the effectiveness of their behavior change programs. However, as with our discussion on behavioral observation, measurement, and recording procedures in the previous chapter, we hope to demonstrate that teachers may employ these simple research designs in the classroom with little difficulty and some exciting results. We will not go into great detail about these designs. Instead, we will provide teachers with an overview of some basic single-subject designs, discuss their importance and application, and refer our readers to other sources where these and other more complicated research designs are discussed in far greater detail (e.g., Barlow & Hersen, 1984; Tawney & Gast, 1984).

## THE PURPOSE OF SINGLE-SUBJECT DESIGNS

When people think about research, they usually imagine large samples of "subjects" participating in one of two groups: an *experimental group* in which a "treatment" or intervention is presented, and a *control group* in which the intervention is not presented. These *group designs* involve many subjects, and each group's average performance is usually compared in order to evaluate *experimental control.*

Under ideal circumstances, teachers may attribute the differences between the performance of the experimental and control groups to the intervention applied in the experimental group and the absence of the intervention in the control group. These attributions refer to *intervention* or *treatment effects.* By using these research designs, researchers can demonstrate the effectiveness of their interventions (e.g., teaching style, behavior change program, new curriculum) and communicate these findings to others.

Another purpose of single-subject designs is to demonstrate experimental control and intervention effects. However, instead of requiring work with large groups of individuals, single-subject designs allow researchers and teachers to demonstrate experimental control and intervention effects while working with one or a few individuals. As Odom (1988) states, "The term 'single subject' is somewhat of a misnomer because usually more than one subject is involved, although the number of subjects is almost always small" (p. 16).

Sidman (1960), an early proponent of single-subject designs, states that group research designs, in which an average group performance is measured, do not communicate important individual performances. He points out that in many cases, the performance of individual children does not resemble the group average. For example, when a teacher initiates a specific behavior reduction program (such as trying to decrease hitting) for an individual student, an average classroom performance score is unlikely to let the teacher know how effective the program is for that individual student.

Single-subject designs are ideal for teachers who wish to demonstrate a relationship between a behavior change program and behavior changes exhibited by a single child or a small group of children (Martin, 1985). For example, a classroom teacher may want to demonstrate that a behavior program developed for a small group of students within her classroom is likely to be effective with other children in the school. In this case each data point in the single-subject design graph represents the performance of a single class or other intact group of children; the data point represents the total group score or average score. For example, in a program to increase appropriate classroom behavior, a teacher could develop a single-subject design for one student or for the whole class. When charting the frequency of appropriate behavior for one student, the data points on the graph represent the performance of the one student. When charting the frequency of appropriate behavior for the whole class, however, the data points on the graph represent the performance of the whole group. This latter example is demonstrated in Vignette 4.1.

Martin (1985) outlines the following four advantages of single-subject designs over large group research designs:

- They provide a powerful method of studying the effectiveness of an intervention or several interventions on a single subject or small group of subjects.
- The results of single-subject experimental designs are easy to interpret, usually by visually inspecting the charted data points.
- They allow teachers to decide when to initiate or modify interventions.
- The use of statistics, necessary in group research designs, is not usually needed with single-subject designs. (pp. 90–91)

In addition to using single-subject designs for an effective measurement of behavior change, these designs are frequently employed to measure the effectiveness of various academic or instructional methods. For example, Patrick, Mozzoni, and Patrick (2000) found that single-subject designs offer an effective way to establish evidenced-based practice in early intervention programs. Others have used and promote the use of single-subject designs when working on language development for children with autism (Bellon, Ogletree, & Harn, 2000) and to measure the effectiveness of reading and math instruction for students with learning disabilities (Swanson & Sachse-Lee, 2000). But teachers should not get the idea that single-subject designs are helpful only with students receiving specialized instruction. As we hope to demonstrate next, single-subjects designs can be an effective assessment tool in general education and for the assessment of classroom performance.

## VIGNETTE 4.1
●

*Initiating Baseline and Intervention Conditions to Study the Effect of a New Seating Arrangement on Student Interactions*

Marty, a first-grade teacher, wanted to try a new seating plan for her 28 students. Her students' desks were arranged in seven rows of four. After Marty implemented her new seating plan, however, her students were arranged in seven groups of four, with their desks facing each other in a circle. Marty believed that her new seating plan would increase appropriate student interactions and decrease inappropriate interactions (e.g., touching the backs of other students, having to turn away from the teacher to ask a student in the rear a question, etc.).

Before Marty rearranged the classroom, she decided to collect baseline data on the type and number of appropriate student interactions in her classroom. She picked three target behaviors that, in her opinion, indicate appropriate student interactions:

- asking another child for help,
- praising another child's work, and
- working cooperatively on a class assignment with another child.

Marty collected frequency data for each target behavior from 10 A.M. to 11 A.M. for five consecutive days. She then recorded her data on a simple line graph.

On the following Monday, Marty initiated her new seating plan. When the students arrived at school, the desks were arranged according to Marty's new plan. To measure the effect of her new seating plan, Marty continued to collect data on the same target behaviors, from 10 A.M. to 11 A.M. for five consecutive days. She recorded this intervention data on the same graph as her baseline data. She drew a line between the baseline and intervention data points and recorded *Baseline* and *Intervention* on the left and right sides of the graph.

Looking at her graph, Marty noticed that the frequency of the target behaviors had increased significantly since implementing her new seating plan. Although other factors possibly may have made the difference in the students' behavior, Marty is sure that her new seating plan was the significant factor for her students.

## Baseline and Intervention Conditions

With single-subject designs, comparisons are made between *conditions* employed during the behavior change program. A condition refers to the baseline phase and various intervention phases used to modify an individual's behavior; these are called *baseline* and *intervention conditions,* respectively.

1. *Baseline condition:* In a single-subject design, the baseline condition is usually referred to as condition A. During this condition, baseline data are collected on a specific target behavior before an intervention strategy is employed.

2. *Intervention condition:* This condition is usually referred to as condition B. Data collection continues throughout the intervention condition.

In Vignette 4.1, Marty's students were in the "baseline condition" when they were in their old seating arrangement. When Marty initiated her new seating plan, the "intervention condition" began. Each data point on Marty's graph represents the total number of appropriate student interactions, defined by her three target behaviors, from 10 A.M. to 11 A.M. each day.

If variations to the intervention condition were employed or if new interventions were initiated, each of these would be considered a new condition (i.e., conditions C, D, E, etc.). For example, Marty's first intervention can be referred to as condition B. It was her first intervention plan initiated after baseline (condition A). If, after a few weeks, Marty decided to modify her new seating plan, the modified intervention would be called condition C. These variations to the basic baseline/intervention designs will be discussed later in this chapter.

A comparison of data across *conditions* allows teachers to determine the most effective intervention. For example, if Marty looked at her data and found that higher rates of appropriate student interactions occurred during condition B than condition C, she might decide to go back to the seating arrangement used in condition B and delete the modifications made during condition C. When conditions are employed in a predetermined order, as in single-subject designs, teachers can demonstrate cause-and-effect relationships between specific interventions and children's behavior.

## TYPES OF SINGLE-SUBJECT DESIGNS

The type of single-subject design employed depends on the order in which baseline and intervention conditions are presented. In some designs, baseline is followed by several intervention phases. In other designs, the baseline period is repeated while the intervention condition is withdrawn. Teachers may also develop designs to represent intervention effects across subjects, settings, and other conditions. The designs reviewed in this chapter include the A-B, A-B-A, A-B-A-B, alternating treatments, changing criterion, and multiple-baseline designs. Each of these designs, along with examples, is discussed here.

### The A-B Design

In the simplest single-subject design, the A-B design, only two conditions are used: baseline (A) and intervention (B). We have already seen examples of A-B designs in Figure 3.14, discussed in the previous chapter, and Vignette 4.1. In addition to the data trends that may be identified *within* each condition of the A-B design, the most important variable within this design is the change in data recorded from the first condition (baseline) to the second condition (intervention). Small changes in the data recorded across conditions indicate a weak intervention effect. That is, regardless of the implementation of the intervention, the recorded data indicate little change in the child's behavior. A large intervention effect would be reflected by large differences observed in the data recorded during the baseline and intervention conditions. In Vignette 4.1, Marty could determine whether an intervention effect occurred by looking at the changes in data trends across the different seating plans (the original seating plan of condition A and the new seating plan of condition B).

Single-subject designs can be used when changing the behavior of one child or a small group of children.

Teachers may determine whether there is a "small" or "large" change in the data by conducting a simple visual analysis or "eyeballing" the graph for obvious differences. "A visual interpretation of graphed data is the most common form of analysis" (Odom, 1988, p. 14). For example, in Figure 4.1, two A-B designs are presented for two hypothetical programs developed to increase school attendance for two high school students. For the first student (example 1), school attendance was reinforced with special activity passes (e.g., field trips, computer time, other preferred activities). For the second student (example 2), a 1-day in-school suspension followed the student's return to school each time he skipped school. Baseline data were collected for four consecutive weeks followed by 4 weeks of intervention. The students' attendance percentage per week (1 day 20%, 2 days 40%, 3 days 60%, 4 days 80%, and 5 days 100%) was graphed during baseline and intervention conditions. When looking at the differences between conditions A and B for each example, what do you conclude about the intervention effects for each attendance program? Which program would you judge as having the greater impact on school attendance?

In example 1, a visual inspection of the graph seems to reveal an intervention effect. Data collected during the intervention phase indicate that school attendance was higher during the reinforcement program compared to data gathered during the baseline condition. In example 2, an intervention effect is not apparent because significant differences are not seen between baseline and intervention data. As a result, teachers using the two attendance programs may conclude that the reinforcement program is more effective than the in-school suspension program.

Although visually analyzing single-subject design data serves the needs of most educators and parents, "some authors have argued that the poor interrater reliability associated with visual analysis is a major limitation of single subject

**FIGURE 4.1.** A-B design demonstrating a possible intervention effect (Example 1) and no intervention effect (Example 2) on school attendance

Example 1:

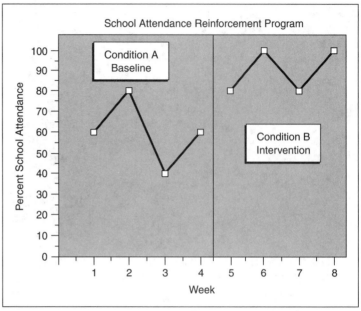

Example 2:

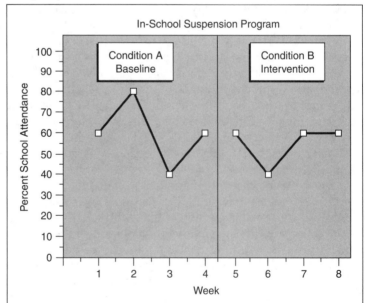

methods" (Ottenbacher & Cusick, 1991, p. 48). More formal estimates than the visual analysis of single-subject design data involve mathematical calculations to determine the stability and changes in the direction of trend lines. These methods are beyond the scope of this text. For more information on visual analysis of single-subject designs and methods that supplement visual analysis, refer to Bailey (1984); Gibson and Ottenbacher (1988); Mueser, Yarnold, and Foy (1991); Parsonson and Baer (1986); and Tawney and Gast (1984).

A considerable limitation with the A-B design is that we can only *presume* that behavior changes noted during the intervention condition are a function of the intervention. Thus, we cannot be assured that the intervention program is responsible for the observed behavior changes (Parsonson & Baer, 1986). Other variables concerning teacher behavior, influences in the home, and other environmental conditions may be more responsible than the reinforcement program for behavior changes during the 4 days of intervention in our hypothetical scenario. For example, suppose the parents of the student in example 1 heard about their son's attendance problems and decided to drive their child to school each day. The change in school attendance may be more closely related to a change in parental behavior than the effects of the reinforcement program implemented by the school. Thus, the A-B design has many internal and external validity problems (Campbell & Stanley, 1966) and is considered a *quasi-experimental design* since an association between the intervention condition and behavior changes may not be made without "major reservations" (Barlow & Hersen, 1984, p. 142). For many teachers, the increase in school attendance would be accepted as a direct outcome of the reinforcement program, and the possibility that other variables are responsible for these changes would not be a primary concern. As Gay (1996) states:

> Single-subject designs are most frequently applied in clinical settings where the primary emphasis is on therapeutic impact, not contribution to a research base. However, if the development of a school-wide attendance program depended upon the results from this research, a stronger research design would be recommended. (p. 296)

Such "stronger" research designs are described in the following sections.

## The A-B-A Design

An important feature of the A-B-A design is the employment of a second baseline condition after withdrawing or terminating the intervention condition. Whereas the A-B design has a baseline and intervention condition, the A-B-A design has a baseline, intervention, and second baseline condition as outlined here:

| *Condition A* | *Condition B* | *Condition A* |
|---|---|---|
| Initial baseline | Initial intervention | Intervention withdrawn; baseline reintroduced |

If Marty from Vignette 4.1 decided that she did not like her new seating arrangement (condition B) and returned her classroom to the original seating plan (condition A), this situation would be an example of an A-B-A design. She would continue to collect data and chart the frequency of appropriate student interactions after the return to condition A. Marty could then evaluate her new seating by comparing her intervention data (condition B) with the data charted during the first and second baseline conditions.

The withdrawal of the intervention and the reintroduction of the baseline condition are referred to as a *withdrawal design* (Gay, 1996) and, sometimes, a *reversal design* (Alberto & Troutman, 1995). However, Gay (1996) argues that the A-B-A design is not a true reversal design:

> *The A-B-A withdrawal designs are frequently referred to as reversal designs, which they are not, since treatment is generally withdrawn following baseline assessment, not reversed. A reversal design is but one kind of withdrawal design, representing a special kind of withdrawal. (p. 302)*

In a reversal design, one intervention is withdrawn and a second intervention, opposite from the first, is implemented. This is called an *A-B-C design.* Both B and C conditions are interventions, but they are opposite to each other. For example, condition B may require a classroom teacher to reinforce *in-seat* behavior, while condition C, the reversal condition, requires the teacher to reinforce *out-of-seat* behavior. In this example, the reversal design may demonstrate the relationship between reinforcement and students' in- and out-of-seat behaviors.

The purpose of the A-B-A design is to demonstrate more clearly the relationship between student performance and an intervention. As previously stated, the change in student performance from condition A to condition B, as in the A-B design, may be coincidental. However, if student performance returns to baseline levels during the *second* baseline condition, teachers may attribute changes in student performance to the implementation and removal of the intervention. Note, however, that a return to baseline may not result in data points that mirror the first baseline condition. Some student learning during the intervention condition may be maintained in the second baseline condition.

While the A-B design tries to establish a relationship between student performance and the implementation of an intervention, the A-B-A design tries to make a relationship between student performance and the implementation *and* withdrawal of an intervention. Thus, the A-B-A design has the potential to demonstrate a more powerful intervention effect than the simpler A-B design: "Whereas the A-B design permits only tentative conclusions as to a treatment's influence, the A-B-A design allows for an analysis of the controlling effects of its introduction and subsequent removal" (Barlow & Hersen, 1984, p. 152).

Continuing with our example from Figure 4.1, suppose that after 4 weeks of the school attendance reinforcement program, the teacher decides to end the reinforcement program but continue to measure the student's attendance for another 4 weeks. In effect, the teacher is deciding to return to the baseline condition in which data on attendance is collected without an intervention program. The A-B-A design has three conditions:

1. *Condition A:* Initial baseline data are collected for four consecutive weeks.
2. *Condition B:* Intervention plan is employed for four consecutive weeks. Student is reinforced for attendance. Attendance data continue to be collected and recorded.
3. *Condition A:* Intervention plan is withdrawn, and baseline data collection condition is reintroduced for four consecutive weeks.

Figure 4.2 provides an example of an A-B-A design using our hypothetical data collected during all three conditions of our school attendance reinforcement program.

The increase in school attendance during the intervention condition and the decrease in school attendance after the intervention was withdrawn demonstrate a strong intervention effect on school attendance. Would you recommend a return to the reinforcement program? If your answer is yes, we agree. Also, a return to the intervention condition leads us to another type of single-subject design—the A-B-A-B design.

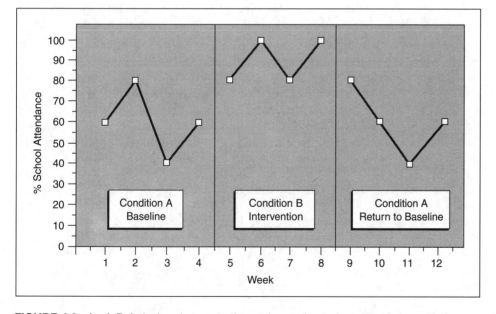

**FIGURE 4.2.** An A-B-A design demonstrating a change in student attendance with the implementation of the intervention (school attendance reinforcement program) and a withdrawal of the intervention

## The A-B-A-B Design

In the A-B-A-B design, the intervention condition is reintroduced after the second baseline condition. The A-B-A-B design has four conditions:

1. *Condition A:* Initial baseline data are collected and recorded.
2. *Condition B:* Intervention plan is initiated. In our example, the student is reinforced for attendance according to the attendance program. Attendance data continue to be monitored and recorded throughout the intervention condition.
3. *Condition A:* Intervention plan is withdrawn and the baseline condition reintroduced.
4. *Condition B:* Baseline condition is withdrawn, and intervention plan is introduced for a second time. Student is again reinforced for attendance. Attendance data continue to be monitored and recorded.

The A-B-A-B design has several advantages over the A-B-A design. First, the A-B-A-B design ends during an intervention condition:

> *While the A-B-A design represents the simplest single subject research paradigm for demonstrating cause-effect relationships, . . . an applied researcher would seldom select this design at the outset to evaluate intervention effectiveness due to the practical and ethical considerations of ending an investigation in a baseline condition.* (Tawney & Gast, 1984, pp. 195–200)

For example, if a teacher was trying to decrease self-injurious behavior exhibited by a child, it would be unethical to withdraw an effective intervention plan in order to demonstrate an intervention effect.

Second, the A-B-A-B design provides three comparisons or opportunities for the intervention, or the lack of intervention, to demonstrate an effect on student behavior (condition A to B, B to A, and A to B). Third, the A-B-A-B design provides a replication of the first A-B sequence or a replication of the introduction of the intervention. Since both A and B conditions are withdrawn and introduced a second time, the efficacy of the intervention, introduced after a baseline condition, may be demonstrated on two occasions (Barlow & Hersen, 1984). This replication is not perfect, however, because some effects from the first A-B experience may remain going into the second A-B experience. While the A-B-A design is an extension of the A-B design, the A-B-A-B design is an extension of the A-B-A design (see Figure 4.3). Note that when the reinforcement program (intervention condition) is reintroduced, the student's attendance increases as it did during the first intervention condition.

## The Alternating Treatments Design

The *alternating treatments design*—also referred to as an *alternating* or *changing conditions design, multiple-schedule design* (Hersen & Barlow, 1976), and a *multielement baseline design* (Ulman & Sulzer-Azaroff, 1975)—involves the relatively rapid alter-

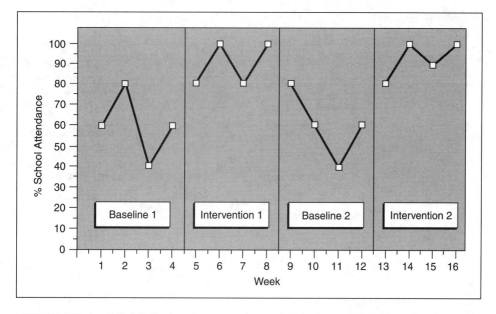

**FIGURE 4.3.** An A-B-A-B design demonstrating a change in student attendance after the reintroduction of the school attendance reinforcement intervention

nating of interventions for a single subject. "Its purpose is to assess the relative effectiveness of two (or more) treatment conditions" (Gay, 1996, p. 299). This design is also an expansion of the basic A-B design. However, instead of withdrawing the intervention and reintroducing the baseline condition, the researcher introduces a second, *different* intervention strategy while continuing to monitor student performance. This second intervention, following conditions A and B, is called condition C. The number of different intervention conditions (D, E, etc.) added to the alternating treatment design depends on the number of interventions the teacher or researcher is interested in testing. Figure 4.4 provides an example of this design using two different intervention conditions (B and C) as follows:

1. *Condition A:* Baseline data are collected on target behavior.
2. *Condition B:* First intervention strategy is employed for a specific period of time.
3. *Condition C:* First intervention strategy is terminated, and a second intervention introduced for a specific period.

Frequently, each new intervention added in an alternating treatment design is a modification of the previous intervention. For example, say that a teacher wants to increase appropriate behavior during a homeroom period. The intervention in condition B may include verbal reinforcement at the end of the class period contingent on appropriate behavior. Condition C may involve using the

**FIGURE 4.4.** The three conditions of an A-B-C design

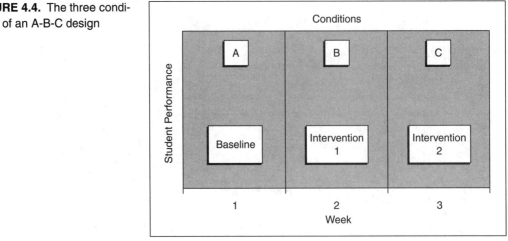

same reinforcement program *plus* a positive note sent home. Condition D may include the reinforcement, a note home, *and* a public announcement regarding the student's outstanding behavior by the school principal.

By reviewing the data collected on student behavior during each intervention condition, teachers can compare the results of each intervention and decide which program *appears* to be the most effective. However, as in the basic A-B design, the alternating treatment design with a single baseline *does not* establish a cause-and-effect relationship between intervention and behavior. Data collected during each intervention may reflect cumulative intervention effects rather than the effects of any one intervention.

Another variation of the alternating research design is the *repeated-baseline alternating research design.* In this design, the teacher decides to return to the baseline condition before introducing each new intervention condition. Thus, one may have an A-B-A-C or an A-B-A-C-A-D design as described here (see also Figure 4.5):

1. *Condition A:* Baseline data are collected on target behavior.
2. *Condition B:* First intervention strategy is employed for a specific period of time.
3. *Condition A:* Intervention is withdrawn, with a return to baseline condition.
4. *Condition C:* Baseline condition is withdrawn, and a second and different intervention is introduced for a specific period.
5. *Condition A:* Second intervention is withdrawn, and a third baseline condition is introduced.
6. *Condition D:* Baseline condition is withdrawn, and a third intervention is introduced for a specific period.

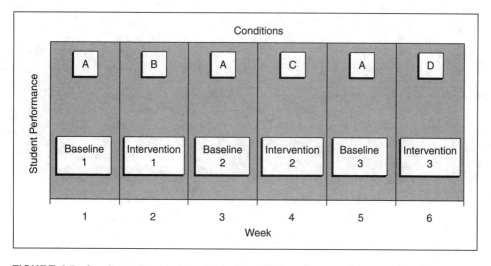

**FIGURE 4.5.** An alternating treatments design with baseline condition employed between each intervention condition

The repeated-baseline variation of the alternating treatment design provides teachers with an opportunity to compare baseline to intervention changes in the child's performance for each intervention tested. This approach somewhat reduces the cumulative treatment effects found in other designs in which treatments are employed consecutively without a baseline period between each intervention.

Another variation of the alternating treatments design is a *repeated* or *rotating design*. For example, in an A-B-C-B-C-B-C design, the interventions B and C are each presented three times in a rotating fashion (see Figure 4.6).

In many of the examples provided earlier, the duration of each condition is 1 week. However, as in all the designs discussed in this chapter, the actual duration of each condition may vary. For example, teachers may employ each individual intervention for 1 day or for several days. Also, the duration of each intervention does not have to be equal. For example, while the duration of condition B may be 1 day, the duration of condition C may be 1 month.

The interpretation of these varied and more complicated designs depends on the same variables described in the basic designs. Teachers need to ask the following questions regarding the data collected across conditions:

- What are the data trends within each condition?
- Regarding the direction of the data trends, how do the data trends differ from baseline to intervention conditions? A change in direction from baseline to intervention conditions may indicate an intervention effect.
- What is the difference between the mean baseline performance and the mean intervention performance? Large differences may be associated with a strong relationship between the intervention and the child's behavior.

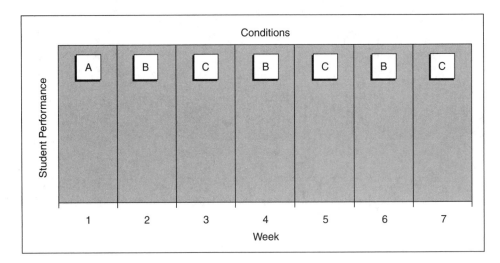

**FIGURE 4.6.** An A-B-C-B-C-B-C alternating treatment design

- How rapid is the change between baseline and intervention conditions? The speed of behavior change may be related to the strength of the intervention effect.
- How do the data trends vary across different intervention conditions? Large differences may indicate different intervention effects across conditions.

## The Changing Criterion Design

First described by Sidman (1960) and named by Hall (1971), the *changing criterion design* is used to increase or decrease the performance of a single behavior by gradually increasing the criterion for reinforcement across several intervals of time. Gay (1996) describes the changing criterion design as follows:

> In this design, a baseline phase is followed by successive treatment phases, each of which has a more stringent criterion for acceptable behavior level. Thus, each treatment phase becomes the baseline phase for the next treatment phase. The process continues until the final desired level of behavior is being achieved consistently. (p. 303)

Like the A-B design, the changing criterion design has two major phases. After the baseline condition, an intervention is initiated. However, the intervention condition is divided into subphases. Within each subphase of the intervention condition, the child must obtain a predetermined level of performance to earn reinforcement. Once that criterion level has been consistently achieved, a new criterion is established. Each increase in the performance criterion brings the student closer to the program objective. According to Hartmann and Hall (1976), "When the rate of the target behavior changes with each stepwise change in the criterion, therapeutic change is replicated and experimental control is demonstrated" (p. 527).

For example, suppose a teacher wants to increase Justin's participation in class discussion to a rate of 10 responses per class period. The first step in a changing criterion design is to assess the child's current performance (baseline) of the target behavior (class discussion). Justin's teacher collected baseline data for four consecutive days and recorded a rate of zero for all 4 days. Since the teacher's goal is 10 responses per class session, the teacher must now determine:

- the number of steps to be implemented between the current performance level (zero) and the ultimate criterion or program objective level (ten),
- the reinforcement to be provided to the child contingent on behavior that meets or exceeds the established criterion, and
- the specific reinforcement criterion for each of the steps.

Justin's teacher decides to divide her program into five steps, to use 15 minutes on the class computer as the reinforcement, and to increase the criterion by two responses per step, as follows:

| | |
|---|---|
| Criterion for step 1: | 2 responses per class |
| Criterion for step 2: | 4 responses per class |
| Criterion for step 3: | 6 responses per class |
| Criterion for step 4: | 8 responses per class |
| Criterion for step 5: | 10 responses per class |

After the baseline period, the intervention condition begins. The teacher begins the intervention condition by telling Justin that he may earn 15 minutes on the computer during class free time by participating in class discussion at a rate of two times per class period. After this criterion is achieved and a stable performance is observed, Justin's teacher changes the criterion to four responses per class period. After this criterion is reached and a stable performance is noted, the next criterion level is implemented, and so on. Justin must be told that the criterion has been changed before the implementation of the next intervention subphase. Figure 4.7 provides an overview of Justin's performance (see data points) per criterion level (indicated by the vertical line per subphase). Note the rapid rate at which Justin's performance increased and the relationship between the increases in his performance and each change in the criterion for reinforcement. Justin's teacher has established a clear relationship between the reinforcement program and the rate of Justin's class participation.

## Multiple-Baseline Designs

In many cases it may be impossible, for practical or ethical reasons, to withdraw an intervention and return to a baseline condition. For example, if an intervention involves some type of academic instruction, returning to a true baseline condition is impossible since the teacher cannot remove information learned during

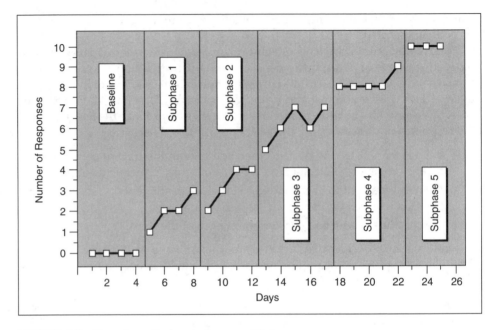

**FIGURE 4.7.** Changing criterion design over 26 days

the intervention condition from the student's memory. In this situation, teachers may incorrectly identify the A-B design as the only alternative.

When a cause-and-effect relationship is desired and it is not possible to extend beyond the simple A-B design with a single subject, teachers should consider a multiple-baseline design. The multiple-baseline design is, in fact, an extension of the A-B design, but in a different way than discussed up to this point. The multiple-baseline design retains the basic concept of the A-B design while extending these principles beyond a single subject. Instead of a sole subject providing replication of intervention effects, replication is achieved across a small sample of subjects, behaviors, or settings. This approach allows teachers to establish a cause-and-effect relationship between the intervention and behavior changes.

The three basic types of multiple-baseline designs are *across subjects, across behaviors,* and *across settings.* In each case, an A-B design is employed across three subjects, behaviors, or settings, and the intervention condition is applied to each subject, behavior, or setting at different intervals.

### The Multiple-Baseline-Across-Subjects Design

In this design, the same intervention is employed across three children. The initiation of the intervention, however, is staggered across the three *subjects,* as demonstrated in Classroom Application 4.1.

## Classroom Application 4.1

## Multiple-Baseline-Across-Subjects Design

Margaret, an elementary teacher who operates an after-school program, has three children (John, Mike, and Julia, ages 8, 8, and 9, respectively) in her program who exhibit hitting behavior. To decrease this behavior, Margaret decides to develop a behavior change program that involves the reinforcement of specific periods of no hitting.

Margaret's first step is to gather 4 days of baseline data on each of the three children's hitting frequency. With the baseline data collected, she is now ready to initiate her intervention plan. Not sure that program will work, Margaret decides to first try her plan only with John while she continues to collect baseline data for the other two students. Margaret observes and charts John's hitting behavior every day. After 4 days, Margaret notices that John's hitting behavior has decreased significantly. At that time she decides to start the same program with Mike while continuing to collect baseline data on Julia's hitting. Then, after four more days, Margaret initiates the same program with Julia. All three students are now involved in Margaret's program.

Margaret notices a significant decrease in the frequency of hitting behavior for all three children, but only after the start of her reinforcement program. She decides that her program was effective in decreasing hitting behavior and feels confident that the program could work with other students with similar behaviors.

The data that Margaret, our teacher in Classroom Application 4.1, collected from observing the hitting behavior of her three students are presented in Figure 4.8. As Figure 4.8 shows, after a baseline condition, the same intervention condition was applied for each of the three children, but at different intervals. Four days of baseline data were collected for each of the three children. For John, the intervention was employed on the 5th day. Meanwhile, Margaret continued to collect baseline data for Mike and Julia. For Mike, the intervention was initiated on the 9th day after 8 days of baseline. Meanwhile, the intervention condition continued for John while the baseline condition continued for Julia. Finally, the intervention was applied for Julia on the 13th day. All three children were now receiving the intervention condition.

### The Multiple-Baseline-Across-Behaviors Design

In this design the same intervention is applied to a single child across three different behaviors. As with other multiple-baseline designs, the initiation of the intervention is staggered. In this case, the start of the intervention is staggered across the three behaviors, as demonstrated in Classroom Application 4.2.

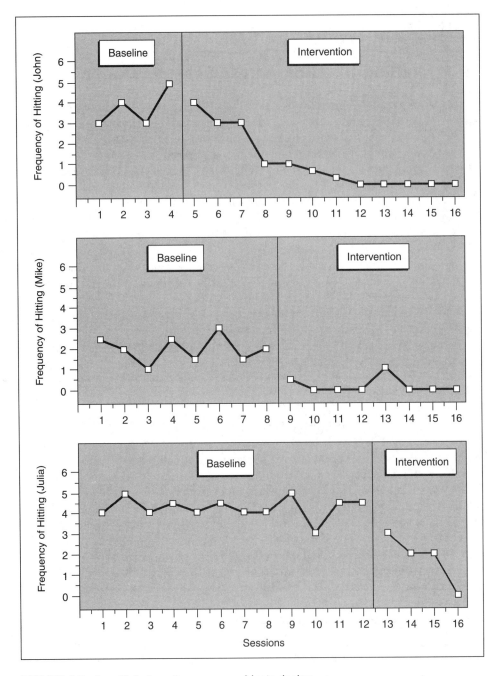

**FIGURE 4.8.** A multiple-baseline-across-subjects design

# Classroom Application 4.2

## Multiple-Baseline-Across-Behaviors Design

Gregg is a third-grade teacher. One of his students, Christopher, exhibits several aggressive behaviors (hitting, yelling, and kicking), and Gregg decides to initiate a new classroom reinforcement program. In this new program, Gregg provides his children with exaggerated verbal reinforcement for appropriate interactions with other children that do not include hitting, yelling, and kicking. He hopes that Christopher will observe the other children receiving attention for appropriate behavior and that Christopher will model his peers. When Christopher is aggressive, Gregg decides to ask Christopher to stand away from the other children for 5 minutes of time-out (usually in a classroom corner).

Gregg does not want to tackle all of Christopher's inappropriate behaviors at the same time. Instead, he decides to complete 4 days of baseline observation on all three behaviors, decide which one was the biggest problem, and initiate his time-out program with one behavior at a time. After the baseline data are collected, he decides to start with Christopher's hitting behavior.

After 4 days of baseline observation and data collection, Gregg initiates his program. Verbal praise is provided following appropriate interactions between students, including Christopher, and Christopher is sent to the time-out corner immediately after he hits another child. Meanwhile, Gregg continues to collect baseline data for Christopher's other two behavior problems (yelling and kicking). By charting the frequency of Christopher's hitting, Gregg notices a significant decrease in Christopher's hitting frequency.

After four more days, Gregg incorporates Christopher's yelling behavior in his program. Thus, hitting and yelling behavior are now followed by 5-minute periods of time-out. Meanwhile, Gregg continues to collect baseline data for Christopher's kicking behavior.

On the 12th day of programming, Gregg includes Christopher's kicking behavior into his program. Now, all three of Christopher's inappropriate behaviors are followed by the 5-minute time-out while appropriate interactions continued to be verbally reinforced.

Gregg continues his program for the rest of the school year because he likes the idea of verbally reinforcing appropriate classroom behaviors. Since Christopher's aggressive behaviors only occur now and then, the occasional use of a 5-minute time-out period provides Gregg with an effective consequence for aggression. In fact, Gregg decides to use this approach as a consequence for aggression exhibited by the other students in his classroom.

The data charted by Gregg during his multiple-baseline-across-behaviors design are given in Figure 4.9. As Figure 4.9 shows, by beginning the same program for the three behaviors at different intervals, Gregg established a relationship between the initiation of his intervention and a deceleration of each of the three behaviors. In this case, as in Classroom Application 4.1, the duration of baseline and intervention conditions was 4 days. The actual number of days for any of the conditions, however, will vary according to the child, behavior, and setting.

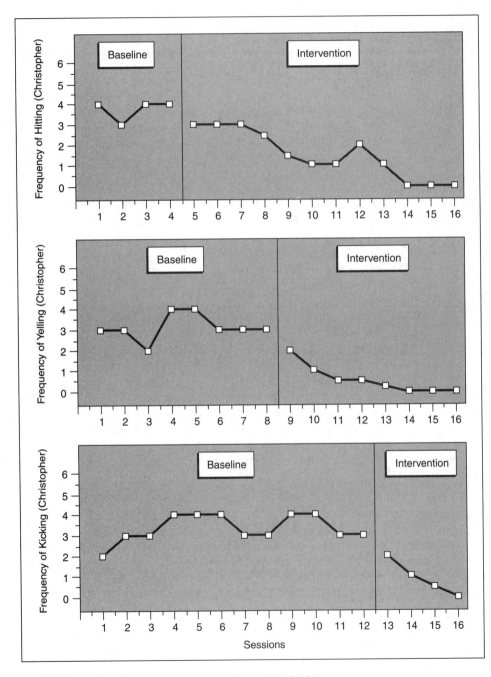

**FIGURE 4.9.** A multiple-baseline-across-behaviors design

# Classroom Application 4.3

## Multiple-Baseline-Across-Settings Design

Brenda, a special education consultant for a large school system, has a meeting with several sixth-grade teachers about a boy named Tommy. Tommy has some attention deficits that resulted in a significant amount of off-task behaviors in his math, science, and English classes.

Baseline measures indicate that Tommy is off-task an average of 30 minutes for each of the 45-minute classes. Brenda recommends a cognitive behavior modification (see Chapter 6) program that includes:

- teaching Tommy how to monitor his own on-task behavior,
- teaching Tommy how to record his own on-task behavior performance,
- teaching Tommy how to evaluate his on-task performance according to specific criteria established by his teachers, and
- developing a reinforcement menu (see Chapter 7) and program for appropriate on-task behaviors.

Brenda suggests that the teachers use a multiple-baseline-across-settings design to evaluate the effectiveness of their program. This design is recommended since they are interested in increasing Tommy's on-task behavior in three different classes.

The program is initiated in Tommy's math class. Tommy's math teacher explains the program to him and starts the program the same day. Meanwhile, Tommy's science and English teachers continue to collect baseline data on his on-task duration data in science and English classes.

On the 5th day, Tommy's science teacher initiates the same program while his English teacher continues collecting and charting baseline data on Tommy's on-task duration in English class. Finally, on the 9th day, Tommy's English teacher tells Tommy that she too will follow the same program used in his other two classes. The on-task program is now being employed across Tommy's three classes. All three teachers communicate daily to ensure that they consistently follow the program.

### The Multiple-Baseline-Across-Settings Design

In the multiple-baseline-across-settings design, the same intervention is applied to a single child across three different settings or environments. As with other multiple-baseline designs, the initiation of the intervention is staggered. In this case, the initiation of intervention is staggered across three settings, as demonstrated in Classroom Application 4.3.

In Classroom Application 4.3, the same behavior change program was initiated by three different teachers across three different settings. By implementing the same on-task program across settings and at different intervals, the teachers demonstrated a relationship between Tommy's on-task behavior and their intervention plan. Data collected and charted by the three teachers are presented in Figure 4.10. Notice that Tommy's on-task behavior remains low across all three settings until the intervention plan is initiated. As the intervention is initiated per setting, Tommy's on-task behavior increases for that setting. A cause-and-effect relationship between Tommy's on-task behavior and the intervention plan is established.

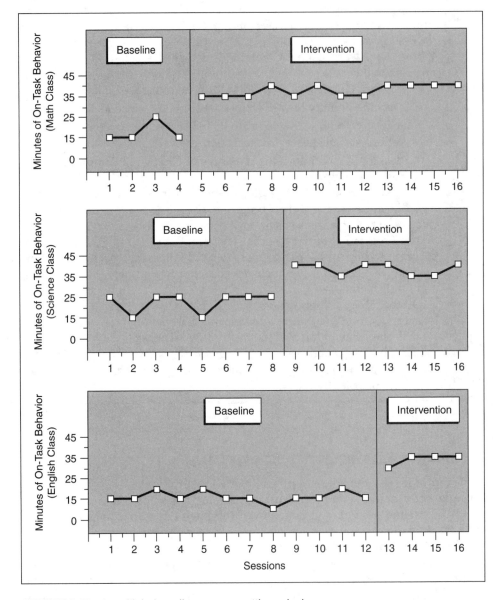

**FIGURE 4.10.** A multiple-baseline-across-settings design

In the Classroom Applications and examples provided here, the intervention condition is applied across three levels of subjects, behaviors, or settings. This approach reflects the most common application of the multiple-baseline designs. Other variations of the multiple-baseline design, however, may employ more than three levels. A minimum of two levels is required. Also, although 4 days (or sessions) per condition were used in all our examples, other variations of this design may include more or fewer than four sessions. Four, however, is usually the minimum number required if a stable data trend is to be established.

Several questions about the recorded data on a multiple-baseline design must be evaluated before a cause-and-effect relationship can be established:

- Are there significant changes from baseline to intervention conditions within each individual A-B design per subject, behavior, or setting? Note these differences in Figures 4.8, 4.9, and 4.10.
- What are the data trends or direction of data during the intervention conditions compared to the baseline conditions per subject, behavior, or setting?
- Do the data improve per subject, behavior, and setting only after the intervention condition is applied? In Figures 4.8, 4.9, and 4.10, note how the baseline data remain stable until the intervention condition is initiated across subjects, behaviors, and settings.
- How rapid did the data change once the intervention condition was initiated?
- Did baseline data remain stable before the intervention condition was introduced per child, behavior, or setting? For example, in Figure 4.8, note how the frequency of hitting remains high during the baseline condition across Mike and Julia even after the intervention program is implemented for John.
- Do the data collected during intervention conditions remain stable across subjects, behaviors, and settings? Note in Figure 4.8 how John's hitting rate remains low during the intervention condition independent of Mike's and Julia's data.

The multiple-baseline designs offer teachers a simple experimental design with the unique feature of testing interventions across several children, behaviors, and settings (Kazdin, 1982). Like the A-B-A-B design, the multiple-baseline design replicates the intervention effect but beyond a single child, behavior, or setting. The design may demonstrate a clear cause-and-effect relationship "by showing that behavior changes when and only when the intervention is applied" (Kazdin, 1982, p. 128).

## SUMMARY

The purpose of single-subject designs is to allow teachers to demonstrate experimental control and intervention effects with a single child or small group of children. Thus, these designs are ideal for classroom teachers, parents, and other teachers who want to demonstrate the effectiveness of their behavior reduction strategies.

When using single-subject designs, comparisons are made between or among conditions employed during different phases of a behavior change program. Baseline and intervention conditions represent the two primary conditions employed in single-subject designs. These are labeled conditions A and B. Intervention conditions may vary and, thus, may be labeled C, D, E, and so on, to indicate a new or modified intervention plan.

Types of single-subject designs include the A-B, A-B-C, A-B-A-B, alternating treatments, changing criterion, and multiple-baseline designs. All of these designs are variations of each other and serve specific functions related to the demonstration of experimental control and intervention effects.

The A-B design is the simplest of the single-subject designs, employing a baseline and one intervention condition. When using the A-B design, we can only presume that behavior changes noted during the intervention condition are a function of the intervention. The A-B-A design employs a withdrawal of the intervention condition and a return to baseline condition. The purpose of the A-B-A design is to demonstrate more clearly the relationship between student performance and the intervention. The A-B-A-B design employs a return to condition B after a short return to baseline as in the A-B-A design. The A-B-A-B design has many advantages over the previously described designs.

The alternating treatment or changing conditions design involves alternating intervention conditions for a single subject or group of subjects. The changing criterion design is used to increase or decrease student performance by gradually increasing the criterion for reinforcement across several intervals of time. Finally, the multiple-baseline designs provide for the replication of intervention conditions across subjects, behaviors, or settings.

## DISCUSSION QUESTIONS

1. Discuss the purpose of single-subject designs and how they may be used in the classroom setting.
2. How is the effectiveness of an intervention demonstrated or not demonstrated in the A-B, A-B-A, and A-B-A-B designs?
3. Describe how the effectiveness of an intervention is demonstrated when using multiple-baseline designs. Give examples of how the multiple-baseline design may be used within a school setting across students, settings, and behaviors.

## REFERENCES

Alberto, P. A., & Troutman, A. C. (1995). *Applied behavior analysis for teachers.* Upper Saddle River, NJ: Merrill/Prentice Hall.

Bailey, D. B. (1984). Effects of lines of progress and semilog-arithmic charts on ratings of charted data. *Journal of Applied Behavior Analysis, 17,* 359–365.

Barlow, D. H., & Hersen, M. (1984). *Single case experimental designs: Strategies for studying behavior change.* New York: Pergamon.

Bellon, M. L., Ogletree, B. T., & Harn, W. E. (2000). Repeated storybook reading as a language intervention for children with autism. *Focus on Autism and Other Developmental Disabilities, 15*(1), 52–58.

Campbell, D. T., & Stanley, J. C. (1966). *Experimental and quasi-experimental designs for research.* Boston: Houghton Mifflin.

Gay, L. R. (1996). *Educational research: Competencies for analysis and application.* Upper Saddle River, NJ: Merrill/Prentice Hall.

Gibson, G., & Ottenbacher, K. (1988). Characteristics influencing the visual analysis of single-subject data: An empirical analysis. *Journal of Applied Behavioral Science, 24,* 298–313.

Hall, R. V. (1971). *Managing behavior—Behavior modification: The measure of behavior.* Lawrence, KS: H & H Enterprises.

Hartmann, D. P., & Hall, R. V. (1976). The changing criterion design. *Journal of Applied Behavior Analysis, 9,* 527–532.

Hersen, M., & Barlow, D. H. (1976). *Single-case experimental designs: Strategies for studying behavior changes.* New York: Pergamon.

Kazdin, A. E. (1982). *Single-case research designs: Methods for clinical and applied settings.* New York: Oxford University Press.

Martin, D. W. (1985). *Doing psychology experiments* (2nd ed.). Pacific Grove, CA: Brooks/Cole.

Mueser, K. T., Yarnold, P. R., & Foy, D. W. (1991). Statistical analysis for single-case designs. *Behavior Modification, 15,* 134–155.

Odom, S. L. (1988). Research in early childhood special education. In S. L. Odom & M. B. Karnes (Eds.), *Early intervention for infants and children with handicaps* (pp. 1–22). Baltimore: Brookes.

Ottenbacher, K. J., & Cusick, A. (1991). An empirical investigation of interrater agreement for single-subject data using graphs with and without trend lines. *Journal of the Association for Persons with Severe Handicaps, 16,* 48–55.

Parsonson, B. S., & Baer, D. M. (1986). The graphic analysis of data. In A. Poling and R. W. Fuqua (Eds.), *Research methods in applied behavior analysis: Issues and advances* (pp. 157–186). New York: Plenum.

Patrick, P. D., Mozzoni, M., & Patrick, S. T. (2000). Evidenced-based care and the single subject design. *Infants and Young Children, 13*(1), 60–73.

Sidman, M. (1960). *Tactics of scientific research: Evaluating experimental data in psychology.* New York: Basic Books.

Swanson, H. L., & Sachse-Lee, C. (2000). A meta-analysis of single subject design intervention research for students with LD. *Journal of Learning Disabilities, 33*(2), 114–137.

Tawney, J. W., & Gast, D. L. (1984). *Single subject research in special education.* Upper Saddle River, NJ: Merrill/Prentice Hall.

Ulman, J. D., & Sulzer-Azaroff, B. (1975). Multi-element baseline design in educational research. In E. Ramp & G. Semb (Eds.), *Behavior analysis: Areas of research and application* (pp. 377–391). Upper Saddle River, NJ: Prentice Hall.

# CURRICULUM-BASED ASSESSMENT

## The Relationship Between Classroom Curriculum and Student Behavior

*Joel Macht*

*Since the beginning of educational measurement no fact has been more frequently revealed, and its implications more commonly ignored, than the great variability in achievement of pupils in the same grade.*

—MCDANIEL (*1994, p. VI*)

**A**rguably, teaching is the most important endeavor an individual can undertake. It may also be the most difficult assignment the individual can accept. Even in the best of worlds (e.g., reasonable class size, highly motivated students with comparable abilities, supportive administration and interested parents, and a well-prepared teacher), the job is ever-taxing, ever-changing, and ever-challenging. But, when the pieces don't fit well, the job can be overwhelming.

While many factors influence a classroom's efficiency and ultimate success, two variables warrant special mention:

- the diversity of a classroom's students, and
- the classroom teacher's curriculum.

Said simply, if the teacher's curriculum is the same for all of his or her students, yet the students differ dramatically in their abilities and academic readiness with respect to that curriculum, success will elude both teacher and students, and student behavior is likely to become an issue of concern.

The converse, however, is more promising and optimistic: If a teacher's classroom curriculum matches the diverse abilities of the classroom's students, everyone is likely to be a winner. To that end, this chapter introduces a methodology that will assist the teacher in reaching each student and, importantly, making the classroom a welcomed and successful place for all its participants.

## WHAT IS CURRICULUM-BASED ASSESSMENT?

*Curriculum-based assessment* (CBA) is a strategy for determining the instructional needs of students in an effort to match the students' needs and abilities with the classroom curriculum. Its primary goal is to eliminate curriculum mismatches between students' skills and teachers' classroom assignments and expectations. The direct result of CBA is increased student performance and a reduction in challenging student behavior within the classroom.

In 1985, James A. Tucker, the guest editor for the journal *Exceptional Children*, wrote:

> *Curriculum-based assessment (CBA) is a new term for a teaching practice that is as old as education itself: Using the material to be learned (in the classroom) as the basis for assessing the degree to which it has been learned. (p. 199)*

A few years later, Shapiro and Derr (1990) succinctly characterized CBA as a method teachers can use to determine the instructional needs of their students.

CBA offers general and special education teachers a means to determine how students are performing within the classroom's curriculum (Macht, 1998).

It provides teachers a strategy to more expeditiously modify their curriculum when it doesn't accomplish what was intended.

## Variations and Similarities

Variations within the CBA model have been clearly described in the professional literature. Shapiro and Derr (1990) have offered in some detail the distinctions attributed to CBA by many of its proponents (Blankenship, 1985; Deno, 1985; Gickling & Havertape, 1981; Idol, Nevin, & Paolucci-Whitcomb, 1986, 1999; Shapiro & Lentz, 1985, 1986.) Additionally, several authors (Choate, Enright, Miller, Poteet, & Rakes, 1992; Howell, Fox, & Morehead, 1993; King-Sears, 1994; Shinn, 1989) have discussed:

   a. the different theoretical underpinnings of CBA (see also Tucker, 1985);
   b. the multiple advantages of CBA over traditional standardized assessment tools (see also Witt, Elliot, Daly, Gresham, & Kramer, 1998); and,
   c. the myriad benefits of CBA when used in classrooms with diverse students.

Despite the seeming large number of differences within the CBA model, the fact remains that most researchers and practitioners see a consistent overlap in the model's value, mechanics, and application (Shinn, 1989).

As the years have passed since CBA first was mentioned as a viable instructional delivery system (Gickling & Thompson, 1985), distinctions within CBA have further blurred, and the CBA model has become a relatively unified approach that provides teachers with strategies to help each student experience a measure of success within the classroom. The following curriculum-based application system has been drawn from the many commonalities presented so thoroughly and effectively by the scholars earlier cited.

### Definition of Terms

We begin our discussion on CBA by clarifying vocabulary often associated with the approach. Afterwards, we will discuss CBA in interrelated sections from purpose to application. The following are frequently used terms in CBA: *present performance level (PPL), error analysis, entering skills, conceptual/motivational errors, curriculum mismatch, curriculum modification, probes, inter-* and *intra-student variability*. Each is discussed here.

A student's *present performance level (PPL)* represents the level of academic work (i.e., reading, math, and writing skills) at which the student succeeds at, or near, 100%. It represents the student's mastery level of the assessed subject area.

A teacher cannot predict a student's PPL or *entering skill* from his or her age, grade level, intelligence quotient, or special education label. A particular third grader can have the same reading entering skills as, let us say, a fifth grader; a particular ninth grader can have the same mathematics entering skills as a twelfth grader. Three students, all labeled with a learning disability, all the same age and all from the same class, can have vastly different entering skills in all subject areas. Don't be surprised to find a student who has tested low on an instrument claiming to measure intelligence who has strong entering skills in one or several subject areas.

Experienced teachers will tell you that it is not uncommon in any class (elementary, middle, or secondary) to have many students with widely varying entering skills. This variability among students is known as *inter-student variability*. As mentioned earlier, if such inter-student variability exists in a classroom where the teacher is using one curriculum strategy for all, the chances are strong there will exist a serious *curriculum mismatch* and related challenging behaviors. Thus, a curriculum mismatch occurs when a teacher's classroom curriculum does not mesh with a student's entering skills (a teacher asks a student to complete an assignment that is either well beyond a student's PPL or is well below a student's present entering skills). In the case where curriculum supercedes a student's entering skills, frustration and other ills are likely to occur; in the case where a student has long since mastered the topic being discussed, boredom can be prevalent. In both instances, behavior problems within the classroom are likely to surface.

Additionally, experienced teachers are well aware of a phenomenon known as *intra-student variability* where an individual student can have dramatically different entering skills in various subjects (e.g., the student may be ready for accelerated mathematics while struggling with the foundations of reading, either its decoding or its comprehension).

Curriculum mismatches can be avoided, although effort is required for that to occur. First, teachers must determine a student's PPL prior to introducing a lesson or an exercise. This is accomplished through vehicles called *probes*. Probes present to students sets of questions and exercises designed to determine what components of the curriculum students have mastered. Probes will help you discover your students' entering skills.

Probes can also be used in conjunction with a technique known as *error analysis*. Error analysis will help you better understand the types of errors your students are making on their assignments. The technique will provide you with a platform from which to modify your curriculum, allowing you the opportunity to design it to fit a student's uniqueness.

## Critical Elements of CBA

Curriculum-based assessment possesses four primary elements that warrant our attention.

   a. CBA is a general education initiative intended to prevent academic problems from escalating. It is used with *all* students, not only with students receiving special services or who have Individual Education Plans (IEP). In fact, the use of CBA reduces the numbers of students designated "special education" by helping general education teachers be more successful with students who present variations in entering skills and learning styles (see Macht, 1998, for a description of an experimental program that provides general education teachers with immediate assistance when students experience academic difficulties). While no precise figures can be known, it is safe to suggest that a huge portion of students eventually labeled "learning disabled" have suffered a curriculum mismatch beginning as early as kindergarten.

b. CBA obtains direct and frequent measures of a student's performance on a series of objectives, ranging from easy to difficult, derived from the curriculum the teacher uses in the classroom. Frequent measures provide a more stable picture of a student's progress, and provide more usable information to teachers and parents than schools' traditional standardized testing that occurs minimally through the school year.

c. CBA requires that teachers focus upon what students can do rather than describe their deficiencies. The phrase "the student can't read" gives way to what the student does read, regardless of the student's entry level. A master teacher always builds upon what students can do.

d. CBA uses a student's classroom performance measured by instruments built from the classroom's curriculum to determine the most effective instructional strategies for that student.

### A "No Fault" Approach

If a student fails to make progress within a teacher's curriculum, it is assumed that the teacher's instructional strategies were unsuccessful and in need of modification. This holds true even for those students assigned to special education. The blaming game (e.g., poor teacher, disinterested parent, disordered brain, or inadequate nervous system) serves little practical purpose. No one individual (or one variable) ever owns a student's particular learning problem. Moreover, teachers are rarely able to affect a change in variables outside their classroom. The significant variable that demands most of our attention is teacher strategies within the classroom. Regardless of a student's predicted innate strength or observed academic weaknesses, a teacher's flexible, efficient, and effective classroom strategy is the tool that will yield success.

### Diverse Learners Need a Broad-Based Curriculum

As a teacher, you will have a classroom composed of highly diverse students presenting highly diverse entering skills and curriculum pacing needs. You will therefore need to have at your disposal a broad-based curriculum to be used within your classroom so all of your students can benefit from their time with you.

It is worth repeating that is is highly unlikely that every student in your classroom will be ready for the same degree of work, either its academic content or the pacing (speed) with which the content is presented. The attitude, voiced by a disgruntled teacher, "I was hired to teach third grade; if one of my students is not ready for third grade, that's not my problem," is counterproductive and far from the best practice. There will be a youngster in third grade who has entering skills that are closer to first or second grade; there will be a student in tenth grade whose entering skills are more in line with seventh grade. The deviation is the teacher's challenge. How the teacher deals with this challenge will greatly affect student performance and classroom behavior.

### Seek Help from Colleagues

In addition to having a working knowledge of curriculum across multigrade levels, you would be well-advised to make friends with teachers whose classroom materials border yours. Such friendships will enable you to "pick the brains" of your colleagues and borrow from them valuable curriculum materials when you are faced with a diversity of entering skills.

You must also be prepared to provide different instruction to those students in need of different experiences. Some students will need direct instruction with the acquisition of new (foundational) skills, while other students, because of advanced entering skills, will benefit more from accelerated instruction and experiences.

The greater your knowledge of the curriculum you use in your classroom, and the sequential curriculum that precedes and follows what you are presenting, the better able you will be to alter your strategies to meet your students' diverse needs. Of course, your ability to match your curriculum to the academic readiness of your students requires that you know what academic skills your students possess.

## CURRICULUM PROBES: ASSESSING A STUDENT'S ENTERING SKILLS

*Probes* are the primary tool for the curriculum-based assessment model. Probes are most often teacher-made, functional, criterion-referenced tests (CRTs) that the teacher builds directly from his or her own curriculum (e.g., math problems, spelling words, reading passages, and writing assignments).

Probes can contain relatively few questions or exercises, or their numbers can be expansive. A piece of paper containing a few strategically chosen math problems is a probe. Having a student decode a line or two from a paragraph probes decoding proficiency. Having a student tell you about the location or setting of a story is a probe. Asking the same student a few comprehension questions, calling for literal or inferential interpretations, is also a probe. Every time you request a student to write a sentence or two, you have conducted a writing probe.

Probes communicate to you what your students can do and at what point on a sequential curriculum to begin your lessons. By comparing the results of the probes you used on Monday with the same probes administered on the following Tuesday or Wednesday, you will know if your teaching strategies have been successful. You will know if you can proceed or if you have to practice further.

Probes provide teachers with invaluable information on students' grasp of classroom curriculum.

## Developing Probes

There are no hard-and-fast rules governing the manner in which probes are developed. As long as your academic probes assess your students' competencies, they will serve their purposes.

Some elementary and middle schools have developed schoolwide probes for reading, writing, and mathematics that are to be used by all the school's teachers at the beginning of the year, and throughout the school year, on a schedule decided by the staff. Other schools have opted to have teachers develop their own probes to be used during the first few days of the school year to see where their students are in relation to the curriculum. In some instances, schools have requested that their special education teams develop probes for regular teachers to use. Other schools have considered using preprinted, standardized tests (e.g., Brigance, for probing basic readiness skills). Again, there is much flexibility.

To build your own probes, consider the following sequence:

  a. Thoroughly analyze the curriculum you are going to use with your students.
  b. Build questions and problems from that curriculum, making sure that your questions and problems sample a wide area (perhaps three full grade levels) of possible entering skills.
  c. Order your questions and problems by difficulty. (Remember, easy is only easy for a student if the student knows the answer). Develop multiple forms with similar items also listed in order of increasing difficulty.
  d. Administer the items.

e. Score the items correct or incorrect, with descriptions of errors in the latter case.

f. Using folders for each student, describe approximate entering skills.

g. Develop simple graphs with which to record student performance (see Chapter 4).

## Examples of Probes

The following probe descriptions are presented to provide you with a structure from which to build your own probes. Consider your own curriculum and goals and preferences when developing your probes. Keep in mind that probes are intended to help you better understand the types of academic experiences your students bring with them into your class.

### *Writing Probes*

Writing probes are the easiest, for they require only that a teacher obtain a sample of a student's writing. Usually, the sample is taken under two circumstances:

a. The teacher provides the student with a concrete topic and asks the student to write about that topic.

b. The teacher provides no identifiable structure; rather, the student is asked to write about any topic of choice.

Writing probes should always have a time limit—one that fits your teaching schedule. Evaluating the probe follows from your particular interests at the moment. Content, punctuation, use of phonics, creativity, spelling, syntax, plot development, and logical flow represent only a few issues that may pique your curiosity. Writing probes can be administered in groups, as well as on an individual basis. In addition to giving you a picture of progress, your writing probes will be used to determine the types of exercises or assignments you will choose to use with a particular student.

### *Math Probes*

When developing math probes, as with any probe, you will need to decide what specific skill you wish to assess. Assuming interest in calculation skills is priority for the moment, your math probes will contain a wide range of problems requiring different types of solutions (e.g., recognition of numbers; which is correct: 3 > 2 or 2 > 3; 23 + 45 = ; 327 − 186 = ; 54 × 30 = ; 144 divided by 6 = ; $1/2 \times 3\ 1/6$ = ; and so on).

When developing math probes, you want to present problems well below and above your students' expected present performance levels. Determine the degree of difficulty the student has mastered, and the level that begins to produce reliable errors. (More than likely, your colleagues already have printed math exercises that can be used as probes for your students. Placing those probes in a folder in a central location within the school would make their access easy.)

You can probe mathematical concepts that go far beyond typical calculations. A problem (which will serve as a probe), such as the following, administered to your entire class, can provide you with a great deal of valuable information regarding your students' readiness to move from concrete calculations to abstract thinking, to understanding of concepts, to application, integration, and generalization:

> Billy ate 1/4 of a candy bar; Mary ate another 1/4 of the same candy bar; and Ms. Smith ate 1/2 of the same candy bar. Questions: (a) How much of the candy bar has been eaten? (b) How much more candy did Ms. Smith have than Billy?

### Reading Probes

Reading probes present the greatest challenge, and you would be well advised to discuss with your school's reading specialists what components warrant assessing for an individual youngster or an entire classroom of students. While reading probes can be conducted in groups, individual probing provides the most valuable information.

Sitting across from a student, determining the level at which reading occurs comfortably and fluidly, having the opportunity to do an immediate miscue or error analysis, being able to gauge a student's literal or inferential comprehension skills with the material at hand, again, is often the most fruitful way of measuring some of a student's reading proficiency.

For group probes, develop multiple, brief paragraphs (3 to 5 sentences or more), ranging from beginning levels to complex reading materials. These paragraphs can be presented to a group of students who are requested first to read each paragraph, beginning at a difficulty level determined by you, and then to answer two or three questions regarding the reading materials. The students should continue this brief reading and answering assignment until the materials end, or until they are no longer able to decode the paragraphs with ease. With younger children in a group, asking them to circle selected sight words, or to circle a picture that begins with a "p" sound, can also serve as a probe to determine roughly what entering or readiness skills the youngsters possess.

## Who Administers Probes?

You and your colleagues will decide who will be responsible for administering subject-area probes. Ideally, classroom teachers will do the majority of the probing since they have the most up-to-date, accurate knowledge of their students' academic successes and difficulties. When necessary, you should request assistance with probing from your school's resource team. Your school may decide that various members of a resource team will assume responsibility for probing all the students.

## When Are Probes Administered?

For very important reasons, CBA probes are administered before, during, and after instruction. Probes administered *prior to instruction* will provide you with data allowing you to make good decisions concerning your students' placement into curriculum materials, thereby reducing, if not eliminating, curriculum mismatches and associated behavior problems. Your initial probe will tell you what materials and exercises your students have mastered.

Probes administered *during instruction* offer you data indicating how your students are doing with your current instruction, thereby providing you with a data-level basis upon which to adjust your instructional strategies. These "on-the-spot" probes reduce the probability that you will continue to use teaching methods that are proving ineffective for various students.

Probes administered immediately *following instruction* and periodically throughout the year will help you know what your students have learned. The post-test probe can be identical to the original probe, or it can contain a slight modification. Probes administered throughout the school year provide useful information on your students' long-term retention abilities, and will assist you when communicating student progress to parents and school officials.

## Where Are Probes Administered?

The ultimate goal of those proponents of CBA is to have all general classroom teachers administer probes in their classrooms daily, perhaps hourly. With practice, this goal is achievable. If you are new to the CBA model, you might consider seeking assistance from members of your school team, from a special education teacher in particular, to help you design and administer the probes in your classroom. You can try the process with one or two students and expand coverage as your confidence increases.

Schools often provide laboratory or study space within the building where students from various classes, struggling with specific components of their studies, meet to receive assistance from a professional assigned by the school's administration. A resource room, a quiet hallway, and a corner of the school's library are possible locations for such brief gatherings where probing PPLs, errors, and measuring effectiveness of teacher strategies occur. Other points to consider include the following:

- *Assess frequently.* If you want to know how a student is doing on a certain skill or academic behavior, administer brief probes frequently. Such repeated assessment will quickly alert you to the fact that you need to modify your instruction.
- *Vary assessment.* Use a variety of student responses to probe a student's accuracy and understanding. Include written and oral answers, fill-in-the-blank answers, multiple-choice answers, finding-error answers, as well as

identification of correct and incorrect answers, correct and incorrect spellings and grammar, and the like.

- *Check generalization* of acquired skills by using assessments outside of the classroom.
- *Prioritize.* Assess the most important and most critical academic behaviors most often. Decide which academic behaviors are most in need of change and then gather as much data about those behaviors as possible.
- *Keep good data.* Have growth-over-time charts and hard copies of students' work to share with teachers and parents, both informally and during meetings pertaining to a student's academic achievement. Help everyone concentrate on what the student is doing correctly.

## Recording Progress: Growth-Over-Time Charts

CBA probes yield data points that can be recorded on students' growth-over-time charts (review single-subject design information in Chapter 4). Plot whatever skill you were working on: the number of addition problems correctly solved, the number of words correctly read, the number of correctly used noun-verb agreements, and so on. The ascending or descending direction of the plotted data lines will tell you if your instructional strategies are working.

A flat data line is most often an indication that your instructional strategy needs to be modified. This is an extremely important point, particularly when you are working with a youngster who is suspected of having learning problems. Without exception, learning problems are only solved with good strategies. If a child is making no (or minimal) progress in any of the subject areas, you must reevaluate your strategies. Once again, seek advice from your school's assistance team to gain fresh ideas as to how to help a youngster over an academic hurdle.

## Probes and Student Errors

Probes should be administered when a student exhibits consistent errors or difficulties with classroom assignments. Anytime a student is struggling with work, a probe is in order. A grade of "C" or worse on an assignment is a sure indicator that a probe is needed. These brief queries are used to analyze possible causes of students' errors.

Two important notes about probes: Probes are not to be used to determine grades, and they are not to be used to compare the performances of students. Instead, probes are used to determine what experiences and instructional strategies individual students need. Probes help teachers modify and improve their curriculum.

## The Value of Student Errors

Kim's errors in Vignette 5.1 provided her dad with valuable information because he used her errors as a means to determine what Kim already knew and what information she had yet to acquire. Indeed, students' errors will provide you with a

## VIGNETTE 5.1

●
_____

*Student Errors Lead to New Student Experiences*

Third grader Kim received her spelling paper back from her teacher. She was upset by the dramatic sad face in the upper right-hand corner, the large "−2" slashed in red ink underneath the face's down-turned lips, and the two "X's" the teacher had marked across sentences 9 and 10. The students were handed their papers without further comment.

At dinner that evening, Kim's mother sensed her daughter's uncharacteristic gloom and gently pressed her for an explanation. Reluctantly, Kim left the table and returned with the crumpled paper she had extricated from her backpack. Her mother promptly shared it with her husband. "I will help you with this after dinner," Kim's father told her.

The assignment consisted of 10 words and 10 sentences, each sentence with a blank to be filled in by one of the words at the top of the page. For several of the young students, Kim including, a few of the words were new. The ninth sentence read; "The fisherman used the _____ to help him catch fish." Kim had two remaining words from which to choose: *bait* and *zebra*. Having not a clue of the meaning of "bait," she chose "zebra," explaining to her father that the zebra went with the fisherman to the river's edge and the zebra, like the Alaskan bears she had seen on television, helped the fisherman grab the fish as they swam close by. (A good answer, her father thought.)

Had the teacher used her exercise as a probe, rather than as a vehicle to grade, Kim and several others in the class who also struggled with the word "bait" would have been the winners. The teacher could have used the students' errors in any number of productive ways: (a) to learn which words were unfamiliar; (b) to ask other students who had experience with fishing for assistance; (c) to show pictures of different fish and explain how the smaller ones were bait for the larger ones; (d) to discuss the differences between a bear's claws and a zebra's hoofs; and (e) to present any number of other growth exercises.

Choosing instead to return the papers to the students with the telling marks, the teacher lost a perfect opportunity to help her students and herself.

_____

window into their thoughts and problem-solving skills. They present golden opportunities for teaching and golden opportunities for learning. Remember these points about student errors:

- Students must feel comfortable making errors and admitting to teachers areas of confusion and difficulty.
- Students must know that, within a teacher's classroom, student errors are not only acceptable, but they are welcomed and encouraged.
- Students need to know that all their answers, even those that are incorrect, are nevertheless very valuable.

Many students believe that errors are bad (they've learned this lesson through lower grades and deprecating marks and notations on assignments), and they are often reluctant to even try to answer a difficult question if they think there is a chance they will make a mistake. You must, therefore, prepare your students to accept that errors are important, and you must prepare them to share with you when they do not understand all or part of an assignment or its instruction.

You'll need a means to keep track of your students' errors. Take notice of reliable, consistent errors. An occasional academic error can be overlooked. A consistent error, or an error with a distinct, repeated pattern, must be recorded and explored. You can use a notebook that you either carry with you or keep close by to record student errors. The notebook should contain each student's name along with sufficient room to describe the student's responses. Your students should see you recording errors. Explain the purpose behind your actions, and assure them that you are keeping a record of the errors so you can develop different strategies. Do not be surprised if the question of grades comes up!

## ERROR ANALYSIS

While we can thank Jean Piaget for much that is good about education, arguably his most important contribution was his interest and resulting research on the cognitive processes students used to arrive at their answers, both correct and incorrect answers. He believed we can learn most about a child (and thus how best to help the child) by investigating the basis for the child's responses and conclusions. The student's exact answer was, for Piaget, quite secondary.

Probes lend themselves to immediate (and very easy) analysis of a student's errors. Asking one of your students to share how he or she arrived at an answer may provide you with just what you need to develop all sorts of innovative ways of helping the student work through the presenting hurdles. Questions for students may include the following:

"How did you arrive at your answer?"

"What were you thinking about when completing the problem?"

"What steps did you use to answer the question?"

These types of questions can illuminate what skills and concepts a student presently possesses and which ones he or she has yet to acquire. Frankly, while error analysis is a marvelous strategy to uncover the basis for a student's problem, it is quite often pure fun for the teacher.

In Vignette 5.2 it took Jack's teacher only moments to develop several "thinking" strategies, involving estimating, to help him understand his errors. A few more exercises, and he understood the concepts of adding groups rather than columns of numbers. A quick probe, with problems similar to the first probe, verified that Jack had learned what addition really meant.

Error analysis is a simple process that will help you identify which components of an assignment are creating difficulty for one of your students. Again, asking the simple question, "How did you arrive at your answer?" will provide you with enormous insights and ideas for new approaches to use with the student.

## VIGNETTE 5.2

●

### *You Don't Know How to Do These?*

Jack loved math. He loved numbers. And he loved putting them together and coming up with all sorts of answers. Unfortunately, his answers were not always correct. Having noticed consistent errors with regrouping, Jack's teacher built a quick probe as a prelude to error analysis. She presented him with the following items:

| 9 | 14 | 24 | 16 | 24 | 34 |
|---|---|---|---|---|---|
| +7 | +3 | +11 | +8 | +27 | +18 |

After looking over the problems, the youngster gave his teacher a full-toothed smile and asked, "You don't know how to do these?" She smiled and asked him to help her out. He did, more than he could have imagined.

| 9 | 14 | 24 | 16 | 24 | 34 |
|---|---|---|---|---|---|
| +7 | +3 | +11 | +8 | +27 | +18 |
| 16 | 17 | 35 | 114 | 411 | 412 |

The teacher watched Jack work over the problems and immediately noticed that he added from left to right, the "tens" first, opening the door for the "ones" to step out rather prominently. It was quite apparent the full concept of addition had eluded him. When he was finished, and satisfied, she asked him to tell her how he arrived at his answers. With an incredulous look, he explained, "You add the top numbers and the bottom numbers. It's simple," he said, pointing to the last problem. "Three plus one is four, four plus eight is twelve." He smiled and let his eyes say, "Obvious, don't you think?"

---

Remember these three important points regarding student errors:

a. The vast majority of student errors are conceptual in nature. The student is missing an important component or two, or an entire conceptualization of the present problem, and unless the confusion or absence of knowledge is rectified, the problems will persist and begin to affect material built upon what is missing.

b. It is tempting to conclude that a student's absence of correct work (or any work!) is a motivational problem. While such is possible, motivational problems are less common that expected. More often, they appear as an issue when in fact a student is experiencing consistent conceptual difficulties. Motivation should never be the first explanation used to account for a student's poor academic work. A strategically asked question of a student might reveal the real felon: A conceptual component is missing.

c. Do not help a student with an erroneous answer without first running an error analysis. Avoid the "Let me show you how to do that" knee-jerk reaction when a student makes an error. Helping the student before you have discovered the confusion or deficiency may not assist the student beyond getting an answer correct.

## CLASSROOM BEHAVIOR AND CBA

The primary purpose of discussing CBA in this text is to understand the relationship between the classroom curriculum and student behavior. In this first section of the text, you are presented with technical skills to measure and chart behavior. However, to simply measure the dimension of a target behavior without looking at the behavior in light of the student's environment, including the student's current relationship with the classroom curriculum, as demonstrated in Vignette 5.3, is inviting a misunderstanding of the real problem.

As educators, we have to guard against the impulse to take a superficial view of children's behaviors. It would have been quicker and maybe easier for Sara's teacher in Vignette 5.3 to have identified a "problem behavior." Sara's teacher might have referred her for screening and testing for a learning or attention deficit disorder. But the real problem underlying the behavior (the curriculum mismatch) would have been missed.

### VIGNETTE 5.3

●

*Another Perspective of a Problem Behavior*

Sara is a lively 12-year-old in a local middle school program. While she is always curious and appears interested in classroom activities, her attention tends to wander. This behavior is particularly noticeable during lectures or when her teacher is providing the class with instructions. Sara usually begins the class sitting attentively, facing the teacher. Within minutes, however, she is more likely to be stretched out in her chair, playing with her pen and notebook or trying to attract the attention of students nearby. These behaviors are disruptive and distracting to her teacher and other students.

One way to look at this situation is to conclude that Sara is controlling, attention seeking and immature. After all, the teacher's lectures provide a valuable learning experience. If Sara is not attentive during the readings or explanations of activities, she obviously has a problem. Or does she?

Sara's teacher chose to look at her behaviors from another perspective: A curriculum issue might be related to Sara's "tuning out." By questioning her, the teacher learned Sara was a precocious reader and had already heard or read many of the facts discussed in class. What was new for the other students was "old stuff" for Sara. A similar situation was occurring when instructions were given by the teacher. Sara could quickly grasp what was being asked for in most instances and did not always need the details or repetitions provided for the sake of the other students.

Sara's teacher modified the classroom assignments to better match Sara's abilities and characteristics. She allowed Sara and other children to begin a task as soon as they could demonstrate they understood the directions. Sara's disruptive behaviors diminished as the teacher's strategies changed.

Sara's teacher responded differently from many of us in that she assumed that there was a purpose and reason for Sara's challenging behavior. In her teacher's mind, Sara's behaviors were not problems in and of themselves; they reflected her response to an environment that was not best suited to her.

Educators are encouraged to seek answers to the following questions when faced with a student's challenging behavior:

- Could the student's misbehavior be a result of a curriculum that is too easy or too difficult?
- Could the student's misbehavior be a result of the student's inability to understand an academic concept being taught?
- Could the student's misbehavior be a result of any other classroom factor over which the teacher has direct control and thus can modify?

## Behavior Problems as Signs of Academic Problems

John, the student in Vignette 5.4, was lucky. Not too many psychologists would consider the classroom curriculum as an antecedent to a problem behavior. Instead, many would focus on identifying John's "problem" or finding a "disability" (e.g., ADD/ADHD) to explain his behavior.

It is hardly a coincidence that many students who present behavior and attention problems while in class are the same students experiencing difficulty with their academically related assignments. Researchers have known of this relationship for a long time. For example, Center, Dietz, and Kaufman (1982) have documented that a mismatch between academic material that the student could not successfully complete usually resulted in higher levels of disruptive classroom behavior. It is also not surprising to discover that for many students, their disruptive behavior is very situation-specific, occurring most often when required to participate in nonpreferred tasks rather than preferred ones.

## Controlling Instructional Difficulty

There has been a significant amount of research on the behavior of students with a history of challenging behaviors while involved in preferred versus nonpreferred tasks (Foster-Johnson, Ferro, & Dunlap, 1994). The variable of choice, or letting students choose their tasks, has also been extensively investigated (Dunlap et al. 1994). While letting students choose their tasks has been shown to increase desirable student behavior, Cole, Davenport, and Bambara (1997) have demonstrated that it is the participation in a preferred activity, not the variable of choice, that seems to have the biggest effect on student behavior.

Students prefer activities that they can complete successfully. These tasks are more reinforcing than tasks that produce consistent errors and, as was the instance with Mrs. Case's student, John, accompanying frustration and embarrassment. When a student says "I love reading," chances are the student is successful at reading. Students generally choose activities they prefer, they prefer activities where success is likely, and their behaviors are more socially acceptable under such conditions.

Realistically, public school teachers can rarely have students choose to spend their entire school day with favorite activities within a curriculum. But, teachers

**VIGNETTE 5.4**

●
───────────────────────────────────────────────

*Working Hard to Avoid Reading*

Reading had always been difficult for John. His first experiences were frustrating and humiliating, and he often feigned sickness when it was his turn to read aloud in front of his classmates. A capable student, John's reading problems emerged center stage in Mrs. Case's third-grade classroom. The teacher had grown increasingly impatient with John's refusal to participate during reading. She required all her students to stand from their desks and read passages from their assigned books to their classmates. John had tried everything he could to avoid the task. His efforts included stomachaches, headaches, dizziness, momentary flu, and nausea. Mrs. Case initially allowed John to visit the nurse when he complained of an infirmity, but she became less lenient and more strident in her demands after learning from the nurse that John was in perfect health. Mrs. Case decided it was time for John to be a responsible member of the class. When the day's reading time arrived, she selected John to be the first reader, catching him completely off guard. She forcefully told him to stand and read from his book. After scanning the passage and realizing he would stumble embarrassingly, he burst into tears, threw over his chair, and ran from the room. He was located quickly and sent to the principal's office. The thought that John had a conduct disorder was seriously considered. The school's psychologist was called, and a consult was established.

The psychologist's precise questions revealed that John was a good student outside of reading class. He also learned that John had never presented any behavior problems prior to the one recent incident. Trained to consider the impact that curriculum can have on the behavior of schoolchildren, the psychologist contacted the special education teacher and suggested that she, John, and he sit down together in an effort to determine the youngster's entering skills with respect to decoding and comprehending written text.

John's strengths and deficiencies were quickly unmasked, and a meeting was immediately established with Mrs. Case. Explaining their findings, the psychologist and special education teacher suggested that Mrs. Case take a few moments to ascertain the reading PPLs for all her students. Not surprisingly, John was not the only student for whom a curriculum mismatch existed. Mrs. Case agreed to provide reading materials and assignments that more accurately fit her students' entering skills. John's confidence (and skills) improved quickly, as did that of others in Mrs. Case's class.

───────────────────────────────────────────────

can make accommodations to the required curriculum in order to assist students in being more successful and lowering their errors and frustration.

For students to have success with their academic requirements, materials must be presented at an instructional level rather than a frustration level. A teacher's instructional demands, therefore, must be tied to each student's academic entering skill and not to group goals or curriculum goals that are unrelated to what the teacher is doing within his or her classroom. Instructional demands must be based on students' present performance level data. A youngster whose reading skills are comfortably positioned in third-grade texts will experience difficulty if a teacher's instructional demands require the same youngster to read and comprehend material designed for students at the sixth- or seventh-grade level.

Curriculum-based assessment can help teachers eliminate many of the educational factors responsible for students' disturbing classroom behavior. As a result, CBA has become one of the strongest tools in many teachers' behavior management portfolios.

## CBA AND EXCEPTIONAL STUDENTS

The term "exceptional" has been purposely chosen to represent all students who, in any number of ways, deviate from the norms of the general education population. Such youngsters may struggle with their work or may excel far beyond predictions. They may have physical and motor issues that interfere with the traditional sit-in-your-chair type of schooling, and they may have cognitive challenges that demand gentle, incremental learning, with constant repetition.

Curriculum-based assessment is as critical for students with IEPs as those without. At the same time, special education labels, including LD, MR, ADD/ADHD, and the myriad of others that have been generated over the past century, provide us with little in the way of academic information. Despite the grouping of same-labeled students in all exceptionality textbooks, students labeled in any manner are unique and, from functional perspective, are not part of any group with shared academic or social/behavioral characteristics. Two children, both labeled with cerebral palsy, are likely to differ to the same degree that any two 10-year-olds will differ. Being told that you have a so-labeled learning disabled child coming into your classroom provides you with nothing upon which to develop curriculum or strategies. The same can be said for any youngster labeled in any fashion.

To know what an exceptional student can do academically, and thus develop a good fit between the student's entering skills and your curriculum, you must put aside

- special education's labels;
- the student's age;
- the student's assigned grade level;
- all derived IQ numbers; and
- all prior professional statements that have foretold what the student will not ever be able to accomplish. Instead, we should follow the same systematic approach we have been discussing in this chapter:
  a. Reexamine your classroom curriculum and consider what student skills are essential to that curriculum.
  b. List those skills in logical order. Write an objective for each skill on the list. Ask, What do I want the student to do?
  c. Prepare items (probes) from your classroom curriculum to assess each listed objective. The items should span from easy to difficult. Reduce the number of items to make the probe administratively manageable. Sequence the items in random order or present items beginning with

the most simple and progressing to the most difficult, stopping when the student no longer answers correctly.

d.  Determine the modality a student will use to express his or her knowledge (oral, ASL, computer-based, written, pointing, and so forth).

e.  Determine the student's entering skills or present performance level with respect to those skills you have selected from your curriculum.

f.  Determine at what point within your curriculum the student begins exhibiting reliable academic errors.

g.  Determine through error analysis the conceptual base for the student's errors.

h.  Build academic assignments and exercises to help the student move beyond the errors that are inhibiting the student's progress.

i.  Develop and implement new strategies to assist the student with the new curriculum.

j.  Identify errors the student is making with the new curriculum.

k.  Select valid indicators of a student's progress (what specific skill— described precisely—you want him or her to learn); develop growth-over-time graphs and monitor slope of curve.

l.  Reevaluate your curriculum strategies and make alterations if they are warranted.

m.  Repeat item "e" from this list and proceed with a continuous loop between items "e" and "h".

## SUMMARY

Know your curriculum. Find colleagues who know more than you do and talk with them about the curriculum. You will need the curriculum to build criterion-referenced tests and probes and sequential lessons to help students move beyond trouble points.

Prior to present performance level (PPL) testing, remind students that they will not be criticized or punished for errors; their errors will tell you where to start the next lesson.

Observe a student's performance on academic assignments to obtain ideas where to begin PPL or entering skill assessment. Administer probes to identify roughly where within curriculum a student succeeds at or near 100%.

During PPL assessment, push the student beyond the point at which he or she makes no errors. A student's errorless performance does not translate to his or her PPL. Push the student beyond achieved success until reliable errors are observed. Watch carefully to determine the general areas that are creating difficulty. Note errors. By looking at the level of academic difficulty where the student's success is probable and then noting where his or her errors are likely, you will know roughly where to begin your lessons.

Avoid the temptation to tell the student what he or she did right or wrong. Do not show the student how to correct errors. You will need an error analysis to know the type of error the student is making.

Carefully analyze the student's responses to your materials. Look for areas of mastery and frequent errors. Look for patterns of errors and initiate error analysis. Based on the student's errors, determine what exercises and practice materials the student needs to move beyond the present error level. Remember, instructional pacing accommodations may be necessary.

Once practice materials and exercises have been chosen, select suitable instructional strategies. Schedule individual and group instructional periods throughout the day. Consider grouping children for brief periods during the day using PPLs and error analyses as the basis for the groupings. Consider cross-grade groupings with fellow teachers. Cross-grade groupings are based on PPLs and error analyses.

Keep track of the student's progress and yield to results. Develop new strategies if the present ones are not working, as indicated by your data.

CBA defines success for each student as growth beyond the student's present performance level. Success is not defined as the attainment of a particular goal or objective used for an entire class of students. It is not defined as being the best in class or scoring high on a standardized test. Success is growth and improvement, measured on an individualized basis.

Used correctly, CBA guarantees all students a measure of sought-after academic success. Since you will have determined through your probes the entering skills for each of your students, you will know each student's individual instructional levels. Do your best to ensure a good curriculum fit between your assignments and your students' varying instructional levels, and you will help your students attain the growth we all want for them.

Remember, if a student leaves your class each day knowing more than when entering, success has been achieved, both for the student and yourself.

## DISCUSSION QUESTIONS

1. What are the advantages of curriculum-based assessment compared to standardized assessment? Consider the following variables: (a) quality of information provided to the teacher, (b) quality of information provided for direct instructional use, (c) student feedback, and (d) parent-teacher communication.

2. For the classroom teacher, what are the benefits of a curriculum-based assessment in regards to the evaluation of student academic performance?

3. What is the difference between a "probe" (as discussed in this chapter) and a typical classroom "test"?

4. Discuss the relationship between an appropriate curriculum match for an individual student and that student's classroom behavior.

5. Discuss how a classroom teacher can employ probe and error analysis strategies in various subjects (math, reading, spelling, writing, etc.) to determine why a student is having difficulty with a specific academic task.

# REFERENCES

Blankenship, C. S. (1985). Using curriculum-based assessment data to make instructional decisions. *Exceptional Children, 52,* 233–238.

Center, D. B., Dietz, S. M., & Kaufman, M. E. (1982). Student ability, task difficulty and inappropriate classroom behavior. *Behavior Modification, 6,* 355–375.

Choate, J. S., Enright, B. E., Miller, L. J., Poteet, J. A., & Rates, T. A. (1992). *Curriculum-based assessment and programming.* Boston: Allyn & Bacon.

Cole, C. L., Davenport, T. A., & Bambara, L. M. (1997). Effects of choice and task preference on the work performance of students with behavior problems. *Behavior Disorders, 22,* 65–74.

Deno, S. (1985). Curriculum-based measurement: The emerging alternative. *Exceptional Children, 52,* 219–232.

Dunlap, G., dePerczel, M., Clark, S., Wilson, D., Wright, S., White, R., & Gomez, A. (1994). Choice making to promote adaptive behavior for students with emotional and behavioral challenges. *Journal of Applied Behavior Analysis, 27,* 505–518.

Foster-Johnson, L., Ferro, J., & Dunlap, G. (1994). Prerferred curricular activities and reduced behaviors in students with intellectual disabilities. *Journal of Applied Behavior Analysis, 27,* 493–504.

Gickling, E. E., & Havertape, J. F. (1981). Curriculum-based assessment. In J. A. Tucker (Ed.), *Non-test based assessment.* Minneapolis: University of Minnesota.

Gickling, E. E., & Thompson, V. P. (1985). A personal view of curriculum-based assessment. *Exceptional Children, 52,* 205–218.

Howell, K. W., Fox, S. L., & Morehead, M. K. (1993). *Curriculum-based evaluation: Teaching and decision making.* Pacific Grove, CA: Brooks/Cole.

Idol, L., Nevin, A., & Paolucci-Whitcomb, P. (1986). *Models of curriculum-based assessment.* Rockville, MD: Aspen.

Idol, L., Nevin, A., & Paolucci-Whitcomb, P. (1999). *Models of curriculum-based assessment: A blueprint for learning.* Austin, TX: Pro-Ed.

King-Sears, M. E. (1994). *Curriculum-based assessment in special education.* San Diego, CA: Singular.

Macht, J. E. (1998). *Special education's failed system: A question of eligibility.* Westport, CT: Bergin & Garvey.

McDaniel, E. (1994). *Understanding educational measurement.* Madison, WI: WCB Brown & Benchmark.

Shapiro, E. S., & Derr, T. F. (1990). Curriculum-based assessment. *The handbook of school psychology* (2nd ed.) (pp. 365–387). New York: John Wiley & Sons.

Shapiro, E. S., & Lentz, F. E. (1985). Assessing academic behavior: A behavioral approach. *School Psychology Review, 14,* 325–338.

Shapiro, E. S., & Lentz, F. E. (1986). Behavioral assessment of academic behavior. In T. R. Kratochwill (Ed.), *Advances in school psychology* (Vol. 5, pp. 87–139). Hillsdale, NJ: Lawrence Erbaum.

Shinn, M. (1989). *Curriculum-based measurement: Assessing special children.* New York: Guilford.

Tucker, J. A. (1985). Guest editor comments. *Execeptional Children, 52,* 199–204.

Witt, J. C., Elliot, S. N., Daly, E. J., III, Gresham, F. M., & Kramer, J. J. (1998). *Assessment of at-risk and special needs children.* Boston, MA: McGraw-Hill.

# chapter 6

# FUNCTIONAL BEHAVIORAL ASSESSMENT

## Joel Macht

*The goal is to make the system work, not simply to adjust something inside the head of the child.*

—HOBBS *(1966, p. 1109)*

Some form of a behaviorally based program is needed when a student's classroom behavior (a) consistently interferes with the student's own learning, (b) consistently interferes with other students' learning, or (c) consistently interferes with a teacher's ability to conduct class. As a teacher, if you conclude that one or more of the above conditions have been met, you will need to put into action a behavior management plan that will help the student learn a more desired way of behaving.

There are several steps you should take before drafting a behavior management program. Trite as it sounds, you need to relax. Keep in mind that the student's disruptive behavior was not acquired in a day; neither will be its solution. Rushed decisions rarely produce effective strategies. Next, carefully examine the student's academic skills to ensure an absence of any curriculum mismatch (see Chapter 5). There are few, if any, behavior management programs that can succeed in the face of continued curriculum mismatches. Finally, initiate a thorough assessment referred to as a Functional Assessment (FA).

Without a careful analysis of the conditions that appear to be associated with a student's undesired behavior, and without knowing the precise effect the environment's consequences are having upon that behavior, a developed behavioral strategy could easily make matters worse both for the student and his or her teacher. Approaching a student's behavioral difficulties with patience and keenly focused eyes will prove more effective than a hurried program built upon an (understandably) urgent need for immediate change.

**VIGNETTE 6.1**

●

*Making Matters Worse*

Daniel had worn out his welcome after only three weeks of the new school year. When Mr. Thompson requested the class open their books to the assigned page, Daniel would slam his book against his desk and sit back in his chair, his arms folded belligerently. When Mr. Thompson repeated his request, his frustrated voice aimed at the youngster, Daniel would remain defiant and tell his teacher that the work was stupid. Mr. Thompson frequently provided the youngster one more opportunity to get to work before sending him to the school's study center, which was euphemistically called a cool-down room. Had anyone looked closely at the room, they would have discovered it had become a cool gathering spot for several veteran visiting students who had learned they could meet and enjoy each other's company in the loosely monitored time-out room. The same students, of course, had also discovered how to avoid classroom work, hardly the intent of the school's hardworking teachers. While Daniel's absence provided Mr. Thompson with a moment's respite, the teacher's poorly fashioned behavioral program guaranteed Daniel's future disruptiveness.

# WHAT IS A FUNCTIONAL ASSESSMENT?

As described by O'Neill et al. (1997), *functional assessment* is a "process for gathering information that can be used to maximize the effectiveness and efficiency of behavioral support" (p. 3). It is a general term used to systematically describe situations in a student's environment that not only reveal when a student's problem behaviors are most likely to occur, but clarify what consequences within that environment might be maintaining the very behavior creating difficulties for that student and school personnel.

Gresham, Quinn, and Restori (1999) describe the same methodology through different nomenclature: Functional assessment is an effective means to identify the antecedents and consequences associated with the occurrence of a student's undesired behaviors. In Vignette 6.1, Mr. Thompson would have employed an entirely different behavioral approach to Daniel's disruptiveness had he a better understanding of the classroom events or antecedents that set the stage for Daniel's behavior, as well as knowledge of the consequences that were maintaining Daniel's actions. This became evident when it was discovered during a later functional assessment that when Mr. Thompson requested his students get ready for a movie, young Daniel turned rapidly compliant. He even chided his friends to listen to the teacher.

If you have ever been involved in an A-B-C analysis (see Chapter 3 for a review), where A stands for antecedents, B stands for a student's behavior, and C represents the consequences used by the student's teacher, then you have had exposure to the technology known as functional assessment.

The U.S. Department of Education (1999, p. 45) outlined five steps for conducting a functional behavioral assessment:

*Step 1.* Define the problem behavior: Create a concrete definition of the problem behavior and the conditions under which it typically occurs.

*Step 2.* Gather information regarding environment and behavior: Use interviews, questionnaires, record reviews, and direct observations to determine what environmental events tend to precede and follow behavior.

*Step 3.* Hypothesize the function of the behavior: Use collected information and data to hypothesize the function or purpose the behavior serves for the student.

*Step 4.* Develop a behavioral intervention plan: Determine and teach an appropriate behavior that serves the same function for the student. Arrange the environment to prompt desired behavior and develop plans for providing consequences for both desired and undesired behavior.

*Step 5.* Monitor behavior to verify hypothesis and validate intervention: When monitoring indicates that the intervention is successful, the functional behavioral assessment is completed. When intervention is unsuccessful, return to step 2 and continue gathering data toward a more valid hypothesis.

# HISTORY OF FUNCTIONAL ASSESSMENT

The history of functional assessment is rich and worthy of considerable study. Its tenets can be traced back to the 1920s with the work of John Watson (1924), the 1930s with the work of Edward Thorndike (1932), and the 1940s and 50s with the work of B. F. Skinner (1953). Later in the 1950s and early in the 1960s, two seminal works (Ayllon & Michael, 1959; Michael & Meyerson, 1962) were published in the first of a series of three books on human behavior (Ulrich, Stachnik, & Mabry, 1966) that introduced a perspective on applied behavior analysis that was the precursor to functional assessment. More recently, Sulzer-Azaroff and Mayer (1991) have written an essential strategies book describing the essence of functional assessment and applied behavior analysis. Lastly, O'Neill and his colleagues (1997) have fashioned a comprehensive and highly pragmatic perspective of functional assessment, including exercises that are ideal for the student beginning or refining his or her studies in the area.

In recent years, teachers have been encouraged to complete functional analyses of student behavior to assess antecedent factors (e.g., task difficulty) and contextual factors (e.g., classroom environment) within the classroom. In fact, the Individuals with Disabilities Act (1997) now requires functional behavioral assessments for students with disabilities who have challenging behaviors (Boyajian, DuPaul, Handler, Eckert, & McGoey (2001).

## Behaviors Never Occur in Isolation

In one manner or another, all the authors just cited urged their readers to move beyond focusing entirely on a student's behavior, no matter how undesirable or unacceptable. The authors cautioned that a student's behavior never occurs in isolation, and they emphasized the importance for viewing a student's behavior within the larger context in which it occurs. Without viewing behavior in its context, it is easy to think that the student owns the behavior (i.e., has a conduct disorder or is disturbed). That bias tends toward identifying a disability within the student. Doing so may well produce very ineffective interventions. O'Neill and his colleagues (1997) put it this way:

> If we consider problem behaviors as occurring in people, it is logical to try to change the people. If we consider problem behaviors as occurring in contexts, it becomes logical to change the context. Behavior change occurs by changing environments, not trying to change people. (p. 5)

# INFORMATION DERIVED FROM A FUNCTIONAL ASSESSMENT

A thorough functional assessment of a student's behavior will yield the following valuable information:

a. a description of the student's problem behaviors

   b. the discovery of the setting events, in and out of school, that trigger the
      occurrence of the student's undesired behavior
   c. the identification of the consequences used by teachers and school
      officials that may be maintaining the problem behaviors

## Identify the Target Behavior

The initial component of functional assessment sets the rhythm for the subsequent
steps. You need to define precisely what the student is doing, the target behavior,
that is interfering with the teaching/learning process. It is also necessary to determine what target behavior(s) (see Chapter 3) you prefer the student to exhibit.

## Identify the Setting Events

After you've defined the student's behaviors, determine when those behaviors are
most (and least) likely to occur. As the name implies, setting events (or antecedents) set the stage for the behaviors. A red traffic light is a familiar example.
The traffic light sets the stage for you to brake your car; it doesn't guarantee you

Teachers have to
think about why
students behave or
the function of their
behavior before they
can change the
behavior.

## VIGNETTE 6.2
●
### *Building a Cushion*

Most of the time, Lucy's teacher enjoyed having her in the classroom. Most of the time, Lucy was a delightful student—focused, ready with an answer, and polite. She was none of those, however, when seated next to Jessica. The two girls, the closest of friends, were also each other's best and worst distractions. When only hands apart, they were a symphony's cymbals. To deal with this challenging behavior, Lucy's teacher gave the two girls new seat assignments, placing them three rows apart. No longer a distraction to each other, the two were able to concentrate on their classroom tasks.

will do so, of course. You can predict with a good deal of certainty that in the presence of a red traffic light, most people, most often, will depress the brake pedal. Notice the term "predict." It plays a very important role in functional assessment.

Functional assessment seeks to determine what antecedent events might be setting the stage for a student's disruptiveness (as well as desired alternative behaviors). If a simple event, such as setting, can be determined, intervention is often successful.

### Proximate Setting Events

*Setting events* can occur in close proximity to a student's disruptive behavior. Often these events occur inside the classroom. This was the case in Vignette 6.2 with Lucy and Jessica. *Proximate setting events* can include the time of the day, the day of the week, a classroom's activities or their cancellation, and the adult in front of the room (a substitute teacher, for example).

Questions that help identify immediate antecedent/stage-setting events include the following:

1. What academic or nonacademic activities during a school day seem strongly associated with a student's problem behavior?
2. What changes in routines seem to set the stage for the problem behaviors?
3. What times of the day seem to increase the likelihood of the problem behaviors?
4. Does the disruptive behavior occur more often during particular classrooms or classroom assignments or in the presence of particular teachers?
5. Where, when, and with whom are the student's problem behaviors most and least prevalent?

### Distant Setting Events

*Distant setting events* occur well before school begins, usually at home, as in Vignette 6.3, but occasionally in transit to school. They can be related to physical or

**VIGNETTE 6.3**

●

*Solving the Problem Early*

Jason was a puzzle. Some days his entire school experience was exemplary; other times he presented problems for his teachers from the school day's first moments. His school's community representative wondered if some event at home might be associated with the student's changeable school behaviors. A phone call verified the representative's hypothesis. Jason's mother, a single parent, was having difficulty juggling all her responsibilities, including caring for her two children as well as getting herself ready for work. She was admittedly sharp-tongued on various mornings, threatening Jason with afternoon punishment for a mild transgression occurring before the youngster was transported by bus to school. Advising the young mother that it would be best to avoid such threats, the representative asked the woman to give him an early morning call if she believed Jason was coming to school in an angry mood. The strategy was very effective. Receiving the call, the representative met young Jason at the bus and spent several minutes with him, walking the playground and talking about ways to avoid the morning confrontations with his mom. The two built a strong relationship that helped Jason relinquish his anger and plan better how to follow his mom's requests.

---

emotional conflicts that upset the child and influence his or her behavior long before reaching school. Parental notification may help school personnel deal with an unsettled student the moment he or she arrives at school. Concerns include illness, arguments with siblings and parents, as well as unexpected changes in routines.

## CRITICAL DETERMINATIONS

While determining the proximate and distant events that seem to set the stage for a student's undesired behavior, there's an additional determination that carries equal if not greater importance. When observing a student exhibiting undesired behaviors, identify as many conditions as possible where the student's undesired behaviors are *least likely* to occur. If a student misbehaves in Mr. Smith's class, but cooperates and participates in Ms. Jones's class, a trip to Ms. Jones's class might reveal for Mr. Smith what he needs to do. In Vignette 6.4, the fact that Ben does fine with schoolwork he enjoys tells us that there are antecedent conditions under which no attention difficulties have been observed. In place of medication, a change in the teacher's academic structure should be the essential first strategy.

### What Purpose Does the Behavior Serve?

Once you have determined the target behaviors, and have documented, when possible, the setting events that predict when those behaviors are most and least likely to occur, you need to turn your attention to two questions: "What purpose does the disruptive behavior serve?" and "What is the student gaining or avoiding from the undesired behavior?"

**VIGNETTE 6.4**

●
_____

*Finding the Exception*

Given Ben's recent behaviors in her class, his teacher raised concern over the possibility that the youngster had an attention problem that was interfering with his schoolwork. The teacher suggested that perhaps a trial dosage of medication might be beneficial. To help with the decision, the school's prereferral team brought together several personnel involved with the youngster. The concerned teacher responsible for the youngster's basic academics shared that Ben was particularly unfocused and disoriented during assignments involving reading and writing. The head of the team pressed the teacher to describe Ben's behavior outside the domains of reading and writing. Perhaps without realizing the significance of her own words, the teacher said that when Ben was asked to involve himself in work that he enjoyed, he had no attention difficulties.

_____

The philosophy upon which functional assessment is based holds that a student's behavior occurs for one of two reasons:

1. The student's behavior, desired or undesired, produces for the student something he or she finds of value.
2. The student's behavior, desired or undesired, enables the student to avoid (or be removed from) something the student finds unpleasant or frustrating.

## No Universal Reinforcers or Punishers

As demonstrated in Vignette 6.5, there are no universal reinforcers or punishers. As stated in Chapter 7, what is reinforcing to one student may not be reinforcing to another. The fact that Joe liked the conference room doesn't guarantee that another student would be so enamored. The same can be said for punishers. Joe didn't appreciate the nurse's station, but there are students who would have found the quiet, isolated space enjoyable.

These facts hold importance when you are considering the purpose behind one of your student's behavior. Just as not all students work to avoid time away from class, not all students work hard for extra recess. If a youngster persists with a behavior that produces a time-out or suspension, that persistence likely means he or she is working hard to gain it. If a student seems to continuously get into trouble when it's time for recess, perhaps recess is something he or she prefers to avoid.

## Student-Directed Interviews

When you consider purposes for behavior, don't be hesitant to think "outside the box." For example, O'Neill and his colleagues (1997) discuss the advantages for interviewing students about their own disruptive behaviors. Asking students why they are misbehaving may provide you with some very interesting information, particularly if they trust you and are willing to reveal an important part of themselves.

## VIGNETTE 6.5

●

### *Fun with the Hard Hats*

Katie was determined to make her classroom as enjoyable as it was educational. Almost without exception she succeeded, and her students enjoyed her animated presentations and their puzzle-oriented assignments. Two boys, however, Buster and Joe, occasionally got out of hand, pushing and shoving each other when moving from one of the classroom's work-stations to another. After warning them several times, Katie decided that a few minutes out of class might teach the boys to watch their manners and be more attentive to the rule of keeping hands to self. With permission from the school's principal, Buster was required to visit the unoccupied nurse's station when he roughhoused with his friend. (The principal's of-fice was a backup if the nurse's station was in use.) The nurse's station was a windowless room with a dim ceiling light. It was hardly as much fun as Katie Smith's classroom. Buster needed only one visit to the nurse's station to learn the lesson that his teacher desired.

Joe was sent to the school's conference room, a larger room with a long table and a win-dow that was covered by a heavy curtain. Although more attractive than the nurse's station, it was quiet and boring and very lonely. Despite all that, Joe seemed bent on revisiting the room many times. As soon as the opportunity presented itself, he would push either Buster or any other student in close proximity. He always made certain his teacher was a witness to his actions.

Katie requested assistance from the school's counselor. The counselor suggested Katie send Joe to the conference room as soon as he initiated his rowdiness. Watching at a distance, the counselor gave the youngster a few minutes inside the conference room before quietly en-tering. She discovered that the creative youngster had opened the room's curtains and had po-sitioned a chair directly against the window. The school was building an addition that was connected near the conference room's window, and while Joe watched the builders move about, they frequently came over and played with the youngster from the other side of the glass.

Having learned of the purpose for Joe's unacceptable behavior, Katie changed her strat-egy. The following morning when the youngster repeated his antics, she sent him to the nurse's station. Ever on her toes, Katie immediately added visiting the conference room and watching the construction workers as a reward for her students. She, of course, explained pre-cisely what they needed to do to gain access to the activity. Joe quickly learned the new rules.

O'Neill et al. (1997) found that interviewing a student can provide a teacher with the student's perception of the following:

 a. the times and situations during the day where problems are most likely to happen;

 b. the setting events that best predict when the disruptive behaviors are likely to occur; and

 c. the possible purposes for the behavior.

The student is asked to judge the degree of difficulty he or she has with main-taining desired behavior during the day, with an opportunity to make that judg-ment vis-à-vis teachers, subject areas, free time periods, and lunch periods, as well

## VIGNETTE 6.6

### *Getting the Teacher to Notice*

The school psychologist walked into the room and sat quietly to the side of the students. He had been asked to observe a youngster who was creating problems for his teacher. Before entering, he knew only the student's name. He didn't need an introduction, however. There was one little boy in the very back of the room, alone at a long table.

The teacher was actively moving about the room, working with all the students except the youngster, who couldn't have been more isolated had a wall separated him from his classmates. The psychologist recorded a full 5 minutes before the teacher moved rapidly to the secluded youngster. Then she was demonstratively angry, and filled with reminders of what he would lose if he continued to misbehave.

The psychologist reviewed his notes: For the first 5 minutes, the child was quiet in his seat, leaning back, the chair on its rear two legs. He had a piece of paper in front of him with questions of an undisclosed nature. Shortly before the 5-minute period expired, he casually threw his pencil toward the back of a boy who was seated at a table some 10 feet away. The pencil hit the floor, close to the boy. The teacher saw the pencil's flight and moved rapidly to the youngster. After admonishing him, she glared toward the psychologist as if to say, "See what I mean?"

The psychologist took the boy with him into the hallway, and they sat on a permanent bench in between metal lockers. "Do you like to get into trouble?" the psychologist asked. Hearing the answer no, the man asked, "Then why did you throw your pencil?" The youngster responded perhaps a drop too wisely, "I got her to come over, didn't I?"

---

as during possible unstructured time before and after school. A few carefully crafted questions might help the youngster divulge what payoffs he or she receives for the undesired actions.

Recall that a functional assessment provides you with the following information:

a. a description of the student's problem behaviors

b. the discovery of events, in and out of school, that seem to trigger the occurrence of the student's undesired behavior

c. the identification of the consequences used by teachers and school officials that may be maintaining the problem behaviors

Read the following three paragraphs and see if you can find the previous points in each example.

1. When John is part of a large group and is getting little attention from his teacher, he is most likely to yell an obscenity in order to have his teacher remind him that obscenities are not nice.

2. When Mary has difficulty with her reading assignment, she closes her book and puts her head on her desk in order to avoid having to complete her work. Seeing Mary with her head down, the teacher chooses not to call on her.

3. When Paul is with Mr. Smith in language arts, he is always ready with an answer to a comprehension question and always willing to read a passage from an assigned chapter. Mr. Smith calls on Paul often.

# DISRUPTIVE BEHAVIOR: IS IT ALWAYS INAPPROPRIATE?

It's easy to suggest that a student's disruptive behavior is inappropriate and/or maladaptive—both terms are widely used in special education's professional literature. IDEA counts the following among its component definitions of emotionally disturbing behavior: "Inappropriate types of behaviors...under normal conditions," and Armstrong and Kauffman (1999) invoke the term "maladaptive" when describing behaviors that are the targets for a functional assessment.

Both terms, it turns out, are judgments driven by theoretical preferences, and neither term is necessary or correct. This assertion is particularly important when viewing behavior in light of a functional assessment.

## Purposeful Behavior

We've known for years that students' behaviors are influenced dramatically by the consequences they produce. Slipping hard when running on ice generally slows our subsequent steps. Walking slower reduces the chances that we will slip again. Walking slower serves a purpose.

Historically, we have classified behaviors that produced identifiable consequences as instrumental behaviors (Hilgard, 1948; Thorndike, 1898). As the term "instrumental" suggests, the behaviors are instrumental (read useful or perhaps necessary) in producing their consequences. Domjan and Burkhard (1986, p. 110) provided the following clarification:

> [T]here are many circumstances in which events are a direct result of the individual's behavior. By studying hard, a student can learn the material in a course and get a good grade; by turning the car key in the ignition, a driver can start the engine; by putting a coin in a vending machine, a child can obtain a piece of candy. In all these instances, some aspect of the [person's] behavior is instrumental in producing [the consequences] and the behavior[s] occur because of the consequences [they produce].

They further point out:

> Students would not study if studying did not result in the learning of interesting information or in good grades; drivers would not turn the ignition key if this did not start the engine; and children would not put coins in a candy machine if they did not get something in return.

As we have discussed in this chapter, students' behaviors are designed to produce one of two outcomes:

    a. to gain access to something they value, or

    b. to avoid something that they perceived as unpleasant. Student behavior, therefore, disruptive and disturbing as it may be, can easily be viewed as

---

**VIGNETTE 6.7**

●

*To Be Quiet or Noisy? That Is the Question*

Eddie was bright, articulate, and considerate of his teacher (he had learned the importance of the latter from his parents). But Eddie was a youngster who preferred to be part of the mix and not part of a passive audience. Ms. Sandburg, his teacher, was bright, articulate, fun, and overwhelmed. She had a larger than usual class, among them several needy and demanding students. The easier students, those who remained quiet, hardworking, and considerate, were assigned, without intent, to the classroom's sidelines, a location Ms. Sandburg rarely visited.

Tired of the solitary life, Eddie stirred up the sidelines with jokes and distracting noises. A surprised Ms. Sandburg visited him briefly, requesting that he refrain from his antics. Eddie did, and found himself alone once again.

---

purposive and thus appropriate rather than inappropriate; it can also be viewed as efficient and thus adaptive rather than maladaptive.

## Behaviors' Payoffs

When considering a student's behavior that is bothersome and interfering with your goals as classroom teacher, concentrate on what the student might be gaining from his behavior. Consider Eddie's situation in Vignette 6.7. If we were to step inside Eddie's head, we might hear the following self-talk:

> This is nuts. When I'm quiet, I'm ignored. When I make a fuss, my teacher comes to me and tells me not to make a fuss. Since I like her to come by and say hi to me every once in a while, I guess I'll make a bunch of small fusses. She's told me my behavior is inappropriate. I don't know, but I think it's kind of smart!

Suggesting the student's behavior is inappropriate or maladaptive implies an inherent failing on the part of the student (and might spur you toward looking for a disability you believe will explain or account for the undesired behavior). Conversely, looking at a behavior's payoff and purpose, rather than its deviation from what is perceived as normal or expected, might suggest to you that something in the classroom environment (or how someone in the classroom environment is or is not responding to target behaviors) needs evaluating.

## SUMMARY

A functional assessment is a general term used to determine possible consequences within the environment that might be maintaining the very behavior a teacher wishes to eliminate. Several steps are outlined to guide teachers through the important elements of a functional assessment within the classroom environment:

1. Calmly identify what the student is doing that you perceive as undesired and interfering.

2. Determine what active behavior you wish the student to do instead. If at all possible, avoid using the term "not" to precede the undesired behavior. Remember, telling a student not to fight doesn't tell him or her what you would prefer.

3. Determine the conditions and circumstances when both the desired and undesired behaviors are most and least likely to occur.

4. Determine how the environment is responding to both the desired and undesired behaviors.

5. Determine what you need to do to provide desired payoffs to the desired behaviors.

6. As suggested by O'Neill and his colleagues (1997, p. 5), always ask yourself the following question: "What desired behavior on the part of the student could produce the same consequences that appear to be maintaining the undesired behavior?"

## DISCUSSION QUESTIONS

1. Discuss the differences between a functional assessment of a student's challenging behavior and a standardized behavioral assessment. What may be the useful outcomes of each for the classroom teacher?

2. What does the statement "Behaviors never occur in isolation" mean?

3. What kind of information may be collected about a student's environment when completing a functional assessment of a target behavior?

4. Discuss how the data collection tools outlined and described in Chapter 3 may be used to help teachers complete a functional analysis.

5. Based upon your previous observations of student behavior, discuss examples where a student exhibited undesirable behavior that served a functional purpose for the student. How were these situations resolved?

6. Are there really no universal reinforcers or punishers?

7. What can be learned by conducting student interviews about challenging behavior?

8. Are there examples in your school where undesirable behavior has a payoff for students? How can this be resolved?

## REFERENCES

Armstrong, S. W., & Kauffman, J. M. (1999). Functional behavioral assessment: Introduction to the series. *Behavior Disorders, 24*(2), 167–168.

Ayllon, T., & Michael, J. (1959). The psychiatric nurse as a behavior engineer. *Journal of Experimental Analysis of Behavior, 2,* 323–334.

Boyajian, A. E., DuPaul, G. J., Handler, M. W., Eckert, T. L., & McGoey, K. E.(2001). The use of classroom based brief functional analyses with preschools at-risk for Attention Deficit Hyperactivity Disorder. *School Psychology Review, 30*(2), 278–294.

Domjan, M., & Burkhard, B. (1986). *The principles of learning and behavior* (2nd ed.). Montery, CA: Brooks/Cole.

Gresham, F. M., Quinn, M. M., & Restori, A. (1999). Methodological issues in functional assessment: Generalizability to other disability groups. *Behavior Disorders, 24*(2), 180–182.

Hilgard, E. R. (1948). *Theories of learning.* New York: Appleton-Century-Crofts.

Hobbs, N. (1966). Helping disturbed children: Psychological and ecological strategies. *American Psychologist, 21,* 1105–1115.

Michael, J., & Meyerson, L. (1962). A behavioral approach to human control. *Harvard Educational Review, 32,* 382–402.

O'Neill, R. E., Horner, R. H., Albin, R. W., Sprague, J. R., Storey, K., & Newton, J. S. (1997). *Functional assessment and program development for problem behavior.* Pacific Grove, CA: Brooks/Cole.

Skinner, B. F. (1938). *The behavior of organisms.* New York: Appleton.

Skinner, B. F. (1953). *Science and human behavior.* New York: MacMillan.

Sulzer-Azaroff, B., & Mayer, G. R. (1991). *Behavior analysis for lasting change.* Fort Worth, TX: Harcourt Brace College.

Thorndike, E. L. (1898). Animal intelligence: An experimental study of the association processes in animals. *Psychological Review Monograph, 2*(Whole Number 8).

Thorndike, E. L. (1932). *The fundamentals of learning.* New York: Teachers College.

Ulrich, R., Stachnik, T., & Mabry, J. (1966). *Control of human behavior.* Glenview, Il: Scott, Foresman & Company.

U.S. Department of Education. (1999). *Twenty-first annual report to Congress on the implementation of the Individuals with Disabilities Education Act.* Washington, DC: Author.

Watson, J. (1924). *Behaviorism.* New York: Norton.

# PART II

# POSITIVE SUPPORTS FOR INCREASING BEHAVIOR

**7** Establishing a Reinforcement Program

**8** Cognitive Behavior Modification

# chapter 7

# ESTABLISHING A REINFORCEMENT PROGRAM

## Thomas J. Zirpoli

*There are a number of advantages to using (positive) programming as a strategy for the reduction of behavior problems in applied settings. Together, these advantages make programming the most preferable alternative to the use of punishment. They include its positive and constructive nature; its long term and lasting effects; its potential for the prevention of future problems; its efficiency; its social validity and the contribution it makes to the learner's dignity.*

—LaVigna and Donnellan *(1986, p. 32)*

All students exhibit at least some appropriate behaviors throughout each day. Too often, however, teachers ignore students when they behave appropriately and are doing what they were asked to do. To increase or maintain appropriate behaviors, students should be reinforced when they engage in desired behavior, rather than receive attention only when they misbehave. Research has demonstrated that when students are reinforced for appropriate behaviors, they will exhibit such behavior more frequently (Skinner, 1938, 1969; Tankersley, 1995). In spite of this evidence, Beaman and Wheldall (2000, p. 431) found that "there is little evidence to suggest that teachers, universally, systematically deploy contingent praise as positive reinforcement" and that "praise for appropriate classroom social behavior is only rarely observed."

Students who get most of their attention after they have behaved inappropriately will soon learn to behave poorly in order to gain attention (Bandura, 1973; Beaman & Wheldall, 2000; Maag, 2001). Indeed, students quickly learn what behaviors—appropriate and inappropriate—will get the most attention from others.

Within a classroom, reinforcement of appropriate behavior may be provided based upon individual or group behavior. Entire classroom reinforcement strategies, such as The Good Student Game (Babyak, Luze, & Kamps, 2000), can make teaching classroom social skills fun for both teachers and students. Simple, positive discipline techniques, employed at the classroom level by classroom teachers, can have a significant influence on the social climate of an entire school (Willert & Willert, 2000).

# REINFORCEMENT

## Definition

*Reinforcement* is any stimulus that maintains or increases the behavior exhibited immediately prior to the presentation of the stimulus. However, a stimulus takes on the value of a reinforcer only if it has been demonstrated that the behavior it followed was maintained (at the current rate, duration, or intensity) or increased (from the current rate, duration, or intensity). If the rate, duration, or intensity of the behavior is not maintained or increased after a stimulus, then that stimulus cannot be considered a reinforcer. For example, when a classroom teacher provides her students with social praise following appropriate behavior in the cafeteria, the social praise (a potentially reinforcing stimulus) may be defined as an effective reinforcer if the praise maintains or increases the students' appropriate cafeteria behavior in the future. However, if the teacher notes that appropriate cafeteria behaviors have not been maintained or improved, then the teacher's social praise cannot be considered an effective reinforcer in that case. The teacher may need to consider another, more powerful reinforcer, or a variation to her social praise. In summary, teachers cannot assume that an item, activity, or other stimulus will be reinforcing to a student; this can only be determined by testing the effect of the potential reinforcer on the student's behavior, as discussed later in this chapter.

It is also important to note that a stimulus may act as a reinforcer for one behavior but not for a second behavior, even if both behaviors are exhibited by the same student. For example, while a young student may maintain appropriate classroom behavior in response to social praise, other more powerful reinforcers, such as positive notes home or a token economy program, may be necessary to maintain acceptable academic performance. Also, items and activities considered reinforcing for one student may not be so for another student, even if they are the same age or in the same grade.

Reinforcement may be positive or negative. Both *positive reinforcement* and *negative reinforcement* increase behavior. The word *positive* refers to the *presentation* of a stimulus following a behavior, not the nature of the stimulus itself. In turn, the word *negative* refers to the *removal* of a stimulus; it does not describe the quality of the stimulus. Also, as discussed later, reinforcers may be *primary* or *secondary*. Both primary and secondary reinforcement increase or maintain target behaviors.

Reinforcement is most effective in maintaining or increasing a target behavior when it is individualized for a particular child and when it is presented contingent on the target behavior (Keyes, 1994). Other factors associated with the effective use of reinforcement include these:

- *Immediacy of the reinforcement.* As the interval between the behavior and reinforcement increases, the relative effectiveness of the reinforcer decreases. At least initially, an effective reinforcement program provides reinforcement immediately after the target behavior. Later, the latency between the behavior and reinforcement may be increased.

- *Combining verbal praise with the reinforcement.* When presenting the reinforcer, remind the student of the behavior that entitled him or her to the reinforcer so that an association is built between the appropriate behavior and reinforcer. Also, the learned association between the reinforcer and verbal praise will increase the reinforcement properties of verbal praise.

- *Schedule of reinforcement.* During the initial phase of the reinforcement schedule, reinforce the student after every occurrence of the target behavior. This also develops a link between the appropriate behavior you want to increase and reinforcement. Later in the program, continuous schedules of reinforcement should be faded to intermittent schedules. These schedules are discussed later in this chapter.

- *Type of reinforcement.* Some reinforcers will be more effective than others depending on the child's individual preferences. By asking the student and testing different potential reinforcers, teachers can generate a reinforcement menu.

- *Quality and quantity of reinforcement.* The quality of a reinforcer refers to its freshness and the immediacy of its effect on behavior. Teachers need to determine the right quantity of reinforcers to deliver—just enough to make the program interesting yet not too much so that the student becomes satiated.

- *Who provides the reinforcement.* Reinforcers are more effective when they are given by significant others or by people the student likes or admires. When provided by people the student does not like or trust, they may lose some or all of their reinforcing properties.

- *Consistency.* The reinforcement program should be followed consistently. Moreover, all other teachers who come in contact with the student should understand and implement the program consistently.

## Positive Reinforcement

*Positive reinforcement* (R1) is the contingent *provision* of a stimulus (such as a treat, an object, or an activity) following a target behavior, which results in an increase or a maintenance of the frequency, duration, and/or intensity of the target behavior (Skinner, 1938, 1969). For example, letting a student spend extra time playing with the classroom computer (stimulus) after the student completes specific classroom tasks (response) may be considered positive reinforcement *if* the future rate of the target behavior (completing specific classroom tasks) is increased or maintained. Positive reinforcement is recommended as the intervention of first choice when trying to teach new behaviors, increase appropriate behaviors, or decrease inappropriate behavior.

## Negative Reinforcement

*Negative reinforcement* (R2) is the contingent *removal* of a stimulus following a target behavior, which results in an increase or a maintenance of the frequency, duration, and/or intensity of the target behavior (Pfiffner & O'Leary, 1987). Usually, the removed stimulus is an aversive stimulus. Negative reinforcement is *not* punishment; again, the effect of negative reinforcement is an *increase* in the target behavior, not a *decrease,* which would be the effect of a punishing stimulus. Unfortunately, negative reinforcement plays an important role in reinforcing many problematic behaviors from food refusal (Kitfield & Masalsky, 2000; Levin & Carr, 2001) to self-injurious behaviors (Iwata et al., 1994). As stated by Cipani and Spooner (1997):

*Addressing all problem behaviors as if they are a function of positive reinforcement omits a vast array of behavioral strategies that can potentially control behavior that is maintained by negative reinforcement. (p. 339)*

Two variations of negative reinforcement can be used. In the first variation, the student performs the target behavior to escape an *ongoing* aversive stimulus (Iwata, 1987). For example, when a teacher tells a student he must remain in the time-out corner until tantrum behavior is no longer exhibited, that teacher is using negative reinforcement. The purpose here is to teach the student to perform a target behavior (nontantrum behavior) in order to have the aversive stimulus (remaining in the time-out corner) removed. In a second variation, the student performs the target behavior in order to avoid a *potential* or *likely* aversive stimulus. For example, when a student performs a target behavior (studying a history lesson) in order to avoid a threatened, aversive stimulus (receiving a failing grade), then the target behavior is maintained by negative reinforcement.

Negative reinforcement is quite different from positive reinforcement, with numerous disadvantages. It involves removing an aversive event contingent on a specific target behavior. Thus, the students focus their attention on avoiding the aversive event. Another significant disadvantage of negative reinforcement in applied settings is the escape and avoidance behavior produced when children are trying to behave appropriately in order to avoid an aversive stimulus. For example, consider the differences between two classrooms. In classroom A, the students behave appropriately because their teacher recognizes their good behavior and the students enjoy her attention (positive reinforcement). The students in classroom A are likely to enjoy school and have a healthy attitude about learning. In contrast, the students in classroom B behave appropriately only to avoid their teacher's aversive behavior (negative reinforcement). The students in classroom B probably do not like going to school and are not motivated, except by fear and anxiety, to do well. Some of the students may try to avoid or escape this situation by skipping school or dropping out of school altogether. These side effects represent the primary reasons why negative reinforcement is not recommended as a preferred intervention. The relationships among the type of reinforcement, stimulus, and outcome for target behavior are as follows:

| *Reinforcement* | *Stimulus* | *Target Behavior* |
| --- | --- | --- |
| Positive | Presented | Increases |
| Negative | Removed | Increases |

## Types of Reinforcers

The list of potential reinforcers for students is limited only by a teacher's imagination. Reinforcers may be verbal statements, foods and drinks, objects, time to participate in preferred activities, and so on. Teachers should not limit their understanding of reinforcers to giving candy. In fact, young children will quickly become satiated when food, especially candy, is used as a reinforcer. *Satiation* refers to a condition in which a current reinforcer loses its reinforcement value. That is, the target behavior is no longer maintained by the reinforcer. For example, when food is used as a reinforcer, a child may become too full to want additional reinforcers. Thus, teachers are encouraged to consider other types of reinforcers before edibles; more attention should be given to the use of praise (McVey, 2001), reinforcing activities, and other social opportunities students enjoy. These types of reinforcers may serve both as reinforcers and learning opportunities for students of all ages.

### Primary Reinforcers

*Primary reinforcers* are stimuli that are naturally reinforcing to individuals—food, liquids, warmth, and sex, for example. In other words, they are unlearned or unconditioned. Individuals do not have to be taught that eating tasty food or drinking refreshing drinks will make them feel good (naturally reinforcing).

### Secondary Reinforcers

*Secondary reinforcers* are stimuli that are *not* naturally reinforcing. Their value to the individual has been learned or conditioned through an association, or a *pairing*, with primary reinforcers. For example, when a preschool teacher pairs giving verbal praise (a potential secondary reinforcer) with delivering a glass of juice (a primary reinforcer) to a young child, the verbal praise takes on some of the reinforcement value associated with the glass of juice. The purpose here is to *fade out*, or decrease, the use of juice as a reinforcer and *fade in*, or increase, the value of verbal praise. If successful, verbal praise will become a secondary reinforcer capable of maintaining or increasing the target behavior.

*High-preferenced activities* (e.g., a computer game, free time, recess) frequently serve as excellent secondary reinforcers. Premack (1959) promotes the idea of using high-preferenced activities as reinforcement for the completion of low-preferenced activities. A classroom example of using the *Premack principle* was demonstrated by Keyes (1994), who reinforced fourth and fifth graders with increasing amounts of time on the classroom computer as they completed increasingly higher levels of academic tasks.

### Socially Valid Reinforcers

A reinforcer is considered socially valid when its provision is congruent with the norms of the student's social setting. The variables that determine what is socially valid include culture, setting, age of the student, the specific situation, and the relationship between the teacher and the student. For example, patting a child on the buttocks may be a socially acceptable form of reinforcement among football players on the playing field (setting); in a different setting (a classroom), this same form of reinforcement is not socially acceptable. In a second example involving the student's age, using stickers may be socially acceptable for young children but socially unacceptable for older children. Social praise, rather than stickers, would be more valid for older students. Thus, considering all these variables is important when selecting reinforcers and developing a reinforcement menu. The following list provides some suggestions for reinforcers:

| *Tangible* | *Social* | *Activities* |
|---|---|---|
| Stars | Verbal recognition | Choice time |
| Rubber stamps | Verbal praise | Spend time with teacher |
| Check marks | Student of the day | Read a story |
| Points | First in line | Pass out materials |
| Toys | Leader of the day | Feed class pet |
| Edibles | Phone call home | Use computer |
| Magazines | Note home | Run errands |
| Puzzles | Activity leader | Listen to tape |

As stated, a reinforcer is considered socially valid when it is consistent with the norms of the student's social setting. Sometimes, however, effective reinforcement means using reinforcers, at least temporarily, that may not be consistent with the "typical" social behavior of a setting. For example, giving students points for completing classroom tasks may not be a natural consequence or socially congruent with the "real" world. In fact, many teachers refuse to reinforce students for expected behaviors. Used temporarily, however, as an initial step to manage behavior and with the objective of eventually fading the point system to a more natural or typical social reinforcement (verbal praise), the use of extrinsic reinforcement is clearly a worthy investment.

## Identifying Reinforcers

Research has demonstrated that high-preference reinforcers serve as the most effective reinforcers in behavior management programs (Piazza, Fisher, Hagopian, Bowman, & Toole, 1996). And researchers have found several ways to identify high-preference reinforcers. Using the most functional approach, teachers can simply observe and record what students do during both instructional and free-time activities (Mason & Egel, 1995).

A more systematic method of developing a list of effective reinforcers is through trial and error or *preference assessment.* A systematic assessment, conducted by direct observation, of different reinforcers for both their preference and influence on behavior, is likely to produce the most potent list of reinforcers. Pace, Ivancic, Edwards, Iwata, and Page (1985) outlined one of the first procedures for the assessment of stimuli as potential reinforcers. In the Pace procedure, potential reinforcers are presented, one at a time, and the student's interest in each stimulus is measured by direct observation. In a second step of the Pace procedure, the reinforcement properties of the high and low preference stimuli are tested.

Piazza et al. (1996) found that *a choice assessment* was a more accurate method of identifying preferred reinforcers than the single-item presentation found in the

Pace procedure. During a choice assessment each potential reinforcer is paired once with every other stimulus. Student approach responses to one or the other stimuli are then measured. This is repeated until the high-preference stimuli are identified. The reinforcment value of these high-preference stimuli is then evaluated. This second phase is referred to as *reinforcer assessments.*

Green et al. (1988) found that the results of a systematic trial-and-error assessment of potential reinforcers did not always correlate with a list generated by teachers alone. Others, using different assessment methods, have also found that a systematic assessment of student preferences for reinforcers was more accurate than teacher predictions (Datillo, 1986; Mason & Egel, 1995). Northrup (2000) and Northrup and George (1996) found that surveying students' preferences yielded effective reinforcers.

### Preventing Satiation

Having a reinforcement menu is important because a single reinforcer may quickly lose its appeal. Children become satiated when the same reinforcement is used too frequently. Moreover, teachers should note that what may be reinforcing one day may not be reinforcing another day, even with the same student. Having a variety of reinforcers to select from allows teachers to keep the reinforcement program fresh and exciting for teachers and students (Egel, 1981).

Too often, teachers blame a reinforcement program for "not working" instead of evaluating the effectiveness of the selected reinforcers. Children's reinforcement preferences change across time and activities. When a teacher suspects that a student is satiated on a single reinforcer, changing to an alternative reinforcer or varying the reinforcers may stimulate the student's interest. Egel (1981) compared the effects of using the same reinforcer against a variety of reinforcers to increase the responsiveness of students in a classroom setting. He found that when the same reinforcer was presented, correct responses and on-task behavior declined over time. Varying the reinforcers, however, produced significantly improved and consistent responding. Egel's study "provides further documentation of the importance of providing variation within the teaching situation" (p. 345).

Teachers may prevent satiation by:

- varying the reinforcer or using a different reinforcer for each target behavior,
- monitoring the amount of reinforcement delivered and using only enough to maintain the target behavior,
- avoiding edible reinforcers (if you must use them, do so minimally and offer a variety),
- moving from a constant to an intermittent schedule of reinforcement as soon as possible, and
- shifting from primary to secondary reinforcers as soon as possible.

Implementing a reinforcement system does not have to be a significant change to an already established program. Rosen, Taylor, O'Leary, and Sanderson (1990) surveyed 137 elementary teachers (grades K–6) and found that the following procedures were used by at least 50% of the teachers to reinforce appropriate social and academic behavior: praise or compliment (100%); hug, pat on back, wink (92%); friendly/encouraging teasing (84%); show others the good work (78%); send note or call parents (72%); special time with teacher (69%); use special materials or objects (67%); give happy face, star, or other symbolic reward (65%); give sticker, food, or other material reward (63%); allow to run errands (63%); allow child to tutor (55%); and show movies, read stories, or have parties (50%).

Classroom reinforcement strategies may include simple changes in activity schedules or a simple commitment on the part of teachers to increase their attention to appropriate behaviors. Teachers should review the schedule of typical activities in which students participate within the educational setting and ask the following questions:

- How may some of these activities, which are known reinforcers to the students, be used to reinforce appropriate behaviors?
- How may some students, as a result of appropriate behaviors, have greater access to preferred activities within the educational setting?
- How may students' schedules be manipulated so that less desirable tasks and activities are followed by more desirable activities?

As we mentioned at the beginning of the chapter, teachers may easily fall into the habit of ignoring appropriate behaviors and instead focus on inappropriate behaviors. Developing a reinforcement program may help busy teachers ensure that they will pay attention to appropriate behaviors.

## ESTABLISHING A REINFORCEMENT PROGRAM

When developing a reinforcement program, teachers need to balance spontaneity and structure. That is, although the program must be planned and systematically applied, teachers also need to be spontaneous in delivering reinforcers. We will outline some important elements in developing a reinforcement program in the following sections.

### Establishing Clear Rules and Guidelines

Teachers need to be clear and direct in outlining which behaviors are expected and which behaviors are not acceptable within the different school environments (Hardman & Smith, 1999). Clear instructions outline behavioral expectations in *specific* and *observable* terms. For example, the rule "Respect others" does have an appealing sound and is certainly a worthy goal for all individuals. However, the rule fails to outline the specific behaviors that demonstrate respect for others and the specific behaviors that violate this rule. Teachers need to be more specific, such as "Never hit other children," "Say 'excuse me' before interrupting others," "Ask permission before taking things that don't belong to you," "Say 'please' and 'thank you,'" and so on. These examples are specific and observable.

Rules and guidelines for behavior should be stated in positive terms whenever possible. Instead of saying, "Don't take things without permission," say, "Ask permission before taking things." Small differences such as this make significant differences in the student's environment by creating a positive, affirming atmosphere. When most rules state what students *cannot* do, then the focus of adult attention will likely be on the punishment of inappropriate behaviors. When the rules state what students *can* do, then teachers will tend to focus on the reinforcement of appropriate behaviors. Rules concerning some inappropriate behaviors, however, such as hitting, need to be stated directly. As a guideline, plan to state at least three appropriate-behavior rules for every inappropriate-behavior rule.

Rules and behavioral guidelines are taught through direct instruction. In addition, rules are likely to be followed more consistently if they are posted somewhere in the educational setting and if the students are reinforced for following them. Also, a periodic (such as daily or weekly) review ensures that all the students understand the rules and, therefore, know what is expected of them (Rosenberg, 1986).

## Setting the Example

Once rules are established, teachers need to be consistent in following them, acting themselves as models of appropriate behavior. If teachers ask children to say "please" and "thank you," then the teachers should use "please" and "thank you" when talking to the students. If the rule says "No hitting," then parents should set the example. If parents spank children, they should not be surprised if their children are aggressive and attempt also to solve their problems by hitting. Remember, children learn from watching others, especially significant others such as parents and teachers.

## The Delivery of Reinforcers

After you have established some behavior guidelines, discussed them with the students, and outlined a reinforcement menu, the next step is to develop a reinforcement delivery program. Reinforcers are most effective in increasing behaviors when they are delivered:

- immediately after the behavior you intend to increase,
- when they are fresh (the child is not satiated with the reinforcer), and
- by significant adults whom the student admires.

The methods of delivering reinforcers to students are as endless as the selection of reinforcers. Again, teachers are encouraged to use their imaginations. The important guidelines here are for teachers to be *consistent* and to *make it fun*. If the reinforcement program is developed for an entire classroom, teachers may want to establish a token economy reinforcement program as described later in this chapter. When this program is targeted to change a specific behavior for one child, then the following steps will be helpful.

First, as previously stated, try to describe the behavior you want to change in positive terms. For example, Robert will not sit in his chair for longer than a few seconds at a time. Instead of stating the program goal in terms of *decreasing* Robert's out-of-seat behavior, state it in terms of *increasing* Robert's in-seat behavior. In this way, teachers will more likely focus on reinforcing the appropriate behavior (Robert's in-seat behavior) instead of the inappropriate behavior (Robert's out-of-seat behavior).

Second, collect baseline data on how often the student currently stays in his seat. Baseline data, as outlined in Chapter 3, measure a student's behavior before the introduction of a behavior change program. This involves measuring, for 30 to 60 minutes per day, for about 4 days, the number of seconds or minutes (duration) the student is currently staying in his seat. Calculate the average duration (total duration of sitting divided by number of observation periods), and this average will serve as the baseline for the student's sitting behavior. An example of baseline data would be to determine, through direct observation, that Robert currently averages 90 seconds of in-seat behavior per 30 minutes of classroom observation.

Third, the teacher should establish an appropriate *program goal.* That is, given the student's age and program needs, how many minutes is it reasonable to expect him or her to sit? Consistent with the earlier example, say the program goal is to teach Robert to stay in his seat for 15 consecutive minutes. Baseline data, the program goal, and the overall behavior change program should be shared with Robert. His teacher should explain to him why his in-seat behavior needs to increase and how he will be reinforced for longer periods of in-seat behavior.

Fourth, given the gap between the baseline data or current level of performance (90 seconds of in-seat behavior) and the program goal (15 minutes of in-seat behavior), the teacher should determine a *reinforcement schedule* to reinforce behaviors (i.e., longer periods of sitting) that will bring the student closer to the program goal. Given our example, phase 1 of the reinforcement schedule may include reinforcing Robert each time he stays in his seat for two consecutive minutes. Phase 2 may include reinforcing him each time he stays in his seat for three consecutive minutes. Phase 3 may include reinforcing him for five consecutive minutes of in-seat behavior, and so on. The last phase of the reinforcement schedule would include reinforcing Robert for 15 consecutive minutes, the program goal.

The speed of progression from one phase to the next will depend on the child's progress for each phase. A *performance criterion* for moving from one phase of the reinforcement schedule to the next should be established. For example, the criterion for moving from phase 1 to phase 2 may state that "Robert must meet the objective of phase 1, staying in his seat for two consecutive minutes, for two consecutive observation periods." When this criterion is reached, the reinforcement schedule changes as outlined in phase 2.

Several other reinforcement schedule variations are available. Understanding these different reinforcement delivery schedules will help caregivers develop effective and individualized reinforcement delivery plans.

# SCHEDULES OF REINFORCEMENT

A reinforcement schedule refers to the frequency or timing of the delivery of reinforcement following a specific target behavior or general appropriate behavior. The specific schedule of reinforcement delivery has been found to have significant effects on the target behavior. For example, Cuvo, Lerch, Leurquin, Gaffaney, and Poppen (1998) found that while young children tended to maximize reinforcement and minimize work when given a choice, they switched to the greater work choice when reinforcement on the easier choice was thinned. Thus, they were willing to engage in a greater workload associated with a richer reinforcement schedule.

A reinforcer may be delivered on a *continuous* or *intermittent* schedule. When a student is reinforced each and every time the target behavior is exhibited, a continuous schedule of reinforcement is being employed. Although not always the case, the initiation of a continuous reinforcement program is usually best until an association between the target behavior and reinforcement is established. For example, Newman and Buffington (1995) found that a continuous schedule was more effective in teaching students to follow instructions. A continuous schedule is recommended for working with young children or teaching a new behavior. As discussed earlier, this schedule should then be faded to an intermittent, or more natural, socially acceptable schedule (as described next).

When a student is reinforced after some occurrences, but not each and every one of the specific target behaviors, an intermittent schedule of reinforcement is being employed. An intermittent schedule is used after the child has learned that there is an association between the target behavior and the reinforcer, and the teacher wants to fade (sometimes referred to as *thinning*) to a more natural reinforcement schedule. We will outline variations of the continuous and intermittent schedules of reinforcement.

## Ratio Reinforcement Schedules

A ratio reinforcement schedule consists of reinforcing a person contingent on an established *number of occurrences* of the target behavior. Although the specific number of occurrences may be fixed or variable, a ratio schedule is always based on the number of behavior occurrences exhibited. For example, reinforcing a student after a specific number of tasks is completed means that a ratio schedule of reinforcement is being employed.

Allowing extra time on the computer and offering other desired classroom activities may serve as effective, functional reinforcers.

### Fixed Ratio Schedules

Reinforcing a student each and every time the target behavior occurs is called a *fixed ratio of one* (FR1) schedule of reinforcement (also called a *continuous schedule of reinforcement*). If, however, a teacher reinforces a student every second time the target behavior is exhibited, then this would be considered a *fixed ratio of two*, or FR2, schedule of reinforcement. Reinforcing a child every third time the target behavior is exhibited would be an example of a *fixed ratio of three* (FR3), and so on. An advantage of fixed ratio schedules is that they provide a systematic schedule of reinforcement; caregivers know exactly when to reinforce the target behavior based on a fixed number of behaviors.

### Variable Ratio Schedules

When a student is reinforced following a variable ratio schedule, reinforcement is delivered following an *average* number of behavior occurrences. For example, when a student is reinforced on an average of every third time she says "please," the schedule would be considered a *variable ratio of three*, or VR3. Variable ratio schedules of reinforcement are not recommended because the delivery of reinforcers for appropriate behavior may become less systematic and consistent. Some teachers may find it difficult to monitor the delivery of reinforcement based on an average number of behaviors. Because a fixed ratio schedule is easier to monitor, it will probably result in a more consistent application of the reinforcement program.

## Interval Reinforcement Schedules

An interval schedule of reinforcement provides reinforcement after an established *interval of time* has elapsed, contingent on a target behavior occurring during the interval. Although the specific interval or length of time between reinforcers may be fixed or variable, an interval schedule is always based on the passage of time. Delivering reinforcement following a specific period of time is best for behaviors that can be measured in terms of duration. In-seat and on-task behaviors, for example, can be measured by duration as well as frequency. Thus, when trying to decrease a student's out-of-seat behavior, teachers will find that reinforcing periods of in-seat behavior with an interval reinforcement schedule, as demonstrated in Classroom Application 7.1, is more functional and effective than with a ratio schedule.

Two primary applications exist for interval reinforcement schedules. In the first application, the student is reinforced after a specific interval of time contingent on the appropriate behavior. For example, when trying to increase in-seat behavior, Ann reinforced Paul after a set interval of time. During the first week of Ann's reinforcement program, Paul was reinforced after five consecutive minutes of in-seat behavior. At the end of each time interval, Ann had to decide whether Paul earned the promised reinforcement (extra tokens). If Paul did not remain seated during the previous interval, reinforcement was not provided.

In a second application, teachers could decide to begin a new time interval every time the targeted inappropriate behavior (e.g., getting out of seat) is exhibited. If, in Classroom Application 7.1, Ann wanted to use this second application, she would reset the interval each time Paul got out of his seat. For example, if Paul got out of his seat at 2:31 and returned to his seat at 2:32, his next reinforcement opportunity would be 5 minutes later at 2:37. A new 5-minute interval would begin once Paul returned to his seat.

### Fixed Interval Schedules

When a student is reinforced following a specific interval of time (e.g., for every 10 consecutive minutes of appropriate behavior), a *fixed interval of 10 schedule*, or FI10, of reinforcement has been applied. Reinforcement for every five consecutive minutes of appropriate behavior is a *fixed interval of 5*, or FI5, and so on. As with fixed ratio schedules, fixed interval schedules provide teachers and parents with a systematic reinforcement schedule; they know exactly when to reinforce the target behavior. In Classroom Application 7.1, Paul was reinforced on a fixed interval of 5 minutes of in-seat behavior during phase 1, a fixed interval of 10 minutes during phase 2, and a fixed interval of 15 minutes during the last phase of his in-seat behavior program.

## Classroom Application 7.1

# Example of Using an Interval Schedule of Reinforcement

Ann, a seventh-grade teacher, has a student named Paul who frequently gets out of his seat and walks around the classroom during a 30-minute study hall period, from 2:30 to 3:00 each school day. This behavior is disruptive to the other students trying to study or complete homework assignments. After collecting some baseline data, Ann discoverers that Paul remains in his seat an average of five consecutive minutes before getting out of his seat. Ann decides that since Paul is already on a token economy program (discussed later in this chapter), she will reinforce Paul's in-seat behavior on an interval schedule of reinforcement. Her goal is to teach Paul to remain seated (except when he receives permission to get out of his seat) for 15 consecutive minutes.

Ann has a meeting with Paul and tells him that he could earn an extra token whenever he stays in his seat for five consecutive minutes. In this new program, she explains, time in-seat will start at 2:30 (the beginning of study hall), and Paul will have opportunities to earn an extra token at 2:35, 2:40, 2:45, 2:50, 2:55, and 3:00. She explains to Paul that during this first phase of the program, he could earn a total of six extra tokens per day. Ann will use the classroom clock to keep track of the time. Ann starts the program and reinforces Paul with a token at the end of each 5-minute interval if he remains seated during the previous 5-minute interval.

After the first week of programming, Ann tells Paul that he is doing very well and that he now needs to remain seated for 10 consecutive minutes to earn extra tokens. However, Ann also raises the number of tokens Paul can earn from one to three. During this second phase, Paul is told that he can now earn a total of nine extra tokens (three at 2:40, 2:50, and 3:00).

After another week on phase 2, Ann has another meeting with Paul and tells him that he now has to remain seated for 15 consecutive minutes to receive extra tokens. She also raises the number of extra tokens Paul can earn to six, giving Paul two opportunities to receive reinforcement at 2:45 and 3:00. Paul does very well with this program and frequently earns the full 12 extra tokens during the 30-minute study hall period. Throughout this program, Ann makes it a point to pair the provision of tokens to Paul with social praise.

### Variable Interval Schedules

When a student is reinforced following a variable interval schedule, reinforcement is delivered following an *average* interval of time. For example, reinforcing a student for staying on-task for an average of every 10 minutes would be considered a *variable interval of 10,* or VI10. As with variable ratio schedules, variable interval schedules of reinforcement are not recommended at the beginning of a behavior change program when consistency is especially important. Again, it may be difficult for some teachers to monitor the delivery based on an average interval of time

**TABLE 7.1 • Summary of Reinforcement Schedules**

|  | **Fixed** | **Variable** |
| --- | --- | --- |
| **Ratio** | Reinforcement is delivered contingent on a *fixed* number of occurrences of the target behavior. | Reinforcement is delivered contingent on an *average* number of occurrences of the target behavior. |
| **Interval** | Reinforcement is delivered after a *fixed* interval of time has elapsed, contingent on the occurrence of target behavior during the interval. | Reinforcement is delivered after an *average* interval of time has elapsed, contingent on the occurrence of a target behavior during the interval. |

and to maintain a consistent program of reinforcement delivery. Once a new behavior has been established, however, more intermittent reinforcement schedules, interval and ratio, are very effective (Baer, Blount, Detrich, & Stokes, 1984). A summary of reinforcement schedules is provided in Table 7.1.

# SHAPING AND CHAINING NEW BEHAVIORS

## Shaping

*Shaping* refers to the reinforcement of *successive approximations* of a terminal behavior. Generally, shaping is used to teach *new* behaviors and skills—behaviors that are not already part of the student's repertoire. A successive approximation to a terminal behavior may be any intermediate behavior that, when combined with other intermediate behaviors, forms the topography of the terminal behavior. Within each step, or successive approximation, responses that meet the criteria for that step are reinforced, while other responses are not (see the differential reinforcement discussion in Chapter 9). As the student moves from one step to the next, the criterion for reinforcement changes as expectations increase. Each step in the shaping process brings the student's behavior closer to the terminal behavior. Vignette 7.1 demonstrates how shaping was used to teach a student how to walk independently from her classroom to a resource room.

In Vignette 7.1, each of the three steps has two substeps—walking with, then without, supervision. Each of the steps and substeps is a successive approximation to the new terminal behavior of walking independently from point A to point D without supervision. The appropriate performance of successive approximations of the terminal behavior was reinforced to shape Aldy's behavior according to the topography of the terminal behavior.

The process of shaping includes several steps:

1. Determine the terminal behavior or behavioral goal.

**VIGNETTE 7.1**

●

*The Use of Shaping to Teach Independent Travel*
*from Classroom to Resource Room*

Aldy, a first grader, was a new student at Luke Elementary. Born and raised in Indonesia, she was attending school in America for the first time. Because of her poor English language skills, Aldy was scheduled to attend an ESL (English as a second language) class every day in the school's resource room. Unfortunately, Luke Elementary is a large school, and the resource room is a significant distance from Aldy's classroom. Aldy, not used to large school buildings, was very anxious about getting lost. Aldy's teacher, Marie, decided to use shaping to teach Aldy how to walk independently from the classroom (point A) to the resource room (point D).

Marie noted that on the way to the resource room, Aldy would have to pass the rest rooms (point B) and the school cafeteria (point C). To teach Aldy how to walk independently from point A to point D, Marie first showed Aldy how to walk from point A to B with supervision, then without supervision. Correct performance of this behavior was practiced and reinforced for 5 days (the time it took for Aldy to learn how to walk independently from the classroom to the rest rooms).

In a second step, Marie showed Aldy how to walk from point A to point C with supervision, then without supervision. In this second step, the criterion for reinforcement was changed. Aldy was now required to walk all the way to point C without supervision, not just point B. This was also practiced until Aldy could independently walk from the classroom to the cafeteria. Correct responses were reinforced.

In the last step, Marie showed Aldy how to walk from point A to point D with supervision, then without supervision. Within 3 weeks Aldy learned to independently walk from her classroom to the resource room.

---

2. Determine the successive approximations or steps necessary to complete the terminal behavior.

3. Identify a "starting point" or behavior that the student currently performs that approximates either the terminal behavior or the first step to the terminal behavior (Aldy already walks to the rest room, point B, with the rest of her class).

4. Reinforce closer approximations of the terminal behavior until the behavioral criterion for each successive approximation, or step, has been achieved (reinforce improvement, not perfection) (Panyon, 1980).

5. Move from one step to the next until the terminal behavior has been learned/shaped (withhold reinforcement for behaviors that are not clear steps toward the terminal behavior) (Panyon, 1980).

Shaping is generally thought of as a method of teaching *new* behaviors or skills. It may be used to *modify* the rate, duration, or intensity of current behaviors. Thus, while the basic topography of the behavior remains the same, the dimensions of the topography are gradually modified. Examples of this second application of shaping include increasing motor activities, in-seat behavior, the number of correct responses per specific time interval, and so on.

Shaping may also be used to *decrease* the rate, duration, or intensity of current behaviors. Again, the student is not learning a new response (the purest application of shaping); the student is learning a new topography of a current response. For example, by reinforcing small decreases in the volume of a student's talking within a classroom setting, shaping may be used to modify a current behavior (talking too loud) to a more socially acceptable level of performance.

One of the primary advantages of shaping is the emphasis on reinforcing appropriate behaviors (successive approximations) as a strategy for teaching new or modified behaviors. Also, the process involved in shaping new behaviors forces teachers to evaluate the student's current performance (baseline), to review the topography of the terminal behavior, and to establish a systematic program for the delivery of reinforcement.

## Chaining

*Chaining* refers to the performance of a series or sequence of behaviors rather than just one independent behavior. For example, if a classroom teacher wants students to walk into the classroom, hang up their coats, put their lunch boxes into their lockers, and sit at their desks, these four behaviors may be taught separately or together as one *behavior chain*. Each of the four behaviors serves as a link in the behavior chain. Each link serves as the SD for the performance of the next link (response) and as a conditioned reinforcer for the previous link:

Step 1: Walking into the classroom
Step 2: Hanging up their coats
Step 3: Putting their lunch boxes into their lockers
Step 4: Sitting at their desks

In our example, walking into the classroom serves as the SD for the students to hang up their coats. Hanging up their coats serves as the SD for putting their lunch boxes in their lockers, and putting their lunch boxes away serves as the SD for sitting at their desks.

The development of a behavior chain, or any chain of skills, is called a *task analysis*. In the previous example, the four behavior links make up a task analysis of the teacher's expectations for her students when they walk into the classroom. Later we provide a task analysis for washing hands. Notice how much more detail is provided in the washing hands task analysis compared with the first example (teacher's expectations). The amount of detail contained in the behavior chain must depend on the complexity of the behavior and the characteristics of the child. More difficult tasks and behaviors may require a more detailed task analysis.

In the initial stages of teaching a behavior chain, teachers should reinforce the student for correctly completing each behavior *and* for completing each behavior in the correct sequence. After the student has learned the appropriate sequence of behaviors, reinforcement may be faded from after the performance of each link to after the performance of the whole chain of behaviors. In addition, this behavior chain can be linked to other behavior chains and serve as the S$_D$ for a second chain. For example, the completion of the behavior chain for coming into the classroom may serve as the S$_D$ for the beginning of another behavior chain (e.g., stop talking, establish eye contact with the teacher, and wait for directions). There are two primary variations to teaching behavior chains: forward chaining and backward chaining.

### Forward Chaining

*Forward chaining* refers to the teaching of each behavior link, starting with the first link and moving "down" to the next link in the chain, until all the behaviors in the chain have been learned and can be performed in the appropriate sequence. A basic decision to be made in using forward chaining is whether to use serial training, concurrent task training, or total task training. In *serial training*, behaviors are taught in order, one at a time, to a set of criteria before the next behavior is added and taught. For example, when teaching students the sequence of behaviors for coming into the classroom, step 1 (walking into the classroom) would be taught to a specific performance criterion before step 2 (hanging up their coats) is taught. In *concurrent task training*, two or more behaviors in the behavior chain are taught at the same time (Snell & Zirpoli, 1987). Thus, step 1 and step 2 of the behavior chain would be taught concurrently. Research has found that concurrent training may be more effective than serial training (Waldo, Guess, & Flanagan, 1982) as well as more interesting and motivating to both the student and teacher. It also may be more readily integrated into the daily routine because training is conducted within the context of other tasks (Dunlap & Koegel, 1980). *Total task training* refers to teaching all steps in the behavior chain simultaneously. Total task training is actually an extension of concurrent training, has the same advantages of concurrent training, and is considered the most effective method for less difficult behavior chains (Johnson & Cuvo, 1981; Spooner & Spooner, 1984).

### Backward Chaining

*Backward chaining* refers to teaching each behavior link in a behavior chain, starting with the *last* link and moving "up" the behavior chain, until all the behaviors in the chain have been learned and can be performed in the appropriate sequence. For example, if a preschool teacher were teaching a young child a simple behavior chain for washing hands, as outlined in the following list, the teacher would physically assist the child through all the steps in the chain until the last step (step 10—hang up the towel). At that point, the teacher begins instruction on step 10. This sequence continues until the child can complete step 10 independently. After the criterion for step 10 is achieved, the teacher begins instruction on the second-to-the-last step (step 9—dry your hands with the towel) in the sequence. At this point, the teacher would assist the child through all of the preceding steps (1–8), provide instruction for step 9, and let the child complete the last step independently. Each preceding step becomes the S$_D$ for the next step in the behavior chain and serves as the conditioned reinforcer for the previous step. For example, step 9 becomes the S$_D$ for step 10 and the conditioned reinforcer for step 8.

Stimulus: Teacher states that it is time to eat lunch.

Step 1: Turn on the water.

Step 2: Wet your hands.

Step 3: Pick up the soap.

Step 4: Rub soap on your other hand.

Step 5: Put the soap down.

Step 6: Rub your hands together.

Step 7: Rinse your hands.

Step 8: Turn off the water.

Step 9: Dry your hands with the towel.

Step 10: Hang up the towel.

Research on which method is better, forward or backward chaining, is mixed. Spooner and Spooner (1984) remind us that "different learners do better with different procedures" (p. 123). In general, forward chaining is recommended because it presents a more natural teaching sequence than backward chaining and allows more effective use of concurrent and total task training. When making these programming decisions (i.e., forward or backward chaining and serial, concurrent, or total task training), teachers should consider the difficulty level of the behavior chain and the child's intellectual ability.

## TOKEN ECONOMY REINFORCEMENT PROGRAMS

A *token economy* program is a symbolic reinforcement system (Kazdin, 1977; Kazdin & Bootzin, 1972). It is called an economy system because it is based on a monetary system, with money as the most common form of tokens. Just as one who has a job receives money for the completion of specific tasks, which can then be exchanged for food, housing, and other material objects, the same principle applies in a token economy reinforcement program. Students receive tokens for specific appropriate behaviors, which they may exchange for objects or activities that have been identified as reinforcing. After the students have learned to associate the tokens with the purchase of reinforcers, the tokens become valuable and desirable. Token economy reinforcement programs have been used successfully with many different ages and populations including preschoolers (Blanding, Richards, Bradley-Johnson, & Johnson, 1994); students with hearing impairments (Buisson, Murdock, Reynolds, & Cronin, 1995); persons with mental illnesses (Corrigan, 1995); students in bilingual education settings; and students with various behavioral challenges (Lucker & Molloy, 1995).

Several advantages of token economy programs exist, especially for classroom teachers or day-care providers who work with large groups of students:

- Tokens can be distributed to large groups of students with minimum effort. Throughout the day, teachers can give tokens to individual students or small groups of students as a simple but effective method of displaying positive attention to appropriate behaviors (Lloyd, Eberhardt, & Drake, 1996).

- Tokens allow teachers to delay the provision of reinforcers during busy periods of the day.
- Tokens let teachers offer a single reinforcer (the token) to many students who may have different reinforcer preferences. The students learn, however, that accumulating tokens throughout the day will allow them to purchase the reinforcer of their preference at a later time.
- Since the provision of tokens is followed by students choosing from a variety of reinforcers, tokens are seldom subject to satiation.
- Tokens can be given to students without interrupting teaching and other activities (Lloyd, Eberhardt, & Drake, 1996).

## Characteristics of Tokens

Tokens may be tally marks or points recorded on the board or check marks recorded on a piece of paper at the child's seat. Tokens may also be plastic chips, points, happy faces, stickers, stars, pennies, pieces of colored paper, pieces of cloth, ribbons, marbles, or any small, attractive object. Tokens should be something that the students can see, touch, and count. With the exception of tally and check marks, tokens should not be so large or small that young children are unable to handle, store, and save them for later purchases. Also, teachers want to be sure that tokens cannot be obtained from other sources via counterfeiting or stealing.

Most important, students must understand that they can exchange the tokens for various reinforcers and how many tokens they will need to purchase each reinforcer. Initially, teachers may need to guide young children through the exchange system to demonstrate how the program works.

## Establishing a Token Economy Program

Several important steps are necessary to establish a token economy reinforcement program. Each of these steps is described in Classroom Application 7.2.

For a token economy to be most effective in increasing appropriate behavior, a student should never experience a zero token balance by the exchange period. Teachers should make an effort to identify at least one appropriate behavior, in even the most challenging child, to enable that child to participate in the token economy program. Finally, students should have the opportunity to purchase something small, even if they have earned only one token. In Marge's program in Classroom Application 7.2, several items could be purchased for one token. An effective token economy program includes several characteristics:

- Tokens should be something students can see, touch, and count.
- Tokens should not be so small or large that young children cannot store them, handle them, and count them. Tally marks or checks may be effective with some, especially older, students.
- Students must be able to exchange the tokens for actual reinforcers.

# Classroom Application 7.2

## Example Token Economy Program

Marge, a fifth-grade teacher, has a class of 30 students. Several of her students demonstrate challenging behaviors such as noncompliance, running around the classroom, hitting, interrupting others, yelling, and so on. Marge is thinking about starting individual behavior reduction programs for each of her "problem students" but decides instead to initiate a classroom-wide token economy program. In this way, she thinks that she can focus her attention and energy on reinforcing children for appropriate behaviors and thus indirectly decrease most of the inappropriate classroom behaviors at the same time.

Marge's first step is to identify the target behaviors she wants to increase. She tries to think of appropriate behaviors that are incompatible with many of the challenging behaviors her students are exhibiting. She develops a list of five target behaviors that will be reinforced within her token economy program:

- following the teacher's directions,
- walking in the classroom,
- keeping hands to self,
- raising hand to be recognized before speaking out, and
- talking in a quiet voice.

Marge's second step is to *identify the medium of exchange,* or what will serve as tokens for her program. She decides to use colored strips of construction paper (1 inch wide and 5 inches long).

Her third step is to *identify reinforcers the children will be able to purchase with the tokens they earn.* To develop this list, Marge wisely decides to talk with her students about her plan and asks them for reinforcement suggestions. Her students are very helpful and have many ideas for reinforcers. Several of their ideas, however, are not acceptable, which Marge communicates to the students. She also includes many activities as reinforcers. With her students' help, Marge develops a list of 15 reinforcers for the reinforcement menu: 5 minutes' extra time on the computer, 5 minutes' extra free time, being first in line for 1 day, being the class leader for 1 day, a pad of stationery paper (several were donated), one baseball card (donated), a new ballpoint pen (donated), picking a game during gym class, a positive note home, serving on a panel of judges for the next class competition, an extra show-and-tell session, pick your own seat assignment for 1 day, extra trip to the water fountain, pick and read a story to the class, and an extra trip to the library.

Marge writes the five target behaviors and the reinforcement menu on two big sheets of cardboard. Each list is hung on the front classroom wall for everyone to see.

Having decided that a student will earn one token each time she observes him or her exhibiting any of the target behaviors, Marge's next step is to *identify the price or number of*

*(continued)*

*tokens necessary to purchase each reinforcer on the reinforcement menu.* To do this, she follows these simple guidelines:

- The greater the supply of an item listed on the reinforcement menu, the lower the price, or the fewer number of tokens necessary to purchase that reinforcer. For example, Marge had hundreds of baseball cards, so these could be purchased for only one token.
- The lower the supply of the item, the higher the price. Marge had only 10 stationery pads, for instance, so she decided that these could be purchased for 10 tokens.
- The greater the demand for an item, the higher the price. Many students, for example, wanted to buy extra time on the class computer. The cost, Marge decided, would be 10 tokens.
- The lower the demand for an item, the lower the price. For example, the students were not very interested in picking and reading a story to the class. Because this was an activity Marge wanted to promote, she charged only one token for it.
- The greater time required (for an activity), the higher the price. Since extra free time removed the students from 5 minutes of academic time, Marge required 15 tokens for this item on the reinforcement menu.
- The less time required, the lower the price. For example, it took little time to write a positive note home, and, besides, Marge viewed this as an effective strategy for promoting positive teacher-parent relationships. Thus, the positive note home cost only one token.

Marge's next step is to *pick a time when the students will have the opportunity to exchange their tokens for reinforcers.* She decides that the classroom exchange period will be every Friday, after lunch. Marge explains to the students that they do not have to exchange their tokens; they can save them if they want. She also tells her students that she will modify the price of each reinforcer after each exchange period, based on supply and demand, but that price changes will not be made between exchange periods.

- Students should not be able to obtain tokens from sources other than their teacher. If stealing is a potential problem, the teacher may choose to store the tokens.
- Students must understand that the tokens they earn can be exchanged for various reinforcers. To learn how the system works, some students, especially young children, may have to be "walked" through the exchange process immediately after earning tokens.
- Teachers must respect the differences in their students' spending habits. Some students will prefer to save their tokens; some will prefer to spend all their tokens at each exchange.
- Each student should have the opportunity to earn at least one token per exchange period. Also, no maximum should be placed on the number of tokens a student may earn.
- Students who earn only a few tokens, or even just one, should have the opportunity to exchange their tokens for small reinforcers.

# CONTINGENCY CONTRACTING

*Contingency contracting* involves the establishment of a written behavioral contract between a student and teacher regarding the performance of specific target behaviors and the exchange of specific consequences. Used with individual students or a group of students, written contracts can provide teachers with a positive approach to reducing inappropriate behaviors (DeRisi & Butz, 1975).

Contracts are useful tools that may be employed in a variety of settings to teach a variety of skills. Contingency contracting has been successfully used to improve classroom behavior (Roberts, White, & McLaughlin, 1997); improve on-task behavior (Allen, Howard, Sweeney, & McLaughlin, 1993; Miller & Kelley, 1994); increase homework performance (Miller & Kelley, 1994); increase homework accuracy (Miller & Kelley, 1994); teach self-control (Raubolt, 1983); modify assaultive and disruptive behaviors (Bagarozzi, 1984); decrease alcohol abuse (Vannicelli, Canning, & Griefen, 1984); treat bulimia (Brisman & Siegel, 1985); and modify personal hygiene and grooming behaviors (Allen & Kramer, 1990).

Raubolt (1983) recommends using individual behavioral contracts over group psychotherapy. He outlines significant flaws in group psychotherapy, including the length of treatment, the difficulty of meeting the needs of a diverse group of children, the complex and delicate problem of choosing and grouping children, and the constraints that must be placed on the behavior of aggressive individuals in group settings. Others have found that contingency contracts can be used to facilitate self-monitoring and to help students gain more control over their own learning (Brisman & Siegel, 1985; MacKinnon-Slaney, 1993; White & Greenwood, 1992).

Contracts provide a means for teachers and students to place in writing behavioral expectations, reinforcers, and other consequences.

DeRisi and Butz (1975, p. 7) outline several steps in establishing a behavioral contract, which have been modified and expanded on here:

- Select the target behavior(s) you want to increase. Limit the number of target behaviors to two or three.
- Describe the target behavior(s) in observable and measurable terms so that the student's progress may be effectively monitored.
- Identify reinforcers that the student will find motivating.
- Establish general guidelines and timelines of the contract—who will do what and what will be the consequences.
- Write the contract so that all individuals involved can understand it; use age-appropriate wording.
- Require the individuals involved to sign the contract indicating their understanding and agreement to its terms.
- Consistently reinforce the performance of the target behavior in accordance with the terms of the contract.
- Monitor and collect data on the performance of target behavior(s).
- Discuss and rewrite the contract when data do not show an improvement in the performance of the target behavior. Contract modifications should be signed by all individuals involved.

## Advantages of Contracts

Contracts have many advantages when used to modify behavior. Behavioral contracts encourage teachers to communicate their expectations clearly and provide students with a good understanding of the rewards and consequences available for their behavior. Teachers are encouraged to use their imagination in developing behavioral contracts and to make them positive tools for changing behavior. Other advantages of contingency contracts are as follows:

- They are easy to use in natural environments and do not restrict the student's participation in normal educational activities (Bagarozzi, 1984; Kerr & Nelson, 1989).
- The teacher's focus is on giving positive reinforcement for appropriate behaviors agreed on in the contract.
- The behavioral expectations of both student and teacher are outlined in writing.
- Reinforcement is presented in a systematic manner.
- Consequences for the performance or nonperformance of the target behavior are specific and clearly understood by the student and teacher.
- Contracts may be modified and rewritten as necessary to meet current needs.
- Contracts may be employed with an individual student, with a group of students, or for an entire classroom.

Examples of simple behavioral contracts that may be used in educational settings are provided in Figures 7.1, 7.2, 7.3, and 7.4.

# GENERALIZATION

*Generalization* refers to the degree to which a behavior change transfers to other settings, situations, or behaviors in addition to the setting, situation, or target behavior involved in the behavior change program. Haring (1988) refers to generalization as "appropriate responding in untrained situations" (p. 5). The two primary types of generalization are *stimulus generalization* and *response generalization*.

## Stimulus Generalization

*Stimulus generalization* describes the degree of behavior change in settings or situations other than the training setting, even when no training occurred in the new setting (Carr, Robinson, Taylor, & Carlson, 1990). If, during science class, for example, the teacher reinforces a student for reading directions on written assignments before asking questions, and then, in math class, the student begins to read directions before asking questions, the new behavior (reading directions before asking questions) has generalized from the science to the math class.

**FIGURE 7.1.** Sample contract between a student and teacher

**Contract**

I _____
  Student's name here

will _____ _____
  _____
  _____
  _____

I _____
  Teacher's name here

will _____
  _____
  _____
  _____

_____     _____
Student's signature                              Teacher's signature

_____
Date

**FIGURE 7.2.** Sample contract between a student and teacher

**Contract**

Contract between _____ and _____
If I do _____
_____
_____

Then I can _____
_____
_____

_____          _____
Student's signature                        Teacher's signature

                    _____
                            Date

**FIGURE 7.3.** Sample contract between a student and teacher

**Contract**

This is an agreement between _____
                                        Student's name

and _____ .
        Teacher's name

This contract begins on _____ and ends on _____ .

The terms of this contract are as follows:
Student will _____
_____
_____

Teacher will _____
_____
_____

If student completes his/her part of the agreement, teacher will provide student with reinforcement as outlined in the teacher part of the agreement above. If student does not complete his/her part of the agreement, teacher will withhold reinforcement.

_____          _____
Student's signature                        Teacher's signature

                    _____
                            Date

**FIGURE 7.4.** Sample contract between a student and teacher

**CONTRACT**

_____ will demonstrate the following
(Student's name)

appropriate behaviors in the classroom:

1. Come to school on time.
2. Come to school with homework completed.
3. Complete all assigned work in school without prompting.
4. Ask for help when necessary by raising hand and getting teacher's attention.

_____ will provide the following reinforcement:
(Teacher's name)

1. Ten tokens for the completion of each of the above four objectives. Tokens for the first two objectives will be provided at the beginning of class after all homework assignments have been checked. Tokens for objectives 3 and 4 will be provided at the end of the school day.
2. Tokens may be exchanged for activities on the Classroom Reinforcement Menu at noon on Fridays.

_____        _____
Student's signature                          Teacher's signature

_____
Date

## Response Generalization

*Response generalization* refers to the degree to which a behavior change program influences other behaviors in addition to the target behavior (Carr et al., 1990). For example, if a teacher develops a reinforcement program to increase a child's use of "please," and the child also exhibits an increase in the use of "thank you," then the behavior change program shows a response generalization. In a second example, if a teacher develops a behavior change program to decrease physical aggression (the target behavior), and the child also demonstrates a decrease in verbal aggression (not the target behavior), then the behavior change program shows a response generalization.

In these cases, response generalization is credited with changing behaviors other than the target behavior in the same direction (increasing or decreasing a response) as the target behavior. Response generalization may, however, change behaviors in the opposite direction of the target behavior. For example, a program resulting in a *decrease* in self-injurious behavior may also result in an *increase* in other prosocial behaviors. Also, an *increase* in on-task behaviors may result in a *decrease* of disruptive behaviors. Although the evidence tends to suggest that these behavior changes result from response generalization (Kazdin, 1989), few would disagree that they may also represent some spread of treatment effects.

## Promoting Generalization of Behavior Change

Haring (1988) states that "generalization is, perhaps, the most important phase of learning" (p. 5). In most cases, however, generalization does not occur spontaneously. To ensure that new behaviors are used in natural settings, generalization must be integrated into the acquisition phase of teaching (Snell & Zirpoli, 1987). Several methods are used to accomplish this objective.

### Teaching in Natural Settings

The term *natural setting* refers to the setting in which a behavior is most likely to occur or should occur (Gaylord-Ross & Holvoet, 1985). For example, if a preschool teacher wants to establish a reinforcement program to increase "sharing" behavior, the best place to teach this behavior is within the environments where students are expected to share. Pulling students out of the classroom for individualized training by a behavior therapist, for example, is usually not recommended. Behaviors that are learned in the pull-out environment are unlikely to generalize automatically to the classroom or other functional environments. The behavior therapist, teacher, and parents must collaborate to integrate skill acquisition and generalization successfully into the student's natural environments (e.g., classroom, playground, home).

### Selecting Natural Antecedents for Stimulus Control

*Natural antecedents* are events or situations that should act as natural prompts or cues for a specific target behavior (Ford & Mirenda, 1984; Snell & Zirpoli, 1987). For example, several situations occur within a classroom setting in which students are expected to stop talking and listen (e.g., when the teacher is talking, reading to the class, or giving instructions). Teaching students to stop talking and listen, following these naturally occurring situations, is another example of integrating skill acquisition and generalization. The most effective way for teachers to identify the natural antecedents or stimuli for behaviors is through direct observation of students within the natural environment of the classroom.

At times artificial stimuli (prompts and cues) are necessary to teach appropriate behaviors or to increase the opportunity for reinforcing a target behavior. For many students, the use of artificial prompts is a necessary, important element during the initial stages of behavior acquisition. Using a tone sound from a tape recorder during the initial stages of a self-instruction program to teach in-seat behavior (see Chapter 8) is an example of an artificial prompt. These artificial prompts clearly have a useful place in behavior management. It is also important, however, to pair artificial prompts with natural stimuli and to fade them as soon as possible (Wolery & Gast, 1984). Students who learn to stop talking only when they hear an artificial prompt may not learn to stop talking in response to natural stimuli.

### Selecting Natural Consequences as Reinforcers

In addition to teaching within natural settings and associating appropriate behaviors with natural antecedents and stimuli, teachers should employ natural consequences for behaviors (Snell & Zirpoli, 1987). Thus, although a token economy program—or any other program using artificial reinforcers—may be appropriate and necessary for many students, one of the goals of reinforcement programs should be to fade artificial reinforcers (e.g., from tokens to praise) and schedules (e.g., from continuous to intermittent) and to teach students to respond to natural reinforcers. Natural classroom reinforcers include receiving positive statements made by the teacher or other students, having completed artwork or other assignments hung on the classroom bulletin board, and getting a good grade on an assignment. Such reinforcement may not be possible in all cases, however, and the long-term use of artificial reinforcers (e.g., tokens, extra attention) may be necessary to maintain appropriate behavior with some students. In addition to selecting natural reinforcers, Gregory, Kehle, and McLoughlin (1997) found that teaching students self-management techniques also promoted generalization and maintenance of appropriate behavior in regular education settings.

### Reinforcing Generalization

As with other behaviors discussed in this chapter, the generalization of learned behaviors for one stimulus, setting, or situation is likely to increase when generalization is systematically reinforced. Generalization may be increased by reinforcing the child for exhibiting target behaviors outside the training setting or situation or, more directly, by training *for* generalization. In a procedure referred to as *sequential modification* (Stokes & Baer, 1977), a skill or behavior is taught in one setting or situation; then additional settings or situations are systematically added to the training program until generalization is achieved in all targeted settings or situations. For example, a behavior change program may begin and continue within a specific classroom setting until the target behavior is achieved. Then teachers gradually expand the program to other settings within the school until complete generalization (within the school) is achieved.

## MAINTENANCE

*Maintenance* refers to the degree to which a behavior change is maintained over time after a behavior change program has been completed. For example, in-seat behavior is said to be maintained when a teacher terminates the behavior change program used to increase in-seat behavior in the first place, and in-seat behavior remains at an acceptable level. If, at the end of the behavior change program, the duration of in-seat behavior decreases to an unacceptable level, then the behavior change was not maintained and the program may have to be reinstated.

## Promoting the Maintenance of Behavior Change

The methods for promoting maintenance are similar to those used to promote generalization. When training is conducted within natural settings, using natural antecedents and consequences, behavior changes are likely to be maintained after artificial stimuli and consequences (and other training conditions) are faded.

The following methods are likely to promote the generalization and maintenance of learned behaviors:

- *Teach within settings where the behavior is likely to occur and within multiple settings; avoid artificial training areas or pull-out training.* Teaching a student appropriate classroom behaviors within a resource room (artificial environment) is unlikely to generalize to the regular classroom or to be maintained after the student leaves the resource room unless the same behaviors are taught and reinforced in the regular classroom.
- *Implement the behavior change program with a variety of teachers across multiple settings.* All teachers who have contact with a student should consistently follow the behavior change program.
- *Identify common elements between the teaching environment and other environments within which behavior is to be generalized.* This tip is especially important when students change classes throughout the school day. Collaboration, cooperation, and consistency are important elements for effective behavioral generalization and maintenance across school personnel and environments.
- *Gradually shift from artificial stimulus controls to natural stimulus controls that occur in the student's natural environment.* Be flexible, however, to the student's individual needs.
- *Shift from continuous to intermittent schedules of reinforcement as soon as possible.* These decisions, as outlined in Chapter 3, should be based on the student's progress as outlined in your program data.
- *Pair artificial reinforcers (e.g., tokens) with natural reinforcers and consequences (social praise) provided within the natural environment.*
- *Phase out artificial reinforcers that are unlikely to be provided in the natural environment.*
- *Introduce delays in the provision of reinforcement that would be likely to occur in the natural environment.* For example, while initially students may exchange tokens at the end of each day, weekly exchange intervals will teach students to plan and save for future consequences. Again, teachers

must, however, be sensitive to what works for their students and be flexible enough to modify the behavior change plan as necessary.

- *Reinforce generalization and maintenance.* Don't forget to tell your students when you notice the generalization of skills across different environments, and verbally reinforce them when appropriate behaviors are maintained after the "official" program is completed.

## SUMMARY

Reinforcement increases the probability that a behavior will reoccur, or at least be maintained, at the current rate, duration, or intensity. Reinforcing appropriate behavior is the most effective method of increasing appropriate and decreasing inappropriate behaviors. Reinforcers may be tangible, social, or physical (activities). Primary reinforcers are naturally reinforcing, while secondary reinforcers are learned or conditioned through their association with primary reinforcers. Teachers must be sure that reinforcers are socially valid and age-appropriate.

It is important that teachers identify effective reinforcers through preference and reinforcement assessments. High-preference reinforcers have been found to be more effective than low-preference reinforcers in behavior change programs.

A *reinforcement menu* is a list of potential reinforcers that may be used for an individual student or a group of students to reinforce appropriate behavior. By having a variety of reinforcers to select from, students will not become satiated with a single reinforcer.

Factors associated with effective reinforcement programs include the immediacy of presentation; consistency; pairing with verbal praise; schedule of presentation; and the type, quality, quantity, and presenter of the reinforcement to the student. Teachers are encouraged to establish clear rules and guidelines, model the target behavior, and consistently reinforce behaviors targeted for increase.

Reinforcement may be delivered on a continuous or an intermittent schedule. A *continuous schedule* involves the delivery of reinforcement each and every time the target behavior is observed. When an *intermittent schedule* is employed, a student is reinforced after some occurrences, but not each one, of the target behavior. Reinforcement may also be delivered on a fixed ratio, variable ratio, fixed interval, and variable interval schedule.

*Shaping* refers to the reinforcement of successive approximations of a terminal behavior. It is generally used to teach new behaviors and skills. *Chaining* is the performance of a series or sequence of behaviors rather than of one behavior independently. Chaining may be presented in a forward or backward sequence.

A *token economy reinforcement* program is a symbolic reinforcement system. Students are presented with tokens for objects or activities that are reinforcing. Tokens, which may take many forms, allow teachers to delay giving reinforcers during busy periods of the day and are effective with individuals or large groups of students. Establishing a token economy program includes identifying the target behavior, medium of exchange, price of each item on the reinforcement menu, and time when the students will exchange their tokens for reinforcers.

*Contingency contracting* involves the development of a written agreement between a student and teacher(s) regarding the performance of target behaviors and the exchange of specific consequences. Contracts are highly recommended because they are easy to use in natural environments, do not restrict the student's participation in educational activities, focus on the reinforcement of appropriate behaviors, outline behavioral expectations in writing, may be used with individuals or groups of students, and may be modified to meet the needs of different students and situations.

*Generalization* refers to the degree to which a behavior change transfers to other settings, situations, or behaviors beyond the training environment. There are two types of generalization—stimulus and response. *Stimulus generalization* describes the degree of behavior change from training to other settings. *Response generalization* refers to the degree to which a behavior change program generalizes to other behaviors.

*Maintenance* is the degree to which a behavior change is maintained over time after the completion of a behavior change program. Teachers may promote generalization and maintenance by teaching in natural environments, selecting natural antecedents for stimulus control, selecting natural consequences as reinforcers, shifting from continuous to intermittent schedules of reinforcement, introducing delays in reinforcement similar to the natural environment, and reinforcing generalization.

## DISCUSSION QUESTIONS

1. What are the different types of reinforcement teachers may use in various environments (school, home, etc.) to increase appropriate behavior?
2. Describe the factors associated with the effective use of reinforcement.
3. List the different types of reinforcement schedules, and give examples of the use of each reinforcement schedule within a classroom environment.
4. Discuss the process of shaping new behaviors. Give an example of shaping a series of behaviors within a classroom setting.
5. What are the important elements of an effective contingency contracting program? Give examples of when contracts might be effective within the classroom settings.
6. What do we mean when we talk about program generalization and maintenance? How can they both be facilitated during and after a behavior management program?

## REFERENCES

Allen, L. J., Howard, V. F., Sweeney, W. J., & McLaughlin, T. F. (1993). Use of contingency contracting to increase on-task behavior with primary students, *Psychological Reports, 72*, 905–906.

Allen, S., & Kramer, J. (1990). Modification of personal hygiene and grooming behaviors with contingency contracting: A brief review and case study. *Psychology in the Schools, 27*, 244–251.

Babyak, A. E., Luze, G. J., & Kamps, D. M. (2000). The good student game: Behavior management for diverse classrooms. *Intervention in School and Clinic, 35*(4), 216–224.

Baer, R. A., Blount, R. L., Detrich, R., & Stokes, T. F. (1984). Using intermittent reinforcement to program maintenance of verbal/nonverbal correspondence. *Journal of Applied Behavior Analysis, 20*, 179–184.

Bagarozzi, D. A. (1984). Applied behavioral intervention in rural school settings: Problems in research design, implementation, and evaluation. *Clinical Social Work Journal, 12*, 43–56.

Bandura, A. (1973). *Aggression: A social learning analysis.* Upper Saddle River, NJ: Prentice Hall.

Beaman, R., & Wheldall, K. (2000). Teachers' use of approval and disapproval in the classroom. *Educational Psychology, 20*(4), 431–447.

Blanding, K. M., Richards, J., Bradley-Johnson, S., & Johnson, C. M. (1994). The effects of token reinforcement on McCarthy Scale Performance for white preschoolers of low and high social position. *Journal of Behavioral Education, 4*(1), 33–39.

Brisman, J., & Siegel, M. (1985). The bulimia workshops: A unique integration of group treatment approaches. *International Journal of Group Psychotherapy, 35*, 585–601.

Buisson, G. J., Murdock, J. Y., Reynolds, K. E., & Cronin, M. E. (1995). Effects of tokens on response latency of students with hearing impairments in a resource room. *Education and Treatment of Children, 18*(4), 408–421.

Carr, E. G., Robinson, S., Taylor, J. C., & Carlson, J. I. (1990). *Positive approaches to the treatment of severe behavior problems in persons with developmental disabilities: A review and analysis of reinforcement and stimulus-based procedures* (Monograph No. 4). Chicago: Association for Persons with Severe Handicaps.

Cipani, E., & Spooner, F. (1997). Treating problem behavior maintained by negative reinforcement. *Research in Developmental Disabilities, 18*(5), 329–342.

Corrigan, P. W. (1995). Use of a token economy with seriously mentally ill patients: Criticisms and misconceptions. *Psychiatric Services, 46*(12), 1258–1262.

Cuvo, A. J., Lerch, L. J., Leurquin, D. A., Gaffaney, T. J., & Poppen, R. L. (1998). Response allocation to concurrent fixed-ratio reinforcement schedules with work requirements by adults with mental retardation and typical preschool children. *Journal of Applied Behavior Analysis, 31*, 43–63.

Datillo, J. (1986). Computerized assessment of preference for severely handicapped individuals. *Journal of Applied Behavior Analysis, 19*, 445–448.

DeRisi, W. J., & Butz, G. (1975). *Writing behavioral contracts.* Champaign, IL: Research Press.

Dunlap, G., & Koegel, R. K. (1980). Motivating autistic children through stimulus variation. *Journal of Applied Behavior Analysis, 13*, 619–627.

Egel, A. L. (1981). Reinforcer variation: Implications for motivating developmentally disabled children. *Journal of Applied Behavior Analysis, 14*, 345–350.

Ford, A., & Mirenda, P. (1984). Community instruction: A natural cues and correction decision model. *Journal of the Association for Persons with Severe Handicaps, 9*, 79–87.

Gaylord-Ross, R. J., & Holvoet, J. F. (1985). *Strategies for educating students with severe handicaps.* Boston: Little, Brown.

Green, C. W., Reid, D. H., White, L. K., Halford, R. C., Brittain, D. P., & Gardner, S. M. (1988). Identifying reinforcers for persons with profound handicaps: Staff opinion versus systematic assessment of preferences. *Journal of Applied Behavior Analysis, 21,* 31–43.

Gregory, K. M., Kehle, T. J., & McLoughlin, C. S. (1997). Generalization and maintenance of treatment gains using self-management procedures with behaviorally disordered adolescents. *Psychological Reports, 80,* 683–690.

Hardman, E., & Smith, S. W. (1999). Promoting positive interactions in the classroom. *Intervention in School and Clinic, 34*(3), 178–180.

Haring, N. G. (1988). *Generalization for students with severe handicaps: Strategies and solutions.* Seattle: University of Washington Press.

Iwata, B. A. (1987). Negative reinforcement in applied behavior analysis: An emerging technology. *Journal of Applied Behavior Analysis, 20,* 361–378.

Iwata, B. A., Pace, G. M., Dorsey, M. F., Zarcone, J. R., Vollmer, T. R., Smith, R. G., et al. (1994). The functions of self-injurious behavior: An experimental-epidemiological analysis. *Journal of Applied Behavior Analysis, 27,* 215–240.

Johnson, B. F., & Cuvo, A. J. (1981). Teaching mentally retarded adults to cook. *Behavior Modification, 5,* 187–202.

Kazdin, A. E. (1977). *The token economy: A review and evaluation.* New York: Plenum.

Kazdin, A. E. (1989). *Behavior modification in applied settings.* Pacific Grove, CA: Brooks/Cole.

Kazdin, A. E., & Bootzin, R. R. (1972). The token economy: An evaluative review. *Journal of Applied Behavior Analysis, 5,* 343–372.

Kerr, M. M., & Nelson, C. M. (1989). *Strategies for managing behavior problems in the classroom.* Upper Saddle River, NJ: Merrill/Prentice Hall.

Keyes, G. (1994). Motivating reluctant learners. *Teaching Exceptional Children, 27,* 20–23.

Kitfield, E. B., & Masalsky, C. J. (2000). Negative reinforcement based treatment to increase food intake. *Behavior Modification, 24*(4), 600–609.

LaVigna, G. W., & Donnellan, A. M. (1986). *Alternatives to punishment: Solving behavior problems with non-aversive strategies.* New York: Irvington.

Levin, L., & Carr, E. G. (2001). Food selectivity and problem behavior in children with developmental disabilities: Analysis & intervention. *Behavior Modification, 25*(3), 443–471.

Lloyd, J. W., Eberhardt, M. J., & Drake, G. P. (1996). Group versus individual reinforcement contingencies within the context of group study conditions. *Journal of Applied Behavioral Analysis, 29*(2), 189–200.

Lucker, J. R., & Molloy, A. T. (1995). Resources for working with children with attention-deficit-hyperactive-disorder (ADHD). *Elementary School Guidance & Counseling, 29,* 260–266.

Maag, J. W. (2001). Rewarded by punishment: Reflections on the disuse of positive reinforcement in education. *Exceptional Children, 67*(2), 173–186.

MacKinnon-Slaney, F. (1993). Theory to practice in co-curricular activities: A new model for student involvement. *College Student Affairs Journal, 12,* 35–40.

Mason, S. A., & Egel, A. L. (1995). What does Amy like? *The Council For Exceptional Children, 61*(1), 42–45.

McVey, M. D. (2001). Teacher praise: Maximizing the motivational impact. *Journal of Early Education and Family Review, 8*(4), 29–34.

Miller, D. L., & Kelley, M. L. (1994). The use of goal setting and contingency contracting for improving children's homework performance. *Journal of Applied Behavior Analysis, 27,* 73–84.

Newman, B., & Buffington, D. M. (1995). The effects of schedules of reinforcement on instruction following. *Psychological Record, 45*(3), 4663–4677.

Northrup, J. (2000). Further evaluation of the accuracy of reinforcer surveys: A systematic replication. *JABA, 33*(3), 335–339.

Northrup, J., & George, T. (1996). A comparison of reinforcer assessment methods. *JABA, 29*(2), 201–213.

Pace, G. M., Ivancic, M. T., Edwards, G. L., Iwata, B. A., & Page, T. J. (1985). Assessment of stimulus preference and reinforcer value with profoundly retarded individuals. *Journal of Applied Behavior Analysis, 18,* 249–255.

Panyon, M. V. (1980). *How to use shaping.* Austin, TX: Pro-Ed.

Pfiffner, L. J., & O'Leary, S. G. (1987). The efficacy of all positive management as a function of the prior use of negative consequences. *Journal of Applied Behavior Analysis, 20,* 265–271.

Piazza, C. C., Fisher, W. W., Hagopian, L. P., Bowman, L. G., & Toole, L. (1996). Using a choice assessment to predict reinforcer effectiveness. *Journal of Applied Behavior Analysis, 29,* 1–9.

Premack, D. (1959). Toward empirical behavior laws: I. Positive reinforcement. *Psychological Review, 66,* 219–233.

Raubolt, R. R. (1983). Treating children in residential group psychotherapy. *Child Welfare, 62,* 147–155.

Roberts, M., White, R., & McLaughlin, T. F. (1997). Useful classroom accommodations for teaching children with ADD and ADHD. *Journal of Special Education, 21*(2), 71–84.

Rosen, L. A., Taylor, S. A., O'Leary, S. G., & Sanderson, W. (1990). A survey of classroom management practices. *Journal of School Psychology, 28,* 257–269.

Rosenberg, M. S. (1986). Maximizing the effectiveness of structured classroom management programs: Implementing rule-review procedures with disruptive and distractible students. *Behavioral Disorders, 11,* 239–248.

Skinner, B. F. (1938). *The behavior of organisms.* New York: Appleton-Century-Crofts.

Skinner, B. F. (1969). *Contingencies of reinforcement: A theoretical analysis.* New York: Appleton-Century-Crofts.

Snell, M. E., & Zirpoli, T. J. (1987). Intervention strategies. In M. E. Snell (Ed.), *Systematic instruction of persons with severe handicaps.* Upper Saddle River, NJ: Merrill/Prentice Hall.

Spooner, S. B., & Spooner, D. (1984). A review of chaining techniques: Implications for future research and practice. *Education and Training of the Mentally Retarded, 10,* 114–124.

Stokes, T. F., & Baer, D. B. (1977). An implicit technology of generalization. *Journal of Applied Behavior Analysis, 10,* 349–367.

Tankersley, M. (1995). A group-oriented contingency management program. *Preventing School Failure, 40*(1), 19–23.

Vannicelli, M., Canning, D., & Griefen, M. (1984). Group therapy with alcoholics: A group case study. *International Journal of Group Psychotherapy, 34,* 127–147.

Waldo, L., Guess, D., & Flanagan, B. (1982). Effects of concurrent and serial training on receptive labeling by severely retarded individuals. *Journal of the Association for the Severely Handicapped, 6,* 56–65.

White, G., & Greenwood, S. (1992). Empowering middle level students through the use of learning contracts. *Middle School Journal, 23,* 15–20.

Willert, J., & Willert, R. (2000). An ignored antidote to school violence: Classrooms that reinforce positive social habits. *American Secondary Education, 29*(1), 27–33.

Wolery, M., & Gast, D. L. (1984). Effective and efficient procedures for the transfer of stimulus control. *Topics in Early Childhood Special Education, 4,* 52–77.

# COGNITIVE BEHAVIOR MODIFICATION

*Mitchell L. Yell, Todd Busch, and Erik Drasgow*
*University of South Carolina*

*Self-management interventions encompass a heterogeneous group of procedures, which have been used with children of all ages to remediate a wide variety of academic and behavior problems. With a focus on skill building, each of these self-management strategies attempts in some way to teach students to be more independent, self-reliant, and responsible for their own behavior.*

—SHAPIRO AND COLE (1994, *p.* 11)

Cognitive behavior modification (CBM) is not a specific type of intervention. Rather, it is a term that refers to a number of different but related interventions. Problem-solving, anger control, self-instruction, alternate response, self-control, self-management, self-monitoring, self-evaluation, and self-reinforcement training are all interventions that are included under the rubric of CBM.

This chapter begins by examining the conceptual basis, purpose, advantages, and origin of CBM. Next, we review specific interventions. Our review of each intervention begins with a definition, followed by a summary of relevant research, and ends with guidelines for using the intervention.

## WHAT IS COGNITIVE BEHAVIOR MODIFICATION?

All CBM interventions share three basic assumptions (Hughes, 1988):

1. Behavior is mediated by cognitive events (e.g., thoughts, beliefs).
2. A change in cognitive mediating events results in a change of behavior.
3. All persons are active participants in their learning.

CBM is based on the reciprocal relationship between one's thoughts and behaviors. Thus, interventions attempt to modify thoughts and beliefs to change behavior. Teachers who use CBM interventions with their students teach them how to control their behavior by teaching them how to regulate their thoughts and beliefs. The major goal of CBM, therefore, is to teach students to manage their own behavior through cognitive self-regulation.

CBM interventions have been used with a wide variety of students and behaviors. Table 8.1 lists examples of the application of CBM to diverse populations and behaviors.

Proponents of CBM believe that sole reliance on externally controlled behavioral interventions makes a student overly dependent on a teacher. But if a teacher uses the techniques and procedures of CBM to teach a student self-management, then the student becomes less dependent on the teacher and on external control. Several researchers have discussed the advantages of teaching students to manage

**TABLE 8.1 ● Selected Studies Using Cognitive Behavioral Interventions**

| *Subjects or Behaviors* | *Study* |
| --- | --- |
| Students with Autism | Koegel & Koegel, 1990 |
| Students with Behavioral Disorders | Carr & Punzo, 1993; Clark & McKenzie, 1989; Kern, Dunlap, Childs, & Clark, 1994; McLaughlin, Krappman, & Welsh, 1985; Rhode, Morgan, & Young, 1983; Smith, Young, West, Morgan, & Rhode, 1988 |
| Students with Learning Disabilities | Lloyd, Hallahan, Kosiewicz, & Kneedler, 1982; Lloyd, Bateman, Landrum, & Hallahan, 1989; Rooney, Polloway, & Hallahan, 1985 |
| Students with Mental Retardation | Osborne, Kosiewicz, Crumley, & Lee, 1987 |
| Students with Severe and Multiple Disabilities | Shapiro, Browder, & D'Huyvetter, 1984 |
| Students with Visual Disabilities | Storey & Gaylord-Ross, 1987 |
| Nondisabled Students | Olympia, Sheridan, Jenson, & Andrews, 1994 |
| Students with Attention Deficit Hyperactivity Disorder (ADHD) | Barkley, Copeland, & Sivage, 1980; Kendall & Finch, 1979 |
| Aggressive Behavior | Christie, Hiss, & Lozanoff, 1984 |
| Anger | Christie, Hiss, & Lozanoff, 1984 |
| Noncompliance | O'Brien, Riner, & Budd, 1983 |
| Social Skills | Kilburtz, Miller, & Morrow, 1985 |
| Depression | Reynolds & Coats, 1986 |
| Academic Deficits | Symons, McGoldrick, Snyder, & Pressley, 1990; Harris & Graham, 1992; McGoldrick, Carigula-Bull, Symons, & Pressley, 1990; Burkell, Schneider, & Pressley, 1990 |
| Attributions | Tollefson, Tracy, Johnsen, & Chatman, 1986 |

their behavior (e.g., Alberto & Troutman, 1999; Cooper, Heron, & Heward, 1987; Schloss & Smith, 1998). These advantages include the following:

1. Self-management represents a proactive rather than reactive approach to behavior management. Teaching students to control their behavior will *prevent* behavior problems from occurring.

2. Students with self-management skills can learn and behave more appropriately without the constant supervision of the teacher.

3. Self-management may enhance the generalization of behavior change. When behaviors are under external control by the teacher, the behaviors may not occur in situations and settings where the teacher is absent. When

students manage their own behaviors, however, these behaviors are more likely to endure and to carry over to different situations and settings.

4. Behavioral improvements established through self-management procedures may be more resistant to extinction than behavioral improvements established through external control procedures. When behavioral improvements are established through external control procedures, these improvements may disappear when the external reinforcers are removed. However, some researchers have suggested that this is less of a problem when behaviors are improved through self-management and reinforcement may be internal.

# THE ORIGINS OF COGNITIVE BEHAVIOR MODIFICATION

CBM represents a synthesis of cognitive psychology and behavior modification. Kendall and Hollon (1979) describe it as "a joining of forces rather than a break for independence" (p. 6). According to Kendall and Hollon:

> *The cognitive-behavioral approach . . . is a purposeful combination of the performance-oriented and methodologically rigorous behavioral techniques with the treatment and evaluation of cognitive-mediational phenomena. Thus internal as well as environmental variables are targets for treatment and are scientifically evaluated as contributors to behavior change. (1979, p. 3)*

Although scholars have identified additional forces that contributed to the development of CBM, the primary forces were behavioral psychology and cognitive psychology. We will briefly summarize the forces that led to the development of CBM intervention.

## Trends in Behavioral Psychology

The traditional behavioral approach has modified behavior by altering environmental events (i.e., antecedents and consequences). The environment is altered through the application of the principles of behavior. Behavioral principles include reinforcement, punishment, and extinction. These principles are used to establish behaviors, increase or maintain behaviors, or reduce or eliminate behaviors.

The 1970s were a time of growing dissatisfaction with behaviorism. Kazdin (1982) argued that conceptual stagnation was occurring within behaviorism. Little in the way of new theory was developed, and the applied research seemed merely to catalog the same behavioral interventions with new populations, problems, or settings. Another source of dissatisfaction was that behavior management procedures were not fostering changes that were durable or that generalized to other settings, across behaviors, or across subjects (Meichenbaum, 1980).

The conceptual stagnation and the growing dissatisfaction with the behavioral model may have helped to foster the shift toward more cognitively oriented interventions (Kazdin, 1982). The shifting view acknowledged that behavior modification involved cognitive processes and that cognitions were involved in the learning process (Craighead, 1982).

In 1978 Bandura advanced his concepts of reciprocal determinism by suggesting that environmental, cognitive, and behavioral variables interact with each other. Moreover, he highlighted the importance of observation in learning and the influence that a person's beliefs in his or her capabilities has on behavior (Bandura, 1977). His work served as the basis of social-learning theory, which was the foundation of what was to become the cognitive-behavioral model (Meyers, Cohen, & Schlester, 1989).

Research on self-control and self-regulation was also an important contribution to the movement toward CBM (Harris, 1982). Homme (1965) stated that cognition was subject to the same laws as other behavior and that changing these cognitions could change behavior. Kanfer and Karoly (1972) developed a model of self-regulation that included self-monitoring, self-evaluation, and self-reinforcement. According to Kanfer and Karoly, self-regulation occurred when a student observed his or her performance, compared it to some criterion, and reinforced him- or herself. These and other events within the behavioral field began to acknowledge the interaction between cognitive and environmental events in human behavior.

## Trends in Cognitive Psychology

Cognitive psychologists believe that behavior is influenced by what we think (i.e., cognitions). Cognitive psychologists believe the main determinants of human behavior are within the individual. Thus, interventions are aimed at directly altering thoughts, perceptions, beliefs, and attributions. An important influence on cognitive behavior modification was the development of cognitive therapy.

According to Craighead (1982), Ellis and Beck began the development of cognitive interventions. Beck (1976) believed that many problems were due to misinterpretations and that identifying faulty perceptions and teaching them more accurate ones could help people who had problems. Individuals progressed through four stages in Beck's cognitive therapy: First, the individual had to become aware of his or her thoughts; second, the individual had to recognize that the thoughts were inaccurate; third, the individual had to substitute accurate judgments for inaccurate ones; and, finally, he or she needed feedback as to the correctness of the changes.

Similarly, Ellis believed that it is an individual's inaccurate perceptions of events that cause disturbances. To modify these inaccurate perceptions, Ellis (1973) developed rational-emotive therapy (RET). In RET, individuals are taught that it is not what happens to them that makes them upset and causes them to behave counterproductively. Rather it is what they *think* about what happens to them that causes them to be upset.

The theories of Beck and Ellis share two primary assumptions. First, dysfunctional behavior is the result of inappropriate cognitive processes (what individuals thought about events). Second, intervention must modify these inappropriate cognitions (Craighead, 1982).

Theories concerning the relationship between private speech and behavior have also influenced the development of CBM. Private speech refers to overt or covert speech that is directed at oneself. Theories about the role of private speech have their roots in the work of Vygotsky and Luria. Vygotsky (1962) proposed that the internalization of a verbal system was a crucial step in a child's control over his or her behavior. Vygotsky's student Luria (1961) proposed a normal developmental sequence by which the child came to regulate his or her behavior. In this developmental sequence, the child's behavior was first controlled by verbalizations of adults. The next stage involved the child controlling his or her own behavior through overt verbalizations. Finally, by the age of 5 or 6, the child's behavior was controlled by his or her own covert verbalizations.

Jenson referred to verbal control of behavior as "verbal mediation." He defined verbal mediation as "talking to oneself in relevant ways when confronted with something to be learned, a problem to be solved, or a concept to be attained" (1966, p. 39). This developmental sequence generally results in the verbal mediation ability becoming automatic. These theories led to the development of interventions that attempted to modify behaviors through self-statements.

# THE PROCEDURES OF COGNITIVE BEHAVIOR MODIFICATION

All CBM interventions share the common element of stressing procedures that teach students to manage their own behaviors. That is, teachers use behavioral principles with their students (e.g., reinforcement) to teach them cognitive strategies. The strategies use some form of self-instruction or verbal mediation to control behavior. CBM procedures are varied and concentrate on different types of verbal mediation. For example, some CBM procedures teach monitoring and evaluate their behavior, whereas others teach students to respond to provocation by following certain cognitive steps. We now examine the different interventions that fall under the rubric of CBM.

## Self-Instructional Training

### Definition

In self-instructional training, students are taught a generic set of statements that they say to themselves when confronted with various situations. For example, when confronted with a mathematics assignment requiring long division, the student may be taught a self-instructional strategy to solve long-division problems. Similarly, when confronted with a situation that may lead to anger, the student may be taught a self-instructional strategy to keep him- or herself calm. Self-instruction is the use of personal verbal prompts. Teachers training students in self-instruction teach them to guide their behavior using these prompts.

### Research Basis

Luria's (1961) developmental theory serves as the basis of self-instructional training. Although most children follow a normal developmental sequence in which they acquire self-regulation, there are children for whom this does not occur or only partially occurs. These children are deficient in the ability to use *internal speech to control behavior.* Similarly, students that have not developed mediational skills will have difficulties in solving problems.

### Research on Self-Instruction Training and Problem Behavior

Meichenbaum and Goodman (1971) investigated hyperactive and impulsive children. They found that many of the children in their studies had deficiencies in internal speech and verbal mediation abilities. Because of their verbal mediation problems, these children did not use self-talk to control their behavior. In a series of investigations, Meichenbaum and his colleagues (Meichenbaum, 1977; Meichenbaum & Asarnow, 1979; Meichenbaum & Goodman, 1971) used Luria's developmental sequence to teach these children to use self-instructions to control their behavior. In other words, the children were taught to talk to themselves as a method to learn to control their impulsive behaviors.

Meichenbaum and Goodman taught the impulsive children to ask themselves a series of questions when confronted with tasks that would typically lead to impulsive behavior. The four types of statements or questions the children were taught to say to themselves were:

1. *Problem definition:* For example, "What do I need to do?"
2. *Attention focusing* and *response guidance:* For example, "What should I do to solve this problem?"
3. *Self-reinforcement:* For example, "I did a good job."
4. *Self-evaluative,* coping skills, and error correction: For example, "I didn't do so well, but that's okay. I can start over again."

Meichenbaum and Goodman's study proved to be very successful. Based on their work with impulsive children, the researchers developed the following generic self-instructional training protocol. Teachers should use the steps listed in Table 8.2 when training students to use self-instruction.

Self-instructional training has also been used with aggressive children. Aggressive children tend to react to problem situations with anger, not taking time to "stop and think" or consider alternatives in responding to provocative situations.

Camp, Blom, Herbert, and Van Doornick (1977) conducted some of the earliest studies examining the use of self-instruction training with aggressive children. The primary purpose of these researchers' studies was to teach aggressive children to engage in coping self-instructions when responding to provocations. *Coping* refers to the child's ability to deal with perceived aversive events in a constructive rather than negative manner (e.g., walking away from a perceived insult rather than starting a fight). Camp and her colleagues developed the *Think Aloud* program to teach aggressive boys to use coping self-instructions. The self-instructional training methods were very similar to those developed by Meichenbaum and Goodman. The Think Aloud program attempted to train the aggressive boys in using self-instructions in a problem-solving sequence. The children were taught a generic format of instructional prompts to (a) identify a problem, (b) generate a solution, (c) monitor their use of the solution, and (d) evaluate their performance. The in-

**TABLE 8.2 • Steps in Teaching Students to Use Self-Instructions**

| | |
|---|---|
| Step 1: *Cognitive modeling* | The teacher models task performance while using self-instructions. This stage requires the teacher to model aloud. The child observes in this stage. |
| Step 2: *Overt external guidance* | The student performs the same task under the teacher's direction. The teacher says the self-instructions aloud while the student performs the task. |
| Step 3: *Overt self-instructions* | The student performs the same task, while saying the self-instructions aloud. The teacher observes and provides feedback. |
| Step 4: *Faded self-instructions* | The student performs the task while whispering the instructions to him- or herself. The teacher observes and provides feedback. |
| Step 5: *Covert self-instructions* | The student performs the task using covert self-instructions. |

structional prompts were questions the children would use when confronted with a provocative situation. The questions the children asked themselves were (a) What is my problem? (b) What is my plan? (c) Am I using my plan? and (d) How did I do? The researchers' goal was to teach these aggressive children to talk to themselves when confronted with situations that would often lead to aggression. The procedures were very successful in achieving the desired results.

## Research on Self-Instructional Training and Academic Problems

Interventions using self-instructional procedures were originally devised for the purpose of altering behavior problems in children. However, these procedures have also been extended to academic interventions, particularly in the area of academic strategy training (Lloyd, 1980). Self-instructional procedures, when applied to academic performance, are designed to help learners improve their academic problem-solving behaviors.

It has been theorized that many behavior problems actually stem from learning problems. Torgeson (1982) has stated that learning problems in children might be due to a failure to apply basic abilities efficiently by using effective task strategies. Children who manifest these failures have been referred to as inactive learners (Torgeson, 1982). To remediate these inefficient learning strategies, teachers should assess the cognitive task strategies needed for competence in a particular area. For example, if a student is being taught long division, the teacher should teach the student the steps necessary to complete a long-division problem. If these steps are then taught to children, and they use them appropriately, they will become more active, self-regulating learners.

In designing CBM strategies, researchers conduct a cognitive task analysis of the processes involved and determine what processes are used by academically successful students. Researchers then develop a training procedure that will enhance the use of these processes (Wong, 1989). The purpose of these training procedures is to help learners improve their academic performance by using cognitive mediation strategies.

The basic procedures in many of these interventions are similar. The teacher models the processes while using self-instructions, students then follow the examples, first overtly, and then covertly (Meichenbaum, 1977). According to Meichenbaum, the teacher modeling provides a window on the thinking processes. Eventually by learning the strategies through modeling and self-instructions, the students take over their own learning.

A few examples will illustrate this process. Rinehart, Stahl, and Erickson (1986) taught summarization to grade school students using modeling and self-instructional training. The students were taught to produce summaries of reading material that included main and supporting ideas. The researchers found that the students trained in the procedure, when compared to students not trained, improved their recall of main ideas.

The teachers in this study used the self-instruction developed by Meichenbaum and Goodman (1971) to teach their students the verbal prompts that they should use when summarizing materials (see Table 8.2). There were three steps to this process:

Step 1: The teachers explained the purpose of summarization to the students.

Step 2: The teachers modeled writing summaries of sample paragraphs. The teachers used overt self-instructions while producing the summaries. The children did similar self-instructing. The teachers would model monitoring of the summaries using the following instructions: "Have I found the overall idea that the paragraph or group of paragraphs is about? Have I found the most important information that tells more about the overall idea? Have I used information that is not directly about the overall idea? Have I used any information more than once?" Students then completed summaries while the teacher provided feedback.

Step 3: When the students became proficient in summarizing short paragraphs using this strategy, the teachers extended the summarization procedure to longer paragraphs.

Graham and Harris (1985) reported another example of using a self-instructional program to teach writing skills to students with learning disabilities. These researchers developed an instructional program based in part on Meichenbaum's (1977) self-instructional training. In teaching the writing program to students, the researchers assessed the student's level of performance, described the learning strategy, and modeled the strategy using self-instructions. When modeling the strategy, the teacher used the self-instructions listed in Table 8.3.

After modeling the story, the teacher and student discussed the importance of using self-instructions. The student was asked to identify the self-instructions and to write examples of self-instructions in his or her own words. The self-control strategy training resulted in increases in student performance above baseline lev-

**TABLE 8.3 • Teaching Students to Use Self-Instructions**

*Problem definition:* What is it I have to do? I have to write a good story. Good stories make sense and use many action words.

*Planning:* Look at the picture and write down good action words. Think of a good story. Write my story—make good sense and use good action words.

*Self-evaluation:* Read my story and ask "Did I write a good story? Did I use action words?" Fix my story—can I use more good action words?

*Self-reinforcement:* That was a great story.

els. The authors concluded that self-control strategy training improved and maintained composition skills among children with learning disabilities.

When using self-instructional training to teach academics, teachers do not need to adhere precisely to any formula. Instead, teachers should follow the general procedural outline provided by Meichenbaum and Goodman to teach the strategy. Whether teaching a child to do long division or to do a household chore, the teacher or parent can use cognitive behavior modification by modeling the task and self-instructing while modeling. Through self-instructions the child is taught to do a kind of thinking they could not, or would not, otherwise do (Meichenbaum & Asarnow, 1979). The child's internal dialogue is used to facilitate performance.

## Application

Teachers should use the following guidelines based on Meichenbaum and Goodman's work when using cognitive behavior modification to teach children skills or strategies. First, the teacher should determine what it is the child needs to know and what is the current level of performance. Second, the teacher must describe the strategy to be taught and model it to the child while using self-instructions. Third, the child should practice the strategy using self-instructions under the guidance of the teacher. The self-instructions are spoken aloud. It is important at this stage that the child has as many opportunities to practice as possible. Fourth, when the child can successfully perform the strategy under controlled practice conditions using overt self-instructions, the child is allowed to independently practice using covert self-instructions. Students should be encouraged to monitor their use of strategies and to continue to use them. Explaining that the skills that are being taught will help to decrease problem behaviors or increase performance in academic subjects can increase student motivation.

For example, if the teacher had determined that the child could not do long division, he or she would decide on a strategy for teaching the skill to the child. If the teacher decided to use the divide, multiply, subtract, bring down, check model (Burkell, Schneider, & Pressley, 1990) to teach the child, he or she would explain the model and how it is used. The teacher would then model the strategy using self-instructions (first I divide, the next step is to multiply, etc.) while doing a long-division problem to successful completion. The next step would involve having the child practice long-division problems while the teacher gives the self-instructions.

**TABLE 8.4 • Generic Self-Instructions Protocol**

1. *Problem definition instructions:* The child first learns to define the problem.
2. *Problem approach instructions:* The child verbalizes potential strategies to solve the problem.
3. *Attention focusing instructions:* The child focuses his or her attention on the problem by asking if he or she is using the strategy.
4. *Coping statement instructions:* If a mistake is made, the child uses statements to cope with the error and to encourage another try.
5. *Self-reinforcement instructions:* The child reinforces him- or herself for doing a good job.

The child would then practice long division using self-instructions (still under the teacher's guidance) until he or she had mastered the strategy. When the teacher is satisfied that the child has mastered the self-instructional procedure, the child should independently practice the skill using the self-instructional strategy covertly. Evaluation of the success of the cognitive-behavioral procedures must take place during training and on completion of training.

Whatever the purpose and content of training, the methods of training will be similar. Whatever the type of self-instructional training, there are five basic components that should be included. These components, listed in Table 8.4, should be followed for teaching both behavior and academic strategies.

When using self-instructional training to teach students to be more reflective and deliberate in their responses to problems, the following guidelines will be helpful.

*First,* it is important that teachers model the self-instruction process. Teachers should perform the task and verbally self-instruct while the child is observing. It is important in modeling that teachers use the same self-instructional process as the child will be using.

*Second,* teachers must consider the ability of the child. It has been shown that if children need practice prior to performing a task or if they are unable to perform a task, self-instructions can actually interfere with their performance. Self-instructions will not enable children to perform tasks that are not in their repertoires. Similarly, children must be capable of understanding the statements to be used.

*Third,* teachers should systematically fade their presence in the process. If self-instructional training is to be effective, the child must be able to self-instruct independently of the teacher.

*Fourth,* teachers must systematically reinforce the child's accurate use of self-instructions and demonstrations of target behaviors.

## Self-Management Training

Self-management is a cognitive-behavioral intervention. As such, the goal of a self-management intervention is to teach the child to manage his or her behavior. The primary advantage of self-management training allows teachers to teach children techniques that will make them less dependent on the teacher's environmental manipulations. In this section we will discuss three procedures often used in self-management training: self-monitoring, self-evaluation, and self-reinforcement. Although each of these procedures is often discussed separately, in reality they are often combined and taught as self-management packages.

## Self-Monitoring

When using self-monitoring or self-recording procedures, students record the frequency of a particular behavior or behaviors. Self-monitoring has been used to improve students' behavior (DiGangi & Maag, 1992) and academic achievement (Webber, Scheuermann, McCall, & Coleman, 1994). Reid (1996) reviewed the research on self-monitoring and found that these procedures had been proven to be effective with diverse populations and behaviors. Moreover, Reid found that these procedures could easily be used in classroom settings.

There are two aspects to self-monitoring. First, a student must be aware of the behavior that he or she is counting. Second, he or she must make a record of what they have done. For example, students may count the number of times they raise their hand to volunteer in class or talk out in class without permission by observing the behavior and then marking the occurrences on a piece of paper.

It has been demonstrated that just the act of having a child collect self-monitoring data may often result in increases in desired behavior. This may be because self-monitoring procedures force the child to monitor his or her behavior. Baer (1984) stated that a reason for behavioral improvement is that self-monitoring provides cues that increase the child's awareness of potential consequences for a particular behavior. Researchers have noted that behavior often improves simply because the student is collecting the behavioral data. Broden, Hall, and Mitts (1971) investigated the effects of self-monitoring on two disruptive students. They found that the act of recording their disruptive behaviors dramatically decreased these behaviors. This has been termed a *reactive effect*. This means that the behavior may change in the desired direction simply as a function of self-monitoring (Alberto & Troutman, 1999).

*Accuracy in self-monitoring.* Teachers may be concerned with children's accuracy in self-monitoring. In a number of investigations children have accurately recorded their behaviors; however, in other investigations children have not been accurate. An important question is whether accuracy is a significant variable during self-monitoring. O'Leary and Dubay (1979) demonstrated that the accuracy of a child's self-collected data did not necessarily correlate with the child's behavior or academic performance. That is, when trying to increase appropriate behaviors, the act of self-monitoring alone may be more important than the accuracy of the child's data.

*Reinforcement for accurate self-monitoring.* If a student is to be reinforced on the basis of self-monitoring data, some researchers believe that contingencies regarding the accuracy of the data should apply. Otherwise, children may rate their behavior as appropriate to receive reinforcement even when inappropriate (Gross & Wojnilower, 1984). Thus children may be reinforced for inaccurate self-monitoring. When accuracy is a concern, matching procedures may be employed to check the child's data. When using matching procedures, a child's data are

Self-monitoring teaches students how to measure and evaluate their own program.

matched with the recorded data of independent observers. The child is reinforced when his or her self-monitoring data closely match the data collected by the independent observer. For example, a student could be reinforced when his or her self-monitoring data matched the data recorded by teachers. The teacher could tell the student that he or she would give the student bonus points if the self-monitoring data were within one point of the teacher's recording. In addition to reinforcing the child for matching, the child should also be reinforced for appropriate behavior exhibited during the self-monitoring program.

In a review of the self-monitoring research, Webber et al. (1994) concluded that self-monitoring could be used successfully with special education students of various ages in various settings to increase attention to task, positive classroom behaviors, and some social skills. Self-monitoring was also successful in decreasing inappropriate classroom behaviors. Additional benefits of self-monitoring included the enhanced likelihood of generalization and the ease of teaching the procedures to students.

*Teaching students to self-monitor.* To teach self-monitoring, the teacher must train the student to collect data on his or her behavior. First, the student must be aware of the particular behavior that will be counted. To assist the student to identify the behavior of concern, the teacher must have a precise, operational definition. Second, the student must be taught how to record occurrences or nonoccurrences of the behavior. The collected data provide the child and the teacher with feedback regarding the frequency of the behavior. Teachers may find it useful to

**TABLE 8.5 • Teaching Self-Monitoring**

| Teaching Steps | Description |
|---|---|
| 1. Select a target behavior. | Choose a behavior that interferes with teaching, the student's education, or the education of others. |
| 2. Operationally define the target behavior. | Precisely define the target behavior so both the student and the teacher agree when it occurs. |
| 3. Monitor the target behavior. | Set up a monitoring system to ensure accuracy (e.g., random student-teacher matches). |
| 4. Evaluate progress. | The student and the teacher should have frequent evaluation meetings so that the teacher can provide feedback and monitor progress. |
| 5. Fade self-monitoring. | When the student's behavior approaches desired levels, the self-monitoring procedure should be faded (e.g., increasing the intervals between self-monitoring periods, using self-monitoring less frequently). |

teach students how to chart and graph the behavior they count. Students will often find this very motivating (Workman, 1998).

Students will usually have to be taught self-monitoring by teachers. Programs to teach students to use self-monitoring strategies should include the components listed in Table 8.5.

Self-monitoring systems can be used with event recording procedures and time sampling procedures. In event recording, the student counts the number of times a particular behavior occurs. An example of event recording would be if the teacher taught a student to record the number of times the student raised his or her hand to ask a question or make a comment during class. Figure 8.1 depicts a self-monitoring form using event recording.

In time sampling recording a student might count the number of occurrences of a particular behavior within a specified period of time. For example, a student may mark if he or she is seated when an audible beep on a tape is heard. This is a more sophisticated type of recording procedure. In addition to requiring that a student can observe his or behavior accurately, the teacher must provide a tape with an audible tone. The tone serves as a cue for the student to record if the behavior occurred. Figure 8.2 is an example of self-monitoring using time sampling.

A classroom example of self-monitoring is presented in Classroom Application 8.1.

## Self-Evaluation

In self-evaluation or self-assessment, the child compares his or her behavior against a preset standard to determine whether the performance meets a particular criterion (Cole, 1987). Maag (1989) referred to self-evaluation as self-monitoring followed by a covert evaluation of the behavior.

Name: _____

Date: _____

Class: _____

Record a "/" each time you talk without permission.

**FIGURE 8.1.** Example of a self-monitoring form using event sampling

**FIGURE 8.2.** Example of a self-monitoring form using time sampling

Name: _____

Date: _____

Environment: _____

Start time: _____ Stop time: _____

Intervals (forty 1-minute intervals)

| | | | | | | | | | |
|---|---|---|---|---|---|---|---|---|---|
| | | | | | | | | | |
| | | | | | | | | | |
| | | | | | | | | | |

Every time you hear the beep, record a "+" if you were paying attention or a "–" if you were not paying attention.

Research has indicated that self-evaluation can be a useful intervention. For example, Smith, Young, West, Morgan, and Rhode (1988) trained four boys with behavior disorders in a self-evaluation procedure. The target behaviors were off-task and disruptive behaviors. The training was conducted in three phases. In the first phase, the children were taught classroom rules. Behavior was rated on a 5-point scale in accordance with how closely they followed the rules. The children rated their behavior on an evaluation card every 10 minutes. Each student was asked to record a "5" or "excellent" if he followed classroom rules and worked on assigned tasks for the entire interval; "4" or "very good" if he followed classroom rules and

# Classroom Application 8.1

## A Classroom Example of Self-Monitoring

Nick, a second-grade student, blurted out answers in class without first raising his hand. He realized that his behavior was disruptive to the class but did not seem to be able to control it. Nick's teacher, Miss Quam, had put Nick on a behavior management system in which he was rewarded with a point every time he raised his hand for permission to speak. The system seemed to work, but Miss Quam wanted Nick to be able to control the behavior himself rather than having it controlled by an external management system. She decided to implement a self-monitoring system with reinforcement.

Miss Quam had a conference with Nick to explain the disruption caused by his blurting out answers in class. She explained that they would be working together to help Nick control this behavior. They talked about the fact that the class would not be disrupted if Nick raised his hand when he knew an answer. Together they practiced the desired behavior. Miss Quam also told Nick that he would be monitoring his own behavior. She explained to Nick that when he became aware of the correct behavior, it would be easier for him to do it.

Nick was given a chart to record his hand-raising behavior. Every time Nick would raise his hand to get permission to answer a question, he was to put a slash mark on the chart. Miss Quam also marked each occasion of Nick raising his hand on a chart at her desk. At the end of each period, Nick and Miss Quam would compare charts. They would count the number of matching slashes, and Nick would be given that number of points. Verbal praise would also be given. Together they practiced marking the chart. When Miss Quam was satisfied that Nick understood the procedure, she told him that they would start doing it in class the next day. Miss Quam told Nick that on Fridays they would review the charts for every day of the week to see if the procedure was helping.

The procedure was in place for two weeks and was very successful. Nick was raising his hand for permission to speak and very seldom blurted out an answer. During the evaluation meetings, Nick expressed a great deal of satisfaction with his newfound control. At this point Miss Quam decided to start fading the procedure. First she withdrew the point reinforcers. The next Monday Nick was told he had to do the procedure only twice a day rather than for each academic period. By Thursday he was told he had to count only once a day. A week later Nick was recording his behavior only on Mondays and Fridays. The hand-raising behavior continued at a high rate, so Miss Quam told Nick they would only do the procedure once in a while. Following the cessation of the program, Miss Quam noted that Nick still raised his hand for permission to talk and seldom blurted out in class.

worked for the entire interval with the exception of one minor infraction; "3" or "average" if he followed the rules and worked without any serious offenses except for receiving two reminders to get to work; "2" or "below average" if he followed the rules and worked for approximately half of the interval; "1" if he followed the rules and worked for half the interval but had to be separated from the group; and "0" or "unacceptable" if he did not follow classroom rules or do any work during the interval. The students were told to rank their behavior on the scale and that their teachers would do the same. The teacher would mark each child's card to indicate her rating at the end of a certain period of time. The two scales would be compared, and the children would receive points for matching or nearly matching the teacher. Points could be exchanged for tangible reinforcers.

In the second phase, the children continued to evaluate their behavior, but they only matched evaluations with the teacher every 15 minutes. During the third phase, children continued to evaluate themselves on the scale; however, they only matched evaluations with the teacher once every 30 minutes. Phase 3 was not as effective in reducing inappropriate behaviors as phases 1 and 2. Results indicated that the self-evaluation procedures paired with teacher matching were effective in reducing off-task and disruptive behavior in the special education classroom. The authors concluded that self-evaluation paired with teacher matching was an effective intervention and that the procedures were effective, even though the behaviors were not first brought under control by an external behavior management procedure. Data collected in regular classrooms did not show *treatment generalization* (see Chapter 5). According to the authors, this was anticipated because regular classroom teachers were unwilling or unable to implement the procedure. They suggested that peers in the regular classroom might be used in the program to match evaluations, thereby freeing the teachers from this responsibility.

Similarly, Nelson, Smith, and Colvin (1995) reported the results of an investigation of a self-evaluation procedure on the recess behavior of students with behavior problems. In the investigation, the authors also reported the effects of using peers to enhance the generalizability of the procedure. Target students were taught the guidelines for appropriate recess behavior using direct instruction and role playing. Next the students were taught to rate their actual recess behavior against the recess guidelines using a 4-point scale with 3 as excellent and 0 as unacceptable. Students rated their behavior on point cards twice during the morning recess period. A peer matched to the target student also rated his or her behavior. Following recess, points were totaled and exchanged for backup reinforcers. Results indicated that the self-evaluation procedure produced clear improvements in the recess behaviors of the target students (e.g., positive social behavior toward peers, isolation, positive social behavior toward adults, appropriate equipment use and game playing). The authors also reported that the improved recess behaviors generalized to the afternoon recess period.

*Teaching students to self-evaluate.* Teaching students to use self-evaluation requires a criterion or goal by which the student can compare his or her performance. Additionally, teaching students to self-evaluate must begin with teaching students to self-monitor. Self-monitoring is a prerequisite for self-evaluation; the student needs data to compare his or her performance against. Once data exists, the student will have information upon which the performance can be evaluated. The end result of self-evaluation is that the student decides whether his or her behavior has reached the desired level.

Perhaps the simplest method of self-evaluation is to include a rating scale at the bottom of a self-monitoring sheet. The student first monitors and records the target behavior and then evaluates his or her behavior against a preset standard. For example, if the student is monitoring talkouts during a one-hour class period, after the monitoring is completed the student tallies the data and compares it to a criterion level. The student then evaluates the behavior monitored against a rating scale. A rating scale may have a range from 1 to 4 with a definition for each point on the scale (e.g., 4=excellent, 3=good, 2=fair, 1=poor). An example of a self-monitoring sheet with an evaluation scale at the bottom of the page is depicted in Figure 8.3.

Figure 8.4 is an example of a self-evaluation rating scale that requires students to make evaluative judgments on their behavior following longer periods of time and without a formal self-monitoring system.

When using self-evaluation training to teach students to evaluate their own behavior, the following guidelines will be helpful:

*First,* students must be able to accurately monitor their own behavior. To perform a self-evaluation procedure, students must be adept at monitoring behaviors; then they may (a) compare the behaviors they monitored to a preset criterion, and (b) evaluate their performance.

*Second,* the teacher and student should set a daily goal. This goal will then serve as a criterion by which the student can self-evaluate. The goal describes the level of performance toward which the student should work.

Name: _____
Date: _____
Class: _____

Every time you hear the beep, record a "+" if you were paying attention or a "–" if you were not paying attention.

| How did I do? | | | |
|---|---|---|---|
| Poor | Fair | Good | Great! |
| 1 | 2 | 3 | 4 |

**FIGURE 8.3.** Example of a self-monitoring form (event) with self-evaluation

**FIGURE 8.4.** Example of a self-evaluation form

Self-Evaluation

Name:

Class:

Date:

1st rating

Time:

| Poor | Fair | Good | Great |
|------|------|------|-------|
| 1    | 2    | 3    | 4     |

Points_____ + Bonus_____ = Total _____

2nd rating

Time:

| Poor | Fair | Good | Great |
|------|------|------|-------|
| 1    | 2    | 3    | 4     |

Points_____ + Bonus_____ = Total _____

*Third*, the student should receive feedback from the teacher. If the student reaches the goal, he or she should receive systematic reinforcement. If the teacher is concerned about accuracy in ratings, he or she may want to include a matching procedure for additional reinforcement.

*Finally*, teachers should systematically fade their presence in the process. If self-evaluation training is to be effective, the student must be able to self-evaluate independently of the teacher.

### Self-Reinforcement

In traditional behavior modification programs, the practitioner specifies the target behavior and delivers the reinforcers for performance of the behaviors. In many self-management packages, the child chooses a reinforcer and delivers the reinforcer following appropriate behavior. This is referred to as self-reinforcement. Research on the use of self-reinforcement is unclear. Some researchers have demonstrated that self-determined reinforcers can be as effective as, or even more effective than, teacher-controlled reinforcers (Hayes et al., 1985) while others contend that there is little empirical evidence to support the efficacy of self-reinforcement (Maag, 1989).

Self-reinforcement, like reinforcement delivered by teachers, must be delivered in a systematic and consistent manner. Research has indicated that initially reinforcement should be teacher managed and delivered. As the child progresses, teacher involvement should be decreased and the child's involvement increased. Wolery, Bailey, and Sugai (1988) offered the following guidelines for self-reinforcement:

1. The child should be fluent at accurate self-monitoring.
2. The child should be involved in setting the criteria for receiving reinforcement and selecting reinforcers.
3. Teachers should provide reinforcement for target behaviors displayed by the child, accurate matches between teacher and child data, and accurate determination by the child of whether the criteria for reinforcement were met.
4. Matching requirements and teacher evaluation should be faded over time.
5. Opportunities for the children to evaluate their performance, determine criteria for reinforcement, select reinforcers, and administer reinforcement should be systematically increased.
6. Naturally occurring reinforcers should be used throughout the process.

Other factors that contribute to the maintenance of desired behavior are continuous teacher praise, peer reinforcement for appropriate behavior, and accurate self-evaluation (Drabman, Spitalnik, & O'Leary, 1973).

While most self-management packages include self-reinforcement, some have investigated the effectiveness of self-punishment. In self-punishment, the student is taught to punish rather than reinforce his or her own behaviors. In several investigations (Humphrey, Karoly, & Kirschenbaum, 1978; Kaufman & O'Leary, 1972), the self-punishment procedure used was response cost in conjunction with a token economy. Humphrey et al. (1978) compared self-punishment to self-reinforcement. The study took place in a chaotic elementary classroom. A self-reinforcement system and a self-punishment system were compared. The students in the self-reinforcement condition reinforced themselves with tokens for accurate performance on reading assignments. The students in the self-punishment condition began each morning with tokens and removed them for inaccurate work or failure to complete work on time. The researchers found that under both conditions the rate of attempted reading assignments was accelerated and accuracy was maintained. The self-reinforcement condition, however, produced slightly better results.

*Teaching students to use self-reinforcement.* When teaching students to use self-reinforcement, three important factors must be addressed. First, the students must be able to monitor their behavior and evaluate their behavior. Students must be able to evaluate their performance, and the evaluation must be positive, before they can self-reinforce. Second, the teacher and student must decide if the self-reinforcement will be external (e.g., tokens, tangibles, preferred activities) or internal (self-praise). Finally the teacher and student should set a criterion level before the student can self-reinforce. Teachers should adhere to the principle of shaping successive approximations when having students use self-reinforcement (see Chapter 7).

## Application

According to Sugai and Lewis (1990), when teaching self-management skills to students, certain conditions must be maintained. During the preintervention phase of training, the student should be involved. Together, the teacher and student should

**TABLE 8.6 • Guidelines for Teaching Self-Management**

- The behavior to be self-managed should first be brought under external control so the student associates the appropriate behavior with reinforcement.
- Behavioral contracts for self-management can be used initially to provide structure.
- The student must have numerous opportunities to practice self-management with immediate feedback given.
- The student must be motivated to participate; this can be encouraged by involving the student in the procedure from the initial stages.
- To involve the student in the process and to increase motivation, teachers should record and post the student's behavioral performance.
- The teacher should periodically monitor the procedure and provide "booster" sessions if necessary.

develop the goals of the self-management program as well as the criteria and contingencies necessary to meet the goals. The recording instrument must be developed at this time and should be simple and easy to use. The student must be trained in the use of the recording procedure. The training should include direct instruction and numerous opportunities for practice. Prior to implementing the procedure, the child must be as fluent as possible in self-monitoring. If a self-reinforcement component will be used, the teacher should involve the child in selecting reinforcers. The student must then be trained in the use of the self-reinforcement procedure.

During the intervention phase of the procedure, a matching strategy is suggested. During this phase, the student is reinforced for appropriate behavior and accurate self-monitoring. Prompts should be provided to cue the child when to self-monitor and record (e.g., beeps on a recorder). The matching procedure, as well as the actual self-monitoring procedure, should be faded when the behavioral criteria are reached. Following the fading of the intervention, teachers should continue to collect data to ensure that behaviors continue at appropriate levels in all settings. If the target behaviors fall below criteria, the procedure may have to be reimplemented. Guidelines for increasing the effectiveness of self-management are included in Table 8.6.

## Problem-Solving Training

### Definition

Children are faced with conflicts, choices, and problems daily. Successful problem solving is necessary for effective coping and independence. The ability to confront and solve these problems successfully is an important factor in social and emotional adjustment. The inability to solve problems in an effective manner can lead to future social and emotional difficulties. Researchers have attempted to remediate difficulties in problem solving through formal training. The training represents a form of self-instruction to teach procedures for systematically approaching, evaluating, and solving interpersonal problems (Braswell & Kendall, 1988). Training in problem solving has been effective in reducing behavior problems and aggression, controlling impulsivity, and increasing appropriate social interaction (Harris, 1982).

## Theoretical Foundation and Research Base

Goldstein (1999) stated that problem solving typically involves a stepwise sequence of problem definition, identification of alternative solutions, choice of an optimal solution, implementation of the solution, and evaluation of the solution's effectiveness. D'Zurilla and Goldfried (1971) presented five steps that could be used to teach problem solving ability:

*Step 1:* Orientation to the problem. Help the child learn to recognize problems and to realize that one can deal with problems in appropriate ways.

*Step 2:* Definition of the problem. Clearly define the problem and any factors related to it.

*Step 3:* Generation of alternatives. The teacher and child should think of as many solutions to the problem as possible.

*Step 4:* Decision making. The teacher and the child should consider all alternatives generated in the previous step and devise a plan for implementing the chosen alternative.

*Step 5:* Verification. Implement the plan and monitor the results. If the problem is not solved, the teacher and child should start over at step 1.

The seminal work in problem solving was done by Spivak, Shure, and colleagues in the mid- to late 1970s. The training program developed by Spivak and Shure (1974) was called *interpersonal cognitive problem solving* (ICPS). The program was designed to teach children *how* to think, not *what* to think (Goldstein, 1999). Spivak and Shure believed that many teachers did not effectively teach problem solving. For example, in dealing with a young child who hits another child, teachers might typically respond with one of the following actions: (1) They might demand that the behavior stop ("Stop because I said so"). (2) They might explain why an action is inappropriate ("You might hurt your brother"). (3) They might try to help the child understand the effect of the situation ("That hurts your brother's feelings"). (4) They might isolate the child ("Stay in your room until you're ready to play appropriately"). These responses have serious limitations if the teacher's goal is to help the child develop effective ways of handling personal and interpersonal problems because the teacher does the thinking for the child.

In ICPS children are taught a problem-solving process rather than solutions to problems. The core of the program is six specific problem-solving skills that are taught to children. The ICPS attempts to train children to be competent in these six skill areas listed in Table 8.7.

Siegel and Spivak (1973) also developed an ICPS training program for older adolescents and adults. It is designed to teach basic problem-solving skills. The program teaches four problem-solving steps: (1) recognition of the problem, (2) definition of the problem, (3) alternative ways of solving the problem, and (4) deciding which solution is the best way to solve the problem.

### TABLE 8.7 • Guidelines for Teaching Problem Solving

1. *Alternative solution thinking:* The ability to generate different options or potential solutions to a problem
2. *Consequential thinking:* The ability to consider consequences that a behavior might lead to; this goes beyond the consideration of alternatives to the consideration of the consequences of potential solutions
3. *Causal thinking:* The ability to relate one event to another over time with regard to why a particular event happened or will happen
4. *Interpersonal sensitivity:* The ability to perceive that an interpersonal problem exists
5. *Means-ends thinking:* The step-by-step planning done in order to reach a given goal. Means-ends thinking involves insight, forethought, and the ability to consider alternative goals
6. *Perspective taking:* The ability of the individual to recognize and take into account the fact that different people have different motives and may take different actions

Goldstein (1999), drawing on the work done by Spivak and Shure, developed a problem-solving training program as part of the *Prepare Curriculum.* The *Prepare Curriculum* is a series of courses designed to teach adolescents and younger children prosocial competencies. It is specifically designed for youngsters demonstrating prosocial deficiencies that fall toward either end of a continuum defined at one extreme by chronic aggressiveness, antisocial behavior, and juvenile delinquency and at the other extreme by chronic withdrawal, asocial behavior, and social isolation. The problem-solving course is taught to groups of students over an 8-week period. Group structure is provided by a set of rules and procedures explained at the beginning of a session. During each session, a poster that shows the problem-solving process being covered during that session is displayed. The program also uses a "problem log." Students fill out the problem log. The logs are to be an accurate record of any problems that students encounter. The purpose of the problem log is to help students determine what their problem situations are and to assist them to begin thinking about ways of handling the problems. An example of a problem diary similar to Goldstein's problem log is provided in Figure 8.5.

Problem logs are also used in role plays. Skills taught in the program include the following:

- *Stop and think.* Students in the program are taught that when a problem is encountered, they must stop and think or they might decide too quickly. They are to use this time to think of alternate ways to handle the problem.
- *Problem identification.* Once the students realize a problem exists and have stopped to think, they have to state the problem clearly and specifically.
- *Gathering information from their own perspective.* Students have to decide how they see a problem and gather information about the problem before acting. If all the information is not available, trainees are taught to ask for it.

**FIGURE 8.5.** Problem diary

**Problem Diary**

What was the problem? Describe the problem.

What did you do to stop the problem?

Did your choice solve the problem?

How would you rate your solution (circle one)?

Poor        Fair        Good        Great

How will you handle this problem if it happens again?

- *Gathering information from others' perspectives.* Students learn the necessity of looking at situations from other people's points of view.
- *Alternatives.* Students are taught that to make a good choice in any situation requires more than one way of acting.
- *Evaluating consequences and outcomes.* Once trainees are taught to consider a number of alternatives, they are told they must consider the consequences of each. Once a decision is made, it must be evaluated.

In a review of research on interpersonal problem-solving training, Coleman, Wheeler, and Webber (1993) found that although researchers were generally successful in demonstrating cognitive gains as a result of the training, they were far less successful in demonstrating generalization. The authors stated that the generalization problems called into question the basic premise of problem-solving training—that students would rely on the trained skills in real-life situations. Based on their review, the authors offered recommendations for teachers in using problem-solving training. Their recommendations were as follows: (a) try to individualize training by including only those students who demonstrate problem-solving deficits, (b) assess the quality and quantity of alternative solutions that students generate as a result of the training, (c) pair problem-solving training with social skills training and other behavioral interventions to remediate problem-solving deficits, and (d) evaluate the success of the program by choosing appropriate outcome measures such as problem-solving tasks, behavior ratings, and behavior observations.

### Application

The work of D'Zurilla and Goldfried (1971), Spivak and Shure (1974), and Goldstein (1999) present useful models teachers can use to teach problem solving to students. The following guidelines based on the work of these researchers should be followed when using cognitive behavior modification to teach children problem-solving skills.

First, the teacher should direct instruction to teach the fundamental concepts of problem solving. We cannot assume the students will pick up these important skills by merely observing others. Important concepts should be presented using lecture, discussion, examples, and nonexamples. When appropriate, role-playing situations involving problem solving should be part of instruction. Additionally, students should be reinforced for appropriate participation in classroom activities.

Second, whenever possible, problem situations should be taken from students' real-life experiences. In this way the instruction is much more likely to be socially valid. This means that the situations will be more meaningful for the students because they are congruent with the their social setting and age. The use of a problem diary can be used as a springboard to class discussions (see Figure 8.5). Having students brainstorm during group discussions can also be used to generate lists of potential problems.

Third, problem-solving training should include the following components: (a) recognizing the problem, (b) defining the problem and the goal, (c) generating alternative solutions, (d) evaluating the solutions, and (e) making a plan to solve the problem. This can be done individually or during group discussions. Also discuss the relevance of problem solving for students' lives.

Fourth, provide your students with numerous opportunities to practice problem solving. This should be done in and outside of the classroom (e.g., home setting).

Finally, be a model of effective problem solving. When a problem arises, deal with it in an effective manner and share your methods of arriving at a solution with the students. Additionally, if you observe students using effective problem-solving strategies outside of the classroom, reinforce them.

## Anger-Control Training

### Definition

In anger-control training, children are taught to inhibit or control anger and aggressive behavior through self-instructions. Three well-known anger training procedures are those developed by Novaco (1975), Feindler and her colleagues (Feindler & Fremouw, 1983; Feindler, Marriott, & Iwata, 1984), Goldstein and Glick (1987), and Goldstein (1999). These programs train children to respond to internal or external provocations with anger-control procedures rather than anger and aggression.

## Theoretical Foundation and Research base

Novaco defined anger arousal as an affective stress reaction. He stated:

> [A]nger arousal is a response to perceived environmental demands—most commonly, aversive psychosocial events. Anger arousal results from particular appraisal of aversive events. External circumstances provoke anger only as mediated by their meaning to the individual. (1975, pp. 252–253)

Novaco noted the importance of the individual's appraisal of events. Because Novaco believed that anger was created, influenced, and maintained by self-statements, he designed a program based on Meichenbaum's self-instructional training. The purpose of the training was to develop an individual's ability to respond appropriately to stressful events. The goals of the program were to (a) prevent maladaptive anger from occurring, (b) enable the individual to regulate arousal when provocation occurred, and (c) provide the person with the skills to manage the provocation.

Anger-control intervention consisted of three stages: (1) cognitive preparation, (2) skill acquisition, and (3) application training. In the cognitive preparation phase, trainees were educated about anger arousal and its determinants, the identification of circumstances that trigger anger, the positive and negative functions of anger, and anger-control techniques as coping strategies. In the skill acquisition phase, trainees learned cognitive and behavioral coping skills. Trainees were taught to recognize anger and to use alternative coping strategies. The self-instructional element of training was emphasized in this phase. In the final phase, application training, the trainee practiced the skills taught through role playing and homework assignments.

The self-instructional component of this intervention consisted of self-statements in the four stages of the provocation sequence: (1) preparation for provocation, (2) impact and confrontation, (3) coping with arousal, and (4) reflecting on the provocation. Examples of self-instructions are listed in Table 8.8.

In the late 1970s and early 1980s, Feindler and her colleagues researched and refined the techniques of anger-control training. In a series of investigations, support was provided for the cognitive preparation and skill acquisition phases and self-instructional training developed by Novaco. The investigations refined the three processes of Novaco's training (i.e., cognitive preparation, skill acquisition, and application training) to include five sequences to be taught to students:

1. *Cues:* The physical signals of anger arousal
2. *Triggers:* The events and internal appraisals of those events that serve as provocations
3. *Reminders:* Novaco's self-instructional statements that were used to reduce anger arousal
4. *Reducers:* Techniques such as deep breathing and pleasant imagery that could be used along with reminders to reduce anger arousal
5. *Self-evaluation:* The opportunity to self-reinforce or self-correct

### TABLE 8.8 • Self-Instructions for an Anger-Control Training Program

**Preparing for provocation**

This could be a rough situation, but I know how to handle it. I can work out a plan to deal with this problem.

Easy does it; stick to the issues and don't take it personally.

There won't be any need for an argument. I know what to do.

**Impact and confrontation**

As long as I keep my cool, I'm in control of the situation.

I don't need to prove myself.

Don't make more out of this than you have to.

There is no point in getting mad. Think of what you have to do.

Look for positives and don't jump to conclusions.

**Coping with arousal**

My muscles are getting tight. Relax and slow things down.

Time to take a deep breath.

He probably wants me to get angry, but I'm going to deal with it constructively.

**Subsequent reflection—Conflict unresolved**

Forget about the aggravation. Thinking about it only makes you upset. Try to shake it off. Remember relaxation. It's a lot better than anger.

Don't take it personally. It's probably not as serious as I think.

**Subsequent reflection—Conflict resolved**

I handled that one pretty well. That's doing a good job.

I could have gotten more upset than it was worth.

My pride can get me into trouble, but I'm doing better at this all the time.

I actually got through that without getting angry.

Goldstein and Glick (1987) added to the work of Meichenbaum, Novaco, and Feindler in developing *Anger Control Training*. The goals of anger-control training were to teach children and adolescents to understand what caused them to become angry and aggressive and to master anger reduction techniques. According to Goldstein:

*Many youngsters believe that in many situations they have no choice: The only way for them to respond is with aggression. Although they may perceive situations in this way, it is the goal of Anger Control Training to give them the skills necessary to make a choice. By learning what causes them to be angry and by learning to use a series of anger reduction techniques, participating trainees will become more able to stop their almost "automatic" aggressive responses long enough to consider constructive alternatives. (1999, p. 256)*

Anger-control training consists of modeling, role playing, and performance feedback. Group leaders describe and model the anger-control techniques and conflict situations in which they may be used. In role playing, the students take part in role plays in which they practice the just modeled techniques. Role plays are of actual provocative encounters provided by the students. Each role-playing session is followed by a brief performance feedback period. In this phase the group leaders point out to the child involved in the role playing how well he or she used the technique. Group leaders also provide reinforcement following role plays.

A unique aspect of the program used in the role-play situations is the "hassle log." The hassle log is a structured questionnaire that students fill out on actual provocative encounters. The trainees have to answer questions concerning where they were when the hassle occurred, what happened, who else was involved, what the trainees did, how they handled themselves, and how angry they were. The log is constructed so that even young children can fill it out; written responses are not required and children simply check off options on the form. The trainees complete a form for each provocative encounter, whether they handle it in an appropriate manner or not. The advantages of the hassle log are that it provides accurate pictures of actual provocative encounters that occur, it helps trainees to learn about what makes them angry and how they handle themselves, and it provides role-playing material. An example of a similar anger diary is shown in Figure 8.6.

During the 10-week training period, the group leaders also teach (1) the A-B-Cs of aggressive behavior (A—What led up to the behavior? B—What did you do? C—What were the consequences?); (2) how to identify cues and triggers; (3) the use of reminders and anger reducers; (4) the importance of thinking ahead (the consequences of anger); and (5) the nature of the angry behavior cycle (identifying anger-provoking behavior and changing it).

It is difficult to draw reliable conclusions about the effectiveness of interventions designed to modify behavioral responses to anger without repeating techniques used in previous investigations. Lochman and his colleagues (see e.g., Lochman, 1985; Lochman, 1992; Lochman, Burch, Curry, & Lampron, 1984; Lochman, Coie, Underwood, & Terry, 1993; Lochman & Curry, 1986; Lochman & Lampron, 1988; Lochman, Lampron, Gemmer, Harris, & Wyckoff, 1989) have begun to build the necessary foundation that enables practitioners to make informed decisions about programming and provides researchers with sufficient information to replicate investigations.

**FIGURE 8.6.** Anger diary

---

**Anger Diary**

Describe the problem that led to your anger.


What did you do?


Did your anger solve the problem?


How would you rate your anger control (circle)

Poor        Fair        Good        Great


How will you handle your anger next time?

---

A study by Etscheidt (1991) examined the effectiveness of the anger control training program developed by Lochman, Nelson, and Sims (1981) in reducing aggressive behavior and increasing self-control in 30 adolescents with behavioral disorders. In the program students were taught to use a five-step sequential strategy in problem situations. The steps were as follows:

*Step 1.* Motor cue/impulse delay - stop and think before you act; cue yourself.

*Step 2.* Problem definition - say exactly what the problem is.

*Step 3.* Generation of alternatives - think of as many solutions as you can.

*Step 4.* Consideration of consequences - think ahead to what might happen.

*Step 5.* Implementation - when you have a solution, try it!

Results indicated that students participating in the training had significantly fewer aggressive behaviors and were rated as having greater self-control than the control group. Although offered, incentives did not seem to enhance the effectiveness of the training program. The author concluded that the program did have a positive effect on the behavior of students and that maintenance and generalization of behavior change should be a component of any anger control training program.

Smith, Siegel, O'Conner, and Thomas (1994) investigated the effectiveness of an anger-control training program in reducing the angry and aggressive behaviors of students with behavior problems. Students were taught a cognitive behavioral strategy called ZIPPER. ZIPPER is a mnemonic for Zip your mouth, Identify the problem, Pause, Put yourself in charge, Explore choices, Reset. The strategy was directly taught to students, modeled, role-played, and rehearsed. Additionally, the instructors gained the students' commitment to using the strategy outside of the training. Results indicated that the students were able to learn the strategy and that the intervention resulted in a decreased level of the targeted behaviors. Data on maintenance indicated that the students were able to maintain the decreased levels of anger and aggression over time. The students enjoyed learning the strategy, and the teacher and paraprofessional in the classroom were very satisfied with the procedure. There was also some indication of generalization—a lunchroom monitor noted that the trained students seemed less angry and aggressive and were able to get along with other students.

## Application

Students with problem behavior often have difficulty controlling their anger. Teaching students to control anger will be extremely valuable to their long-term adjustment. The work of Novaco (1975), Feindler et al. (1984), and Goldstein (1999) presents important models teachers can use to teach anger control to students. The following guidelines based on the work of these researchers should be followed when using cognitive behavior modification to teach students anger-control skills.

First, the teacher should direct instruction to teach the fundamental concepts of anger-control. Important concepts in controlling anger should be presented using lecture, discussion, and role-playing situations. Additionally, students should be reinforced for appropriate participation in classroom activities.

Second, whenever possible, real-life situations involving students' anger should be taken from students' experiences. In this way the instruction is much more likely to be socially valid. This means that the situations will be more meaningful for the students because they are congruent with the their social setting and age. The use of an anger diary can generate individual or class discussions (see Figure 8.6).

Third, anger-control training should include the following components: (a) recognizing anger (e.g., cues and triggers), (b) coping with anger (e.g., using reminders and reducers), (c) generating alternative solutions to anger, (d) practicing self-evaluation. This can be done individually or during group discussions. Also discuss the relevance of anger control for students' lives.

Fourth, provide your students with numerous opportunities to discuss anger control. Because anger control should be practiced in the school and home setting, students' parents should be aware of, and participate in, their child's anger-control program.

Finally, be a model of effective anger control. When a problem arises that could lead to an angry confrontation, manage the situation in an effective manner. Moreover, share your methods of arriving at a solution with the students. Additionally, if you observe students using effective anger-control strategies outside of the classroom, reinforce them.

## Alternate Response Training

### *Definition*

In alternate response training a child is taught an alternative or competing response that interferes with opportunities for an undesirable response to be emitted (Wolery et al., 1988). If an alternative response already exists in the child's repertoire, it can be strengthened as the child is taught to use the alternative behavior. In using alternate response training, a child must first be taught to self-monitor.

Relaxation training procedures designed to relieve stress and calm children have been investigated by researchers as an alternative response procedure. A widely used relaxation training procedure is progressive muscle relaxation (Maag, 1989). The training involves having children tense and relax muscles while focusing on the relaxation of particular parts of the body. Eventually the child focuses on relaxing the entire body. Muscle relaxation is a form of alternate response training that has been used to decrease disruptions and aggression and increase social skills and academic performance.

### *Theoretical Foundation and Research Base*

Robin, Schneider, and Dolnick (1976) developed an alternate response intervention called the *turtle technique.* The turtle technique is a procedure that was developed to teach aggressive students to manage their aggressive impulses. The procedure consists of teaching the students to pull their arms and legs close to their bodies, put their heads on their desks, and imagine that they are turtles withdrawing into their shells. The children were taught to do this when they perceived that a provocative situation was about to occur, they felt frustrated or angry, or a teacher or classmate called out "turtle." The children were also taught a muscle relaxation procedure. Once children mastered this technique, they were taught to relax while doing the turtle. Eventually, the children learn to relax and imagine withdrawing from the situation rather than actually going into the turtle position. Robin et al. (1976) found that children who had been taught the procedure behaved less aggressively. Morgan and Jenson (1988) stated that the turtle technique and other similar approaches are worthy of consideration in selecting interventions.

Knapczyk (1988) reduced aggressive behaviors by students in regular and special class settings by using alternative social response training. Participants in the study were two male junior high school students in special education programs. Both had been referred because of aggressive behavior. The treatment involved training the students in social skills that could be used as alternatives to the aggressive behavior. The students learned alternate responses through modeling and rehearsal. Videotapes were prepared and shown to the students that provided examples of events that often led to aggressive behavior. The tapes had two male students (of high social status in the school) demonstrating alternative responses to the aggression. One of the actors played the part of the participant. In response to a particular event, the student actor would first simulate aggressive behaviors. The student would then demonstrate an acceptable alternative response rather than the aggressive response. The other student actor represented the reactions of peers. The teacher and participant viewed the videotapes together. Following a discussion, the participant was asked to demonstrate the appropriate behavior and provide additional alternatives. Results indicated that the treatments reduced the level of aggressive behaviors and led to an increase in peer-initiated interactions.

## Application

When instructing students to use alternate responses to anger or other maladaptive behaviors, teachers must address three important factors. First, the students must be able to monitor their behavior. Specifically they must be able to recognize when the behavior that the teacher hopes to eliminate is occurring. For example, students must recognize when they are becoming angry (e.g., stomach muscles tighten, fists clench). Teaching self-monitoring, therefore, is an essential prerequisite to alternate response training. Second, after the student has become adept at self-monitoring, the student is taught a specific technique that will compete with the maladaptive behavior. For example, Robin et al. (1976) taught students to respond when they were getting angry by imagining they were turtles pulling into their shells so that they could not be bothered. It is important that this technique is directly taught to students, that the teacher models the specific technique, and that students are given many opportunities to practice the procedure. When the technique is used appropriately, the teacher must reinforce the student. A classroom example of alternative response training is presented in Classroom Application 8.2.

## Attribution Retraining

### Definition

The cognitive-behavioral procedure of attribution retraining is based on attribution theory. Attribution theory posits that individuals seek causes for events in their environment and that these perceived causes influence subsequent behavior (Palmer & Stowe, 1989). Performance attributions can be influenced by a child's current performance, his or her history of performance, and the performance of others. A number of researchers have examined the consequences of repeated failure on a child's attributions and the subsequent effects on the child's motivation and achievement (Palmer & Stowe, 1989). Attribution theorists believe that children with positive attributions impute successes to their effort and ability and failure to a lack of effort. When children experience repeated failure, however, they may impute failure to their lack of ability and success to good luck. As a result of these attributions, the child becomes less likely to attempt or persist at accomplishing tasks. This lower level of persistence and effort can lead to additional failures.

### Theoretical Foundations and Research Base

Attribution retraining attempts to replace negative attributions with positive attributions and thereby increase task persistence. The positive attributions are effort-oriented statements concerning students' successes and failures (Maag, 1989).

## Classroom Application 8.2

## Alternate Response Training

Jerry is a fourth-grade student in a self-contained classroom for children with learning disabilities. Jerry also has problems controlling his temper. His temper tantrums frequently follow requests to do academic work. The special education teacher had implemented a point system with a response cost component in an attempt to reduce the tantrums. The program had succeeded in reducing the tantrums but did not eliminate them. Because the tantrums were so disruptive to the class and Jerry became so upset following them, the teacher referred the problem to Mr. Cleveland, the school behavior specialist.

Mr. Cleveland observed Jerry at various times during the next week. He was present during two of Jerry's tantrums. He observed that prior to a tantrum Jerry grew tense, grimaced, and frequently chewed on his fingernails. This behavior would escalate into tantrums in which Jerry would swear, throw books, damage objects, etc.

In a conversation with the special education teacher and Mr. Cleveland, Jerry expressed frustration with his tantrums. He said he didn't like to "blow up" but he couldn't help it. He also said that the tantrums made it hard for him to learn, that kids were afraid of him, and that his parents were upset about Jerry's violent temper. Jerry also said he wanted to be able to control his behavior.

Because Jerry was motivated to change his behavior and the tantrum behavior had been controlled with external management procedures, Mr. Cleveland felt that a cognitive behavioral intervention might be effective. He chose to try a form of alternate response training with Jerry.

Jerry was first taught to recognize when a tantrum was about to occur by becoming aware of the tension in his body and his angry feelings. The next step was to teach him an alternate response to the tension and anger. Together Jerry and Mr. Cleveland decided on a technique using deep breathing, self-instruction, and visualization. When Jerry felt angry and tense, he was to fold his arms on his desk, put his head on his arms, breathe deeply 10 times, and say to himself "stop and think." While saying this to himself, he was to think of a red stop sign with the words "stop and think" on it. Jerry was also told to go through this procedure when the teacher told him to stop and think. If Jerry performed the procedure correctly and didn't have a tantrum, he received social praise from the teacher. Following the procedure, the teacher was to reissue the original request if it was an academic or behavioral direction.

Within a few weeks of using the procedure, Jerry significantly reduced his temper tantrums. The instances of the teacher having to remind Jerry to stop and think also were almost entirely eliminated. Jerry felt more in control of his behavior.

Dweck (1975) investigated attributional retraining with children who had difficulty solving math problems. The children were taught to make an effort-oriented statement, such as "Failure makes you try harder," when working on math problems. Results indicated that the children persisted longer on the problems. Borkowski, Weyhing, and Turner (1986) stated that attributions can also influence a child's use of learning strategies. Schunk (1983) indicated that attribution retraining may not work when a child has a specific skill deficit. However, attribution retraining is more likely to be successful when the child is not using the skills that he or she possesses.

### Application

Attribution retraining usually consists of two phases (Licht & Kistner, 1986). In the first phase, the child is set up to experience some degree of failure. The failure is not severe and might consist of a few problems among a set that are too difficult for the child. In the second phase, the child is taught to make statements that attribute the failures to insufficient effort. According to Licht and Kistner (1986), the following is of crucial importance when teaching attributional statements: The teacher must convey to the children that increased effort leads to success rather than simply that they are not trying hard enough. It is also important that the child in attribution retraining does experience some success. Self-statements that "increased effort will lead to increased success" will be more readily accepted when the child does experience some success. If the child does experience success, this will validate the self-statements. Attribution retraining is likely to be successful if the child believes that the use of the strategy will contribute to future success.

Concerns have been raised about having children attribute their failures to lack of effort because this might convey to the children that they are lazy. Anderson and Jennings (1980) suggested that children be taught to attribute their difficulties to ineffective task strategies. This would lead to less blame on the child's part. Licht and Kistner (1986) have suggested that attribution retraining be coupled with problem solving and strategy training. It might be advisable for the teacher to teach attributional statements and strategies as an integrated approach.

## DEVELOPMENT AND GENERALIZATION OF CBM PROGRAMS

Developing cognitive-behavioral programs requires more than choosing a strategy and following a program of implementation. Harris (1982) outlined a three-stage process for constructing and implementing cognitive-behavioral interventions.

The first stage is *task analysis*. In this stage the teacher must determine the cognitions and strategies necessary for successful performance in whatever is being taught. In determining the necessary strategies, the teacher might perform the task him- or herself and note the strategies used or observe those who do well on a task to determine necessary strategies. According to Meichenbaum (1976), determination of strategies involved in a task, the production of appropriate strategies, and the application and monitoring of these strategies are important considerations.

The second stage is *learner analysis.* In analyzing the learner, a variety of characteristics (e.g., age, cognitive capabilities, language development, learning ability, initial knowledge state, etc.) must be considered. These characteristics will influence the development of the training procedure. It is very important that the cognitive-behavioral training procedures and requirements be matched to the learner's characteristics if the training is to be successful.

The third stage is *development* and *implementation.* The teacher must establish the goals of training. The next step is to select the cognitive-behavioral procedures that are appropriate given the results of the task and learner analysis. In designing the intervention, the teacher must tailor the learning activities to the desired goals (Brown, Campione, & Day, 1981). Following the development of the cognitive-behavioral procedure, the teacher initiates training.

Previous chapters have documented powerful behavioral strategies that have been used successfully by teachers to modify behaviors in children and adolescents. The effects of behavioral change programs, however, often are not generalized to other settings or maintained in treatment settings when the intervention procedures are withdrawn (Kerr & Nelson, 2001). Morgan and Jenson (1988) referred to self-management strategies as being among the more promising strategies to facilitate generalization. When behaviors are under external control by the teacher, the behaviors might not be controlled in situations and settings in which the teacher is not able to apply the external control procedures. When persons are able to manage their behaviors, these behaviors will be more likely to last and to carry over to different situations and settings, even without external control by teachers. However, in a review of self-management strategies, Nelson, Smith, Young, and Dodd (1991) found that treatment effects of self-management procedures do not automatically generalize. They suggest that treatment effects will generalize if generalization is systematically programmed.

Kaplan (1995) offered several suggestions that could be used by teachers to encourage children to use CBM strategies outside of the training environment. The following is a list of some of the suggestions:

1. *Model the strategies.* The teacher should model the strategies taught when appropriate. Students should be able to observe the strategies in action. Teachers should share how they are using the strategies to help modify their behavior.

2. *Teach the strategies to mastery.* The teacher should teach the skills and subskills in the CBM strategy to mastery. Periodic assessments may be necessary to determine if a child has achieved mastery. When mastery is achieved, a child is much more likely to use the strategy. According to Kaplan (1995), a child has achieved mastery of a strategy when he or she is both fast and accurate in its use.

3. *Reinforce appropriate use of strategies.* Whenever the practitioner observes a child using a CBM strategy outside of the training context, it is important that the teacher reinforce him or her. Teachers should also encourage the child's peers to reinforce appropriate behavior.

4. *Program for generalization by giving homework assignments.* Give homework assignments that will require the CBM strategies to be used in environments outside of the training context.

5. *Discuss the relevance of each strategy when it is taught.* Students must be taught how the particular strategy is relevant to them and their situations. An effective way to do this is for the teacher to discuss the relevance of the strategy prior to training.

## SUMMARY

In this chapter we have examined a number of interventions that fall under the general category of cognitive behavior modification. The review was not exhaustive but only meant to give the reader a flavor of the number of different strategies available for affecting the teacher's desired outcomes. Cognitive-behavioral strategies have been used to modify behavior, facilitate academic performance, train problem-solving ability, and foster self-control. The major aim of cognitive-behavioral training is to teach children to be their own agents of change, in control of their behavior and learning.

## DISCUSSION QUESTIONS

1. What is cognitive behavior modification? List and explain the three basic assumptions and goals of CBM.
2. Discuss some advantages of teaching individuals to manage their own behavior using CBM.
3. Discuss problem-solving and anger-control training.
4. Discuss the three components of self-management training: self-monitoring, self-evaluation, and self-reinforcement.
5. List and explain guidelines for increasing the effectiveness of self-monitoring strategies.
6. Discuss procedures for encouraging the generalization of CBM strategies.

## REFERENCES

Alberto, P. A., & Troutman, C. A. (1999). *Applied behavior analysis for teachers* (5th ed.). Upper Saddle River, NJ: Merrill/Prentice Hall.

Anderson, C. A., & Jennings, D. L. (1980). When experiences of failure promote expectations of success: The impact of attributing failure to ineffective strategies. *Journal of Personality, 48,* 393–407.

Baer, D. M. (1984). Does research on self-control need more control? *Analysis and Intervention in Developmental Disabilities, 4,* 211–284.

Bandura, A. (1977). *Social learning theory.* Upper Saddle River, NJ: Prentice Hall.

Bandura, A. (1978). The self system in reciprocal determinism. *American Psychologist, 33,* 344–358.

Beck, A. T. (1976). *Cognitive therapy and emotional disorders.* New York: International Universities Press.

Borkowski, J. G., Weyhing, R. S., & Turner, L. A. (1986). Attributional retraining and the teaching of strategies. *Exceptional Children, 53,* 130–137.

Braswell, L., & Kendall, P. C. (1988). Cognitive-behavioral methods with children. In K. S. Dobson (Ed.), *Handbook of cognitive-behavioral therapies* (pp. 167–213). New York: Guilford.

Broden, M., Hall, R. V., & Mitts, B. (1971). The effect of self-recording of the classroom behavior of two eighth-grade students. *Journal of Applied Behavior Analysis, 4,* 191–199.

Brown, A. L., Campione, J. C., & Day, J. D. (1981). Learning to learn: On training students to learn from text. *Educational Researcher, 10,* 14–21.

Burkell, J., Schneider, B., & Pressley, M. (1990). Mathematics. In M. P. Pressley & Associates (Eds.), *Cognitive strategy instruction that really improves children's academic performance* (pp. 147–177). Cambridge, MA: Brookline Books.

Camp, B., Blom, G., Herbert, F., & Van Doornick, W. (1977). "Think aloud": A program for developing self-control in young aggressive boys. *Journal of Abnormal Child Psychology, 5,* 157–169.

Cole, C. L. (1987). Self-management. In C. R. Reynolds & L. Mann (Eds.), *Encyclopedia of special education* (pp. 1404–1405). New York: John Wiley & Sons.

Coleman, M., Wheeler, L., & Webber, J. (1993). Research on interpersonal problem-solving training: A review. *Remedial and Special Education 14,* 25–37.

Cooper, J. O., Heron, T. E., & Heward, W. L. (1987). *Applied behavior analysis.* Upper Saddle River, NJ: Merrill/Prentice Hall.

Craighead, W. F. (1982). A brief clinical history of cognitive-behavior therapy with children. *School Psychology Review, 11,* 5–13.

DiGangi, S. A., & Maag, J. W. (1992). A component analysis of self-management training with behaviorally disordered youth. *Behavioral Disorders, 17,* 281–290.

Drabman, R. S., Spitalnik, R., & O'Leary, K. D. (1973). Teaching self-control to disruptive children. *Journal of Abnormal Psychology, 82,* 10–16.

Dweck, C. S. (1975). The role of expectations and attributions in the alleviation of learned helplessness. *Journal of Personality and Social Psychology, 31,* 674–685.

D'Zurilla, T. J., & Goldfried, M. R. (1971). Problem solving and behavior modification. *Journal of Abnormal Psychology, 78,* 107–126.

Ellis, A. (1973). Rational-emotive therapy. In R. Corsini (Ed.), *Current psychotherapies* (pp. 313–323). Itasca, IL: F. E. Peacock.

Etscheidt, S. (1991). Reducing aggressive behavior and improving self-control: A cognitive-behavioral training program for behaviorally disordered adolescents. *Behavioral Disorders, 16,* 107–115.

Feindler, E. L., & Fremouw, W. J. (1983). Stress inoculation training for adolescent anger problems. In D. Meichenbaum & M. E. Jaremko (Eds.), *Stress reduction and prevention* (pp. 434–462). New York: Plenum.

Feindler, E. L., Marriott, S. A., & Iwata, M. (1984). Group anger control training for junior high school delinquents. *Cognitive Therapy and Research, 8,* 299–311.

Goldstein, A. P. (1999). *The prepare curriculum: Teaching prosocial competencies* (rev. ed.). Champaign, IL: Research Press.

Goldstein, A. P., & Glick, B. (1987). *Aggression replacement training: A comprehensive intervention for aggressive youth.* Champaign, IL: Research Press.

Graham, S., & Harris, K. H. (1985). Improving learning disabled students' composition skills: Self-control strategy training. *Learning Disability Quarterly, 8,* 27–36.

Gross, A. M., & Wojnilower, D. A. (1984). Self-directed behavior change in children: Is it self-directed? *Behavior Therapy, 15,* 501–514.

Harris, K. R. (1982). Cognitive-behavior modification: Application with exceptional students. *Focus on Exceptional Children, 15,* 1–16.

Hayes, S. C., Rosenfarb, I., Wulfert, E., Munt, E. D., Korn, Z., & Zettle, R. D. (1985). Self-reinforcement effects: An artifact of social standard setting? *Journal of Applied Behavior Analysis, 18,* 201–214.

Homme, L. E. (1965). Perspectives in Psychology: XXIV. Control of coverants, the operants of the mind. *Psychological Record, 15,* 501–511.

Hughes, J. N. (1988). Cognitive behavior therapy. In L. Mann & C. Reynolds (Eds.), *The encyclopedia of special education* (pp. 354–355). New York: John Wiley & Sons.

Humphrey, L. L., Karoly, P., & Kirschenbaum, D. S. (1978). Self-management in the classroom: Self-imposed response cost versus self-reward. *Behavior Therapy, 9,* 592–601.

Jenson, A. (1966). The role of verbal mediation in mental development. *Journal of Genetic Psychology, 118,* 39–70.

Kanfer, F. H., & Karoly, P. (1972). Self-control: A behavioristic excursion into the lion's den. *Behavior Therapy, 3,* 398–416.

Kaplan, J. S. (1995). *Beyond behavior modification: A cognitive-behavioral approach to behavior management in the schools* (3rd ed.). Austin, TX: Pro-Ed.

Kaufman, S. K., & O'Leary, K. D. (1972). Reward, cost, and self-evaluation procedures for disruptive adolescents in a psychiatric hospital school. *Journal of Applied Behavior Analysis, 5,* 293–309.

Kazdin, A. E. (1982). Current developments and research issues in cognitive-behavioral interventions: A commentary. *School Psychology Review, 11,* 75–82.

Kendall, P. C., & Hollon, S. D. (1979). *Cognitive-behavioral interventions: Therapy, research and procedures.* New York: Academic Press.

Kerr, M. M., & Nelson, C. M. (2001). *Strategies for managing behavior problems in the classroom* (4th ed.). Upper Saddle River, NJ: Merrill/Prentice Hall.

Knapczyk, D. R. (1988). Reducing aggressive behaviors in special and regular class settings by training alternative social responses. *Behavioral Disorders, 14,* 27–39.

Licht, B. G., & Kistner, J. A. (1986). Motivational problems of learning disabled children: Individual differences and their implications for treatment. In J. K. Torgeson & B. Y. L. Wong (Eds.), *Psychological and educational perspectives on learning disabilities* (pp. 225–249). New York: Academic Press.

Lloyd, J. W. (1980). Academic instruction and cognitive behavior modification: The need for attack strategy training. *Exceptional Education Quarterly, 8,* 53–63.

Lochman, J. E. (1985). Effects of different treatment lengths in cognitive behavioral interventions with aggressive boys. *Child Psychiatry and Human Development, 16,* 45–56.

Lochman, J. E. (1992). Cognitive behavioral intervention with aggressive boys: Three-year follow-up and preventative effects. *Journal of Consulting and Clinical Psychology, 60,* 426–432.

Lochman, J. E., Burch, P. R., Curry, J. F., & Lampron, L. B. (1984). Treatment and generalization effects of cognitive-behavioral and goal-setting interventions with aggressive boys. *Journal of Consulting and Clinical Psychology, 52,* 915–916.

Lochman, J. E., Coie, J. D., Underwood, M. K., & Terry, R. (1993). Effectiveness of a social relations intervention program for aggressive and nonaggressive, rejected children. *Journal of Consulting and Clinical Psychiatry, 61,* 1053–1058.

Lochman, J. E., & Curry, J. F. (1986). Effects of social problem-solving training and self-instruction training with aggressive boys. *Journal of Clinical Child Psychology, 15,* 159–164.

Lochman, J. E., & Lampron, L. B. (1988). Cognitive-behavioral interventions for aggressive boys: Seven-month follow-up effects. *Journal of Child and Adolescent Psychotherapy, 5,* 15–23.

Lochman, J. E., Lampron, L. B., Gemmer, T. C., Harris, R., & Wyckoff, G. M. (1989). Teacher consultation and cognitive-behavioral interventions with aggressive boys. *Psychology in the Schools, 26,* 179–188.

Lochman, J. E., Nelson, W. M., & Sims, J. (1981). A cognitive-behavioral program for use with aggressive children. *Journal of Clinical Child Psychology, 19,* 146–148.

Luria, A. (1961). *The role of speech in the regulation of normal and abnormal behaviors.* New York: Basic Books.

Maag, J. W. (1989). Use of cognitive mediation strategies for social skills training: Theoretical and conceptual issues. In R. B. Rutherford, Jr., & S. A. DiGangi (Eds.), *Severe behavior disorders of children and youth* (Vol. 12, pp. 87–100). Reston, VA: Council for Children with Behavioral Disorders.

Meichenbaum, D. (1976). Cognitive factors as determinants of learning disabilities: A cognitive functional approach. In R. M. Knights & D. J. Baker (Eds.), *The neuropsychology of learning disorders: Theoretical approaches* (pp. 216–282). Baltimore, MD: University Park Press.

Meichenbaum, D. (1977). *Cognitive behavior modification: An integrative approach.* New York: Plenum Press.

Meichenbaum, D. (1980). Cognitive behavior modification with exceptional students: A promise yet unfulfilled. *Exceptional Education Quarterly, 8,* 83–88.

Meichenbaum, D., & Asarnow, J. (1979). Cognitive-behavioral modification and metacognitive development: Implications for the classroom. In P. C. Kendall & S. D. Hollon (Eds.), *Cognitive-behavioral interventions: Theory, research, and procedures* (pp. 11–35). New York: Academic Press.

Meichenbaum, D., & Goodman, T. J. (1971). Training impulsive children to talk to themselves: A means of developing self control. *Journal of Abnormal Psychology, 77,* 115–126.

Meyers, A. W., Cohen, R., & Schlester, R. (1989). A cognitive-behavioral approach to education: Adopting a broad-based perspective. In J. N. Hughes & R. J. Hall (Eds.), *Cognitive behavioral psychology in the schools: A comprehensive handbook* (pp. 62–84). New York: Guilford.

Morgan, D. P., & Jenson, W. R. (1988). *Teaching behaviorally disordered students: Preferred practices.* Upper Saddle River, NJ: Merrill/Prentice Hall.

Nelson, J. R., Smith, D. J., & Colvin, G. (1995). The effects of a peer-mediated self-evaluation procedure on the recess behavior of students with behavior problems. *Remedial and Special Education, 16,* 117–126.

Nelson, J. R., Smith, D. J., Young, R. K., & Dodd, J. (1991). A review of self-management outcome research conducted with students who exhibit behavioral disorders. *Behavior Disorders, 13,* 169–180.

Novaco, R. W. (1975). *Anger control: The development and evaluation of an experimental treatment.* Lexington, MA: Lexington.

O'Leary, S. D., & Dubay, D. R. (1979). Application of self-control procedures by children: A review. *Journal of Applied Behavior Analysis, 2,* 449–465.

Palmer, D. J., & Stowe, M. L. (1989). Attributions. In C. R. Reynolds & L. Mann (Eds.), *Encyclopedia of special education* (pp. 151–152). New York: John Wiley & Sons.

Reid, R. (1996). Research in self-monitoring: The present, the prospects, the pitfalls. *Journal of Learning Disabilities, 29,* 317–331.

Rinehart, S. D., Stahl, S. A., & Erickson, L. G. (1986). Some effects of summarization training on reading and studying. *Reading Research Quarterly, 21,* 422–438.

Robin, A., Schneider, M., & Dolnick, M. (1976). The turtle technique: An extended case study of self-control in the classroom. *Psychology in the Schools, 12,* 120–128.

Schloss, P., & Smith, M. A. (1998). *Applied behavior analysis in the classroom* (2nd ed.). Boston: Allyn & Bacon.

Schunk, P. H. (1983). Ability versus effort attributional feedback: Differential effects on self-efficacy and achievement. *Journal of Educational Psychology, 75,* 848–856.

Shapiro, E. S., & Cole, C. L. (1994). *Behavior change in the classroom: Self-management interventions.* New York: Guilford Press.

Siegel, J. M., & Spivak, G. (1973). *Problem-solving therapy* (Research report 23). Philadelphia: Hahnemann Medical College.

Smith, D. J., Young, K. R., West, R. P., Morgan, R. P., & Rhode, G. (1988). Reducing the disruptive behavior of junior high school students: A classroom self-management procedure. *Behavioral Disorders, 13,* 231–239.

Smith, S. W., Siegel, E. M., O'Conner, A. M., & Thomas, S. B. (1994). Effects of cognitive-behavioral training on angry behavior and aggression of three elementary-aged students. *Behavioral Disorders, 19,* 126–135.

Spivak, G., & Shure, M. B. (1974). *Social adjustment of young children.* San Francisco, CA: Jossey Bass.

Sugai, G. M., & Lewis, T. (1990). *Using self-management strategies in classes for students with behavioral disorders.* Paper presented at the annual conference of Teacher Educators of Children with Behavioral Disorders, Tempe, AZ.

Torgeson, J. K. (1982). The learning disabled child as an inactive learner: Educational implications. *Topics in Learning and Learning Disabilities, 2,* 45–52.

Vygotsky, L. (1962). *Thought and language.* New York: Wiley.

Webber, J., Scheuermann, B., McCall, C., & Coleman, M. (1994). Research on self-monitoring as a behavior management technique in special education classrooms: A descriptive review. *Remedial and Special Education, 14,* 38–56.

Wolery, M., Bailey, D. B., & Sugai G. M. (1988). *Effective teaching: Principles and procedures of applied behavior analysis with exceptional students.* Boston, MA: Allyn & Bacon.

Wong, B. Y. L. (1989). On cognitive training: A thought or two. In J. N. Hughes & R. J. Hall (Eds.), *Cognitive behavioral psychology in the schools: A comprehensive handbook* (pp. 209–219). New York: Guilford.

Workman, E. A. (1998). *Teaching behavioral self-control to students* (2nd ed.). Austin, TX: Pro-Ed.

# BEHAVIOR REDUCTION STRATEGIES

*Thomas J. Zirpoli*

*School discipline has two main goals: (1) ensure the safety of staff and students, and (2) create an environment conducive to learning.*

—GAUSTAD *(1992, p. 1)*

It is no coincidence that chapters regarding reinforcement and cognitive behavior modification were placed in this text before our discussion of specific behavior challenges and behavior reduction strategies. The use of positive reinforcement is promoted as the intervention of first choice when teachers want to implement a behavior reduction strategy. The most effective intervention strategy for most challenging or inappropriate behaviors is the reinforcement of appropriate behaviors and behaviors that are inconsistent or incompatible with inappropriate behaviors (Donnellan & LaVigna, 1990). Even for severe behavior problems, such as self-injury, there is growing empirical support that positive or nonaversive methods can be effective without the employment of "aversive" punishers (Berkman & Meyer, 1988; Donnellan, LaVigna, Negri-Shoultz, & Fassbender, 1988; Friman, 1990; O'Brien & Repp, 1990; Underwood & Thyer, 1990). Decisions to use behavior reduction procedures, however, must extend beyond the question of effectiveness. Evans and Meyer (1990) state that "clinical interventions must be judged in a variety of ways, and simply because something meets someone's definition of 'effectiveness' does not mean that it is right" (p. 134).

The focus on appropriate behavior and positive reinforcement dramatically changes the atmosphere of any environment where individuals live and work (Meyer & Evans, 1989; Turnbull & Turnbull, 1990), including the home and educational setting, and the quality of interactions among teachers and students (Pfiffner & O'Leary, 1987; Pfiffner, Rosen, & O'Leary, 1985). Additionally, by receiving reinforcement for appropriate behaviors, students may learn effective social skills that will "enhance successful functioning in school and other environments" (Sasso, Melloy, & Kavale, 1990, p. 9).

## TERMINOLOGY

The term *behavior reduction strategies* is used here to identify procedures that, when implemented immediately after a target behavior, reduce the future probability of the target behavior recurring. The use of the term *punishment* is limited in this chapter because it has many meanings for different people and is frequently—though incorrectly—associated only with "aversive" procedures not promoted in this text. By definition, punishment "simply refers to any contingent consequence that decreases the behavior that it follows; thus, the term ought to be a neutral one as such consequences would usually be idiosyncratic to the individual" (Evans & Meyer, 1985, p. 135). The problem of finding the "correct" terminology to describe procedures that reduce the likelihood of challenging or inappropriate behaviors was articulated by Skiba and Deno (1991):

> *By introducing methodologies called punishment, psychologists and educators are placed in the awkward position of using a term that serves as a discriminative stimulus for the*

*very practices they are trying to avoid or reform. It is not surprising that trainers of practitioners are often unsuccessful in shaping nonpunitive practice, when the word they use to describe behavior reduction is derived from the same Latin root* (poena: *fine, penalty*) *as* punitive *(Oxford English Dictionary, 1982, p. 1604). (p. 301)*

## Appropriate Terminology for Challenging Behavior

Another challenge in the area of terminology is what to call the behavior targeted for reduction. The terms *antisocial, challenging, inappropriate, excessive,* and *undesirable* are frequently used. In this chapter, both *challenging* and *inappropriate* will be used to describe behaviors that are targeted for reduction because of either their excessive or antisocial nature. Although the current trend in the field is to use *challenging,* situations exist in which behaviors are less challenging than they are inappropriate. An inappropriate behavior may or may not be challenging. A challenging behavior may or may not be inappropriate.

## Is There Really a Problem?

Behavior must be judged by its function (see Chapters 5 and 6), the social context in which it is exhibited, and the impact on the individual's growth and development across settings. Indeed, perhaps the most important consideration before implementing a behavior change program is to ask the question "Is there really a problem?" (Snell & Zirpoli, 1987). Gaylord-Ross (1980) outlines five questions that should be considered before a decision is made to eliminate or modify a behavior:

1. Is the behavior causing physical harm to the child or others?
2. Is the behavior disruptive to the student's learning or the learning of others?
3. Does the behavior appear to be triggering additional problem behaviors or emotional reactions in the child or others?
4. Is the behavior causing the child to be socially excluded?
5. Is the behavior related to a medical condition (e.g., ear infections in young children, side effects of medication, behavior associated with a genetic condition)?

Teachers also need to complete a curriculum-based assessment, along with a functional assessment (see Chapters 5 and 6), in order to determine if curriculum changes or other modifications of the student's environment may eliminate the inappropriate behavior. After these considerations have been examined and the target behavior is still judged to be a problem, teachers should try to identify positive or alternative behaviors that can be used to decrease or eliminate the inappropriate behavior. These differential reinforcement strategies are outlined in the next section.

# DIFFERENTIAL REINFORCEMENT OF BEHAVIOR

*Differential reinforcement* refers to two primary applications of reinforcement to maintain or increase the occurrence of appropriate behavior. First, a behavior may be reinforced only when it is exhibited following an appropriate *discriminative stimulus* (SD). For example, talking in class may be appropriate under some situations but inappropriate in others. By reinforcing talking only when it follows certain antecedents (e.g., when the teacher asks a question) and not reinforcing talking at other times, teachers can apply differential reinforcement to talking behavior.

A second application of differential reinforcement refers to the reinforcement of one target behavior while other behaviors are ignored. Thus, as the reinforced behavior increases, it becomes differentiated from other behaviors, related or unrelated, that are likely to decrease in the absence of reinforcement. When reinforcing behaviors that are incompatible with, or provide an alternative to, inappropriate behaviors, teachers are using differential reinforcement to increase appropriate behaviors. For example, Drasgow, Halle, and Ostrosky (1998) used differential reinforcement to replace reaching and grabbing behaviors in young children with severe language delays, by teaching them to sign the word "please."

Generally, differential reinforcement increases the rate, duration, or intensity of behaviors that students already have in their repertoire but do not perform at acceptable levels. For example, a student may know how to raise his hand to get a teacher's attention, but he frequently calls out the teacher's name in the middle of an assignment, interrupting the other students. When the teacher responds to the hand-raising instead of calling-out behavior, the student learns which behavior is effective in getting the teacher's attention.

## Differential Reinforcement of Other Behaviors

*Differential reinforcement of other behaviors* (DRO), first described and used by Reynolds (1961), refers to the delivery of reinforcement after the child *has not exhibited* a target behavior during a predetermined interval of time, regardless of other behaviors occurring during the interval. For example, Ramasamy, Taylor, and Ziegler (1996) eliminated out-of-seat behavior of a 14-year-old boy by providing an edible reinforcer or free time contingent upon his staying in his seat. During the first phase of intervention, the boy was reinforced every 15 minutes for staying in his seat. In the second phase, he was reinforced every 30 minutes. In the third phase, he was reinforced every 45 minutes, and in the last phase, he was reinforced every hour.

A DRO schedule may also be used for providing reinforcement contingent on the absence of several inappropriate behaviors during a specific interval. For example, if a child screams and occasionally kicks others, reinforcement may be provided contingent on the absence of both screaming and kicking or contingent on the absence of only screaming or only kicking. Because the DRO procedure entails reinforcing the *omission* of specified inappropriate behaviors, the term *differential reinforcement of the omission* of behavior is sometimes used (Deitz & Repp, 1983).

The primary purpose of this procedure is to target the reduction of a *specific* inappropriate behavior in a student who has perhaps several, less severe, inappropriate behaviors, which are put on hold. Prioritizing inappropriate behaviors and targeting the reduction of one behavior at a time may be an acceptable solution for teachers working with students who have many behavior problems.

### Fixed or Whole-Interval DRO

A DRO schedule has several different applications. In the first application, the DRO schedule is fixed (such as every 10 minutes or every 30 minutes). If the inappropriate behavior does not occur during the predetermined fixed interval, the student is reinforced. If the inappropriate behavior does take place at any time during the interval, the student is not reinforced at the end of the interval; a new interval begins only at the end of the preceding interval. For example, a student who frequently fights with other students may be placed on a DRO with a fixed interval of 30 minutes beginning at 9:00 A.M. and ending at 3:00 P.M. At 9:30 and each 30-minute interval thereafter, teachers would determine whether the student exhibited fighting behavior. If fighting behavior did not occur, the student would qualify for a reinforcer. If fighting behavior showed up at any time during the 30-minute period, the student would not qualify for a reinforcer. With this DRO 30-minute fixed schedule, the student could earn up to 12 reinforcers. Providing reinforcement when a targeted behavior has not been exhibited for an entire predetermined interval has also been referred to as *whole-interval DRO* (Repp, Barton, & Brulle, 1983).

Repp, Felce, and Barton (1991) determined that DRO is more effective when the interval between reinforcement is initially small than when it is large. In fact they found that a shorter DRO was about twice as effective as a longer DRO. They also stated that the specific DRO interval should be related to the rate of behavior during baseline or the number of inappropriate behaviors divided into the duration of the class period. For example, if the average number of target behaviors was 10 within a 60-minute class period, then the DRO interval should be 6 minutes.

### Momentary DRO

A second variation, labeled *momentary DRO* (Repp et al., 1983), also uses a fixed, predetermined interval during which the occurrence of a target behavior is monitored. However, the student is reinforced only if the target behavior is not being emitted at the specific moment of observation—the end of each interval. For example, if a teacher were using a momentary DRO-5 (minutes), the student would be observed every 5 minutes. If, at that moment, the target behavior is not occurring—even if it had occurred at another moment during the interval—the student would be reinforced. If, at that moment, the target behavior is occurring, the student would not earn reinforcement, regardless of the student's behavior during the rest of the interval. The student's next opportunity for earning a reinforcer would be at the end of the next interval (5 minutes).

In a comparison of whole-interval DRO and momentary DRO, Repp et al. (1983) found the whole-interval DRO to be more effective, especially in the initial stages of programming. They suggest that momentary DRO may be used as part of a maintenance program. But in a multiple baseline design, Miller and Jones (1997) found that momentary DRO was more effective than whole-interval DRO in reducing stereotyped behavior in one subject and as effective with a second. They suggested that momentary DRO was easier to use and required less vigilance in applied settings.

### DRO-Reset Interval

In a third variation of DRO, described by Donnellan et al. (1988) as a *DRO-reset* interval, the interval of time is reset, or starts over, each time the targeted inappropriate behavior occurs. Using the previous example, if the student fought with another student at 9:15, the 30-minute interval would immediately be reset at 9:15 and end at 9:45 instead of 9:30. On the DRO-reset schedule, the student is reinforced for every 30 minutes during which no fighting occurs. The clock is always reset after each fight. With the DRO-fixed interval, the student who has a fight at 9:15 would not have another opportunity for reinforcement until 10:00 (45 minutes after his last fight), the end of the next interval.

### DRO-Increasing Interval or DRO-Fading Schedule

In a fourth variation of the DRO schedule, the expected interval of appropriate behavior increases over time in relation to the student's progress. Research has demonstrated that DRO schedules are more effective when the interval is short at the start of the program and gradually increases than when the interval is initially long (Repp et al., 1991; Repp & Slack, 1977). This variation of DRO may be referred to as a *DRO-increasing-interval* schedule or a *DRO-fading* schedule. The purpose of this variation is to fade or decrease the provision of reinforcement gradually from a frequent-opportunity schedule to a less-frequent-opportunity schedule. Using this procedure, the student is reinforced for the absence of a targeted inappropriate behavior for a specific interval (e.g., 30 minutes). However, after a predetermined number of successful intervals (e.g., three 30-minute intervals), the duration of the interval increases (e.g., from 30 to 45 minutes). Now the student must not exhibit the inappropriate behavior for a longer interval to qualify for reinforcement. If the inappropriate behavior does occur, the length of the interval stays the same. In effect, fading the reinforcement delivery schedule is determined by the student's progress. As the student progresses to longer intervals of appropriate behavior, teachers may wish to increase the quantity or quality of reinforcement. Otherwise, the student may feel penalized for making progress (i.e., getting reinforced less often for behaving appropriately for longer periods of time). The four variations of DRO are outlined as follows:

| *Variation* | *Reinforcement (R+) Delivery* |
| --- | --- |
| Whole-interval | R+ is delivered if target behavior does not happen at any time during interval. |
| Momentary | R+ is delivered if target behavior is not occurring at the moment of observation at the end of interval. |
| Reset-interval | R+ is delivered if target behavior is not demonstrated for a full interval period of time; clock is reset after each target behavior. |
| Increasing-interval | R+ is delivered if target behavior is not exhibited at any time during interval. Duration of interval gradually increases as student makes progress. |

Fading reinforcement schedules are an important element in any reinforcement program. Busy teachers are not likely to reinforce target behaviors consistently every 10, 15, or 30 minutes for extended periods. Also, the student needs to learn to behave appropriately in response to a more natural, intermittent schedule of reinforcement. On the other hand, it is important for teachers to understand that all students have different needs and that some students will continue to need more support than others.

LaVigna and Donnellan (1986) list three cautions concerning the use of DRO. First, because reinforcement is provided as a result of the *nonoccurrence* of a targeted inappropriate behavior, a specific appropriate behavior is not reinforced. Other types of differential reinforcement programs may be more effective for teachers increasing specific appropriate behaviors. Second, providing reinforcement contingent on a targeted inappropriate behavior's not occurring may lead to the inadvertent reinforcement of other inappropriate behaviors as well as appropriate behaviors. Last, under a DRO-reset schedule, the student may learn to exhibit the inappropriate behavior *immediately* after the timer is set and, after the timer is reset, still receive reinforcement at the end of the new interval. In effect, the student still receives a reinforcer at the end of each interval, even if the inappropriate behavior occurred. This problem could be eliminated by changing to a DRO-fixed schedule and not resetting the interval after each inappropriate behavior. Then, the student would not receive a reinforcer at the end of the interval because the inappropriate behavior had been exhibited at the beginning of the interval. A new interval would begin only at the end of the previously scheduled interval.

## Differential Reinforcement of Alternative Behaviors

*Differential reinforcement of alternative behaviors* (DRA) refers to reinforcement of a more appropriate *form* of a targeted inappropriate behavior. Unlike DRO, DRA is more specific about the targeted behaviors to be reinforced. For example, when a teacher reinforces a student for politely *asking* for a treat instead of *demanding* a treat, the teacher is reinforcing an alternative, socially appropriate form of a behavior that has the same intent—to get a treat. Piazza, Moes, and Fisher (1996) used DRA to reduce destructive behaviors of an 11-year-old boy. The intervention included differential reinforcement of compliance to staff requests. Following compliance with a specific number of instructions, the boy was allowed free time and social interaction. Over time, the number of demands the boy was required to complete per session was increased. The boy's compliance increased and his destructive behavior decreased.

The DRA procedure has several advantages. First, it emphasizes the reinforcement of specific, appropriate behaviors. Unlike the DRO procedure, in which the teacher must monitor the occurrence or absence of inappropriate behaviors, the DRA procedure forces teachers to focus on the occurrence of appropriate behaviors. Second, the DRA procedure encourages teachers to review alternative behaviors that may be taught (if not already in the student's repertoire) or increased (if already in the student's repertoire). Too frequently, teachers are eager to punish inappropriate behaviors without considering alternative behaviors they could reinforce. Again, focusing on reinforcement instead of punishment will have a significant, positive influence on the student's home and classroom environment. Third, the DRA procedure has a double effect on the student's behavior. Not only does appropriate behavior increase when reinforced, but the targeted inappropriate behavior is likely to decrease (Vollmer, Roane, Ringdahl, & Marcus, 1999). In contrast, when punishment of inappropriate behavior is used alone, decreases in inappropriate behaviors are unlikely to occur in conjunction with increases in appropriate behaviors. Lastly, the DRA procedure is easy to teach and use.

Implementing a DRA procedure can vary in several ways. Appropriate alternative behaviors may be reinforced based on a ratio schedule (number of appropriate behaviors) or an interval schedule (duration of appropriate behaviors). In addition, these ratio and interval schedules of reinforcement may be fixed or variable.

## Differential Reinforcement of Incompatible Behaviors

*Differential reinforcement of incompatible behaviors* (DRI) refers to the reinforcement of behaviors that are topographically incompatible with targeted inappropriate behaviors. *Topographically incompatible* means that it is physically impossible for the incompatible and the target behaviors to occur at the same time. This procedure is also referred to as *differential reinforcement of competing* behaviors (DRC) (Donnellan et al., 1988). Reinforcement of incompatible or competing behaviors is even more specific than DRO or DRA as to what types of behaviors are targeted. For example, keeping your hands in your lap is incompatible with hitting others, and on-task behavior is incompatible with off-task behavior. Thus, when a teacher reinforces hands-in-lap behavior, hitting-others behavior is likely to decrease; and the reinforcement of on-task behavior is likely to reduce off-task behavior.

**TABLE 9.1 • DRO, DRA, and DRI Examples**

| Target Behavior | Behavior Reinforced per Program | | |
| --- | --- | --- | --- |
| | **DRO** | **DRA** | **DRI** |
| Out of seat | Absence of | Asking permission | In seat |
| Off-task | Absence of | — | On-task |
| Hitting | Absence of | Cooperation/talking | Hands in lap |
| Self-stimulation | Absence of | Playing with toys | Keeping still |
| Noncompliance | Absence of | — | Compliance |
| Temper tantrum | Absence of | Taking/asking | — |
| Talking out | Absence of | Raising hand | Being quiet |
| Throwing objects | Absence of | Playing basketball | Writing |
| Hands in mouth | Absence of | Brushing teeth | Hands in lap |
| Running | Absence of | Walking | Standing still |
| Foul language | Absence of | Appropriate language | Being quiet |

Of course, not all inappropriate behaviors have topographically incompatible behaviors that would be appropriate or functional to reinforce. For example, although sitting still (the absence of movement or behavior) is incompatible with overactivity, self-stimulation, and a variety of behaviors identified as inappropriate in certain settings, reinforcing students for not moving is not recommended. Instead, teachers should identify alternative, functional behaviors to increase using a DRA or DRO procedure. Table 9.1 lists examples of differential reinforcement programs.

## Differential Reinforcement of Lower Rates of Behavior

*Differential reinforcement of lower rates of behavior* (DRL) first described by Skinner (1938), refers to the reinforcement of small *decreases* in the rate of a target behavior compared to the baseline rate of that behavior. Unlike the DRA, DRI, and DRO procedures, DRL is especially useful when trying to decrease the frequency of a behavior that occurs often. With a DRA or DRI approach, few appropriate behaviors may occur during the high rate of inappropriate behavior, which thus leaves few opportunities to reinforce alternative (DRA) or incompatible (DRI) behaviors. In addition, when there is a high rate of inappropriate behavior, reinforcement delivered under a DRA or DRI schedule may inadvertently become associated with the inappropriate behavior. A DRO procedure may also be problematic when an inappropriate behavior occurs at a high rate. Since this procedure calls for providing reinforcement contingent on the absence of the targeted inappropriate behavior for a specific interval, the student may never qualify for a reinforcer.

A DRL procedure may also be recommended for a behavior considered appropriate and functional except for a high rate of occurrence. Asking to use the bathroom is an appropriate behavior; however, when it occurs frequently through-out the school day, it may disrupt the classroom and have an adverse effect on the student's academic performance. In this case, the classroom teacher would be in-terested in decreasing the rate of the behavior to an acceptable level rather than try-ing to eliminate the behavior.

The use of DRL may take one of two forms. In the first form, reinforcement is provided contingent on a target behavior as long as a predetermined interval of time has passed since the target behavior last occurred (Skinner, 1938). For in-stance, the teacher would determine that a student could leave the classroom for the bathroom if a certain length of time had passed since the student's previous request. The objective with this form of DRL is to increase the intervals between target behaviors from the current baseline interval to a more socially acceptable level.

In a second form of DRL, reinforcement is provided contingent on a lower rate of the target behavior within a specific interval of time (Dietz & Repp, 1983). In keeping with our example, teachers may decide to monitor the average hourly rate of the target behavior (asking to use the bathroom) and then reinforce the student each hour, contingent on a lower hourly rate of the target behavior. For example, the student may be reinforced for making two or fewer requests to use the bath-room per hour. As the student progresses in reducing the rate of the target behav-ior, reinforcement becomes contingent on a new criterion (an even lower hourly rate of the target behavior), until an acceptable level is achieved.

An important element in both DRL and differential reinforcement of higher rates of behavior is the completion of a baseline measurement of the target behav-ior. Before new criteria or objectives are set for reduced rates of behavior, an accu-rate baseline measurement is a must. Baseline data will reveal a benchmark for expected behavior or behavior change. For example, if teachers did not know the hourly baseline rate (how often the student asked to use the bathroom), they would not know whether the behavior had decreased during intervention or whether the decrease was significant enough for the student to earn a reinforcer. If teachers know that the baseline rate of the target behavior was 10 requests per hour, how-ever, then they know that the first step in their DRL program should be to reinforce the student contingent on an hourly rate of fewer than 10 requests (e.g., 8 or fewer per hour). After the student has consistently (three or four consecutive hours) stayed below the baseline rate, a new and lower rate (such as six per hour) is es-tablished. Now, to earn a reinforcement, the student must exhibit the target be-havior fewer than six times per hour. Additional reductions in the criteria for reinforcement should be made as the student progresses. Figure 9.1 outlines a sam-ple DRL program to decrease cursing behavior.

## Differential Reinforcement of Higher Rates of Behavior

*Differential reinforcement of higher rates of behavior* (DRH; also called a changing cri-terion design) refers to the reinforcement of *increases* in the rate of a target behav-ior compared to the baseline rate of that behavior. DRH is typically used to increase

---

**Child's name:** John (15 years old)

**Target behavior:** Cursing during gym class

**Baseline data:** John was observed for five consecutive days during gym class (45 minutes each). John cursed an average of five times during each 45-minute gym class (range = 4–6).

**Program goal:** John will reduce his cursing rate to one or fewer per 45-minute gym class.

**Reinforcement menu:** John may pick one reinforcement from the list below per reinforcement opportunity.

- Ten minutes of playing with a video game of his choice during study hall
- Ten minutes of listening to an audiotape of his choice (with earphones only) during study hall
- Fifteen minutes of computer time

**Reinforcement schedule:**

**Phase 1:** John may select <u>one</u> reinforcer when his cursing rate is less than five per 45-minute gym class.

**Phase 2:** John may select <u>one</u> reinforcer when his cursing rate is less than four per 45-minute gym class.

**Phase 3:** John may select <u>two</u> reinforcers when his cursing rate is less than three per 45-minute gym class.

**Phase 4:** John may select <u>two</u> reinforcers when his cursing rate is less than two per 45-minute gym class.

**Performance criteria for phase change:** John will move to each new phase of this program after achieving the current phase objective for three consecutive gym periods. For example, after John has achieved the objective for phase 1, reducing the rate of cursing to less than five for three consecutive gym classes, he is moved to phase 2.

---

**FIGURE 9.1.** Example of teacher's DRL program to decrease cursing behavior

behaviors that are already in the student's repertoire but do not occur frequently or consistently enough. A student may know how to say "please" and "thank you" but may use the two terms infrequently. Reinforcing the student for using these expressions more often is likely to increase the use of the behaviors that already exist in the student's repertoire.

The application of DRH is similar to the application of DRL, except that the purpose of DRH is to *increase* the rate of a target behavior within a specific interval of time. As with DRL, teachers must first complete a baseline observation of the target behavior to establish a current rate. Then, they should reinforce increases in the rate, above baseline, until the rate of the target behavior occurs at an acceptable level. Figure 9.2 outlines a sample DRH program to increase a student's use of "please."

---

**Child's name:** Julia (5 years old)

**Target behavior:** Saying "please" when making a request

**Baseline data:** A 4-day baseline measure was taken by caregivers, from 8:30 until 12 noon, on the rate of saying "please" when making a request. Julia averaged 12.5% correct responses by saying "please" two out of sixteen requests (range = 0–4).

**Program goal:** Julia will say "please" when making a request 95% of the time as measured during day care from 8:30 until 12 noon, for three consecutive days.

**Reinforcement menu:** Julia may select from the following reinforcement menu:
- One additional story read by a caregiver
- An extra cup of juice during snack time
- A choice of stickers
- Five minutes playing with a computer game

**Reinforcement schedule (criteria for reinforcement, per phase):**

**Phase 1:** Julia will say "please" at a rate greater than 13% of total requests made during morning day care.

**Phase 2:** Julia will say "please" at a rate greater than 25% of total requests made during morning day care.

**Phase 3:** Julia will say "please" at a rate greater than 50% of total requests made during morning day care.

**Phase 4:** Julia will say "please" at a rate greater than 75% of total requests made during morning day care.

**Phase 5:** Julia will say "please" at a rate greater than 90% of total requests made during morning day care.

**Performance criteria for phase change:** Julia will move to the next phase of this program after achieving the phase objective for three consecutive sessions. For example, after Julia has achieved the objective for phase 1, saying "please" at a rate greater than 13% of total requests made during morning day care, for three consecutive sessions, she is moved to phase 2.

---

**FIGURE 9.2.** Example of a teacher's use of reinforcement of higher rates of appropriate behavior program to increase a child's use of "please"

# PREVENTIVE STRATEGIES

Perhaps the best behavior reduction strategy, along with the reinforcement of appropriate behavior, is the strategy of prevention. As previously stated, teachers should monitor the environment in order to identify environmental conditions (antecedents and consequences) related to inappropriate behavior. *Antecedents* are the activities or conditions occurring immediately before a behavior. For example, if a student is aggressive, teachers need to identify the activities occurring immediately before the aggressive acts. The teacher may be able to modify the antecedents (change schedule, seating arrangement, etc.) of a behavior and, as a result, decrease the occurrence of the inappropriate behavior. By reinforcing appropriate behaviors and modifying antecedent conditions, teachers are more likely to be effective in reducing inappropriate behaviors rather than just trying to decrease inappropriate behavior.

An excellent example of modifying environmental antecedents was documented by Rosenberg (1986), who added a brief (2-minute) review of the classroom rules before the start of a lesson to an ongoing classroom behavior management program. The teacher asked the students individually or in unison to state the classroom rules orally. Rosenberg found that "daily lessons preceded by a review of rules tend to possess a greater academic focus and are generally conducted with greater efficiency" (p. 246).

It is also important to review the *consequences* of current inappropriate behaviors (see ABC assessment in Chapter 3). The consequences of a behavior are the responses, positive or negative, that occur immediately after a behavior. Consequences may be reinforcing, which tend to increase the occurrence of the behavior, or punishing, which tend to decrease the occurrence of the behavior. Teachers may provide consequences to inappropriate behaviors that actually serve to reinforce and thus increase the likelihood of the behavior occurring again.

Sometimes when teachers think they are providing punishing consequences for inappropriate behaviors, they are actually reinforcing the behaviors they want to decrease. This is usually the case when a positive reinforcement program is *not* in place and the student receives attention only as a consequence of inappropriate behaviors. If students do not get attention for appropriate behaviors, they will probably misbehave for attention—even if the attention is in the form of punishment.

## Interrupting the Behavior Chain

LaVigna and Willis (1991) discuss several strategies related to *interrupting the behavior chain* of inappropriate behavior. These methods are helpful in preventing and de-escalating inappropriate behaviors. Suggestions for interrupting the behavior chain include proximity control, humor, instructional control, problem-solving facilitation, and stimulus change.

### Proximity Control

*Proximity control* is a method of anticipating a student's potential response to an event or a situation and interrupting the usual sequence of behaviors by positioning one's body a certain way, remaining calm, and facilitating communication. For example, a classroom teacher may notice that the students are beginning to talk too loudly during a community library visit, and, anticipating that the students will become louder, the teacher breaks the behavioral chain by reminding the students to talk quietly. By anticipating a potential problem, the teacher was able to position herself among the students, calmly communicate her expectations, and prevent a potential situation in which she might have to yell above the students' noise for them to hear her instructions.

### Injecting Humor

Injecting *humor* into a situation may also interrupt a behavior chain. Humor will often reduce the tension of an explosive situation. A teacher might respond to a student who is ready to lose control by telling the student a story about a similar situation occurring in the past ("Did I ever tell you that that happened to me once?").

### Instructional Control

*Instructional control* or providing instructions on expected behaviors is also useful in interrupting a behavior chain. For example, after a classroom schedule is abruptly changed and the students begin to respond in frustration, the teacher provides clear instructions about what they will do next and what the expectations are for student behavior.

### Problem-Solving Facilitation

*Problem-solving facilitation* involves offering positive alternatives to inappropriate behavior. For example, a teacher may suggest to a student, "Let's sit and talk about what you can do about this" after observing that the student is ready to behave inappropriately in response to a frustrating experience. Problem-solving skills are also facilitated when teachers talk to students about alternatives to the inappropriate behaviors students observe in their everyday environment (e.g., students fighting on the playground, world events students hear on the news). These kinds of problem-solving discussions are easily integrated into both academic and social activities.

### Stimulus Change

*Stimulus change* refers to a range of teacher behaviors that prevent challenging behaviors by modifying environmental stimuli that might precipitate challenging behavior. Stimulus change may include removing objects, relocating people, removing unnecessary demands and requests, changing the location or timing of events, and making other rearrangements of environmental stimuli. For example, teachers frequently modify student seating arrangements in response to disruptive interactions among students. A greater effort to anticipate and prevent inappropriate behaviors through environmental modifications, rather than direct behavior modification, is encouraged. Environmental changes may be temporary while teachers gradually reintroduce the stimulus that elicited the behavior. For example, a toy that children have fought over may be temporarily removed and gradually reintroduced in a more controlled manner.

## Preventive Strategies for School

While there has been significant media coverage of student violence in our nation's public schools, the facts about school violence may not be congruent with the coverage. The National Center for Educational Statistics (1997) of the U.S. Department of Education reported that during the 1996–1997 school year only 10% of U.S. schools reported at least one serious violent crime. Almost half of the schools reported no crimes at all. Vandalism was reported by 38% of schools, and physical attacks or fights without a weapon by 28%.

### Variables Related to School Violence

As would be expected, high schools have more crime than middle schools, and middle schools more than elementary schools. School crime was also more likely in larger schools. While 38% of small schools reported any incidents, this statistic grew to 60% of medium-sized schools and 89% of large schools. City schools were twice as likely to report serious crimes as those in rural schools. Lastly, the proportion of poor students in a school was positively related to the number of crimes reported by a school.

### Current School Efforts to Ensure Security

Schools report a variety of security measures to ensure the safety of their students. The most common method employed is to have visitors sign in before entering the school building. About 96% of schools have this requirement. Many schools close their campus or employ other methods to control access to school grounds during school hours. Drug sweeps were reported in 19% of schools, random metal detector checks in 4%, and 1% of schools had students pass through metal detectors daily (National Center for Educational Statistics, 1997).

### Schoolwide Prevention Programs

Most schools (78%) report having some type of formal, schoolwide, prevention program.

Gaustad (1992) identified additional ways to prevent disruptive behavior in schools:

- Establish school and classroom rules.
- Establish consistent consequences for following and breaking rules.
- Communicate rules to staff, students, and parents frequently.
- Treat minor infractions flexibly.
- Make consequences for serious offenses nonnegotiable.
- Use social reinforcement to increase appropriate behavior.
- Provide a hearing-and-appeal process to increase student and parent perception of fairness.

- Divide large schools into schools-within-schools.
- Increase academic performance for all students.
- Increase student social and school involvement.
- Have principal be a highly visible model of the above.

Lastly, Strain & Smith (1996) and Sugai and Lewis (1996) stress the importance of prevention curriculum and instruction for students on appropriate social skills. As stated by Gaustad (1992), many students simply don't have appropriate social skills because no one ever taught them how to behave appropriately in different social situations.

## *Conflict Resolution and Peer Mediation*

While the terms "conflict resolution" and "peer mediation" are frequently used interchangeably, peer mediation is really a part of an overall, schoolwide, conflict resolution program. Peer mediation is a process by which students volunteer to receive training on how to mediate conflicts between their peers and help their peers find a fair solution to their conflict. Two primary goals of peer mediation are (a) to offer students an opportunity to discuss their feelings and conflicts openly with peers and (b) to provide schools a process to de-escalate disputes before students resort to more violent solutions to their conflicts. Conboy (1994), who coordinates the peer mediation program at Roosevelt High School in Minneapolis, cites four main outcomes of peer mediation:

- Peer mediation offers school officials and other educators a positive alternative to manage conflict.
- Peer mediation helps prevent conflicts from escalating.
- By helping resolve disputes, peer mediation helps create a more positive school climate for educators and students.
- Peer mediation teaches and empowers students to think of alternative ways to solve their own conflicts with peers.

Peer mediation starts with the recruitment of students who are willing to be trained as peer mediators. Students are usually selected by teachers because of their potential to be good listeners and problem solvers. After they are trained, peer mediators are then contacted by a school official when a third party is needed to mediate peer disputes or conflicts.

Students who serve as mediators benefit from their training and experiences, and maintain their conflict resolution skills after school (Carruthers, Sweeney, Kmitta, & Harris, 1996). Also, mediators report improved attitudes towards school, improved academic performance, and a more positive attitude towards dealing with conflict in their own lives. And with students helping to resolve conflict, teachers report less stress in the classroom, more time for academics, and a greater capacity for students to solve their own disputes (Lane & McWhirter, 1992).

Conboy (1994) recommends the following steps during the dispute resolution:

1. All parties are asked by the peer mediator to make a pledge that they will listen to the other person's point of view and honestly try to solve their dispute without name-calling or other put-downs.
2. The peer mediator helps the conflicting parties define the problem, what happened, and how they felt.
3. The mediator repeats what was said in order to ensure that everyone understands what was said and how everyone feels.
4. The mediator asks both parties to brainstorm solutions to their conflict that would be fair to both sides.
5. The agreement to the conflict is developed into a written contract and signed by all parties to the conflict.

Conflicts that are common to mediation include theft or damage to personal property, harassment and put-downs, rumors or gossip, threats, fights, and even student-teacher conflicts. Peer mediation programs frequently include "anger control" or "anger management" training for students. This training may be provided as a course, as part of a course, or as short training sessions, as an elective to all students and/or a requirement for some. For example, students suspended for fighting might be required to complete an anger control training session before returning to the classroom.

Research on the effects of peer mediation is impressive. Decreases in physical violence and increases in cooperation among students have been reported (Johnson & Johnson, 1996). Thompson (1996) found that conflict resolution provides students with alternatives to conflict, involves students in school decisions, increases student self-regulation, and increases student responsibility for their behavior.

### Block Scheduling

Block scheduling is defined as organizing the school day into larger blocks of time (more than 60 minutes) instead of the traditional school schedule of six to eight classes per day (45 to 55 minutes per class) (Black, 1998). The main case for block scheduling is that longer class periods will allow teachers to cover subject matter in greater depth and that fewer course periods will significantly decrease transition periods throughout the school day.

There are various models of block scheduling. The most common and successful form is the "4 × 4" where students take four courses (90 minutes in length) during each of two semesters per academic year. The big advantage to block scheduling is that students do indeed spend more time focused on academic work within the classroom, and less time changing classes and socializing with others in the hallways. Teachers can spend more time on a topic before students have to run to their next class. When compared with schools using the standard five- to seven-class daily schedule, some schools using the block schedule report fewer discipline problems, suspensions, tardy referrals, and student fights (Eineder & Bishop, 1997;

Kramer, 1997). Other studies found that block scheduling reduced both teacher and student stress, and increased student academic performance (Nichols, 2000; Peterson, Schmidt, Flottmeyer, & Weincke, 2000).

Disadvantages of block scheduling include the following:

a. Transition from traditional to block scheduling involves logistical preparation and teacher/staff training.
b. Teachers must change their teaching style to accommodate longer teaching periods.
c. Students may not be able to focus for 90 minutes of instruction, which requires teachers to be more creative in their instruction strategies.
d. Longer instructional periods may work better for some course material (biology lab) than others (math instruction) (Howard, 1998).

### School Uniforms

Many schools are mandating school uniforms as a way of decreasing behavior problems. While the evidence that uniforms decrease behavior problems is mostly anecdotal, some data suggest that uniforms do make a difference. For example, schools in Long Beach, California, became the first to require public school students to wear uniforms and report a significant decrease in assaults, thefts, vandalism, and weapon and drug violations (Ritter, 1998). Schools in Birmingham, Alabama, report a 30% decrease in drug and weapon incidents in the two years after the school board required uniforms. School principals report that school uniforms

- bolster security because outsiders are easy to spot on school grounds,
- decrease fights over clothing,
- decrease gang influence since students can't wear gang colors or attire,
- blur socioeconomic lines as all the students dress the same,
- decrease student distraction caused by some clothes, and
- communicate to students that they are dressed for work.

## Preventive Strategies for the Classroom

Several authors suggest applying preventive strategies in order to promote the use of socially acceptable classroom behavior (DeLuke & Knoblock, 1987; Sabatino, 1987; Stainback, Stainback, & Froyen, 1987). Many of these strategies are based on the earlier work of Long and Newman (1976). Long and Newman discuss three categories of ecological manipulation that can be incorporated into classroom management strategies to prevent challenging behaviors: classroom environment, classroom activities, and teacher behavior. By monitoring and modifying the classroom environment (Sabatino, 1987), classroom activities, and teacher behavior (DeLuke & Knoblock, 1987), teachers may facilitate acceptable student behavior and prevent unacceptable behavior. Long and Newman list several strategies for classroom teachers:

- *Inform students of what is expected of them.* Teachers are encouraged to develop classroom rules and to review the rules frequently with students. Rules may even be posted to serve as a reminder for teachers and students.
- *Establish a positive learning climate.* Teachers can establish a positive learning climate by reinforcing students for appropriate behavior, by interacting with the students in a consistent manner, and by being flexible enough to accommodate the individual needs of all the classroom students. In addition, teachers need to make learning a fun experience so that students will want to come to school and will arrive motivated to learn.
- *Provide meaningful learning experiences.* Relating academic lessons and tasks to the daily lives of students will increase student interest and provide for effective generalization of skills.
- *Avoid threats.* When rules are clearly stated and understood, threats are unnecessary. Instead of threats, teachers should remind students of the classroom rules and other behavioral expectations and consistently provide consequences for both appropriate and inappropriate behaviors.
- *Demonstrate fairness.* Teachers are more likely to interact with all students equally and consistently when classroom rules are clearly stated and understood.
- *Build and exhibit self-confidence.* Students who feel good about themselves and their schoolwork are likely to interact with others appropriately. Teachers have many opportunities to model self-confidence (e.g., "I know I can do this") and encourage student self-confidence throughout the day.
- *Recognize positive student attributes.* All students have positive attributes that may be recognized to build self-esteem and self-confidence. Also, teachers should recognize, be sensitive to, and celebrate individual student differences.
- *Use positive modeling.* Students are likely to model the behavior of teachers and other significant adults. This provides teachers with many opportunities to teach students how to deal appropriately with anger, mistakes, and everyday frustrations.
- *Pay attention to the physical arrangement of the classroom.* The classroom should allow for a smooth flow of student traffic and visual monitoring of student behavior. An organized teacher and classroom environment may encourage students to be better organized.
- *Limit downtime.* The more time students spend in downtime, the more opportunities are available for inappropriate behaviors. Both teacher and students should be prepared for the day. The time a teacher spends preparing for class will be time saved when students are busy and challenged (and not engaged in inappropriate behavior).

Figure 9.3 provides additional strategies for classroom teachers to prevent inappropriate behavior and encourage socially appropriate behavior.

*Number 1: Provide Appropriate Supervision.*

Students who know that their teachers know where they are and what they are doing are less likely to get into trouble than students whose whereabouts and behavior are not monitored. Indeed, supervision is one of the most important factors that researchers use to predict future behavioral problems in children. For example, it has been demonstrated that the lack of supervision is a major contributor and predictor of delinquency in adolescents. How are students supervised before and after school? How about during lunch and recess?

*Number 2: Provide Appropriate Structure and Routines.*

Contrary to the popular myth, structure and routines do not stifle a student's creativity. In fact, structure provides children with the security to explore and learn within a safe environment. Rules, guidelines, and daily routines help children develop organization in their lives and an understanding of what is acceptable and unacceptable behavior. Routines add predictability to a child's busy schedule. Teachers should provide students with rules regarding acceptable and unacceptable behavior. Communicate to students your expectations regarding their behavior. Establish daily routines. Give students jobs and responsibilities.

*Number 3: Model Appropriate Behavior.*

Parents and teachers are the most important models for children, and they must model the behavior they want to see in children. So, if teachers want their students to say "Please" and "Thank you," they must set the example. If teachers want their students to say "I am sorry," they must provide the model. Also, if teachers do not want their students to be aggressive when expressing anger, they must learn to express their feelings in nonaggressive ways. Teachers provide students with important models when they deal with anger, hurt, pain, and disappointment in an appropriate, socially acceptable manner. Think about the models of behavior you provide for your students on a daily basis. Think about what your students are learning from these models. If necessary, provide more appropriate models.

*Number 4: Reinforce Appropriate Behavior.*

Whoever started the rumor that children should learn to behave appropriately because "it is the right thing to do" should be sentenced to life with a boss who never says an encouraging word. Even we grown-ups need to hear we are doing a good job. The bottom line is that everyone needs to feel appreciated. As the saying goes, "Catch them being good" and let your students know that you notice the good things they do. Students who need the attention will resort to inappropriate behavior in order to get your attention. Remember, you can't say too many nice things about the good things they do.

*Number 5: Provide Predictable and Consistent Discipline.*

Once teachers understand the importance of rules and guidelines, it is time to decide what to do when the rules are not followed. The bottom line is this: DO SOMETHING! If teachers establish a rule and do not have a consequence for breaking the rule, students will learn not to take teachers or their rules seriously. In the future, they will learn that their teachers do not mean what they say and that it is not important to listen to them. In other words, they will learn to be noncompliant. So say what you mean and mean what you say. Praise students for following the rules and making good choices. Have a consequence for breaking the rules and other inappropriate behaviors. Remember, be consistent!

*(Continued)*

**FIGURE 9.3.** Top-Ten List for Effective Classroom Management

*Source:* By Thomas J. Zirpoli.

*Number 6: Maintain Regular Contact with Parents.*

When teachers and parents maintain regular contact with each other, students are more likely to perform better in school. When parents and teachers talk to one another, students get the message that both care about their schoolwork, that their schoolwork is being monitored by teachers and parents, and that their teachers and parents are working together. Encourage parents to attend parent-teacher conferences. Call and send notes home. Reinforce parents who participate.

*Number 7: Avoid Looking for Biological Causes of Behavior.*

Very little research links typical, everyday, inappropriate behavior (such as tantrums, noncompliance, aggression) to biological causes. The fact is, most of these behaviors are learned and appropriate behaviors can be learned in their place. Medications, while sometimes necessary, do not change the child's environment and conditions under which the inappropriate behavior was learned. Medications should be a last resort, not a quick fix for common behavior problems. When confronted with behavior problems, evaluate your own behavior and ask what you can do to change the student's behavior. For example, is the child noncompliant because sometimes you do not follow up on your requests? Are you consistent with your stated consequences?

*Number 8: Be a Teacher, Not a Friend.*

Some teachers think that they need to be a good "friend" to their students. The most important thing children need in life is effective parenting and teaching, not another friend. Someday, if teachers are very lucky, their students will grow up, look back, and appreciate the fact that they had good teachers. Listen to your students and they will talk to you. If you jump on them every time they approach you, they will stop talking to you. Let your students know that you value their opinion. Allow them to have and make choices, but you limit the choices.

*Number 9: Let Students Know You Like Them and Are Interested in Their Interests.*

Children need to know that they are loved and that the significant adults in their lives like them regardless of the stupid mistakes that they are likely to make. For example, while parents may not like their children's behavior, it is important for children to know that they are loved. At the same time, teachers need to separate the behavior from the child. Show students that you care about the things that are important to them. Ask about and encourage their extracurricular activities and hobbies. Speak to students with respect.

*Number 10: Have Fun!*

Students sense teachers' mood, and their behavior frequently reflects their teachers' frame of mind. When teachers are happy and having fun, their students are usually happy and having fun. When teachers are in a foul mood, aren't their students usually moody and restless? Ask yourself: Am I having fun with my students? If not, how is this affecting both your behavior and the behavior of your students?

**FIGURE 9.3.** (*Continued*)

Teachers should always evaluate environmental variables, especially antecedents and consequences, along with their own behavior, as the first step in reducing inappropriate behavior. When behavior reduction strategies are still necessary, teachers are encouraged to familiarize themselves with some generally acceptable guidelines and procedural safeguards.

# GENERAL BEHAVIOR REDUCTION GUIDELINES

When behavior reduction strategies are employed, several general guidelines are available that will assist teachers in implementing an effective behavior change program.

## The Fair Pair Rule

Coined by White and Haring (1976), the *fair pair rule* states that when a teacher targets a behavior for reduction, "an alternative behavior is selected to replace the challenging behavior" (Wacker, Berg, & Northrup, 1991, p. 11). Snell and Zirpoli (1987) state that when one behavior is targeted for reduction, an appropriate behavior should be targeted for positive reinforcement. Preferably, the behavior targeted for increase is an appropriate substitute for, or at least incompatible with, the challenging behavior targeted for decrease. "This procedure results in a repertoire of appropriate behaviors, providing the student with alternative responses rather than merely eliminating behavior. More opportunities to reinforce the student positively are also created" (Snell & Zirpoli, 1987, p. 136).

## Be Consistent

When students are provided with rules and behavioral guidelines, teachers must be consistent about enforcement and reinforcement. For example, if the rule states that Robert must sit in the corner for 2 minutes when he hits other students, teachers must implement the consequence each time the rule is broken. Mild inappropriate behaviors, such as an occasional rude comment or noncompliance, may be followed by a verbal warning—as long as this is stated in the rules. Severe inappropriate behaviors, such as hitting or other acts of aggression, should not be followed only by a warning. Consistency teaches children that there is a relationship between following the rules and reinforcement. Also, it teaches the children that there are consequences when the rules are not followed. When teachers are not consistent, students tend to become confused about the rules and teacher expectations. This confusion will be demonstrated by their behavior. For example, if a teacher is inconsistent with the enforcement of a classroom rule (such as "Students must receive permission from the teacher before leaving the class"), some students may think that the rule is not very important or that it is not important *always* to obey the rule. Some students may generalize this attitude to other classroom rules. Thus, teachers should not establish rules they are unable or unwilling to enforce consistently.

## Avoid Reinforcing Inappropriate Behavior

Teachers must be careful that students do not get more attention following inappropriate behaviors than they would following appropriate behaviors. Inappropriate behavior should be calmly followed with the provision of a specific consequence as outlined in the behavior change program. It is important that "the challenging behavior never results in the desired consequence" (Wacker et al., 1991, p. 11).

Teachers should avoid long lectures and excessive one-to-one interaction with students after inappropriate behavior. This type of attention may be reinforcing to some students, especially when done in the other students' presence. For example, a high school student may enjoy a teacher reprimand conducted in full view of classmates if he perceives the incident as a way of increasing his status among his peers. The teacher can deliver the same comments, quietly at the student's desk, without drawing a significant amount of attention to the student's inappropriate behavior. This approach may be called a "soft" reprimand.

The greatest danger in implementing a behavior reduction procedure without a reinforcement component is that children may learn to associate adult attention only with the behavior reduction procedure. A child who is "hungry" for adult attention will soon learn to act inappropriately for the attention he or she cannot gain through appropriate behavior.

## Consequences for Inappropriate Behavior

The consequences a child experiences for acting inappropriately should be short and to the point. Whether we are talking about time-out or the removal of a toy or other preferred object, a short period of time is usually as effective as longer intervals. Taking a toy away from a child for an hour or, at most, for the day following an inappropriate behavior is long enough. Consequences for inappropriate behavior should seldom be carried over into the next day. Indeed, the next day will provide teachers with new opportunities to identify and reinforce appropriate behavior. In behavior management, longer (such as longer time-out periods, longer periods of restriction or "grounding," etc.) does not necessarily mean better. For example, if a student breaks a rule in school and the consequence is the removal of recess, the removal of one to a few recess periods should be sufficient if the student considers recess reinforcing. Taking away recess for weeks or months is counterproductive and will likely lead to further inappropriate behavior (Harris, 1985).

## Deal with Inappropriate Behavior Immediately

When teachers send students to the principal's office for inappropriate behavior or when a mother says, "Wait 'til your dad comes home," the stated consequence for the inappropriate behavior will probably not be immediately or consistently applied. In addition, children of these caregivers will learn that it is not necessary to behave appropriately in the absence of the threatened adult (e.g., the principal or dad). By teaching the child that the first caregiver either will not or cannot deal with the inappropriate behavior, the caregiver is, in effect, teaching the child that it is safe to behave inappropriately with that caregiver.

## Avoid Ineffective Procedures

Yelling or shouting at children is not an effective manner in which to communicate or control inappropriate behavior. The same is true with spanking or other forms of corporal punishment, which will be discussed at greater length later in this chapter. Instead of controlling inappropriate behavior, these behaviors simply provide children with inappropriate models of behavior. When a caregiver resorts to the use of corporal punishment, chances are that the caregiver is out of control. In this case, the caregiver should take a break and, if possible, let someone else take over for a while. These kinds of caregiver behaviors are not only ineffective in changing the behavior of children but also damaging to children's self-esteem. In the end, nothing worthwhile has been accomplished, and the potential for negative outcomes is great.

## Restrictiveness and Social Acceptability

Another important factor that teachers must consider when selecting a behavior change procedure is the perceived restrictiveness and social acceptability of the procedure by others. Least restrictive procedures are always preferred over more restrictive procedures. Researchers have found general agreement among professionals regarding the restrictiveness of various behavior change procedures. For example, Morgan and Striefel (1988) studied how educators viewed the restrictiveness of various behavior change procedures, including those discussed in this chapter. They surveyed the perceptions of school psychologists, administrators, teachers, and specialists. The perceived restrictiveness of the procedures evaluated in their study, and discussed in this chapter, is outlined in Figure 9.4.

The focus of any behavior program should be reinforcement of appropriate behaviors.

**FIGURE 9.4.** Restrictiveness of procedures to decrease behaviors as viewed by school teachers and specialists

*Source:* Adapted from "Restrictiveness of Procedures to Decrease Behavior: Views of School Psychologists, Administrators, Teachers, and Specialists," by R. L. Morgan and S. Striefel, 1988, *Journal of Special Education; 21,* 108–119.

| Level of Restrictiveness | Behavioral Procedure |
|---|---|
| Least Restrictive | Changing antecedent events |
| | Planned ignoring |
| | Response cost |
| | Nonexclusionary time-out |
| | Positive practice overcorrection (with physical guidance) |
| | Positive practice overcorrection (without physical guidance) |
| | Exclusionary time-out |
| Most Restrictive | Application of discomforting stimuli |

Morgan and Striefel speculated that the restrictiveness of a procedure depended on several variables, including the amount of physical contact or restraint from the teacher and the student's level of discomfort when the procedure is applied. They also found that the "social acceptability" of each procedure was influenced by the "suitability of the procedure for classroom use, risk to the student, teacher time and skill required for intervention, and effects on other students" (p. 119).

## ESTABLISHING SAFEGUARDS AND PROGRAM REVIEW PROCEDURES

Once the decision is made to implement a behavior reduction program, several procedural safeguards should be put in place. Wolery and Gast (1990) outline several "conditions under which all behavior reduction procedures, aversive or nonaversive, should be implemented":

- "A decision model should be employed to ensure that individuals' rights are protected, appropriate planning is completed, best-practice implementation occurs, and appropriate review is obtained" (p. 137).
- There should be an assessment of motivational factors related to the target behavior.
- Assessment of the target behavior should be data based.
- Behavior reduction strategies should be used in conjunction with strategies to teach and reinforce appropriate and adaptive behaviors.
- There should be reliable measurement of the target behavior and treatment implementation.
- Side effects of the intervention should be monitored periodically.

- Attention should be given to the maintenance and generalization of program outcomes.
- Informed consent from parents and administrative authorities must be obtained.
- There should be peer review of the intervention plan to ensure "that the proposed procedure reflects best-practice and has a base in the empirical literature" (p. 139).
- The program must be implemented in an "open" environment in which interested parties may "observe, evaluate and comment" on the implementation of the program (p. 139).
- The program must be implemented by a competent team of professionals.

Decisions about the management of children's behaviors should be made in collaboration with many caregivers involved. Any decision to implement a behavior reduction procedure should be a team decision rather than an individual one. Parents are very important members of this team, and educators should make every effort to include parents in important discussions about their children. None of the behavior reduction strategies discussed in this chapter should be implemented before talking about the child and his or her behaviors with all significant caregivers.

## Program Review and Human Rights Committees

Within educational settings, the establishment of a program review committee (PRC) or human rights committee (HRC) is recommended. These committees may serve to review general behavior management policies and specific behavior reduction program plans for individual students. Members of the committee may include administrators, teachers, parents, and community experts in behavior management. The PRC/HRC may serve:

- as a sounding board for educators regarding individual students, challenging behaviors, or programming ideas;
- as a source of fresh programming ideas for specific behavior problems;
- as a way to monitor and review ongoing behavior management programming for individual students; and
- as a review board for general policy guidelines regarding the use of behavior management strategies within the educational setting.

While some may view the PRC/HRC as intrusive (Axelrod, 1990), these committees should be regarded as both a resource and a group concerned with providing students with appropriate, positive learning experiences. When behavior reduction procedures are used, the PRC/HRC should ensure that responsible professionals are monitoring student progress and that decisions about program effectiveness are made based on reliable data.

# SPECIFIC BEHAVIOR REDUCTION STRATEGIES

A number of behavior reduction strategies are available to teachers to decrease inappropriate behavior. While some strategies are recommended, others are advised only with modifications, and some not at all. These recommendations will be communicated within the discussion of each procedure. Some common strategies used to reduce inappropriate behavior include *reviewing environmental influences, extinction, time-out, response cost, restitution, positive practice,* and *overcorrection.* Other more intrusive interventions (including some we do not recommend), such as *medications, restraints,* and *corporal punishment,* will also be discussed because they are frequently used and abused as behavior reduction procedures. Again, it must be stressed that none of these techniques should be used in isolation. They should always be used in conjunction with interventions that are designed to increase appropriate behavior. Teachers should incorporate techniques to decrease behavior only when reinforcement strategies alone are not effective.

## Review Environmental Influences

All of the behavior reduction strategies discussed in this section correctly assume that most challenging behavior exhibited by a student is influenced by his or her environment. So one must understand that the teacher's behavior within the classroom and the parents' behavior in the home are significant variables in the teaching of appropriate behavior and the modification of inappropriate behavior. If teachers and parents are not willing to evaluate their own behavior as a contributing factor to both appropriate and inappropriate behavior in their children, there is little hope of helping the student. Zirpoli (2003) states that many parents suffer from Parental Wimp Syndrome (PWS), which is associated with a lack of supervision, expectations, rules, and consistent consequences. Unless these parents are willing to learn how to become stronger parents (see Zirpoli, 2003), their children will continue to fail regardless of interventions provided by the child's school.

## Extinction

Frequently, students engage in behaviors to elicit teacher or peer attention. *Extinction* is a procedure that gradually reduces the frequency and/or intensity of a target behavior by withholding reinforcement from the previously reinforced behavior. Extinction requires teachers to ignore behavior that, under normal circumstances, would typically lead to attention, a form of reinforcement. By withholding this reinforcement, "extinction can be used to eliminate the connection between the behavior and the positive consequences that follow it" (Kazdin, 1989, p. 174). Gilliam (1989) states that "to discontinue the effect the behavior has on the environment (extinction)" is one of "the most fundamental" ways to eliminate behavior (p. 5).

Extinction is only effective in reducing behaviors that are motivated by attention or some other form of reinforcement. For example, in what may be the first published article regarding the withholding of reinforcement to reduce an inappropriate behavior, Williams (1959) outlines an extinction program to eliminate temper tantrums in a 21-month-old boy. The boy had been sick for the first 18 months of life and had learned to associate crying behavior with parental attention. Although he had recovered, he still used the crying behavior as a way to gain significant amounts of parental attention and to avoid going to bed at night. By ignoring this behavior, the parents helped gradually eliminate the child's crying at bedtime.

As demonstrated by the Williams study, extinction has been effective with very young children. Others have demonstrated the effectiveness of extinction with older preschoolers (3 to 5 years old) (Higgins, Morris, & Johnson, 1989) and young adults (Barrett, Deitz, Gaydos, & Quinn, 1987).

Extinction will not be effective for behaviors that are intrinsically reinforcing. Examples of behaviors that are intrinsically reinforcing include thumb sucking, daydreaming, and self-stimulatory behaviors. Also, extinction should not be used for physical aggression, even if attention seems to be the motivating factor. Physical aggression is a behavior that should never be ignored. Also, some behaviors, such as severe self-injury or those that may hurt others, may require a more direct intervention approach than extinction.

## Extinction and Consistency

Consistency is the most important factor related to the efficacy of extinction. For extinction to be effective in reducing a target behavior, teachers must be willing to ignore the behavior each and every time the behavior is observed. Teachers must alert other teachers and caregivers about the extinction program so that everyone who has contact with the student consistently withholds reinforcement following the target behavior. Accidental reinforcement must be prevented.

Teachers must determine whether the student's primary source of reinforcement is from teachers or peers. If the primary source of reinforcement is from the student's peers, teachers may not be in a position to control the delivery of reinforcement, and extinction is unlikely to be an effective procedure in reducing the target behavior. For example, if a student exhibits disruptive behavior within an educational setting in order to gain recognition from friends, an extinction program initiated by the teacher without the cooperation of the student's friends is unlikely to be effective.

As with other behavior reduction procedures, extinction should not be used in isolation and must be paired with the reinforcement of appropriate behaviors. When the inappropriate behavior is consistently ignored, it will be extinguished over a period of time. Like Leon in Classroom Application 9.1, the student will learn that inappropriate behaviors are ignored and that only appropriate behaviors will yield the desired attention or reinforcement.

## Classroom Application 9.1

## Using Extinction in the Classroom

Ann has a class of 12th graders who are fairly bright. One day she notices that one of her students, Leon, is acting very silly, which is disruptive to the other students. She also notices that the other students are giving him a lot of attention for his silly behavior. After class, several of her students talk to her about Leon's behavior and how disruptive it is to them. She advises them that Leon is probably seeking their attention and that if they would ignore him, Leon will eventually stop. She also warns them that once they start extinction, Leon's behavior will become more disruptive before it gets better. Sure enough, during the next few days, as the students do a good job ignoring him, Leon becomes even more disruptive then ever. After several days, however, Leon realizes that the other students no longer find his silly behavior funny and he settles down. Ann is sure to call on him and draw attention to Leon when he is acting appropriately. She wants to ensure that Leon learns that he can receive her attention following appropriate, not inappropriate, behavior.

### Other Factors Affecting Extinction

Kazdin (1989) cites several factors that may influence a behavior's resistance to extinction:

- The schedule of reinforcement that previously maintained the behavior (continuously reinforced behaviors decrease more rapidly than intermittently reinforced behaviors)
- The amount or strength of reinforcement that previously maintained the behavior (the greater the amount or strength of reinforcement associated with the behavior, the more resistance to extinction)
- The length of time the reinforcement was previously associated with the target behavior (the longer the association between the reinforcement and the behavior, the more resistance to extinction)
- The frequency of extinction used in the past to disassociate the reinforcement and the behavior (the greater the number of times, the more rapid the extinction)

### Extinction Burst

Extinction is an effective procedure for reducing inappropriate attention-getting behavior in children. However, one aspect of the procedure may make extinction very difficult for some teachers to use. Often a student has learned that demands will eventually be met if he or she is persistent and engages in the inappropriate behavior until teachers "give in" or "give up."

What happens when a teacher decides to ignore behavior that has previously been reinforced? The student is likely to repeat the behavior with greater frequency and intensity in hopes that the teacher will eventually give in (again). This is called an *extinction burst*. An extinction burst is a temporary increase in the frequency or intensity of a target behavior immediately after the introduction of extinction. For example, when a teacher decides to ignore a student's talking-out behavior, which previously resulted in getting the teacher's attention, the student's behavior may initially increase. By being consistent and reinforcing the student for appropriate methods of getting the teacher's attention (raising hand), the student's talking-out behavior will decrease.

Unfortunately, many teachers do not know about extinction bursts and, at this point, incorrectly judge the extinction program as ineffective. On the contrary, the extinction burst demonstrates that the teacher has identified at least some of the primary reinforcements maintaining the target behavior, that these reinforcers have been effectively withheld, and that the extinction procedure is having an impact on the student's behavior. With a little persistence and patience on the part of the teacher, once the extinction burst period is over, the student's behavior will improve. Teachers must decide *before* using extinction whether they will be able to ignore the inappropriate behavior through the extinction burst phase. If this is not possible, then another procedure is recommended.

## Spontaneous Recovery

*Spontaneous recovery* refers to the temporary recurrence of a target behavior during extinction even though the behavior has not been reinforced. The frequency or intensity of the behavior is usually not significant during spontaneous recovery. The biggest danger during this time is that the behavior will receive significant teacher attention or other forms of reinforcement. This, of course, will increase the likelihood of the behavior's recurring in the future. However, if teachers are consistent with the extinction procedure, the behavior is less likely to recur. Figure 9.5 demonstrates an example of both an extinction burst and spontaneous recovery during an extinction program used to reduce the frequency of a student's tattling behavior.

## Advantages of Extinction

Extinction has many advantages over other behavior reduction procedures, especially those considered "intrusive" or "aversive." First, extinction may be effective in reducing inappropriate behavior without the use of any physical or verbal consequences (e.g., repeatedly telling the student, "No!") that may decrease the student's self-esteem or establish a "battle" between the teacher and the student. Second, since extinction does not involve the use of any aversive punishments, negative side effects from these procedures are avoided. Third, while the effects of extinction may be gradual, the duration of effects is usually long-lasting. Last, the reinforcement of appropriate behaviors, while ignoring the inappropriate target

**FIGURE 9.5.** Demonstration of extinction burst and spontaneous recovery during extinction program for reduction of tattling behavior

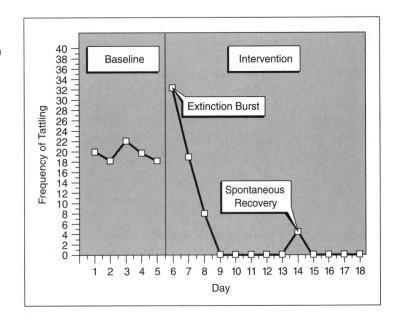

behavior, is a critical element of extinction. Next to positive reinforcement, this point makes extinction, in our opinion, a procedure of first choice when teachers are trying to reduce minor inappropriate behaviors.

### Potential Side Effects and Disadvantages of Extinction

Except for the temporary increase in the target behavior that occurs during the extinction burst, the extinction procedure has only minor potential side effects. For example, the student may become frustrated when teachers no longer provide attention that has come to be expected following a target behavior. This may lead to a significant extinction burst and the demonstration of other inappropriate behaviors (e.g., aggression) as well. As long as teachers provide reinforcement for other appropriate behaviors and are consistent with the extinction procedure, these side effects should be only temporary setbacks.

In summary, extinction may be effective when teachers are able and willing to:

- identify all reinforcers that typically follow the target behavior;
- withhold all reinforcers that typically follow the target behavior;
- be consistent, ignoring the target behavior every time it is exhibited;
- identify and reinforce appropriate behaviors during the extinction program;
- maintain the procedure through the expected extinction burst and spontaneous recovery periods beyond; and
- teach and demonstrate to the student that teacher attention follows appropriate behavior.

Extinction may not be effective or should not be used when:

- the reinforcers that typically follow the target behavior cannot be identified,
- the withholding of reinforcement following the target behavior is not possible,
- other teachers who come in contact with the student are not willing or able to follow the extinction procedure,
- peer reinforcement in maintaining the target behavior cannot be controlled,
- there is a high probability of accidental reinforcement,
- an extinction burst of the behavior cannot be tolerated given the student's behavior or other factors within the environment, or
- it is inappropriate or dangerous to ignore the target behavior (e.g., aggression, severe self-injury).

## Time-Out from Positive Reinforcement

Time-out from reinforcement entails removing an individual's access to sources of reinforcement for a specific period of time contingent on inappropriate behavior. Teachers may deny access to reinforcement in two primary ways: Teachers can remove the student from the reinforcement or remove the reinforcement from the student. Time-out from positive reinforcement has proven effective in reducing many kinds of behaviors (Onslow, Packman, & Stocker, 1997; Skiba & Raison, 1990).

Note that if the initial environment or activity is *not* reinforcing to the student, then removing the student's access to that reinforcement would *not* be considered time-out or a behavior reduction procedure. In fact, if a student does not want to be in an environment to begin with, removing the student may actually be reinforcing. For example, if a student does not like his or her classroom and wants to get out of the classroom (e.g., sending the student to a time-out area outside the classroom), contingent on inappropriate behavior, may serve as a reinforcer, not a punisher (Costenbader & Reading-Brown, 1995). The use of time-out in this case may, in fact, increase the student's inappropriate behavior. Shriver and Allen (1996) urge teachers to consider the reinforcing value of the time-in environment compared with the time-out environment. Again, the time-out environment must be less reinforcing than the time-in environment.

As with any behavior reduction procedure, the effectiveness of time-out is measured by the reduction of the target behavior for which the time-out serves as a consequence. By monitoring the target behavior, teachers should be able to determine whether the time-out procedure is effective. Unfortunately, many teachers continue to use time-out with individual students even when the evidence is clear that time-out has not been an effective behavior reduction procedure for those individuals. Because some types of time-out involve removing a challenging student from the environment, some teachers use time-out as a method of taking a temporary "break" from the student. This, however, is not time-out from positive reinforcement and is unlikely to serve as an effective behavior reduction procedure. In fact, the temporary "break" from the student may be negatively reinforcing for teachers, and, despite a lack of effectiveness, they continue to use the procedure.

One of the primary issues regarding time-out is the length of the time-out period. Two- to 8-minute time-out periods are suggested for young children contingent on inappropriate behavior. Time-out periods should be given in increments of 1 minute per year of age (e.g., 2 years = 2 minutes of time-out) for children 10 years old and younger. Longer periods are not more effective and may even lead to an increase in inappropriate behavior (Harris, 1985). Teachers should use an alarm clock, a timer, or other method to act as a cue to end the time-out period and to ensure that the student does not spend more time in time-out than scheduled. Several types of time-out procedures are available. There are also some terminology issues concerning other procedures incorrectly identified under the heading of "time-out." These will be discussed next.

### Nonexclusion Time-Out

*Nonexclusion time-out* is discussed in several texts and articles as a procedure in which the student is *not* removed from the reinforcing environment, but in some way or another, attention and other forms of reinforcement are taken from the student (Alberto & Troutman, 1995; Cooper, Heron, & Heward, 1987; Kazdin, 1989). At first reading, some readers may be confused by the similarity of nonexclusion time-out and extinction. While extinction involves withholding reinforcement previously associated with a target behavior, nonexclusion time-out refers to the temporary removal of *all* reinforcement for a short period. For example, as a result of an extinction program, Julia is ignored by her teacher when she speaks in class without first raising her hand. While Julia was previously able to receive her teacher's attention in this manner, her teacher now calls on Julia only when she raises her hand. If the same teacher were using a nonexclusion time-out procedure, the teacher would remove all attention and other reinforcement from Julia for a specific period of time (e.g., 2 minutes) each time Julia speaks in class without first seeking recognition by raising her hand. With extinction, a specific reinforcement (teacher's attention) previously associated with the target behavior (speaking out) is withheld. With nonexclusion time-out, all attention and reinforcement are removed for a limited period contingent on the target behavior.

Several variations of nonexclusion time-out are possible. The three most common variations are planned ignoring, removal of a specific reinforcer, and the time-out ribbon.

**Planned ignoring.** *Planned ignoring* refers to the removal of any social attention for a short period of time contingent on the occurrence of an inappropriate behavior. For example, when working with a student or a group of students, a teacher may look away from the student/students for 30 seconds contingent on inappropriate behavior.

*Removal of specific reinforcers.* *Removal of specific reinforcers* refers to taking away such reinforcers as food, toys, or materials for a short time contingent on the occurrence of an inappropriate behavior. For example, a parent may remove a child's food for 60 seconds contingent on inappropriate behavior during mealtime, or a teacher may remove a toy from a student for 2 minutes after the student throws the toy at another student.

*The time-out ribbon.* The *time-out ribbon* refers to a procedure first used by Foxx and Shapiro (1978) in which all the students in a classroom were given a ribbon to wear. In addition, the students received edibles and praise for appropriate behavior and for wearing their ribbon. When targeted inappropriate behavior occurred, a teacher removed the ribbon and attention from the student for 3 minutes or until the inappropriate behavior was terminated. Inappropriate behavior decreased from 42% during baseline to 6% during the time-out ribbon program.

The time-out ribbon procedure has been effective with both groups and individuals. For example, McKeegan, Estill, and Campbell (1984) used the time-out ribbon procedure to eliminate stereotypic behavior of a single student. The student learned that, contingent on stereotypic behavior, the ribbon, along with any associated attention or reinforcement, was removed. Yeager and McLaughlin (1994) effectively used a time-out ribbon program to significantly increase compliance within a classroom. Salend and Gordon (1987) used one large ribbon for a whole group of students and demonstrated the effectiveness of an interdependent, group-oriented time-out ribbon procedure. While the class had possession of the ribbon (on display in front of the class), a token system was employed in which the group received one token for every 2 minutes they refrained from inappropriate verbalization. However, when a group member engaged in inappropriate verbalization, the ribbon was removed for 1 minute. The students could not earn tokens during this 1-minute period. Inappropriate verbalizations were significantly reduced.

Teachers may employ many variations to the time-out ribbon. For example, Fee, Matson, and Manikam (1990) used a wristband covered with smiling-face stickers, instead of a ribbon, with preschool students. The wristband was removed for three consecutive minutes contingent on targeted inappropriate behaviors.

## Exclusion Time-Out

*Exclusion time-out* refers to the *physical removal* of a student from a reinforcing environment or activity for a specific period of time. In our opinion, exclusion time-out is the only "true" time-out procedure since, by definition, time-out is the removal of the student from reinforcement. Within exclusion time-out, there are three widely accepted subtypes.

*Contingent observation time-out.* A *contingent observation time-out* is a type of exclusion time-out that involves removing the student from a reinforcing activity (e.g., story time, game) to the "sideline" contingent on the target behavior (Porterfield, Herbert-Jackson, & Risley, 1976). Rather than being isolated, the student is allowed to remain on the periphery of the group and observe the other

## Classroom Application 9.2

### The Use of Contingent Observation Time-Out to Decrease Aggressive Behavior in a Third-Grade Classroom

Susan is a third-grade teacher in a large school with a diverse population of students. Her most common complaint about her students is the frequency of aggressive play she observes throughout the day. Some examples of aggressive play observed by Susan include children pushing each other, pretending to shoot each other with make-believe guns, verbal aggression ("I'm going to kill you!"), and other acts of violence against classmates. Susan decides to have a talk with her students one morning and tells them that from now on any acts of aggression observed in the classroom will result in the student being placed in a time-out corner for 5 minutes. Susan gives her students examples of the types of aggression she is talking about and shows them where the time-out corner will be. Soon after her talk Susan observes one of her students (Michael) hitting another student for getting in his way. She immediately directs Michael to the time-out corner and tells him that he must stay there for 5 minutes for hitting. Michael tries to explain his behavior and talk his way out of his consequence, but Susan ignores him and sets the timer for 5 minutes. During the 5 minutes, Susan goes about her work with the other students. When the timer rings, she directs Michael to return to his activity. In order for this new program to work, Susan knows that she must be very consistent. After several days, her children learn that Susan will be consistent and that aggressive behavior in her classroom is not tolerated. She verbally praises her students for their improved classroom behavior, and they talk about how the class is both safer and more fun for all of them. Susan understands, however, that the continued success of her program depends upon the consistent implementation of her time-out program throughout the school year.

students participating in the activity and behaving appropriately (Skiba & Raison, 1990). After a short time, the student is allowed to return to the group. For example, when a hockey player commits a foul, he or she must sit on the sideline for a specific time period. The hockey player may observe other members of the team play, but he or she may not rejoin the activity until the time-out period is over. White and Bailey (1990) used a contingent observation time-out procedure called "sit and watch" to decrease disruptive behaviors (noncompliance, aggression, and throwing objects) with elementary students during physical education classes. An example of contingent observation time-out is presented in Classroom Application 9.2.

*Isolation time-out.* *Isolation time-out* is a procedure that requires the teacher to remove the student totally from the reinforcing activity contingent on the target behavior. This procedure is one step beyond contingent observation, and the student is *turned away* from the reinforcing activity. An isolation time-out area may be a designated corner or other isolated space in the environment. The students need to know beforehand that they are placed or sent to this area as a result of their inappropriate behavior.

This technique is especially effective in decreasing physically aggressive behavior in young children. When the student exhibits the target behavior (e.g., hitting others), he or she is immediately removed from the activity and placed in the time-out area for a predetermined period. For young students, teachers should gently but firmly take the student to the predetermined area, then briefly tell the student why he or she is being placed in time-out, and how long he or she must remain there (e.g., "You may come out of time-out when the timer goes off"). Older students may simply be instructed, "You [committed the target behavior]. Go to time-out." Other general guidelines for using isolation time-out include these:

- The time-out area should be set up so that the teacher can clearly observe the student but the student cannot observe the activity from which he or she was just removed. Isolation time-out may include placing the student behind a partition within the environment or other open space next to the environment. School hallways are usually not good time-out areas since the classroom teacher may not be able to monitor the student during the time-out period.

- The isolation time-out area may contain a chair for the student to sit on so that expectations for what the student will do while in the time-out area are clear (i.e., sit on the chair).

- The teacher should set a timer for the amount of time the student is to spend sitting in the time-out area. Using a timer clearly delineates to the student how long he or she must stay in time-out and also eliminates the possibility that the teacher will lose track of how long the student has been in time-out. Again, it is important to note that longer time-out periods do not mean that the student will be less inclined to engage in the inappropriate behavior in the future. Time-out periods that last longer than 10 minutes are unlikely to be any more effective than 2-minute periods. As stated earlier, 1 minute of time-out per year of the age of the student is a good guideline to follow (D. Wacker, personal communication, January 9, 1989).

- The most important factor regarding the effectiveness of time-out is the reinforcement value of the environment from which the student has been removed. Students should not be allowed to play with toys or interact with others while in the time-out area. Remember, the purpose of time-out is to remove the student from reinforcement.

- If the student refuses to remain in the time-out area, the teacher should return him or her to the area and tell the student that he or she may not return to the group until the time in time-out is completed. If this does not work, the student may be given a choice between sitting in the time-out area or being completely removed from the environment. This step may be enough of a deterrent that the student will choose to stay in the less restrictive area. Also, other backup consequences may be employed to reinforce appropriate time-out behavior. Keep in mind that the student will want to return to the activity if he or she has learned that reinforcement may be earned through appropriate behavior.

*Seclusion time-out.* *Seclusion time-out* involves the complete removal of the student to a separate, usually closed, room or cubicle (i.e., time-out room) "outside the individual's normal educational or treatment environment that is devoid of positive reinforcers and in which the individual can be safely placed for a temporary period of time" (Cooper et al., 1987, p. 445). An example of seclusion time-out is sending a student to his or her bedroom or to a time-out room within the educational setting. Some may argue that sending a student to the bedroom is not an appropriate time-out room because it is not devoid of positive reinforcers. However, if the student does not want to be in his or her bedroom and would rather be playing with friends, the bedroom may be appropriate. If not, other less reinforcing areas of the house, such as a parent's bedroom, the stairway, or a chair placed in an isolated area of the home may be used. Small areas (e.g., closets) that are too confining and poorly ventilated or lit are *not* recommended and may be considered abusive. In the classroom environment, where an appropriate time-out room is not available, a special chair or carpet square placed in an isolated area of the classroom may compose a form of seclusionary time-out.

From our personal observations, the use of seclusion time-out has been and continues to be misused and abused in many educational settings. First, students are being removed from environments or activities they do not find reinforcing. By removing a student from an unpleasant environment contingent on inappropriate behavior, teachers may be negatively reinforcing inappropriate behavior. Second, students are frequently sent to seclusion time-out for periods of time that are too long and serve only to provide teachers with a break from the student. Third, in many cases time-out continues to be used despite data indicating its ineffectiveness in reducing specific inappropriate behavior in individual students. Fourth, time-out is frequently used across schools and other educational settings with disregard for individual differences across students and behaviors. A procedure perceived as punishing for one student may be perceived as reinforcing for another and vice versa.

## Advantages of Time-Out

Time-out from positive reinforcement has several advantages:

- It is easy to integrate a time-out procedure with a positive reinforcement program to increase appropriate behaviors.
- Effects from time-out procedures are usually rapid, and the duration of effects is usually long-lasting.

- The nonexclusion time-out process may be employed without removing the student from the educational environment.
- Nonexclusion time-out involves little or no physical contact with the student following inappropriate behavior.
- Time-out gives teachers an alternative to more intrusive behavior reduction strategies.
- Time-out provides students with the opportunity to regain control of their own behavior (Taylor, 1997).

## Potential Side Effects and Disadvantages of Time-Out

A primary concern about the use of time-out is the removal of students from the instructional setting, which may affect the student's academic performance. Skiba and Raison (1990) examined the relationship between time-out usage with elementary students and academic achievement. They found that "considerably less instructional time was lost to time-out than to other sources of classroom absence, such as suspension or truancy" (p. 36). The amount of time-out usage was stated as "low to moderate for the majority of students," or an average of seven time-out periods (74 minutes) per month per student. When time-out usage is high, teachers should begin to question not only the impact on educational performance but the effectiveness of the time-out procedure for the individual students (Costenbader & Reading-Brown, 1995). In addition, some courts and the U.S. Office of Civil Rights have ruled that excessive and prolonged use of time-out, especially if it interferes with the student's appropriate education, may be a violation of Section 504 and IDEA (Yell, 1998).

In summary, time-out from positive reinforcement may be an effective behavior reduction procedure if the following result:

- The use of time-out is paired with a positive reinforcement program for appropriate behaviors.
- Teachers make the student's environment and activities reinforcing so that the student will want to remain in the current environment and activities. That is, the student perceives the current environment and activities as more reinforcing than the time-out area.
- Teachers monitor the effectiveness of time-out and discontinue its use when data indicate no effect on behavior.
- Teachers do not abuse time-out as a method of removing a student with challenging behavior.

Potential disadvantages and side effects of time-out include these:

- Time-out may be abused, especially the duration of the time-out period.
- Some teachers may use it as a break.
- Some students may view time-out as more reinforcing than the time-in environment.

- Frequent time-out usage removes the student from educational settings and may affect academic performance.
- The student may exhibit other inappropriate behaviors when teachers remove positive reinforcement or remove the student from a reinforcing environment.

## Response Cost

*Response cost* is the systematic removal of reinforcers, sometimes in the form of tokens, points, money, or check marks, contingent on inappropriate behavior. Often used in conjunction with a token economy program (described in Chapter 7), this intervention requires systematically removing tokens as a consequence of inappropriate behavior (Walker, 1983). The number of tokens lost per inappropriate behavior is predetermined and usually depends on the severity of the behavior.

The response cost system should be explained to the student prior to implementation; moreover, it is a wise idea to list and post both the behaviors that will result in a removal of reinforcers and the number of reinforcers that will be lost per inappropriate behavior. A response cost program should always be employed in conjunction with a token economy program. Thus, along with a list of inappropriate behaviors that will lead to the removal of reinforcers, a list of appropriate behaviors that will warrant the earning of additional reinforcers should also be posted. Research has repeatedly indicated that the combination of response cost with other reinforcement programs is more effective than response cost alone (Phillips, Phillips, Fixsen, & Wolf, 1971; Walker, 1983; Walker, Hops, & Fiegenbaum, 1976).

Teachers should be sure that a student does not have all reinforcers removed or "go in the hole." For example, a student on a response cost program should not owe teachers 10 tokens at the end of the day. This is ensured by reinforcing appropriate behavior more often than removing tokens for inappropriate behavior. Teachers should reinforce appropriate behavior four times for every response to inappropriate behavior. In this way, the primary focus of the educational setting will be on reinforcing appropriate behaviors rather than punishing inappropriate behaviors.

Walker (1983, p. 52) outlines several guidelines for implementing response cost (RC) programs:

- RC should be implemented immediately after the target behavior occurs.
- RC should be applied consistently.
- The student should not be allowed to accumulate negative points.
- The ratio of points earned to points lost must be controlled.
- The subtraction of reinforcers should not be punitive or personalized.
- The student's appropriate behavior should be praised frequently.

**TABLE 9.2 • Comparison of Extinction, Time-out, and Response Cost Procedures**

| Procedure | Definition | Example |
|---|---|---|
| Extinction | Removal of attention and other reinforcement previously associated with a target behavior | Caregiver ignores child during tantrum behavior. |
| Time-out | Removal of all reinforcement for short, specific time period contingent on a target behavior | Caregiver removes child from activity contingent on hitting others. |
| Response cost | Removal of predetermined number of reinforcers (tokens, points, check marks) contingent on a target behavior | Caregiver removes one token from child contingent on off-task behavior. |

Table 9.2 provides a comparison of response cost with extinction and time-out. While all three involve the removal of reinforcement, response cost removes a specific reinforcement in increments. Also, the amount of the reinforcement removed is directly proportional to the frequency of inappropriate behavior. As explained by Pazulinec, Meyerrose, and Sajwaj (1983, p. 71):

> In both extinction and timeout procedures, the reinforcing consequence following a response is withheld. In contrast, response cost involves the removal of a positive stimulus contingent upon the occurrence of an undesirable behavior. . . . [I]n timeout the individual is restricted from receiving reinforcement or from participating in ongoing setting activities, whereas the response cost condition imposes no restrictions.

Pazulinec et al. (1983) outline several variations to response cost. In the first variation, a student is noncontingently provided with reinforcers at the beginning of a specific period of time (e.g., day, class period). Then, the student must give back reinforcers contingent on the occurrence of specific target behaviors. This variation may also be used with a group of students. For example, a classroom teacher may give the students 10 points and state that if the class still has 5 points by the end of the day, the students will receive a special reinforcement. Points would be removed throughout the day contingent on inappropriate target behaviors. This first variation is not recommended for several reasons:

- By providing the students with reinforcers noncontingently, this approach does not allow for teaching appropriate behaviors through the contingent presentation of reinforcers.
- A program that removes tokens without a procedure for students to earn tokens increases the chance that a student will develop a negative balance of tokens. Moreover, after a teacher has taken away all of a student's tokens, what will he or she do following the next inappropriate behavior?
- This variation provides attention only for inappropriate behaviors.

In a second variation of response cost, students earn reinforcers throughout the response cost program. Thus, unlike the first variation, students are not provided with "free" reinforcers, which may be taken away contingent on inappropriate behavior. Rather, reinforcers must be earned contingent on appropriate behavior, and, at the same time, reinforcers may be taken away contingent on inappropriate behavior. This second variation may be considered a combination token economy and response cost program, and it may also be employed with a group or classroom of students. Walker (1983, p. 48) reports that the two variations of response cost described so far are "equally effective" in school settings.

In a third variation, teachers may divide their students into smaller groups and give each group opportunities to earn reinforcers and, contingent on inappropriate behavior, lose reinforcers. Special reinforcers may be provided to the group of students who ended the day with the most tokens or points. For example, many classroom teachers have activities (e.g., a companion reading program) throughout the day when students are divided into several small groups. These group periods provide teachers with opportunities to use a group token economy and response cost program to manage classroom behavior. Each group could earn or lose tokens contingent on behavior. At the end of the lesson, the group with the most tokens could earn a special reinforcer (e.g., extra time on the computer). An example of a combination token economy and response cost classroom program is provided in Classroom Application 9.3.

### Advantages of Response Cost

There are many advantages to using response cost programs to modify behavior. However, the advantages listed here assume the use of response cost in conjunction with a positive reinforcement program:

- Response cost programs are easily integrated with token economy or other positive reinforcement programs.
- Response cost programs are easily implemented in both home and classroom settings.
- Response cost programs may be employed with very young or older students (Reynolds & Kelley, 1997).
- The effects of response cost programming on target behaviors are usually rapid and long-lasting.
- During response cost programs, teacher attention is directed at specific target behaviors that need modification.
- During response cost programs, there is little delay between inappropriate behavior and teacher-produced consequences.

### Potential Side Effects and Disadvantages of Response Cost

Since the major element of response cost is the removal of reinforcers as a consequence of inappropriate behavior, too much teacher attention may be directed toward inappropriate behavior rather than appropriate behavior.

## Classroom Application 9.3

# Example of a Combination Token Economy and Response Cost Classroom Program

Marie is a first-grade teacher in a classroom of 28 students. As part of her classroom behavior management program, Marie divides her students into groups of four. She varies group membership throughout the school year in an effort to find the best student combination per group. The desks of the four students are placed in a circle. For each group, Marie places a clear plastic jar on one of the group members' desks. Contingent on appropriate behavior demonstrated by either an individual member of a group or a whole group, Marie drops a token into the jar. Also, when inappropriate behavior is observed, a token is removed from the jar. Because the jars are made of clear plastic, the students can see the tokens accumulate in (or disappear from) their group jars. Marie tries to maintain a higher rate of giving tokens than removing tokens. A special pencil is provided to each member of the group who ends the day with the most tokens. Marie provides an extra special reinforcer to the group who ends the week with the most tokens.

A second disadvantage of response cost programs is the potential for some students to lose all reinforcers and then "give up." Both of these disadvantages may be avoided when opportunities to earn positive reinforcers are also available whenever response cost programs are employed.

## Restitution, Positive Practice, and Overcorrection

In many behavior management references, restitution and positive practice are considered subtypes or components of overcorrection (Foxx & Azrin, 1972, 1973; Foxx & Bechtel, 1983). Thus, the terms *restitutional overcorrection* and *positive practice overcorrection* are frequently used in the literature to describe procedures designed to decrease inappropriate behavior (Alberto & Troutman, 1995; Cooper et al., 1987). In this chapter the terms are presented separately in order to clarify their definitions and expand on their practical applications.

### Restitution or Simple Correction

*Restitution,* also known as *simple correction,* refers to a procedure that requires an individual to return the environment to its state prior to a behavior that changed the environment (Azrin & Besalel, 1980). The classic example is asking a student who spills a glass of milk to clean up the spill. Whether the child spilled the milk deliberately or accidentally, restitution teaches students to be responsible for their behavior. Restitution should not be employed punitively but rather in a matter-of-fact

**TABLE 9.3 ● Examples of Restitution and Restitution Overcorrection**

| If the Child: | Restitution Only—Ask Child to: | Restitutional Overcorrection—Ask Child to: |
|---|---|---|
| Damages family car | Pay for repair. | Pay for new car. |
| Throws things | Pick up the items thrown and return to appropriate storage place. | Pick up all items in environment and return to appropriate place. |
| Makes a mess during play or other activities | Clean play area to condition prior to activity. | Clean play area and beyond. |
| Writes on the wall | Wash the writing from the wall. | Wash the entire wall. |
| Drops food on the floor during lunch | Sweep up food after lunch. | Sweep entire floor. |
| Damages school materials | Repair or replace materials. | Repair or replace materials plus repair other damaged materials. |
| Damages school property | Repair property to condition prior to behavior. | Repair property damaged and perform additional service to school property. |
| Throws litter on the playground | Pick up the litter thrown on the playground. | Pick up all litter on the playground and around the school. |

way, especially if the behavior was an accident. Examples of restitution are provided in Table 9.3.

Very young children may not be able to complete the restitution of the environment independently. However, it is important that teachers ask the child to help as much as possible, depending on age and ability, while the teacher repairs the environment. For example, a teacher may ask the student to put the wet paper towels in the trash after the spill is wiped up. This approach may be called *assisted restitution.*

### *Restitutional Overcorrection*

*Restitutional overcorrection* is defined by Foxx and Azrin (1973) as a step beyond simple correction of the environment. Contingent on inappropriate behavior, the student is required not only to perform restitution but to "restore the situation to a state vastly improved from that which existed before the disruption" (Foxx & Azrin, 1973, p. 2). Restitutional overcorrection should not be used as a consequence of unintentional spills or other accidents. Rather, restitutional overcorrection is intended to serve as a "punishing" consequence for deliberate inappropriate behaviors. Table 9.3 provides examples of restitution overcorrection.

Foxx and Bechtel (1983, p. 213) list the following conditions for the overcorrection procedure:

- The response required of the student should be "directly related" to the student's "misbehavior."
- The student should experience "the effort normally required of others to correct the products of his misbehavior."
- The overcorrection procedure should be "instituted immediately following the misbehavior."
- The student should be required to perform the overcorrection procedure "rapidly so that consequences constitute an inhibitory effort requirement."
- The student "is instructed and manually guided through the required acts, with the amount of guidance adjusted on a moment-to-moment basis according to the degree to which he/she is voluntarily performing the act."

Foxx and Bechtel (1983) later reduced the procedures of restitution overcorrection to three steps:

- Identify the specific and general disturbances created by the misbehavior.
- Identify the behaviors needed to vastly improve the consequences of the disturbance.
- Require the individual to perform these corrective actions whenever the misbehavior occurs. (p. 135)

The use of restitutional overcorrection has been mentioned most often in the literature as a procedure to decrease inappropriate behaviors with individuals having disabilities (Foxx & Bechtel, 1983). Frequently cited behaviors targeted with this procedure include aggression and disruption (Foxx & Azrin, 1972), toileting accidents (Azrin & Foxx, 1971; Hagopian, Fisher, Piazza, & Wierzbicki, 1993), and self-stimulatory behaviors (Zirpoli & Lloyd, 1987). With nondisabled populations, restitutional overcorrection is most often cited in the literature as an intervention for toileting accidents and aggression and/or disruption (Adams & Kelley, 1992; Foxx & Bechtel, 1983). For example, a child who has a toileting accident may be required to clean the entire room where the accident occurred. In a second example, a child may be required to apologize to all students in a classroom as a consequence for aggression directed at one student.

Restitutional overcorrection has been extensively documented as effective in the elimination of many inappropriate behaviors. Yet, while the use of restitution is recommended, restitutional overcorrection is not advised as an acceptable behavior reduction procedure for the following reasons:

- Overcorrection has questionable educational value beyond the lessons learned during the restitution phase of the student's response (Carey & Bucher, 1986).
- Overcorrection places a great deal of attention on the student's inappropriate rather than appropriate behaviors.

- It may be difficult or impossible to force a student to perform an overcorrection procedure.
- Overcorrection may require a teacher to use physical force if a student refuses to participate or cooperate in the overcorrection procedure. As a result, the student may become aggressive.
- Forcing a student to perform overcorrection may provide the student with opportunities for inappropriate attention, especially if completed in the presence of peers.
- Because the overcorrection procedure will probably require considerable teacher effort, teachers will find the procedure disruptive to their teaching and to the other students within the educational setting.

### Positive Practice

*Positive practice* is practicing an appropriate behavior as a consequence for inappropriate behavior. The behavior practiced is the correct, or positive, behavior the student should have exhibited instead of the observed inappropriate behavior. "It means stopping all activities, whenever an error occurs, and then carefully performing the correct behavior several times" (Azrin, Besalel, Hall, & Hall, 1981). For example, when a student throws a piece of paper across the classroom toward a wastepaper basket, the teacher may ask the student to pick up the paper, walk to the wastepaper basket, place the paper into the basket, and return to his seat. On the completion of this appropriate behavior, the teacher should reinforce the student ("Thank you") for performing the behavior correctly. This example provides a nonpunitive approach to positive practice. The teacher corrects the inappropriate behavior, informs the student of an appropriate alternative, allows the student to practice the appropriate behavior, and praises the student for correct performance of the behavior.

Positive practice is not meant to be a positive consequence for inappropriate behavior. Forcing the student to practice the correct response is intended to be a punitive procedure. Also, Foxx and Azrin (1972) and Foxx and Bechtel (1983) state that the use of reinforcement for correct responses during positive practice may encourage the student to behave inappropriately (in order to have additional opportunities for positive practice and reinforcement). Foxx and Bechtel (1983) recommend that the term *positive practice* be discontinued since the word *positive* gives the wrong impression about the procedure. Lenz, Singh, and Hewett (1991) suggest that the term *directed rehearsal* be used "instead of the generic term *overcorrection*" (p. 71).

### Positive Practice Overcorrection

While many texts do not distinguish between positive practice and positive practice overcorrection, a distinction is made here between the use of positive practice as described earlier and positive practice overcorrection. While positive practice may be completed with a nonpunitive, educational intent, positive practice overcorrection is clearly intended as a punishing consequence for inappropriate behavior. With overcorrection, the student is required to perform the correct or appropriate behavior repeatedly. The operative word here is *repeatedly*. Using our previous example, the student may be required to repeat the steps of putting the paper in the wastepaper basket 10 times. The student is not reinforced for correct responses during the positive practice overcorrection procedure.

In another example, Ollendick, Matson, Esveldt-Dawson, and Shapiro (1980) used positive practice overcorrection to decrease spelling errors. In keeping with the original intent of positive practice, Ollendick et al. did not reinforce students for correct spelling during positive practice. Asking a student simply to repeat the spelling of a word correctly is an example of positive practice. Asking a student to repeat the spelling of a word 100 times (orally or in writing) is an example of positive practice overcorrection.

Carey and Bucher (1986) compared the use of positive practice overcorrection with and without the reinforcement of correct responses during the procedure. They found that reinforcing correct performance during the procedure was effective for increasing appropriate behavior and for reducing inappropriate behavior. Carey and Bucher conclude that nonreinforced positive practice "showed no advantages over the reinforced variation, and resulted in a greater incidence of undesirable side effects such as aggression and emotionality" (p. 85).

Foxx and Bechtel (1983) voice some concerns about the reinforcement of students for correct responses during positive practice. Their primary concern was that students might choose to behave inappropriately in order to receive reinforcement during the positive practice procedure. However, we hope that students will be reinforced for appropriate behavior outside the positive practice procedure and not have to depend on the positive practice procedure for teacher attention. Using positive reinforcement during positive practice makes both variations of positive practice less punitive and increases the educational value of the procedures. While not consistent with the initial intent of positive practice, the procedure may be employed in a less punitive manner to teach and reinforce appropriate social skills. These variations are outlined in Figure 9.6.

## Medications

The use of medications to control inappropriate behavior has recently received a significant amount of public attention. This attention has focused on the use of methylphenidate (Ritalin) and other stimulants used to control the behavior of

**FIGURE 9.6.**
Punitiveness of different variations of positive practice with and without the use of positive reinforcement

|  | With Reinforcement | Without Reinforcement |
|---|---|---|
| Positive practice | Least punitive | Punitive |
| Positive practice overcorrection | Punitive | Most punitive |

children diagnosed as hyperactive or having attention-deficit hyperactivity disorder (ADD or ADHD). Clearly, medication is helpful for some children (Swanson et al., 1993; Tannock, Schachar, Carr, Chajczyk, & Logan, 1989). It is also clear, however, that medications such as Ritalin are significantly overprescribed and that many children are taking medication when less intrusive behavior management interventions would prove much more effective (DuPaul, Guevremont, & Barkley, 1992; Maag, 1990; Reid, Maag, & Vasa, 1994). Berry (1998) of Duke University Medical Center, in a report issued by the National Institute of Health, stated that mind-altering medications are prescribed too often to children and criticized the lack of studies on their long-term effects. In the same report, Baltimore (1998) stated that since there is no standard for therapy, it is difficult to look at the prescribing practice and say what is appropriate or not appropriate.

Nonmedical interventions include teaching appropriate social skills to students, effective parenting skills to parents, and classroom management skills to teachers. Unfortunately, it continues to be the case that the overwhelming majority of general education teachers do not complete even a fundamental behavior management course at the preservice level. As a result, ADHD is being overdiagnosed, and many children are "then prescribed medication that cannot help them and could harm them" (Wicks-Nelson & Israel, 1991, p. 203).

In a review of the literature, Taylor (1995) found that "as many as 25% of pediatric visits are for evaluation of children with behavioral challenges" (p. 87). Many of these children are labeled ADHD, and medication remains the primary intervention for at least 80% of them (Hoza, Pelham, Sams, & Carlson, 1992). Reid, Maag, Vasa, and Wright (1994) found that over 90% of a sample of 136 students labeled ADHD were taking medication. Teachers frequently look for quick solutions when faced with inappropriate behaviors, and the use of medication appears to offer teachers fast results. As a result, Goodman and Poillion (1992) have suggested that *ADD* has become an acronym for Any Dysfunction or Difficulty.

While sometimes necessary, medicating a student does not change the antecedents and consequences within the student's environment—an environment that may be reinforcing inappropriate behaviors or that seldom teaches and reinforces appropriate behaviors. In this case, the effects of medication may only mask the real problems, which remain unsolved. As stated and outlined in Part I of this text, identifying the real issues related to inappropriate behavior is a complicated task that includes the assessment of antecedents and consequences of the target behavior. This assessment includes an evaluation of the student's environment and the behaviors of significant adults within the student's environment (see Maag & Reid, 1994, for a functional approach to assessment and treatment of ADHD).

## *Categories of Medications*

The medications most frequently used to alter the behavior of children are categorized by Epstein and Olinger (1987) into three types: stimulants, antidepressants, and antipsychotics. Stimulants are used most frequently to increase attention span and decrease hyperactive, disruptive, and impulsive behavior. Reid, Maag, Vasa, and Wright (1994) found that of students taking medication for ADHD, 79.7% were taking Ritalin and 12.2% Cylert.

Antidepressants are frequently used for enuresis, childhood depression, and anxiety (Gadow, 1986). Antipsychotics are frequently used to treat severe behavioral disorders in children such as psychosis and childhood schizophrenia. Gadow (1986) states that antipsychotics are also used to treat self-injurious and aggressive behaviors in individuals who have mental and emotional disorders. Examples of each of these categories of medications are listed here:

| *Type of Medication* | *Examples* |
|---|---|
| Stimulants | Methylphenidate (Ritalin) |
| | Dextroamphetamine (Dexedrine) |
| | Pemoline (Cylert) |
| Antidepressants | Amitriptyline (Elavil) |
| | Imipramine (Tofranil) |
| Antipsychotics | Chlorpromazine (Thorazine) |
| | Haloperidol (Haldol) |
| | Thioridazine (Mellaril) |

Of the three medication categories discussed here, Epstein and Olinger (1987) state that stimulants are considered the mildest and antipsychotic medications the strongest, with the most side effects. However, the use of stimulant medication is not recommended for children under the age of 3 years and is questionable for children between 3 and 5 years (Barkley, 1989).

Teachers should be knowledgeable about the potential side effects associated with any medication prescribed to the students placed in their care. A text by Gadow (1986), titled *Children on Medication: Epilepsy, Emotional Disturbance, and Adolescent Disorders,* provides a more complete understanding of medications and their use with children and adolescents. Also, works by Pelham (1993) and Greenhill (1992) are recommended for information regarding the use of medication with students labeled ADHD. The following list outlines potential side effects for all three categories of medications—stimulants, antidepressants, and antipsychotics (Epstein & Olinger, 1987; Gadow, 1986):

*Stimulants*

- Loss of appetite
- Insomnia
- Growth inhibition
- Nervous tics
- Motor restlessness

*Antidepressants*
- Loss of appetite
- Insomnia
- Dry mouth
- Nausea
- High blood pressure
- Heart problems
- Poisoning

*Antipsychotics*
- Increased appetite and weight gain
- Lethargy/apathy
- Dry mouth
- Impaired cognition
- Motor disorders (may be temporary or permanent)

*Other precautions include:*
- monitoring and documenting observed side effects;
- requesting periodic blood tests to determine whether the amount of medication is too high or low for the child's body weight; and
- using periods of "drug holidays" to reassess the student's behavior without the medication and to give the student's body a "rest" from the medication's side effects.

Throughout this text, teachers have been encouraged to review and evaluate their own behavior and the student's overall environment and to seek professional advice on modifying these variables before trying to change the student's behavior. The same approach should be followed before placing a student on medication. Teachers are advised to question professionals who are quick to prescribe medications before environmental variables have been thoroughly evaluated and proven behavior management techniques have been explored.

## Physical Restraint

There are two categories of physical restraint. *Manual restraint* involves the use of person-to-person physical contact between a teacher and the individual being restrained. In this procedure, the student is physically restrained by a teacher or other caregivers. *Mechanical restraint* involves the use of some apparatus used by teachers to restrain the individual. Straps, belts, and blankets are just a few examples of mechanical restraints.

Schloss and Smith (1987) outline four primary limitations of manual restraint. First, manual restraint, when used in isolation, does not promote the acquisition of prosocial skills that may be learned through positive strategies such as modeling, direct instruction, and so on. Second, the physical contact and social interaction involved in a manual restraint procedure may serve as reinforcement for inappropriate behavior. Placing an individual in a mechanical restraint may also draw significant attention to the individual. A student who does not have the social skills to gain attention through positive behavior may find the restraint procedure very reinforcing. Third, the restraint procedure is very likely to produce additional inappropriate behaviors, such as aggression, which may be reinforced by teachers during the restraint procedure. In this case, the student's overall inappropriate behavior may increase. Finally, restraint procedures may lead to physical injury to the student and/or teacher. Schloss and Smith state that manual restraint may be the most "potentially dangerous behavior management procedure practiced in educational programs" (p. 211).

An additional limitation is the significant physical and emotional trauma caused to children who are restrained. Teachers who are using or considering using physical restraint are encouraged to think about how they would feel if a similar procedure were employed against them.

It is important to understand the difference between using restraints as a temporary, emergency measure and as a planned consequence for inappropriate behavior within a behavior reduction procedure. While there may be situations when restraining a student is necessary in an emergency situation, the use of restraints as a behavior reduction strategy or planned consequence for inappropriate behavior is not recommended. Programming limitations and side effects overwhelmingly condemn the use of restraints as an acceptable behavior management strategy. Using manual or physical restraints as a planned behavior reduction strategy may also be considered physically and emotionally abusive. In the rare emergency situations when restraints are necessary, only teachers who have received appropriate training in the proper and safe use of restraints should participate in restraining a student.

## Corporal Punishment

"If there is one discipline method that's sure to inspire heated debate, it's spanking. Indeed, a 'spare the rod, spoil the child' mentality is making a comeback" (Samalin, 1995, p. 35).

*Corporal punishment* involves hitting an individual with a hand or an object (e.g., belt, paddle) with the intent to cause pain or injury. Corporal punishment continues to be a common, although unacceptable, consequence for inappropriate behavior in the United States (Baker, 1987; Gunnoe & Mariner, 1997; National Committee to Prevent Child Abuse, 1995). While other less aversive procedures have been proven significantly more effective, corporal punishment has very little empirical support regarding its effectiveness as a behavior reduction procedure.

While some teachers may view the short-term punitive effects of corporal punishment as beneficial, the long-term problems and negative side effects of corporal punishment are numerous. The National Committee to Prevent Child Abuse (1995) listed six reasons to stop spanking:

- Spanking teaches children the moral correctness of hitting.
- Spanking teaches children that those who love you are those who hit you.
- Spanking does not teach kids self-control; rather, it teaches them not to get caught.
- Adults spanked as children show an increased tendency toward alcoholism, depression, and thoughts of suicide.
- Spanking erodes the trust bond between parents and children, teachers and students.
- When spanking is used to control behavior, physical and verbal child abuse is more likely to occur.

Other problems related to corporal punishment include these:

- As a behavior reduction procedure, corporal punishment does not involve the reinforcement of appropriate behavior and places the focus of teacher attention on the child's inappropriate behavior.
- Emotional reactions from corporal punishment may interfere with academic learning and appropriate social skill development (Kazdin, 1989).
- Corporal punishment decreases the victim's self-esteem (Bayless, 1986).
- Corporal punishment provides an inappropriate model for behavior and teaches children to solve problems through aggression (Bandura, 1969).
- The victim of corporal punishment may become aggressive toward the punishing teacher (Kazdin, 1989).
- The use of corporal punishment may lead the victim to avoid or escape the punishing environment (Kazdin, 1989).
- The use of corporal punishment may elicit a fear response in the child when interacting with the punishing teacher (Newsom, Favell, & Rincover, 1983).

The side effects of corporal punishment certainly outweigh any short-term benefits. Corporal punishment is not only an ineffective behavior reduction strategy, but given all the other more positive alternatives, it is unnecessary.

The following is a sample list of some of the professional organizations that have condemned the use of corporal punishment:

- American Bar Association
- American Psychological Association
- National Association of School Psychologists

- American Public Health Association
- American Educational Association
- National Education Association
- National Parent and Teachers Association
- Council for Exceptional Children
- American Association on Mental Retardation
- The Association for Persons with Severe Handicaps

Teachers are urged to resolve against the use of corporal punishment in all settings and support efforts to ban the hitting of children under any circumstances.

## SUMMARY

The term *behavior reduction strategies* is used in this chapter instead of *punishment* because of the perceived association between punishment and aversive procedures. Punishment is technically any response that reduces the occurrence of preceding behaviors. However, the punishing response does not have to be aversive or even punitive to reduce target behaviors effectively.

The use of positive reinforcement is promoted as the intervention of first choice for the reduction of inappropriate behaviors. Differential reinforcement of behavior refers to the reinforcement of behavior following an appropriate discriminative stimulus, or the reinforcement of a target behavior while other behaviors are ignored. Differential reinforcement schedules include the differential reinforcement of other behaviors, differential reinforcement of alternative behaviors, differential reinforcement of incompatible behaviors, and differential reinforcement of lower and higher rates of behaviors.

General guidelines for behavior reduction strategies include following the fair pair rule, being consistent, avoiding too much child-focused attention after inappropriate behavior, providing consequences that are effective, and immediately delivering consequences. Teachers are urged to consider environmental modifications before trying to modify the behavior of students within the environment. In addition, establishing internal and external committees to safeguard students' rights is strongly recommended before teachers attempt to modify or eliminate a student's behavior.

A number of behavior reduction strategies are available to teachers. These include extinction, time-out, response cost, restitution, positive practice, and overcorrection.

Extinction is the withholding of reinforcement from a previously reinforced behavior. Time-out refers to taking away an individual's access to sources of reinforcement for a specific period of time. Response cost is the systematic removal of reinforcers, such as tokens and points, contingent on inappropriate behavior. Note that all of these interventions should be used in conjunction with the positive reinforcement of appropriate behaviors.

Restitution is the act of returning the environment to the condition prior to inappropriate behavior. Restitutional overcorrection, a step beyond simple restitution, refers to vastly improving the environment contingent on inappropriate behavior. The nonpunitive use of restitution is supported, while the use of restitutional overcorrection is not.

Positive practice refers to the required practice of appropriate behaviors contingent on inappropriate behavior. Positive practice overcorrection is the punitive, repeated practice of appropriate behavior. Although not part of the historic or technical definition of positive practice or overcorrection, reinforcing correct performance of behaviors during and outside of the practice procedures is recommended.

Medications are frequently employed to modify the behavior of children. The most common medications used include stimulants to control aggressive and disruptive behaviors, antidepressants, and antipsychotics to treat children with severe behavior disorders. Teachers are encouraged to become knowledgeable about the associated side effects of any medications prescribed to their students. Medications should not serve as a treatment of first choice or a quick fix to behavior challenges that may be remedied by environmental modifications or the employment of basic behavior management strategies.

Manual and mechanical restraints are not recommended, except for rare emergency situations, for the management of inappropriate behaviors. Restraints should never be used as a planned strategy or consequence for inappropriate behavior. Because of the potential physical and emotional trauma restraints may cause to children, the use of restraints as a behavior reduction strategy is considered abusive.

Corporal punishment involves the hitting of children with the intent to cause pain or injury. While many parental and professional organizations have condemned the use of corporal punishment, it continues to be a common consequence for inappropriate behavior. The use of corporal punishment has many negative side effects, has no educational value, and interferes with learning and social development. Thus, the practice of hitting children in any setting or situation is not an acceptable behavior management strategy.

## DISCUSSION QUESTIONS

1. Discuss the differences between programs that focus teacher attention on the reinforcement of appropriate behaviors and those that focus teacher attention on inappropriate behaviors. What are the advantages and disadvantages of each?

2. Discuss the different variations of differential reinforcement, giving examples of each for both school and home settings.

3. Discuss the importance of establishing internal and external review committees when teachers attempt to change or eliminate students' behavior. What procedures are in place within your local school district regarding internal and/or external review of behavior change programs?

4. List and discuss the general guidelines for behavior reduction strategies as outlined in this chapter.

5. Discuss the following behavior reduction strategies, and give examples of each for both school and home environments: extinction, time-out, response cost, restitution, positive practice, and overcorrection. What are your school district's policies regarding these procedures?

6. Discuss the reasons that mechanical restraints and corporal punishment are not recommended strategies for teachers and parents. Investigate and discuss your state's and local school district's policies regarding these procedures.

## REFERENCES

Adams, C. D., & Kelley, M. L. (1992). Managing sibling aggression: Overcorrection as an alternative to time-out. *Behavior Therapy, 23*, 707–717.

Alberto, P. A., & Troutman, A. C. (1995). *Applied behavior analysis for teachers.* Upper Saddle River, NJ: Merrill/Prentice Hall.

Axelrod, S. (1990). Myths that mis(guide) our profession. In A. C. Repp & N. N. Singh (Eds.), *Perspectives on the use of nonaversive and aversive interventions for persons with developmental disabilities* (pp. 59–72). Sycamore, IL: Sycamore.

Azrin, N. H., & Besalel, V. A. (1980). *How to use overcorrection.* Austin, TX: Pro-Ed.

Azrin, N. H., Besalel, V. A., Hall, R. V., & Hall, M. C. (1981). *How to use positive practice.* Austin, TX: Pro-Ed.

Azrin, N. H., & Foxx, R. M. (1971). A rapid method of toilet training the institutionalized retarded. *Journal of Applied Behavior Analysis, 4*, 89–99.

Baker, J. N. (1987, January). Paddling: Still a sore point. *Newsweek,* p. 62.

Baltimore, R. S. (November, 1998). *Report on ADHD.* Washington, DC: National Institute of Health.

Bandura, A. (1969). *Principles of behavior modification.* New York: Holt, Rinehart & Winston.

Barkley, R. A. (1989). Attention deficit-hyperactivity disorder. In E. J. Marsh & R. A. Barkley (Eds.), *Treatment of childhood disorders.* New York: Guilford.

Barrett, D. H., Deitz, S. M., Gaydos, G. R., & Quinn, P. C. (1987). The effects of programmed contingencies and social conditions on response stereotype with human subjects. *Psychological Record, 37*, 489–505.

Bayless, L. (1986). *Discipline: The case against corporal punishment.* King George, VA: American Foster Care Resources.

Berkman, K. A., & Meyer, L. H. (1988). Alternative strategies and multiple outcomes in the remediation of severe self-injury: Going "all out" nonaversively. *Journal of the Association for Persons with Severe Handicaps, 13*, 76–86.

Berry, D. A. (November, 1998). *Report on ADHD.* Washington, DC: National Institute of Health.

Black, S. (1998). Learning on the Block. *American School Board Journal, 185*(1), 32–33.

Carey, R. G., & Bucher, B. D. (1986). Positive practice overcorrection: Effects of reinforcing correct performance. *Behavior Modification, 10,* 73–92.

Carruthers, W. L., Sweeney, B., Kmitta, D., & Harris, G. (1996). Conflict resolution: An examination of the research literature. *The School Counselor, 44,* 5–17.

Conboy, S. M. (1994). *Peer mediation and anger control: Two ways to resolve conflict.* St. Paul, MN: University of St. Thomas.

Cooper, J. O., Heron, T. E., & Heward, W. L. (1987). *Applied behavior analysis.* Upper Saddle River, NJ: Merrill/Prentice Hall.

Costenbader, V., & Reading-Brown, M. (1995). Isolation timeout used with students with emotional disturbance. *Exceptional Children, 61*(4), 353–363.

Deitz, S. M., & Repp, A. C. (1983). Reducing behavior through reinforcement. *Exceptional Education Quarterly, 3,* 34–46.

DeLuke, S. V., & Knoblock, P. (1987). Teacher behavior as preventive discipline. *Teaching Exceptional Children, 19*(4), 18–24.

Donnellan, A. M., & LaVigna, G. W. (1990). Myths about punishment. In A. C. Repp & N. N. Singh (Eds.), *Perspectives on the use of nonaversive and aversive interventions for persons with developmental disabilities* (pp. 33–57). Sycamore, IL: Sycamore.

Donnellan, A. M., LaVigna, G. W., Negri-Shoultz, N., & Fassbender, L. L. (1988). *Progress without punishment: Effective approaches for learners with behavior problems.* New York: Teachers College Press, Columbia University.

Donnellan, A. M., Mirenda, P. L., Mesaros, R. A., & Fassbender, L. L. (1984). Analyzing the communicative functions of aberrant behavior. *Journal of the Association for Persons with Severe Handicaps, 9,* 201–212.

Drasgow, E., Halle, J. W., & Ostrosky, M. M. (1998). Effects of differential reinforcement on the generalization of a replacement mand in three children with severe language delays. *Journal of Applied Behavior Analysis, 31,* 357–374.

DuPaul, G. J., Guevremont, D. C., & Barkley, R. A. (1992). Behavioral treatment of attention deficit hyperactivity disorder in the classroom. *Behavior Modification, 16,* 204–225.

Eineder, D. V., & Bishop, H. L. (1997). Block scheduling the high school. *NASSP Bulletin, 81,* 45–54.

Epstein, M. H., & Olinger, E. (1987). Use of medication in school programs for behaviorally disordered pupils. *Behavioral Disorders, 12,* 138–144.

Evans, I. M., & Meyer, L. H. (1985). *An educative approach to behavior problems: A practical decision model for interventions with severely handicapped learners.* Baltimore: Brookes.

Evans, I. M., & Meyer, L. H. (1990). Toward a science in support of meaningful outcomes: A response to Horner et al. *Journal of the Association of Persons with Severe Handicaps, 15,* 133–135.

Fee, V. E., Matson, J. L., & Manikam, R. (1990). A control group outcome study of a nonexclusionary time-out package to improve social skills with preschoolers. *Exceptionality, 1,* 107–121.

Foxx, R. M., & Azrin, N. H. (1972). Restitution: A method of eliminating aggressive-disruptive behaviors of retarded and brain damaged patients. *Behavior Research and Therapy, 10,* 15–27.

Foxx, R. M., & Azrin, N. H. (1973). The elimination of autistic self-stimulatory behavior by overcorrection. *Journal of Applied Behavior Analysis, 6,* 1–14.

Foxx, R. M., & Bechtel, D. R. (1983). Overcorrection: A review and analysis. In S. Axelrod & J. Apsche (Eds.), *The effects of punishment on human behavior* (pp. 133–220). New York: Academic Press.

Foxx, R. M., & Shapiro, S. T. (1978). The time-out ribbon: A nonexclusionary time-out procedure. *Journal of Applied Behavior Analysis, 11,* 125–136.

Friman, P. C. (1990). Nonaversive treatment of high-rate disruption: Child and provider effects. *Exceptional Children, 57,* 64–69.

Gadow, K. D. (1986). *Children on medication: Epilepsy, emotional disturbance, and adolescent disorders.* San Diego, CA: College-Hill.

Gaustad, J. (1992). School discipline. Eugene, OR: ERIC Clearinghouse on Educational Management (ED350727).

Gaylord-Ross, R. (1980). A decision model for the treatment of aberrant behavior in applied settings. In W. Sailor, B. Wilcox, & L. Brown (Eds.), *Methods of instruction for severely handicapped students* (pp. 135–158). Baltimore: Brookes.

Gilliam, J. E. (1989). Positive reinforcement and behavioral deficits of children with autism: C. B. Ferster's thoughts versus current practice. *Focus on Autistic Behavior, 4,* 1–16.

Goodman, G., & Poillion, M. J. (1992). ADD: Acronym for any dysfunction or difficulty. *Journal of Special Education, 26,* 37–56.

Greenhill, L. (1992). Pharmacologic treatment of ADHD. *Psychiatric Clinics of North America, 15,* 1–25.

Gunnoe, M. L., & Mariner, C. L. (1997). Toward a developmental contextual model of the effects of parental spanking on children's aggression. *Archives of Pediatrics & Adolescent Medicine, 151,* 768–775.

Hagopian, L. P., Fisher, W., Piazza, C. C., & Wierzbicki, J. J. (1993). A water-prompting procedure for the treatment of urinary incontinence. *Journal of Applied Behavior Analysis, 26,* 473–474.

Harris, K. R. (1985). Definitional, parametric, and procedural considerations in time-out interventions and research. *Exceptional Children, 51,* 279–288.

Higgins, S. T., Morris, E. K., & Johnson, L. M. (1989). Social transmission of superstitious behavior in preschool children. *Psychological Records, 39,* 307–323.

Howard, E. (1998). The trouble with the block. *American School Board Journal, 185*(1), 35–36.

Hoza, B., Pelham, W. E., Sams, S. E., & Carlson, C. (1992). An examination of the dosage effects of both behavior therapy and methylphenidate on the classroom performance of two ADD/ADHD children. *Behavior Modification, 16,* 164–191.

Johnson, R. T., & Johnson, D. W. (1996). Conflict resolution and peer mediation programs in elementary and secondary schools: A review of the research. *Review of Educational Research, 66,* 459–473.

Kazdin, A. E. (1989). *Behavior modification in applied settings.* Pacific Grove, CA: Brooks/Cole.

Kramer, S. L. (1997). What we know about block scheduling and its effects on math instruction. *NASSP Bulletin, 81,* 18–42.

Lane, P., & McWhirter, J. J. (1992). A peer mediation model: Conflict resolution for elementary and secondary school children. *Elementary School Guidance and Counseling, 27,* 15–21.

LaVigna, G. W., & Donnellan, A. M. (1986). *Alternatives to punishment: Solving behavior problems with non-aversive strategies.* New York: Irvington.

LaVigna, G. W., & Willis, T. J. (1991, February). *Nonaversive behavior modification.* Workshop presented by the Institute for Applied Behavior Analysis, Minneapolis, MN.

Lenz, M., Singh, N. N., & Hewett, A. E. (1991). Overcorrection as an academic remediation procedure. *Behavior Modification, 15,* 64–73.

Long, N. J., & Newman, R. G. (1976). Managing surface behavior of children in school. In N. J. Long, W. C. Morse, & R. G. Newman (Eds.), *Conflict in the classroom: The education of the emotionally disturbed children* (3rd ed., pp. 308–317). Belmont, CA: Wadsworth.

Maag, J. W. (1990). Social skills training in schools. *Special Services in the Schools, 6,* 1–19.

Maag, J. W., & Reid, R. (1994). Attention-deficit hyperactivity disorder: A functional approach to assessment and treatment. *Behavior Disorders, 20,* 5–23.

McKeegan, G., Estill, K., & Campbell, B. (1984). Use of nonseclusionary time-out for the elimination of stereotypic behavior. *Journal of Behavior Therapy and Experimental Psychiatry, 15,* 261–264.

Meyer, L. H., & Evans, I. M. (1989). *Nonaversive intervention for behavior problems: A manual for home and community.* Baltimore: Brookes.

Miller, B. Y., & Jones, R. S. (1997). Reducing stereotyped behaviour: A comparison of two methods of programming differential reinforcement. *British Journal of Clinical Psychology, 36,* 297–302.

Morgan, R. L., & Striefel, S. (1988). Restrictiveness of procedures to decrease behavior: Views of school psychologists, administrators, teachers, and specialists. *Journal of Special Education, 21,* 108–119.

National Center for Educational Statistics (1997). *Principal/School disciplinarian survey on school violence.* Washington, DC: U.S. Department of Education.

National Committee to Prevent Child Abuse (1995). *Seven good reasons to stop spanking.* Washington, DC: Author.

Newsom, C., Favell, J. E., & Rincover, A. (1983). The side effects of punishment. In S. Axelrod & J. Apsche (Eds.), *The effects of punishment on human behavior* (pp. 285–316). New York: Academic Press.

Nichols, J. D. (2000, April). *The impact of block scheduling on various indicators of school success.* Paper presented at the Annual Meeting of the American Educational Research Association, New Orleans, LA.

O'Brien, S., & Repp, A. C. (1990). Reinforcement-based reductive procedures: A review of 20 years of their use with persons with severe or profound retardation. *Association for Persons with Severe Handicaps, 15,* 148–159.

Ollendick, T., Matson, J., Esveldt-Dawson, K., & Shapiro, E. (1980). Increasing spelling achievement: An analysis of treatment procedures utilizing an alternative treatment design. *Journal of Applied Behavior Analysis, 13,* 645–654.

Onslow, M., Packman, A., & Stocker, S. (1997). Control of children's stuttering with response-contingent timeout. *Journal of Speech, Language, and Hearing Research, 40,* 121–131.

Pazulinec, R., Meyerrose, M., & Sajwaj, T. (1983). Punishment via response cost. In S. Axelrod & J. Apsche (Eds.), *The effects of punishment on human behavior* (pp. 71–86). New York: Academic Press.

Pelham, W. (1993). Pharmacotherapy for children with ADHD. *School Psychology Review, 22,* 199–227.

Peterson, D. W., Schmidt, C., Flottmeyer, E., & Weincke, S. (2000, November). *Block scheduling: Successful strategies for middle schools.* Paper presented at the National Middle School Association Conference, St. Louis, MO.

Pfiffner, L. J., & O'Leary, S. G. (1987). The efficacy of all positive management as a function of the prior use of negative consequences. *Journal of Applied Behavior Analysis, 20,* 265–271.

Pfiffner, L. J., Rosen, L. A., & O'Leary, S. G. (1985). The efficacy of an all-positive approach to classroom management. *Journal of Applied Behavior Analysis, 18,* 257–261.

Phillips, E. L., Phillips, E. A., Fixsen, D. L., & Wolf, M. (1971). Achievement place: Modification of behaviors of pre-delinquent boys within a token economy. *Journal of Applied Behavior Analysis, 4,* 45–59.

Piazza, C. C., Moes, D. R., & Fisher, W. W. (1996). Differential reinforcement of alternative behavior and demand fading in the treatment of escape-maintained destructive behavior. *Journal of Applied Behavior Analysis, 29,* 569–572.

Porterfield, J. K., Herbert-Jackson, E., & Risley, T. R. (1976). Contingent observation: An effective and acceptable procedure for reducing disruptive behavior of young children in a group setting. *Journal of Applied Behavior Analysis, 9,* 55–64.

Ramasamy, R., Taylor, R. L., & Ziegler, E. W. (1996). Eliminating inappropriate classroom behavior using a DRO schedule. *Psychological Reports, 78,* 753–754.

Reid, R. T., Maag, J. W., & Vasa, S. F. (1994). Attention deficit hyperactivity disorder as a disability category: A critique. *Exceptional Children, 60,* 198–214.

Reid, R. T., Maag, J. W., Vasa, S. F., & Wright, G. (1994). Who are the children with attention deficit-hyperactivity disorder? A school-based survey. *Journal of Special Education, 28,* 117–137.

Repp, A. C., Barton, L. E., & Brulle, A. R. (1983). A comparison of two procedures for programming the differential reinforcement of other behaviors. *Journal of Applied Behavior Analysis, 16,* 435–445.

Repp, A. C., Felce, D., & Barton, L. E. (1991). The effects of initial interval size of the efficacy of DRO schedules of reinforcement. *Exceptional Children, 57,* 417–425.

Repp, A. C., & Slack, D. J. (1977). Reducing responding of retarded persons by DRO schedules following a history of low-rate responding: A comparison of ascending interval sizes. *Psychological Record, 27,* 581–588.

Reynolds, G. S. (1961). Behavioral contrast. *Journal of the Experimental Analysis of Behavior, 4,* 57–71.

Reynolds, L. K., & Kelley, M. L. (1997). The efficacy of a response cost-based treatment package for managing aggressive behavior in preschoolers. *Behavior Modification, 21*(2), 216–230.

Ritter, J. (1998, October 29). School uniforms changing culture of classroom. *USA Today.*

Rosenberg, M. S. (1986). Maximizing the effectiveness of structured classroom management programs: Implementing rule-review procedures with disruptive and distractible students. *Behavioral Disorders, 11,* 239–248.

Sabatino, D. A. (1987). Preventive discipline as a practice in special education. *Teaching Exceptional Children, 19*(4), 8–11.

Salend, S., & Gordon, B. (1987). A group-oriented time-out ribbon procedure. *Behavioral Disorders, 12,* 131–137.

Samalin, N. (1995, May). What's wrong with spanking? *Parents,* pp. 35–36.

Sasso, G. M., Melloy, K. J., & Kavale, K. A. (1990). The effects of social skills training through structured learning: Behavioral covariation, generalization, and maintenance. *Behavioral Disorders, 16,* 9–22.

Schloss, P. J., & Smith, M. A. (1987). Guidelines for ethical use of manual restraint in public school settings for behaviorally disordered students. *Behavioral Disorders, 12,* 207–213.

Shriver, M. D., & Allen, K. D. (1996). The time-out grid: A guide to effective discipline. *School Psychology Quarterly, 11*(1), 67–74.

Skiba, R. J., & Deno, S. L. (1991). Terminology and behavior reduction: The case against "punishment." *Exceptional Children, 57,* 298–312.

Skiba, R., & Raison, J. (1990). Relationship between the use of timeout and academic achievement. *Exceptional Children, 57,* 36–46.

Skinner, B. F. (1938). *The behavior of organisms.* New York: Appleton-Century-Crofts.

Snell, M. E., & Zirpoli, T. J. (1987). Instructional strategies. In M. E. Snell (Ed.), *Systematic instruction of persons with severe handicaps* (pp. 110–149). Upper Saddle River, NJ: Merrill/Prentice Hall.

Stainback, W., Stainback, S., & Froyen, L. (1987). Structuring the classroom to prevent disruptive behaviors. *Teaching Exceptional Children, 19,* 12–16.

Strain, P. S., & Smith, B. J. (1996). Developing social skills in young children with special needs. *Preventing School Failure, 41,* 24–27.

Sugai, G., & Lewis, J. (1996). Preferred and promising practices for social skills instruction. *Focus on Exceptional Children, 29*(4), 1–16.

Swanson, J. M., McBurnett, K., Wigal, T., Pfiffner, L. J., Lerner, M. A., Williams, L., et al. (1993). Effect of stimulant medication on children with attention deficit disorder: A "review of reviews." *Exceptional Children, 60,* 154–163.

Tannock, R., Schachar, R. J., Carr, R. P., Chajczyk, D., & Logan, G. D. (1989). Effects of methylphenidate on inhibitory control in hyperactive children. *Journal of Abnormal Child Psychology, 17,* 473–491.

Taylor, C. (1995). Vignette 4.1: A physician's perspective on behavioral assessment. In T. J. Zirpoli (Ed.), *Understanding and affecting the behavior of young children* (pp. 87–89). Upper Saddle River, NJ: Merrill/Prentice Hall.

Taylor, J. (1997). When timeout works some of the time. *School Psychology, 12,* 4–22.

Thompson, S. M. (1996). Peer mediation: A peaceful solution. *The School Counselor, 44,* 151–154.

Turnbull, A. P., & Turnbull, H. R. (1990). A tale about lifestyle changes: Comments on "Toward a technology of 'nonaversive' behavior support." *Association for Persons with Severe Handicaps, 15,* 142–144.

Underwood, L., & Thyer, B. (1990). Social work practice with the mentally retarded: Reducing self-injurious behaviors using non-aversive methods. *Arete, 15,* 14–23.

Vollmer, T. R., Roane, H. S., Ringdahl, J. E., & Marcus, B. A. (1999). Evaluating treatment challenges with differential reinforcement of alternative behavior. *Journal of Applied Behavior Analysis, 32,* 9–23.

Wacker, D., Berg, W., & Northrup, J. (1991). Breaking the cycle of challenging behaviors: Early treatment key to success. *Impact, 4,* 10–11.

Walker, H. M. (1983, February). Application of response cost in school settings: Outcomes, issues and recommendations. *Exceptional Education Quarterly,* pp. 47–55.

Walker, H. M., Hops, H., & Fiegenbaum, E. (1976). Deviant classroom behavior as a function of combinations of social and token reinforcement and cost contingency. *Behavior Therapy, 7,* 76–88.

White, A. G., & Bailey, J. S. (1990). Reducing disruptive behaviors of elementary physical education students with sit and watch. *Journal of Applied Behavior Analysis, 23,* 353–359.

White, O. R., & Haring, N. G. (1976). *Exceptional teaching.* Upper Saddle River, NJ: Merrill/ Prentice Hall.

Wicks-Nelson, R., & Israel, A. C. (1991). *Behavior disorders of childhood.* Upper Saddle River, NJ: Prentice Hall.

Williams, C. D. (1959). The elimination of tantrum behavior by extinction procedures. *Journal of Abnormal and Social Psychology, 59,* 266–272.

Wolery, M., & Gast, D. (1990). Defining the role of social validity. In A. C. Repp & N. N. Singh (Eds.), *Perspectives on the use of nonaversive and aversive interventions for persons with developmental disabilities* (pp. 129–143). Sycamore, IL: Sycamore.

Yeager, C., & McLaughlin, T. F. (1994). Use of time-out ribbon with and without consequences as procedures to improve a child's compliance. *Perceptual and Motor Skills, 79*(2), 945–946.

Yell, M. L. (1998). *The law and special education.* Upper Saddle River, NJ: Merrill/Prentice Hall.

Zirpoli, T. J. (2003). *Cures for parental wimp syndrome: Lessons on becoming a stronger parent.* Westminster, MD: Zirpoli Publishing and Consulting.

Zirpoli, T. J., & Lloyd, J. W. (1987). Understanding and managing self-injurious behavior. *Remedial and Special Education, 8,* 46–57.

# chapter 10

# SPECIFIC BEHAVIOR CHALLENGES

*Kristine J. Melloy and Thomas J. Zirpoli*

*You can't make anyone do anything.*

—Johnson, Agelson, Macierz, Minnick, and Merrell (1995)

The previous chapters of this book provided information for teachers who wish to understand and better manage the behavior of children and adolescents. Once we realize, however, that we can manage only our own behavior and teach others how to do the same, the better behavior managers we become. In other words, the key to changing a student's behavior is likely to be a change in the teacher's behavior.

Another key consideration related to managing challenging behaviors in children is to think of problematic behavior in terms of opportunities to teach new behaviors rather than opportunities to punish misbehavior.

Using the interventions described in previous chapters, we can teach children to manage their own behavior. Teaching children to manage their own behavior can assist them in learning and demonstrating more appropriate, prosocial behaviors.

In order to address specific behavior challenges, we must understand that children demonstrate problematic behavior in order to achieve the same outcomes that are experienced when they demonstrate prosocial, appropriate behavior. A typical example of a classroom challenging behavior is demonstrated by a student who calls out an answer to a teacher's question, even though the teacher has asked students to raise their hands to answer a question. If the teacher acknowledges the student who calls out, the student may have achieved the desired outcome of getting the teacher's attention, even though he or she did not follow the teacher's directions. If successful, the student is likely to engage in that behavior in the future.

In this chapter we discuss specific challenging behaviors that are commonly seen in school settings, typical antecedents and consequences that motivate and maintain these behaviors, and effective interventions for changing challenging behavior to more desirable behavior.

More and more, children and adolescents come to school with poor social skills. In fact, it has become quite common for school personnel to be faced with problematic behaviors among students. According to one source, 160,000 children miss school daily in order to avoid peers who are mean to them (Garrity, Jens, Porter, Sager, & Short-Camili, 1994–1996). Some of the students who present challenging behaviors receive special education services related to an emotional/behavioral disorder (E/BD). Emotional/behavior disorders are characterized by problem behaviors that are demonstrated more frequently, intensely, and of longer duration than those of peers. These children may be at risk of exclusion from typical school settings (Sasso, Peck, & Garrison-Harrell, 1998). However, many more children than the 1–2% labeled E/BD demonstrate challenging behaviors in the school setting (Yell, 1998).

Federal legislation has also put challenging behaviors in the limelight since educators are now required to consider IDEA and ADA regulations (see Chapter 11) when considering disciplinary methods for students with and without disabilities (Katsiyannis & Maag, 1998; Yell, 1998).

In actuality, the daily newspaper brings to the fore the seriousness of school violence and the frequency with which our children and their teachers are placed in jeopardy (e.g., Steinberg, 1999). Fortunately, many of the challenging behaviors that children and adolescents demonstrate in school and other settings are not at the severe levels described. This provides educators and others hope in being able to be effective in managing their own behavior and assisting others in managing their behavior.

Specific externalizing challenging behaviors discussed in this chapter include disruptiveness, noncompliance, impulsivity, inattention, hyperactivity, aggression, temper tantrums, and stereotypy. Depression, a common internalizing behavior problem will also be discussed. Each of the challenging behaviors will be discussed in terms of (a) typical observable, measurable behaviors; (b), common causes and/or antecedents; (c) acceptable replacement behaviors; and (d) effective interventions. Chapters 7, 8, and 9 of this text provide further information on interventions for increasing appropriate behaviors and decreasing inappropriate behavior.

Before each of the challenging behaviors is discussed, it is important to note that the majority of children who demonstrate challenging behaviors engage in seemingly more than one of these behavior problems at the same time. One of the problems teachers experience in completing functional assessment is related to identifying a target behavior when more than one behavior is demonstrated. However, when we realize that many demonstrated behaviors are related, it becomes easier to figure out the most salient behavior, or in other words, the one to work on first. For example, a student who is considered disruptive in a classroom may also be described as someone who does not follow teacher directions (i.e., noncompliant behavior) and as a child who trips his classmates when they walk by his desk (i.e., aggressive behavior). In this case, the disruptive behavior looks like noncompliance and aggressive behavior.

When we identify challenging behavior, we need to make sure that we describe what exactly the child does when, for example, he or she is being disruptive. This description will be helpful in identifying the most salient target behavior and thereby assist in determining an effective intervention. Ask yourself, of the three challenging behaviors described in the previous example, which one seems to be the most serious? If you said tripping classmates, give yourself a pat on the back. Hurting others or causing potential danger to others is often the most salient behavior and the type of behavior that warrants immediate intervention. Fortunately, once we intervene with one behavior, other behaviors may change without direct intervention because of multiple effects on behavior (e.g., entrapment, collateral effects, covariation effects; McMahon, Wacker, Sasso, & Melloy, 1994). In our example, the student who learns a replacement behavior for getting his peers' attention by tripping them will probably be less likely to disrupt the class. Perhaps the student will learn that he can get the teacher's attention more appropriately when he engages in compliant, rather than noncompliant, behavior.

## Classroom Application 10.1

# Brian: A Student to Think About . . .

Brian is a student in Mrs. Romano's freshman Spanish class. Brian attends class every day but does not participate in class. When Mrs. Romano directs the students to work in the language lab, Brian refuses to work and tells her he isn't going to work today. Instead, Brian sits in his desk with his legs stretched out and his arms crossed, refusing to put on the headphones that would assist him in completing the language lesson. Whenever Mrs. Romano stands in front of the class to present a lesson, Brian sits in his desk with his arms crossed over his chest and yells out obscenities directed at the teacher and at other students in the class. Mrs. Romano has talked to Brian about his behavior, and he has told her he really doesn't want to take Spanish but he knows it is required if he wants to go to college. Brian promises Mrs. Romano that he will follow the class rules for respecting others and participating in class. However, after two weeks he still demonstrates inappropriate behavior by not being respectful and not participating in class. Mrs. Romano has been documenting Brian's behavior by writing anecdotal reports each day that describe his inappropriate behavior. She presents Brian's case to the Teacher Assistance Team. The members of the team suggest that Mrs. Romano conduct a functional behavioral assessment of Brian's behavior. Once the FBA is complete, the team will assist Mrs. Romano in developing interventions that will assist Brian in changing his behavior and help him to stay in the Spanish class. Think about the following as you read the rest of the chapter:

1. Describe Brian's behavior in terms of characteristics of challenging behavior.
2. Once Mrs. Romano and her colleagues complete the functional behavioral assessment, what do you think they will find out in terms of the function of Brian's behavior?
3. What do you think will be effective interventions to assist Brian in changing his behavior so that he is able to respect others and participate in class?

Children who exhibit one or more of these challenging behaviors do not typically demonstrate these behaviors at a level that would warrant a disability label. On the contrary, intervention in the form of behavior management for challenging behaviors would assist most children in modifying their behavior before the problem becomes so serious that more intensive intervention (e.g., medication or special education) would be necessary. In the following sections we hope to provide educators an overview of these challenging behaviors and urge them to consult other sources for more in-depth information (e.g., Hennggeler, Schoenwald, Borduin, Rowland, & Cunningham, 1998; Kauffman, 1997; Mash & Barkley, 1998; Zionts, 1996).

# DISRUPTIVE BEHAVIOR

Disruptive behavior has been described as any behavior that "serves to disrupt the ongoing learning process in a classroom" (Kerr & Nelson, 1998, p. 192). The functions of disruptive behavior typically include gaining positive or negative attention, escaping from work, and self-gratification. Disruptive behavior covers a wide range of behaviors demonstrated in school and other settings. Teachers and peers commonly describe children who engage in disruptive behaviors ranging from those demonstrated by the "class clown" to aggressive and violent behavior. Common sense tells us that the intervention used to decrease inappropriate clowning behavior will be quite different from an intervention designed to prevent or decrease aggressive behavior. However, the effect of the consequences will be the same: If the behavior is reinforced, it will increase or be maintained; if the behavior is punished, the behavior will decrease. Several examples of disruptive behaviors and definitions written in observable, measurable terms follow:

1. *Off-task talking:* The child speaks out without permission or interrupts others who are talking.
2. *Getting out of seat:* The child lifts his or her buttocks off the chair and walks around the classroom without permission. He or she may stop to chat with peers or may just continue to walk around with no purpose related to an academic task.
3. *Making noises:* The child creates sounds, either verbally or physically, that are clearly not related to the task (e.g., tapping a pencil repeatedly, tipping chair back until it falls over).
4. *Playing with objects:* The child engages in play with things, such as pens, pencils, or small toys, that may be related or unrelated to the task. To constitute an inappropriate behavior, the play must not be part of the task and clearly not appropriate for the time.
5. *Throwing objects:* The child projects things, such as pencils, paper airplanes, or furniture, into the air or across the floor when this behavior is not related to an educational task.
6. *Climbing:* The child ascends to the top of furniture or other objects/persons in the room for no reason related to a classroom task.

Often these behaviors are more annoying than anything and can be effectively managed using the behavior management interventions described next.

## Common Causes and Antecedents of Disruptive Behavior

### Curriculum and Teaching Strategies

Daniels (1998) suggests that inappropriate curriculum or teaching strategies, individual learning styles, and student disability could contribute to student misbehavior (see Chapter 5 on curriculum-based assessment). Students often experience feelings of frustration related to the classroom curriculum and the strategies teachers use for instruction. For example, a middle school student who is a poor reader is likely to struggle through classes that require a significant amount of reading (e.g., social studies and science). The student's frustration may lead to misbehavior. At the same time, curriculum that is not interesting or seems irrelevant to the student's life experience can create situations that result in disruptive behavior. Disregard for individual learning style and poor instructional delivery also serve as antecedent stimuli for disruptive behavior. For example, a child who has trouble taking notes in a class where the teacher uses overheads instead of handouts may exhibit disruptive behavior. Teachers who present appropriate curriculum in a style that addresses individual student strengths and needs report that they experience more appropriate classroom behavior among their students.

## Inappropriate Classroom Management

Another common cause of disruptive behavior appears to stem from inappropriate behavior management strategies within the classroom. Students who demonstrate disruptive behaviors (e.g., talking out, being noisy, playing with things) are often reinforced for this behavior by teachers (McMahon, 1989; White & Bailey, 1990) and peers (Smith & Fowler, 1984). The reinforcement may be in the form of laughter from peers or attention from teachers. Of course, when the disruptive behavior is reinforced, it is likely to be repeated.

Unfortunately, students who are described as "class clowns" often say and do funny things, but usually at an inappropriate time. When the student is laughed at, this serves to reinforce and maintain the behavior. Rather than develop interventions that squelch the student's sense of humor, it would be better to teach him or her to manifest the behavior at appropriate times (e.g., when the class is waiting in line to go to the lunchroom), in an appropriate manner (e.g., not meant to hurt others' feelings), and in appropriate places (e.g., on the playground).

As stated in Chapter 7, research has found that teachers tend to provide students with more attention following misbehavior than appropriate behavior. To avoid this pitfall, teachers are encouraged to develop a comprehensive classroom management plan that promotes positive social behavior and discourages disruptive behavior (e.g., Francois, Harlacher, & Smith, 1999).

## Deficits in School Readiness Skills

Children who lack competence in classroom social skills often demonstrate disruptive behavior (McGinnis & Goldstein, 1997). If children don't have the opportunity to learn school readiness skills, such as raising their hand, asking permission, and listening to others, at home or in a preschool setting, they will be at a disadvantage in kindergarten. However, when these children are taught these skills, become competent in them, and are reinforced for demonstrating these prosocial behaviors, their disruptive behavior decreases significantly (Melloy, Davis, Wehby, Murry, & Lieber, 1998).

## Effective Interventions for Disruptive Behavior

### *A Functional Assessment of Disruptive Behavior*

Part I of this text, especially Chapter 6, describes methods used to determine the function of behavior through functional assessment. Knowing the function of a student's behavior will assist the teacher in developing effective interventions for teaching replacement behaviors that can be reinforced. As previously stated, a common function for disruptive behavior is getting others' attention (i.e., peers and teachers). Thus, if teachers want to teach and reinforce acceptable replacement behaviors for disruptive behavior, a classroom plan to increase on-task behaviors, following directions, cooperating with others, participating in class, raising hand to ask or answer a question, using a quiet voice, keeping hands to self, and staying in seat is recommended. Students will learn that engaging in prosocial behavior can achieve the same outcome or function as disruptive behavior, and that they are considered more favorably by their peers and teachers when they engage in these behaviors. The following section describes several effective interventions for disruptive behavior.

### *Schoolwide and Classroom Rules*

A number of authors discuss the effectiveness of interventions based on behavioral, cognitive, psycho-educational, and social learning theories in teaching, promoting, and supporting replacement behavior for disruptive behavior in children and adolescents. Nelson, Martella, and Galand (1998) describe the effects of establishing, teaching, and reinforcing schoolwide rules and routines on the disruptive behavior of elementary school students. A 4-year study revealed that children who were taught and expected to follow school rules and routines were more likely to demonstrate prosocial behavior in the school setting. In addition, the authors found that providing a plan for a systematic response to disruptive behavior resulted in fewer formal office referrals for disciplinary action. Malone, Bonitz, and Rickett (1998) confirm these research findings with their study on teacher perceptions of disruptive behavior. The teachers in the study believed that having classroom rules and expecting students to follow them was the best way for disciplining students.

One of the most common interventions thought to be effective in decreasing disruptive behavior and consequently increasing more appropriate classroom behavior is in-school suspension. However, the effects of this type intervention have repeatedly been proven to have little or no effect on students' disruptive behavior. Stage (1997) completed a study on the effects of in-school suspension on the disruptive behavior of 36 twelve-to-seventeen-year-old students with emotional behavioral disorders. The results of this study revealed that students' disruptive behavior did not decrease as a result of in-school suspension. A number of alternative interventions to in-school suspension are available that were more effective in decreasing disruptive behavior and increasing appropriate replacement behaviors, such as being on task, asking permission, and getting others' attention. These procedures included sound educational programming and preventive discipline, which served to promote and reinforce acceptable behavior. When punishment procedures were needed in addition to proactive approaches, interventions such as Saturday School were suggested. These interventions were also effective in decreasing noncompliance, a challenging behavior that is discussed in the following section.

### Teaching Self-Discipline Skills

Several authors report that teaching children self-discipline resulted in decreased disruptive behavior and increased self-management (Hoff & DuPaul, 1998; Schmid, 1998; Shapiro, DuPaul, & Bradley-Klug, 1998). For example, Hoff and Du-Paul found that three elementary-aged children were able to learn self-management strategies and consequently decreased their disruptive behavior. Schmid (1998) taught children a three-step self-discipline procedure that resulted in improved self-management and less disruptive behavior. The three-step strategy involved teaching the children to:

1. say "Stop, I don't like that,"
2. try to ignore the objectionable behavior, and
3. report to a responsible adult if steps 1 and 2 didn't work.

These strategies are excellent examples of placing the focus on students managing their own behavior rather than relying heavily on others for behavior management.

## NONCOMPLIANCE

Children who engage in disruptive behavior frequently demonstrate behaviors that are described as noncompliant. Teachers often report that children will not do what they have been asked. Skiba, Peterson, and Williams report that the primary reasons students are referred to the office for discipline are related to noncompliant and disrespectful behavior (1997). Adults get frustrated with children who seem to know what they are supposed to do but won't perform the appropriate behavior on cue (Maag, 1997).

Compliance is generally described as obedience to adult directives and prohibitions, cooperation with requests and suggestions, and/or the willingness to accept suggestions in a teaching situation (Rocissano, Slade, & Lynch, 1987). *Noncompliance,* then, is defined as oppositonal or resistant behavior, such as disobedience to directives, uncooperativeness with requests and suggestions, and unwillingness to accept suggestions. One facet of compliance/noncompliance is the issue of teaching children how to become independent and make appropriate choices regarding their own behavior—characteristics that are admired in U.S. society. Regardless, noncompliant behavior becomes challenging when a child is frequently defiant and this behavior is expressed in an unpleasant, negative manner. Moreover, the function of noncompliant behavior has been identified as gaining power and control over a situation, escaping from a task, and/or getting the attention of others. Again, the function of the behavior is not what causes the problem; rather the noncompliant behavior appears to be at fault.

Kuczynski, Kochanska, Radke-Yarrow, & Girnius-Brown (1987) describe four categories of noncompliance in a study with young children and their mothers. A child was described as engaging in *passive noncompliance* when she did not overtly refuse or defy the request, but rather went on about her business as if she had not been addressed. A child who overtly refused requests with angry, defiant, or negative facial, body, and/or verbal expressions was described as behaving with *direct defiance.* Children who replied "No" or "I don't want to" with no apparent negative verbal or body language were described as engaging in *simple refusal* behavior. Finally, *negotiation behavior* was defined as attempts by the child to convince the parent to issue a new directive through bargaining. A case example, in which Beth's teacher asks her to put her science project away and get ready for math, shows each of these types of noncompliance.

1. *Passive noncompliance:* Beth continues working on her science project.
2. *Direct defiance:* Beth throws her pencil to the floor, yells at her teacher that she isn't finished with her project, and looks away from her teacher.
3. *Simple refusal:* Beth tells her teacher that she is not going to stop work on her science project. Beth is smiling and doesn't raise her voice.
4. *Negotiation:* Beth asks her teacher if she can work on her science project for 10 more minutes before doing math. When her teacher says "No," Beth asks for 5 minutes, then 3 minutes, and so on.

## Common Causes and Antecedents of Noncompliance

### Teacher-Student Interactions

The reader is reminded of the opening statement for this chapter: "You can't make anyone do anything." Unfortunately, children are considered oppositional and noncompliant when they resist our efforts to make them do things. Think about how often you have experienced the following scenario:

> The students in Mrs. Nice's class are exuberantly working on a group project for which there is a high amount of interest and activity. However, all good things must come to an end, and Mrs. Nice announces that in a few minutes it will be time to change to another class. In an effort to be polite to her students, Mrs. Nice approaches each small group to warn them of the impending transition and ask them if they would like to put their materials away and get ready for the next class. Mrs. Nice is surprised when students in several groups tell her "No, I don't want to stop what I'm doing" and then continue with their project.

Why is Mrs. Nice surprised? She did give the impression that the students had a choice about continuing or stopping the project when she asked them rather than told them what was expected. If you expect students to do something, tell them what it is you want and then reinforce the students for being compliant. Also, if the student does not follow your directions, you must have a discipline plan that is employed fairly and consistently.

Adults also promote noncompliant behavior by their own, sometimes stubborn, refusal to change their behavior to better meet the needs of their students. Teachers and others who personalize behaviors demonstrated by their students will set themselves up for resistance. Let us illustrate with an example of a teacher and a group of high school students.

> The students had finished using their calculators for an assignment, and the teacher walked around the room to collect them. One student looked the teacher in the eye, and then held onto his calculator when she reached for it. Rather than struggling with the student, who obviously wanted to battle her for the calculator, the teacher walked on and ignored his comment about taking his calculator by force. In less than a minute, the student raised his hand, asked the teacher to come to his desk when she acknowledged him, and gave her the calculator with no further problem.

In minimizing the amount of attention given to the student for noncompliant behavior, the teacher was able to promote compliant behavior with very little effort on her part.

### Parent-Child Interactions

Holden and West (1989) also offer information on parent factors that contribute to compliant and noncompliant behavior. They observed the interactional styles of mothers and their children and the consequences of those styles within a play setting. The mothers were given directions to be either "directors" or "forbidders" in separate trials in which the mother and child were placed in a setting with toys that were either out of bounds or in bounds. In the proactive trial, mothers were instructed to direct their child's attention to objects, suggest activities, or play games. In the reactive trial, mothers were not allowed to direct their child in play and were instructed to interact with their child only when the child needed to be prohibited from playing with a toy that was out of bounds.

The authors reported that children were more likely to comply with requests and suggestions for play in the proactive trial than in the reactive trial. This research has important implications related to the causes of noncompliance in children. It provides confirmatory data for the idea that attending to the child for appropriate behavior (i.e., compliance) will prevent the need for the child to engage in inappropriate behavior (i.e., noncompliance) in order to get the attention of the adult. These findings also offer important information related to the function of compliant versus noncompliant behavior since getting others' attention has been found to be a typical outcome of compliance and noncompliance.

Wahler and Dumas (1986) report that noncompliant behavior may be maintained by an adult's indiscriminant attention. When children cannot predict how an adult will react to their behavior (i.e., the adult sometimes attends, other times ignores), they have no way of knowing what is expected of them. Wicks-Nelson and Israel (1991) also suggest that adults who are not consistent in follow-up on commands/requests realized a higher incidence of noncompliance. In other words, the child learns that it is not necessary to comply since there is not a consequence for noncompliance. The opposite effect was experienced when adults positively reinforced children for compliance.

### Functional Assessment of Noncompliant Behavior

Educators who completed functional assessment for target behaviors defined as noncompliance found that noncompliant or resistant behavior often resulted in power and control over the situation or escape from tasks. For example, Jose became very resistive when he was given a writing assignment. Assessment revealed that, although Jose had good ideas for writing and was able to physically produce written work, he had quite a bit of trouble with spelling. Rather than risk being embarrassed by misspelling words, Jose sat back at his desk and refused to write. Teaching Jose to ask for assistance in spelling and providing him with a word list for each writing assignment resulted in completion of writing assignments.

## Interventions for Noncompliant Behavior

### Teaching Compliance

If teachers want their students to be compliant, they need to mean what they say and say what they mean. In other words, when you tell your students to do something, you must follow through with a "Thank you" if the student complies or a consequence if the student does not comply. If you don't say "Thank you," you are not reinforcing the student's appropriate behavior. If you don't have a consequence when the student does not comply, you are teaching the student that it is not important to listen to you. Consistent follow-through is the key to teaching compliance. Again, you must teach your students that when you ask them to do something, you expect them to respond in an appropriate manner. Unfortunately, many students report to school without ever learning at home to follow directions from their parents. Thus, they are not in the habit of following directions from adults. But children can quickly learn that, at least in school, they need to be compliant, regardless of poor parenting at home.

Pfiffner and O'Leary (1987) investigated the effects of an all-positive behavior management program on the noncompliant behavior of eight first through third graders. Prior to the study, these children had no experience with negative consequences for their inappropriate behavior, which was operationally defined as off-task and academic inaccuracy. Using an alternating treatments design, the authors applied interventions within three conditions (Pfiffner & O'Leary, 1987, p. 266):

1. *Regular positives alone condition:* Children earned positive consequences for on-task behavior in the form of social praise, bonus work, and public posting of completed work.

Teacher praise for on-task student behavior often results in increased on-task behavior.

2. *Enhanced positives alone condition:* The teachers increased the frequency and quality of positive consequences (described previously).
3. *Enhanced positives and negatives condition:* The teachers administered positive consequences for appropriate behavior and reprimands for off-task behavior.

The results of this study indicated that children in the third condition improved their on-task behavior significantly when they were positively reinforced for appropriate behavior and received negative consequences for inappropriate behavior. The all-positive behavior management conditions were not effective in changing the behavior of these children. These findings are critical because, in many education settings, "discipline" and "punishment" seem to be dirty words. This is especially the case in pre-K and elementary-level classrooms, where many teachers have been encouraged to rely on positive reinforcement and redirection as their only consequence. While positive consequences are strongly encouraged throughout this text, Pfiffner and O'Leary (1987) offered empirical evidence that at times it is more effective to use reinforcement and punishment procedures together versus reinforcement alone.

## Cognitive Behavior Management

An intervention that is effective in increasing compliant behavior and reducing noncompliant behavior is cognitive behavior management (see Chapter 8). For example, Rhode, Morgan, and Young (1983) observed positive behavior changes in six children with behavior disorders who were served in a resource room. Children in this elementary classroom were taught to use self-evaluation to monitor their classroom rule-following behavior. A token reinforcement program was implemented to reinforce children for compliance. The intervention consisted of modeling, role playing, feedback, correction, and clarification of classroom rules. Initially, the teacher awarded points for following rules and the children tallied these points on a point card. Points were traded for secondary reinforcers. In the next phase of the study, the children were asked to evaluate their academic work and behavior by awarding themselves points. The teacher also continued to rate the children. Eventually, the children were taught to evaluate their performance without the teacher matching the ratings. The program was successful in increasing compliant behavior. In addition, the children generalized their compliant behavior and the self-evaluation strategy to regular classroom settings.

### Schoolwide and Classroom Rules

Suspension is a punishment procedure that has been used to assist in decreasing noncompliant behavior. Costenbader and Markson (1998) reported findings for suspension's effect on noncompliant behavior similar to those reported by Stage (1997) for disruptive behavior. In fact, these authors quoted 32% of the students surveyed as saying that suspension was not helpful and that they would probably be suspended again for similar behaviors. These findings present further evidence that even though some punishment procedures are helpful in decreasing noncompliant behavior and increasing compliant behavior, suspension is not effective. Since escape is sometimes a common function of noncompliant behavior, suspending students for noncompliant behavior may actually reinforce the behavior rather than punish noncompliance.

# IMPULSIVITY

Teachers who refer to a child as being impulsive usually conjure up images of children who rarely stop to think before they act, who attempt tasks before they fully understand the directions, who often demonstrate remorse when their actions have led to errors or mishaps, who call out frequently in class (usually with the wrong answer), and who have difficulty organizing their materials. Impulsivity, although difficult to define as a separate construct of behavior (Campbell & Werry, 1986; Olson, Bates, & Bayles, 1990), is often referred to when persons consider the types of behavior that cause problems for adults and children. Common functions of impulsivity include gaining attention and self-gratification.

Kauffman (1989) points out that impulsive behavior is normal in young children, but that as children grow older, they are able to learn alternative responses. Olson and colleagues point out that 2-year-old children will begin to "inhibit prohibited actions owing to remembered information" (1990, p. 318), but state that "self-regulation does not develop until the 3rd or 4th year of life" (p. 318). Campbell and Werry define impulsivity as "erratic and poorly controlled behavior"

(1986, p. 120). Kauffman defines impulsivity as behavior demonstrated by children who are "unable to keep from responding quickly and without thinking to academic tasks and to social situations. Typically, these children's impulses are wrong, and they get them into trouble" (1985, pp. 198–199). In other words, children who act impulsively are often observed to fail to inhibit their response to target stimuli.

Shafrir and Pascual-Leone (1990) report that children who have deficits in postfailure reflective behavior make more errors than children who stop and reflect on the errors they made in initial efforts to complete academic tasks. Likewise, children who make errors on academic tasks and reflect on them right away will learn from their mistakes, therefore reducing the probability of making further errors on the task. On the other hand, Shafrir and Pascual-Leone found that children who did not reflect on errors made even more errors on the subsequent tasks.

Children who manifest impulsive behavior often get into trouble in social situations such as games and play activities (Melloy, 1990). Since they demonstrate poor impulse control, these children are apt to take their turn before its time, or to respond incorrectly to game stimuli (e.g., questions). Some children who have poor impulse control may respond to teasing, for example, by hitting the person who teases them. They are often sorry for their actions and can discuss what they should have done had they taken time to think about their action. Children who manifest impulsive behavior are also described as not being able to delay gratification (Shafrir & Pascual-Leone, 1990).

## Common Causes and Antecedents for Impulsive Behavior

### Multiple Factors

According to a number of authors, no one actually knows what causes impulsivity (Campbell & Werry, 1986; Kauffman, 1997). Kauffman (1997) suggests that impulsivity is most likely caused by multiple factors, including biological, psychological, environmental, and social learning factors. Assessment of impulsivity is usually achieved through the use of behavioral checklists, behavior ratings, mazes, match-to-sample tasks, and behavioral observations (Campbell & Werry, 1986; Olson et al., 1990; Shafrir & Pascual-Leone, 1990; Vitiello, Stoff, Atkins, & Mahoney, 1990). Many children who exhibit impulsive behaviors are also disruptive and noncompliant. Many of the same variables that are associated with these two previously discussed behaviors apply to impulsive behavior.

### Failure to Self-Monitor

Shafrir and Pascual-Leone (1990) conducted a study with 378 children 9, 10, 11, and 12 years of age. The purpose of the study was to determine the effect of attention to errors on academic tasks and the relationship to reflective/impulsive behavior. Shafrir and Pascual-Leone administered a number of measures, including mazes and match-to-sample tasks, to determine response behavior, and tests of academic achievement to evaluate arithmetic abilities. The authors report that children who completed tasks quickly and accurately tended to take time to check their answers. If an error occurred, they took time to correct the error and used the information learned in correction of the error to assist them in completing the rest of the task. This resulted in fewer errors overall and completion of the task in a more timely fashion. They call these children *postfailure reflective* (Shafrir & Pascual-Leone, 1990, p. 385).

In comparison, children who are referred to as *postfailure impulsive* (Shafrir & Pascual-Leone, 1990, p. 385) were found to complete tasks slowly and inaccurately. These children plodded through the task without checking answers for correctness. They simply went on to the next problem with no reference to previously completed tasks. Shafrir and Pascual-Leone concluded that the lack of postfailure reflection by this group led to more errors because they did not learn from their previous errors. The implications of the results of this study are that children possess some type of "reflection/impulsivity cognitive style" (Shafrir & Pascual-Leone, 1990, p. 386), which was first proposed by Kagan (1966). Also, children who appear to be taking their time (slow thinkers) in actuality make more errors than the children who complete the tasks quickly (reflective thinkers).

### Parent-Child Interactions

Olson and his colleagues (1990) attempted to identify the antecedents of impulsivity in children. They assessed parent-child interactions through behavioral observation to determine if parental interaction style was a predictor of impulsive behavior. According to Olson et al., the purpose of their study was to "identify the relative contributions of different parent-child interaction antecedents to children's later self-regulatory abilities" (1990, p. 320). This longitudinal study involved 79 mother-child dyads. Their findings indicate that "responsive, sensitive, and cognitively enriching mother-child interactions are important precursors of childhood impulse control" (p. 332). Children, especially boys, were more likely to develop impulsivity if their mothers manifested punitive and inconsistent behavior management styles.

## Interventions for Impulsive Behavior

### Waiting and Self-Control Skills

Impulsivity may be decreased by teaching students appropriate waiting behaviors, and by a reinforcement plan for appropriate responding behavior. For example, after an assignment has been given, a teacher may teach a student to place her hands on her desk, establish eye contact with the teacher, and listen for directions. The teacher should praise the student for demonstrating waiting behaviors.

Students who manifest impulsive behavior will benefit from training in social skills such as self-control. At the same time, students may be taught relaxation techniques. Reinforcement will increase the possibility that a student will demonstrate behaviors that are alternatives to impulsivity. The student just described learned social skills through direct instruction and reinforcement for use of the skills to replace impulsive behavior. Schaub (1990) also found that targeting behaviors for intervention that were positive and incompatible with undesirable behaviors was effective with children who demonstrated impulsive behavior. Bornas, Servera, and Llabres (1997) suggest that teachers use computer software to assist students in preventing impulsivity. The authors describe several software products that are effective in preventing impulsivity through instruction in problem solving and self-regulation

### Smaller and Shorter Tasks at One Time

A student who hurries through an assignment without stopping to read the directions or to check for errors could be given smaller amounts of a task to accomplish at one time, rather than the whole task at once. This would give the student a smaller chunk of the problem to deal with and more opportunities for reinforcement since the student would be more likely to solve the problem correctly.

Sometimes, a student can handle solving only one problem at a time. In this case, the student should be allowed to solve the problem and receive feedback immediately. As the student becomes more confident and is able to pace himself or herself more efficiently, then he or she may be able to handle larger portions of projects and assignments.

## INATTENTION

Attention has been defined as the ability to remain oriented to a task for the length of time required to complete the task, or for an amount of time that seems socially acceptable (Kounin, 1970; Ruff, Lawson, Parrinello, & Weissberg, 1990). McGee, Williams, and Silva identify three behavioral dimensions associated with inattention: "planning, organization, and execution of tasks or activities" (1985, pp. 487–488). Children who manifest inattentive behavior will often have problems that fall along three dimensions:

  a. coming to attention,
  b. making decisions, and
  c. giving sustained attention (Brown & Wynne, 1984; Hallahan, Kauffman, & Lloyd, 1985).

Parents and teachers often describe these children as having trouble starting and/or finishing things, and being easily distracted. These children may become off task at even the slightest noise (e.g., someone's pencil dropping on the floor) or change in the environment (e.g., someone coming to the door of the classroom to talk to the teacher). These children often have trouble getting back to work once they have been distracted. As a result, they may have difficulty completing academic tasks, possibly resulting in poor academic achievement.

In a study on social skills, McMahon (1989) observed children on a playground and found that one of the children seemed easily distracted. This child rarely initiated play activities with other children. When he did become involved in a game or an activity, he switched groups every few minutes. For instance, the child started playing kickball with one group of children, then moved to another group playing on the swings before the kickball game was over.

Children who have attention problems are also described as poor listeners. For example, 15-year-old Matthew rarely uses any body language (e.g., eye contact) to indicate that he is listening to another person. At school, the students have been instructed to look at a person who is talking (e.g., a peer giving a speech in front of the class). During these situations, Matthew is often observed to stare out the window. In Matthew's home, where he is expected to stand or sit in close proximity to the person speaking, but not to make eye contact, Matthew often looks away while someone talks to him. He reports that he can concentrate better on what is being said when he is not distracted by looking at people and noticing something about what they are wearing or their hairstyle.

Inattention is a problem that often exists with other behavioral deficits such as impulsivity and hyperactivity. Its existence as an independent construct has been debated (Kauffman, 1997). Regardless of its definition, inattention is a problem that seems to be a common characteristic among children with challenging behaviors.

## Common Causes and Antecedents for Inattention

Ruff and Lawson (1990) investigated the development of attention in preschoolers. Two studies of attention involved 67 children, ages 1 through 5. The studies were conducted using observations of free play as the measure of focused attention. They found that as children got older, their attention became more focused when they were presented with a variety of activities that involved complex problem-solving aspects. Effective intervention of children and adolescents with attention problems usually involves the presentation of novel and interesting tasks at a pace that is age-appropriate and geared toward motivating children (Kerr & Nelson, 1989).

### *Learning to Be Attentive*

Teachers frequently talk about children who don't sit and listen. These children have not learned how to sit and listen, typically taught at home, starting at a young age, when parents have their children sit and listen to them read a story. But many children do not have this early childhood experience and come to school without the skills of "sitting and listening." These children must be taught these skills at school, hopefully at the preschool or kindergarten level.

## Effective Interventions for Inattention

DuPaul, Stoner, Tilly, III, & Putnam, Jr. (1991) offered some guidelines for developing behavior change interventions to assist children increase attention skills:

1. A functional analysis should be used to assess problem behaviors.
2. The children should receive more frequent and specific feedback than their peers.
3. Both positive and negative consequences should be incorporated into behavior management programs.
4. Tasks should be broken down into specific instructions and delivered to the student a few steps at a time.
5. The focus of behavior change programs should be based on "concrete results of appropriate behavior rather than on specific task-related behaviors" (p. 690).
6. Preferred activities should be used as reinforcers, rather than tangible rewards such as candy.
7. "Priming" children with discussion of privileges that can be earned prior to the assignment of academic tasks will increase task completion (p. 691).

Behaviorally based strategies that have been effective in changing behavior of children with poor attention skills include token reinforcement programs, contingency contracting, and response cost. These strategies are described in Chapters 7 and 9 of this text.

Self-instructional training with children who demonstrate inattentive behavior has been very effective in reducing this behavior (Davis & Hajicek, 1985; Lloyd, Bateman, Landrum, & Hallahan, 1989). During a self-instruction program, students would receive a prompt (usually a recorded tone) throughout class. Each time they hear the prompt, the students would ask themselves if they were paying attention and completing their task. Self-instruction usually includes self-monitoring, in which a student would record if he or she was (+) or was not (−) paying attention or completing his or her work. Davis and Hajicek (1985) found that seven children who had problems attending to tasks were able to learn self-instructional verbalizations. In this strategy, a self-instructional verbalization program might have a student remind him- or herself to "Pay attention" or "Do your work" after a recorded tone was sounded every 60 seconds. This strategy helped the children significantly improve their attending and accuracy rate on academic tasks.

Lloyd and his colleagues (1989) assisted five upper elementary children in changing their attending behavior through self-recording. Using self-recording, the children's arithmetic productivity and attention to task improved significantly. Self-monitoring and self-recording provide studends with the opportunity for direct feedback as they review their own recorded data. The self-recording strategy is explained in Chapter 8 of this text.

# HYPERACTIVITY

Hyperactivity has to be one of the most overused terms in education. Controversy has arisen over whether or not hyperactivity exists as an independent behavioral construct, and it is often associated with inattention and impulsivity in children's behavior (e.g., Gaynor, 1990; Kauffman, 1985, 1989, 1997; Kohn, 1989). Like impulsivity and inattention, the function of hyperactivity seems to be to gain attention, to escape from tasks, or to provide self-gratification. Hyperactivity may refer to behaviors that include developmentally inappropriate levels of activity, out-of-seat behavior, moving about without permission, talking out of turn to others, and excessive talking. Most of these behaviors are expected of young children in many environmental contexts. These same behaviors, however, may prove troublesome for school-age children and adolescents in home, school, and community environments.

Interestingly, symptoms of many children labeled hyperactive often seem to disappear when the child is engaged in something he or she likes to do such as playing/working on the computer, playing video games, watching TV, or engaging in free play. This should tell us much about the etiology of the behavior. If it were biological, hyperactivity would be either constant or random. But if the behavior follows environmental antecedents, the etiology is environmental (and medications will not solve the primary problem).

The following is a list of behaviors that are often associated with hyperactive behavior in children and adolescents:

1. *Problems in school:* The child is disruptive, aggressive, constantly out of seat, and often off task.
2. *Restlessness:* The child does not sit still for more than several minutes at one time.
3. *Childish or immature behavior:* The child may choose to play with or spend time with younger children.
4. *Problems keeping friends:* The child does not know how to join a group for play.
5. *Self-overassertiveness:* The child goes overboard trying to please adults with offers to help.
6. *Perfectionism:* The child erases answers on a math worksheet so often that holes appear in the paper or rarely completes an assignment or project because he or she just can't get it right.

## Common Causes and Antecedents for Hyperactive Behavior

### Multiple Factors

There is not one definitive cause of hyperactivity, though a number of theories have been researched. Brain damage, biological factors, food additives, difficult temperament, and psychoanalytic factors have all been proposed as explanations for hyperactivity (Kauffman, 1989). None of these explanations, however, have been supported by sufficient scientific research to conclude that any one of them alone or in combination is a cause for hyperactivity.

Other explanations for hyperactive behavior revolve around theories of modeling, imitation, and environmental interaction (Campbell & Werry, 1986; David &

Wintrob, 1989; Kauffman, 1985, 1989; Kohn, 1989). Clearly, the most plausible explanation for hyperactive behavior is that it is caused by a combination of factors, including learned behavior.

Bussing, Zima, and Belin (1998) revealed data that suggest that students in grades 2 and 4 who demonstrated hyperactivity, inattention, and impulsivity also received special education services for learning disabilities and emotional/behavioral disorders. This suggests a link between these disorders, including the possibility that the causative factors of each disorder are shared. It may also be the case that children who have not learned to pay attention and other school-readiness skills at home do poorly at school and, thus, are more likely to be labeled learning disabled by educators. That brings us to environmental factors.

### Environmental Factors Associated with Hyperactivity

Kohn (1989) suggests that hyperactive behavior is caused by environmental factors such as classroom dynamics and/or family dynamics. He states that children demonstrate hyperactive behavior in classrooms where the work is not stimulating and where the pace of instruction is not conducive to the child's ability. Kohn also suggests that hyperactive behavior may be the result of academic failure, rather than the cause of that failure.

Kohn further reports that some "family patterns often accompany hyperactivity" (1989, p. 94). These patterns are described in terms of mental health issues among family members, a heavy emphasis on punitive and authoritative approaches to behavior management, and marital problems between the child's parents. In a later article, Harden (1997) suggests that children who demonstrate hyperactivity when in a boring, nonstimulating situation can be helped to engage in more appropriate behavior with interventions such as restricting television watching and establishing family routines (e.g., mealtimes and bedtime).

### Parent-Child Interactions

David and Wintrob (1989) studied the role of mother-child communication patterns in the development of hyperactive/conduct-disturbed behavior. The authors conducted research with 30 boys, who had been diagnosed as hyperactive/conduct-disordered, and their mothers. Mothers and their sons were given pictures to discuss while their interactions were videotaped. Examples of the exchanges that were taped included an interaction about a picture that could have been described as a type of flying animal. The following interaction was considered to demonstrate a disturbed communication pattern between a mother and her son:

*Son:* "That's a bat."

*Mother:* "Don't be stupid! That's not a bat; that's a butterfly."

In comparison, this interaction was considered to be a positive interaction between the mother and her son:

*Son:* "That is a bat."

*Mother:* "Very good! That's what it looks like."

David and Wintrob (1989) found that mothers' communication with sons labeled hyperactive was socially inappropriate in comparison to the communication patterns of mothers and their sons without hyperactivity. They stated that even though their study was conducted with mothers and sons, there is a possibility that others who communicate with children may influence children's behavior (e.g., fathers, siblings, teachers). They pointed out that "in most instances the primary caretaker will be most influential in this regard" (p. 390).

## Effective Interventions for Hyperactivity

A number of effective strategies are available for decreasing hyperactivity, but few studies are available in current literature that focus solely on hyperactivity. Most of the research focuses on hyperactivity combined with inattention and impulsivity as constructs of attention deficits. This section describes the literature that is available on behavioral interventions that were effective in decreasing hyperactive behavior. The most popular of these interventions include consistent reinforcement consequences, social skills training, and cognitive behavior management.

### Teach Appropriate Social Skills

Children who are hyperactive will respond best in settings where the rules for behavior have been clearly established. In addition, the rules must be consistently enforced, and children should be reinforced for following the rules. Children with hyperactivity are most successful in structured classroom settings where the rules are obvious and consistently enforced (Gordon, 1991; Schaub, 1990).

Children with hyperactivity also respond well in educational programs that include positive reinforcement. Children who are positively reinforced using praise and tokens for appropriate behavior (e.g., staying in seat, asking permission, following rules) are more likely to engage in behaviors incompatible with hyperactivity (DuPaul & Eckert, 1997; Melloy, 1990). Paniagua, Morrison, and Black (1990) report on the effective use of positive reinforcement to reduce the hyperactive behavior of a 7-year-old boy. They found that offering a toy as positive reinforcement for promising to inhibit behavior and actual inhibition of the behavior was effective in reducing hyperactive behavior.

Children labeled hyperactive often receive low social status ratings from their peers and deviant scores on teacher ratings of behavior (McConnell & Odom, 1986). These children benefit from training in social skills using a structured learning approach (McGinnis & Goldstein, 1997). Social skills that are incompatible with hyperactive behavior include staying in seat, task completion, joining in a group, and offering help to others. Modeling, role playing, receiving feedback, and generalization training in these skills can reduce hyperactive behavior in children.

Mathes and Bender (1997) report that self-monitoring of behavior and psychostimulant medication were helpful to three boys, ages 8 through 11 years, in improving their on-task behavior. Maag and Reid (1994) also have suggested that self-monitoring is effective in helping children with hyperactive behavior engage in more appropriate classroom behavior.

Involvement in sports and arts activities is another type of intervention that resulted in development of replacement behaviors for hyperactivity and in more academic and social success for children who are challenged by hyperactivity. Participation in a sport with a team may help a child to develop social skills for getting along with others and give him or her an appropriate means for exerting energy.

## AGGRESSIVE BEHAVIOR

Whenever the term *aggressive* is used to describe a child's behavior, images of physical injury to another automatically come to mind. Violent and bullying behavior are specific types of aggressive behavior that result in similar outcomes or functions of aggressive behavior. These functions include power and control, affiliation, escape, gaining attention, and self-gratification. There is no one globally accepted definition of aggressive behavior (e.g., Bandura, 1973; Kerr & Nelson, 1998; Lancelotta & Vaughn, 1989). Some consensus seems to exist, however, that aggressive behavior is meant either to injure another, to gain something for the aggressor, or to result in both injury and extraneous gains. Bandura distinguishes instrumental and hostile aggression. He describes *instrumental aggression* as those actions "aimed at securing extraneous rewards other than the victim's suffering" (1973, p. 8). A child who steals a pair of tennis shoes out of another child's locker is an example of someone who engages in instrumental aggression. *Hostile aggression*, on the other hand, is defined as actions that are "used to produce injurious outcomes rather than to gain status, power, resources, or some other types of results" (Bandura, 1973, p. 8). Long and Brendtro (1993, p. 3) define aggression as

> a spontaneous, impulsive act of anger. Aggression is observable behavior which can depreciate, threaten, or hurt a person or destroy an object. It is unplanned and usually occurs during times of stress. Aggression is viewed as a loss of self-control or an impulse break-through. After an aggressive act, the individual may feel guilty or escalate the situation to the point where he can become enraged.

In this chapter, aggressive behaviors refer to those behaviors—verbal, nonverbal, or physical—that injure another indirectly or directly and/or result in extraneous gains for the aggressor. These behaviors are typically described in terms such as those that appear frequently in the literature (Hunt, 1993; Kerr & Nelson, 1998; Lancelotta & Vaughn, 1989; Long & Brendtro, 1993; Sasso, Melloy, & Kavale, 1990). The child's body language for all of these aggressive behaviors is a stance that clearly communicates anger, rage, frustration, humiliation, and/or other feelings that motivate aggressive behavior. For example, the children's faces may become red, they may be crying, their breathing may become faster and harder, and their muscles may be tensed. In instances where verbal aggression is manifested, children will not always demonstrate the body language described (e.g., tattling), but the intent of the behavior is still clearly to hurt another person or to gain something for the aggressor. It is also important to keep in mind that even playful hits, kicks, and punches and sarcastic statements are forms of aggressive behavior. Educators and others should encourage children and reinforce them for using alternative behaviors to express affection and liking for others.

## Target Behaviors Involving Physical Aggression

The following is a list of common physically aggressive behaviors and their observable, measurable characteristics:

- *Kicking:* A child uses his or her foot/feet to make contact with another's body in a manner that inflicts discomfort, pain, and/or injury.
- *Hitting:* A child uses his or her hand(s) (i.e., open or in a fist) to strike another person's body with the intention of inflicting discomfort, pain, and/or injury.
- *Spitting:* A child projects saliva onto another person, which causes the other person's body parts or clothing to become wet. (Note that sometimes children may pretend to spit on another. Even though no saliva is actually projected, the behavior is considered aggressive because it may result in the same effect—degradation and discomfort on the part of the other person.)
- *Biting:* The child's teeth make contact with another's skin and cause discomfort, pain, and/or injury.
- *Grabbing/holding:* A child forcibly takes another person with his or her hand(s) and then inhibits the movement of the other in a manner that results in discomfort, pain, and/or injury.
- *Fighting:* Two or more children are engaged in hitting, kicking, grabbing, and/or holding behavior, which may result in one or more children falling to the ground or being shoved against a structure (e.g., wall, door, ledge, cupboard). This behavior results in discomfort, pain, and/or injury to the aggressor and aggressee. (Note that wrestling behavior in which one or more children are engaged in grabbing and holding each other while they roll on the ground is not considered physical aggression unless the prerequisite body language is present and/or physical injury or pain results.)
- *Throwing:* A child directs materials (e.g., book, pencil, objects, furniture, papers) towards a person by sending the object through the air with a motion of the hand or arm. This is considered aggressive behavior (a) if the prerequisite body language is present and (b) whether or not the object actually strikes the targeted person causing pain or injury—the intention is enough to consider the behavior to be aggressive.

## Target Behaviors Involving Verbal Aggression

Some examples of verbal aggression and their observable behavior characteristics are as follows:

- *Bossy verbal behavior:* The child commands others in a demanding tone.
- *Teasing others:* The child makes fun of another person(s) by verbally expressing words that result in emotional discomfort, pain, and/or injury of the other person. The other person demonstrates his or her feelings of hurt by crying, running away, verbal aggression, and/or pretending to ignore the aggressor.
- *Tattling:* The child repeatedly reports on trivial behaviors of others that are not endangering others to an adult who is in authority (e.g., teacher, paraprofessional). An example would be a child who reports to the teacher that "Billy is pulling Susan's hair" in an exaggerated tone of voice.
- *Nonconstructively criticizing the work of others:* The child puts down the work of others using condescending terms (e.g., "That's a stupid idea"), which results in the other person expressing hurt feelings or anger.
- *Picking on others:* The child says things to another person that emphasize a perceived fault of the other (e.g., "Hey, Angela, look at Jose. He can't even do these baby math problems!"), which results in the person feeling humiliation, hurt, and/or anger. Behaviors of the person being picked on that demonstrate these feelings include a dejected look, verbal retorts, and/or anger outbursts.
- *Making sarcastic remarks:* The child uses phrases to comment on another's appearance, performance, and so on, that are derogatory in nature and result in emotional discomfort and/or pain in the person to whom the remarks were directed. The remarks are generally made in a sarcastic tone of voice (e.g., words exaggerated, nasty tone). An example of a sarcastic remark is "Don't count on Barbara to show up. She always has more important things to do," which is voiced in a nasty tone of voice. Sarcastic remarks can also be made in a pleasant tone of voice, but the result is that the other person is hurt or humiliated by the remark (e.g., a teacher remarks, "Wow, isn't it nice that Lori could join us again?" after a child returns from time-out for behaving aggressively). Hurt and humiliation are demonstrated by behaviors such as putting one's head down, getting a red face, or crying.

## Patterns of Aggression

Hunt (1993, pp. 16–18) describes five patterns of aggressive behavior: over-aroused aggression, impulsive aggression, affective aggression, predatory aggression, and instrumental aggression.

- *Over-aroused aggression:* Children engage in behavior that is characterized by high levels of activity that result in frequent accidents and aggressive incidents. Children who push and shove their peers often provoke or initiate an aggressive response from their peers. Unlike motivation for other types of aggressive behavior, children who demonstrate over-aroused aggression rarely select their victims.

- *Impulsive aggression:* Children are generally quiet and passive in their demeanor but seemingly have a low tolerance for frustration. When frustrated, the child may burst into a flurry of activity and violence that can be uncharacteristically destructive.
- *Affective aggression:* Children demonstrate rageful aggression. Their behavior is described as appearing to be chronically angry, resentful, and hostile.
- *Predatory aggression:* Children seem to be seeking revenge. Individuals who demonstrate predatory aggression are described as persons who wait for a chance to get back at another person in a hurtful, harmful manner.
- *Instrumental aggression:* Children act as the intimidating bully. Children who engage in instrumental aggression demonstrate behaviors that allow them to get their own way through intimidation of others.

## Stages of Aggressive Behavior

Smith Myles and Simpson (1994, 1998) describe four stages that precede and follow aggressive behavior:

1. the frustration stage,
2. the defensiveness stage,
3. the aggression stage, and
4. the self-control stage (1994, pp. 371–372).

The authors suggest that knowing the behaviors that a child demonstrates for each stage is important since this information can then be used to intervene early on in the aggression cycle, consequently preventing aggressive behavior.

Typical behaviors that demonstrate the *frustration stage* include biting nails and tensing muscles. Warning behaviors for the *defensiveness stage* are withdrawing from others or lashing out at teachers and peers. Smith Myles and Simpson caution that if the behaviors are not attended to in the early stages, children may engage in physically and/or verbally aggressive behavior similar to the behaviors described earlier. Finally, following the aggressive behavior, the child will engage in the *self-control stage.* During this stage the child may become quiet and even huddle on the floor. Unfortunately, teachers and others take this as a sign that the incident has passed, when in actuality, the child will engage in further aggressive behavior unless the child learns, through reinforcement of appropriate behavior and discipline following aggressive behavior, more appropriate social skills.

## Common Causes and Antecedents for Aggressive Behavior

### Modeled Aggressive Behavior

On any given day, children are faced with many instances that result in feelings of anger, frustration, and/or humiliation. These feelings often result in children reacting aggressively. The most commonly accepted cause for aggressive behavior is that these behaviors are learned through modeling (e.g., Bandura, 1973; Wicks-Nelson & Israel, 1991; Widom, 1989). For example, children observe aggressive behavior models when adults and others engage in verbally abusive or physical punishment of children. Hyman and Perone (1998) studied victimization of students in school settings and found that teachers, administrators, and other school personnel consistently used aggressive behavior toward students in the name of discipline. A common example of adult-modeled aggressive behavior is when a child is slapped or spanked as a consequence of hitting another person. When a child is hit in response to his own hitting behavior, the child learns that it is acceptable to hit others when you are upset or angry. Children cannot be expected to expand their repertoire of responses to anger if they see only a limited number of inappropriate responses modeled. Teachers and parents can model appropriate alternatives to aggressive behavior by remaining calm in anger-inducing situations, talking out the problem, or walking away from the problem until they feel calm enough to discuss the situation. This alternative to aggression can be modeled and practiced in a formal social skills training.

Rudo, Powell, and Dunlap (1998) report on a review of the literature related to the effects of modeled aggressive behavior and children's social, emotional, and behavioral functioning. They reviewed 27 studies that were published within the last 20 years. Their review reveals that children who live in violent homes where they are abused themselves, watch parents or their partners being abused, or witness both types of abuse are more likely to develop behavioral and emotional problems. The authors offer compelling evidence that children exposed to violence in their homes are at greater risk for development of behavior and other problems.

### *Developmental Perspective on Aggressive Behavior*

Other research findings indicate that antisocial behavior, including aggression, "appears to be a developmental trait that begins early in life and often continues into adolescence and adulthood" (Patterson, DeBaryshe, & Ramsey, 1989, p. 329). According to a number of researchers, antisocial behavior develops as a result of the child's behavior and interaction with the social environment (Finkelhor, 1995; Landy & Peters, 1992; Patterson, 1992). Patterson and colleagues maintained that these behaviors occur in stages and that behaviors of one stage will result in certain predictable reactions from the child's social environment, leading to further actions from the child.

During the first stage of aggressive behavior development, family variables, such as harsh parental discipline and poor adult supervision, result in the child being "trained" to engage in aggressive behavior such as hitting. These behaviors become functional in the sense that the child may be allowed to escape from tasks when he or she acts aggressively. For example, a child may be sent to her room after hitting her brother while they do dishes. Also, aggressive behaviors may be positively reinforced through laughter, attention, and approval, which results in maintenance of the behaviors. Children in these situations do not learn socially skillful responses to others, but they learn aggressive behavior that results in meeting their needs.

Following this stage, children who are aggressive often find themselves rejected by their peer group and experiencing academic failure (Patterson et al., 1989). Having learned aggressive behaviors in early childhood, these children become rejected because they do not demonstrate the social skills that allow them to be socially competent with peers. This idea is in contrast to that of others who believe that children become aggressive after they are rejected by their peers and/or fail academically.

Patterson et al. (1989) report that children who engage in aggressive behaviors spend less time on academic tasks and have more difficulty with classroom survival skills (e.g., staying in seat, answering questions). These behaviors result in a higher incidence of academic failure. Once children have learned aggressive behavior and experienced peer rejection and academic failure, they are at a higher risk for developing delinquent behavior (Lancelotta & Vaughn, 1989; Patterson et al., 1989; Wahler & Dumas, 1986). These children have a tendency to become involved with deviant peer groups who also engage in aggressive behaviors (e.g., fighting, property damage). The members of the groups positively reinforce these actions, thus increasing the probability of their repeated occurrence. Unfortunately, long-term outcomes for children who seemingly follow this developmental sequence of aggressive behavior are not generally desirable.

These findings have important implications for children and their parents and teachers. Reports have found that children who engage in antisocial behavior throughout childhood and adolescence are at an extremely high risk for becoming school dropouts, having difficulty maintaining employment, committing crimes, and having marital difficulties.

### *Media Influence on Aggressive Behavior*

The media also offer plenty of aggressive models for children through TV programs geared to the interest of young persons (Hughes, 1996; Lieberman cited in Walker, Colvin, & Ramsey, 1995). Lieberman suggests that children who are exposed to media violence become desensitized to aggressive and violent behavior. This factor has led to increased levels of violent and aggressive behavior among youth (Walker et al., 1995). Widom (1989) reviewed the literature on the relationship of TV violence to aggressive behavior in children and concluded that television violence was clearly related to aggressive behavior. One has to watch only a few minutes of professional wrestling on TV, a popular show for young boys, to understand the problem. Unfortunately, many parents, especially fathers, don't realize the negative influence these shows have on their sons' behavior at home and school. But teachers see the effects every day.

Friedrich-Cofer and Huston (1986) reviewed studies that focused on the relationship of viewing TV violence and subsequent manifestation of aggressive behavior in children. Their review included laboratory studies that generally demonstrated a causal link between TV violence and aggressive behavior. Friedrich-Cofer and Huston also reviewed field experiments and found a relationship between children's viewing of TV violence and the demonstration of aggressive behavior. They reported that this was more often the case with children who demonstrated a high rate of aggression before viewing the TV show. In these children, the rate of aggressive behavior increased after viewing the shows. A review of longitudinal studies revealed that viewing TV violence at one age correlated with aggressive behaviors demonstrated at a later age. "Of a large number of parent, family, and socioeconomic variables measured at age 8, television was the single best predictor of aggression in 18-year-olds" (Friedrich-Cofer & Huston, 1986, p. 367).

Findings also indicate that children who demonstrate a predisposition for aggressive behavior are likely to choose a diet of violent television programs. Friedrich-Cofer and Huston (1986) note that in their study, viewing of television violence generalized to serious forms of aggression including "firing a revolver at someone, attacks with a knife, setting fire to a building, hitting someone in the face with a broken bottle, and knocking someone off a bike" (p. 369). These findings present serious implications for our society in the face of the expanding and increasingly violent television available to children through cable television and videotape rentals.

Violence and aggression are also apparent in video computer games, which are easily accessed by children and teenagers. Producers of these games say that blaming school-yard killings such as those experienced in Jonesboro, Arkansas, on video games is society's way of taking the focus off of other causes of aggression such as poverty and access to guns. However, Grossman (cited in Cummins, 1999) suggests that video and computer games may condition youngsters and others to kill without thinking.

### Peer Reinforcement

Research offers other explanations for the cause of aggressive behavior. Several authors propose that the likelihood that aggressive behavior will be repeated is strengthened through peer reinforcement of the behavior (Fremont, Tedesco, & Trusty, 1988; Quay, 1986). In this case, the probability of engaging in aggressive behaviors is increased when children are given attention for their behavior.

### Social Skills Deficits

Others have proposed that children act aggressively because they lack alternative skills that would allow them to choose a socially acceptable behavior to deal with a provocative situation in an assertive rather than aggressive manner (Dubow, Huesmann, & Eron, 1987; Hollinger, 1987; Strain, Guralnick, & Walker, 1986). Dubow and others (1987) report the need for children to develop social competence before they experience a history of reinforcement for solving problems with aggressive behavior. Strain and his colleagues (1986) outline a number of reasons for aggressive behavior in children that focus on development of social behavior. They maintain that children often have a limited repertoire of social problem-solving behaviors. Often, due to environmental interactions and opportunities for modeling, aggressive behaviors are manifested as the only choice for situations that require problem-solving skills.

Neel, Jenkins, and Meadows (1990) found results that conflict with those of researchers who report that aggressive behavior was caused by deficits in social skills. In their study of 19 preschoolers, ages 3 to 4, Neel and his colleagues found that children who were aggressive demonstrated similar usage of social skills compared to their nonaggressive peers. They conclude that children who were aggressive used a number of social problem-solving strategies just as their nonaggressive counterparts did. The difference was that children who were aggressive used more intrusive types of strategies (e.g., barging into a game) compared to the more socially acceptable strategies used by their nonaggressive peers (e.g., asking for information and questioning before joining the group). A number of authors have suggested this in previous research (e.g., Melloy, 1990; Strain et al., 1986). The findings of Neel and others suggest that the development of social competence in children who are aggressive should concentrate on strategy content rather than on the number of strategies within the child's repertoire. For example, a child who demonstrates intrusive group joining-in skills will need to learn social skills that are more acceptable. Children who manifest aggressive behaviors with their peers do not always fail in their social goals—the child may be allowed to join the group even if he or she uses intrusive means. However, these children more often earn a reputation that results in deviant peer acceptance.

Melloy (1990) describes several types of peer acceptance of children who demonstrate aggressive behavior. Some children who are aggressive are accepted as leaders by their peers because their peers are afraid to reject them. In other words, a child who is aggressive may threaten his or her peers with taunts such as "If you don't let me play, I'll beat you up." On the other hand, children who are aggressive are often rejected by their peers. A common scene on a playground is for a group of children to terminate their play and move to another area when they see a peer who is aggressive approaching the group.

In the long run, a history of rejection by one's peers can lead to a dependence on less desirable peers and membership in deviant subcultures, which often leads to social maladjustment (Center, 1990; Weinberg & Weinberg, 1990). Children in these subcultures are frequently reinforced for engaging in aggressive behaviors.

## Effective Interventions for Aggression

Sasso and his colleagues (1990) have demonstrated that social skills training could assist elementary and junior high students in acquiring, maintaining, and generalizing social skills as alternatives to aggression. The authors report a study that took place over an entire school year with three children, ages 8, 10, and 13, who were behaviorally disordered. The subjects were part of a larger class of eight students in a large, midwestern elementary and junior high school. The children were all integrated into regular classes for at least one class period per day. Students were taught social skills using the structured learning approach and the curriculum from *Skillstreaming the Elementary School Child* (McGinnis & Goldstein, 1984). Pertinent to the Sasso et al. study was the training of replacement behaviors for aggression. These alternative behaviors included accepting consequences, dealing with accusations, negotiating, responding to teasing, asking permission, and staying out of fights.

Following intervention, all of the children in the study reduced levels of aggressive behavior in comparison to baseline levels. During the maintenance phase

Establishing rules, reinforcing appropriate behavior, and having consistent consequences for inappropriate behavior make up the most effective intervention plan.

of the study, the children maintained intervention levels of appropriate behaviors and generalized these behaviors to their regular classroom settings and other school settings. Use of social skills training along with positive reinforcement for appropriate behaviors are among the current promising practices in teaching children alternative behaviors to aggression.

Using cognitive behavior management (CBM) intervention, children are taught to use techniques such as self-talk and self-instruction to deal with stressful situations. Etscheidt (1991) used CBM with 30 adolescents, ages 13 to 18, who demonstrated aggressive behavior. The purpose of the study was (a) to determine the effectiveness of cognitive behavior management on the reduction of aggressive behavior and increases in prosocial behavior, and (b) to determine if the addition of positive consequences would increase the effectiveness of cognitive training.

One group of students was exposed to cognitive training from the *Anger Control Program Model* (Lochman, Nelson, & Sims, cited in Etscheidt, 1991). The intent of the program was to assist students "in modifying their aggressive behaviors by altering their cognitive processing of events and response alternatives" (Etscheidt, 1991, p. 110). During training, children in Group 1 participated in 12 lessons with these goals:

1. self-awareness
2. exploration of reactions to peer influences

3. identification of problem situations
4. generation of alternative solutions to problems
5. evaluation of solutions
6. recognition of physiological awareness of anger arousal
7. integration of physiological awareness
8. self-talk and social problem-solving techniques to reduce aggressive behavior

The students were taught to use the following strategy in problem situations:

*Motor Cue/Impulse Delay:* Stop and think before you act; cue yourself.
*Problem Definition:* Say how you feel and exactly what the problem is.
*Generation of Alternatives:* Think of as many solutions as you can.
*Consideration of Consequences:* Think ahead to what might happen next.
*Implementation:* When you have a really good solution, try it! (Etscheidt, 1991, p. 111)

The students in Group 2 received cognitive training and were positively reinforced for use of the skills taught. A control group received no cognitive training or positive consequences for use of the training strategy.

The results of the study indicate a significant decrease in aggressive behavior and a significant increase in self-control behavior in Group 1 and Group 2 students compared to the control group. No significant differences between Group 1 and 2 were noted. The author attributes this to the fact that, prior to cognitive training, a behavior management program existed in the students' classroom. Adding additional positive consequences may not have been as effective because of this factor.

Use of cognitive behavior management intervention strategies is highly recommended for treatment of aggressive behavior in children. Descriptions of cognitive behavior management curricula that are available for use in school settings are outlined in Chapter 8.

In the preceding paragraphs we discussed social skills instruction and cognitive behavior management as strategies for teaching alternative behaviors to aggression. It is also important to support use of new behaviors by the children targeted for intervention. The major portion of this text was designed to provide the reader with ideas for proactive behavior management. You may find that these ideas are the most useful to you in trying to help students change aggressive, antisocial behavior into prosocial behavior.

Children were found to be more responsive in terms of behavior change when they were reinforced for acceptable behavior than when they were merely punished upon engaging in unacceptable behavior (Meadows, Melloy, & Yell, 1996). Building relationships with students and providing meaningful curriculum in a positive classroom climate were also effective in reducing aggressive behavior and increasing acceptable school behavior (Abrams & Segal, 1998). Goal setting, behavioral contracts, and token economies were other behaviorally based interventions that teachers used effectively in promoting and supporting acceptable replacement behavior for aggression (Ruth, 1996). Behavior reduction strategies including suspension and exclusionary time-out were not effective in assisting children (especially older children) to change aggressive behavior to prosocial behavior (Costenbader & Markson, 1998; Maag, 1996).

# TEMPER TANTRUMS

Temper tantrum behavior is often included in literature regarding the characteristics of aggressive and/or noncompliant behavior (e.g., Kerr & Nelson, 1989; Kuczynski et al., 1987; McMahon & Wells, 1989; Sasso et al., 1990). Temper tantrums have been defined as noxious behavior demonstrated by children when their demands are not met or when they are tired (Sasso et al., 1990). Blechman defines temper tantrums as taking place "when a child, who has not been mistreated, is out-of-control for at least 1 minute, screaming, crying, throwing things, or hitting" (1985, p. 89). Although tantrum behavior is exhibited by persons of all ages, it is usually affiliated with toddlers and young children. Temper tantrums are characterized by a variety of acting-out behaviors including crying, stamping, throwing self, screaming, kicking, clinging, jumping up and down, shouting, pounding, and other annoying behaviors. Temper tantrums are among the most common challenging behaviors of young children (Blechman, 1985).

Children manifest tantrums most often when their wishes for edibles or privileges are not met. For example, 2-year-old Tyler requests to go to the store with his mother. When he is told he cannot go, he throws himself to the ground, screams and cries, demanding in a loud voice that he be allowed to go along. This behavior may be manifested from a few seconds to several hours depending on the child's history of reinforcement for tantrum behavior.

## Common Causes and Antecedents for Tantrum Behavior

### Inconsistent Reinforcement Consequences

Children have temper tantrums for one primary reason: They work! Temper tantrum behavior can often be traced directly to an adult's pattern of giving in to the child's wishes as soon as he or she begins to tantrum. The most common function of tantrum behavior is to gain attention, usually from an adult (e.g., parent, grandparent). In the case of Tyler, his mother did not like the tantrum behavior, so she let Tyler accompany her to the store. Tyler promptly stopped his tantrum, got his coat, and smilingly accompanied his mother. By giving in to Tyler's behavior, his mother reinforced his behavior. In the future, Tyler will be more likely to engage in tantrum behavior when he is told no as a result of the positive consequences he experienced for his tantrum behavior.

A more common scenario is the battle that young children and parents engage in at bedtime. Children may manifest tantrum behavior when they are told it is time to go to bed. The tantrum may begin when the parent and child attempt to put on the child's pajamas. The parent may let the child get out of bed (for just a little while longer) when the child engages in tantrum behavior. Unfortunately, this only exacerbates the problem as the child will continue to engage in tantrums whenever the parents try to put the child to bed. Parents who are consistent in their behavior (i.e., not allowing the child to get out of bed once he or she has gone to bed), will be more successful in helping the child comply with behavioral expectations. Of course, it is helpful if the child is properly prepared for bed (such as brushed teeth, glass of water, snack, bedtime story) using a regular routine. Otherwise the child's protests or expressions of needs may be warranted.

Recently, a father told me that the thing about his son's temper tantrums that drove him wild was the screaming. Anyone who has been in a closed space with a small child engaged in a screaming tantrum knows exactly what this father was talking about. All of us have been tempted to give the child anything he or she wanted just to get the child to stop the screaming. Children are masters at this. A more appropriate alternative to a tantrum, and the inevitble screaming that often accompanies tantrum behavior, is to teach children to use their words or to show you what they want. More importantly, is is very important for the child to learn to accept the word "no" from parents and other significant adults.

## Interventions for Tantrum Behavior

Temper tantrums occur most frequently when a child does not get his or her own way or when he or she is very tired. Ironically, both of these factors exist at bedtime—a time when some children manifest tantrum behavior. According to Edwards (1991), one out of four preschoolers exhibits tantrums at bedtime. The problem is that children want to stay up, but they are often too tired to stay up. Occasionally, however, parents will experience problems with their child when the child has had a late nap and is not tired at bedtime. It is extremely important for adults to be consistent when trying to decrease tantrum behavior. When a child is told "no," adults must be prepared to follow through with the command. If the parents do not really mean "no" then they should not say "no."

Tantrum behavior can be significantly decreased through the use of extinction. When reinforcement for tantrum behavior is withdrawn, and the child's behavior is ignored, the tantrum behavior will probably be greatly reduced or eliminated. To avoid tantrum behavior at bedtime, a routine for getting to bed should be established and then consistently followed (Edwards, 1991). Generally, the child is given a warning that bedtime is in a specific number of minutes. This gives the child a chance to finish what he or she is doing before the bedtime routine begins and lets the child know that a pleasant time with a parent or other adult is soon to take place. Consistent bedtime routines are effective in reducing tantrum and noncompliant behaviors at bedtime, and in making bedtime a pleasant time for children and parents (Edwards, 1991). An example of a bedtime routine for a 5-year-old child follows:

1. Tell the child that bedtime is coming about 15 minutes before bedtime.
2. Offer the child a small snack "before you go to bed."

3. Tell the child, "It is time to brush your teeth."
4. Help the child put on his or her pajamas.
5. Tell the child to "use the bathroom and wash your hands."
6. Read the child a story from a book the child selects.
7. Offer the child a drink of water.
8. Exchange good-night hugs and kisses while tucking the child into the bed.
9. Turn on the night-light and turn off the room lights.
10. Leave the room.

If the child gets out of bed following the routine, the parent should gently and quietly lead the child back to bed. It is important that the parent be firm, but gentle, in efforts to assist the child back to bed. Additional interactions with the child, especially reinforcing interactions, should be kept to a minimum.

We stated earlier that the function of temper tantrum behavior is to gain attention for the person engaged in the tantrum. Stereotypic behaviors comprise a group of behaviors that also seem to serve the function of getting the attention of others. In fact, children and adults who engage in stereotypic behavior provide the earliest clues to understanding the functions of behavior including attention, escape, tangible reinforcement, and sensory reinforcement (Durand & Carr, 1985). Although stereotypic behavior is considered challenging when demonstrated at levels that interfere with academic and social achievement, it is observed among a relatively small population. Because stereotypic behavior is so amenable to behavioral interventions, however, we will discuss it briefly in the next section.

## STEREOTYPY

Children who demonstrate stereotypic behavior typically engage in repetitious, invariant responses that occur at an excessively high rate and do not appear to have any adaptive function (Baumeister, 1978). Specific responses vary from child to child and include self-injurious behavior and self-stimulatory behavior. The major implication for children is that these behaviors often interfere with the child's level of attention to environmental stimuli. This often limits the effectiveness of educational and other programming efforts. Stereotypic behaviors that interfere with educational goals are most commonly observed in children who are autistic or severely mentally disabled. In fact, however, we all engage in stereotypic behavior whenever we flip a pencil repeatedly or shake a leg or foot for no apparent reason.

*Self-injurious behaviors* (SIB) inflict harm on the person exhibiting them. Behaviors of this type include "striking oneself, biting or sucking various body parts, pinching, scratching, poking or pulling various body parts, repeatedly vomiting, or vomiting and reingesting food, and consuming nonedible substances" (Favell cited in Kerr & Nelson, 1998, pp. 298–299). These behaviors are often of such high intensity that they inflict permanent tissue damage to the person's body or even death (Berkman & Meyer, 1988; LaVigna & Willis, 1991).

*Self-stimulatory behaviors* (SSB) are stereotypic behaviors that are repetitive and frequent but do not cause physical injury to the child exhibiting them. These behaviors are often manifested as "screaming, running, hopping, finger wiggling, looking out the corner of the eye, public masturbation, rocking and other repeated movements" (Kerr & Nelson, 1998, p. 302). Lovaas, Newsom, and Hickman report that SSB "takes the form of prolonged body-rocking, head-nodding, flapping the hands at the wrist, tapping or shaking objects, gazing at lights, and jumping up and down" (1987, p. 45). Self-stimulatory behaviors are not always intrusive behaviors for the person engaging in them or others around them. For this reason, professionals and parents need to consider two rules in order to make decisions about treatment of SSB: (a) If the behavior has developed into SIB, there should be no question of intervention, and (b) if SSB is interfering with the child's progress in educational programming, then intervention is warranted.

## Common Causes and Antecedents for Stereotypic Behavior

### Reinforcement, Sensory Arousal, or Organic Origination

Bellfiore and Dattilio (1990) reviewed the literature on SIB from the past 30 years. They report that the literature reveals three explanations for the "onset, maintenance, and continuance of self-injury" (1990, p. 29). According to Bellfiore and Dattilio's review, SIB seems to originate from one of the following sources:

1. SIB is learned behavior that is maintained by operant contingencies of either the "positive reinforcement paradigm" (p. 24) or the "negative reinforcement paradigm" (p. 25). In other words, children learn to manifest self-injurious behaviors, which are maintained by positive reinforcement (e.g., attention from others) or negative reinforcement (e.g., withdrawal of parent/teacher abuse) contingent on eliciting SIB.

2. SIB is elicited as an attempt to increase or decrease sensory arousal. It has been theorized that persons who engage in SIB have a need to provide neurological stimulation and that these behaviors assist in meeting this need. Others suggest that SIB is manifested as an attempt to reduce aversive stimuli. For example, children who suffer from otitis media (i.e., inner ear infection) may resort to head banging as an attempt to reduce or replace the pain experienced from the ear infection (Demchak & Halle, 1985).

3. SIB is related to organic origination such as is present in genetic anomalies or biochemical imbalances. SIB has been manifested by some persons who experience genetic flaws that are present in Lesch-Nyhan syndrome or Cornelia de Lang syndrome. Individuals who exhibit Lesch-Nyhan syndrome engage in SIB characterized by "severe repetitive mutilation of fingers, lips, and tongue" (Bellfiore & Dattilio, 1990, p. 27). Persons experiencing Cornelia de Lang syndrome exhibit

irregular patterns of SIB that are characterized as "eye picking, face hitting, and [sic] self-biting" (Bellfiore & Dattilio, 1990, p. 28). It should be noted that these types of syndromes are very rare and affect a very few people who engage in SIB.

Bellfiore and Dattilio (1990) note that although each of these causative factors all have some empirical backing, none has been identified as the primary etiology for SIB.

## Functions of Self-Injurious Behavior

Durand and Carr (1985) offer supported evidence that SIB has four functions or outcomes. Their theories have received support in the literature (e.g., Favell, McGimsey, & Schell, 1982; Iwata, Dorsey, Slifer, Bauman, & Richman, 1982; Northup et al., 1994; Sasso & Reimers, 1988). According to Durand and Carr (1985), SIB serves four main functions for the person engaged in the behavior. These functions include the following:

*Social attention:* SIB appears to be shaped and maintained by attention (e.g., from others) as a consequence.

*Tangible consequences:* Some children exhibit SIB in order to gain access to tangible rewards such as playing with a desired toy.

*Escape from aversive situations:* Children who engage in SIB in order to remove themselves from an unpleasant task (e.g., an academic task) are said to be motivated by escape.

*Sensory consequences:* Sensory feedback (e.g., auditory, visual, tactile), which reinforces the child, appears to be another motivating condition that maintains SIB.

A number of authors have completed a functional analysis of SIB by exposing children who exhibit SIB to analogue conditions in which hypotheses related to each function are tested (Iwata et al., 1982; Northup et. al., 1994; Sasso & Reimers, 1988; Wacker et al., 1990). They report that interventions based on findings from the functional analysis were effective in reducing SIB in children. These results lend credence to Durand and Carr's theories of motivation for SIB.

## Functions of Self-Stimulatory Behavior

Lovaas and others (1987) report that SSB is learned behavior that is maintained by *perceptual reinforcers* or *automatic reinforcers* (Iwata, Vollmer, & Zarcone, 1990). Considerable controversy surrounds the operant learning theory as a cause for SSB. Lewis, Baumeister, and Mailman (1987) argue that Lovaas and his colleagues' theory of SSB is flawed and failed to take into account biological factors.

Demchak and Halle (1985) report that SSB is maintained by the level of stimulation received by the individual during the behavior. The individual, according to this theory, is unable to receive this stimulation through other, more appropriate methods. They concluded that SIB may be "an extreme type of sensory self-stimulation" (p. 30).

Horner (1980) hypothesizes that SSB is exhibited within environments that are not enriched with activities, materials, and manipulatable toys. Horner concludes that, when individuals are exposed to enriched versus austere environments, SSB and SIB decrease in the enriched environment and increase in the austere environment.

### Frequently Related to Disabilities

Children and adolescents who typically engage in severe stereotypic behavior are autistic or severely developmentally disabled. A number of these children are successful in inclusive classroom settings because they respond to interventions designed to assist them in adopting more appropriate behavior for those settings. For example, children who communicate their wants, needs, and desires through stereotypic behavior are successfully taught to use sign language to replace self-injurious behavior. Through social skills instruction and reinforcement for engaging in prosocial behavior, stereotypic behavior is replaced by increased levels of social interaction behavior. Interventions that are effective in effecting these changes are described next.

## Interventions for Stereotypic Behavior

Of all the challenging behaviors described in this chapter, stereotypic behavior has been described more often in the literature as being responsive to behavior management-based interventions (e.g., Crnic & Reid, 1989; Day, Horner, & O'Neill, 1994; Northup et al., 1994; Zarcone, Iwata, Smith, Mazaleski, & Lerman, 1994). Durand and Carr (1985) describe intervention ideas that consider the teaching of social skills to increase interactive skills and decrease stereotypic behavior.

Durand and Carr (1985) outline several intervention guidelines that have been used to treat the self-injurious behavior of children. These guidelines include the teaching of appropriate social skills and interactive behaviors depending on the function that seems to be maintaining the child's SIB. For example, Durand and Carr suggest that if the SIB is maintained by social attention, the teacher should teach the child appropriate attention-seeking behavior. Children have been taught to ask if they are doing good work, and other appropriate phrases, for gaining teacher attention. Children who are nonverbal have been taught to use sign language or to play a taped message that is an alternative to seeking teacher attention. This appropriate communication behavior has increased and been maintained as a result of communication skills training and positive reinforcement of appropriate behavior versus SIB (e.g., Day et al., 1994; Northup et al., 1994).

For example, Northup and his colleagues (1994) provided teacher training and support for using functional analysis to determine antecedents and maintaining factors for SIB in five children ages 5 to 11 years, who were severely disabled. Teachers were trained to conduct functional assessment in a school setting. Following training, they were able to identify positive or negative reinforcers and/or punishers that appeared to maintain the children's behavior (e.g., access to music, escape from a task). The teachers were also trained to provide intervention that would assist children in increasing appropriate behaviors and decreasing SIB (e.g., activate a micro switch to get the teacher's attention versus handmouthing). These strategies were effective in increasing appropriate communication skills and decreasing SIB in all five children.

Before persons responsible for educational programming decide to reduce a child's SSB, they should first determine that this behavior is interfering with the child's educational performance and social interactions with others. Also, a functional assessment of the SSB will likely lead professionals and parents to the conclusion that environmental variables, not the child's behavior, should be the focus of an intervention plan. Teachers are encouraged to first modify the environment before trying to reduce the child's behavior directly. Increasing environmental stimulation by providing a greater array of stimulating activities and materials is likely to prove effective in reducing these behaviors. Also, children who engage in SSB may be redirected to other incompatible behaviors with verbal and physical prompts. These appropriate behaviors should then be reinforced. For a more extensive review of SSB and SIB, and related interventions, readers are referred to Repp and Singh (1990) and Kerr and Nelson (1998).

Externalized behavior problems are discussed in previous sections of this chapter. In the remainder of the chapter, we will discuss a common internalized behavior challenge: depression. Depression is generally considered an internalized behavior problem even though there are a number of observable, measurable behaviors associated with it. Also, recently, depression has been found to appear in individuals along with other challenging behaviors such as aggression, hyperactivity, and noncompliance (Bussing et al., 1998; Dubuque, 1998; Forness, 1998).

# DEPRESSION

Many children experience feelings of depression and demonstrate behaviors associated with depression. In most cases these feelings and behaviors are considered normal human behavior. However, in some cases these feelings and behaviors become serious enough for the child to receive a diagnosis of clinical depression (Carmanico et al., 1998; Maag, 1998). Miller (1994) indicates that depression has often been correlated with suicide in adolescents. It is extremely important that teachers and others become familiar with the behaviors associated with depression and effective interventions.

Kazdin (1990) points out that there is a difference between depressed mood, which commonly occurs in everyday life, and depression as a disorder (i.e., a group of symptoms that comprise depression). Teachers and parents can play a significant role in identifying depressed mood and depression in children and applying consequent interventions to assist the child in overcoming the problem. Powers (cited in Maag & Forness, 1991, p. 5) noted that "school personnel may be the first professionals to notice developing problems."

The *Diagnostic and Statistical Manual of Mental Disorders* (American Psychiatric Association, 1994, p. 349) lists the following behaviors that are typically linked to depression in children and adolescents:

1. sadness and/or irritability
2. poor appetite or overeating
3. insomnia or hypersomnia
4. low energy or fatigue
5. low self-esteem
6. poor concentration or difficulty making decisions
7. feelings of hopelessness

Maag and Forness (1991) describe behaviors associated with depression based on developmental levels of children. For example, infants may "express depression through eating and sleep disorders" (p. 6). Toddlers may have problems expressed as night terrors and elimination problems. School-age children may demonstrate more aggressive, anxious, and/or antisocial behaviors. Finally, adolescents may verbalize their feelings of low self-esteem and guilt associated with their feelings of depression.

Children who demonstrate these behaviors in varying levels of intensity and/or duration may be experiencing normal feelings associated with events such as loss or change. However, if the problems persist for longer than might be expected (e.g., several days or weeks), the child may need help such as that provided by school personnel and mental health professionals.

## Common Causes and Antecedents for Depression

Depression in children and adolescents seems to be caused by a number of factors related to biological and/or environmental factors (Kauffman, 1997). Ostrander, Weinfurt, and Nay (1998) conducted a study of 102 children between the ages of 7 and 18. The purpose of the study was to determine if the way a person thought about himself or herself and/or a nonsupportive family would have anything to do with development of depression. They found that in younger children, either factor contributed to depression, but in older children, both factors were typically present.

In truth, there is no sure way to know the cause of depression in many cases. A number of authors offer explanation of depression based on several theoretical models (Kauffman, 1997; Kazdin, 1989; Maag & Forness, 1991; Reynolds, 1991), which are summarized in Figure 10.1.

Most people who live with a teenager know the definition of moody. Moodiness seems to be normal behavior for most adolescents going through puberty. However, moodiness that is associated with behaviors such as depressed mood, unpopularity, social withdrawal, disobedience, inattentiveness, poor school performance, being bullied, and other behaviors may indicate depression, not just a depressed or "bad" mood (Puura, Almqvist, & Tamminen, 1998). Teenagers are not the only ones subject to depression. More and more, parents, teachers, researchers,

| Model | Description |
|---|---|
| Social skills deficits | Depression results from a lack of social skills necessary to obtain reinforcement from the environment. Youth who do not engage in positive interactions with others may not receive positive reinforcement from others or be punished for their social skills deficits / excesses. This may lead to symptoms of depression. |
| Self-control model | Youth who demonstrate maladaptive or deficient strategies in coping with stress using self-regulatory processes may cause depression. Self-regulatory processes include self-monitoring, self-evaluation, and self-reinforcement. Individuals with self-regulatory deficits focus on negative events, set overly stringent criteria for evaluating their performance, and administer little reinforcement to themselves. |
| Learned helplessness | Depression results from individuals' experiences and expectations that their responses do not influence events in their lives. Youth who feel that they have no control over what happens to them may demonstrate depression due to feelings of learned helplessness. |
| Cognitive triad of depression | Depressed individuals have a systematically negative bias in their thinking, which leads them to have a negative view of themselves, the world, and the future. Youth who view their circumstances negatively have tremendous difficulty seeing the positive side of things that occur and therefore become depressed, feeling there is no hope of things getting better. |
| Interpersonal problem-solving deficits | Inability to generate alternative solutions to social problems, engage in means-end thinking, and make decisions exacerbates effects of negative events. Depression emerges in response to problems of daily living. |

**FIGURE 10.1.** Theoretical models accounting for depression

*Source: Adapted from "Depression in Children and Adolescents: Identification, Assessment, and Treatment," by J. W. Maag and S. R. Forness, 1991, Focus on Exceptional Children, 24(1), 1–20.*

and mental health professionals have come to recognize sadness, even aggressiveness, in young children as symptoms of depression.

So what are acceptable replacement behaviors for these behaviors that are often quite normal? The key is determining if the level of the behavior is normal or deemed unacceptable by the child, his or her peers, family, and school personnel. Working with children and adolescents who were depressed and who were clinically depressed resulted in positive outcomes (Maag & Forness, 1991). These outcomes were noticeable since the children and adolescents renewed an interest in things they liked, became more outgoing, did better in school, and got along better with their peers, teachers and families. One of the most positive outcomes of intervention for a child who becomes suicidal is the change from suicide ideation to thoughts of a more positive nature—mainly a desire to live. We offer some ideas for interventions for teaching, promoting, and supporting alternative behavior for depression in the next section.

## Interventions for Depression

Maag and Forness (1991) and Kazdin (1989) offer information on interventions for depression in children based on behavioral, psychodynamic, and medical models of treatment. Several behavior management interventions are discussed in this section. It should be noted that the most effective intervention for depression in children has resulted from combinations of interventions including behavioral, pharmocological, and psychological strategies (e.g., Kazdin, 1989; Reynolds, 1991).

Kazdin (1989) describes effective social skills interventions that focus on teaching the child with depression the skills necessary to interact with peers and adults. Improvement in interaction skills led to more positive reinforcement for the child, who became more assertive in communicating desires, initiating conversations, and responding to others. Maag (1996) also suggests that children with depression be taught social skills so that they will experience greater levels of reinforcement for interaction from peers and others.

Reynolds (1991) describes a number of studies that effectively utilized cognitive-behavioral interventions to treat depression in children. In one study with fifth- and sixth-grade children who were mildly and moderately depressed, children received either social skills training or cognitive restructuring intervention. Children in the intervention groups were compared to a control group. The results of the study indicate that children who received either of the interventions showed significant decreases in depression compared to children in the control group (Butler, Miezitis, Friedman, & Cole cited in Reynolds, 1991).

Stark, Reynolds, and Kaslow (cited in Reynolds, 1991) studied the effects of intervention with 20 moderately depressed children, ages 9 through 12. Children who received cognitive-behavioral treatment were taught strategies in self-control and attribution retraining. Other children received intervention in the form of problem-solving strategies. They were taught to self-monitor their behavior and to become involved in pleasant activities. Both of these interventions resulted in significant decreases in depressed behavior among the children who received intervention as compared to a control group.

In Classroom Application 10.2, we return to the case of Brian, and his teacher, Mrs. Romano.

## SUMMARY

Throughout this chapter we have attempted to give you a brief overview of common challenging behaviors that teachers and others are confronted with in the school and other settings. Typical challenging behaviors demonstrated by children and adolescents include disruptiveness, noncompliance, inattention, hyperactivity, impulsivity, aggressiveness, temper tantrums, stereotypy, and depression. For each of these challenging behaviors we provided discussion on (a) typical observable, measurable behaviors; (b) common causes and antecedent stimuli; (c) acceptable replacement behaviors; and (d) ideas for interventions to teach, promote, and

## Classroom Application 10.2

### Brian . . . A Solution

Brian's teacher, Mrs. Romano, and the school psychologist completed the functional behavioral assessment of Brian's behavior. They were able to develop a hypothesis, which stated that whenever Brian was in Spanish class and the class was given directions or the teacher gave a lecture, he would call out obscenities and sit at his desk, refusing to do work in order to escape from the class. Once his teacher determined the function of Brian's behavior, she was able to develop interventions to teach him replacement behaviors for being disrespectful and for not participating in class. The replacement behaviors of demonstrating respect and participating in class were taught using social skills instruction lessons presented in the first 10 minutes of class for a period of 2 weeks. Reminder sessions were presented once a week during the first 5 minutes of class for the remainder of the quarter. Whenever Brian was able to demonstrate the replacement behaviors throughout the class period, he was able to spend the last 5 minutes of class sitting at his desk doing nothing. If Brian did not engage in appropriate behavior, he did not earn the escape time and was ignored by his teacher and peers.

Throughout class, Brian and his classmates received social praise and attention from the teacher for engaging in rule-following behavior. Ironically, once Brian started participating in class and being respectful to the teacher and his peers, he began to learn Spanish and found that he actually enjoyed learning a foreign language. In fact, after earning his "escape time" at the end of class for 2 weeks, Brian was observed to spend the last 5 minutes of class continuing to participate in class and being respectful. Teacher praise and attention continued, but eventually the escape time was eliminated from the intervention designed to assist Brian in changing his behavior. It should be noted that once an intervention plan was developed to teach Brian replacement behaviors, and the plan was explained to Brian, his inappropriate behavior decreased almost immediately and he consistently earned his 5 minutes of escape time at the end of the class period.

support acceptable behaviors. It is suggested that effective interventions be designed based on data from functional assessment since all behavior has a purpose. Once the function of behavior has been determined, teachers and parents will find their work to develop an effective intervention simplified.

In general, students are observed to engage in prosocial behavior. Nearly everyday, however, educators and others witness inappropriate, challenging behavior exhibited by their students. In this chapter we hoped to pull together ideas that are geared to assisting all of us in managing our own behavior better. Also, we hoped to provide teachers with ideas for helping their students to learn how to manage their own behavior and consequently experience academic and social success.

## DISCUSSION QUESTIONS

Read the following paragraph; then answer the questions that follow.

> Carla, a 13-year-old seventh grader, is repeatedly truant from school. When asked what she does when she does not attend school, Carla replies that she has a tough time getting out of bed in the morning. She figures that since she will be late for her first class and will get a tardy slip, she may as well just blow off the entire school day. Her teachers and counselors have tried to talk to her about this and maintain that it is in fact better to be late for the first hour than to miss the whole day. Her homeroom teacher has even tried to help Carla by calling her in the morning to get her out of bed. Carla answers the phone, says "Thanks for calling," replies that she will get up, and then goes back to sleep. Punishing Carla with detention and failing grades has not been effective in helping her to change her behavior.

1. What do you suppose is the main behavior problem demonstrated by Carla? Which category of behavior problem does this behavior fall under?
2. If you were to conduct a functional assessment of Carla's behavior, what might the hypothesis statement look like?
3. Develop a list of possible interventions that you would predict to be effective in helping Carla to develop replacement behaviors for her truant behavior.

## REFERENCES

Abrams, B. J., & Segal, A. (1998). How to prevent aggressive behavior. *Teaching Exceptional Children, 30,* 10–15.

American Psychiatric Association (1994). *Diagnostic and statistical manual of mental disorders* (4th ed.). Washington, DC: Author.

Bandura, A. (1973). *Aggression: A social learning analysis,* Upper Saddle River, NJ: Prentice Hall.

Baumeister, A. A. (1978). Origins and control of stereotyped movements. In C. E. Meyers (Ed.), *Quality of life in severely and profoundly mentally retarded people* (pp. 353–384). Washington, DC: American Association on Mental Deficiency.

Bellfiore, P. J., & Dattilio, F. M. (1990). The behavior of self-injury: A brief review and analysis. *Behavioral Disorders, 16*(1), 23–31.

Berkman, K. A., & Meyer, L. H. (1988). Alternative strategies and multiple outcomes in the remediation of severe self-injury: Going all out nonaversively. *Journal of the Association of Severely Handicapped, 13*(2), 76–86.

Blechman, E. A. (1985). *Solving child behavior problems at home and at school.* Champaign, IL: Research Press.

Bornas, X., Servera, M., & Llabres, J. (1997). Preventing impulsivity in the classroom: How computers can help teachers. *Computers in the Schools, 13,* 27–40.

Brown, R. T., & Wynne, M. E. (1984). An analysis of attentional components in hyperactive and normal boys. *Journal of Learning Disabilities, 17*(3), 162–167.

Bussing, R., Zima, B., & Belin, T. (1998). Children who qualify for LD and SED programs: Do they differ in level of ADHD symptoms and comorbid psychiatric conditions? *Behavioral Disorders, 23,* 85–97.

Campbell, S. B., & Werry, J. S. (1986). Attention deficit disorder (hyperactivity). In H. C. Quay & J.S. Werry (Eds.), *Psychopathological disorders of childhood* (3rd ed., pp. 111–155). New York: John Wiley & Sons.

Carmanico, S. J., Erickson, M. T., Singh, N. N., Best, A. M., Sood, A. A., & Oswald, D. P. (1998). Diagnostic subgroups of depression in adolescents with emotional and behavioral disorders. *Journal of Emotional and Behavioral Disorders, 6,* 222–232.

Center, D. B. (1990). Social maladjustment: An interpretation. *Behavioral Disorders, 15*(3), 141–148.

Clarizio, H. F., & Payette, K. (1990). A survey of school psychologists' perspectives and practices with childhood depression. *Psychology in the Schools, 27,* 57–63.

Costenbader, V., & Markson, S. (1998). School suspension: A study with secondary school students. *Journal of School Psychology, 36,* 59–82.

Crnic, K. A., & Reid, M. (1989). Mental retardation. In E. J. Mash & R. A. Barkley (Eds.), *Treatment of childhood disorders* (pp. 247–285). New York: Guilford Press.

Cummins, H. J. (1999, January 2). War games: Are video games no different than military training simulations? Are we teaching our children to kill? *Minneapolis Star Tribune.*

Daniels, V. I. (1998). How to manage disruptive behavior in inclusive classrooms. *Teaching Exceptional Children, 30,* 26–31.

David, O. J., & Wintrob, H. L. (1989). Communication disturbances and hyperactive/conduct disordered behavior. *Psychiatry, 52,* 379–392.

Davis, R. W., & Hajicek, J. O. (1985). Effects of self-instructional training and strategy training on a mathematics task with severely behaviorally disordered students. *Behavioral Disorders, 10,* 275–282.

Day, H. M., Horner, R. H., & O'Neill, R. E. (1994). Multiple functions of problem behaviors: Assessment and intervention. *Journal of Applied Behavior Analysis, 27,* 279–289.

Demchak, M. A., & Halle, J. W. (1985). Motivational assessment: A potential means of enhancing treatment success of self-injurious individuals. *Education and Training of the Mentally Retarded, 20*(1), 25–38.

Dubow, E. F., Huesmann, R., & Eron, L. D. (1987). Mitigating aggression and promoting prosocial behavior in aggressive elementary schoolboys. *Behavioral Research Therapy, 25*(6), 527–531.

Dubuque, S. E. (1998). Fighting childhood depression. *The Education Digest, 63,* 65–69.

DuPaul, G. J., & Eckert, T. L. (1997). The effects of school-based interventions for attention deficit hyperactivity disorder: A meta-analysis. *The School Psychology Review, 26,* 5–27.

DuPaul, G. J., Stoner, G., Tilly, W. D., III, & Putnam, D., Jr., (1991). Interventions for attention problems. In G. Stoner, M. R. Shinn, & H. M. Walker (Eds.), *Interventions for achievement and behavior problems* (pp. 665–713). Silver Spring, MD: National Association of School Psychologists.

Durand, V. M., & Carr, E. G. (1985). Self-injurious behavior: Motivating conditions and guidelines for treatment. *School Psychology Review, 14*(2), 171–176.

Edwards, V. N. (1991). Changes in routine can ease bedtime tantrums. *Growing Child Research Review, 9*(1), 5.

Etscheidt, S. (1991). Reducing aggressive behavior and improving self-control: A cognitive-behavioral training program for behaviorally disordered adolescents. *Behavioral Disorders, 16*(2), 107–115.

Favell, J. E., McGimsey, J. F., & Schell, R. M. (1982). Treatment of self-injury by providing alternate sensory activities. *Analysis and Intervention in Developmental Disabilities, 2,* 83–104.

Finkelhor, D. (1995). The victimization of children: A developmental perspective. *American Journal of Orthopsychiatry, 65,* 177–193.

Forness, S. (1998, October). *ADHD: Special education implications and interdisciplinary treatment.* Presented at the 1998 Minnesota Council for Children with Behavioral Disorders/Minnesota Educators of Children with Emotional Disorders Annual Conference, University of St. Thomas, St.Paul, MN.

Francois, R., Harlacher, G., & Smith, B. (1999). *Improving student behavior in the classroom by using assertive discipline strategies.* Masters Action Research Report, St. Xavier University, Chicago, IL. (ED431550)

Fremont, T., Tedesco, J. F., & Trusty, N. (1988). Understanding conduct problems. *Behavior in Our Schools, 2*(2), 17–19.

Friedrich-Cofer, L., & Huston, A. C. (1986). Television violence and aggression: The debate continues. *Psychological Bulletin, 100*(3), 364–371.

Garrity, C., Jens, K., Porter, W., Sager, N., & Short-Camili, C. (1994–1996). *Bully proofing your school: A comprehensive approach for elementary schools.* Longmont, CO: Sopris West.

Gaynor, J. (1990). Attention deficit hyperactivity disorder may be etched in sand. *Beyond Behavior, 2*(1), 17–18.

Gordon, M. (1991). *ADHD/Hyperactivity: A consumer's guide for parents and teachers.* DeWitt, NY: GSI Publications.

Hallahan, D. P., Kauffman, J. J., & Lloyd, J. W. (1985). *Introduction to learning disabilities* (2nd ed.). Upper Saddle River, NJ: Prentice Hall.

Harden, G. D. (1997). Is it going to be boring? *Principal, 76,* 43–44.

Hennggeler, S. W., Schoenwald, S. K., Borduin, C. M., Rowland, M. D., & Cunningham, P. B. (1998). *Multisystemic treatment of antisocial behavior in children and adolescents.* New York: The Guilford Press.

Hoff, K. E., & DuPaul, G. J. (1998). Reducing disruptive behavior in general education classrooms: The use of self-management strategies. *The School Psychology Review, 27,* 290–303.

Holden, G. W., & West, M. J. (1989). Proximate regulation by mothers: A demonstration of how differing styles affect young children's behavior. *Child Development, 60,* 64–69.

Hollinger, J. D. (1987). Social skills for behaviorally disordered children as preparation for mainstreaming: Theory, practice and new directions. *Remedial and Special Education, 8,* 17–27.

Horner, R. D. (1980). The effects of an environment enrichment program on the behavior of institutionalized profoundly retarded children. *Journal of Applied Behavior Analysis, 13,* 473–491.

Hughes, J. N. (1996). Television violence: Implications for violence prevention. *The School Psychology Review, 25,* 134–151.

Hunt, R. D. (1993). Neurobiological patterns of aggression. *Journal of Emotional and Behavioral Problems, 27,* 14–19.

Hyman, I. A., & Perone, D. C. (1998). The other side of school violence: Educator policies and practices that may contribute to student misbehavior. *Journal of School Psychology, 36,* 7–27,

Iwata, B. A., Dorsey, M. F., Slifer, K. J., Bauman, K. E., & Richman, G. S. (1982). Toward a functional analysis of self-injury. *Analysis and Intervention in Developmental Disabilities, 2,* 3–20.

Iwata, B. A., Vollmer, T. R., & Zarcone, J. H. (1990). The experimental (functional) analysis of behavior disorders: Methodology, applications, and limitations. In A. C. Repp & N. N. Singh (Eds.), *Perspectives on the use of nonaversive and aversive interventions for persons with developmental disabilities* (pp. 301–330). Sycamore, IL: Sycamore.

Johnson, S., Agelson, L., Macierz, T., Minnick, M., & Merrell, T. (1995, March/April). *Leadership training institute: Interventions for youth with emotional/behavioral disorders who engage in violent and aggressive behavior.* University of St. Thomas, St. Paul, MN.

Katsiyannis, A., & Maag, J. W. (1998). Disciplining students with disabilities: Issues and considerations for implementing IDEA. *Behavioral Disorders, 23,* 276–289.

Kauffman, J. M. (1985). *Characteristics of children's behavior disorders* (3rd ed.). Upper Saddle River, NJ: Merrill/Prentice Hall.

Kauffman, J. M. (1989). *Characteristics of children's behavior disorders* (4th ed.). Upper Saddle River, NJ: Merrill/Prentice Hall.

Kauffman, J. M. (1997). *Characteristics of emotional and behavioral disorders of children and youth* (6th ed.). Upper Saddle River, NJ: Merrill/Prentice Hall.

Kazdin, A. E. (1989). Childhood depression. In E. J. Mash & R. A. Barkley (Eds.), *Treatment of childhood disorders* (pp. 135–166). New York: The Guilford Press.

Kazdin, A. E. (1990). Childhood depression. *Journal of Child Psychology & Psychiatry, 31,* 121–160.

Kerr, M. M., & Nelson, C. M. (1989). *Strategies for managing behavior problems in the classroom.* Upper Saddle River, NJ: Merrill/Prentice Hall.

Kerr, M. M., & Nelson, C. M. (1998). *Strategies for managing behavior problems in the classroom.* Upper Saddle River, NJ: Merrill/Prentice Hall.

Kohn, A. (1989, November). Suffer the restless children. *The Atlantic Monthly,* 90–97.

Kounin, J. (1970). *Discipline and group management in classrooms.* New York: Holt, Rinehart, & Winston.

Kuczynski, L., Kochanska, G., Radke-Yarrow, M., & Girnius-Brown, O. (1987). A developmental interpretation of young children's noncompliance. *Developmental Psychology, 23*(6), 779–806.

Lancelotta, G. X., & Vaughn, S. (1989). Relation between types of aggression and sociometric status: Peer and teacher perceptions. *Journal of Educational Psychology, 81*(1), 86–90.

Landy, S., & Peters, R. D. (1992). Toward an understanding of a developmental paradigm for aggressive conduct problems during the preschool years. In R. D. Peters, R. J. McMahon, & V. L. Quinsey (Eds.), *Aggression and violence throughout the life span* (pp. 1–30). Newbury Park, CA: Sage Publications.

LaVigna, G. W., & Willis, T. J. (1991, February). *Nonaversive behavior modification.* Workshop presented by the Institute for Applied Behavior Analysis, Minneapolis, MN.

Lewis, M. H., Baumeister, A. A., & Mailman, R. B. (1987). A neurobiological alternative to the perceptual reinforcement hypothesis of stereotyped behavior: A commentary on self-stimulatory behavior and perceptual reinforcement. *Journal of Applied Behavior Analysis, 20,* 253–258.

Lloyd, J. W., Bateman, D. F., Landrum, T. J., & Hallahan, D. P. (1989). Self-recording of attention versus productivity. *Journal of Applied Behavior Analysis, 22,* 315–323.

Long, N. J., & Brendtro, L. K. (1993). Encountering rage. *Journal of Emotional and Behavioral Problems, 2,* 3.

Lovaas, I., Newsom, C., & Hickman, C. (1987). Self-stimulatory behavior and perceptual reinforcement. *Journal of Applied Behavior Analysis, 20,* 45–68.

Maag, J.W. (1996). *Parenting without punishment: Making problem behavior work for you.* Philadelphia: The Charles Press.

Maag, J.W. (1997). Managing resistance: Looking beyond the child and into the mirror. In P. Zionts (Ed.), *Inclusion strategies for students with learning and behavior problems, perspectives, experiences, and best practices.* Austin, TX: Pro-Ed.

Maag, J. W. (1998). *When existence is painful: A contextually-based approach to treating depression.* Presented at the 1998 Minnesota Council for Children with Behavioral Disorders/Minnesota Educators of Children with Emotional Disorders Annual Conference, University of St. Thomas, St.Paul, MN.

Maag, J. W., & Forness, S. R. (1991). Depression in children and adolescents: Identification, assessment, and treatment. *Focus on Exceptional Children, 24*(1), 1–20.

Maag, J. W., & Reid, R. (1994). Attention-Deficit Hyperactivity Disorder: A functional approach to assessment and treatment. *Behavioral Disorders, 20,* 5–23.

Malone, B. G., Bonitz, D. A., & Rickett, M. (1998). Teacher perceptions of disruptive behavior: Maintaining instructional focus. *Educational Horizons, 76,* 189–194.

Mash, E. J., & Barkley, R. A. (1998). *Treatment of childhood disorders* (2nd ed.). New York: The Guildford Press.

Mathes, M. Y., & Bender, W. N. (1997). The effects of self-monitoring on children with attention-deficit hyperactivity disorder who are receiving pharmacological interventions. *Remedial and Special Education, 18,* 121–128.

McConnell, S. R., & Odom, S. L. (1986). Sociometrics: Peer-referenced measures and the assessment of social competence. In P. S. Strain, M. J. Guralnick, & H. M. Walker (Eds.), *Children's social behavior: Development, assessment, and modification* (pp. 215–284). Orlando, FL: Academic Press.

McGee, R., Williams, S., & Silva, P. A. (1985). Factor structure and correlates of ratings of inattention, hyperactivity, and antisocial behavior in a large sample of 9-year-old children for the general population. *Journal of Consulting and Clinical Psychology, 53*(4), 480–490.

McGinnis, E., & Goldstein, A. (1984). *Skillstreaming the elementary school child.* Champaign, IL: Research Press.

McGinnis, E., & Goldstein, A. (1997). *Skillstreaming the elementary school child* (Rev. ed.). Champaign, IL: Research Press.

McMahon, C. (1989). *An evaluation of the multiple effects of a social skills intervention: An interactionist perspective.* Unpublished doctoral dissertation, University of Iowa, Iowa City.

McMahon, C. M., Wacker, D. P., Sasso, G. M., & Melloy, K. J. (1994). Evaluation of the multiple effects of a social skill intervention. *Behavioral Disorders, 20,* 35–50.

McMahon, R. J., & Wells, K. C. (1989). Conduct disorders. In E. J. Mash & R. A. Barkley (Eds.), *Treatment of childhood disorders* (pp. 73–132). New York: Guilford Press.

Meadows, N. B., Melloy, K. J., & Yell, M. L. (1996). Behavior management as a curriculum for students with emotional and behavioral disorders. *Preventing School Failure, 40,* 124–129.

Melloy, K. J. (1990). *Attitudes and behavior of non-disabled elementary-aged children toward their peers with disabilities in integrated settings: An examination of the effects of treatment on quality of attitude, social status and critical social skills.* Unpublished doctoral dissertation, University of Iowa, Iowa City.

Melloy, K. J., Davis, C. A., Wehby, J. H., Murry, F. R., & Lieber, J. (1998). Developing social competence in children and youth with challenging behaviors. L. M. Bullock & R. A. Gable (Eds.), *The second CCBD mini-library series: Successful interventions for the 21st century.* Reston, VA: The Council for Children with Behavioral Disorders.

Miller, D. (1994). Suicidal behavior of adolescents with behavior disorders and their peers without disabilities. *Behavioral Disorders, 20,* 61–68.

Neel, R. S., Jenkins, Z. N., & Meadows, N. (1990). Social problem-solving behaviors and aggression in young children: A descriptive observational study. *Behavioral Disorders, 16*(1), 39–51.

Nelson, J. R., Martella, R., & Galand, B. (1998). The effects of teaching school expectations and establishing a consistent consequence on formal office disciplinary actions. *Journal of Emotional and Behavioral Disorders, 6,* 153–161.

Northup, J., Wacker, D. P., Berg, W. K., Kelly, L., Sasso, G. M., & DeRaad, A. (1994). The treatment of severe behavior problems in school settings using a technical assistance model. *Journal of Applied Behavior Analysis, 27,* 33–47.

Olson, S. L., Bates, J. E., & Bayles, K. (1990). Early antecedents of childhood impulsivity: The role of parent-child interaction, cognitive competence, and temperament. *Journal of Abnormal Child Psychology, 18*(3), 317–334.

Ostrander, R., Weinfurt, K. P., & Nay, W. R. (1998). The role of age, family support, and negative cognitions in the prediction of depressive symptoms. *The School Psychology Review, 27,* 121–137.

Paniagua, F. A., Morrison, P. B., & Black, S. A. (1990). Management of a hyperactive-conduct disordered child through correspondence training: A preliminary study. *Journal of Behavior Therapy and Experimental Psychiatry, 21*(1), 63–68.

Patterson, G. R. (1992). Developmental changes in antisocial behavior. In R. D. Peters, R. J. McMahon, & V. L. Quinsey (Eds.), *Aggression and violence throughout the life span* (pp. 52–82). Newbury Park, CA: Sage.

Patterson, G. R., DeBaryshe, B. D., & Ramsey, E. (1989). A developmental perspective on antisocial behavior. *American Psychologist, 44,* 329–335.

Pfiffner, L. J., & O'Leary, S. G. (1987). The efficacy of all-positive management as a function of the prior use of negative consequences. *Journal of Applied Behavior Analysis, 20,* 265–271.

Puura, K., Almqvist, F., & Tamminen, T. (1998). Children with symptoms of depression—what do adults see? *The Journal of Child Psychology and Psychiatry and Allied Disciplines, 39,* 577–585.

Quay, H. C. (1986). Conduct disorders. In H. C. Quay & J. S. Werry (Eds.), *Psychopathological disorders of childhood* (3rd ed., pp. 35–72). New York: John Wiley & Sons.

Repp, A. C., & Singh, N. N. (1990). *Perspectives on the use of nonaversive and aversive interventions for persons with developmental disabilities.* Sycamore, IL: Sycamore.

Reynolds, W. M. (1991). Psychological interventions for depression in children and adolescents. In G. Stoner, M. R. Shinn, & H. M. Walker (Eds.), *Interventions for achievement and behavior problems* (pp. 649–683). Silver Spring, MD: National Association of School Psychologists.

Rhode, G., Morgan, D. P., & Young, K. R. (1983). Generalization and maintenance of treatment gains of behaviorally handicapped students from resource rooms to regular classrooms using self-evaluation procedures. *Journal of Applied Behavior Analysis, 16,* 171–188.

Rocissano, L., Slade, A., & Lynch, V. (1987). Dyadic synchrony and toddler compliance. *Developmental Psychology, 23*(5), 698–704.

Rudo, Z. H., Powell, D. S., & Dunlap, G. (1998). The effects of violence in the home on children's emotional, behavioral, and social functioning: A review of the literature. *Journal of Emotional and Behavioral Disorders, 6,* 94–113.

Ruff, H. A., & Lawson, K. R. (1990). Development of sustained, focused attention in young children during free play. *Developmental Psychology, 26*(1), 85–93.

Ruff, H. A., Lawson, K. R., Parrinello, R., & Weissberg, R. (1990). Long term stability of individual differences in sustained attention in the early years. *Child Development, 61,* 60–75.

Ruth, W. J. (1996). Goal setting and behavior contracting for students with emotional and behavioral difficulties: Analysis of daily, weekly, and total goal attainment. *Psychology in the Schools, 33,* 153–158.

Sasso, G. M., Melloy, K. J., & Kavale, K. A. (1990). Generalization, maintenance, and behavioral covariation associated with social skills training through structured learning. *Behavioral Disorders, 16*(1), 9–22.

Sasso, G. M., Peck, J., & Garrison-Harrell, L. (1998). Social interaction setting events: Experimental analysis of contextual variables. *Behavioral Disorders, 24,* 34–43.

Sasso, G. M., & Reimers, T. M. (1988). Assessing the functional properties of behavior: Implications and applications for the classroom. *Focus on Autistic Behavior, 3,* 1–15.

Schaub, J. M. (1990, March). *ADHD: Practical intervention strategies for the classroom.* Presentation to the East Metro Special Education Cooperative, Edina, MN.

Schmid, R. (1988). Three steps to self-discipline. *Teaching Exceptional Children, 30,* 36–39.

Shafrir, U., & Pascual-Leone, J. (1990). Postfailure reflectivity/impulsivity and spontaneous attention to errors. *Journal of Educational Psychology, 82*(2), 378–387.

Shapiro, E. S., DuPaul, G. J., & Bradley-Klug, K. L. (1998). Self-management as a strategy to improve the classroom behavior of adolescents with ADHD. *Journal of Learning Disabilities, 31*(6), 545–556.

Skiba, R. J., Peterson, R. L., & Williams, I. (1997). Office referrals and suspension: Disciplinary intervention in middle schools. *Education and Treatment of Children, 20,* 295–315.

Smith, L. K., & Fowler, S. A. (1984). Positive peer pressure: The effects of peer monitoring on children's disruptive behavior. *Journal of Applied Behavior Analysis, 17,* 213–227.

Smith Myles, B., & Simpson, R. L. (1994). Prevention and management considerations for aggressive and violent children and youth. *Education and Treatment of Children, 17,* 370–384.

Smith Myles, B., & Simpson, R. L. (1998). Aggression and violence by school-age children and youth: Understanding the aggression cycle and prevention/intervention strategies. *Intervention in School and Clinic, 33,* 259–264.

Stage, S. A. (1997). A preliminary investigation of the relationship between in-school suspension and the disruptive classroom behavior of students with behavioral disorders. *Behavioral Disorders, 23,* 57–76.

Steinberg, J. (1999, January 3). The coming crime wave is washed up. *The New York Times.*

Strain, P. S., Guralnick, M. J., & Walker, H. M. (1986). *Children's social behavior: Development, assessment and modification.* New York: Academic Press.

Vitiello, B., Stoff, D., Atkins, M., & Mahoney, A. (1990). Soft neurological signs and impulsivity in children. *Developmental and Behavioral Pediatrics, 11*(3), 112–115.

Wacker, D., Steege, M., Northup, J., Reimers, T., Berg, W., & Sasso, G. (1990). Use of functional analysis and acceptability measures to assess and treat severe behavior problems: An outpatient clinic model. In A. C. Repp & N. N. Singh (Eds.), *Perspectives on the use of nonaversive and aversive interventions for persons with developmental disabilities* (pp. 349–359). Sycamore, IL: Sycamore.

Wahler, R. G., & Dumas, J. E. (1986). A chip off the old block: Some interpersonal characteristics of coercive children across generations. In P. S. Strain, M. J. Guralnick, & H. M. Walker (Eds.), *Children's social behavior: Development, assessment, and modification* (pp. 49–91). Orlando, FL: Academic Press.

Walker, H. M., Colvin, G., & Ramsey, E. (1995). *Antisocial behavior in school: Strategies and best practices.* Pacific Grove, CA: Brooks/Cole.

Weinberg, L. A., & Weinberg, C. (1990). Seriously emotionally disturbed or socially maladjusted? A critique of interpretations. *Behavioral Disorders, 15*(3), 149–158.

White, A. G., & Bailey, J. S. (1990). Reducing disruptive behaviors of elementary physical education students with sit and watch. *Journal of Applied Behavior Analysis, 23,* 353–359.

Wicks-Nelson, R., & Israel, A. C. (1991). *Behavior disorders of childhood* (2nd ed.). Upper Saddle River, NJ: Merrill/Prentice Hall.

Widom, C. S. (1989). Does violence beget violence? A critical examination of the literature. *Psychological Bulletin, 106*(1), 3–28.

Yell, M. (1998). *The law and special education.* Upper Saddle River, NJ: Merrill/Prentice Hall.

Zarcone, J. R., Iwata, B. A., Smith, R. G., Mazaleski, J. L., & Lerman, D. C. (1994). Reemergence and extinction of self-injurious escape behavior during stimulus fading. *Journal of Applied Behavior Analysis, 27,* 307–316.

Zionts, P. (1996). *Teaching disturbed and disturbing students* (2nd ed). Austin, TX: Pro-Ed.

# DISCIPLINING STUDENTS

## Legal Issues
## for Schools

### Mitchell L. Yell
**University of South Carolina**

*Discipline and order is essential (in our schools) if the educational function is to be performed.*

JUSTICE BYRON R. WHITE, *GOSS V. LOPEZ* (1975, p. 584)

Administrators and teachers have been challenged by student discipline problems since the beginning of public education in the United States. In fact, one of the earliest education textbooks published was on classroom management (Bagley, 1907). Recently, efforts to address the problem of student discipline in schools have taken on a greater sense of urgency because of the increases in aggressive and violent behavior.

Moreover, opinion polls of the general public and polls of professional educators indicate that both believe that student behavior problems are the major issue facing our schools (Harris, 1996; Rose & Gallup, 1998). These polls indicate that the public and teachers believe that schools are no longer able to effectively discipline students, and that we are losing control of our schools. Clearly, to maintain discipline, and to operate efficiently and effectively, schools must have rules that regulate student conduct. This means that students should clearly know which behaviors are acceptable and which are prohibited. If students violate reasonable school rules, by behaving in ways that are prohibited, they should be held accountable. Student accountability to rules usually implies that violators will be subject to disciplinary sanctions or consequences.

Courts have recognized the crucial importance of schools maintaining a safe and orderly educational environment and have granted great latitude to teachers to exercise this control through the use of discipline. Courts, however, have also recognized that students, while at school, have rights that must be respected. Such rights include the right to (a) reasonable expectations of privacy, (b) due process procedures, and (c) free expression. School officials and teachers, therefore, must balance these students' rights with the need to maintain safety and order in the school environment.

The purpose of this chapter is to examine teachers' rights and responsibilities with respect to disciplining students in public schools. First is an examination of the basis of a teacher's authority over student behavior. Next is provided a brief overview of students' rights in public schools with respect to disciplinary issues. Addressed separately is disciplining students with disabilities and those without disabilities. This is because there is very little federal law regarding disciplining nondisabled students, whereas federal law specifically addresses the discipline of students with disabilities in the Individuals with Disabilities Education Act of 1997 (hereafter IDEA '97). In fact, students with disabilities must have proactive behavior programming included in their individualized education programs (IEPs). There is a brief discussion of schoolwide discipline. The chapter ends with recommendations for teachers and school officials to follow when disciplining students.

## TEACHERS' DUTY TO ENFORCE DISCIPLINE

The courts recognize the importance of giving teachers and school administrators authority over student behavior. This authority originates from the English common law concept of *in loco parentis* (i.e., in place of the parent). According to this concept, parents grant a measure of control over their children to teachers and school personnel when they place their children in school (Yell, 1998). The principal and the teacher have the authority not only to teach, but also to guide, correct, and discipline the child. Clearly, such control is necessary to accomplish the mission of schools. *In loco parentis* does not mean, however, that the teacher has the same control over a child when at school as a parent would when the child was at home. It does mean that school officials and teachers, acting with knowledge of appropriate laws and regulations, have a duty to maintain an orderly and effective learning environment through reasonable and prudent control of students. Although the concept does not have the importance it once did, it is, nonetheless, an active legal concept that helps to define the school-student relationship. In relation to the use of disciplinary procedures, *in loco parentis* implies that the teacher has the duty to see that school order is maintained by requiring students to obey reasonable rules and commands, respect the rights of others, and behave in an orderly and safe manner when at school.

All students, disabled and nondisabled, have rights in disciplinary matters based on the Due Process Clause of the Fifth and Fourteenth Amendments to the U.S. Constitution. Both the Fifth and Fourteenth Amendments prohibit states from depriving any person of life, liberty, or property without due process of law. This means that prior to taking an action that may lead to such a deprivation, individuals have the right to, at a minimum, be notified of the charges against them and be able to attend a hearing in which they can tell their version of the facts. The next section addresses the rights of students in situations involving disciplinary actions by school officials.

## STUDENTS' DUE PROCESS PROTECTIONS

The Supreme Court in *Goss v. Lopez* (1975; hereafter *Goss*) held that students have the constitutional protection in the form of due process rights when school officials use disciplinary procedures such as suspension. The due process protections afforded students, however, are limited by the state's interest in maintaining order and discipline in the schools. The courts, therefore, have had to strike a balance between student rights and the legitimate needs and interests of the schools.

The two general areas of due process rights afforded students are procedural and substantive. In terms of discipline, *procedural due process* involves the fairness of methods and procedures used by the schools; *substantive due process* refers to the protection of student rights from violation by school officials and involves the reasonableness of the disciplinary processes (Valente & Valente, 2001). School authorities, however, are vested with broad authority for establishing rules and procedures to maintain order and discipline. Unless students can show that they are deprived of a liberty or property interest, there is no student right to due process. According to a federal district court in Tennessee, "teachers should be free to impose minor forms of classroom discipline, such as admonishing students, requiring special assignments, restricting activities, and denying certain privileges, without being subjected to strictures of due process" (*Dickens v. Johnson Board of Education*, 1987, p. 157).

## Procedural Due Process: The Right to Fair Procedures

In 1954 the Supreme Court stated that

> it is doubtful that any child may reasonably be expected to succeed in life if he is denied the opportunity of an education. Such an opportunity, where a state has undertaken to provide it, is a right that must be made available to all on equal terms. (Brown v. Board of Education, *1954, p. 493)*

The importance of education to a student's future certainly requires that disciplinary actions that result in the student being deprived of an education (e.g., suspension, expulsion) be subjected to the standards of due process. The purpose of due process procedures is to ensure that official decisions are made in a fair manner. Due process procedures in school settings do not require the full range of protections that a person would get in a formal court trial (e.g., representation by counsel, cross-examination of witnesses). Due process procedures in school settings do, however, include the basic protections such as notice and hearing.

The U.S. Supreme Court in *Goss* outlined the due process protections, which must be extended to all students. This case involved nine high school students who had been suspended from school without a hearing. The students filed a lawsuit claiming that they had been denied due process of law under the Fourteenth Amendment. The Supreme Court agreed, ruling that the students had the right to at least minimal due process protections in cases of suspension. The high court stated: "Having chosen to extend the right to an education . . . [the state] may not withdraw the right on grounds of misconduct absent fundamentally fair procedures to determine whether the misconduct had occurred (p. 574).

The Court noted that schools have broad authority to prescribe and enforce standards of behavior. However, in their decision, the Supreme Court held that students are entitled to public education as a property interest, which is protected by the Fourteenth Amendment. Because education is protected, it may not be taken away without adhering to the due process procedures required by the Constitution. The school's lawyers had argued that a 10-day suspension was only a minor and temporary interference with the student's education; the high court disagreed, stating that a 10-day suspension was a serious event in the life of the suspended child. When school officials impose 10-day suspensions, therefore, they must grant the suspended student the fundamental requisite of due process of law, the opportunity to be heard.

The opportunity to be heard, when applied to the school setting, involves the right to notice and hearing. The right to notice and hearing requires that students are presented with the charges against them and have an opportunity to state their case (Yudof, Kirp, & Levin, 1992). These protections will not shield students from properly imposed suspensions. The protections will, however, protect them from an unfair or mistaken suspension. The court in *Goss* recognized the necessity of order and discipline and the need for immediate and effective action, stating that suspension is a "necessary tool to maintain order [and] a valuable educational device" (p. 572). The prospect of imposing lengthy and cumbersome hearing requirements on every suspension case was a concern to the Court. However, the majority believed that school officials should not have the power to act unilaterally, free of notice and hearing requirements. The Court held that when students are suspended for a period of 10 days or less, therefore, the school must give them oral or written notice of the charges, an explanation of the reasons for the suspension, and an opportunity to present their side of the story.

The notice and hearing requirement does not mean that a formal notice to a student and a meeting must always precede suspension. It is permissible to a have reasonable delay between the time the notice is given and the student's hearing. For example, if the behavior poses a threat to other students or the academic process, a student can be immediately removed from school. The notice and hearing should then follow within 24 to 72 hours. A teacher or an administrator who is disciplining the student could also informally discuss the misconduct with the student immediately after the behavior occurred. This would give the student notice and an opportunity to explain his or her version of the facts before the teacher or administrator carried out the disciplinary sanction. In this case, the notice and hearing would precede the discipline.

It is important to remember that the basic due process protections outlined by the Supreme Court in *Goss* only apply to short suspensions of under 10 school days. According to the Court, longer suspensions, or expulsions, require more extensive and formal notices and hearings. Disciplinary procedures such as time-out, deten-

Legal considerations provide for the education of all students.

**TABLE 11.1 • Students' Due Process Protections**

*Short-Term Suspension (may be a formal or informal meeting)*

❑ Written or oral notice of charges
❑ Opportunity to respond to charges

*Long-Term Suspension and Expulsion (must be a formal meeting)*

❑ Written notice specifying charges
❑ Notice of evidence, witnesses, and substance of testimony
❑ Hearing (advance notice of time, place, and procedures)
❑ Right to confront witnesses and present their own witnesses
❑ Right to a written or taped record of the proceedings
❑ Right of appeal
  • Brief in-school sanctions do not require a due process hearing
  • Dangerous students may be immediately removed

*Source: The Law and Special Education*, by M. L. Yell (Upper Saddle River, NJ: Merrill/Prentice Hall (1998). Adapted with permission.

tion, response cost, and overcorrection do not require that due process procedures be extended to students. It is a reasonable assumption that when using in-school suspension the notice and hearing procedures should be followed. Table 11.1 lists the due process protections that teachers and administrators must follow when using short-term suspensions and expulsions. These procedures apply to all students, disabled and nondisabled alike.

## Substantive Due Process: The Right to Reasonableness

The courts have tended to give great authority to teachers and school officials to write rules that govern student behavior in school. Additionally courts have granted school officials the authority to develop and impose consequences on students who break their rules. There is a limit to this power, however. These rules and consequences must not violate students' constitutional principles discussed earlier (e.g., privacy, due process, expression). Generally, rules and consequences will not violate students' constitutional rights when they are reasonable. Reasonable rules and consequences have a carefully considered rationale and a school-related purpose. Schools may not prohibit or punish behavior that has no adverse affect on the school environment. Furthermore, schools cannot use disciplinary penalties or restraints that are unnecessary or excessive to achieve safety and order in school. In other words, reasonable rules and consequences are rational and fair and they are not excessive for a school environment.

Rules must be sufficiently clear and specific to allow students to distinguish permissible from prohibited behavior. School rules that are too vague or general may result in the violation of students' rights because students will not have a clear understanding of them. Appropriate school rules are specific and definitive. They provide students with information regarding behavioral expectations.

A federal district court in Indiana addressed the issue of the reasonableness of a school's use of discipline in *Cole v. Greenfield-Central Community Schools* (1986). The plaintiff, Christopher Bruce Cole, was diagnosed as emotionally disturbed under Indiana state law. The student exhibited management and adjustment problems. The school had attempted, and documented, numerous positive behavioral procedures that they had used to improve Christopher's behavior. When these procedures failed, school officials decided to use behavior reduction strategies. The student's teacher began to use time-out, response cost, and corporal punishment. The plaintiff sued the school, contending that in using these procedures the school had violated his civil rights.

The court recognized that Christopher, although he had a disability covered by the IDEA, was not immune from the school's disciplinary procedures. The court held that the validity of the plaintiff's claim, therefore, rested on the "reasonableness" of the disciplinary procedures used by the school in attempting to manage Christopher's behavior. The court analyzed four elements to determine if the rules and consequences were reasonable. They were (a) Did the teacher have the authority under state and local laws to discipline the student? (b) Was the rule violated within the scope of the educational function? (c) Was the rule violator the one who was disciplined? and (d) Was the discipline in proportion to the gravity of the offense? Finding that all four elements of reasonableness were satisfied, the court held for the school district.

## Summary of Due Process Protections and Discipline

All students in public schools, disabled and nondisabled, have constitutional rights. However, students in public schools do not possess the same rights as people do in the community setting. This is because educators must maintain a safe and orderly environment. To maintain such an environment school officials and teachers need to impose rules of conduct on their students. Moreover, if students break these rules, teachers may impose consequences in the form of disciplinary sanctions on the students.

There are two fundamental prerequisites that teachers and school officials must adhere to in developing rules and imposing disciplinary procedures. First, the rules must be clear to all students and their parents. Furthermore, the rules must have a school-based rationale. Similarly, disciplinary procedures that will serve as consequences for rule violation must be clearly stated and understood by all students and their parents. Consequences must be applied on a fair and consistent basis. Furthermore, if the disciplinary sanctions involve suspension, students must be given notice of the offenses they committed and have an opportunity to tell their side of the story.

Many states have laws regarding disciplinary procedures that may be used with students. Teachers need to be aware of their state laws and regulations. There are very few federal laws affecting discipline of nondisabled students in public schools. This is not the case with students who are disabled, however. The next section is an examination of the federal law that addresses the discipline of students in special education. It is extremely important that teachers and school officials understand their rights and responsibilities in this area.

Also following are a discussion of the disciplinary requirements of IDEA '97, a brief review of the provisions of the federal law that directly address discipline, and recommendations for teachers and administrators to follow when disciplining students with disabilities.

## DISCIPLINING STUDENTS WITH DISABILITIES

Since the passage of the Education of All Handicapped Children Act in 1975, disciplining students with disabilities has been a very controversial and confusing issue. This law, renamed the Individuals with Disabilities Education Act (IDEA) in 1990, created a detailed set of rules and guidelines to ensure the appropriate education of students who were eligible for special education programs. However, the IDEA contained no specific federal requirements regarding discipline. Administrators and teachers, therefore, have had little guidance with respect to their rights and responsibilities when having to discipline students with disabilities. Because of this lack of federal guidance, the discipline of students with disabilities has been governed by the rulings in numerous court cases that examined this issue, including the U.S. Supreme Court. The rulings in these cases have resulted in the formation of a body of case law that has brought some clarity to this issue. Generally, this case law indicated that disciplinary actions against students with disabilities were subject to different rules and limitations than the same disciplinary procedures used with students who were not disabled (Katsiyannis & Maag, 1998; Yell, 1998). One area of difference was that the courts viewed suspensions and expulsions of students with disabilities as changes in placement, even in instances of dangerous behavior, if these suspensions exceeded 10 days. Because such procedures were changes in placement, they had to be conducted in accordance through the IEP procedures of the law (Mead, 1998). Courts also created a rule that became known as the manifestation determination. Prior to considering expulsion, a group of persons knowledgeable about the student and the student's disability had to determine whether the student's misbehavior was related to his or her disability. If no relationship was found, a student could be expelled. However, courts differed in their rulings regarding the provision of educational services following an expulsion. These rulings provide some guidance regarding discipline; however, many believed a federal standard was needed.

In hearings that preceded the reauthorization of the IDEA, Congress heard testimony regarding the difficulties educators faced when having to use disciplinary sanctions with students in special education. Seeking to strike a balance between educators' duty to maintain safe classrooms and schools and special education students' right to receive a free appropriate public education, Congress included provisions regarding discipline in the IDEA Amendments of 1997 (hereafter IDEA '97).

The disciplinary provisions clarified a number of the issues previously considered by the courts.

## Disciplinary Provisions of IDEA '97

Prior to discussing IDEA '97, it is important that we understand two major points regarding the discipline sections of the law. First, IDEA '97 emphasizes the use of positive behavior programming for students with disabilities to increase the likelihood of success in school and in postschool life. Congress was clearly concerned about preserving safety and order in the school environment, yet they also stressed including this proactive behavioral programming in students' IEPs. The purpose of proactive programming is to teach appropriate behaviors, rather than merely eliminate inappropriate behaviors. Second, school officials may discipline a student with disabilities in the same manner as they discipline students without disabilities, with a few notable exceptions. For example, procedures such as verbal reprimands, warnings, contingent observation, exclusionary time-out, response cost, detention, in-school suspension, or the temporary delay or withdrawal of goods, services, or activities (e.g., recess, lunch) are permitted as long as these procedures do not interfere significantly with the student's IEP goals and are not applied in a discriminatory manner (Yell, 1998). The disciplinary provisions of IDEA '97 only address suspensions and expulsions in excess of 10 school days. Figure 11.1 is a disciplinary flowchart that meets the requirements of IDEA '97. The remainder of this section addresses specific issues in more detail.

### Suspensions and Expulsions

*Short-term suspensions.*  IDEA '97 authorizes school officials to suspend students with disabilities to the extent that suspensions are used with students without disabilities. There is no specific amount of time that school officials must adhere to in suspending students with disabilities. However, when a student is suspended for more than 10 school days, educational services must be provided. A comment to the regulations further clarifies this issue (IDEA Regulations, 1997). The comment provides the example of a student with disabilities who is suspended for two 5-day suspensions in the fall term. If that student is then suspended for a third time in the spring term, educational services must be provided from the first day of the third suspension. Therefore, school officials may implement additional short-term suspensions for separate incidents of misconduct, as long as the school provides educational services. If a student is suspended for less than 10 school days, a school district is not required to continue educational services (OSEP Discipline Guidance, 1997).

Schools should use out-of-school suspensions judiciously. Martin (1999) contends that the frequency and amount of short-term removals, if they are excessive, may be indicative of a defective IEP. He argues that the greater the number of short-term disciplinary removals, the greater the likelihood that a hearing officer will find that the behavior portion of the IEP is inappropriate and a deprivation of the student's right to a free appropriate public education.

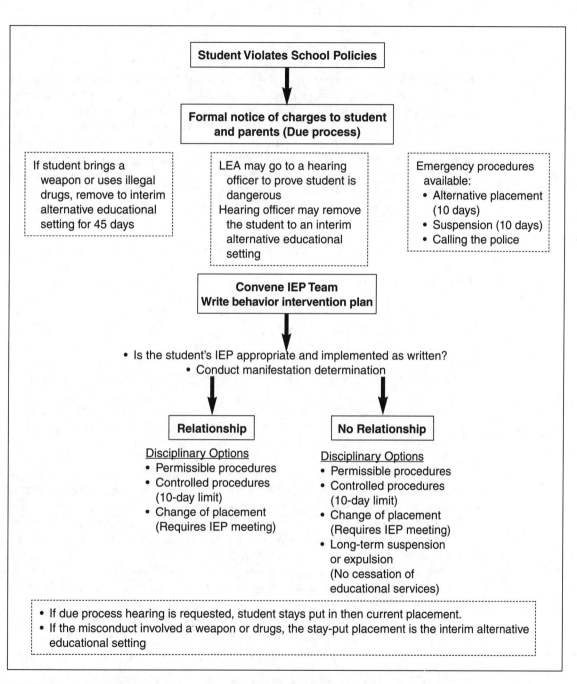

**FIGURE 11.1.** Discipline flowchart under the IDEA Amendments of 1997

*Source: The Law and Special Education,* by M.L. Yell (Upper Saddle River, NJ: Prentice Hall/Merrill (1998). Adapted with permission.

***Serial suspensions.***   When using suspension, school officials may not remove a student for a series of short-term suspensions if these suspensions constitute a pattern of exclusion. Such a pattern constitutes a unilateral change of placement and is illegal under IDEA '97. However, not all suspensions in excess of 10 days would constitute a change in placement. The law and regulations are not clear regarding when suspensions in excess of 10 days become a change in placement. To determine if a series of suspensions constitute such a change, school officials must determine the circumstances surrounding the suspension. In making this determination regarding suspensions, the team should consider factors such as length of each removal, the total amount of time that the student is removed, and the proximity of the removals to one another (IDEA Regulations, § 300.520, Note 1). Thus, determination of when a series of suspensions become a change in placement can only be decided on a case-by-case basis. The IEP team, therefore, is the most qualified team to conduct this inquiry.

***Long-term suspensions and expulsions.***   School officials may unilaterally place a student with disabilities in an appropriate interim alternative educational setting for up to 45 days if the student (a) brings, possesses, or acquires a weapon at school or a school function or (b) knowingly possesses, uses, or sells illegal drugs, or sells a controlled substance at school or a school function (IDEA, 20 USC § 1415(k)(1)). A weapon is defined as a "weapon, device, instrument, material, or substance . . . that is used for, or is readily capable of, causing death or serious bodily injury" (Federal Criminal Code, 20 U.S.C. § 615(k)(10)(D)). In this situation, a controlled substance refers to a legally prescribed medication (e.g., Ritalin) that is illegally sold by a student.

Until the passage of IDEA '97, school districts had to seek a temporary restraining order from a court to remove a student with disabilities who presented a danger to him- or herself or others. The IDEA now authorizes school officials to seek temporary removal of a dangerous student by requesting that a hearing officer order the student removed to an interim alternative educational setting for 45 days (IDEA 20 U.S.C. § 1415 (k)(2)). Therefore, if school officials believe that a student may present a danger to self or others and seek to have the student removed from school, they must convince a hearing officer that (a) should the student remain in the current placement, he or she is substantially likely to injure him or herself or others; (b) the school district has attempted to minimize the risk of harm; (c) the student's current IEP and placement were appropriate; and (d) the school's interim alternative educational setting is appropriate. The hearing officer may then change the student's placement to the interim alternative educational setting for up to 45 days. During this time period the IEP team should meet to determine what actions will be taken regarding the situation (e.g., change placement, rewrite the IEP, move to expel the student).

## The Manifestation Determination

IDEA '97 clarifies a procedure long required by the courts, referred to as the manifestation determination. A *manifestation determination* is a review of the relationship between a student's disability and misconduct. It must be conducted when

**TABLE 11.2 • The Manifestation Determination**

1. Were the IEP—including special education services, supplementary aids and services, and behavior intervention strategies—and placement appropriate?
2. Were the IEP, including all of the preceding components, and placement implemented as written?

   If the answer is "no" to either of the first two questions, the behavior is considered a manifestation of the disability, and the determination ends. If the answers to both of the first two questions are "yes," the team may answer the final two questions.
3. Did the student's disability impair the student's ability to understand the impact and consequences of his or her behavior? and
4. Did the student's disability impair the student's ability to control the behavior in question?

   If the answers to questions 1 and 2 are "yes" and the answers to questions 3 and 4 are "no" (i.e., the student's disability did not impair the student's ability to understand the consequences of the behavior or his or her ability to control the behavior), there is no manifestation between the disability and the misconduct, and the student may be disciplined in the same manner as would a child without disabilities.

school officials seek a change of placement, including suspension, or expulsion, in excess of 10 school days. In situations in which a student has been suspended in excess of the 10 days, the review should take place no later than 10 days following the disciplinary action.

The manifestation determination must be conducted by a student's IEP team and other qualified personnel. When conducting the review, the IEP team must consider all relevant information regarding the misbehavior including evaluation and diagnostic results, observations, and the student's IEP and placement. The team's task is to then determine if the student understood the consequences of his or her behavior and was capable of controlling it. The specific questions the team must answer are depicted in Table 11.2.

If the team determines there is no relationship between the misconduct and disability, the same disciplinary procedures as would be used with students who are not disabled may be imposed on a student with disabilities, including long-term suspension and expulsion. Educational services, however, must be continued. The parents of the student may request an expedited due process hearing if they disagree with the results of the manifestation determination. The student's placement during the hearing will be in the interim alternative educational setting. If, however, the team determines that a relationship did exist, the student may not be suspended or expelled. Change of placement procedures may still be initiated using the IEP process.

## The Interim Alternative Educational Setting

When a student is suspended in excess of 10 cumulative days in a school year or expelled, the school district must continue to provide a free appropriate public education. That is, educational services must continue in an interim alternative educational setting (IAES; IDEA, 20 U.S.C. § 1415(k)(3)). The IEP team determines the IAES. Although the IAES is usually not in the current educational setting, the student must be able to continue to participate in the general education curriculum and continue to receive the services and modifications listed in the IEP. In this placement students must continue to work toward the goals and objectives of the IEP, including goals that address the behavior problems that led to the placement.

Using homebound instruction or tutoring as an IAES is not specifically prohibited by the IDEA; nevertheless, homebound placements are problematic. School districts must continue to provide the special education and related services listed in a student's IEP while he or she is in the IAES. This would include access to all special education and related services as well as access to the general education curriculum. Clearly, providing these services in a homebound setting would be difficult. Furthermore, a comment in the proposed regulations suggests that a homebound placement will usually be appropriate for a limited number of students, such as those who are medically fragile and not able to participate in a school setting (IDEA Regulations § 300.551, Note 1). In answers to a series of questions regarding discipline, the Office of Special Education and Rehabilitative Services (OSERS) noted that in most circumstances homebound instruction is inappropriate as a disciplinary measure; however, appropriateness would have to be determined on a case-by-case basis ("Department of Education Answers Questions," 1997).

## Proactively Addressing Behavior Problems of Students with Disabilities

IDEA '97 requires that if a student with disabilities has behavior problems (regardless of the student's disability category) that impedes his or her learning or the learning of others, the team that writes the IEP shall consider strategies to address these problems (IDEA, 20 U.S.C. § 1414 (d)(3)(B)(i)). This includes (a) conducting an assessment of the problem behavior, (b) writing measurable annual goals and benchmarks or short-term objectives to address the problem behaviors, and (c) providing the appropriate special education and related services, including supplementary aids and services, that are required to allow the student to meet the goals and objectives. For such students, a proactive behavioral intervention plan (BIP) may be developed and included with the IEP. The purpose of the BIP is to address the behavior problems through the consideration of strategies, including positive behavioral interventions, strategies, and supports to ameliorate the problems. This plan is clearly more than a management plan delineating disciplinary procedures to be used with a student. The BIP should be based on a functional behavioral assessment and developed with the intent of positively intervening to ameliorate the problem behavior and teaching appropriate behavior ("Senate Report," 1997). When a student is suspended for more than 10 school days, or a manifestation determination is conducted, a functional assessment of behavior must be conducted and the BIP must be revised or developed if it does not exist.

IDEA '97 does not detail the components of a functional behavioral assessment (FBA) beyond stating that when conducting an FBA following a 10-day suspension or 45-day removal, the assessment must address the behavior that led to the removal. Failure to comply with the FBA requirement has led to hearing officers overturning school districts' disciplinary actions because they violated IDEA '97 (*Board of Education of the Akron Central School District,* 1998).

## Summary of Disciplining Students with Disabilities

The disciplinary provisions of the IDEA Amendments have been the subject of much controversy. While some have argued that the law makes the task of schools more difficult in disciplining students with disabilities, others assert that the law merely codifies much of the existing case law ("Understanding Discipline," 1997). It is certain, however, that these provisions will lead to increased litigation. Until the courts begin to clarify some of the ambiguities and gaps within the law, the discipline of students with disabilities will remain unclear. Finally, administrators and teachers should consult state laws and regulations prior to developing discipline policies. States will be required to bring their statutes and regulations into compliance with the IDEA Amendments, but they may be more prescriptive than the federal law. In such cases, educators must adhere to the laws and guidelines of their states.

IDEA '97 is consistent in that it emphasizes *proactive, positive behavioral supports and interventions* for students experiencing behavioral challenges. This textbook describes the procedures that teachers should use to effect behavior change. We must remember that the intent of law is to address and ameliorate behavior that impedes student learning and teach socially appropriate replacement behaviors.

# SCHOOLWIDE DISCIPLINE

One approach to reducing discipline problems in school is to adopt schoolwide discipline plans that focus on teaching appropriate behavior while preventing misbehavior from occurring. These efforts are aimed at the prevention of both disruptive (e.g., noncompliance) and violent behavior (e.g., physical assault) through schoolwide discipline programs rather than through merely focusing on reacting to discipline problems after they have occurred (Horner, Sugai, & Horner, 2000; Walker & Epstein, 2001). Schoolwide discipline programs refer to strategies that schools develop both to prevent and to respond to problem behavior. Such programs have been shown to have great promise as an effective way to define, teach, and support appropriate behaviors and address disruptive behavior in the schools.

One such effort was the U.S Department of Education's publication, *Early Warning, Timely Response: A Guide to Safe Schools* (Dwyer, Osher, & Warger, 1998). In late 1998, every school administrator in the United States received a copy of this report. The purpose of the guide was to help school districts develop comprehensive violence prevention plans. The guide summarized the research on violence prevention, interventions, and crisis response in schools. According to the guide, well-functioning schools had a strong focus on learning and achievement, safety, and socially appropriate behaviors (Dwyer et al., 1998). Additionally, Horner and others (2000) noted that if schools are to be safe, effective environments, proactive behavior support must become a priority.

Although there is no one model of schoolwide discipline used in schools, there are three basic practices that are often followed in effective disciplinary systems (Horner et al., 2000; Walker, Colvin, & Ramsey, 1995). First, schools with effective policies invest in preventing problem behavior by defining, teaching, and supporting student behavior. This means that school personnel develop important expectations or rules about student behavior and clearly communicate these expectations to students. Moreover, school officials recognize students who adhere to these expectations, and respond effectively when students do not. Second, effective schoolwide discipline systems have rapid, effective support systems for identifying and addressing needs of students who are at risk of developing problem behavior. According to Lewis and Sugai (1999), these procedures often involve increased adult monitoring and group behavior support. Third, schools using effective discipline systems have support for high-intensity problem behavior. Such systems focus on a small number of students who display high rates of disruptive behavior and include specialized individual behavior programs (e.g., FBAs and BIPs).

## Developing Schoolwide Discipline Policies

According to Sugai, Sprague, Horner, and Walker (2000), from 85% to 90% of students begin school having already learned the social skills necessary to be an effective learner. That is, they (a) pay attention, (b) are actively engaged in learning, and (c) follow school rules and procedures. The most important part of any schoolwide discipline procedure is to ensure that these skills become a part of the school's culture (Horner et al., 2000). One way for schools to ensure that such behaviors become ingrained in a school's culture is through the development and systematic use of universal interventions. The key idea behind universal interventions is reducing the number of new cases of problem behavior. Sugai and others (2000) refer to universal interventions as systemic interventions in which school personnel develop a system of rules and consequences that focus on improving the overall level of appropriate behavior of most students in a school. The most important components of universal interventions are that (a) behavioral expectations in the form of rules are defined and taught to all students and (b) inappropriate behaviors are corrected through the systematic application of consequences.

## Rules and Consequences

When developing universal interventions, schools must define, teach, and support expected student behaviors. To maintain discipline, and to operate efficiently and effectively, schools must have rules that regulate student conduct. This means that students should clearly know which behaviors are acceptable and which behaviors are prohibited. Schools recognize and reinforce students who follow the rules regarding acceptable behaviors. Additionally, if students violate reasonable school rules by behaving in ways that are prohibited, they should be held accountable.

Student accountability to rules implies that violators will be subject to disciplinary sanctions or consequences. School officials have long known that students are more likely to conduct themselves appropriately when they understand (a) the types of behavior that are expected of them when they are in school, (b) the consequences of engaging in behaviors that meet these expectations, and (c) the consequences of engaging in prohibited behavior. A number of courts have addressed the issue of schoolwide discipline policies, and have tended to give great authority to teachers and school officials to write rules that govern student behavior when they are in school (Yell, Katsiyannis, Bradley, & Rozalski, 2000).

When developing school policies regulating student conduct, rules and consequences should have a carefully considered rationale and a school-related purpose. This means that rules should be clear enough to allow students to distinguish permissible from prohibited behavior. Appropriate school rules are specific and definitive. School rules that are too vague or general may result in the violation of students' rights because students will not have a clear understanding of them. In fact, if a court finds that a school rule is so vague that students may not understand what behavior is prohibited, it is likely that that rule would be legally invalid (Gorn, 1999). Thus, teachers and administrators must take care that their school rules are sufficiently clear and are communicated to students. Furthermore, rules must be school-related. This means that school officials may not prohibit or punish conduct that is not related to their school's educational purposes.

As previously noted, an important legal requirement for developing schoolwide discipline policies is that rules and consequences must be reasonable. From a legal perspective, this means that the rules should be rational and fair. Rules that are vague and consequences that are excessive and unsuitable to the particular circumstances may be legally invalid. Additionally, disciplinary procedures that are harsh or excessive are also likely to be ruled legally invalid if they are challenged in court. This means that school officials must use reasonable means to achieve compliance with a school's rules. Reasonable rules and consequences are rational and fair and not excessive or unsuitable to the educational setting.

When schools focus on improving the overall level of appropriate behavior by developing schoolwide rules and consequences, they can expect that problem behavior will be prevented in 80% to 90% of all students (Sugai et al., 2000). However, there are 10% to 20% of students who will not respond to such interventions. For these students more intensive interventions are required.

## Programming for Students with Serious Behavior Problems

Lewis and Sugai (1999) found that the level and intensity of interventions must be increased for students at risk for developing serious problem behavior (5% to 15% of the student population) and for students who already have chronic and intense problem behavior (1% to 7% of the student population). Unfortunately, for many students who may fall into these categories, there are no legal guidelines to guide school districts in developing these more intensive and individualized interventions for problem behavior. Although there are federal laws and programs that fund the development of violence prevention programs in schools (e.g., the Safe and Drug Free Schools and Communities Act of 1994), unless students have a disability, laws address only reactive and exclusionary practices (e.g., zero tolerance policies, searches of students and their property; for a review of these laws see Yell & Rozalski, 2000). For students with disabilities, however, the Individuals with Disabilities Act (hereafter IDEA) is very specific and exact when directing schools to address problem behavior (see previous discussion on students with disabilities).

# IMPLICATIONS FOR TEACHERS AND ADMINISTRATORS

Maintaining a safe and orderly education environment is one of the most important duties teachers face. Certainly it is one of the most difficult. If our schools are to be places where students can learn, we have to adopt rules to indicate which behaviors will be rewarded and which behaviors will not be tolerated. When we have to use disciplinary procedures, it is important that we understand our rights and responsibilities as well as those of our students. Those who teach students in special education face an even more complex situation when applying disciplinary procedures. It is also important that school officials fashion school district policies and procedures that comport with the law. Following are suggested guidelines that will help to ensure that administrators and teachers meet federal, state, and court requirements when using discipline with public school students.

## Developing School District Disciplinary Policies and Procedures

School district administrators should develop written policies and procedures for teaching appropriate behavior and disciplining students when they violate school rules. These policies and procedures must ensure that schools maintain safe and orderly environments while continuing to provide students with an appropriate public education. These policies should include rules of student conduct, and disciplinary sanctions when those rules are broken. Developing the policies with the participation of administrators, teachers, parents, and students will help to ensure that they are reasonable and related to a legitimate educational function. Teachers, administrators, staff, and parents should have access to, and understand, information in the school district's discipline policy. Methods to ensure parental access include mailing discipline policy brochures to district parents and having teachers explain the procedures in parent-teacher conferences. It is important that policies and procedures apply equally to all students and that they be administered in a fair and consistent manner.

When a student is in special education, the teacher should inform the parents of the district policies and procedures. Furthermore, the district's discipline policies should be appended to the IEP. This will ensure that they are discussed and understood by all parties. If there are any changes to this policy (e.g., teachers use in-school suspension instead of out-of-school suspension), the changes should be noted in the IEP.

## Proactively Address Problem Behavior

We must remember that the purpose of discipline is to teach. As educators our goal should not be solely the elimination of problem behavior. Rather it should be the elimination of problem behavior and the teaching of positive prosocial behaviors. Positive behavioral programming (e.g., conflict resolution training, anger control training) should be an important part of our school district practices.

In the case of students with disabilities who have a history of misbehavior, the problem behavior must be addressed in their IEP. The IDEA requires that "in the case of a child whose behavior impedes his or her learning or that of others (the IEP team must) consider, where appropriate, strategies, including positive behavioral interventions, strategies, and supports to address that behavior." In an OSEP memorandum (OSEP Discipline Guidance, 1997), Judith Huemann, the assistant secretary of the Office of Special Education and Rehabilitative Services in the Department of Education, states that as part of the IEP process, teams have a responsibility to consider a child's behavior. Additionally, she writes that school districts should take prompt steps to address misconduct *when it first appears*. She suggests that when a student exhibits problem behavior, the IEP team should conduct a functional behavioral assessment and determine the needed programming to properly address the behavior. This requirement applies to all students in special education, regardless of their disability category. Additionally, because these elements will be discussed at an IEP meeting, the plan would have an increased probability of success because of parental support and participation. The plan is also less likely to be legally challenged (Hartwig & Ruesch, 2000). Clearly positive behavior intervention should be used. If behavior reduction strategies are part of the student's program, they should also be included in the IEP.

## Provide Training in Behavioral Interventions to Teachers.

Teachers must be trained in the use of positive behavioral programming (e.g., developing rules and consequences reinforcing appropriate behavior) and using consequences when students violate rules (e.g., time-out, response cost). Additionally, special education teachers should receive intensive training in (a) conducting functional behavioral assessments, (b) writing behavioral goals and objectives, and (c) developing behavioral intervention plans. Such training should include the appropriate use of disciplinary procedures as well as legal ramifications of these procedures. A policy letter from the Department of Education noted the importance of training teachers and staff in the effective use of behavior management strategies, indicating that the appropriate use of these strategies is essential to ensure the success of interventions to ameliorate problem behavior (OSEP Discipline Guidance, 1997).

According to Drasgow and Yell (2002), appropriate training is especially important for school personnel who conduct FBAs and develop BIPs because failure of IEP teams to translate the law's requirements to students' educational programs will likely result in inappropriate IEPs and, thus, the denial of a free appropriate public education (FAPE). The denial of a FAPE may, in turn, lead to due process hearings, litigation, and application of the law's sanctions against the offending school districts. Preservice and inservice educational opportunities should be provided, therefore, to ensure that members of IEP teams thoroughly understand their responsibilities under IDEA 97 and have the skills to carry them out. Public schools must ensure that personnel involved in implementing FBAs and BIPs have the necessary training and expertise. Public schools will be well served if this technology is implemented in a proactive manner to address serious and chronic maladaptive behaviors.

### Document Disciplinary Actions.

When using disciplinary procedures with students with and without disabilities, teachers must keep thorough written records of all disciplinary actions taken. An examination of court cases and administrative rulings in disciplinary matters indicates that in many instances, decisions turned on the quality of the school's records (Yell, 1998). That is, when a school district is sued over a particular disciplinary incident, the court will examine the rules and consequences of the school to determine whether they are fair and reasonable. Often they will also examine the records that were kept, if any, on the particular behavior incident. Records on emergency disciplinary actions are also important. Such records should contain an adequate description of the incident, disciplinary action taken, and the signatures of witnesses present.

### Evaluate the Effectiveness of Interventions.

Finally, it is crucial that school officials and teachers evaluate the effectiveness of the schoolwide policies and procedures and individual students' discipline plans. If schoolwide discipline plans, classroom rules and consequences, and individualized student programs are to be effective, school personnel should develop and implement a set of procedures for monitoring program effectiveness (Drasgow & Yell, 2002). The collection of meaningful data will allow school officials and teachers to determine the efficacy of the schoolwide policies and to maintain effective components of the program while eliminating the ineffective components.

There are a number of reasons for collecting data on an ongoing basis. To make decisions about whether an intervention is reducing target behaviors in the school or in a student, teachers need data collected during the course of the intervention. If formative data is not collected, school officials and teachers will not know with certainty if the procedures they use are actually achieving the desired results (Yell & Shriner, 1998).

Teachers and administrators are accountable to supervisors, parents, and communities; data collection is useful for these purposes. From a legal standpoint it is imperative that school officials and teachers collect such data. Courts do not readily accept anecdotal information; data-based decisions certainly would be viewed much more favorably (Yell & Drasgow, 2001).

## SUMMARY

School districts, administrators, and teachers have legal rights and responsibilities to ensure that their students attend safe and orderly environments where they can receive a meaningful education. To do this, educational personnel need to develop schoolwide discipline plans and behavior support programs that define, teach, and reinforce appropriate behaviors while discouraging and reducing inappropriate behaviors. Schoolwide discipline programs eschew the traditional discipline methods of reducing inappropriate behaviors through punishment and exclusion, and instead focus on a positive, proactive, problem-solving model for promoting appropriate behavior and discouraging inappropriate behavior. For students with the most serious problem behavior, the IDEA requires adoption of a similar problem-solving approach using FBAs and BIPs to address these students' problems.

Schoolwide discipline plans that are properly developed and implemented will result in safe and orderly schools where teachers can teach and students can learn. Such programs should begin with positive educational programming that does not rely on punitive reductive procedures to change behavior, but rather develops skill-based programming and discipline systems designed to improve the education of their students.

## DISCUSSION QUESTIONS

1. The Individuals with Disabilities Education Act of 1997 (IDEA) and case law since 1997 require school-based teams to use positive behavior interventions and supports, and to move away from reliance on punishment when addressing problem behavior. What are positive behavior interventions and supports and why does the law encourage their use?

2. What are the due process protections for students? How can schools ensure that due process protections are available to all students?

3. What does IDEA require when using short-term suspensions with students who are receiving special education services?

4. What discipline procedures can schools use for students receiving special education services? Specifically, what action can a school take when a student receiving special education services brings a weapon to school?

5. What is an interim alternative educational setting? What must schools do to ensure these settings are appropriate?

6. What is a manifestation determination?

## REFERENCES

Bagley, W. C. (1907). *Classroom Management.* Norwood, MA: MacMillan.

Board of Education of the Akron Central School District, 28 IDELR 909 (SEA NY 1998).

Brown v. Board of Education, 347 U.S. 483 (1954).

Cole v. Greenfield-Central Community Schools, 657 F.Supp. 56 (S.D. Ind. 1986).

Department of Education answers question on regulations (1997, November 21). *The Special Educator, 1.*

Dickens v. Johnson Board of Education, 661 F. Supp. 155 (ER.D. TN 1987).

Drasgow, E., & Yell, M. L. (2002). School-wide behavior support: Legal implications. *Child and Family Behavior Therapy, 24,* 129–145.

Dwyer, K. P., Osher, D., & Warger, W. (1998). *Early warning, timely response: A guide to safe schools.* Washington, DC: U.S. Department of Education.

Gorn, D. (1999). *What do I do when . . . The answer book on discipline.* Horsham, PA: LRP.

Goss v. Lopez, 419 U.S. 565 (1975).

Harris, L. (1996). *Violence in America's public schools: A survey of the American teacher.* New York: Metropolitan Life Insurance Company.

Hartwig, E. P., & Ruesch, G. M. (2000). Disciplining students in special education. *Journal of Special Education, 33,* 240–247.

Horner, R. H., Sugai, G., & Horner, H. F. (2000). A school-wide approach to student discipline. *The School Administrator, 24,* 20–23.

Individuals with Disabilities Education Act, 20 U.S.C. § 1401–1485.

Individuals with Disabilities Education Act Regulations, available at http://www.ed.sc.edu/spedlaw/lawpage.htm.

Katsiyannis, A., & Maag, J. (1998). Disciplining students with disabilities. *Behavioral Disorders, 23,* 276–289.

Lewis, T. J., & Sugai, G. (1999). Effective behavior support: A systems approach to proactive school-wide management. *Focus on Exceptional Children, 31*(6), 1–24.

Martin, J. L. (1999, May). *Current legal issues in discipline of disabled students under IDEA: A section by section comment on § 1415(k), discipline regulations, and initial case law.* Paper presented at the Annual Conference on Special Education Law, San Francisco: LRP.

Mead, J. F. (1998). Expressions of congressional intent: Examining the 1997 amendments to the IDEA. *Education Law Report, 127,* 511–531.

OSEP Discipline Guidance, 26 IDELR 923 (OSEP 1997).

Rose, L. C., & Gallup, A. M. (1998). The 30th annual Phi Delta Kappa/Gallup poll of the public's attitudes toward the public schools. *Phi Delta Kappan, 80,* 41–56.

Senate report of the Individuals with Disabilities Act Amendments of 1997, available at wais.access.gpo.gov.

Sugai, G., Sprague, J. R., Horner, R. H., & Walker, H. M. (2000). Preventing school violence: The use of office discipline referrals to assess and monitor school-wide discipline interventions. *Journals of Emotional and Behavioral Disorders, 8*(2), 94–102.

Understanding discipline under the new IDEA (1997, July). Special issue. *The Special Educator, 1.*

Valente, W. D., & Valente, C. M. (2001). *Law in the schools* (5th ed.). Upper Saddle River, NJ: Merrill/Prentice Hall.

Walker, H. M., Colvin, G., & Ramsey, E. (1995). *Antisocial behavior in school: Strategies and best practices.* Pacific Grove, CA: Brooks/Cole.

Walker, H. M., & Epstein, M. H. (2001). *Making schools safer and violence free: Critical issues, solutions, and recommended practices.* Austin, TX: Pro-Ed.

Yell, M. L. (1998). *The law and special education.* Upper Saddle River, NJ: Merrill/Prentice Hall.

Yell, M. L., & Drasgow, E. (2001). Litigating a free appropriate public education: The Lovaas hearings and cases. *Journal of Special Education, 33,* 205–214.

Yell, M. L., Katsiyannis, A., Bradley, R., & Rozalski, M. (2000). Ensuring compliance with the disciplinary provisions of IDEA '97: Challenges and opportunities. *Journal of Special Education Leadership, 13,* 3–18.

Yell, M. L., & Rozalski, M. E. (2000). Searching for safe schools: Legal issues in the prevention of school violence. In H. M. Walker & M. H. Epstein (Eds.), *Making schools safer and violence free: Critical issues, solutions, and recommended practices.* Austin, TX: Pro-Ed.

Yell, M. L., & Shriner, J. G. (1998). The discipline of students with disabilities. *Education and Treatment of Children, 19*(3), 282–298.

Yudof, M. G., Kirp, D. L., & Levin, B. (1992). *Education policy and the law* (3rd ed.). St. Paul, MN: West.

# PART IV

# SPECIAL CONSIDERATIONS FOR SPECIAL POPULATIONS

# chapter 12

# ISSUES IN EARLY CHILDHOOD BEHAVIOR

*Thomas Zirpoli*

*Children's experiences during early childhood not only influence their later functioning in school but also can have effects throughout life. Positive, supportive relationships . . . appear essential not only for cognitive development but also for healthy emotional development and social attachment. Research on the long-term effects of early childhood programs indicates that children who attend good-quality child care programs, even at a very young age, demonstrate positive outcomes.*

—NATIONAL ASSOCIATION FOR THE EDUCATION OF YOUNG CHILDREN *(1997)*

The importance of understanding and effectively managing the behavior of young children cannot be overemphasized for several reasons. First, many early caregivers (in this chapter, the term *caregiver* will be used to described parents, early educators, preschool teachers, aides, and other adults who care for young children) report that their biggest challenge in the preschool setting is behavior management. Yet, many early childhood caregivers have had little or no behavior management education during their preservice training.

Second, appropriate social behaviors are positively correlated with academic performance. Children who stay on task, listen to their teachers, and follow classroom rules are more likely to be liked by both adults and peers, and succeed in the classroom. Indeed, researchers have identified significant relationships between children's individual characteristics and how adults evaluate children's intelligence, personality, and other attributes (Zirpoli & Bell, 1987). These findings are especially significant when one studies the relationship between children's social behaviors and caregiver-child interaction patterns (Kilgore, Snyder, & Lentz, 2000; Zirpoli, Snell, & Loyd, 1987).

Children who have learned appropriate social behaviors have significant educational advantages over children who have not learned these basic skills. For example, children who have learned at home how to sit quietly and listen when a story is being read are likely to sit and listen to a story read by educators within the preschool setting. If these skills are not learned at home, they need to be learned at preschool. Regardless of where they learn them, children who know how to sit and listen will have the social readiness skills that will help make them ready to learn and be successful in school.

Third, caregivers should have a good understanding of young children's behavior because of the significant role they play in the development of those behaviors. Young children learn appropriate and inappropriate social skills from many sources. For many children, the educational setting may provide the only structured setting in which prosocial behaviors are modeled and reinforced. Thus, the caregiver's role in the educational setting may take on additional significance for many children. Also, many early childhood programs are becoming less center based and more home based. Caregivers must be able to model and teach effective behavior management skills to the families they visit and serve.

Last, the best time to teach appropriate social behaviors effectively and prevent the development of inappropriate behaviors is when children are young. During these critical years of early development, children establish behavioral patterns while they learn the response value of appropriate and inappropriate behaviors. For example, children who learn at a young age that tantrum behaviors "work" are likely to use them throughout childhood and into adolescence. Thus, it is important to teach children when they are young which behaviors are considered appropriate and which are not, and that appropriate behaviors are reinforced and inappropriate behaviors are not. We will talk more about the efficacy of early intervention later in this chapter.

All children misbehave at times. This, of course, is normal. A caregiver's response to inappropriate behaviors, however, will frequently determine the future course for both the misbehavior and the child. As mentioned, when a teacher provides attention to a child during a temper tantrum, the child is likely to exhibit tantrum behavior in the future as a means of getting adult attention and having demands met. In fact, the frequency and intensity of tantrums will increase over time as the child learns how to use tantrums to manipulate adult behavior. On the other hand, when a teacher refuses to give in to a child's demands during and immediately following a temper tantrum, the child is unlikely to demonstrate tantrum behavior in the future. Thus, the relationship is clear between the rate of children's misbehavior and the response they receive from significant caregivers.

When children misbehave, parents and teachers frequently focus on assessing and identifying what may be wrong with the *child*, what treatment or intervention might be best for the *child*, and so on. This focus-on-the-child approach fails to recognize the significant role of the child's *environment* and the people in that environment in shaping the child's behavior. In our fast-paced, busy world, parents seem to have less time to devote to the needs of their children than in previous times. Frequently, both teachers and parents look for quick and easy answers to questions regarding children's inappropriate behavior. We believe that the blame-the-victim syndrome places too great an emphasis on how to "fix" children; instead, we need greater emphasis on improving the quality of children's environments.

Much of the information in this text regarding understanding and managing behavior is applicable to children of all ages. Special understandings, however, apply to young children. Young children are exposed to a variety of environmental variables that place them at risk. Understanding these variables will help caregivers understand the influences affecting children and their behavior.

## ENVIRONMENTAL INFLUENCES ON YOUNG CHILDREN'S BEHAVIOR

Today, more children are considered to be at risk for developing antisocial behaviors than ever before. Although this situation may seem impossible in view of the significant advances we have made in general health care and education, a growing population of children does not have access to the opportunities these advancements offer. For example, the National Association for the Education of Young Children (1997) found that 12% to 20% of children were in child care settings described as "dangerous to their health and safety and harmful to their social and cognitive development" (p. 7). For infants and toddlers specifically, these numbers were estimated at between 35% and 40%. Other factors that place children at risk are discussed next.

## Poverty

According to the Illinois State Board of Education (2001), poverty is the single greatest predictor of academic and social failure in U.S. schools. An analysis of state data in Illinois and Kentucky found that income level alone accounted for 71% of the variance in standardized achievement scores. Additional variables such as student attendence, English proficiency rates, student race, class size, and several teacher-related variables (including race and education) accounted for only an additional 7% to the predictability of student performance. And, as pointed out by Kauffman (2001), academic failure in school is directly related to social failure and problem behavior.

In 1974, children replaced the elderly as the poorest subgroup of our nation's population. By 1980, the rate of poverty among children was six times that of the elderly (Schorr & Schorr, 1989) and peaked at 22.7% in 1993. The rate has declined since, and the U.S. Census Bureau (2000) reported that 16.9% of children under 18 years of age lived in poverty in 1999. Table 12.1 shows child poverty rates over a 10-year period.

Interestingly, in 1999 only 31% of children in poverty lived in a family that received public cash assistance (Annie E. Casey Foundation, 2001). Children raised within impoverished environments are at great risk for academic failure

**TABLE 12.1 • Child Poverty Rates, 1989–1999**

| | |
|---|---|
| 1989 | 19.6% |
| 1990 | 20.6% |
| 1991 | 21.8% |
| 1992 | 22.3% |
| 1993 | 22.7% |
| 1994 | 21.8% |
| 1995 | 20.8% |
| 1996 | 19.9% |
| 1997 | 19.9% |
| 1998 | 18.9% |
| 1999 | 16.9% |

*Source:* United States Census Bureau (2000).

and challenging behavior problems. These children are living and developing in neighborhoods where there are limited positive role models for appropriate social behaviors. In 1998, nearly 19 million children lived in a household where no parent worked full-time, year-round (Annie E. Casey Foundation, 2001). Frequently, the only adults they see who are making a "decent" living are making it in illegal activities, such as selling drugs and prostitution.

## Single-Parent Families

The percentage of births to unmarried mothers in the United States has increased steadily from 26.6% in 1990 to 33.0% in 1999. Between 1960 and 1999 the number of children living with a single parent rose from 5.8 to 19.8 million (Annie E. Casey Foundation, 2001). While the rate of births to unmarried mothers continued to rise, the percentage of children in single-parent families fell to 27.8% in 2000 after peaking at 29.1% in 1996. Most of these families are headed by mothers who are likely to drop out of high school, and the poverty cycle will continue for another generation. Schorr and Schorr (1989) suggest, however, that this cycle of poverty and "rotten outcomes" can be broken; we only need the will and resources to support the social programs that have proven effective both in cost and effect for at-risk children. For example, the Children's Defense Fund (1995) reports that only 67% of 2-year-olds are fully immunized against childhood diseases. Compared to the cost of hospitalization for millions of young children, community-based immunization programs are very cost effective.

## Low Birth Weight Babies

Infants who are born premature (too soon) or dysmature (low birth weight) are likely to be especially challenging (i.e., cry frequently, have poor sleeping patterns, are difficult to feed). About 2% of all babies born in the United States were born prematurely, and about 7.6% were classified as low birth weight (less than 2,500 grams or 5.5 pounds) in 1998 (Annie E. Casey Foundation, 2001). This is a 9% increase over the 1990–1998 period linked to (a) an increase in twins and triplets, and (b) an increase in health insurance and medical care provided to women living in poverty (Annie E. Casey Foundation, 2001). The majority of women in this second group do not receive adequate nutritional and prenatal care.

The prematurity rate for babies born to teenage mothers is about 20%. These infants frequently have trouble establishing regular sleeping patterns. They may be especially difficult to feed and, in general, to comfort. Crying behavior may be constant and irritating due to the high-pitched nature of the premature child's cry. It is no wonder that these infants are at risk for maltreatment by caregivers.

Early educators need to know that these behaviors will decrease as the infant develops beyond the normal 9th month of gestation. Patience, support from others, and a sense of humor will get most caregivers through this difficult time. The behavior of most children born prematurely will be consistent with their peers before their second birthday.

## Fetal Alcohol Syndrome

The American Academy of Pediatrics (AAP) states that prenatal exposure to alcohol is one of the leading preventable causes of disabilities in young children (Fritz, 2000). The National Academy of Sciences (1996) estimates that the occurrence of Fetal Alchol Syndrome ranges from 0.5 to 3 cases per 1,000 births, with some communities having much higher rates. For example, within the native American Indian population, 25% of all babies are reportedly alcohol damaged (Rosenthal, 1990). According to Howard (1990), approximately one-third of these children are born prematurely.

The long-term detrimental consequences on these children may include permanent neurobehavioral and affective disorders and many other developmental disabilities (Randall, 2001). The AAP (Fritz, 2000) lists the following problems associated with children exposed to excessive alcohol in utero:

a. central nervous system abnormalities,

b. impaired motor skills,

c. behavior and cognitive abnormalities, and

d. various physical problems, including heart abnormalitites, scoliosis, and hearing impairments.

Schonfeld, Mattson, Lang, Delis, and Riley (2001) documented significant deficits in verbal and nonverbal fluency among children with heavy prenatal alcohol exposure.

## Lead Poisoning

"Lead poisoning is the most common environmental health problem affecting children in the United States" (Enders, Montgomery, & Welch, 2002, p. 20). The National Health/Education Consortium (1991) reports that "one American child in six has toxic levels of lead in his or her blood. Each year, 400,000 newborns are delivered with toxic levels of lead" that can be transferred from mother to fetus (p. 4). The most common sources of lead poisoning today include lead-based paint found in older homes; lead-laden dust and soil found around old buildings; and lead-based materials such as old plumbing systems, which affect water supplies (Enders, et al., 2002). Unfortunately, young children are at greatest risk from lead poisoning "because of the impact on (their) developing central nervous system" (p. 20). Children who have elevated lead levels demonstrate a variety of problems including developmental disabilities and behavioral difficulties.

The increase in the number of children exposed to drugs, alcohol, and lead—placing them at risk for developmental and behavioral problems—is not occurring in isolation. Indeed, this increase is interrelated with more general societal problems, especially the problem of so many children living and developing within impoverished environments. "One in every five children lives in an environment characterized by substandard housing, poor nutrition, high social stress, and inadequate or nonexistent primary/preventive health care" (Baumeister, Kupstas, &

Klindworth, 1990, p. 5). The effects on children's social behavior are significant. Again, early educators face far greater challenges from the young children they serve than ever before.

## Child Maltreatment

*Child maltreatment*, a generic term, may be used to describe negligence, physical injury, emotional or psychological injury, and sexual molestation by caregivers (parents and educators). Clearly, child maltreatment is the ultimate example of a dysfunctional interaction between caregivers and the children in their care. More than 3 million cases of child maltreatment are reported in the United States each year. This figure compares to 1 million cases reported in 1980 and half a million reported in 1976 (Children's Defense Fund, 1995; Zirpoli, 1990).

The study of child maltreatment allows researchers to understand the many and interacting variables associated with caregiver-child relationships and interaction patterns. These variables include social and cultural factors, environmental factors, characteristics of the caregiver (parent or early educator), and the characteristics of the child or victim.

### Social-Cultural Variables

Social and cultural factors have been noted as a significant contributing variable in the maltreatment of children in the United States. Straus, Gelles, and Steinmetz (1980) refer to the culturally sanctioned violence within families in which spouse and child maltreatment are learned and are acceptable forms of interaction. Zigler and Hall (1989) and Rose (1983) reviewed the acceptance of physical punishment of children and found that the willingness of caregivers to employ physical punishment is the most significant determinant of child maltreatment in America. Violence seems to be embedded in U.S. society, and this social acceptance of violence is directly related to the high prevalence of child maltreatment in America (Zirpoli, 1986).

### Environmental Variables

Environmental conditions are frequently thought of as trigger variables in child maltreatment. That is, maltreatment is likely to occur under certain environmental conditions, which, given an already dysfunctional caregiver-child relationship, trigger inappropriate and abusive caregiver behavior. These conditions may include unemployment, household poverty, frustration, a lack of social support, and a general lack of family structure (Straus et al., 1980).

Environmental conditions are especially problematic when there is little or no support system to help buffer the caregiver against the effects of these conditions. Neighborhood support groups, quality day care and preschool programs, and other community services may assist caregivers and reduce environmental burdens to a tolerable level. Garbarino (1982) and Belsky and Vondra (1989) discuss the importance of social support systems for healthy families and note that, as society has become more mobile, many caregivers find themselves separated from the natural support systems of their extended family and long-term friendships.

## Caregiver Variables

Child maltreatment research has historically focused on the characteristics of the abusive caregiver. Current research, however, views the caregiver as a single, although significant, variable within a model of many interacting variables that cannot be separated and understood in isolation from each other (Pianta, Egeland, & Erickson, 1989).

Many abusive caregivers have unrealistic expectations about children and their behavior. This sort of opinion is especially true with new caregivers (e.g., adolescent parents) who have little or no knowledge of child development or of effective parenting. When combined with their own immaturity and the lack of appropriate social support, new caregivers may not be able to cope with the responsibilities of parenthood, and the children in their care may be considered at risk for maltreatment.

Caregivers who abuse their children have often been victims of maltreatment themselves (Straus et al., 1980). Many caregivers have only their own abusive caregivers from which to model and learn the skills of caring for children and how caregivers and children should interact. For example, Egeland, Jacobvitz, and Papatola (1984) followed 47 women who were physically maltreated as children and found that 70% were maltreating their children at 2 years of age. As long as other environmental and sociocultural factors persist, the cycle of maltreatment is likely to continue.

## Child Variables

Although children who are maltreated should never be blamed for the maltreatment they receive from caregivers, it is helpful to understand the variables that may place some children at greater risk. The idea that children affect caregiver behavior (known as *child effects*) has received considerable attention during the past two decades beginning with Richard Bell's review of the parent-child relationship as a reciprocal relationship (Bell, 1968; Bell & Harper, 1977). As professionals began to realize the significant contribution children make toward caregiver-child interactions, interest in the characteristics of children maltreated by caregivers has increased considerably (Rusch, Hall, & Griffin, 1986; Zirpoli, 1986; Zirpoli et al., 1987).

Research has shown that younger children are at greater risk for maltreatment than older children. Premature infants, representing less than 10% of all births, have been reported to represent up to half the cases of child maltreatment (Fontana, 1971). Pianta et al. (1989) report that toddlers are more likely to be maltreated than school-age children.

Premature infants present an excellent example for understanding child effects. These infants are prone to colic, irritability, and restlessness. They have irregular sleeping and eating patterns and may be difficult to feed. Premature infants may have an annoying and irritating cry and usually require additional parental care and attention. Combined with certain caregiver, environmental, and sociocultural factors, one can easily understand how premature infants may be at greater risk for maltreatment by caregivers who are already stressed by other family and environmental challenges.

Some debate exists concerning the extent or degree of child effects on caregiver behavior, specifically concerning the role of child effects in child maltreatment. Some professionals believe that child effects are short-term and situational and do not account for the quality of caregiving over time (Starr, 1982). Researchers generally agree, however, that some child characteristics have been associated with maltreatment but they alone are not enough to predict future child maltreatment. The following statement reinforces this point:

> To the extent that the child with extreme individual differences is placed in a family which may not be ready to parent, characteristics of that child may exacerbate an already difficult situation. This child may become the victim of maltreatment, not because of its own behavior, but because the child places added burdens upon an already stressed or incapable family system, resulting in a breakdown in the processes of good parenting. (Pianta et al., 1989, p. 203)

Some predictors and outcomes of child maltreatment, as documented by Egeland (1990), with high-risk mothers and their children through sixth grade, are provided in Table 12.2.

## Breaking the Cycle of Child Maltreatment

Given the variables associated with child maltreatment, how can we help break the cycle? Some solutions require significant changes in national priorities and attitudes. Early educators, however, are in the best position to advocate for these changes.

First, we must put an end to the widespread tolerance of physical punishment of children. As professional educators, we can start in our own educational settings. Second, we must advocate a highest-priority status for children and the issues related to their protection and enrichment (physical, mental, and emotional). This stance means full funding for Head Start; the Women, Infants and Children (WIC) program; and other effective programs that serve impoverished children. Third, we must ensure that all caregivers, regardless of background or income, have the appropriate, necessary community support to provide their children with a protecting, healthy, and enriching environment. Such support means that appropriate prenatal care for *all* women, appropriate medical care for *all* children, and quality educational settings for *all* children are available, regardless of family income or ability to pay. These are sound investments for the future of our nation's children and for the future of our nation.

**TABLE 12.2 • Selective Antecedents/Predictors and Outcomes of Maltreatment**

*Antecedents/Predictors Related to Mothers:*

- Low socioeconomic status/poverty.
- Mean age of mothers at birth of their child was 20.5, range 12 to 37 years.
- 62% of mothers were single.
- Only 13% of the biological fathers were in the home at 18 months.
- 40% of mothers had not completed high school.
- Many of the mothers had a history of having been abused as a child.

*Outcomes Related to Children by Sixth Grade:*

- The consequences of maltreatment were severe.
- None of the children were invulnerable to the negative effects of maltreatment.
- At each assessment from infancy through the sixth grade, there were increasing numbers of children who were having problems.
- By third grade, 60% of the children were receiving some form of special education services. Despite receiving services, these children continue to fall further behind.
- The problems these children bring to school make it difficult for them to profit from special services regardless of how good the teacher or curriculum is.
- Intervention with these children must include a comprehensive, intensive approach that also involves their families.
- The effects of neglect and emotionally unresponsive caretaking were as devastating as physical abuse.
- The child's environment (e.g., an organized, predictable home environment, secure attachment between mother and infant) was associated with resilience in the early elementary grades.
- Most parents of the children who were having difficulty in school had little involvement with the school.
- To some degree, an organized classroom, where the teacher provided clear expectations for the child, served as a protective factor for the child.

# THE EFFICACY OF EARLY INTERVENTION

More and more young children are attending some type of preschool setting outside the home. The increase in maternal employment outside the home, single-parent families, and families with two working parents are the primary reasons for the greater demand for early childhood programs. For many children, these programs provide early, quality intervention with many beneficial outcomes—for example, the opportunity to develop appropriate social skills necessary for success in elementary school and beyond. Weikart (1990) says that the demand for greater quality programs is directly related to the growing recognition that good early childhood programs produce positive outcomes for children's development.

Although more children are attending preschool than ever before, the number of children entering kindergarten or first grade without basic readiness skills is also increasing. These readiness skills include basic social behaviors such as listening, compliance, following directions, and staying-in-seat and on-task behaviors. Caregivers, especially educators and pediatricians, report a significant increase in children who are considered "behavior problems," especially children considered hyperactive, aggressive, and having attention deficits (Newacheck, Budetti, & Halfon, 1986; Reid, Maag, & Vasa, 1993). Also, the number of preschool children labeled with some type of disability, especially a behavioral disability, is increasing at an alarming rate.

At least some of the increase in behavior problems may be attributed to both the growing number of children living in impoverished environments and the number of children exposed to alcohol and drugs. These children, along with a growing number of homeless children, represent a new population of preschoolers and young elementary school children with challenging behaviors and other potential disabilities not yet totally understood (Yamaguchi, Strawser, & Higgins, 1997). Although the long-term outcome for these children is unknown, educators must now be prepared to serve this new and challenging population.

Children considered at risk because of prematurity, dysmaturity, alcohol and drug effects, and general poverty are best served early in life. The earlier intervention begins, the better the short- and long-term outcomes for children and their families. Early childhood intervention programs such as Head Start have had and continue to have dramatic effects on the lives of children considered at risk for developmental problems and antisocial behaviors (Gallagher & Ramey, 1990; Smith, 1990). Unfortunately, due to a lack of federal funding, less than half of eligible children receive services (Coeyman, 1998). However, between 1982 and 2002, the number of children served by Head Start increased from 395,800 to 912,345 (Children's Defense Fund, 2003).

Long-term studies have found that high-risk children who participated in quality preschool programs had a 40% to 60% reduction in crime, a 50% reduction in teenage births, a 50% reduction in welfare payments, a 30% to 50% increase in high school graduation and college attendance, and a 50% increase in employment compared to their high-risk peers who did not have the same early intervention opportunities (Hodgkinson, 1989; Miller, 1989). Weikart (1990), in a review of eight long-term studies on the effects of quality early childhood programs, also found a reduction in crime, teen pregnancy, and welfare utilization, as well as an increase in high school graduation rates and employment.

In a 4-year study of 985 premature babies who weighed 5 ½ pounds or less at birth, the children from families that received early intervention and services were found at the age of 3 to have IQ scores that averaged 13 points higher than those who did not participate in an early intervention program. Babies in the control group were nearly three times more likely to be mentally disabled (Sparling et al., 1991).

Ramey and Ramey (1992) found significant long-lasting (through age 12) differences between children who received intensive early intervention and control group children. Following children who participated in the Abecedarian Project, they note the following results:

- Only 28% of the Abecedarian Project children failed a grade during elementary school compared to 55% of the control group children.
- Only 13% of the Abecedarian Project children had an IQ less than 86 compared to 44% of the control group children.

Children who receive early intervention perform better on achievement tests, are less likely to need special education services or be retained in a grade, and have more positive attitudes toward achievement and school (Scarr & Weinberg, 1986). The following list by Smith (1990) summarizes numerous research studies relating to the impact of the Head Start program:

- *Cognitive effects:* Children involved in Head Start make substantial gains in all cognitive components during their Head Start experience. They demonstrate a test score advantage over control groups of children who did not attend Head Start.
- *Socioemotional effects:* Children in Head Start make meaningful gains in self-esteem, achievement, motivation, and especially social behaviors during their Head Start experience.
- *Health effects:* Children involved in Head Start are healthier as a result of their participation. They have a level of general pediatric and dental health comparable to more advantaged children. Their nutritional intake is better than children who do not attend. Significant improvements can be seen in the motor coordination and development of all participating children, particularly among children with physical handicaps.
- *Family effects:* Parents are generally positive about their children's experience and are satisfied with the benefits they receive from Head Start. Parents who actively participate in the program feel better about themselves, improve their economic and social status, and have children with high levels of developmental achievement. Head Start programs also link families with a wide range of health and social services. Head Start has also had mixed success in influencing parents' child-rearing practices in the home.
- *Community effects:* Head Start has a positive impact on providing increased social and health services for the poor and affecting more responsive educational programs among public school institutions.

## Variables Associated with Effective Early Intervention

Quality early childhood programs have several major components. First, in addition to serving children during their early development, effective programs aim to serve children at the prenatal and early infancy periods—and, again, the earlier services are provided, the better the outcome for child and family. Research has clearly demonstrated that mothers who receive quality prenatal care have babies who are at lower risk for developmental and behavioral disorders (Gallagher & Ramey, 1990; Schorr & Schorr, 1989). Second, effective programs have a low caregiver-to-child ratio, with no more than sixteen to twenty 3- to 5-year-olds for every two adults (National Association for the Education of Young Children, 1997). Third, parental participation and education is essential to the effective early childhood program (Mahoney & Kaiser, 1999). Professional caregivers must work with parents as *partners* in their children's development, and effective programs provide services to the *family* in addition to the children (Egeland, 1990; Weikart, 1990). Finally, research has also found that home-based programs are more effective than center-based ones (Smith, 1990).

The National Association for the Education of Young Children (1997) outlines 12 principles of child development and learning for developmentally appropriate early childhood practice:

- Domains of children's development—physical, social, emotional, and cognitive—are closely related. Development in one domain influences, and is influenced by, development in other domains.
- Development occurs in a relatively orderly sequence, with later abilities, skills, and knowledge building on those already acquired.
- Development proceeds at varying rates from child to child as well as unevenly within different areas of each child's functioning.
- Early experiences have both cummulative and delayed effects on individual children's development. Optimal periods exist for certain types of development and learning.
- Development proceeds in predictable directions toward greater complexity, organization, and internalization.
- Development and learning occur in, and are influenced by, multiple social and cultural contexts.
- Children are active learners, drawing on direct physical and social experience as well as culturally transmitted knowledge to construct their own understandings of the world around them.
- Development and learning result from interaction of biological maturation and the environment, which includes both the physical and social worlds that children live in.
- Play is an important vehicle for children's social, emotinal, and cognitive development, as well as a reflection of their development.

- Development advances when children have opportunities to practice newly acquired skills as well as when they experience a challenge just beyond the level of their present mastery.
- Children demonstrate different modes of knowing and learning and different ways of representating what they know.
- Children develop and learn best in the context of a community where they are safe and valued, their physical needs are met, and they feel psychologically secure.

# UNDERSTANDING THE BEHAVIOR OF YOUNG CHILDREN

By the time of birth, an infant's brain, at two-thirds the size of an adult brain, is remarkably complete. Recent research has found that 3 months before birth, a fetus has already developed 10 billion neurons, nearly the full complement of brain maturity. Neurons are the single nerve cells that serve as the functional unit of the nervous system. They are created at the average rate of 40,000 every minute for the first 180 days after conception (National Health/Education Consortium, 1991).

Newborns are totally dependent on others. For the most part, their behavior is directly related to their physical condition and environment. Newborns cry when they need to be changed, when they are hungry, or when they are in some sort of discomfort (Pomeranz, 1986). Newborns do not cry in order to manipulate their parents into giving them excessive attention. A newborn's crying is not a learned behavior that will increase if parents or other caregivers respond to the child's needs. In other words, you cannot spoil a newborn. The newborn needs lots of caregiver attention, warmth, and love. He or she will develop a sense of security knowing that there are caregivers willing and able to care for his or her basic needs.

Attachment in infants has been studied extensively by Ainsworth (1979) and Bowlby (1982). Ainsworth found that mothers of securely attached infants were more responsive to their infants' basic needs and that the infants were more cooperative and less aggressive in their interaction with their mothers than "anxiously attached" infants.

Between the 3rd and 6th months, infants begin to develop an understanding of the relationship between their behavior and responses from others (Ensher & Clark, 1986). About this time, infants may begin to use a variety of behaviors, including crying, simply to seek the attention of others, especially significant others such as parents. At this time, caregivers may begin to regulate their response to these behaviors so that appropriate behaviors are reinforced and inappropriate behaviors are not.

At around 6 months of age, children may exhibit several inconvenient or even irritating behaviors that represent a passage through normal cognitive and motor stages of development. For example, the child may enjoy dropping things from the high chair and looking to see where the object goes. With this simple behavior, the child begins to learn about cause and effect and object permanence. Thus, a 6-month-old child should not be punished for these learning behaviors.

A significant milestone for the 7- to 8-month-old infant is the development of anxiety toward strangers. During this time the infant demonstrates a strong attachment to the primary caregiver, usually the mother. Parents frequently feel the need to apologize for their child's crying and clinging during separation. Caregivers should be assured that the child is developing normally and understand that, especially during this period, the child needs reassurance and comfort (Woolfolk, 1987). By the time the infant approaches 18 months, he or she will be able to cope with separation from the primary caregiver. Attachment to many others is evident in their ease at being with other familiar caregivers.

At 6 to 8 months, children want to crawl around and explore (learn). Caregivers should provide safe places for the child to explore rather than confine the child to a playpen or crib for long periods. At 9 to 12 months, the child will be cruising furniture and, by 12 to 18 months, walking. Again, providing a safe environment allows children to explore and develop new cognitive and motor skills.

Feeding time for infants and young children is likely to be challenging for caregivers. At 6 months of age, infants may push the spoon away from the feeder to show that they are finished. Nine-month-olds begin to feed themselves crackers and toast. By 15 months, finger feeding is typical. Being able to use a cup without spilling may be seen by 18 months. The point is that learning to eat and drink is part of normal development and that opportunities for self-feeding should be allowed. Young children are not neat eaters, but rather than punishing them for their messes and spills, caregivers should make cleanup easier by pouring only small amounts of liquids into cups, putting drop cloths under high chairs, and using appropriate child-sized utensils. If children start to throw food or drop it on the floor, remove the food for a short time (2 to 3 minutes) and say, "No throwing food on the floor." Children will soon get the message that this is unacceptable behavior.

By the end of the 1st year, children begin to show interest in other children. They frequently enjoy being around other children and playing beside them. Expecting a 1-year-old to play with other children, however, is unrealistic. They delight in exploring other children, which may take the form of hair pulling, poking (particularly around the face), and grabbing toys. Putting objects in their mouth is still a primary means of exploration for the 1-year-old—and that may include biting other children. Although these actions may appear to be aggressive, they are simply children's way of exploring their environment.

Language development is a critical component of early development. By the end of the 1st year, the child typically speaks one-word utterances (which consist primarily of nouns) and can name familiar objects such as "bottle," "cup," "milk," "ball," and "mommy." By the second birthday, children are usually capable of speaking two-word utterances such as "mommy go," "kitty run," "bite finger," and "dolly hat." Parents frequently understand the language of their young children even when no one else can. For example, a child who points to the refrigerator and says "milk" is understood by the parent to mean "Mommy, I'm thirsty. Could you please give me a glass of milk?" Unfortunately, because of limited language development, children are often unable to communicate their wants and needs to caregivers. Young children who are tired, unhappy, wet, or in need of a hug may become frustrated and express themselves through crying, tantrums, or other means that caregivers judge inappropriate. But they must understand that children may not possess the words to express themselves. Caregivers are usually on the right track to comfort distressed toddlers and try to read the body language that may be saying "I'm tired" or "I'm wet." Providing basic needs such as warmth, food, sleep, and physical contact should be the first intervention when comforting young children.

By the time children reach their second birthday, they should be on the way to developing an awareness of some basic behaviors considered appropriate and inappropriate. Behavior rules may apply to the home, car, preschool, grocery store, and so on. The toddler learns these rules when caregivers verbally repeat the rules and praise compliance. On the other hand, toddlers learn not to follow rules if they do not clearly understand them and when caregivers are inconsistent with enforcement. For example, young children learn that they must always sit in the car seat when traveling by hearing about the importance of the car seat, consistently using the car seat, and never, under any circumstances, traveling in the car without using the car seat (regardless of crying or other tantrum behaviors).

Young children are quick to learn their limits and their ability to amend the limits established by early educators. It is up to caregivers to set clear limits and be consistent in enforcing them. Children develop an understanding of no by their first birthday. Caregivers should avoid saying no when they do not really mean it. Children quickly learn that the word *no* may have a different meaning for some caregivers. For example, a child may learn that for some caregivers, no means maybe. Around these caregivers, children are likely to be noncompliant and exhibit other challenging behaviors.

During the first 2 years of life, children progress rapidly in many areas. By the end of the 2nd year, the child is beginning to develop a sense of self; however, young children continue to need structure in their environments as much as they need room and freedom to explore. Some early educators believe the two are incompatible; they are not. In fact, young children who feel secure within a structured environment will feel free to explore and take risks within the boundaries established by loving caregivers.

Table 12.3 provides an overview of some of the important behavioral milestones in young children.

# APPROPRIATE CAREGIVING FOR YOUNG CHILDREN

## Establishing a Caring and Loving Environment

Children need to know that they are loved and accepted. Even very young children develop an understanding about how caregivers feel about them. They listen to what caregivers say to them and to others about them, and they observe how caregivers behave. Children who feel secure in their environment and in

**TABLE 12.3 • Important Behavioral/Social Milestones in Young Children**

| Behavior | Age of Onset Range (months) |
|---|---|
| Responds positively to feeding and comforting | B–1 |
| Looks at another face momentarily | B–1 |
| Shows social smile | 0.6–3 |
| Quiets with sucking | 0.6–3 |
| Shows distress and excitement | 0.6–3 |
| Discriminates mother | 1–5 |
| Responds with vocal sounds when talked to | 1–6 |
| Laughs | 3–5 |
| Shows awareness of strange situation | 3–6 |
| Discriminates strangers | 3–6 |
| Shows interest in mirror image | 5–7 |
| Laughs at games (peekaboo) | 5–7 |
| Cooperates in games | 5–12 |
| Resists having a toy taken away | 5–12 |
| Plays pat-a-cake | 5–12 |
| Imitates facial expressions | 7–9 |
| Shows stranger anxiety | 8–10 |
| Tugs at adult to get attention | 8–12 |
| Offers toy to adult | 12–16 |
| Demonstrates affection toward others | 12–17 |
| Enjoys playing with other children | 12–17 |
| Engages in tantrums | 12–18 |
| Demonstrates mastery pleasure | 12–24 |
| Enjoys listening to simple stories | 18–23 |
| Responds to adult praise and rewards | 18–23 |
| Follows directions related to daily routines | 18–23 |
| Expresses ownership or possession | 18–23 |
| Shows jealousy toward others | 18–24 |
| Enjoys rough-and-tumble play | 18–24 |
| Wants to help with simple jobs | 18–24 |
| Develops a sense of self-importance | 18–24 |
| Engages in parallel play | 18–24 |
| Begins to share toys | 20–26 |
| Attempts to comfort others in distress | 22–24 |
| Initiates own play activities | 24–36 |

| Behavior | Age of Onset Range (months) |
|---|---|
| Participates in group play | 24–36 |
| Shares property with others | 24–36 |
| Engages in dramatic play | 24–30 |
| Relates experiences | 24–36 |
| Demonstrates parallel and role play | 28–32 |
| Helps at little household tasks | 36–48 |
| "Performs" for others | 36–48 |
| Group play takes place of parallel play | 42–50 |
| Shows affection and hostility with peers | 46–50 |
| Has many fantasy fears | 46–50 |
| Plays cooperatively with other children | 48–60 |
| Plays competitive exercise games | 48–60 |
| Calls attention to own performance | 54–62 |
| Relates fanciful stories | 54–62 |
| Shows many real fears | 58–62 |
| Increases in organized play with rules | 68–76 |

*Sources: From Bayley Scales of Infant Development,* by N. Bayley, 1993, San Antonio, TX: Psychological Corporation; *Battelle Developmental Inventory,* by J. Newborg, J. R. Stock, & L. Wnek, 1988, Allen, TX: DLM; *Child Development Inventory,* by H. Ireton, 1992, Minneapolis: Behavior Science Systems; *HELP Checklist: Ages Birth to Three Years,* by S. Furuno, K. A. O'Reilly, C. M. Hosaka, T. T. Inatsuka, T. L. Allman, & B. Zeisloft, Palo Alto, CA: VORT; *Vineland Adaptive Behavior Scales,* by S. Sparrow, D. Balla, & D. Cicchetti, 1985, Circle Pines, MN: American Guidance Service.

their relationships with caregivers are less likely to misbehave as a way of getting inappropriate attention.

When a child misbehaves, caregivers are likely to focus on the child and the child's behavior in an effort to stop the inappropriate behavior and prevent its recurrence. It may be difficult for the caregiver to understand how the environment may be a contributing factor to the misbehavior (Barkley, 1987; LaVigna & Donnellan, 1986). Environmental variables that may contribute to the misbehavior include the following:

- the behavior of the caregiver (e.g., is misbehavior reinforced?);
- the behavior of others in the environment (e.g., how do peers respond to the child's behavior?); and
- factors relating to the environment in which the child exhibits the behavior (e.g., physical environment, cognitive and social demands).

We will look at three suggestions as to how caregivers can demonstrate to young children that they are loved, liked, and accepted.

### Tell Children You Like Them

A caregiver cannot assume that children know someone likes them—you must tell them! Caregivers should get into the daily habit of telling children they are liked. Some caregivers may have a very difficult time saying "I like you" or expressing positive feelings to the children placed in their care. If expressing feelings in this way becomes part of the daily routine, however, caregivers will find it becomes easier to do so. Children should leave their educational setting saying, "My teacher really likes me!"

Families who communicate their feelings about each other when children are young will have an easier time expressing feelings when the children become adolescents. Thus, efforts to communicate affection when children are young provide an investment for future parent-child communication patterns.

Educators can help children establish healthy attitudes about expressing their feelings in the classroom. Talking about feelings and giving children opportunities to talk about how they feel teach children that their feelings are real and part of being a person. They also give educators a chance to teach children how to identify, be sensitive to, and respect the feelings of others. These lessons will help provide a solid foundation for the development of appropriate social skills.

### Set Aside Individual Time

Set aside some special time, if only a few minutes per day, with each child. Use this time to talk and listen to the child and to let that child know how important he or

Most of all, children need to know that they are loved by the significant adults in their lives.

she is. These private conversations also give children a chance to express any feelings, concerns, or reactions to the day's events. Moreover, regardless of how difficult the day has been for both of you, this special time provides an opportunity for at least one positive caregiver-child interaction.

Many children do not have a significant adult in their lives outside the school environment. They may live in a single-parent household with a parent who is busy and preoccupied with trying to support the family. The Annie E. Casey Foundation (2001) found that the number of children living with a single parent rose from 5.8 million in 1960 to 19.8 million in 1999. We all know how important it is for children and adolescents to have one special adult to talk to, share their feelings, and provide positive feedback and support. Often that adult is a teacher or counselor from the child's school. Educators need to be aware of these social needs and willing to give some time (even a few minutes each day) to show a student that someone cares.

### Give Children Affection

With all the attention to and appropriate concern about the sexual abuse of children, some caregivers are hesitant to touch, hug, or otherwise express affection toward the children in their care. Some schools have even told educators not to touch their students. This reaction is very unfortunate. Children need affection to develop normally and to be emotionally happy and secure. Children in today's society spend more and more time out of their homes and away from loving parents. Thus, the affection of other caregivers becomes even more crucial, especially for infants and young children. Schools are encouraged to develop policies that also outline acceptable touching (e.g., pats on the shoulders, handshakes).

## Building Self-Esteem

Children who have healthy self-esteem are usually happy children who feel good about themselves and others. Happy, self-assured children are likely to interact positively with caregivers and other children. In addition to its social and behavioral benefits, healthy self-esteem is positively related to academic achievement.

Demonstrating to children that they are loved, liked, and accepted is the first step to building their self-esteem. We can now look at some specific suggestions for increasing children's self-esteem.

### Allow and Enable Children to Be Competent

Hendrick (1990) states that "the purpose of early education is to foster competence in young children" (p. 4). *Competence* is the self-assured feeling that one is capable of doing something "all by myself." Teachers and parents alike can help children participate in competence-building activities by allowing them to do things for themselves. Caregivers who provide opportunities for children to wash dishes after snacks or meals at low sinks or who give preschoolers jobs (e.g., feeding the family dog, being the leader at school) are providing children with opportunities to feel competent.

### Tell Children About the Good Things They Do

Too often caregivers focus on children's *inappropriate* behaviors instead of *appropriate* behaviors. When this happens, children are taught to associate caregiver attention with inappropriate behaviors. As a result, inappropriate behaviors increase. Unfortunately, it seems easier to focus on inappropriate behaviors than appropriate behaviors. Caregivers must make every effort to give greater attention to the appropriate things children do. This can be accomplished by telling children, "You're such a good worker" or "I like the way you played with John," or "I like the way you solved that problem with Mary." Make it a point to attend to the good things children are doing. Teach the children that there is an association between caregiver attention and *appropriate* behavior.

### Speak to Children Appropriately

Many caregivers do not understand how their own behaviors teach appropriate and inappropriate behaviors to children. Caregivers influence children's learning every time they interact with them. Two things are important to keep in mind when speaking to children. First, *what* you say is important. Sarcastic, negative statements promote feelings of worthlessness. If a child does something inappropriate and you must say something, talk about the *behavior,* not the child. Although their behaviors may sometimes be bad, *children* are never bad. To maintain a child's dignity and self-worth, describe what the child did that you dislike, but do not criticize the child as a person. Inappropriate statements from a significant caregiver may severely damage a child's self-esteem.

Second, *how* you speak to children is very important. Some caregivers believe that the louder they shout, the more effective they will be in changing children's behaviors. However, talking to children firmly, but calmly, is more effective in both the short and long term. In addition, when caregivers stop shouting, the environment becomes a calmer place for children to learn and develop. Children exhibit less inappropriate behavior within calm, positive environments where they are getting lots of attention for appropriate behaviors (Hetherington & Martin, 1986).

### Teach Children That Mistakes Are Normal

Everybody makes mistakes. When children make mistakes, tell them that everyone errs and that no one is perfect. Caregivers have opportunities to model appropriate ways to deal with mistakes whenever they commit an error—for example, by saying, "I was wrong and I am sorry." Children who observe this behavior are more likely to say "I was wrong" or "I am sorry" when they make mistakes because they will feel confident that it is all right to make errors. Also, children will not be afraid to try new things when they are not worried about successful outcomes (Woolfolk, 1987).

Teaching young children that it is normal to make mistakes and to talk about them will help them confront and talk about mistakes as adolescents and adults. Being able to say "I was wrong and I am sorry" will serve as a functional behavior throughout the child's life and across all social settings.

## Allow Children to Have Limited Choices

Children will learn how to make good choices if they are allowed to practice making choices from an early age. Some choices young children can make include selecting books or stories to read before bedtime, choosing juice to drink during snack time, deciding what clothes to wear, and so on. Giving children choices is an excellent way to reduce power struggles. Caregivers frequently feel that, to be in control of children's behavior, they must resort to giving directives. Sometimes, directives are appropriate; however, young children who are struggling to develop their independence may respond negatively to a lack of choices, leading to a cycle of caregiver-versus-child battles. Of course, caregivers should limit the range of choices. For example, when we say that children may decide what to drink, the caregiver first limits the choice ("Do you want orange juice or apple juice?"). In this way, mature adults remain in control while providing opportunities for children to make safe choices.

Everyday events provide opportunities to discuss choices. For example, when children fight over a toy, caregivers can use the event to help children think about alternative behaviors and choose appropriate behaviors on their own. Asking questions about their behaviors (such as "Can you think of another way of telling John that you want to play with that toy?") and giving them an opportunity to explore alternatives and consider the consequences of their behaviors ("How do you think John would feel about that?") are other ways to teach children how to make choices about their behaviors.

Hendrick (1990) notes that children who are allowed to make choices are more creative. She says that "for an experience to be creative for children, it must be generated from within them, not be an experience 'laid on' from outside" (p. 250). For example, rather than providing children with coloring books during art activities in a classroom, the teacher could provide collage materials for children to create their own original artwork. Sometimes, caregiver-directed activities provide limited opportunities for problem solving. Indeed, children who are given choices may have an advantage when it comes to solving problems related to their social behavior. For example, the child who divides and shares blocks with a friend is able to plan a solution to the problem (i.e., both children wanting to play with blocks), rather than acting on the immediate impulse to be possessive.

## Let Children Know You Value Their Opinions

When children are reinforced for expressing their own opinions, they learn the value of their personhood, in addition to the value of their feelings, beliefs, and opinions. Children can be encouraged to develop their own feelings and ideas and

# Classroom Application 12.1

## Fighting over Toys

Kelly has been a preschool teacher for 3 years. She has learned that fighting over toys is usually the result of a lack of desirable toys within the preschool environment, a crowded room and/or a disorganized room. In Kelly's program, she limits the number of children in each play zone. This is done in several ways. For example, she places only four chairs around the Lego table. The Play-Doh table has three chairs, three rolling pins, and three cutters. Kelly's book center has five carpet squares for children to sit on while reading. The children in her class know that if the chairs or carpet squares are taken, they must move to another play area. Also, the children are encouraged to move from one play center to another.

Kelly sets up her play areas differently each day to allow her to introduce a variety of play materials. She places herself and her assistants throughout the room to allow adequate supervision. With this arrangement, Kelly's preschoolers have opportunities to play with many different toys and materials that are desirable.

Still, fights over toys may occur. Kelly encourages the children to ask for toys when another child has something they want. She also teaches them the concept of trading one toy for another. If a child is aggressive, however, Kelly removes the child from the play area for a specific time period (a few minutes) and remembers to reinforce the child when he or she is observed playing appropriately. Most importantly, Kelly remembers to verbally reinforce all the children when they are playing appropriately. In Kelly's class, you will frequently hear her say, "I like the way you guys are sharing with your friends!"

to express their own opinion when caregivers ask, "What do you think?" or "How do you feel about that?" These kinds of queries let children know that they (and their feelings) are important, too. In addition, this is a great way to teach and practice how to interact and converse appropriately with adults and other children.

### *Respect Individual Differences*

Caregivers must teach that all children are unique, that their own differences should be recognized and appreciated, and that they should recognize and appreciate the differences in others. Lyle (1990) suggests the following activities to encourage children to recognize and appreciate their differences:

- Ask the children to talk about things that make their families special.
- Have the children develop and share their autobiographies.
- Have the children interview each other about their backgrounds, physical differences, and so on.
- Encourage children to express their ideas, even when they are different from their peers'.

# VARIABLES ASSOCIATED WITH APPROPRIATE BEHAVIOR IN YOUNG CHILDREN

Several variables are associated with appropriate behavior in young children, including the level of adult supervision, consistency of consequences, readiness for academic achievement, and environmental considerations. The absence of these variables has been found to place children at risk for antisocial behaviors.

## Supervision

The strongest predictor of appropriate behavior in children is the quantity and quality of caregiver supervision (Kauffman, 2001; Lewis, Colvin, & Sugai, 2000; Patterson, 1982). When caregivers monitor children's behavior—where the children play and whom their children play with—they are showing children that they care about their well-being, that there are specific physical and behavioral boundaries, and that there are caregivers who will monitor their safety. Caregivers must strive for a healthy balance between restrictiveness and permissiveness. When caregivers are overly restrictive, children tend to be submissive, dependent, and unable to take risks. When caregivers are overly permissive, children tend to be noncompliant, delinquent, and careless. A lack of caregiver supervision is also related to children's association with property destruction (e.g., breaking toys) (Patterson, 1982) and student misbehavior during school transition periods (Colvin, Sugai, Good, & Lee, 1997). Hetherington and Martin (1986) state that children will have positive outcomes when parental discipline is firm and consistent, yet loving and responsive.

## Consistency

Perhaps the most significant variable in managing young children's behavior is consistency. "Consistency helps make an environment predictable" (Bailey & Wolery, 1984, p. 242). Consistency builds understanding and trust between caregivers and children. Children learn what to expect and what is acceptable and unacceptable behavior when caregivers are consistent in what they say and how they respond. Children learn the likely consequences for their behaviors when caregivers consistently follow through.

In the absence of consistency, children are likely to be rebellious when caregivers finally do try to respond to inappropriate behaviors. Research has shown that caregivers who are inconsistent when disciplining children tend to be harsh and hostile in responding to inappropriate behaviors (Doke & Flippo, 1983). This inconsistent and hostile relationship is associated with children's aggressive, noncompliant, and delinquent behavior (Martin, 1975). Zirpoli (1986) found that inconsistent discipline is associated with dysfunctional and abusive caregiver-child interactions.

## Readiness Skills

When young children enter school, at either the preschool or elementary level, educators have certain expectations about their skills and behavior. Unfortunately, many young children do not have the skills or behaviors to meet even minimal teacher expectations. The percentage of young children entering educational settings without basic readiness skills is increasing (Hodgkinson, 1989). The potential outcome for these children includes social and academic failure, poor relationships with educators and peers, and the risk of falling further and further behind the norm throughout their school years.

Parents and early childhood caregivers can improve the chances of success for young children entering school by teaching them basic readiness skills and behaviors, such as these:

- appropriate social interactions with caregivers (listening, compliance, following directions),
- appropriate social interactions with peers (sharing, playing, turn taking), and
- appropriate environmental behaviors (use of toys and other materials, in-seat behavior, attention to environmental cues).

Caregivers teach these skills through verbal instructions and practice. We have already provided the example of children who have been read to from an early age; they are likely to sit and listen when caregivers read a story within an educational setting. Sitting and listening are not just behaviors; they are skills that children must learn. Children who learn to share and cooperate from an early age are likely to get along with their peers in later years. Children who learn to take care of their toys and not to be destructive are likely to generalize these skills and behaviors to the school environment. These children will be ready to learn and ready to expand their social relationships with new caregivers and peers.

## Environmental Considerations

Both teachers and parents alike need to realize the importance of environmental influences on young children's behavior. The purpose of considering these influences is to establish an environment that serves to *prevent* inappropriate behaviors in preschoolers (McEvoy, Fox, & Rosenberg, 1991; Nordquist & Twardosz, 1990). Of course, prevention is the best form of intervention. While structuring the physical environment, one should keep in mind that the preschool child is struggling to become independent yet still requires caregivers' close support and guidance. Although the preschool setting is the most typical educational environment outside the home, the passage of Public Law 99-457 in 1989 has promoted the provision of early childhood services within the context of the family. Thus, many early childhood intervention programs are home based.

# THE EDUCATIONAL SETTING FOR YOUNG CHILDREN

Zirpoli (1995) lists several variables related to the environment's influence on behavior within educational settings: social density, the physical layout, appropriate use of materials, effective scheduling, transitions, and staffing qualifications and ratios.

## Social Density

*Social density* refers to the number of children within the educational setting. Crowded settings are associated with less caregiver availability and responsiveness (Dunst, McWilliam, & Holbert, 1986). Also, crowded settings result in children being physically and socially withdrawn, as well as acting aggressively (Greenman, 1988). While most states have minimum space requirements for early childhood settings, these requirements provide only minimum standards, not recommended or state-of-the-art standards.

Throughout the day, many children feel overwhelmed by high levels of activity, noise, or ongoing contact with other children and caregivers. Providing safe, cozy areas for time alone is encouraged. Beanbag chairs, rocking chairs, cushioned areas with tape recorders and earphones, book nooks, and lofts can provide a great escape for young children. Sand and water tables are frequently effective for calming an overstimulated child. The soothing, tactile sensation of warm water on the hands is a great stress reducer for many children.

## Physical Layout

The physical layout should be safe, obviating too many restrictions set by the teacher. It should be divided into activity areas or learning centers, which include areas for art, dramatic play, science, language arts, sand and water play, music, manipulatives, and other games. Also, preschool programs must have areas for nap time, toileting, and eating, and space for children's personal belongings.

The physical layout should include separate active and quiet activity spaces, which will prevent play from one area affecting activities in other areas. At the same time, quiet activities should be in close proximity of other quiet activities. Quiet activity areas provide a place where children can retreat or pull themselves together when feeling overwhelmed from too much activity or involvement with many others. These include spots for reading, listening to tapes, and art activities.

By separating and defining play spaces, caregivers can eliminate many inappropriate behaviors. Tables, shelving, room dividers, and other furniture can create physical boundaries as the simplest way of defining separate activity areas. Importantly, caregivers should avoid large open spaces which invite children to run around within the classroom. These activities, of course, should be promoted in more appropriate settings such as the gym or playground.

The behaviors of young children are shaped by a variety of internal and environmental influences.

Zirpoli (1995) also recommends that caregivers limit the number of children per activity area to decrease the incidence of children fighting over space, toys, or other materials. Zirpoli (1995) suggests using the following methods for limiting the number of children per activity area:

- *Chairs:* Place a specific number of chairs at an activity table that corresponds to the number of children allowed at that table at a time.
- *Tickets:* Use tickets to limit the number of children allowed to enter an activity area. For example, four tickets could be placed in slots at the bottom of the ladder of a loft. If a ticket is available at the bottom of the stairs, the child may enter the loft. The child must take the ticket at the bottom of the ladder, take it to the top of the ladder, and place the ticket in the appropriate slot provided before entering the loft. When the child leaves the loft, the child returns the ticket in the original slot at the bottom of the ladder, indicating to other children that they may enter the loft.
- *Carpet squares:* The number of carpet squares may correspond to the number of children allowed to play in a specific activity area. For example, a block area designed for two children would have only two carpet squares on the floor within this play space. When both carpet squares are occupied, other children understand that they must select another activity.
- *Pictures:* Pictures of children playing paired with a corresponding number of children who may enter an area can be laminated and placed on the

wall or table near an activity. For example, a playhouse door may have a picture of two children playing alongside the number "2," indicating that a maximum of two children are allowed in the playhouse at a time.

• *Small rugs:* A bucket of small rugs may be used to define individual work and play spaces. A child may roll out a rug on the floor where she intends to play with a toy or other material. Other children understand that when a child is on one of these rugs, she wishes to be alone. When the individual play is finished, the child returns the materials to the appropriate place and the rug to the bucket. This is a great way to give children permission to play alone while a variety of group activities are available throughout the classroom. (p. 130)

## Appropriate Use of Materials

The appropriate use of materials within the preschool environment means providing opportunities for children to explore the environment independently with challenging yet age-appropriate materials. Young preschoolers are usually just beginning to share toys at playtime. Caregivers who expect children to share toys without guidance have unrealistic expectations. Children in a preschool class typically sit alongside one another but play by themselves. The teacher can facilitate the children's learning to respect others and their playthings.

Many schools use small carpet squares or rugs on which children sit and place their play materials (Bailey & Wolery, 1984). The children are taught that they must wait for materials to be placed back on the shelf or ask permission to play with materials. Children are more likely to ask or allow other children to share playthings on "their" rug if they are not forced to share and if they are given time when they may play with the materials alone. With limited and preferred items, caregivers may use timers. Children are usually compliant in turning over playthings to others when their time is up as long as the same rule applies to the other children as well.

Specific materials may be selected to promote desired behaviors. For example, playing with Play-Doh, Silly Putty, or fingerpaint and listening to story tapes or quiet music are calming activities. Calming activities may be used prior to circle or story time to encourage appropriate behavior.

## Effective Scheduling

One cannot discuss environmental factors in the classroom without addressing the issue of scheduling. Young children are likely to be more comfortable in the preschool classroom if they know what to expect. By following routines, children learn to expect snacks, free time, group times, stories, outdoor play, lunch, nap time, and so on. McEvoy et al. (1991) recommend that the preschool schedule "be divided into short time segments, depending on the length of the child's attention span and the nature of the activity" (p. 21). Schedules should follow the child's natural rhythm. Active play and group times should occur when children are well rested and fed. Passive and quiet activities, such as story time, should be utilized when children are tired or as a means of entertaining children during transition times (e.g., waiting for parents to pick up the child from school).

In the typical preschool classroom, a great portion of the child's day is spent waiting for an activity to begin, waiting for an activity to end, waiting in line to go to the bathroom, and waiting for others to settle down quietly for group times. These frequent transitions are one of the high-risk periods for behavior problems. Young children have great difficulty sitting quietly and waiting for long durations. Finding ways to reduce transition periods can significantly lessen behavioral problems in the classroom.

Rather than insisting that children be seated quietly before beginning group activities such as story times, teachers should instruct children to join the group for story time and begin reading when most are seated. Beginning a group activity with familiar songs or active finger plays will entice most children. When young children demonstrate a lack of interest in an activity, the teacher should be flexible and change the activity. McEvoy and Brady (1988) suggest that children rotate through activities independently rather than as a group. McWilliam, Trivette, and Dunst (1985) note a positive relationship between the level of a child's engagement with the environment and the efficacy of early intervention, including appropriate behavior. Small-group, child-directed activities rather than large-group, teacher-directed activities generally are recommended when trying to reduce the amount of transition time and to prevent disruptive behavior during the transition.

## Transitions

Transition periods can be a source of problem behaviors. Hurrying children during transition times is likely to cause some behavior problems, so planning and giving children warnings will be helpful. For example, when moving children from one situation (e.g., a play activity) to another (getting ready for lunch), scheduling time for putting toys away and washing hands will save caregivers the need to rush the children, and will be a warning to children that they are about to move to a different activity. Caregivers must be sensitive to the needs of children who, based on their developmental age, will need varying degrees of time to move from one activity to another. Allowing for some transition time and advance preparation will decrease the challenges.

## Staffing Qualifications and Ratios

Early childhood caregivers must be knowledgeable about young children's physical, cognitive, and social-behavioral development. They must understand the difference between inappropriate and age-appropriate behaviors. Most importantly, they must be knowledgeable about responding to children's behaviors. Teachers' expectations for young children are often too high. For example, teaching readiness skills, such as sitting and listening, are frequently overdone during the traditional "circle time" or group activities.

## Classroom Application 12.2

# Making Transitions Fun with Young Children

Susan is a preschool teacher who knows that transition periods are difficult for young preschoolers. Thus, she tries to prepare her students in advance of any transition. For example, when it is getting close to the time when the children must clean up after a play period, she shows them that she is setting the timer and tells them, "When the bell rings in 5 minutes, it will be cleanup time."

When the timer bell rings, Susan uses a song to indicate that it is cleanup time. Like most young children, her children love to sing. By singing through the transition time, Susan gives the children something to do while they put their materials away. She frequently includes the children's names in the songs. For example, "I like the way that Julia is cleaning and I like the way that Josh is putting his toys away" are made part of the song. Susan tries to ignore the children who are not following the directions, and, by including them in the song, she gives the children who are following directions lots of attention.

Susan also plays games with students to make transitions fun. For example, after a storytelling period about a caterpillar turning into a butterfly, she has the children pretend that they are caterpillars who are asleep in their cocoons waiting to become butterflies and fly away. She then tells the students that when she touches their them on their shoulders, they become butterflies and they can fly away to the snack table—the next activity. One by one, she touches each student, and they fly away to the next activity.

Classrooms should be active places where young minds can explore and young bodies can exercise. Group times should be fun but optional. If activities are inviting and stimulating, young children will readily join in song or story time. In many settings, however, there is considerable variance in children's developmental levels. Hence, not all children will be able to sit or be interested in the same materials. Small groups, whenever possible, are recommended. Reading times should not only be shared during large group times but also incorporated throughout the day on a one-to-one basis.

As with space density discussed earlier, minimum standards for child-caregiver ratios do not match state-of-the-art standards. They are what they are called: minimum standards. In many states, these standards are, at best, inappropriate. The National Association for the Education of Young Children (1997) recommends the following maximum child-caregiver ratios and class sizes per age of children:

| | |
|---|---|
| Infants | 1:3 ratio (maximum group 6) |
| 24–36 months | 1:6 ratio (maximum group 12) |
| 3 years | 1:8 ratio (maximum group 16) |
| 4–5 years | 1:10 ratio (maximum group 20) |
| 6–8 years | 1:12 ratio (maximum group 25) |

Supervision is one of the most important variables related to appropriate and inappropriate behavior in young children. The quantity and quality of staff supervision is a variable that may be manipulated to prevent inappropriate behaviors. In comparisons of one-to-one and zone staffing patterns, the zone arrangement was found to be superior (Dunst et al., 1986).

> *Caregivers are assigned activities or areas within the environment to supervise. Children are free to move to different activities within the classroom rather than wait for other children to finish activities. In the zone method, it is advisable to space staff throughout the classroom unless a group activity is scheduled.* (Zirpoli, 1995, p. 148)

Other recommendations for setting up the preschool environment to prevent inappropriate behavior are provided in Classroom Application 12.3.

In summary, environmental modifications suggested for the prevention of inappropriate behaviors include these:

- Allow adequate room for children to move within activity areas and from one area to the next. Children should not feel that they have to fight for their physical space.
- Employ rules that will reduce fighting over materials.
- Reduce transition or waiting times for activities—plan for transition.
- Keep children busy—busy children have little time for inappropriate behaviors (Bailey & Wolery, 1984).
- Provide a predictable and consistent environment through effective scheduling (McEvoy et al., 1991).
- Engage children in interesting activities at their developmental levels (Bailey & Wolery, 1984).
- Employ the Premack principle (see Chapter 7).
- Reinforce appropriate behaviors (see Chapter 7).
- Maintain a safe environment for children. Such a setting reduces the frequency of having to say, "No," "Don't touch that," "Stay away from there," and so on.
- Allow children to rotate through activities independently rather than as a group (McEvoy & Brady, 1988).
- Promote competence, confidence, and independence.
- Give children simple, age-appropriate responsibilities.
- Use daily rituals and routines to help make the home setting predictable and comforting.
- Allow children to have special things they do not have to share. Encourage—do not force—children to share.

# Classroom Application 12.3

## Organization for the Preschool Environment

Lisa is a preschool teacher and with school about to begin in a couple of weeks, organizing her classroom is her top priority. Lisa wants to arrange her classroom setting so that it is inviting and supportive. Most importantly, she wants to arrange the classroom setting so that the room encourages appropriate behavior.

She starts by putting compatible interest centers near each other. For example, she makes sure that the block area is not next to the quiet book/music area. Next, she makes sure that each area is well defined, as it is important that her children know where the art area begins and ends. Lisa decides to use small room dividers, carpet squares, and tape on the floor to designate her areas. Her children will have these cues to assist them in remembering to keep the crayons, blocks, and other materials in their assigned area.

Finally, Lisa sets up the room so that she can easily scan the room and see all of the children at all times. This is important to her because she wants to be able to intervene immediately in situations where she is needed.

After her room is set up, Lisa makes a schedule of activities. The schedule is important to her for two reasons. First, it will help her structure the day, as much as possible, for the children. Second, it will help her and her aides know where they should be and when. Free-play activities are the primary activity on her schedule. In addition, small- and large-group activities are also scheduled.

Lisa will allow her children to move through activities individually. For example, during a small-group activity such as pasting or coloring, some children will finish before other children, and she believes that they should be allowed to leave an activity as they finish. In addition, during free play she will encourage her children to practice skills that were introduced to them during the small- and large-group activities.

Next, Lisa orders materials to support her scheduled activities. She tries to select many materials that are pro-social or that require children to play cooperatively. For example, she orders lots of puzzles and building blocks. Lisa plans to rotate the toys in her classroom to keep them fresh and interesting. Thus, only some of the toys will be out on the shelves at the same time. Finally, she will place some very desirable materials on a shelf out of the children's reach. She knows that while the children will be able to see the toys, they will have to ask us for the toy or find a friend with whom to share a toy. This is one of her strategies to encourage language and social skills development.

Lastly, Lisa will assign her staff to certain areas of the classroom rather than assigning children to staff. By using a "zone" coverage strategy, Lisa and her staff will be able to work with an individual child when he or she enters a certain area of the classroom. In this way, Lisa and her aides will be able to work with all the children.

*(continued)*

Lisa knows that not all of her children's inappropriate behaviors will disappear in a well-organized classroom. However, she is determined to eliminate many problems related to classroom disorganization. She will do everything she can to reduce or eliminate waiting time or downtime. She plans to be ready for her children when an activity begins. In addition, while her free-play setting may look like "free choice" to the children, Lisa will set up each area to help children practice important skills. For Lisa, having an organized classroom environment helps her and her staff work more effectively with all the children, regardless of their behavioral needs.

## PARENT-TEACHER RELATIONSHIPS

The role of professional caregivers in facilitating positive and effective parent-child interactions cannot be overstated. When teachers and others make positive comments to parents regarding their children, parents tend to feel good about their child and to interact with him or her more frequently and positively. On the other hand, when teachers make many negative comments to parents about a child, parents tend to feel negatively about their child and interact with him or her less frequently and positively (Bell & Harper, 1977; Zirpoli & Bell, 1987).

Unfortunately, teachers tend to regard parents and parental involvement in mainly negative terms. Instead of viewing parents as partners in the challenge of educating children, teachers tend to perceive parents as an obstacle to their work (Williams & Chavkin, 1985). Teachers must understand, however, that there are significant gains to be had from encouraging parental involvement. In one inter-city study, Walberg (1980) found that when parents were encouraged to provide a work space at home for their child, praise their child's schoolwork, and cooperate with the teacher, students achieved twice the grade level gain of those in a control group. Sattes (1985) found that, as parents became more interested and involved in their children's school and achievement, their children's attitudes and achievement also improved.

Parents tend to reduce contact with teachers who always have "bad" news about their child's current performance or behavior. For example, parents may stop attending teacher-parent conferences if they consistently hear only negative news about their child. A good rule of thumb for teachers is to balance negative statements to parents with at least an equal number of positive statements. For example, when talking to parents about their child's inappropriate behavior, mention situations during which the child's behavior was appropriate. Try to make parents feel good about their children. Be supportive. Parenting is a difficult job even with well-behaved children. Parenting a child who has challenging behaviors may be all that a parent can handle. Adding to the parents' already stressful feelings and anxiety about the child's behavior will not be helpful.

When parents do not maintain contact with teachers or are not supportive, teachers should take the initiative to contact parents. These initiatives may go un-rewarded, and parents may continue to be unresponsive; nonetheless, it is still the

Children need strong parents to guide their social development.

teacher's professional responsibility to maintain regular, positive contact with the students' home environments. Although teachers may not realize or perceive any significant outcomes from these efforts, they must understand the potential positive influence these efforts have on parent-child relationships.

## SUMMARY

With more and more young children attending some form of day-care service, preschool, or early childhood intervention program, an understanding of some special behavioral considerations for newborns, infants, and young children is necessary. In addition, a new and growing problem with premature infants and infants born addicted to drugs (and related behaviors) is emerging. Research has demonstrated the effectiveness of early intervention in helping children develop academic readiness and appropriate social skills. Effective early intervention programs are integrated, comprehensive, normalized, adaptable, family referenced, and outcome based.

For the most part, the behavior of newborns is directly related to their physical situation and environment. Their cry is their primary means of communication to significant others. As infants develop, their understanding of the relationship between their behavior and the behavior of others increases. By their second birthday, young children are developing an awareness of appropriate versus inappropriate behavior. Much of their behavior is shaped by caregivers who establish limits and guidelines.

Premature and dysmature infants may be especially challenging for caregivers. Drugs, alcohol, and lead also place children at risk for developmental and behavioral problems. Poverty is, perhaps, the greatest handicap facing children in the United States. Indeed, 20% of all American children live in poverty.

Child maltreatment, a significant problem in the United States, is influenced by social-cultural, environmental, caregiver, and child variables. Breaking the cycle of child maltreatment involves terminating the widespread acceptance of physical punishment and making children's needs a national priority through the provision of early intervention to all at-risk children and families.

Appropriate caregiving for young children includes the establishment of a caring and loving environment for children as they develop. This atmosphere is accomplished by letting children know they are liked and loved, setting aside individual time, and giving children affection. Self-esteem may be developed in children by allowing and enabling children to be competent, telling children about the good things they do, speaking to children appropriately, teaching children it is all right to make mistakes, allowing children to make choices, letting children know their opinions are valued, and teaching children to respect individual differences.

Variables associated with appropriate behavior in young children include providing appropriate supervision, establishing a consistent and predictable environment, and teaching readiness skills for academic success. A greater emphasis must be placed on the prevention of inappropriate behaviors through a sensitivity to children's developmental stages, environmental considerations, and special attention to daily routines and children's physical needs.

Teachers are encouraged to facilitate parent-child-teacher relationships by making frequent contacts with parents and having positive comments to share about their children. Negative statements to parents about their children should always be balanced with positive comments to make parents feel good about their children and reinforce parent-teacher contacts.

## DISCUSSION QUESTIONS

1. Describe some of the social problems placing newborns and young children at greater risk than ever before.
2. Discuss the effectiveness of early intervention and the long-term benefits, especially with regard to costs.
3. What factors are related to child maltreatment?
4. List and discuss the elements of effective caregiving for young children.
5. Discuss some of the variables of classroom environments and associated influences on young children's behavior. With these variables in mind, design a preschool classroom setting.
6. Discuss the components of a preschool schedule that facilitate appropriate behavior. With these variables in mind, develop a preschool schedule for 4-year-olds.
7. How may teachers and parents facilitate effective parent-child-teacher relationships? Discuss the importance of effective parent-child-teacher relationships.

# REFERENCES

Ainsworth, M. D. S. (1979). Attachment as related to mother-infant interaction. In J. S. Rosenblatt, R. A. Hinde, C. Beer, & M. C. Busnel (Eds.), *Advances in the study of behavior* (Vol. 9, pp. 1–51). New York: Academic Press.

Annie E. Casey Foundation. (2001). *Kids count data book.* Baltimore: Author.

Bailey, D. B., & Wolery, M. (1984). *Teaching infants and preschoolers with handicaps.* Upper Saddle River, NJ: Merrill/Prentice Hall.

Barkley, R. A. (1987). *Defiant children: A clinician's manual for parent training.* New York: Guilford.

Baumeister, A. A., Kupstas, F., & Klindworth, L. M. (1990). New morbidity: Implications for prevention of children's disabilities. *Exceptionality, 1,* 1–16.

Bell, R. Q. (1968). A reinterpretation of the direction of effects in studies of socialization. *Psychological Review, 75,* 1171–1190.

Bell, R. Q., & Harper, L. V. (1977). *Child effects on adults.* Hillsdale, NJ: Erlbaum.

Belsky, J., & Vondra, J. (1989). Lessons from child abuse: The determinants of parenting. In D. Cicchetti & V. Carlson (Eds.), *Child maltreatment: Theory and research on the cause and consequences of child abuse and neglect* (pp. 203–253). New York: Cambridge University Press.

Bowlby, J. (1982). *Attachment.* New York: Basic Books.

Children's Defense Fund. (1995). *The state of America's children yearbook.* Washington, DC: Author.

Children's Defense Fund. (2003). *The state of America's children yearbook.* Washington, DC: Author.

Coeyman, M. (1998, August). Head Start loses some elbow room. *The Christian Science Monitor.*

Colvin, G., Sugai, G., Good, R. H., III, & Lee, Y. (1997). Using active supervision and precorrection to improve transition behaviors in an elementary school. *School Psychology Quarterly, 12,* 344–363.

Doke, L. A., & Flippo, J. R. (1983). Aggressive and oppositional behavior. In T. H. Ollendick & M. Hersen (Eds.), *Handbook of child psychopathology.* New York: Plenum.

Dunst, C. J., McWilliam, R. A., & Holbert, K. (1986). Assessment of preschool classroom environments. *Diagnostique, 11,* 212–232.

Egeland, B. (1990). Summary of findings from the Mother-Child Project and implications for program and policy. In *Crossing the boundaries between health and education* (pp. 1–2). Washington, DC: National Health/Education Consortium.

Egeland, B., Jacobvitz, D., & Papatola, K. (1984, May 20–23). *Intergenerational continuity of parental abuse.* Proceedings from the Conference on Biosocial Perspectives on Child Abuse and Neglect, Social Science Research Council, York, ME.

Enders, J., Montgomery, J., & Welch, P. (2002). Lead poison prevention. *Journal of Environmental Health, 64*(6), 20–26.

Ensher, G. L., & Clark, D. A. (1986). *Newborns at risk.* Rockville, MD: Aspen.

Fontana, V. J. (1971). *The maltreated child.* Springfield, IL: Thomas.

Fritz, G. K. (2000). Keep your eye on fetal alcohol syndrome. *Child and Adolescent Behavior Letter.* Providence, RI: The Brown University.

Gallagher, J. J., & Ramey, C. T. (1990). *The malleability of children*. Baltimore: Brookes.

Garbarino, J. (1982). *Children and families in the social environment*. New York: Aldine.

Greenman, J. (1988). *Caring spaces, learning spaces: Children's environments that work*. Redmond, WA: Exchange.

Hendrick, J. (1990). *Total learning: Developmental curriculum for the young child*. Upper Saddle River, NJ: Merrill/Prentice Hall.

Hetherington, E. M., & Martin, B. (1986). Family factors and psychopathology in children. In H. C. Quay & J. S. Werry (Eds.), *Psychopathological disorders of childhood*. New York: Wiley.

Hodgkinson, H. L. (1989). *The same client: The demographics of education and service delivery systems*. Washington, DC: Institute for Educational Leadership.

Howard, J. (1990, May 29). Substance abuse. In *Crossing the boundaries between health and education*. Washington, DC: National Health/Education Consortium.

Illinois State Board of Education. (2001). *Predicting the school percentage of ISAT scores that are below state standards*. Washington, DC: U.S. Department of Education.

Kauffman, J. M. (2001). *Characteristics of behavior disorders of children and Youth* (7th ed.). Upper Saddle River, NJ: Merrill/Prentice Hall.

Kilgore, K., Snyder, J., Lentz, C. (2000). The contribution of parental discipline, parental monitoring, and school risk to early-onset conduct. *Developmental Psychology, 36*(6), 835–845.

LaVigna, G. W., & Donnellan, A. M. (1986). *Alternatives to punishment: Solving behavior problems with non-aversive strategies*. New York: Irvington.

Lewis, T. J., Colvin, G., & Sugai, G. (2000). The effects of pre-correction and active supervision on the recess behavior of elementary students. *Education and Treatment of Children, 23*(2), 109–121.

Lyle, C. (1990). *The impact of hearing impairment on children's self-concept and strategies for building self-esteem*. Unpublished manuscript, University of St. Thomas, St. Paul, MN.

Mahoney, G., & Kaiser, A. (1999). Parent education in early intervention. *Topics in Early Childhood Special Education, 19*(3), 131–141.

Martin, B. (1975). Parent-child relations. In F. D. Horowitz (Ed.), *Review of child development research* (Vol. 4, pp. 463–540). Chicago: University of Chicago Press.

McEvoy, M. A., & Brady, M. P. (1988). Contingent access to play materials as an academic motivator for autistic and behavior disordered children. *Education and Treatment of Children, 11*, 5–18.

McEvoy, M. A., Fox, J. J., & Rosenberg, M. S. (1991). Organizing preschool environments: Suggestions for enhancing the development/learning of preschool children with handicaps. *Topics in Early Childhood Special Education, 11*, 18–28.

McWilliam, R. A., Trivette, C. M., & Dunst, C. J. (1985). Behavior engagement as a measure of the efficacy of early intervention. *Analysis and Intervention in Developmental Disabilities, 5*, 59–71.

Miller, K. (1989, January 15). Are we doing enough? *Sunday Magazine: Star Tribune* [Minneapolis], pp. 6–7.

National Academy of Sciences. (1996). *Fetal Alcohol Syndrome*. Washington, DC: National Academy Press.

National Association for the Education of Young Children. (1997). *Standards.* Washington, DC: Author.

National Health/Education Consortium. (1991). *Healthy brain development: Precursor to learning.* Washington, DC: Author.

Newacheck, P. W., Budetti, P. P., & Halfon, N. (1986). Trends in activity-limiting chronic conditions among children. *American Journal of Public Health, 76,* 178–184.

Nordquist, V. M., & Twardosz, S. (1990). Preventing behavior problems in early childhood special education classrooms through environmental organization. *Education and Treatment of Children, 13,* 274–287.

Patterson, G. R. (1982). *Coercive family process.* Eugene, OR: Castalia.

Pianta, R., Egeland, B., & Erickson, M. F. (1989). The antecedents of maltreatment: Results of the mother-child interaction research project. In D. Cicchetti & V. Carlson (Eds.), *Child maltreatment: Theory and research on the cause and consequences of child abuse and neglect* (pp. 203–253). New York: Cambridge University Press.

Pomeranz, V. E. (1986, January). You're going to spoil that child. *Parents,* 100.

Ramey, C. T., & Ramey, S. L. (1992). Effective early intervention. *Mental Retardation, 30,* 337–345.

Randall, C. L. (2001). Alcohol and pregnancy: Highlights from three decades of research. *Journal of Studies on Alcohol, 62*(5), 554–562.

Reid, R., Maag, J. W., & Vasa, S. F. (1993). Attention deficit hyperactivity disorder as a disability category: A critique. *Exceptional Children, 60,* 198–214.

Rose, T. L. (1983). A survey of corporal punishment of mildly handicapped students. *Exceptional Education Quarterly, 3,* 9–19.

Rosenthal, E. (1990, February). When a pregnant woman drinks. *New York Times Magazine,* p. 7.

Rusch, R. G., Hall, J. C., & Griffin, H. C. (1986). Abuse-provoking characteristics of institutionalized mentally retarded individuals. *American Journal of Mental Deficiency, 90,* 618–624.

Sattes, B. (1985). *Parent involvement: A review of the literature.* Appalachia Educational Laboratory.

Scarr, S., & Weinberg, R. (1986, November). The early childhood enterprise: Care and education of the young. *American Psychologist, 41,* 140–146.

Schonfeld, A., Mattson, S., Lang, A. R., Delis, D. C., & Riley, E. P. (2001). Verbal and nonverbal fluency in children with heavy prenatal alcohol exposure. *Journal of Studies on Alcohol, 62*(2), 239–247.

Schorr, L. B., & Schorr, D. (1989). *Within our reach: Breaking the cycle of disadvantage.* New York: Anchor Books.

Smith, A. N. (1990). Summary impact of Head Start on children, youth, and families. In *Crossing the boundaries between health and education.* Washington, DC: National Health/Education Consortium.

Sparling, J., Lewis, I., Ramey, C. T., Wasik, B. H., Bryant, D. M., & LaVange, L. M. (1991). Partners: A curriculum to help premature, low birthweight infants get off to a good start. *Topics in Early Childhood Special Education, 11,* 36–55.

Starr, R. H., Jr. (1982). A research-based approach to the prediction of child abuse. In R. H. Starr, Jr. (Ed.), *Child abuse prediction: Policy implications* (pp. 105–134). Cambridge, MA: Ballinger.

Straus, M. A., Gelles, R. J., & Steinmetz, S. K. (1980). *Behind closed doors: Violence in the American family*. New York: Anchor.

United States Census Bureau. (2000). *Current Population Survey, March 1999.* Washington, DC: Author.

Walberg, H. J., Bole, R. E., & Waxman, H. C. (1980). School-based family socialization and reading achievement in the inner city. *Psychology in the Schools, 17,* 509–514.

Weikart, D. P. (1990, May 29). Early childhood programs for disadvantaged children. In *Crossing the boundaries between health and education.* Washington, DC: National Health/Education Consortium.

Williams, D., & Chavkin, N. (1985). *Guidelines and strategies to train teachers for parent involvement.* Austin, TX: Southwestern Educational Development Laboratory.

Woolfolk, A. E. (1987). *Educational psychology.* Upper Saddle River, NJ: Prentice Hall.

Yamaguchi, B. J., Strawser, S., & Higgins, K. (1997). Children who are homeless. *Intervention in School and Clinic, 33,* 90–97.

Zigler, E., & Hall, N. W. (1989). In D. Cicchetti & V. Carlson (Eds.), *Child maltreatment: Theory and research on the cause and consequences of child abuse and neglect* (pp. 203–253). New York: Cambridge University Press.

Zirpoli, S. B. (1995). Designing environments for optimal behavior. In T. J. Zirpoli (Ed.), *Understanding and affecting the behavior of young children* (pp. 122–151). Upper Saddle River, NJ: Merrill/Prentice Hall.

Zirpoli, T. J. (1986). Child abuse and children with handicaps. *Remedial and Special Education, 7,* 39–48.

Zirpoli, T. J. (1990). Physical abuse: Are children with disabilities at greater risk? *Intervention in School and Clinic, 26,* 6–11.

Zirpoli, T. J., & Bell, R. Q. (1987). Unresponsiveness in children with severe disabilities: Potential effects on parent-child interactions. *Exceptional Child, 34,* 31–40.

Zirpoli, T. J., Snell, M. E., & Loyd, B. H. (1987). Characteristics of persons with mental retardation who have been abused by caregivers. *Journal of Special Education, 21,* 31–41.

# ADOLESCENT BEHAVIOR

## Understanding Influences and Modifying Outcomes

### Stephanie D. Madsen

*The young are permanently in a state resembling intoxication; for youth is sweet and they are growing.*

ARISTOTLE, NICOMACHEAN ETHICS (4TH C.B.C.), 7.14, TR. J. A. K. THOMSON

*Young people are thoughtless as a rule.*

HOMER, ODYSSEY (9TH C.B.C.), 7, TR. E. V. RIEU

Adolescence has long been both idolized as a youthful, idealistic time, and vilified as a period fraught with problem behavior and insolent attitudes. Our perceptions are shaped, in part, by the media's attention to the risky behaviors for which adolescents are known. Teenage pregnancy, school and street violence, underage drinking, and school dropouts are frequent stories on the evening news. Popular culture further influences our perceptions by portraying adolescents as self-absorbed, moody, and apathetic toward their families and futures. But are these portrayals accurate?

Research on adolescence suggests that although it can be a challenging period, these portrayals fail to capture the richness of the adolescent period. For example, we know that many individuals with trouble-free childhoods engage in antisocial behavior (e.g., vandalism, petty theft) in adolescence. However, most people do not continue this behavior beyond adolescence, but rather report emerging into adulthood relatively unscathed. In addition, some of the most troubling statistics, such as the teen birthrate, rate of teen deaths by homicide and suicide, and rate of high school dropouts, actually have been declining in recent years (Kids Count Data Book Online, 2002). Furthermore, although it is true that relationships with families are more conflict-filled in adolescence (Laursen & Collins, 1994), most teens remain close to their families throughout adolescence and continue to adhere to parental values on moral issues (Collins, 1997; Smetana, 1988). Still, adolescence remains a time when youth are at an increased risk for problem behavior (Arnett, 1999).

Since our culturally bound beliefs about adolescence tell only part of the story, it may be useful to limit our value judgments on the behaviors of these developing individuals. If we instead try to understand how these behaviors function within the teenager's present developmental and environmental contexts, we may be able to effectively shape these behaviors and promote alternate behaviors that are likely to lead to better current and future outcomes. Advancing this understanding of adolescent behaviors and reviewing adolescent behavior modification programs and issues will be the major focus of this chapter.

Adolescence is commonly considered to span the ages of 12–18. Youth at this age are no longer children in need of our constant guidance, nor are they fully mature, with all of the rights and responsibilities of adulthood. This period is defined by the many transitions that characterize it. Adolescents change physically, cognitively, emotionally, and socially. Their environmental contexts change (e.g., school and work), and as they gain independence their decisions seem to have greater consequences for their lives compared to when they were children. Adolescents are sometimes considered to be a difficult group to work with because of their rapidly fluctuating moods, attitudes, and resulting behaviors. At the same time, adolescents can be a highly rewarding group with which to work. The sheer transitory nature of this period means that adolescents are open to change. In effect, a window is open, and interventions begun in this period have the potential of effecting long-lasting and meaningful change. Teachers are in a unique position of having regular access to adolescents in a structured setting. Adolescents continue to value relationships with adults and continue to need their guidance. Teachers in middle and high schools are asked not only to teach their lesson plans and prepare students to pass exams, but also to equip students with a repertoire of behaviors that will allow them to avoid risky behavior, interact successfully in social situations, and achieve their goals in life. It appears that the developmental status of these students and the environmental context of school make ideal partners to accomplish these objectives.

The purpose of this chapter is to provide you with a solid background for how teachers might apply behavioral modification techniques to adolescent populations. First, this chapter will introduce you to the key developmental changes of adolescence by emphasizing the resulting changes in adolescents' behavior. Individual adolescents are changing physically, cognitively, emotionally, and socially. The greater contexts surrounding adolescents (e.g., educational setting, others' expectations) are changing simultaneously. Second, factors that promote adolescents' optimal development will be explored. Third, research on current behavioral modification foci will be reviewed. Although there is some overlap with the kinds of behaviors elementary school teachers wish to modify, adolescents' growing maturity presents new opportunities and challenges for interventions. Finally, issues particular to adolescent interventions will be discussed. For example, what types of programs are most successful and what are some potential pitfalls of using them with adolescent populations? It is hoped that by understanding the developmental changes inherent in adolescence and the pathways to optimal developmental outcomes, you will be better able to use the tools of behavior modification to effectively alter adolescent behavior.

## UNDERSTANDING THE CHANGING BEHAVIOR OF ADOLESCENTS

Although people are constantly developing throughout their lives, the changes that take place during the second decade of life are striking. Physical, cognitive, social, and relational changes intersect with contextual changes. In understanding adolescent behavior, you should take note of not only the great advances that are made in these areas, but also the limitations that remain.

## Physical Changes

The physical changes the body goes through in adolescence are the most rapid it has seen since infancy. The major physical changes, and some of the ways they affect behavior, are outlined here.

### Puberty

The most salient physical change during adolescence is puberty. Puberty marks the onset of the capability of reproduction. In the United States, the average age for girls to begin menstruating is 12.5 years, with European American girls typically starting a bit later than African American girls do (Brooks-Gunn & Reiter, 1990). Most girls (95% of the population) reach puberty between the ages of 9 and 16. Boys lag behind girls by a few years; boys' average age for reaching sexual maturity is 14 years. Most boys (95% of the population) enter puberty between the ages of 10 and 19 (Brooks-Gunn & Reiter, 1990).

The ways in which puberty impacts adolescent behavior are related, in part, to the reactions of others. Once a child looks physically mature, he or she may be assumed to have greater mental and emotional maturity too, regardless of whether or not this is true. The timing of puberty—whether one matures early, late, or on time with respect to peers—has been shown to play an important role in whether pubertal changes are a positive or negative force in adolescents' lives. For boys, maturing early has some benefits. Early-maturing boys are perceived as adultlike and may be given greater leadership roles. In addition, their greater strength and speed are valued by their peers in athletic arenas. For girls, maturing early seems to carry some costs. These girls often report feeling awkward around their peers, tend to hang out with an older crowd, begin dating earlier than their peers, and may be pressured into sexual experiences before they are ready (Stattin & Magnusson, 1990). Boys who mature later than their peers might find that situation to be personally challenging, as it is for Justin in Vignette 13.1, but research has not revealed any long-term negative effects. Maturing late may actually be advantageous for girls, as they are given more time to be children, and are somewhat protected from body image problems stemming from cultural perceptions of the weight gain that accompanies puberty.

Historically speaking, the average age for reaching puberty is decreasing. This secular trend may be due to better nutrition, sanitation, and control of infectious disease. Although the average age for girls to begin menstruating is unlikely to dip far below 12 years, a significant minority of girls may show one or more signs of puberty by age 7. Therefore, the effects of puberty may begin well before adolescence, often to the surprise of parents, teachers, peers, and the child herself.

### Brain Development

Students are sometimes surprised to learn that the brain is still developing in adolescence. Changes that happen during this period make the brain more efficient: (1) unnecessary connections among brain cells are eliminated; (2) the formation of

## VIGNETTE 13.1
●

### *Boys and Puberty*

Justin is a 15-year-old boy with a slight build. Last year, when Justin was in 8th grade, his teachers described him as being full of energy, helpful to other students, and well liked in his small circle of friends. However, over summer vacation most of his peers reached puberty, and Justin now experiences considerable teasing due to his short stature, high voice, and childlike features. Justin lacks the social skills to cope with his friends when they tease him. He is clearly hurt by their words and actions, yet Justin has not been able to effectively communicate this in a way that will end the teasing.

Justin's older brother suggests that he just try to ignore the teasing, and to draw attention elsewhere. Justin takes this advice to heart and decides to build on his strengths. He joins a mixed-sex peer group and starts some cross-sex friendships with girls who do not join in with the teasing. To win respect among his male peers, he focuses on his soccer-playing abilities. Justin is quick on the soccer field, while his developing peers are sometimes clumsy with their newly long limbs. When his peers occasionally do tease him, he makes a joke and teases back in a nonthreatening way. Eventually Justin reaches puberty, but is already well accepted among his peers.

---

myelin sheaths around nerve fibers is completed, allowing messages to travel faster in the brain; and (3) brain functions become more localized on either the right or the left side of the cerebral cortex. These changes are reflected in adolescents' greater memory and problem-solving abilities. But as its efficiency increases, the brain looses the ability to easily take on new functions. The brain does not recover from trauma as easily, and if certain experiences haven't happened before adolescence, the skills associated with them may be more difficult to acquire. For example, although most secondary language instruction happens during adolescence, our brains would actually be more receptive to learning this material before adolescence.

One of the last parts of the brain to finish developing is the prefrontal cortex, or the area at the front of the brain. We use this area for planning and anticipating the consequences of our actions. Because teenagers are still developing these neurological capabilities, they may have trouble thinking of the long-term impact of their risky behavior on their own. Similarly, some of the impulsiveness we see in teens may be partly attributed to their still-developing brains.

### *Changes in Moods*

Teenagers are noted for their rapid mood swings and general moodiness. Hormones are thought to be partially responsible for these emotional changes, especially among younger adolescents. Early in the pubertal process, when the hormonal system is being turned on, hormones fluctuate rapidly and result in fluctuating moods. In early adolescence boys tend to become more irritable, aggressive, and impulsive, whereas girls tend to react with more depressed moods.

But beyond early adolescence, the direct link between hormones and moods is relatively weak. Stressful changes in adolescents' environments may be just as important as biological factors in influencing their moods. Using a method known as the Experience Sampling Method, researchers outfitted adolescents with beepers in order to track the effect of contextual factors on moods. Adolescents carried the beepers with them everywhere they went for a week. The adolescents were beeped at random times. When they were beeped, adolescents recorded where they were, what they were doing, whom they were with, and whether their mood was positive or negative. The researchers found that adolescents experienced emotional extremes (both positive and negative) more often than adults did. However, changes in moods were linked to what the teen was doing rather than biological changes (Larson, Czikszentmihalyi, & Graef, 1980). Since adolescents change contexts and activities quite frequently, they may be moodier than adults or children.

### Sleep Requirements

Researchers have also suggested that adolescents' moodiness might be due to their failure to get enough sleep. In fact, most adolescents (and many adults) operate in a state of sleep deprivation (Maas, 2002). Teenagers' preferences for staying up late and then sleeping in are actually tied to biological changes. When allowed to determine their sleep schedules, most teens stay up until 1:00 A.M. and sleep until 10:00 A.M. However, school schedules often force teens to adhere to sleep schedules more suited for children or adults, leaving adolescents sleepy during school hours (Carskadon, Wolfson, Acebo, Tzischinsky, & Seifer, 1998). In fact, adolescents are sleepiest between 8:00 A.M. and 9:00 A.M. and most alert after 3:00 P.M., posing obvious challenges to those trying to maintain their attention during class!

## Cognitive Changes

Middle schools and high schools offer a bevy of classes not available in elementary schools. Adolescents can now take classes in areas such as higher level math (e.g., algebra, calculus), foreign languages, sciences, and civics. Each of these classes takes advantage of advances in adolescents' expanding cognitive abilities. Compared to students in elementary schools, adolescents have a greater capacity to think systematically, employ their memorization and attention abilities, and consider abstract concepts.

### Hypothetico-Deductive Reasoning

The scientific method involves developing a series of hypotheses or predictions and then testing them in an orderly fashion by isolating the relevant variables and excluding the irrelevant ones. In his classic pendulum problem, Jean Piaget gave children strings of different lengths and objects of different weights and asked them to determine what influences the speed of the pendulum. Children usually failed this test because they randomly tested different combinations, and ended their testing before they had exhausted all possibilities. Adolescents were able to systematically test the different factors and determine that only the length of the string makes a difference. This ability to reason systematically is considered a hallmark of adolescent cognitive development, and is referred to as *hypothetico-deductive reasoning*. Older adolescents are better at consistently using formal reasoning, whereas younger adolescents appear to use this ability in some situations, but not others. The use of formal reasoning does not appear to be universally present in all cultures, but rather is heavily tied to participation in a schooling system that promotes this type of thinking.

Adolescents' advances in reasoning abilities can also pose new challenges to parents and teachers. Adolescents are now capable of developing more sophisticated arguments promoting their preferences. The standard adult response of "because," or other weak arguments are unlikely to go unchallenged by an adolescent. On the other hand, cognitive reasoning skills may be useful in developing social skills. For example, adolescents could generate a list of hypotheses why another student didn't say hello to them in the hall (e.g., she didn't see me, he was absorbed in thought) rather than jumping prematurely to a negative conclusion (e.g., she hates me, he is avoiding me).

### Abstract Thinking

When they do reason, younger children tend to reason more about the concrete world—the things that they can see and touch. Adolescents are able to reason about abstract concepts or ideas (e.g., justice, peace, the environment). This ability creates a more complex world for adolescents to think about. For example, consider two siblings, David (age 9) and Kimberly (age 17), who watched a documentary about the problems of pollution. The documentary left both of them concerned and anxious to do their part to help the environment. David, focusing on the concrete world, organizes his friends to clean up the neighborhood park. Kimberly has the advanced cognitive capabilities to consider the long-term implications of pollution, the moral obligations of corporations with poor environmental practices, and the difficulties associated with seemingly simple, obvious solutions such as outlawing all industry. After a little thought, Kimberly organizes her friends to help out with the political campaign of a local candidate who supports environmental reform. Both David and Kimberly are reasoning about the environment, but Kimberly is able to conceptualize the problem in a more abstract way, and deal with the issues on a deeper level.

The ability to reason about abstract issues can raise difficult philosophical, religious, and identity-based questions for adolescents. Although teenagers are sometimes thought to be superficial in their concerns with their friends and appearance, they actually are confronted with a whole new set of complex issues to make sense of, right at a time when they are immersed in a host of physical and social changes. It can sometimes feel overwhelming for them to tackle all of these issues at once.

The ability to think abstractly can serve adolescents well in their social interactions; these abilities allow adolescents to consider possible behaviors without actually acting them out. For example, if a girl feels her friend is neglecting her for her boyfriend, she might think through possible ways of approaching this issue with her friend, and then select the one that is likely to result in the best outcome. Many behavioral interventions aimed at adolescents capitalize on these newly advanced cognitive abilities.

### Social Cognitive Beliefs

Cognitive developments intersect with social ones, altering ways adolescents think about themselves and those around them. Teens sometimes feel as though they are the focus of everyone's attention, creating an *imaginary audience* that is watching them and taking note of their every behavior. Though adolescents frequently engage in social comparison and are attentive to their peers' behaviors, teens often take their concern about others' attentions to an unjustified extreme. For example, note the reaction of the young man who slipped in front of his art class (see Classroom Application 13.1). In adolescence, teens spend more time alone than they did in childhood (Larson, Richards, Moneta, & Holmbeck, 1996). Part of adolescents' desire to spend time alone might reflect the tremendous energy that is required to act in an environment where they feel as though they are constantly under surveillance.

The *personal fable* is the belief that your experiences, thoughts, and feelings are totally unique. Teenagers reflect this belief with feelings that they are invulnerable, and actions that seem foolish to more mortal-feeling adults (e.g., fast driving, excessive drinking). The personal fable stems, in part, from adolescents' relative unfamiliarity with their changing world and their changing selves. For example, when a teenager first falls in love, this feeling might be stronger than any he or she has ever experienced before. Given this overwhelming feeling, the adolescent might feel it is reasonable to conclude that there has never been a love like this before, and that risky behaviors (e.g., unprotected sex) are warranted by the situation. Feelings of uniqueness and invulnerability might lead the teenager to believe he or she is immune from unwanted outcomes (e.g., pregnancy or disease). The *personal fable* diminishes as the adolescent builds up more experiences and learns from the experiences of those around him or her.

## Social and Relational Changes

### Search for Identity

When asked to describe themselves, very young children tend to mention their possessions ("I am the owner of a red tricycle") or their appearances ("I am tall"). By elementary school, children include social group membership ("I am a Boy Scout"), relationships ("I am Malika's friend"), and some psychological traits ("I am nice") in their definitions (Livesley & Bromley, 1973). By adolescence, descriptions become more complex. Adolescents realize that who they are might change with different settings or relationships ("I am shy at school but outgoing with my friends"). They also can imagine who they might be ("I am going to become a better athlete by practicing harder"). Compared to children in middle childhood, adolescents view themselves in

## Classroom Application 13.1

# Junior High Concerns

This fictitious letter illustrates the seemingly extreme reactions teenagers sometimes have to ordinary situations. What cognitive changes might be responsible for the student's reaction to this situation? What advice would you offer this teacher?

Dear Advice Columnist:

I teach junior high school students and my students' behaviors baffle me at times. It seems that students reapply their makeup between classes and inspect each other's outfits daily. Changing clothes for gym and getting the perfect school photo are big topics of discussion.

I'm concerned about one student in particular, though. The other day this student slipped during art class and got paint all over his clothes and in his hair. The other students laughed at him, but were quickly quieted. This student didn't come to school the next day, and now I hear that he is talking to the counselor about switching schools. Can you help me understand how he could arrive at such an extreme response to such an ordinary accident?

Troubled Teacher

terms of what makes them different or unique from their peers, showing that they value their individuality. Adolescents also are capable of reflecting on and evaluating themselves, which leads them to believe that they should be able to make their own decisions and create their own set of values.

These changes in thinking about the self are tied to the broader issue of developing an identity, which is the integration of all the different aspects of the self. Adolescents form their identities by trying on different ideas, appearances, behaviors, and relationships. Adults may sometimes be frustrated by a teenager who wants to attend a service of a different religion, dress in a nontraditional way, or hang out with a different set of friends. Although teenagers still need adult guidance, this experimentation and exploration of different possibilities of the self is considered essential in forming a healthy identity. Once an identity is established, it can be used to guide the individual's future actions.

### *Growing Autonomy and Parent-Adolescent Relationships*

At one time, it was believed that adolescents needed to deindividuate from their parents and to completely separate from the family to be emotionally healthy. Now researchers realize that a more appropriate goal is for adolescents to become autonomous, gaining ownership over their thoughts and behaviors, but to remain emotionally connected to their families (Ryan & Lynch, 1989). Still, parents and teenagers must negotiate the timing and extent of this independence.

In his expectancy-violation model, Collins (1990) suggests that the handing over of authority from parent to teenager is a gradual process. Both parents and teenagers carry expectancies about how the other should behave (e.g., an expectation that the child will follow rules set by the parents). Times of rapid change, such as adolescence, lead to violations of expectations (e.g., a curfew is broken), resulting in conflict. In order to maintain the relationship (and any hope of influencing the teenager in the future), the parent and teenager need to resolve their conflict, and realign their behavior (e.g., teenager resolves never to break curfew again), or, more commonly, their expectations (e.g., a new rule is created, stating that the teenager must phone for a curfew extension). In this way, the relationship is maintained, and more and more control is gradually relinquished to the teenager.

Much of the conflict surrounding issues of autonomy concerns rather mundane issues such as hairstyle, clothing, and curfew (Steinberg, 1990). In a study of autonomy, Judith Smetana (1988) asked teenagers in the 6th, 8th, and 10th grades, and their parents, to think about 24 hypothetical situations, and to decide whether the teenager or the parent should be in control of the issue. Some of these issues concerned friendship (e.g., when to see friends, who your friends are), personal matters (e.g., watching television, choosing clothes), and prudential matters (e.g., smoking, eating junk food, drinking), while others

Adolescents who are supported by significant adults in their lives have a better chance for coping with the major changes that occur during the teen years.

## Classroom Application 13.2

# Earning Autonomy and Free Time

Ms. Knutson teaches seventh-grade language arts. Her classes run smoothly, for the most part, and she is able to get through her lessons as planned. However, she finds that the students in her eighth-hour section just cannot seem to get things together to finish their work on time. This class spends more time chatting and moves slower than the other sections.

Ms. Knutson wants to bring this section up to speed. She considers how a behavioral approach might make use of the developmental issues already at play in adolescents' lives. She knows that adolescence is a time of striving for greater autonomy; being granted a little autonomy in the classroom might be a strongly motivating factor for these students. She also knows that her students are just learning to use their increased metacognitive skills; they can set longer-term goals and plan for how to manage their time to meet these goals.

Using this information, Ms. Knutson announces to her eighth-hour group that she is going to start posting each day's "agenda" on the board. Students can see exactly what they need to accomplish each day. Agenda items that are not completed will be assigned as homework. She tells them that they will be responsible for keeping the class on schedule, granting them greater autonomy in the process. The class also discusses time management issues.

Under this new system, students encourage each other to complete their tasks on time. Ms. Knutson is careful to post agendas that are manageable so that the class will be negatively reinforced (i.e., by receiving no homework) for staying on task. Occasionally, Ms. Knutson will post an entire week's agenda on the board. If students finish all of the items on Tuesday's agenda, she asks if they would like to get started on Wednesday's agenda. At the end of the week, if the class has met its posted agenda, students are allowed to have a bit of free time or to do something else that they enjoy. By giving the students greater responsibility and by making use of their growing cognitive abilities, Ms. Knutson is able to get her class back on track.

concerned moral issues (e.g., taking someone else's money). Not surprisingly, parents and teens each believed that they should retain control of most of the issues, with teens tending to view the issues as a matter of personal choice. However, both parents and teens agreed that parents should retain jurisdiction when the issue was a moral one. So although adolescents' striving for autonomy creates conflict within the family, most teenagers retain the values of their family and wish to maintain those relationships. In fact, very few teenagers (about 3% of girls and 5–9% of boys) reject their parents outright (Rutter, Graham, Chadwick, & Yule, 1976). Instead, parents remain important figures in adolescents' lives, and are valued for the aid and advice they provide (Furman & Burmester, 1992).

Adolescents' desire for autonomy extends beyond the reach of the family and into the classroom. Classroom Application 13.2 illustrates how one teacher made use of adolescents' desire for autonomy as a positive source of change.

### Peer Relationships

During adolescence, teenagers begin to spend more time with their friends than they do with their parents (Larson, et al., 1996). Friendships are a source of mutual understanding, intimacy, and commitment.

Although friendships can be a positive force in adolescents' lives, adults have expressed concern about the role of peer pressure in adolescent behavior. Research shows that conformity to peers peaks in early adolescence to midadolescence and it greatly diminishes by late adolescence (Berndt, 1979). In all stages of adolescence, however, the identity of one's friends influences behaviors (Hartup & Stevens, 1997). Adolescents who have delinquent friends are much more likely to participate in delinquent acts than are other teens. It seems that delinquent teenagers not only select each other as friends, but also "train" each other in how to behave delinquently (Dishion, Andrews, & Crosby, 1995). Alternatively, having a group of friends who value academics may lead a teenager to improve his or her academic performance.

Dating and romantic relationships have only recently begun to receive attention as important peer relationships in adolescents' lives (Furman, Brown, & Feiring, 1999). Most adolescents have had some experience with dating by age 15 (Feiring, 1996). These relationships are brief, lasting an average of four months at age 15, but intense (Feiring, 1996). Adolescents with boyfriends or girlfriends typically have wider mood swings than teens without romantic partners (Larson, Clore, & Woods, 1999).

## Contextual Changes

In addition to all of the changes occurring within the adolescent, there are a host of contextual changes with which teenagers must contend:

- School transition: Middle school and high school have far less structure and support than elementary school.
- Changing legal status: Adolescents are granted adult status in some arenas (e.g., driving, voting), but not others (e.g., drinking alcohol).
- Entry into employment: Almost all adolescents are employed at some point while attending high school, exposing them to a context with greater responsibilities, and possibly more mature peers.
- Broader sociocultural factors: Assumptions fueled by stereotypes affect how the public responds to teenage behaviors.

## Cumulative Effect of Changes

Clearly adolescence is a time wrought with change. Simmons and her colleagues (1979) studied the cumulative effect of multiple changes in adolescence. They followed 800 young people at the transition from elementary school to junior high school and found that girls who began menstruating, started dating, and changed schools during the same year experienced the greatest declines in self-esteem across the transition to junior high. It appears that the *number* of stressful events going on in adolescents' lives may be more important than any one specific stressful event. Other researchers have supported this idea that we should be most concerned about adolescents who are experiencing multiple changes at once, and that we should be especially concerned about adolescents who lack the resources to deal with all of these changes simultaneously.

# PREDICTING POSITIVE OUTCOMES FOR ADOLESCENTS

What do we know about factors in adolescents' lives that promote optimal behavioral outcomes? Although high self-esteem, low feelings of anxiety or alienation, and frequent participation in extracurricular activities are commonly assumed to protect adolescents from problem behaviors, in fact these factors do not predict fewer problem behaviors in adolescence (Gottfredson, 2001). Instead, research shows that the internal and external assets described next relate to positive outcomes; they protect adolescents from high-risk behaviors, enhance the likelihood of engaging in positive behaviors, and promote resilience in the face of adversity. The more protective factors a teenager has working to his or her advantage, the more likely he or she is to avoid problem behaviors. Adolescents without the benefit of these protective factors are not doomed to poor outcomes, but may face greater challenges. To illustrate, consider the stories of Amy and Nick in Vignette 13.2 on pages 457–458. Both teenagers were arrested for their behaviors, but differ in terms of the protective factors they can draw upon to recover from their delinquent behavior.

## Internal Assets

Some of the most important assets for youth are the ones they carry within themselves. Four key internal assets identified by the Minneapolis Search Institute (Benson, Scales, Leffert, & Roehlkepartain, 1999) include the following:

- a commitment to lifelong learning and education
- positive values that guide future choices
- social competencies to build relationships and make wise decisions
- positive identity in the form of a strong sense of self-worth

These assets result from a community's commitment to actively promote them. When families, schools, media, religious institutions, and neighborhoods work together continuously, youth have the greatest chance of benefiting from these supportive features.

# External Assets

The remaining assets, or predictors of positive outcomes, may be considered external assets since they reside outside the adolescent. They are tied together in that they all offer support, feelings of empowerment, boundaries and expectations, and a constructive use of time.

## Supportive Relationships

Peers and friends provide important sources of self-validation, cooperation, mutual respect, and security (Newcomb & Bagwell, 1996). They are especially important in adolescents' lives because they represent voluntary relationships where members are on equal levels. This context is ideal for providing mutual support, and also for developing important conflict resolution skills within a safe environment.

Parents can also be developmental assets for adolescents. Extensive research has shown that authoritative parenting, or parenting that combines warmth with structure and rules, is related to the best outcomes for adolescents (Steinberg, 2001). Adolescents with authoritative parents are less likely to engage in problem behavior, including drug and alcohol use, and delinquency. These adolescents also enjoy better mental health, including higher self-esteem and lower rates of anxiety and depression. Furthermore, they achieve more in school than adolescents with parents who do not employ this combination of warmth and structure.

Although adolescents generally view teachers with greater mistrust and find fewer opportunities to establish relationships with teachers than they did as elementary school students, teachers remain important influences in adolescents' lives. Support from teachers is unique from both parent and peer support in that it relates to interest in attending class, pursuing academic goals, and adhering to rules and norms (Wentzel, 1998). Furthermore, adolescents who perceive their teachers as supportive are more likely to behave prosocially and to engage in behaviors that promote their learning (Wentzel & Battle, 2001).

Other adults in adolescents' lives may also act as developmental assets. Grandparents, mentors, or neighbors can all provide guidance for teenagers. Especially in the absence of a strong parent-adolescent relationship, other adults may fill this gap and provide important support.

## Balancing School and Work Roles

Given that most American adolescents are employed at some point during high school, how might work experiences in adolescence contribute to positive outcomes? Working teens' perceptions of the effects of their employment are overwhelmingly positive (Mortimer, Harley, & Aronson, 1999). Adolescents cite gains in responsibility, money management, and acquiring social skills as key benefits. Hours worked per week do not have a significant effect on time spent doing homework (Mortimer et al., 1999), in large part because working adolescents spend significantly less time watching television. Adolescents appear to benefit most from employment that is limited to part-time work. Minor delinquency is greater for teens who work long hours, or who do not work at all, than it is for teens occupied by part-time work (Wofford, 1988). Similarly, working excessive hours limits educational attainment, while part-time work encourages adolescents to balance their roles as students and employees (Mortimer et al., 1999). Beyond the number of hours worked, it is important that the level of the job be appropriate to the adolescents' capabilities. Adolescents who work in highly stressful jobs are more likely to experience depression (Shanahan, Finch, Mortimer, & Ryu, 1991), whereas those working in jobs with high autonomy and clearly defined roles experience gains in self-esteem (Barling, Rogers, & Kelloway, 1995).

### Community Factors

One often overlooked but important developmental asset for youth is the value that communities place on youth. Unfortunately, only one in five youths feels that his or her community values youth (Benson et al., 1999). Sixty percent of adolescents feel that they are part of a caring neighborhood and only twenty-five percent feel that their schools provide a caring environment. Furthermore, reports of perceived caring decline from middle to high school. These factors may be particularly important because they represent the influence of relationships beyond the immediate family. Such relationships are important for building self-esteem, transmitting cultural customs, developing social competencies, and, perhaps most critically, compensating for suboptimal familial relationships.

## Avoiding Developmental Deficits

In a study of 99,462 6th- through 12th-grade youth, the Minneapolis Search Institute uncovered five key correlates of poor outcomes for adolescents:

- being home alone
- attending parties where there is drinking
- being a victim of violence
- overexposure to television
- experiencing physical abuse

Engaging in or experiencing these behaviors increases the likelihood that adolescents will also engage in high-risk behaviors such as drinking, gambling, use of drugs, and acts of violence. On average, an adolescent will experience approximately two of these five deficits (Benson et al., 1999). Measures that help teens to avoid these deficits (e.g., greater parental monitoring of activities, youth centers providing structured after-school activities, violence prevention programs) are likely to promote positive developmental outcomes for adolescents.

## VIGNETTE 13.2

### Amy and Nick: Do You Know Them?

Amy and Nick are 17-year-old juniors at Central High School. Amy, an honors student and basketball player, was arrested over the weekend for possession of alcohol. She was released into the custody of her parents after paying a $500 fine. This was Amy's first encounter with the law for delinquent activity. As a result of Amy's arrest, she was suspended from extracurricular activities for the remainder of the semester in compliance with her school's discipline policy and athletic rules. She also met with the guidance counselor once a week to discuss the potential problems associated with drinking, ways to refuse alcohol without alienating her friends, and alternative activities teenagers might enjoy without alcohol. Amy was also disciplined at home. She put in many hours baby-sitting her younger sister to pay back her parents for the fine. Her parents sat down with her and discussed problems associated with underage drinking. They clearly expressed that they did not approve of her recent behavior, and that they wanted to discuss ways that Amy and her friends might avoid activities where there would be alcohol present. Amy and her parents agreed that when Amy went out with her friends, she would check in by cell phone during the evening. If there was alcohol present, she would use her parents as an excuse for needing to leave the party early, and they would come and get her, if needed.

At first, Amy was angry about the consequences for her behavior and her grades began to slip. With encouragement from her parents and teachers, however, Amy was able to bring her grades back up and maintain them. After 6 months, Amy told her school counselor that she no longer chose drinking as a weekend activity. She and her friends took turns having alcohol-free parties at each others' houses as one alternative to drinking parties.

Nick, a classmate of Amy's, experienced many run-ins with the law for delinquent behavior. Nick was bright and noted for his great sense of humor and his artistic talent. Nick's teachers reported that he had the potential for good grades, but that he didn't seem to try very hard. As a result, Nick was on the verge of failing two classes, and barely making C's in three others.

Nick wanted to go out for football in the fall, but his father said that he needed to get a job to help support his three younger siblings. Nick's mother had died of cancer the year before, and it was necessary for Nick to work to supplement the family's income as his mother had. Nick's father already worked 60 hours a week and could not add on another job if he was going to be around to spend time with his children. Nick told his father that if he took on more adult responsibilities, he ought to be able to be allowed more adult privileges. This topic was a frequent source of conflict, and eventually resulted in a later curfew. However, Nick often broke his new curfew, staying out past 3:00 A.M. with friends he met at work. These friends were a few years older than Nick and had dropped out of school. Several nights, Nick stayed overnight with his friends without telling his father. Nick and his friends often drank heavily on the weekends, and began vandalizing property when they were drunk. Nick was arrested several times for his behavior.

Each time, Nick's father bailed him out of jail by paying his fine and then grounded him from use of the family car for 2 weeks. One night, Nick's father told the police to keep him overnight—thinking that would teach him a lesson. When Nick's father picked him up the next morning, neither of them talked to each other, except to say how betrayed they each felt. When Nick got home, he went to his room, and didn't emerge until evening to go out with his

*(continued)*

friends. He walked out of the house without looking at his father, who didn't even try to enforce the punishment of grounding he had set. Nick's school recommended that he meet with the school counselor on a weekly basis to talk about his behavior and his grades. Nick showed up for his session once and then didn't return. His grades continued on their downward slide and he failed two classes. He maintained his job, but was rarely home. After work his friends and he would go out and vandalize property. Nick eventually ended up in a correctional facility after he stole a car and took it for a joyride.

Amy and Nick could both be described as typical teenagers—both preferred the company of their friends, both were involved in school activities, and both experimented with alcohol. Amy, however, received support from significant adults in her life, and was able to get back on track despite making some mistakes. Nick, on the other hand, did not have the necessary level of support from family and school personnel. As a result, he made some choices in behavior that led to serious consequences—alienation of his father and spending time in a correctional facility.

*Source:* Ramona A. de Rosales, a founder of Academia Cesar Chavev and the Executive Director.

## BEHAVIORAL INTERVENTIONS FOR ADOLESCENT POPULATIONS

Our society has a critical interest in socializing our children into becoming effective citizens and socially competent individuals. Part of this process involves equipping students with the social skills they will need to avoid problematic behavior and to promote social relationships. The school setting is seen as an optimal arena for teaching these skills for two main reasons. First, school is compulsory, thus making it possible to reach most of the youth population at once. Ninety-seven percent of youth ages 14–17 attend high school and 83% stay through graduation (U.S. Census Bureau, 2000). Second, interventions conducted in the school setting reach children during their formative years, and can optimally teach appropriate behaviors before inappropriate ones are learned.

Although schools have long been interested in shaping the behaviors of their students, the contributions of the behavioral approach are relatively recent. In the 1950s and 1960s, schools often relied on scare tactics to prevent adolescents' problem behaviors. Alternatively, schools sometimes taught students about the underlying causes of problem behaviors. However, neither of these approaches has been shown to be effective (Forman & Neal, 1987). In the mid-to-late 1970s, the humanistic approach was popular. This approach focused on raising students' self-esteem and teaching stress management. In the 1980s, programs drew from social influence models and taught students to "Just Say No" in order to avoid peer influence. Like their earlier counterparts, these programs were not highly effective in helping adolescents to avoid problem behaviors (Herrmann & McWhirter, 1997). The introduction of behavior modification-based programs, with their emphasis on teaching and maintaining critical social skills, appears to have had greater success. However, such programs need to be implemented with care when working with adolescent populations.

Behavioral interventions aimed at adolescent populations typically address common risky behaviors in which adolescents participate (e.g., unprotected sex, drugs, gambling, violence, and tobacco use). Effective interventions either improve adolescents' resistance and refusal skills or bolster their social skills.

## Resistance and Refusal Skills

Interventions that offer resistance and refusal skills (RRS) typically follow a common outline. First, they invite students to identify types of social pressure. Students might discuss the types of situations where they feel tempted to drink, for example. Second, they offer a demonstration of resistance techniques. Videotaped vignettes or live skits may be used to model a variety of effective refusal behaviors. Third, students are asked to rehearse refusal through role play with other students or the instructor (Rohrbach, Graham, Hansen, Flag, & Johnson, 1987).

One example of a typical RRS program is the *Say It Straight* program, which is aimed at preventing alcohol and drug use by adolescents (Englander-Golden, Elconin, & Miller, 1985). This program asks students to role-play situations where they encounter friends pressuring them to use drugs. These role plays are videotaped as adolescents replay the scenario several times, practicing a variety of different communication styles. For example, an adolescent might behave passively in the first scene, aggressively in the second, and assertively in the third. A group of the "actor's" peers then watch the videotape and offer feedback about the messages (verbal and nonverbal) that were sent with each interaction. Once the most effective approach is determined, the adolescent then repeats the role play by practicing that approach.

Of course, having the skills to resist does not automatically mean that the adolescent will change his or her behavior when faced with a real-life situation (Hovell et al., 2001). Acquiring these skills is merely the first step. The true measure of the effectiveness of an intervention program is the change in adolescents' behaviors.

The most effective school-based RRS programs are likely to be those that are highly comprehensive in addressing all possible factors that contribute to the adolescents' risky behaviors (Farmer, Farmer, & Gut, 1999). For example, teacher behavior might be examined to ensure that discipline strategies are not unintentionally negatively reinforcing students' behaviors. The social goals of the students should be considered (e.g., will new RRS interfere with the support teenagers receive from their friends?). Finally, the social roles of peer groups at a school might be evaluated. Perhaps influencing the values and behaviors of a particular clique is necessary to engender far-reaching effects in students' behaviors.

## Social Skills Training

Social skills training programs take the view that adolescent problem behaviors, such as violent solutions to interpersonal difficulties, are actually a result of social skills deficits. The logical way to address problem behaviors, then, is to provide training in the relevant social skills. In particular, social skills training programs target decision-making skills, assertiveness skills, building relationships, and effective conflict resolution.

As with resistance and refusal skills programs, social skills training is often done in groups of peers. Adolescents are asked first to identify or define their goal. For example, a shy adolescent might set a goal of joining a group of students for lunch. Second, adolescents are asked to generate alternative solutions for reaching this goal. The student might just sit down with a group, try to set up a lunch meeting in advance with an existing group, or ask a few students to join her. Third, each of the alternatives is evaluated. Younger adolescents' limitations in abstract thought can sometimes hinder their progress in this step without outside guidance (Halford, 1989). Finally, a plan for implementation is generated (D'Zurilla & Goldfried, 1971).

In recent years social skills training programs have gone beyond the basic provision of skills to promote (1) generalization of these skills to situations outside of the training setting, and (2) maintenance of these skills over time (Christopher, Nangle, & Hansen, 1993). In addition, most social skills programs do not stop at one skill, but hope to provide adolescents with a broad repertoire of skills upon which they might draw.

One example of a social skills training program that embodies these goals is the Social-Competence Promotion Program for Young Adolescents (Weissberg, Barton, & Shriver, 1997). This 45-session comprehensive program enhances adolescents' cognitive, emotional, and behavioral skills so that they can effectively address social tasks. In the first phase of the program, students are taught to use a problem-solving process, much like the one previously outlined. In the second phase of the program, students are exposed to information specifically targeting substance use. For example, students are given accurate information about consequences of substance use, learn about social and media influences on substance use, and discuss ways to involve students and the larger community in prevention efforts. In the third and final phase, students learn about human growth and development, AIDS prevention, and teen pregnancy. Students are encouraged to apply problem-solving skills to situations involving social relationships and sexuality. Teachers are asked to model problem-solving skills spontaneously as opportunities arise in the classroom, increasing the likelihood that adolescents will transfer these skills to situations outside of the intervention effort.

## ISSUES PARTICULAR TO BEHAVIORAL INTERVENTIONS WITH ADOLESCENTS

### Is It Ever Too Late to Intervene?

In recent years there has been a push to intervene in children's lives as early as possible. For example, in 1997 the White House held a conference to discuss ways to intervene in children's lives between the ages of zero and three in the hopes that early intervention would effect long-lasting change. Programs like Head Start aim to set children on a good developmental pathway even before they enter school. At the same time, it seems that more adolescents are being tried as adults in our court systems, suggesting that our society holds little hope for rehabilitating them in the juvenile system.

Given these trends, is it possible that it is too late to really affect students' behaviors by the time they reach adolescence? Fortunately the answer is no. Behavior is modifiable at any point, though the techniques that worked with younger children may not always be optimal for adolescent populations. In fact, it may be especially important to continue intervention programs into middle school and high school, as that is when students are at a greater risk for problem behaviors, and the negative consequences of poor decisions become more serious. Adolescence also brings new issues to consider and heightens the salience of issues raised in elementary school. For example, teenagers need to be provided with the skills to resist drugs and alcohol and to practice safe sex. Although younger children might be instructed in conflict resolution skills, adolescents' greater propensity for violence creates a new urgency for needing these skills.

## Who Should Lead the Intervention—Teachers or Peers?

Most interventions are led in groups, but vary in terms of whether a teacher or peer(s) leads the sessions. Who is most effective with adolescent populations—teachers or peers? The answer appears to depend on your goals. If the goal of the intervention is to change students' behaviors when interacting with teachers, it is beneficial to have teachers lead the training. For example, Pentz (1980) found that teachers, parents, and peers were all effective at increasing students' self-reported and observed assertiveness. However, teacher-led groups were most effective in producing assertiveness when students were actually interacting with teachers in real-life situations. If the goal of the intervention is to alter students' interactions with peers, it is important to include peers in the intervention. Although teachers are viewed as more credible sources of factual information than peers are, peers have greater social credibility among students than teachers do. Furthermore, peers provide more opportunities for rehearsing new skills in training sessions, and can model appropriate behavior outside of the training sessions (Perry & Murray, 1989).

The use of peers in behavioral interventions is becoming more widespread. The chief advantage appears to be in facilitating the training and in helping students to generalize their skills to the situations beyond the training sessions. Three caveats should be kept in mind. First, there is little research available on how the training experience affects the peer-trainers. Second, it may be more difficult to honor students' rights to confidentiality when peers are involved in the training. Third, while peers can be effective models and teachers, not all peers are equally suited for this task. Classroom Application 13.3 gives an example of how a teacher may need to guide the use of peer learning in a classroom setting.

## Classroom Application 13.3

## Learning from Peers

Mr. Storey teaches 10th-grade geometry. He usually provides his students some time in class to work on problem sets. When a student asks if he or she can get help on a particular proof, Mr. Storey often encourages that student to ask a peer, saying, "If you didn't get it from my first explanation, you might not get it from my second one." He then asks the student to think about whom he or she would like to ask to get "good" advice. This strategy tends to be effective for most students. Even students performing at C and D levels in his class opt to ask the students getting A's, even if they are not their friends.

However, Mr. Storey has noticed a difference when it comes to his students who are failing geometry. These students do not turn to the A-level students for help; rather, they turn to their friends. He knows that all people are likely to select friends who are similar to themselves on important characteristics; these students have selected friends who are equally poor at geometry. Mr. Storey's solution is to occasionally assign groups of students to work together. In these groups, Mr. Storey is careful to pair students at different ability levels, and to include peers, but not friends.

### Could Interventions Ever Have Unintended Harmful Effects?

Educators initiate interventions with the intention of improving the lives of adolescents by decreasing adolescents' rates of risky behaviors and promoting their social skills. However, under certain circumstances, behavioral interventions may do more harm than good. Unintended, harmful effects, known as *iatrogenic effects*, are apparent when control groups, receiving no intervention, function better than groups who took part in the intervention.

When and how do iatrogenic effects occur in interventions serving adolescent populations? Grouping deviant peers together in interventions has been flagged as a potential problem (Arnold & Hughes, 1999; Dishion, McCord, & Poulin, 1999). Adolescents who engage in antisocial behavior may already be highly susceptible to peer influences. Providing these youth with ready access to other antisocial adolescents encourages friendships. These friends then "train" each other in deviant behavior (Dishion et al., 1995). One possible solution is to include diverse groups of adolescents in intervention efforts, rather than just including those with problem behaviors. This approach may encourage more diverse friendships after the intervention ends.

Some interventions aimed at teaching resistance and refusal skills have been shown to actually *increase* the rate of problem behavior among adolescents participating in the intervention. Purely educational approaches (failing to incorporate any skills training) can lead to greater familiarity with drugs or alcohol and have been associated with increased substance use (Arnold & Hughes, 1999). Furthermore, when schools launch an all-out attack on a problem such as underage drinking, adolescents may conclude that this behavior must be extremely prevalent at their school to warrant the intense intervention. If adolescents believe this behavior is normative among their peers, they may be more likely to take part in it, thereby increasing the very behaviors the educators had hoped to decrease. Programs that focus purely on resistance skills (e.g., Just Say No) can backfire by sensitizing students to difficulties of saying no to friends—something about which they may not have previously worried. The best approach for avoiding these types of iatrogenic effects is to combine normative education about the incidence of problem behaviors (e.g., how many students drink) with resistance skills (e.g., rehearsing how a student might turn down a drink without alienating his or her friends) (Donaldson, Graham, Piccinin, & Hansen, 1995).

The only way to truly know if an intervention is causing more harm than good is to include a control group in the intervention. This group of students should be identical to those receiving the intervention in every way, except that they do not receive the intervention. Unfortunately, many researchers and program developers fail to include a control group in their studies of interventions. You should question the validity of the claims made for those interventions, even if it appears that the intervention was beneficial. It is possible that the intervention had no effect, and that the adolescents' problem behavior simply decreased with time or due to a change in environment unrelated to the intervention. In the worst case, it is possible that an intervention actually *increased* problem behavior by unintentionally reinforcing the very behavior you had hoped to decrease.

## How Can We Run Interventions and Cover Required Course Material?

Behavioral interventions were once relegated to clinicians who worked only with the most troubled teens. Today we realize that all adolescents can benefit from instruction in social skills and resistance and refusal skills, and such interventions are conducted within our schools. But schools are also responsible for preparing students to meet high school graduation requirements and to be successful at college and in the workplace. How can schools take time away from their academic agenda to help students succeed in the social realm? In fact, schools are less likely to adopt and maintain special programs that stand alone from regular subject matter (e.g., English or history) or that do not increase achievement.

Although such approaches are rare, Stevahn and her colleagues offer one promising way of accomplishing both academic and social behavior goals (Stevahn, Johnson, Johnson, Green, & Laginski, 1997). In their study, one group of ninth-grade students received over 9 hours of training in conflict resolution skills that was integrated into the study of literature. Students were asked to identify the conflicts in their readings, write about the conflicts, write scripts for what each character would say using the negotiation procedure to reduce conflict, and act out their scripts in role plays. The control group spent the same amount of time studying the identical literature, without conflict resolution training. At the end of the study, the first group not only showed better knowledge of and willingness to use the conflict resolution procedure, but they also demonstrated a greater command of the literature compared to the control group. This finding is particularly impressive since the control group devoted their entire study time to learning the literature, rather than dividing their time between conflict resolution skills and studying the literature. Psychologists have long known that the greater depth and elaboration you use to process information (as was used by the first group), the better able you are to recall that information later (Craik & Tulving, 1975). Therefore, interventions that encourage deeper processing of course material may carry an added benefit of improving students' scholastic performance. Given the importance of both academic and behavioral agendas to the well-being of adolescents, more programs that successfully integrate behavioral interventions into course curriculums would be beneficial to our youth.

## SUMMARY

Adolescents' changing behavior reflects rapid biological, cognitive, social, and contextual developments to which they must adapt. As a group, adolescents are both a highly challenging and a highly rewarding population with which to work.

Youth in adolescence are at a higher risk of engaging in problem behavior than they are as children or adults. Adolescents who encounter many changes at once, who experience developmental deficits, and who lack developmental assets may be at the greatest risk for problem behavior.

Behavioral interventions for adolescents typically try to stem risky behaviors by teaching resistance and refusal skills, or by bolstering adolescents' social skills. Such programs assume that problem behaviors reflect a skills deficit, and that providing adolescents with the appropriate skills will allow them to avoid risky behavior.

Teachers or peers may effectively lead interventions, though the most effective leader will be the one who most closely reflects the situation in which the adolescent will find himself or herself. Interventions should include control groups to protect against unwanted harmful effects of the intervention. Interventions that incorporate course material are more likely to be adopted by schools.

## DISCUSSION QUESTIONS

1. Think about an adolescent you know who engages in a lot of risky behavior, and one who engages in relatively little risky behavior. Describe each adolescent's balance of protective factors (e.g., developmental assets) and risk factors.

2. Discuss some typical behaviors of adolescents that might seem frustrating to adults, but that actually may be a natural outgrowth of the physical, cognitive, and social transitions adolescents are navigating.

3. In the section on parent-adolescent relations and autonomy, Collins' (1990) expectancy-violation-realignment model is described. Although this model was intended to describe change in parent-parent relations, do you think that it might apply to changing teacher-student relations across adolescence as well? How so?

4. A school principal has asked you to design an intervention/prevention program aimed at reducing school violence. What features would you most want the program to have? What aspects would you be careful to avoid in designing your program?

# REFERENCES

Arnett, J. J. (1999). Adolescent storm and stress, reconsidered. *American Psychologist, 54,* 317–326.

Arnold, M. E., & Hughes, J. N. (1999). First do no harm: Adverse effects of grouping deviant youth for skills training. *Journal of School Psychology, 37,* 99–115.

Barling, J., Rogers, K. A., & Kelloway, E. K. (1995). Some effects of teenagers' part-time employment: The quantity and quality of work makes the difference. *Journal of Organizational Behavior, 16,* 143–154.

Benson, P. L., Scales, P. C., Leffert, N., & Roehlkepartain, E. C. (1999). *A fragile foundation: The state of developmental assets among American youth.* Minneapolis, MN: Search Institute.

Berndt, T. J. (1979). Developmental changes in conformity to peers and parents. *Developmental Psychology, 15*(6), 608–616.

Brooks-Gunn, J., & Reiter, E. O. (1990). The role of pubertal processes. In S. Feldman and G. Elliot (Eds.), *At the threshold: The developing adolescent* (pp. 16–53). Cambridge, MA: Harvard University Press.

Carskadon, M. A., Wolfson, A. R., Acebo, C., Tzischinsky, O., & Seifer, R. (1998). Adolescent sleep patterns, circadian timing, and sleepiness at a transition to early school days. *Sleep, 21,* 871–881.

Christopher, J. S., Nangle, D. W., & Hansen, D. J. (1993). Social-skills interventions with adolescents: Current issues and procedures. *Behavior Modification, 17,* 314–338.

Collins, W. A. (1990). Parent-child relationships in the transition to adolescence: Continuity and change in interaction, affect, and cognition. In R. Montemayor & G. R. Adams (Eds.), *Advances in adolescent development: Vol. 2. From childhood to adolescence: A transitional period?* (pp. 85–106). Thousand Oaks, CA: Sage.

Collins, W. A. (1997). Relationships and development during adolescence: Interpersonal adaptation to individual change. *Personal Relationships, 4,* 1–14.

Craik, F. I. M., & Tulving, E. (1975). Depth of processing and retention of words in episodic memory. *Journal of Experimental Psychology, 104,* 268–294.

Dishion, T. J., Andrews, D. W., & Crosby, L. (1995). Antisocial boys and their friends in early adolescence: Relationship characteristics, quality, and interactional process. *Child Development, 66,* 139–151.

Dishion, T. J., McCord, J., & Poulin, F. (1999). When interventions harm: Peer groups and problem behavior. *American Psychologist, 54,* 755–764.

Donaldson, S. I., Graham, J. W., Piccinin, A. M., & Hansen, W. B. (1995). Resistance-skills training and onset of alcohol use: Evidence for beneficial and potentially harmful effects in public schools and in private Catholic schools. *Health Psychology, 14,* 291–300.

D'Zurilla, T. J., & Goldfried, M. R. (1971). Problem solving and behavior modification. *Journal of Abnormal Psychology, 78,* 107–126.

Englander-Golden, P., Elconin, J., & Miller, K. J. (1985). Say It Straight: Adolescent substance abuse prevention training. *Academic Psychology Bulletin, 7,* 65–79.

Farmer, T. W., Farmer, E. M. Z., & Gut, D. M. (1999). Implications of social development research for school-based interventions for aggressive youth with EBD. *Journal of Emotional & Behavioral Disorders, 7,* 130–136.

Feiring, C. (1996). Concepts of romance in 15-year-old adolescents. *Journal of Research on Adolescence, 6,* 181–200.

Forman, S. G., & Neal, J. A. (1987). School-based substance abuse prevention programs. *Special Services in the Schools, 3,* 89–103.

Furman, W., Brown, B. B., & Feiring, C. (1999). *The development of romantic relationships in adolescence: Cambridge studies in social and emotional development.* New York: Cambridge University Press.

Furman, W., & Burmester, D. (1992). Age and sex differences in perceptions of networks of personal relationships. *Child Development, 63,* 103–115.

Gottfredson, D. C. (2001). *Schools and delinquency.* New York: Cambridge University Press.

Halford, G. S. (1989). Reflections on 25 years of Piagetian cognitive developmental psychology: 1963–1988. *Human Development, 32,* 325–357.

Hartup, W. W., & Stevens, N. (1997). Friendships and adaptation in the life course. *Psychological Bulletin, 121,* 355–370.

Herrmann, D. S., & McWhirter, J. J. (1997). Refusal and resistance skills for children and adolescents: A selected review. *Journal of Counseling & Development, 75,* 177–187.

Hovell, M. F., Blumberg, E. J., Liles, S., Powell, L., Morrison, T. C., Duran, G., et al. (2001). Training AIDS and anger prevention social skills in at-risk adolescents. *Journal of Counseling & Development, 79,* 347–355.

Kids Count Data Book Online. (2002). *Percent of teens who are high school dropouts.* Retrieved August 25, 2002, from the Kids Count Web site: http://www.aecf.org/kidscount/kc2002/summary/summary9.ht

Kids Count Data Book Online. (2002). *Rate of teen deaths by accident, homicide, and suicide.* Retrieved August 25, 2002, from the Kids Count Web site: http://www.aecf.org/kidscount/kc2002/summary/summary6.htm

Kids Count Data Book Online. (2002). *Teen birth rate.* Retrieved August 25, 2002, from the Kids Count Web site: http://www.aecf.org/kidscount/kc2002/summary/summary7.htm

Larson, R. W., Clore, G. L., & Woods, G. A. (1999). The emotions of romantic relationships: Do they wreak havoc on adolescents? In W. Furman, B. B. Brown, & C. Feiring (Eds.), *The development of romantic relationships in adolescence* (pp. 19–49). New York: Cambridge University Press.

Larson, R., Czikszentmihalyi, M., & Graef, R. (1980). Mood variability and the psychosocial adjustment of adolescents. *Journal of Youth and Adolescence, 9,* 469–490.

Larson. R. W., Richards, M. H., Moneta, G., & Holmbeck, G. (1996). Changes in adolescents' daily interactions with their families from ages 10 to 18: Disengagement and transformation. *Developmental Psychology, 32,* 744–754.

Laursen, B., & Collins, W. A. (1994). Interpersonal conflict during adolescence. *Psychological Bulletin, 115,* 197–209.

Livesley, W. J., & Bromley, D. B. (1973). *Person perception in childhood and adolescence.* New York: John Wiley & Sons.

Maas, J. (2002). *What you should know about sleep.* Presentation given at the 24th Annual National Institute on the Teaching of Psychology, St. Petersburg, FL.

Mortimer, J. T., Harley, C., & Aronson, P. J. (1999). How do prior experiences in the workplace set the stage for transitions to adulthood? In A. Booth, A. C. Crouter, & M. J. Shanahan (Eds.), *Transitions to adulthood in a changing economy: No work, no family, no future?* (pp. 131–159). Westport, CT: Praeger.

Newcomb, A. F., & Bagwell, C. L. (1996). The developmental significance of children's friendships. In W. M. Bukowski, A. F. Newcomb, & W. W. Hartup (Eds.), *The company they keep: Friendship in childhood and adolescence* (pp. 289–321). New York: Cambridge University Press.

Pentz, M. A. (1980). Assertion training and trainer effects on unassertive and aggressive adolescents. *Journal of Counseling Psychology, 27,* 76–83.

Perry, C., & Murray, D. (1989). Prevention of alcohol use and abuse in adolescence: Teacher- vs. peer-led intervention. *Crisis, 10,* 52–61.

Rohrbach, L. A., Graham, J. W., Hansen, W. B., Flag, B. R., & Johnson, C. A. (1987). Evaluation of resistance skills training using multitrait-multimethod role play skill assessment. *Health Education Research, 2,* 401–407.

Rutter, M., Graham, P., Chadwick, O., & Yule, W. (1976). Adolescent turmoil: Fact or fiction? *Journal of Child Psychology and Psychiatry, 17,* 35–56.

Ryan, R. M., & Lynch, J. H. (1989). Emotional autonomy versus detachment: Revisiting the vicissitudes of adolescence and young adulthood. *Child Development, 60,* 340–356.

Shanahan, M. J., Finch, M. D., Mortimer, J. T., & Ryu, S. (1991). Adolescent work experiences and depressive affect. *Social Psychology Quarterly, 54,* 299–317.

Simmons, R. (1979). *Transition into adolescence: A longitudinal study, 1974–1979.* Cambridge, MA: Harvard University Press.

Smetana, J. G. (1988). Adolescents' and parents' conceptions of parental authority. *Child Development, 59,* 321–335.

Stattin, H., & Magnusson, D. (1990). *Pubertal maturation in female development.* Hillsdale, NJ: Erlbaum.

Steinberg, L. (1990). Autonomy, conflict, and harmony in the family relationship. In S. Feldman & G. Elliot (Eds.), *At the threshold: The developing adolescent* (pp. 255–276). Cambridge, MA: Harvard University Press.

Steinberg, L. (2001). We know some things: Parent-adolescent relationships in retrospect and prospect. *Journal of Research on Adolescence, 11,* 1–19.

Stevahn, L., Johnson, D. W., Johnson, R. T., Green, K., & Laginski, A. M. (1997). Effects on high school students of conflict resolution training integrated into English literature. *Journal of Social Psycology, 137*(3), 302–315.

U. S. Census Bureau. (2000). *United States Census 2000.* Washington, DC: United States Department of Commerce.

Weissberg, R. P., Barton, H. A., & Shriver, T. P. (1997). The social competence promotion program for young adolescents. In G. W. Albee & T. P. Gullotta (Eds.), *Primary prevention works* (pp. 268–290). Thousand Oaks, CA: Sage.

Wentzel, K. R. (1998). Social support and adjustment in middle school: The role of parents, teachers, and peers. *Journal of Educational Psychology, 90,* 202–209.

Wentzel, K. R., & Battle, A. A. (2001). Social relationships and school adjustment. In T. Urdan & F. Pajares (Eds.), *Adolescence and education: General issues in the education of adolescence* (pp. 93–118). Greenwich, CT: Information Age.

Wofford, S. (1988). *A preliminary analysis of the relationship between employment and delinquency/crime for adolescents and youth adults.* National Youth Survey No. 50. Boulder: Institute of Behavioral Science, University of Colorado.

# CULTURAL INFLUENCES ON BEHAVIOR

*Julia L. Orza and Thomas J. Zirpoli*

*What is normal and acceptable in a child's culture may be regarded as abnormal or unacceptable in school and may result in conflict, mislabeling, or punishment. Along with objective recording of behaviors, a child's social and cultural background should be taken into account when assessing performance.*

—HEWARD *(1996, p. 115)*

There is always the danger of stereotyping when discussing different cultures, and we certainly try to avoid that in this chapter. Each one of us is a unique individual with a unique self-identity shaped by our experiences, values, attitudes, the people we encounter, and the communities that socialize us. As stated by Banks and Banks (1989, p. 13):

*Although membership in a gender, racial, ethnic, social class, or religious group can provide us with important clues about individuals' behavior, it cannot enable us to predict behavior. Knowing one's group affiliation can enable us to state that a certain type of behavior is probable.*

So while we will try to avoid stereotyping, we believe that cultural influences on behavior have largely been ignored in the field of behavior management and must be specifically addressed.

According to the U.S. Census Bureau (2001), 12.3% of the U.S. population is African American, 12.5% Hispanic, 4.2% Asian/Native Hawaiian/Other Pacific Islander, and .90% American Indian/Alaska Native. The census also reports that an additional 5.5% of the U.S. population identified as "Some other race" and another 2.4% of the U.S. population reported as "Two or more races." Of that 2.4% (6.8 million people), the most common combinations of race reported were "White and Some other race," "White and American Indian and Alaska Native," and "White and Asian." The total U.S. population is 281,421,906 and is projected to exceed 400 million by 2050. As Table 14.1 shows, the number of nonwhites will increase from 29.6% to 47.5% of the U.S. population by the year 2050. As outlined in Table 14.2, minorities currently make up 37.2% of students in U.S. elementary and secondary schools (National Center for Educational Statistics, 2000).

**TABLE 14.1 • Percent of United States Nonwhite Population, 1999, and Projected Population for 2050**

|  | African American | Hispanic | American Indian | Asian | Total |
|---|---|---|---|---|---|
| 1999 | 12.8 | 11.9 | .88 | 4.08 | 29.6 |
| 2050 | 14.4 | 22.5 | .90 | 9.7 | 47.5 |
| Projected Increase | 12.5% | 89.0% | 2.3% | 137.4% | 60.4% |

*Source:* U.S. Department of Commerce (1999).

TABLE 14.2 • Percent of United States Elementary and Secondary Schools Nonwhite Population, 1998

| African American | Hispanic | American Indian | Asian | Total |
|---|---|---|---|---|
| 17.1% | 15.0% | 1.1% | 4.0% | 37.2% |

*Source:* National Center for Educational Statistics (2000).

The number of foreign-born citizens in the United States has doubled from 1970 (5%) to 1996 (10%) (Bruce, 1997). In 1998 alone, 660,477 immigrants from 208 countries around the world were granted permanent resident status in the United States. Twenty percent of them came from Mexico. In many cities more than half the population is foreign born. For example, over 60% of the population of Miami is foreign born. As a result, many school systems (e.g., New York, Chicago, Los Angeles) must accommodate over 100 languages or dialects. In 1992, 14.2% of children 5 to 17 years old (6.4 million children) spoke a language other than English at home, and by 1999, that percentage grew to 16.7 (8.8 million children) (U.S. Census Bureau, 2001). While this diversity is not a new experience for the United States (the number of foreign-born citizens from 1910 to 1940 ranged from 10% to 15% of the population), it brings unique needs to America's public schools, along with many opportunities.

Several myths and overgeneralizations are associated with individual racial and ethnic groups. These myths, along with a lack of appreciation for, and celebration of, different cultural norms, contribute to a frequent misunderstanding and misinterpretation of children's behaviors. Often a child who has been reared in a strong cultural environment becomes frustrated when teachers and peers consider him or her backward or slow for following the behavioral traditions of his or her culture—the only behavior the child knows. An examination of individuals within the context of their own cultural background, conducted from a descriptive rather than ethnocentric point of view, is essential for understanding behavior (Hale-Benson, 1987).

Part of the evolution of multicultural thinking and appreciation in the American classroom includes a switch from advocating the 19th-century Americanization model (merging all students into one "American" ideal) and the "melting pot" ideology developed in the early 1900s (which asserts that all immigrants should give up their culture and assimilate into the "better" American culture), to the more recent "salad bowl" analogy—with "various groups maintaining their distinctive identities while contributing to the quality of the whole society" (Tiedt & Tiedt, 1999, p. 4). Both students and educators need to recognize and value individual differences, and acknowledge diverse cultural roots as strengths (Tiedt & Tiedt, 1999). To assist teachers, World Wide Web sites that access knowledge bases for various ethnic and racial cultural identities are included at the end of the chapter.

An additional focus of this chapter is on the cultural background and biases of the teacher. Often overlooked in the training to become a diversity-sensitive educator is the need on the part of the teacher to examine the effects of his or her own cultural identity, bias, and stereotyping on children's behaviors. Lacking awareness of our own values, background, and cultural influences makes it difficult to recognize and value another's unique perspective. As stated by Grossman (1995), teachers do not have to be prejudiced to use biased behavior management techniques:

> Even well-meaning teachers can misperceive and misunderstand students' behaviors when they interpret them from their own perspective. They can perceive behavior problems that do not exist, not notice problems that do exist, misunderstand the causes of students' behaviors, and use inappropriate techniques to deal with students' behavior problems. (p. 358)

All children need to be connected to family, cultural values, and belief systems. Showing respect for these values and beliefs is a way of showing respect for individual children, their families, and their cultures.

## A DEFINITION OF TERMS

> Language is always changing. It responds to social, economic, and political events and is therefore an important barometer and descriptor of a society at any given time. Language also becomes obsolete; it could not be otherwise because it is a reflection of societal changes" (Nieto, 1996, p. 23).

This is important to keep in mind as we attempt to offer definitions of terms related to multicultural education and diverse learners—the reader can find many variations and alternatives to the concepts defined here, especially between the various disciplines. We have chosen the broadest representations of terms most commonly discussed in education.

*Culture* is an umbrella term that "denotes a complex integrated system of values, beliefs, and behaviors common to a large group of people. A culture may include shared history and folklore, ideas about right and wrong, and specific communication styles" (Tiedt & Tiedt, 1999, p. 11) and also includes the ways in which we use and react to our physical environment, symbols, economy, education, information and technology, and sociological and psychological climates. Okun, Fried, and Okun (1999) offer a useful and more complete description of the concept, including common ideas about culture, worldviews, and high- and low-context cultures.

*Ethnicity* is "a group classification in which members believe that they share a common origin and a unique social and cultural heritage such as language or religious belief" (Gladding, 2001, p. 45). This term originates from the Greek *ethnos*, which means "nation."

*Race,* often misused as synonymous with ethnicity or nationality, is "an anthropological concept that classifies people according to their physiological characteristics" (Gladding, 2001, p. 100), such as skin color and facial characteristics. There is much debate in the education literature about how effective knowing one's race is for cultural understanding and about whether race is merely a political classification (Hodgkinson [2000/2001] reports that The Federal Office of Management and Budget Directive 15 states that the racial categories in the census have no scientific validity), and disagreement over which terms to use for the various geographical races/groups (e.g., African American vs. Black, and American Indian vs. Native American). It is important to remember that both race and ethnicity are social constructs, created by a society, affected by a society, and judged by a society. Behavior is learned within the framework of a particular ethnic group or culture and usually taught within a family structure.

The following terms describe additional multicultural principles of behavior:

- *Acculturation:* "The ways people learn the customs, beliefs, behaviors, and traditions of a culture; or the degree to which individuals from minority cultures identify with or conform to the attitudes, lifestyles, and values of the majority culture" (Gladding, 2001, p. 2).
- *Assimilation:* "An approach to acculturation that seeks to merge small ethnically and linguistically diverse communities into a single dominant national institutional structure and culture" (Garcia, 2002, p. 415).
- *Bias:* "This is a personal preference which prevents one from making fair judgments or assessments" (Schwartz, Conley, & Eaton, 1997, p. 36).
- *Bigotry:* "This is a stubborn intolerance of any race, nationality, or creed that differs from one's own" (Schwartz et al., 1997, p. 36).
- *Cultural conflict:* Refers to differences between a child's culture and the culture of the child's immediate community (e.g., neighborhood and school setting).
- *Cultural pluralism:* "The existence within a society of a number of varied groups with distinct values and lifestyles. Also known as *cultural diversity*" (Gladding, 2001, p. 34).
- *Cultural relativity:* "The idea that any behavior must be judged first in relation to the context of the culture in which it occurs" (Randall-David, 1989, p. 2).
- *Ethnocentrism:* "This is the belief that one's cultural ways are not only valid and superior to other people's, but also universally applicable in evaluating and judging human behavior" (Schwartz et al., 1997, p. 22).
- *Multicultural:* "This refers to a number of diverse traditions, customs, arts, languages, values, and beliefs existing side-by-side" (Schwartz et al., 1997, p. 22).
- *Multicultural education:* "A curriculum whose content educates students on the contribution of more than one culture" (Garcia, 2002, p. 417).

- *Racism:* "Prejudice displayed in blatant or subtle ways due to recognized or perceived differences in the physical and psychological backgrounds of people. It is a form of projection usually displayed out of fear or ignorance" (Gladding, 2001, p. 100).
- *Stereotype:* "A concept or representation of a category of persons that can be inaccurate in terms of how it exaggerates real differences and the perception of those differences" (Okun et al., 1996, p. 2).
- *Worldview:* "An individual's perception of the world based on his or her experiences as well as the socialization processes of the person in interaction with members of his or her reference group. Worldviews directly affect and mediate people's belief systems, assumptions, modes of problem solving, decision making, and conflict resolution styles" (Gladding, 2001, p. 129).

## WORLDVIEW

Worldview describes how a person perceives his or her relationship to the world (i.e., nature, people, institutions), and provides a framework from which a person can respond to others. Worldviews of the teacher and the students interact in the classroom and affect the behaviors of each person involved. An effective classroom manager understands his or her own worldview and the worldviews of his or her students. Ibrahim (1991) claims that an understanding of the construct can lead to more effective, sensitive, and ethical interactions and interventions. Although Ibrahim (1991) specifically applies the construct to counseling psychology, she claims it can help address national and international concerns in terms of human growth and development, and training: "Worldviews are a significant contribution of the multicultural counseling and development literature to the generic fields of counseling, education, training, and development" (p. 14).

Worldview is the mediating variable between knowledge of specific cultures, and the knowledge and use of culture-specific interventions. Without consideration of worldview, teachers could misapply both cultural knowledge and techniques, leading to ethical violations and cultural oppression. Since within-group variation is much greater than between-group variation, worldview helps a teacher go beyond applying only general culture information (representative of an entire race, religion, nationality, etc.) to interpret each student's behavior. Ibrahim (1991) explains: "General information provides an important background but does not provide all the answers" (p. 14). Since worldview directly affects our values, assumptions, presuppositions, and modes of problem solving, decision making, and conflict resolution, it becomes clear that one's worldview influences students' and teachers' goals and behavior. Ibrahim's theory, based on an earlier philosophical and existential framework (see Kluckhohn, 1951), "is a cognitive-values perspective that uses worldview and cultural identity as mediational forces in an individual's life" (p. 15). In its application, two things are necessary: The worldviews of both the teacher and the student must be recognized and understood (including an awareness of the cultural identities of both parties), and the worldviews "must be placed within a sociopolitical context, history of migration, acculturation level, languages spoken, and comfort with mainstream assumptions and values" (p. 15).

Ibrahim and Kahn (1984) developed the Scale to Assess World Views (SAWV) to help identify a person's worldview and to use as an evaluation instrument in communication and development. While it is not necessary for teachers to have to administer this instrument to their students or themselves, a general understanding of the categories within the scale will greatly assist teachers in understanding and interpreting their own worldview and that of their students. This information, along with culture-specific knowledge, will increase the chances of accurate and unbiased interpretation of behavior.

The five categories of worldview, with the possible range of assumptions along a continuum in each, are as follows:

1. *Nature:* Examines our "people vs. nature" orientation, including whether we believe people subjugate and control nature, live in harmony with nature, or accept the power and control of nature over people. Questions for this category include these: How do we survive and react to our environment? Does this individual believe in living in harmony with nature? Is nature accepted as all-powerful and controlling? For example, Native Americans often orient more toward the nature end of the continuum, and have a great respect for the power of nature.

2. *Time orientation:* Examines our temporal focus, including whether we value and function according to the past, present, or future. Questions for this category include these: Is the person concerned with the past, present, or future? Is life viewed as finite or eternal? Does the person have a monochronic or polychronic sense of time? For example, Latin Americans consider being late as a sign of respect, and African Americans are generalized to be polychronic.

3. *Activity orientation:* Examines our preferred modality of human activity, including being, being-in-becoming, and doing. Questions for this category include these: Is the client's activity expressive-emotional (affective), detached-meditative (cognitive), or action-oriented (behavioral)? What mechanism does the person use to act and change? For example, women are primarily expressive-emotional and men are action-oriented.

4. *Social relationships:* Examines our "relational orientation" or how we function in human relationships, including linear-hierarchical, collateral-mutual, and individualistic. Questions for this category include these: How does this individual view social relationships and social isolation? Are relationships drawn in terms of lines of authority, rights and rank, subordinate-superior, hierarchy, individualistic, autonomous? Is the collectivism valued over individualism? African Americans are said to

value collectivism, while Anglo Americans are said to identify with individualism and autonomy.

5. *Human nature:* Examines our view of "humankind," including good, bad, or immutable (a combination of good and bad). Questions for this category include these: How does the person feel about him- or herself? How does the person feel about others? Are people viewed as basically evil, neutral, good, or some combination? For example, a troubled, at-risk youth may see everything in his or her world (e.g., school and parents) as "bad."

A teacher can take into consideration a student's worldview as he or she tries to interpret how well the student fits into the culture-specific values, assumptions, and behaviors representative of the primary group. Ibrahim (1991) explains that knowledge of the worldview construct can assist in a better understanding of acculturation level and specific concerns of the student, and increase trust, empathy, rapport, and communication related to modes of student behavior. The following sections include further discussion and examples of behaviors related to the worldviews of African Americans, Hispanics/Latinos, Asian Americans, and American Indians.

# AFRICAN AMERICANS

## Demographics

African Americans, the largest minority group in the United States, include 34.7 million people, or about 12.9% of the total U.S. population (U.S. Census Bureau, 2001). The African American population is projected to reach 14.7% of the U.S. population by 2050 (U.S. Census Bureau, 2001). African Americans are one of the youngest minority groups in the United States. While 28.7% of Americans are under 20 years of age, 34% of African Americans are under 20 years old and make up 17% of students in elementary and secondary schools (U.S. Census Bureau, 2001). Meanwhile, almost one in four (23.6%) African Americans live in poverty (compared to 9.8% of whites) and nearly one of every three (33.1%) African American children under the age of 18 lives in poverty (U.S. Census Bureau, 2001).

The educational status of African Americans has improved over the past 25 years (see Tables 14.3 and 14.4). For example, in 1973 only 24% of African Americans attended college. This increased to 40% in 1998 (U.S. Census Bureau, 2001). However, only 13.6% of African Americans complete at least a college degree compared to 24.3% of whites. The high school graduation rate for African Americans (78.5%) has also gradually increased since school desegregation (U.S. Census Bureau, 2001), but a report by the Civil Rights Project at Harvard University entitled "Race in American Public Schools: Rapidly Resegregating" claims that "virtually all" of the nation's school districts with 25,000 or more students are becoming more segregated for African Americans and Latinos ("City's Schools," 2002).

**TABLE 14.3 • High School Graduate or More by Race and Origin, 1995–2000**

| Year | African American | Hispanic | White |
|------|------------------|----------|-------|
| 1995 | 73.8% | 53.4% | 83% |
| 1998 | 76% | 55.5% | 83.7% |
| 2000 | 78.5% | 57% | 84.9% |

*Source:* Compiled from data from U.S. Census Bureau (2001).

**TABLE 14.4 • High School Graduation Rates for 18-to-24-Year-Olds in 2000**

| Year | African American | Hispanic | White |
|------|------------------|----------|-------|
| 2000 | 83.7% | 64.1% | 91.8% |

*Source:* Compiled from data from U.S. Department of Education (2001).

**TABLE 14.5 • Poverty Rates in the United States**

| | |
|---|---|
| Total for U.S. | 11.8% |
| African Americans | 23.6% |
| American Indians | 25.9% |
| Asians/Pacific Islanders | 10.7% |
| Hispanics/Latinos | 22.8% |
| Whites | 9.8% |

As noted by the U.S. Department of Commerce (1999) in Table 14.5, African Americans have one of the highest poverty rates of any cultural group in the United States.

While the gap between test scores of African Americans and European Americans is narrowing, standardized test scores for African Americans still lag behind all other minority groups (National Center for Educational Statistics, 2000). Almost 64% of African American fourth graders cannot read an age-appropriate book compared to a national average of 38% ("Improving Reading," 2001). African American students are nearly three times as likely as white students to be labeled mentally retarded, and two times as likely to be labeled emotionally disturbed (Losen & Orfield, 2002). High school dropout rates remain higher for African American students, at 6.0%, than for white students, at 4.4% (U.S. Census Bureau, 2001). Based upon current rates of incarceration, an estimated 28% of African American males will enter state or federal prison during their lifetime, compared to 4.4% of white males (Bureau of Justice Statistics, 2001).

Poverty is still a significant variable affecting African American children. For African American children living with both parents, 14% live in poverty compared with 8% for whites. And for African American children living within a female-headed household, the picture is very grim, as 58% live below the poverty level (compared with 40% of white children).

## Cultural Influences on Behavior

The majority of critiques and discussions of African Americans have generally portrayed their families as disorganized, matriarchal, and single-family directed. Ladson-Billings (2000) discovered that literature searches with the descriptor "Black education" directed one to see "culturally deprived" and "culturally disadvantaged." This view has resulted in a deficiency model for studying the culture and behavior of African Americans and devalues or delegitimizes the culture in the classroom. Any explanation of behavior, however, must consider the environmental context and larger social systems.

Gay (2000) states that "teaching is a contextual and situational process. As such, it is most effective when ecological factors . . . are included in its implementation" (p. 21). Low social status, racism, oppression, less respect, and less power and influence on historical and societal levels have certainly made an impact on the culture of the African American community. Most literature suggests that effective teaching of African American students should involve recognition of and attention to the issues of race and racism, and the role these constructs play in the lives of the students (Gopaul-McNicol & Thomas-Presswood, 1998; Ladson-Billings, 2000; Nieto, 2000; Schwartz, 2001).

While African Americans may have much in common with other racial and ethnic groups, and are an extremely diverse group, it is important to understand the unique qualities of the African American culture. Research has characterized several key concepts valued by the African American community: collectivism and the extended family, the adaptability of family roles, strong religious orientation, education and the work ethic, and the use of coping skills in the face of socioeconomic hardships (Gopaul-McNicol & Thomas-Presswood, 1998; Priest, 1991).

Whereas formal school systems often promote individualism and autonomy, and even assess and evaluate students individually, African American culture places more emphasis on the collective (participation as part of a tribe or community). Values such as independence, uniqueness, and individual goal-orientation may be restrained in favor of family care and honor, group solidarity, and social harmony. Often, African American children are raised to believe in the collective view of success and to be concerned with the African American community (including church, clubs, neighborhood, etc.) as a whole. Relationships are viewed in terms of loyalty to the kin, community, and strong interdependence. In terms of worldview, African Americans are considered to engage in relationships that are collateral-mutual and emphasize cooperation, kinship, rituals, and standards, and that operate from "closed" social systems (Okun et al., 1999). Because of historical, socioeconomic, and marital factors, African American familial structures and interactions include immediate and extended relatives, as well as neighbors, friends, godparents, steprelatives, and so forth. A student's "family" may include many different people and roles beyond the transitional "blood relative" definition.

An African-American child learns at an early age that behavioral expectations of the predominantly white school community may vary significantly from those of his or her neighborhood community.

A type of kinship exists in African American culture based on reciprocal social, political, and economic relationships. The term used to convey this kinship is *brotherhood* or *sisterhood.* Simply being African American, however, does not guarantee good standing in the community. A person can be denied membership based on behavior, attitude, and activities if he or she is perceived to be at variance from group (or peer) norms and expectations. This condition is evident in Vignette 14.1 as one 14-year-old student talks about how he tries to balance peer pressure with the demands of school and home. His worldview related to social relationships, family, and time is evident.

At age 5 or 6, children are learning how to make sense of their world from a culture-specific perspective. At a time when African American children are learning who they are, where they are, and how they fit into the world, they are introduced to formal schooling, which promotes acculturation. Many of these youngsters quickly become aware of hostility toward their race at an early age. To succeed in school, some students develop a minimal connection to their own culture or, like T. J. in Vignette 14.1, become creative in their efforts to fit in with their peers while meeting the demands of school and home.

Children who do not develop a strong connection with their school community may find it easier to drop out—intellectually, emotionally, and physically. For many African Americans, the knowledge learned in school has no direct relationship to their own real world and culture if the school system values concepts more in line with

## VIGNETTE 14.1

●

*Balancing Expectations of Peers, School, and Home*

*T.J.**

Growing up in a lower class home with a working mom and no father present creates some dilemmas for me, especially at school. A major problem, one that I think many African American youth share, is trying to juggle the various roles my living environment places me in. I have to be a role model to my younger brother, help provide for my mother and our house, and make friends and fit in with my peer group. Then of course there are classes, teachers, and grades! Peer pressure has come in many different ways: in dealing with relationships, playing sports, acceptable behavior when not at home, school behavior, and so on. Although I know to take my role as student very seriously, I value my family and peer relationships the most right now. Both my friends and my basketball team come first, although I would never tell my mom that!

My mother expects me to do my very best in school. She wants and expects me to succeed academically and go on to college. I, too, want to go to college, and I have been able to do well so far in school (grades K through 10). I love sports and especially basketball, and want to go to college to play hoops. I see basketball as my ticket to a good college because we won't have enough money to send me without scholarships. I know that if I play hard enough I can get college scouts to look at me. I play basketball every chance I get, choosing a game in the gym or park over my homework any day.

Peer pressure makes it difficult to act responsibly all the time. It is hard to be considered cool and be in the "in" groups while doing all your homework and never going to any of the fresh parties or activities. My peers even control what I choose to wear. It's not hard to figure out what I should buy and wear to school—if you wear the wrong thing you hear about it for days! I am luckier than some of my other friends, because I have basketball as an excuse to have to do well in school; if I didn't, I wouldn't be allowed to play. If I didn't have basketball, I would probably have to slack off on doing all my work and get in trouble once in a while, to not show up my friends. Sometimes I purposefully "forget" my books so my friends don't see me walking around with them all the time. It is hard to have to choose between playing basketball, my mom's wishes, and my friends' opinions, so I manage to do a little of each and it is working so far. I don't think my teachers understand that my goals right now are different than what they expect from me. Sure they think school comes first, but it doesn't all the time, and when it does, it is sometimes for reasons that are different from theirs. They want me to always look ahead to my future, but I can tell you that how I get along with everyone each day is more important. I also have my little brother to consider. He has to learn what is right and wrong from me, not some teacher who doesn't know what goes on in our family. My family keeps things private, and I tell him not to talk about our stuff with teachers and guidance counselors. I don't think a lot of people would understand that I have some "fatherly" responsibilities at my age, and that my mom may do things differently, but she does the best she can. So do I.

---

*T.J. is in grade 11 in high school.

traditional Western, white, middle and upper class culture. Frequently, knowledge learned through their cultural environment is not valued by the school. For example, many educators are critical of native dialects and want all students to learn Standard English. As stated by Erickson (1972): "Until recently a major function of the public school was the Americanization of immigrants. Rigid adherence to Standard English in the classroom was one of the school's defensive responses to its inundation by culturally different immigrant children" (p. 19). It is important to understand that additional dialects and communication forms exist (e.g., Ebonics, also called Black English or African American Language is common among urban and working class African Americans) and may be an important part of the student's cultural identity. By not recognizing and respecting a student's use of the dialect, a teacher sends the message that an important part of the student's culture and family is unacceptable.

Franklin (1992) identifies several child-rearing practices common among African American families that may influence children's behavior in other settings. For example, African American children

- have a significant amount of interactions among many family members;
- learn how to be assertive at a young age;
- take on significant family responsibilities at an early age;
- experience "high-energy, fast-paced home environments, where there is simultaneous variable stimulation (e.g., television and music playing simultaneously)" (p. 118); and
- are socialized about racism and poverty at an early age.

Okun et al. (1999) identify seven commonly agreed-upon identities of African Americans: interdependence, emotional vitality, collective survival, oral tradition, rhythm, improvisation, and spirituality.

## Recommendations for Schools and Teachers

Some teachers believe that it is inappropriate to change their behavior or make other accommodations for students from different cultures. They think that all students should be treated in the same way. Part of this attitude may stem from a reliance on the 19th-century "culture neutral" model of schooling that was designed to create one system that merged all students regardless of cultural origins (the melting pot theory mentioned earlier). However, Ladson-Billings (2000) explains the shortfalls of thinking that "equality means sameness" and warns us about the dangers of applying the same remedy to all situations and contexts (p. 208). Those who do make accommodations feel

> that people's behavior . . . is influenced by different cultural veneers. They have different criteria for success. They find different forms of praise and recognition rewarding. They differ in terms of when, where, why, and how they are willing to accept criticism or condemnation. They also express acceptance and rejection in their own culturally determined ways. Therefore, if teachers expect all individuals to behave the same way or interpret everyone's behavior from a single culturally determined point of view, they may

*fail to respond to the unique needs of many of their ethnic minority students. (Grossman, 1995, pp. 122–123)*

## Deal with Feelings of Alienation

Teachers need to understand that parents of color often report higher levels of alienation and isolation in their relationship with public schools than white parents (Jones, 1985). This alienation should be examined in light of the school's culture and the parents' perception of that culture, along with an understanding of the parents' previous experiences within the school system. For example, parents of color may view school regulations as arbitrarily determined and applied according to the prevailing white, middle-class culture. Furthermore, they may perceive the school's organizational policies and procedures as hostile and identify a lack of "friendliness" and overt attempts by teachers not to relate to them positively (Jones, 1985). Schwartz (2001) cites evidence that African American students are suspended much more often than whites. This disciplinary discrepancy can contribute to increased mistrust and alienation.

## Value Extended Family

In a study of teenage parents and their families, Tatum, Moseley, Boyd-Franklin, and Herzog (1995) stress the importance of the "extended family" in the lives of African American children. Tatum et al. describe this extended family as a "complex extended family" or "a closely knit network of households that might include a mother, father, children, grandmother, grandfather, aunts, uncles, and cousins" (p. 19). The extended family may also include many nonblood "relatives," such as "boyfriends, neighbors, friends, godparents, and, in some cases, members of the church family, such as a minister, brothers and sisters in the church" (p. 19). The authors state that it is a serious error for those working with African American children not to learn about the significant others in the child's life because all of these extended family members often play significant roles in "parenting" the child. Tatum et al. also stress that child care frequently takes on an "intergenerational theme" across parents and grandparents. So while teachers may assume that important notes should be mailed "home" to a student's parents, the child may be temporarily staying with grandparents. Teachers are encouraged to view the bonds of the extended family and the adaptability of family roles as strengths of the African American family that provides important coping skills, caretaking, and socialization functions (Gopaul-McNicol & Thomas-Presswood, 1998).

## Facilitate Positive Parent-School Relationship

Teachers often contact family members only when their children are in trouble. Since the teachers become associated with predominantly negative information about their children, the teacher-parent relationship becomes strained. As a result, parent-teacher interactions may become dominated by confrontation rather than mutual respect. This situation frequently occurs when teachers are working with parents of students who have behavioral problems. But teachers can learn how to balance comments about a child's inappropriate behavior with positive remarks that will communicate to the parent that the good things about their child, the child they love, are also recognized by the teacher.

A consistent pattern of discrimination is also established by administrators who make changes in school assignments, policy, or instructional methods without first consulting people, including people of color, from the larger school community. One way to alleviate some of these concerns is to have an active and effective parent-community involvement advisory board for each school that looks at the whole or general needs of the school rather than isolated parts (Banks & Banks, 1989).

Due to disparities in economic conditions, African Americans and their children often are treated as clients and not as consumers by school personnel. Educators often attribute poor academic performance of African Americans to a lack of parental interest, when in fact education is a strong value in the African American culture. Banks (1991) found that African American parents may not want to be passive participants, and their children passive recipients, in the education process. As with other parents, however, many African American parents feel that they lack the personal knowledge or confidence to confront school officials about their concerns.

Jones (1985) found that many African American parents continue to believe school officials covertly maintain discriminatory attitudes that reflect cultural biases against them and their children. Attempts to mask these attitudes have not been successful, and many parents have developed a passive attitude to help their children survive in the public school environment. This passivity may be translated as a "negative attitude" by many educators.

### *Maintain High Expectations*

According to Grossman (1995), teachers tend to have lower expectations for poor, African American students and "tend to evaluate them lower than objective evidence warrants, praise and call on them less often, criticize them more often, and use harsher and more punitive disciplinary techniques with them" (p. 357). Schwartz (2001) claims, "School practices may fail to account for the knowledge, cognitive abilities, culture, and values of African American students. The reasons for differential treatment of students of color and white students are many and complex, but the result is often the same: African American students may feel encouraged to act out" (paragraph 3). McCadden (1998) found that teachers try to control black males more than whites, and that white males are excused for their bad behavior more often than black males.

The following list, adapted from Randall-David (1989) and Berry and Asamen (1989), outlines some behaviors frequently associated with the African American culture and misinterpreted by teachers:

- look away while listening,
- stand close to others when talking,
- are reluctant to talk about family problems and personal relationships,
- are concerned with present more than future goals,
- embrace cultural norms if they are living in low socioeconomic conditions but not if they live in middle- or upper-class conditions,

- believe that most individuals within the white culture do not understand or want to understand their culture, and
- express their emotions more intensely than other students.

Schwartz (2001) recommends that teachers enforce fair and culturally sensitive classroom rules, model knowledge of and respect for diverse cultures, contextualize misbehavior by eliciting reasons and various perspectives before disciplining students, and customize punishments based on promoting responsibility and positive change rather than humiliation and retribution.

# HISPANICS/LATINOS

## Demographics

Hispanics/Latinos may be of any race. They are of European, African, Asiatic, and Native American extraction. Within the various countries and in different areas of each country, the degree and variety of racial mixes change according to the historical realities of the locality (National Catholic Educational Association, 1987). Census 2000 revised its questions on race and Hispanic origin to reflect this diversity. The federal government considers race and Hispanic origin to be two separate and distinct concepts, and uses the Office of Management and Budget (OMB) definition of Hispanic/Latino: "a person of Cuban, Mexican, Puerto Rican, South or Central American, or other Spanish culture or origin regardless of race" (1997, p. 1).

Hispanic/Latino children may prefer working more in cooperative groups than on independent assignments.

The Hispanic/Latino population grew faster than any other racial or ethnic group in the United States between 1980 and 1998. During this time, the Hispanic/Latino population increased at five times the rate of non-Hispanic/Latino populations. The U.S. Census Bureau (2001) reports that Hispanics/Latinos have increased their population from 14.6 million in 1980 to an estimated 35.3 million in 2000 (12.3 million are under the age of 18), and they now comprise 12.5% of the U.S. population. It is projected that by the year 2050, 24.3% of the U.S. population will be Hispanic/Latino. While Hispanic/Latino families typically have a high birthrate, some of the increase in population can be attributed to immigration. Most Hispanics/Latinos come looking for a livelihood denied them in their native land due to poor economic conditions. The illegal immigrant population is estimated at between 8 and 9 million, with almost 50% from Mexico ("Rise Seen," 2002). The largest group within the Hispanic/Latino population consists of Mexican Americans, who account for 65% of Hispanics/Latinos. They are the second largest ethnic minority group in the United States and will soon be the largest. Other groups that make up the Hispanic/Latino people in America and their estimated current population, according to the U.S. Census Bureau (2001), are as follows:

| *Subgroup* | *Percentage of Hispanics/Latinos* |
|---|---|
| Mexican | 65% |
| Puerto Rican | 12% |
| Cuban | 8% |
| Other | 15% |

The Hispanic/Latino population is one of the youngest major ethnic groups in the United States (second only to Native Americans). Thirty-eight percent of Hispanics/Latinos are under 20 years of age compared to 28.7% of all Americans (U.S. Department of Commerce, 1999). Traditionally, Hispanic/Latino families are large, and children are valued as an important part of the extended family system.

While college enrollment of Hispanics grew 68% during the 1990s (compared to a 48% increase for all minorities), they have the highest high school dropout rate (30% in 1996) and the lowest college attendance rate (34.1% in 1998) of all ethnic groups. Census 2000 reported that while almost 85% of whites graduate from high school or more, only 57% of Hispanics/Latinos do the same. However, this percentage doubled from only 28% for Hispanics in 1970. A report from the Pew Hispanic Center says that the gap between rates of high school graduation for Hispanics and the American-born population will continue to narrow as more immigrants get their education in the United States and younger residents outnumber older residents ("Rise Seen," 2002). This also increases the pressure on schools to teach the immigrants the English language. A recent national study found that 60% of Hispanic fourth graders cannot read an age-appropriate book compared to 38% nationally ("Improving Reading," 2001). The situation for foreign-born Hispanics is grimmer. Forty-four percent of foreign-born Hispanics drop out of high school, compared with 17% of U.S.-born Hispanics. According to the Bureau of Justice Statistics (2001), an estimated 16% of Hispanic/Latino males will enter state or federal prison during their lifetime, compared to 4.4% of white males.

## Cultural Influences on Behavior

Because of the immense diversity of the Hispanic/Latino population, and because Mexican Americans make up the majority of Hispanics/Latinos, this section focuses on the Mexican American people. Commonality across Hispanics/Latinos, however, is found in the Spanish background, language (except for the people of Brazil, who speak Portuguese), geographic ancestry, and religion or faith. Although some similarities are found in the behaviors of children from various Hispanic/Latino cultures, teachers are cautioned to recognize the individuality of all their students.

### *The Importance of the Family*

For most Mexican Americans the family represents their highest priority and strongest allegiance. "Familismo" (strong commitment, obligation, and responsibility) is considered one of the most important cultural values of Hispanics/Latinos (McEachern & Kenny, 2002). Traditionally, whenever a child needs to make a choice between school or family, the family holds the stronger position and will likely take precedence over school obligations. When there is a family celebration, special function, or circumstance requiring participation, the family members must be in attendance. Because of the physical proximity of their homeland to the United States, Mexican Americans can return home more easily than other Hispanic/Latino groups and may travel often to support family left in Mexico, help with family affairs, or attend family events. According to Mexican American traditions, family loyalty comes before adherence to any schooling or job obligation.

Bonding and loyalty tie the family together. The Hispanic/Latino extended surrogate family can consist of parents, siblings, grandparents, aunts, uncles, cousins, adopted grandparents, close friends, and in-laws. Especially high regard is awarded grandparents and other elderly adults. Questioning them is interpreted as disrespectful (McEachern & Kenny, 2002). Furthermore, family life stresses dependence on, and involvement with, one another, and sharing the joys and sorrows among family members. Blood relatives and godparents are joined to the family through such events as baptism and confirmation. Godparents are considered to be members of the family and participate in all family events as if they were blood relatives.

Though variations exist in family patterns (especially when acculturation or assimilation is a factor), the Hispanic family is characterized by rigid family, gender, and sex roles: authority on the part of the father, "machismo" (strength, virility, and authoritarian) expectations for men, loyalty and compassion on the part of the mother, female purity, and obedience and submission on the part of the children. The individual gains identity and self-esteem in relation to the family group. The collective interest of the family takes precedence over the individual's goals.

Caring, sharing, obedience, respect, loyalty, responsibility, and interdependence are stressed. (McEachern & Kenny, 2002; National Catholic Educational Association, 1987).

### Religion, Festivals, and Celebrations

Hispanics emphasize spirituality, and religion is often a support system. The majority of Hispanics are Catholics, but numbers for other religions are increasing (McEachern & Kenny, 2002). Church festivals and important family events become major celebrations for Hispanics/Latinos and their communities. The family celebrations are of both life and death. For example, celebrations of life are those of baptism, marriages, or a coming-of-age ceremony for young girls called a *quinceanera*. The last event sometimes occurs early in the young girl's life. Following this celebration and a traditional church ceremony, young women are ready to be courted and married. In some regions of the United States, families have incurred great debt in their dedication to provide a major gala occasion for their daughters. Similarly, men are introduced to society at age 18 when they are supposedly ready to support and care for a wife and family. These ceremonies and celebrations may be held within the home, church, or other community setting.

Celebrations of death are also deeply rooted in the Hispanic/Latino culture and religion. Because the Catholic Church plays such a significant role in the lives and religious beliefs of Hispanic/Latino people, death is viewed as a passage into a new life and, thus, should be celebrated. This celebration, called the Mass of the Resurrection, is usually held at a Catholic church. Another celebration of death among Hispanics/Latinos is the Dia de los Muertos (Day of the Dead). Dia de los Muertos celebrates death as a natural process of life and provides participants with an opportunity to remember those who have died. It includes a community procession in which participants carry candles and may wear skeleton costumes or black clothing. The procession usually concludes with a ceremonial dance.

### Categories of Worldview

Research (Altarriba & Bauer, 1998) suggests that many Hispanics/Latinos share the following beliefs:

- Nature: Hispanics believe people have very little control over nature, and people are one with nature. "Nature is one's partner in life, and if anything, a person must subjugate himself or herself for nature's benefit" (p. 393).
- Time: Most Hispanics/Latinos have a present-centered time orientation. The activity or relationship in the moment takes precedence over past and future behaviors and obligations.
- Activity: Activity and behavior are spontaneous and expressive in emotions and desires.

- Social Relations: Relationships are often hierarchical, linear, and authoritative. The role of subordination is usually clear. Collectivism and personal interdependence are valued.

## Language and Conversation

The majority of first-generation Hispanics/Latinos speak Spanish. Language switching and language mixing may be common in households with different generations and different levels of acculturation. In a recent study by El Hispanic News (1998), 87% of Hispanic adults are more comfortable with Spanish than English and 91% prefer that their children learn to speak Spanish in the home. Children are often asked to translate for parents in a school setting, even though this may violate family rules of authority and respect. Teachers should be aware of the pressure on the child and embarrassment on the part of the parent. When one is accustomed to holding conversations in his or her native language, the communication will be much more animated. Mexican Americans are very visual and prefer to use more of the senses while communicating. A sensual conversational style is intimate and carries more emotion so that conversation is lively when spoken within the native language and familiar vocabulary. Speaking Spanish is also an expression of pride in one's culture and self. In Spanish or in English, conversations may be animated when expressing emotional events or feelings in a trusting situation.

Open participation is the rule for joining a group discussion. One does not need to wait patiently for a timely pause in order to enter the conversation. Interruptions in Hispanic/Latino culture are not considered rude. These conversational expectations are direct opposites to mainstream politeness, along with Asian and Native American modes of correct behaviors. For Hispanics/Latinos, these cultural expectations are meant to bring people together and encourage them to participate in conversations and interactions with one another.

## Relationships with Others

Family relationships, birth order, and duties have an all-encompassing importance. The status of the older sibling, for example, depends on his or her ability to care for the smaller children. Likewise, the well-being of younger siblings depends on the help given by older siblings. The rearing of girls is different from the rearing of boys. All of this can impact a child's behavior in school.

Most Mexican American students and family members are accustomed to sharing and helping one another. Teachers report that their students are frequently busy helping each other instead of listening to the teacher. Many Mexican American children would probably be comfortable in a cooperative and dependent environment (i.e., cooperative learning, sharing tasks, peer teaching). Traditional Mexican American children may perform poorly in situations that emphasize or require individual competition and individual achievement. Thus, teachers are recommended to use more group discussions, group projects, and group reinforcement when possible with these students.

## Recommendations for Schools and Teachers

Okun et al. (1999) identify nine common identities of Hispanics/Latinos: interdependence, conformity, avoidance of interpersonal conflict, strong loyalty and attachment, clearly defined gender roles, obedience to authority, flexible attitudes toward time, support to extended family, and collective identity (p. 263). Altarriba and Bauer (1998) recommend attention to issues surrounding a child's migration and place of residence, socioeconomics, value orientations (including worldview), family characteristics and values, and language.

Recommendations to teachers and other professionals for success when working with Hispanic/Latino Americans include establishing personal rapport, working in groups, and having group discussions. Once trust has been established, tasks can be divided into smaller units. At first, the student must understand the group goal; then he or she can be asked to perform something individually. It is important to define the totality and ensure that each task is well defined and understood before proceeding with smaller units in the lesson. Unfortunately, some teachers may view this group-dependent behavior as immature instead of culturally based (Grossman, 1995). Grossman (1995) recommends that teachers understand the importance of sharing among Hispanic/Latino children. Teachers should know that Hispanic/Latino students are more likely to share their materials and personal belongings and expect others to want to do the same. They may feel rejected or confused when peers talk in terms of what is "mine" versus "yours."

As outlined in Vignette 14.2, the teacher and professional must make personal, caring efforts to attend to the cooperative nature of the Hispanic/Latino. One must know the loyalties and structure of the family along with the ideas and beliefs that are most important to each family.

Once again, teachers must be familiar with the traditional values and belief systems so that they appreciate the various effects they may have on children's behaviors. How much each individual adheres to these values and behaviors will be the mystery discovered in the classroom.

Behaviors associated with the Hispanic/Latino culture are presented in the following list, adapted from Randall-David (1989, pp. 55–59):

- touch people with whom they are speaking; may engage in introductory embrace, kissing on the cheek, or backslapping;
- stand close to people with whom they are speaking;
- interpret prolonged eye contact as disrespectful;
- keep family or personal information from strangers;
- have a high regard for family and extended family;
- treat the elderly with respect;
- help other family members and friends with child care;
- are emotionally expressive;
- have traditionally prescribed sex roles for males and females; and
- expect their children to consult with parents on important issues.

## VIGNETTE 14.2

●
_____

### *Interactions with the School Community:*
### *A Hispanic/Latino Parent's Perspective*

#### ***Rosalind Esteves****

Dear Educators:

What I tell you may not be the same thing that other Hispanic/Latino parents tell you. The Hispanic/Latino population is very diverse. I am writing in an effort to try and make the most of my child's education. I am a mother who is deeply concerned about her children. I don't always perceive that my children are totally understood, or that they are getting the most out of the educational system here in the U.S. I am Latino and I am raising my children to appreciate their cultural identity and the values that are associated with the Latino world. I am not sure this message is being conveyed at their school. Please do not misconstrue my comments for accusations. I understand that many of the manifested biases are deeply ingrained within the very institutions of this country. As teachers you are part of those institutions. I want to let you know what is important to me and my family as Latinos, but ultimately you can make the choice to accept or reject what we feel identifies us as a people.

I appreciate the American way of individualism. We want our children to do the same, but for us there is something more important than individual achievements and individual gain. It is very important for the typical American to "Be all you can be," but this is less important for my family. Our motto would be more like "Be all *we* can be." Our family unit is fairly large and very close-knit. We look out for one another. When a member of the family falters, or when one takes a step backward, we make the necessary adjustments to help out, even at the expense of individual gain. All family members' opinions matter; decisions are not made alone. Autonomy is not what we strive for. Please try and remember this when you talk to a Latino student who is struggling with his or her actions or decisions. Involving the family can go a long way in helping resolve problems. This piece is very important to understanding who we are. Although you may view us as "enmeshed," we are a very close-knit, interdependent unit, and we value and respect each member of the system.

Our children have learned to respect and value their elders. Adults are listened to, and it is considered disrespectful for our children to talk back to any adult. It is also important to take the *consejo* (advice) of adults. It would not be advantageous for a child to contradict any advice that may come from elder members of the family. The child would be considered disrespectful and may alienate the family. If you question decisions or behaviors that my children make or do, invite me to come in and discuss the concerns. Remember that not all Latinos have learned fluent English and may need a translator. This does not make them incapable of understanding, so address them as you would an English-speaking parent.

Our children also have learned to watch out for one another. It is drummed into them from a very young age to take care of one another, and to especially watch out for the younger ones. I can still remember an incident on the school bus when my son was disciplined for fighting with another student. Although I do not condone violence under any circumstances, no one bothered to try and understand that there was a reason for his outburst. This particular student had been picking on my son's cousin for weeks. She had suffered great anguish at the hand of this student and her tears wore on my son's patience. Yes, I believe both boys deserved to be disciplined, but understanding my son's motivation for his actions would have brought about a more productive result for all involved.

*(continued)*

I hope my words help you appreciate what makes our children seem "different" at times. Many of our cultural norms and values are in contrast with what is being taught as "normal," so my hope is that this letter makes you more aware of some aspects of the Hispanic culture. Accepting and respecting who we are will go a long way in understanding our children and creating the proper teaching environment for them. We have many different values and customs that do not always coincide with what you recognize. Because of the many differences, we are sometimes viewed as "not going with the program." As I see it, we are living out the great American dream without losing who we are in the process.

---

*Rosalind Esteves is the mother of four school-age children, and the Director of Affirmative Action for Classified Staff at McDaniel College.

# ASIAN (PACIFIC) AMERICANS

## Demographics

The Asian American population (including Asians, Native Hawaiians, and Pacific Islanders) is one of the fastest growing ethnic groups in the United States and currently represents 38% of all immigrants in the United States (U.S. Census Bureau, 2001). From 1980 to 2000, the number of Asian Americans rose from 3.8 million to over 12.6 million, with a 57% increase since 1990. Since 1980, the Asian American community has grown from 1.7% to 4.5% of the U.S. population (U.S. Census Bureau, 2001). By the year 2050, the Asian American population in the United States is predicted to grow to 9.7% of the population (over 37 million) compared to 22.5% for Hispanics/Latinos, .90% for Native Americans, and 14.4% for African Americans. California and New York are home to almost half of the Asian American population.

The Asian American population (much like the diversity within the Hispanic/Latino population) is far from a homogenous group. The literature has identified over 40 subgroups including Filipino, Korean, Cambodian, Thai, Hmong, Hawaiian, Chinese, Laotian, and Pakistani (Baruth & Manning, 2003). There are four major groups of Asian Americans: East Asian (e.g., Chinese, Japanese, Korean); Southeast Asian (Vietnamese, Thai, Cambodian, Laotian); South Asian (e.g., Indian, Pakistani); and Pacific Islander (e.g., Hawaiian, Samoan). More than 6 million Asian Americans reside in California, New York, Hawaii, and New Jersey. Although many of the subgroups may share similar cultural values and characteristics, each group also has its own history and immigration and cultural patterns that may influence behavior. As we have emphasized for each ethnic group, it is important for teachers not to make overgeneralizations regarding "Asian American" students' academic performance or behavior.

Chinese Americans make up the largest group of Asian Americans (24%) followed by Filipino (19%); Asian Indians (17%); Vietnamese (11%); and Korean (10.5%). Thirteen percent identified themselves as "Other Asian" (U.S. Census Bureau, 2001). While 60% of Asian Americans are foreign born, and 88% of Asian American elementary and high school students have at least one foreign-born parent, the average Japanese American speaks English as his or her native language, while almost no Southeast Asians do (Department of Education, 2001). Because of the increasing Southeast Asian immigration, language problems among Asian American students are expected to increase.

About one in three Asians arrives in America with a college degree, and 85.7% of Asian Americans complete high school (more than any other racial or ethnic group, including whites), while 44% complete college (compared to 26.1% for whites) (U.S. Census Bureau, 2001). While Asian American SAT verbal scores (413) are below the U.S. average (423), their math SAT scores (532) are higher than the U.S. average (476) (U.S. Department of Education, 2001). Because of their competence in math and the physical sciences, Asian Americans represent a disproportionate share of minority students at many colleges and universities (Tollefson, 1986). However, it is important to note that most Asian students are not gifted, and "the wiz-kid" stereotype, often applied to East Asian children, is a gross generalization (Huang, 1996, p. 5). These stereotypes obscure the immense diversity within Asian communities and ignore many existing problems. For example, in Philadelphia, 40% to 50% of Asian American students drop out of high school. And while Vietnamese students in Orange County, California, are disproportionately overrepresented as high school valedictorians, this same group also has the highest rate of truancy and suspensions of any ethnic group (Rumbaut & Kenji, 1988).

Asian Americans are one of the most diverse ethnic groups in the United States today. Four primary subgroups of Asian Americans will be discussed here: the Chinese, Japanese, Koreans, and Southeast Asians.

## Chinese

The Chinese first arrived in the United States in great numbers between 1849 and 1870. Some came from the Toishan district in Guandong, but most came from the provincial area of Kwangtung on the south China coast. This was a commercial port city that routinely gathered news from around the world. When word came about the gold rush in California, many citizens decided to seek new opportunities in America.

After the mining industry slowed, many Chinese found jobs working on the railroad. The owners were so impressed by their efficiency that other Chinese were recruited. When the major railroad construction projects were completed, many Chinese turned to other enterprises in agriculture and fishing. A large number settled in urban areas—the most notable of which was San Francisco, where Chinatown became a social, political, and cultural center for the Chinese. It provided the Chinese immigrants with a community of shared language and tradition. Approximately 37,000 Chinese immigrated to the United States in 1998. Today, there are 1.07 million foreign-born Chinese living in the United States (U.S. Census Bureau, 2001).

## Japanese

In the late 1800s, Japan faced overpopulation, political turmoil, and depressed agricultural conditions. Its citizens began immigrating to Hawaii and the U.S. mainland in search of better opportunities. The largest number of Japanese immigrants arrived in the United States between 1891 and 1924. In the early 1900s, a number of legislative acts were passed that were discriminatory against the Japanese. The most devastating of these was the Executive Order 9066 signed by President Roosevelt in 1942, which resulted in the internment of Japanese Americans.

Compared to other Asian groups, few Japanese have emigrated to the United States in the last 25 years because of the highly developed economy in Japan and its ability to provide necessary employment. As a result, the Japanese in the United States are one of the smallest Asian groups (Kan & Liu, 1986). Approximately 5,100 Japanese immigrated to the United States in 1998 (U.S. Census Bureau, 2001). With a relatively low rate of immigration, structural assimilation into the American mainstream is quite likely.

## Koreans

The number of Koreans in the United States has increased in the past 25 years. The first Koreans came to the United States in 1881, and, later, many more came as students. A significant number of Koreans were also recruited to work on the sugar plantations of Hawaii in the early 1900s. Few Koreans, however, immigrated to the United States until 1965. Many Koreans immigrated as political refugees following the Russo-Japanese war when the Japanese occupied and annexed Korea. The 2000 census reports over 700,000 Koreans now residing in the United States. In 1998 alone, over 14,000 Koreans immigrated to the United States (U.S. Census Bureau, 2001).

## Southeast Asians

The end of the Vietnam War and the fall of Saigon in 1975 sparked a mass immigration of Vietnamese, Laotian, and Cambodian people to the United States. Indeed, in the past two decades, over 1 million Southeast Asian immigrants have settled in the United States (863,000 from Vietnam; and over 500,00 from Laos and Kampuchea, the former Cambodia) (U.S. Census Bureau, 2001). The Vietnamese are one of the fastest growing Asian groups in the United States.

The people of Vietnam, Laos, and Kampuchea have unique but intertwined histories, religions, and cultures. Each country has a national language, as well as several languages of ethnic subgroups. For example, the languages of Vietnam include Vietnamese, French, and Chinese. The Hmong, a subgroup in Laos, speak their own language of Hmong. Consequently, it is incorrect to assume that all Southeast Asian refugees can communicate with each other or share a common culture. Immigrants from Southeast Asia are a diverse group.

The formal education rates for the Vietnamese immigrants are higher than the Laotian or Khmer rates. Three-quarters of Vietnamese refugees have received a high school education or higher. This high education rate has served as a significant factor in the success that the Vietnamese have achieved in the United States.

Laos can be divided into three regions: lowland, midland, and highland. The dominant ethnic Lao occupy the lowland and midland. The Hmong, an ethnic minority, reside in the highlands. The cultures and religions of the Lao and Hmong are different, and the relationship between the two groups can be best described as tumultuous. Since most of the Lao were subsistence farmers, most immigrating to the United States arrived without any formal education.

Approximately 150,000 Hmong have immigrated to the United States. California, Minnesota, and Wisconsin have sizeable populations of Hmong. While in the highlands of Laos, the Hmong practiced slash-and-burn farming techniques. Most arrive in the United States without any formal education and are not literate in their own native language. McInnis (1990) summarizes the plight of the Hmong this way:

> Of all the Southeast Asian refugee groups, the Hmong are the most severely disadvantaged. They arrive in the United States with large numbers of unemployable dependents. Adults were illiterate in their own language, had little occupational experience other than small-scale farming and warfare, and had rarely been exposed to Western culture. (p. 6)

The Khmer (people from Kampuchea) represent all levels of socioeconomic status. While 44% have no formal education prior to their immigration, 56% have, at a minimum, some high school education.

## Cultural Influences on Behavior (East Asia: China, Japan, Korea)

As we have just discussed, Asian Americans are a diverse group. Thus, it is difficult to describe general cultural influences on behavior. In this chapter, cultural influences on the behavior of East Asians (Chinese, Japanese, and Korean Americans) will be outlined separately from the people of Southeast Asia.

One way to begin to understand East Asians from China, Japan, and Korea is to examine their social structure (Kan & Liu, 1986). In China, Japan, and Korea, Confucianism has served for centuries as the essential basis for their ethical, social, cultural, and political life. This structure provides a framework for understanding motivation and behavior, which is essential for communication in education.

The foundation of Confucianism is the dictum of the so-called "five cardinal relationships" between father and son, wife and husband, elder and younger brother, friend and friend, ruler and subject. The dictum decrees that these relationships, except that between friends, are inherently unequal. The husband is superior to his wife by virtue of sex, the father is superior to his son and the elder to the younger brother by virtue of age, and ruler is superior to subjects by virtue of status. In this framework of relationships, where there are only superiors and inferiors, a superior holds absolute authority over an inferior. At least in theory, if not always in practice, an inferior is expected to obey the superior. It is from this absolute premise that Confucian society is organized. This is why the concept of equality before God or supreme law or the value of human rights (or individual rights) has never evolved in the tradition of Confucianism.

In this system, a person's worth is determined primarily by sex, age, or social status, not by the intrinsic value of life or the individual self. A strong emphasis on the hierarchy of a relationship, as well as on the family group rather than the individual, is built into many aspects of Confucian culture. For example, in Korea as in Japan and China, one's family name precedes one's personal name.

Perhaps the most important example of the effects of Confucian culture is language. In Korean and Japanese, it is not essential for a sentence to indicate singular personal pronouns, particularly that of first-person. Thus, these elements are often omitted in daily conversation. The function of a Korean verb is also drastically different from that of an English verb. A Korean verb comes at the end of a sentence and changes forms according to the status of the speaker in relation to the listener. Since language binds cultures to belief systems, this rule has a significant impact on the entire system.

### Issues of Gender and Sexuality

Standards for social behavior between the sexes are probably most contrasting in Confucian and American cultures. In Confucian tradition boys and girls are brought up in strict separation from an early age. This custom is deeply rooted in the Confucian teachings, starting with the Confucian dictum of the five cardinal relationships mentioned earlier. It is further reinforced by the Confucian precept that boys and girls must not sit together after the age of 7.

Although today there are some signs that this custom is changing in some urban segments of the country, the Confucian teaching on the male-female relationships still has a formidable hold on the mind and manner of Asian people and virtually dominates the social fabric of their lives. Traditionally and at the present time, the separation between boys and girls in Asian countries is strictly enforced in elementary school. In the lower grades, boys and girls may share the same classroom, but the boys are seated on one side of the classroom and girls on the other. Some teachers may even try to make a boy sit with a girl as punishment. One 16-year-old girl who came to the United States at age 11 reported that her former teachers would say, "You guys keep quiet, or I'll mix you boys and girls and make you sit by each other." She stated that the students were terrified by this.

In the upper classes, boys and girls are grouped separately in different classrooms. In school or out, boys and girls do not play with one another. One American mother who adopted two sisters age 8 and 10 reported that the girls were uncomfortable in the presence of boys, did not know how to play with boys, and found it difficult to cope with boys' teasing.

Needless to say, the enforcement of strict division between the sexes influences interactions and relationships. For example, when an Asian child sees another child of the opposite sex in school or in the street, one neither greets nor talks to the other, even though they know each other (Spero, 1985). Of course, this behavior exhibited in the United States might be misinterpreted as inappropriate. Some children of mixed parentage, or children who have lived outside the mainstream of Asian culture, may not follow traditional behavior (Overbeck, 1984).

Asian teenagers receive little or no sex education at home or in school, other than the instruction girls receive from their mothers about menstruation. Biological changes in adolescent years, as well as the emotional experiences of young people, are paid little attention. Girls rarely discuss matters of sex with others, although some girls may read about sex or talk about it with their close girlfriends. Discussing sex-related matters is often considered in bad taste. Platonic relationships are much admired and romanticized in Korea and Japan, where open sexual expressions are generally looked on with contempt. This attitude often carries over into social interactions by Asian Americans in the United States. Unless others bring up this subject, married women do not openly talk about their pregnancies or send birth announcements. Pregnancy is accepted as part of the natural course of marriage, just as growing old is.

Dating between the sexes is generally permitted after graduation from high school. At this time girls are allowed to use makeup and face cream or powder, but in a modest manner. They may change their hairstyle from pigtails to permanent waves and wear clothes of their choice instead of school uniforms. However, some girls may be very careful not to expose their bodies.

## Discipline

Since the types of social structure differ between Confucian and American cultures, the methods of discipline used in each culture are correspondingly different. In the United States, where the individual is the most basic social unit, individual rights and responsibilities are emphasized. Accordingly, American parents train their children to stand up for their own rights and the rights of others, to be autonomous, and to become independent of them. In contrast, in Korea and other East Asian countries where the family is the basic social unit, the individual is primarily part of the family. Accordingly, Asian parents teach their children not to think for themselves but to think of themselves as part of the group. They put greater emphasis on teaching their children to be loyal to their group—whether family or nation—than on individual rights or responsibilities. The concept of "our" rather than "my" is emphasized. For example, Asian children say "our mother" or "our family" instead of "my mother" or "my family." In school and at home, the child is exhorted to obey authority and to conform to group norms and be like everyone else (Zhang & Carrasquillo, 1995). The value of uniformity and conformity is strongly instilled in children from an early age.

Some Asian parents often use commanding, exhortation, fear-inspiring tactics, or, as the last resort, physical punishment. During the preschool years, Asian mothers tend to be excessively indulgent and often do not discipline their children. They may believe that the child is too young to know better and that discipline is more appropriate for older children. Instead, mothers may try to pacify their children with candy or toys or scare tactics as a primary method of behavioral control

(Prendergast, 1985; Walker, 1987). As a result, some of these young children may have some problems adapting to the guidelines and structure of the educational setting.

Despite the many differences in culture, values, and behaviors that can be found among Chinese, Japanese, and Korean Americans, they share a belief in the importance of education. In Asia, traditionally and today, the attainment of a good education is a common dream. It is regarded as the ultimate key to success and social status (Zhang & Carrasquillo, 1995). For example, one might hear an Asian mother tell her children to "study hard" or "obey your teacher" when the children go to school. When the children return from school, the mother may ask, "Did you study hard?" Relatives and peers may greet children by asking, "Are you studying hard?"

## Cultural Influences on Behavior (Southeast Asia)

While there are many cultural differences among Southeast Asians, the importance of the extended paternal family is shared by most. The extended family serves as a unit of social organization and economic success of the family. For example, the Hmong extend their concept of "family" to a "clan." There are 18 Hmong clans, which correspond to 18 Hmong surnames. The Vietnamese, Khmer, and Lao have similar connections to distant relatives.

The focus of child rearing among many Southeast Asians is on the family rather than the individual child. Children are generally taught to value and consider the needs of the family and community above their own needs. Thus, children are reinforced for behaviors that "maintain and improve the family name" (Morrow, 1987, p. 290). Additionally, children are expected to have unquestioned loyalty and obedience to parents. This obedience is usually extended to other authority figures, including teachers.

Studies conducted by Baizerman and Hendricks (1988) of women between the ages of 13 and 24 found that Khmer women had career goals reflecting motivation to work outside the home and believed that an appropriate age for marriage is between 18 and 25. For Vietnamese women, results varied more according to their current educational status, but many aspired to continue their education beyond high school. Hmong women, however, expressed significant differences in their hopes for the future. Many of the Hmong were already married and had significant responsibilities at home, especially caring for many young children. Getting married at a very young age is not uncommon in Laos, where women marry as young as age 12. In the United States, these young marriages continue and place many Hmong women at a serious economic disadvantage.

Significant for teachers, Southeast Asians are not accustomed to the idea of parental involvement in their children's school. As stated by Schwartz (1996, p. 2):

> In general, Asians think about social institutions such as schools quite differently from educators, seeing teachers as professionals with authority over their children's schooling. They believe that parents are not supposed to interfere with school processes, and may regard teachers who seek parent involvement as incompetent.

As a result, Asian parents may believe that it is inappropriate to visit a child's school or question teachers about their child, because it may imply that the teacher is not doing an adequate job. Schwartz (1996) recommends the following to facilitate parental involvement of Asian parents:

- Explain that parent involvement is a tradition in American education.
- Encourage involvement without increasing family tension by respecting tradition that demands that the young obey the elderly.
- Offer a family English literacy project to help parents understand how teaching and learning takes place in the United States and to bridge the generational gaps within families.
- Make it clear that a child's psychological or academic problems are not a source of shame, and that cooperation between family and the professionals can solve them.

## Recommendations for Schools and Teachers

Not surprisingly, teachers frequently describe the behavior of Asian children as respectful and obedient, as well as highly motivated to learn. However, because many Asian students may not be as assertive as other students, some teachers may perceive them as unmotivated or unresponsive (Grossman, 1995).

As with other minority groups, conflicts emerge between the values Asian children learn at school and those taught at home. For example, in traditional Indochinese homes, the children are taught to respect older people and to be quiet, polite, modest, and humble. The conflicting behavioral expectations of the home and school sometimes confuse the children and put them in a position of forced choice, which often results in conflict at home and in the school (Zhang & Carrasquillo, 1995). For example, one teacher reported that it took an entire year to convince an Asian student that it was appropriate and important for him to participate in class discussion, ask the teacher questions, and express his own opinion of subjects. Indeed, for some Asian students, asking questions in the classroom is considered an insult to the teacher (Grossman, 1995). This point is demonstrated in Classroom Application 14.1

Luckily for Ha in Classroom Application 14.1, her teacher is sensitive to her educational needs, her culture, and her family. Working with Ha and her family was an effective strategy in changing Ha's classroom behavior.

Teachers should take extra precautions with their language when communicating with Asian parents about their children. Remember that what you say about their children may be perceived as a remark about the whole family. In addition, Asian parents may not understand such concepts as learning or behavior disabilities. An additional list of suggestions for teachers by Schwartz (1996) is provided here:

- Understand that Asian students and parents may regard eye-to-eye contact between strangers as shameful.
- Understand that some Asians' smiles or laugher may express confusion and embarrassment, not pleasure.

# Classroom Application 14.1

## Asking Questions: A Sign of Disrespect?

Ha is an 8-year-old child in third grade and described by her teacher, Ann, as respectful, obedient, and motivated to learn. Although she is fairly proficient in the English language, English is not Ha's primary language. It is the beginning of the school year and Ann reports that Ha is having problems completing classroom and homework assignments. Ann notices that although Ha consistently makes significant efforts to complete the assignment, mistakes in how or when the assignments are completed make Ann believe that Ha is not following directions.

In an effort to solve this problem, Ann asks Ha if she understands the directions whenever Ann gives the class an assignment. Ha always says yes. But the problem continues. Why, Ann wonders, would Ha say she understands the directions when she clearly does not? Ann decides to have a conference meeting with Ha and her parents to discuss possible solutions to Ha's "problem." During the meeting, Ann notices that Ha is very respectful to her parents and agrees with everything Ann and her parents say. Ann is sure, however, that Ha does not understand many of the issues they discussed. Ann also notices that Ha does not ask any questions and, in thinking about Ha's classroom behavior, remembers that Ha seldom asks questions in the classroom. At that time Ann asks Ha why she does not ask questions in the classroom when she does not understand assignments or other directions. Ha's response surprises Ann. "I think you are a great teacher," said Ha. Ann gets the message. She now understands that Ha believes that saying she does not understand Ann's directions by asking questions is, in Ha's mind, not polite and, perhaps, a sign of disrespect.

Ann talks with Ha and Ha's parents about the importance of asking questions in school. In the classroom, Ann's questions to Ha are now more direct. For example, instead of asking Ha whether she understands the assignment, she asks Ha to repeat the directions or certain parts of the directions. In this way, Ann can determine whether Ha really understands her directions. In addition, Ann specially requests that Ha ask at least one question per day during class. Ann verbally reinforces Ha for these questions and makes Ha understand that, as a teacher, she is very happy to hear Ha's questions.

- Understand that Asian culture may consider emotional restraint, formality, and politeness as essential for appropriate social behavior.
- Understand that some Asians may view time as flexible and may not show up for meetings on time.
- Understand that when a teacher reprimands a student, the student may believe that he or she is bringing shame to the family.

- Be patient at meetings and do not interrupt periods of silence.
- Communicate in person, rather than in writing.
- Watch for nonverbal cues.
- Pay particular attention to signs of hearing impairment among Southeast Asian immigrants.

Okun et al. (1999) identify eight commonly agreed-upon identities of Asian Americans: precedence of group interests over individual interests, harmonious relationships, importance of fulfilling obligations, respect for elders, control of undesirable emotions, outward calmness, avoidance of confrontation, and high value on education (p. 263).

# AMERICAN INDIAN/ALASKAN NATIVE

## Demographics

The population of American Indians is small compared to other minorities. The current Native American population stands at approximately 2.48 million people, or 0.94% of the total U.S. population (U.S. Census Bureau, 2001). An additional 1.6 million people reported American Indian/Alaskan Native and at least one other race on the Census 2000. Native American children represent approximately 1% of public school students. While small, their numbers have increased significantly. The U. S. Census Bureau (1993) reported a 72% increase in Native Americans, Eskimos, and Aleut population between 1970 and 1980, and a 38% increase from 1980 to 1990. The 2000 census indicates a 26.4% increase from 1990. This group is predicted to grow to 1.1% of the U.S. population as soon as 2040.

Many Native Americans have recently moved from rural to urban homes. The urban population of Native Americans increased from almost 0% in 1890 to 49% in 1980 (Thornton, 1987). As of 1990 (the Census Report 2000 does not report this information), 62.3% of Native Americans were living in urban areas or lands off the reservations (U.S. Census Bureau, 1993). Almost half of the Native American population lives west of the Mississippi, 29% in the South, 16% in the Midwest, and almost 7% in the Northeast. Six states have Native American populations over 100,000: Oklahoma, North Carolina, Texas, California, Arizona, and New Mexico. The four cities in the United States with the most Native Americans are Tulsa, Oklahoma City, Los Angeles, and Phoenix (U.S. Census Bureau, 2001).

Of the four minority groups discussed in this chapter, Native Americans have the largest proportion of individuals under the age of 20 years (38.5%) (U.S. Department of Commerce, 1999). While the median age for the United States is about 35 years, the median age for Native Americans is 28 years. Native Americans had a 66% high school graduation rate in 1990, compared with only 56% in 1980. Only 9% of Native Americans completed a bachelor's degree or higher in 1990. This information was not available from the Census Report 2000.

## Cultural Influences on Behavior

Considering all the behaviors of all the Native American people and nations across America would be unmanageable because there are approximately 400 different nations, with their own languages, dialects, and customs. In 1990, the United States government formally recognized 542 different tribes. The four biggest tribes include the Cherokee, Navajo, Chippewa, and Sioux. Thus, not all Native Americans share the same culture, look the same, or have the same behavioral traits. Native Americans are conservatives, liberals, urban, rural, traditional, contemporary, and so on; and they raise their children accordingly.

While Native Americans have a unique culture, many individuals have not been exposed to their own tribal customs. Many of the subtleties of Native American behavior, however, can be found in the children regardless of their cultural knowledge. These behaviors are learned and nurtured within Native American families and their communities.

Some traditional cultural behaviors of Native Americans are described next. Again, not all Native Americans will exhibit all these characteristics—it is not the purpose of this chapter to generalize or stereotype Native American behavior. However, there are some cultural influences on Native American behavior of which educators should be aware.

### Respectful Behavior

Although similarities are found in the outward submission conveyed to authority, such as church figures, business leaders, and elderly family members, Native Americans view "respectful behavior" differently than non-Native Americans. For Native Americans, demonstrating respect of elders, with their more powerful spirits and a wealth of knowledge obtained through longevity, is based on religious and cultural values. Respect is an integral part of the Native American culture and transfers into all aspects of life. Respect for others has a significant effect on individual behavior and on social mores within the Native American culture.

One of the most unique expressions of respect is that of "noninterference." This belief includes a tolerance for others that allows family and friends to make their own mistakes and live their own lives without interference. Respect has precedence over all aspects of the Native American child and the family's behavior, underlying the thoughts and actions observed by teachers. Although each Native American nation has its own customs, this powerful value is the foundation of most Native American cultures.

### Eye Contact

Native American children may look away from an adult or hold their heads down during initial interactions with adults. Traditional children will not raise their heads to their teachers because the teacher is an adult who should be respected. Also, adults may gaze away from the person with whom they are speaking as a sign of respect and religious custom. Maintaining eye contact for Native Americans may be considered an act of disrespect, hostility, or rudeness (LaFromboise, 1982).

## Nonaggressive Behavior

Traditionally, and in some homes today, Native American children learn not to argue with or criticize parents or offer views different from parents' views in their presence. For many children, this respect carries into all adult relationships, especially relationships with figures of authority and elders. Consequently, elderly people, who are not to be challenged in public, are treated with respect regardless of their social status. Displays of disrespect of elders may result in a reduction of credibility throughout the Native American community.

In this framework of relationships, traditional Native Americans perform in American society in a nonassertive or passive manner. Native Americans may walk away from a potential problem whenever they feel uncomfortable. For example, one may walk away from a situation that has the potential for aggressive behavior. Also, although they may have strong feelings and emotions about an issue, they may refrain from expressing these feelings in order to keep the human relationships respectful. Opinions and feelings are sometimes better expressed to other perceptive people with the use of body language and other subtle gestures and movements (LaFromboise, 1982, p. 10).

LaFromboise (1982), with the help of many Native American professionals from across the country, has produced a manual called *Assertion Training with Native Americans: Cultural/Behavioral Issues for Trainers.* One of the strategies within this manual provides Native Americans with skills in assertiveness so that they are better prepared to exercise personal rights without denying the rights of others. LaFromboise states:

> *Through effective communication, Indians can protect their heritage, reach compromises acceptable to both Indian and non-Indian cultures, and prosper through self-determination. Indian people can still be quiet and self-disciplined, using bravery (assertiveness) when necessary to stand up for the rights of all Indian people.* (p. 12)

## Sharing Behavior

Traditionally, tribal people worked for the good of the group. Native American tradition teaches that a life well lived should be for the family and others in the clan and tribe—individuals should not stand out from the group. This is a trait or quality not fully understood by many within American society, in which individuals are encouraged to stand out and be the best.

Sharing is an expectation within Native American culture because of the traditional sharing of food, ideas, knowledge, material, wealth, and time. Also, others are expected to reciprocate. If this exchange does not happen, one's cultural heritage may be suspect. Native American women may offer nourishment to guests without concern for their modest homes or furnishings. Mothers and grandmothers worry aloud about their ability to provide for guests. Through this behavior, children are indirectly taught particular cultural mores.

### Speaking Behavior

Privately, Native Americans laugh, gossip, and verbalize as much as anyone else. But, while family siblings and cousins may converse very freely, respectful behavior is maintained with parents and elders. Other guidelines vary from tribe to tribe. For example, Winnebago people have rules about teasing, and other restrictions apply for in-laws and other relatives in the extended family.

Disclaimers are frequently used in Native American conversation—this is an essential method of showing one's humility. Pepper (1986) states, "Many Indian people believe all people are of equal social value, therefore, each person has inherent rights to mutual respect and equal treatment. These values are generally learned in an informal manner and unconsciously applied" (p. 5). Native Americans typically disavow, deny, and repudiate any attempts at bragging or placing themselves above anyone else. Disclaimers may also be used when asked to express their opinion. Again, the purpose here is to nullify any attempt to raise one's status above that of others (LaFromboise, 1982).

Native Americans believe that conversation should not be interrupted. For example, in a Native American home it was observed that the husband would let his dinner get cold when he received a phone call from a salesman. He would not interrupt the sales pitch until it was finished. Then he would politely tell him he was not interested in the product.

When elders or others are speaking, they continually use allegorical phrases, stories, and anecdotes and may speak for long periods of time. The traditional Native American will talk around the point and expect the listener to locate the meaning (LaFromboise, 1982). Many times, elders will refrain from joining the conversation in a school faculty meeting. Instead, they may expect to be asked their opinion and expect others to wait patiently for their full response.

### Observing and Listening Behavior

Observing and listening are essential skills in the Native American culture. Traditionally, children observed their elders working or attending other "adult" activities and meetings. Parents used cradleboards to wrap children securely so they would be immobile and snug, yet transferrable and safe for travel with their parents as they worked. "Although you in Western society may argue that such a method serves to hinder motor-skill development and abstract reasoning, we believe it forces the child to first develop his intuitive faculties, rational intellect, symbolic thinking and five senses" (Lake, 1990, p. 50). Today, Native Americans will frequently bring children along rather than leaving children to the care of relatives or enlisting the services of a baby-sitter. Community events are usually planned with the whole family in mind (Light & Martin, 1985).

Traditionally, Native American children were taught to value stillness and quiet in preparation for learning. Family elders had a certain "look" for children that reminded them their behavior at that moment was not appropriate and they must remain still and quiet, observing and listening. Although some of this attitude has changed, listening still is an important characteristic of Native American people. For example, when involved in a conversation, a Native American may sit with his eyes closed and simply listen and think about what others have to say. This behavior should not be considered a sign of rudeness or inattention.

## Timing Behavior

Native American culture teaches an acute sense of timing. Before speaking or taking action, Native Americans are taught to assess the situation. Non-Native Americans are able to be curt and abrasive with constant interruptions, quick questions, and short answers. This behavior is not congruent with Native American culture. While it is not uncommon for non-Native American people to be abrupt or straightforward in the business world or in a professional setting, this style is offensive to Native Americans because it contrasts with their traditional means of communication and interactions with others (LaFromboise, 1982).

Native Americans are sometimes perceived as having a very relaxed perspective of time. Actually, for Native American people, time has a people-centered focus. They feel that, first and foremost, priority should be given to people and their needs rather than the clock. Native American traditionalists carefully consider the present time and do not worry about the distant future. For example, it would be inappropriate to interrupt an elder's storytelling in order to be on time for a meeting. To the Native Americans, the present is considerably more important than the future. This way of living contrasts with the fast-paced, dominant society.

## Physical Appearance and Behavior

Hair length is important to the Ojibwe Native Americans. Furthermore, this outward appearance has spiritual meaning. Even today, some tribes believe that hair length is a symbol of one's lifeline, while others consider hair length a sign of health, knowledge, and adherence to traditions. Unfortunately, government boarding schools and public schools often did not allow Native American children to wear their hair long. This is another example of how many children of Native American cultures were forced to follow the expectations of the dominant, white society.

Native Americans are respectful of body space. They believe that people need only to be within listening distance and communications do not have to be face-to-face. For example, conversations may be more comfortable when held while members are working side by side, not staring into each other's face. Two or 3 feet is a respectful distance during communications; to be closer may be considered rude. Even the modern adoption of the handshake is done with a very gentle clasping of the hands and one small up-and-down movement. This gesture may also include a tiny up-and-down movement of the head. The gentleness of the handshake is a demonstration of respect. A firm and dynamic handshake may be perceived as an expression of aggression (LaFromboise, 1982).

From a Native American's perspective, body position and movements can reveal a person's feelings and attitudes. Likewise, the fewer movements and expressions on the face, the more successful one is in keeping emotions hidden. This manner is perceived by Native Americans as a respectful way of presenting oneself.

### Social Behavior

Socializing occurs in all community gatherings. Many people incorporate socializing at work. Work can be the place for humor and friendship because Native Americans are functioning as "whole" persons at all times and do not separate their business or religious lives from the rest of their personhood. To be strictly businesslike, or to keep religion separate from education, is incongruent to many Native American cultures.

Language is part of any culture and the language of many native tribes is rapidly disappearing. This has had a profound impact on the Native American culture and negatively affects many aspects of their social behavior.

## Recommendations for Schools and Teachers

Okun et al. (1999) identify 12 commonly agreed-upon identities of Native Americans: privateness, present time orientation, harmony with nature, generosity, cooperation, interrelatedness of all life, belief in a Supreme Creator, power of the spoken word, support of families, shared child rearing to establish bases of collective responsibility, more visual than auditory, and importance of silence (p. 264). Educators may experience children who are very quiet within the school setting, perhaps because of the child's unsure assessment of his or her situation. Silence may also be a way of expressing respect for the teacher as an elder and authority figure. For example, one teacher told the story of a 6-year-old girl who moved from a Native American reservation to Minneapolis. She did not talk aloud in the classroom for many months. During the same period of time, however, she was observed talking to her cousins and sisters on the playground. After 5 months in the school, she began to whisper in her teacher's ear. It was not until the following school year that she was able to participate verbally in classroom discussions. LaFromboise (1982) advises educators to watch for visual clues from Native American children, along with encouraging them to express their feelings and attitudes.

### Coping with Indian Stereotypes

Native American children must still contend with a variety of television and other media presentations that stereotype Native Americans. There is a proliferation of stereotypic materials in traditional texts and media that inaccurately portray the Native American as a savage, violent warrior, among other negative images. Even old history books and other educational materials, still used in many classrooms, contain stereotypic pictures and commentary regarding the Native American. Teachers must screen these materials for offensive stereotypes and be sensitive to situations. There are an increasing number of Web sites that promote Native Americans in a positive and more accurate light, including one on Chief Sitting Bull (*www.indians.org/weker/sttbull.htm*), and one on Sacagawea, the Shosone Native American who guided the Lewis and Clark expeditions (*www.pbs.org/weta/thewest/wpages/wpgs400/*). Teachers are encouraged to examine their materials for a diversity of voices beyond the mainstream, accuracy, and relevancy.

### Teaching with Stories

The use of stories in teaching and everyday conversation is common in Native American culture. Children develop listening skills at an early age. They are encouraged to draw their own conclusions and find the hidden meaning in the rhetoric or allegories often found in the traditional stories. Intense listening skills and analytical powers are needed to find the meanings in an ancient culture with an oral rather than written tradition.

Educators are encouraged to allow for longer waiting periods when questioning Native American students. In a study of children living on a Native American reservation, Tharp (1989) found that Navajo teachers allowed a longer waiting period before an answer was expected of Navajo children than Anglo teachers working with the same children. Native Americans believe that, when given an opportunity to speak, verbalization should not be hurried.

Typically, Native Americans must feel they can succeed at a task before they will initiate it. This view is different from the European-American "try and try again until you succeed" virtue. For example, before participating in a new game, Native American children may spend a significant amount of time just watching and learning how to play. They may not participate in the activity unless they believe they can succeed.

Traditionally, Native American mothers and grandmothers demonstrated skills repeatedly before children were given opportunities to perform the task. When elders were assured the child was ready, then they would provide the opportunity to proceed. In classroom situations, such as the provision of in-class and homework assignments, the use of demonstrations as a teaching tool may be important for some Native American children.

Public displays of affection are a rarity for traditional Native Americans. In school, however, a gentle touch or a pat of encouragement on the student's shoulder is acceptable. Hugging is also acceptable for young children.

## DIVERSE LEARNERS

Thus far in this chapter we have discussed diversity only in terms of race and ethnicity. But sources of cultural identity that can affect a child's behavior can be expanded to include religion, sexual orientation, health, language, and gender, to name a few (Cushner, McClelland, & Safford, 2000). Although these categories are beyond the scope of this chapter, teachers are encouraged to expand their knowledge base of them and become aware of their own values and biases related to them. The Internet is becoming an increasingly abundant source for research, collaboration, interaction, lesson plans, and activities related to all kinds of diversity.

**TABLE 14.6** ● **Percent of Students Receiving Special Education Services by Disability Category**

| Category | % of All Students Ages 6–21 |
| --- | --- |
| Learning Disability | 4.45 |
| Speech or Language Impairments | 1.7 |
| Mental Retardation | .96 |
| Emotional Disturbances | .73 |
| All Other Disabilities | .90 |

*Source:* Council for Exceptional Children (2001).

Teachers will also see a diversity of learners (e.g., exceptional and disabled) and learning styles within their classroom. Teachers must understand, as outlined in Chapter 5, that there is a relationship between a student's ability to interact with the classroom curriculum and his or her classroom behavior.

During the 1998–99 school year, the Council for Exceptional Children (2001) reported that 9% of students age 6–12 received special education services. More importantly, most of these students (75%) were served within the general education classroom. Table 14.6 outlines the four major disability categories that apply to most students receiving special education services.

## INTEGRATING A MULTICULTURAL APPROACH IN THE CLASSROOM

Appropriate behavior is frequently associated with children feeling positive about themselves and others. "If children are to feel good about themselves and develop a positive self-esteem, they must receive positive messages from teachers and children around them" (Zirpoli, 1995, p. 253). These positive messages must also reinforce the child's culture, including the child's language, customs, family traditions, and behaviors related to the child's culture.

Schwartz et al. (1997) state:

> There are few places where a greater probability exists of encountering racial and ethnic diversity than in the classroom. As a teacher, you will be challenged to create harmony from many different voices as you teach respect for diversity while stressing our common human attributes. You will have the task of examining your own attitudes and prejudices as well as those of your students as you cultivate fair and objective attitudes (p. 29).

While many educators state that they strive to recognize individual differences in children and that they respect these differences, research may indicate otherwise. "Research indicates that teachers and administrators often have low expectations for language minority students, low income students, and students of color" (Banks, 1999, p. 17), and most educational practitioners have gone through training programs that require only one course in multicultural education (Gopaul-McNicol & Thomas-Presswood, 1998). "More disturbing, a substantial number of teacher education students do not believe that low-income and minority learners are capable of learning high-level concepts in the subjects they are preparing to teach" (Cushner et al., 2000, p. 12).

Cushner et al. (2000) describe the disturbing discrepancy between the makeup of the average student population (over one third of them are children of color and bilingual) and the teachers (most of the country's teachers are European American, white, females), claiming that many children lack role models of their own background, and teachers with experience with people from other cultures. Half of the country's states do not offer professional credentialing for teachers of culturally diverse students, although "in states that are greatly affected by growing numbers of language minority students, concern for professional teaching standards is developing, but the progress has been uneven" (Garcia, 2002, p. 288). To face the challenges of the culturally diverse classroom, educators must evaluate the effectiveness of the learning environment (including classrooms, activities, and curriculum) for all learners.

Garcia (2002), in addition to schoolwide practices, offers a list of teacher practices, including high expectations of diverse students, treatment of diversity as an asset to the classroom, ongoing professional development on issues of cultural and linguistic diversity and practices that are most effective, and curriculum development that addresses cultural and linguistic diversity (p. 121). Banks (1999) describes the eight characteristics of the multicultural school:

1. The teachers and school administrators have high expectations for all students and positive attitudes toward them. They also respond to them in positive and caring ways.

2. The formalized curriculum reflects the experiences, cultures, and perspectives of a range of cultural and ethnic groups as well as of both genders.

3. The teaching styles used by the teachers match the learning, cultural, and motivational styles of the students.

4. The teachers and administrators show respect for the students' first languages and dialects.

5. The instructional materials used in the school show events, situations, and concepts from the perspectives of a range of cultural, ethnic, and racial groups.

6. The assessment and testing procedures used in the school are culturally sensitive and result in students of color being represented proportionately in classes for the gifted and talented.

7. The school culture and the hidden curriculum reflect cultural and ethnic diversity.

8. The school counselors have high expectations for students from different racial, ethnic, and language groups and help these students to set and realize positive career goals. (p. 18)

Teachers and staff can do many things to recognize and celebrate their students' cultures, making them feel positive not only about themselves but also about the differences observed in others. These methods may be incorporated into the daily activities and materials of the educational setting. Derman-Sparks (1990) and Derman-Sparks, Gutierrez, and Phillips (1993) make these recommendations for teachers:

- Create an environment that celebrates diversity. For example, make wall collages showing young children from many racial and ethnic groups participating in common activities.
- Play music and sing songs from different ethnic groups and in different languages.
- Provide activities to help young children explore their own skin color by having children draw pictures of themselves. Have skin-colored crayons available.
- Provide learning materials (especially books) that reflect diverse images of children. These materials should be sensitive to gender roles, children from different racial and cultural backgrounds, children with different abilities and disabilities, and children who come from a variety of family compositions. (Tiedt and Tiedt [1999] offer a list of age-appropriate multicultural fiction and nonfiction titles.)
- The teachers and staff should model their own value of regard for diversity. For example, teachers and staff should talk positively about each student's cultural heritage.
- Communicate to the students that teasing or rejecting another student based on the child's cultural or racial identity is not acceptable behavior.
- Provide opportunities for students to interact with other children and adults who are racially or culturally different. For example, invite parents of African American children into the classroom to talk about and help celebrate Martin Luther King Day.
- Invite role models into the classroom to talk about their profession (doctors, nurses, firepersons, etc.) who also represent diversity among the community.
- Listen to and answer students' questions about themselves and others. Look for "teachable moments."
- Teach students how to recognize stereotypes of different groups in what they read and see on TV or in the movies. Discuss how these stereotypes may make some people feel about themselves and others.
- Invite students to talk about family traditions, special foods, and customs.

Tiedt and Tiedt (1999) present practical examples of infusing multicultural concepts across the curriculum, including art, language arts, mathematics, music, physical education, science and technology, and social studies lesson plans.

# EXPLORING YOUR CULTURAL IDENTITY AND BIAS

*I have a responsibility to myself to study and understand the lenses through which I see and experience the people and happenings around me. Only when I have a sense for how my own perceptions are developed in relation to my life experiences can I truly understand the world around me and effectively navigate my relationships with colleagues and my students. I also have a responsibility to my students to work toward eliminating my prejudices, examining who is (and is not) being reached by my teaching style, and relearning how my own identity influences their learning experiences. To be an effective multicultural educator, and an effective educator in general, I must be in a constant process of self-examination and transformation. (Gorski, 2001, p. 10)*

In addition to increasing one's multicultural knowledge base and incorporating it into the classroom, it is essential that every educator explore his or her own cultural identity, and become aware of any values or bias that may interfere with validating diversity, interpreting behaviors accurately, and providing a multicultural education. Merely celebrating alternative holidays or including diverse activities in lesson plans does not constitute diversity-sensitive classroom management. Teachers need to make a real and honest connection with students to communicate that they understand and value each child's culture. In order to have this connection and relationship, teachers also need to understand their own culture and its influence on everyone's behavior.

A growing body of literature related to education focuses on the "whiteness" and homogeneity of our teachers (84% of U.S. school teachers are white, and the number was as high as 90.7% in 1996) and education professors (between 87% and 96% are white). The emphasis is on improving teacher education programs by including a focus on the trainee's cultural identities and privilege, becoming multilingual, identifying and challenging bias and racism, providing community-based multicultural immersion experiences, increasing coursework in multiculturalism, and increasing the minority role models in schools and in training programs (Ladson-Billings, 2000; Nieto, 2000; Sleeter, 2001). The next section offers Internet addresses that access a large body of literature on activities and exercises that teachers can do to increase awareness of their own cultural identity and bias.

# INTERNET FOR THE DIVERSE CLASSROOM

Technology and computer use is rapidly increasing across the educational scene, for training, teaching, communication, and so forth. More than 40% of North Americans over the age of 16 use the Internet, an increase of 32% since 1995 (Gorski, 2001). Benefits of the Internet include expanding our informational knowledge base, increasing our access to diverse voices and cultures, increasing our interaction with people across borders and boundaries, and supplementing traditional materials with access to larger databases, collections, artifacts, other classrooms, and archives. One of the challenges of using the Internet in the classroom is ensuring that it is consistent with principles of multicultural education. There exist disparities in Internet use between groups of people: African Americans and Hispanic/Latinos are only 40% as likely as whites to have access to the Internet in their homes (Gorski, 2001). Teachers should be aware of the plethora of resources on the Internet, not only to aid them in their classroom, but to help them learn more about their students' cultures and their own culture. Students can use the Internet to better understand experiences and worldviews of people different than themselves, thus minimizing miscommunication and misunderstandings in the classroom. The following is a sample list of the hundreds of Web sites (adapted from Gorski, 2001) that can help the teacher in this process. See Gorski (2001) for an excellent source on Web sites for classroom use (such as lesson plan banks and exchanges, and interactive pen pal sites).

- iEarn *http://www.igc.apc.org/iearn/*
  The International Education and Resource Network connects young people around the world for collaborative projects related to social and global issues. There is also a section for teachers.

- Multicultural Pavillion *http://curry.edschool.Virginia.edu/go/multicultural*
  This site provides resources for educators to explore and discuss multicultural education, to facilitate opportunities to work toward self-awareness and development, and provides a forum for dialogue on multicultural issues (MCPAVILION is the listserve). This site includes awareness activities, research, and collaborative opportunities for teachers and students.

- Multicultural Supersite *http://www.mhhe.com/multicultural*
  This site is hosted by McGraw-Hill's Higher Education Division and offers activities, a discussion forum, articles, book reviews, and so forth. The site is designed for preservice teachers, in-service teachers, and teacher educators.

- Center for Multilingual Multicultural Research *http://www.usc.edu/dept/education/CMMR/*
  Located at the University of Southern California, this center serves as a starting point for teachers wanting information about bilingual, multicultural, and cross-cultural education.

- Active Learning Principles for Schools *http://learnweb.harvard.edu/alps/*
  This site offers a community of educators working toward the improvement of education. Hosted by The Harvard Graduate School of Education, this site offers educators tools for reflecting on their teaching practice and connects them to others doing the same thing.

- Forum One *http://www.forumone.com/index.flml*
  This bulletin board indexes over 300,000 discussion forums on a variety of diversity topics accessed by keyword searches.

- National Association for Multicultural Education
  *http://www.inform.umd.edu/NAME/*

NAME is the largest organization in the world specifically dedicated to the ideas and principles of multicultural education.

## SUMMARY

Racial and ethnic minorities make up over 37% of elementary and secondary students in the United States, and 29.6% of the overall U.S. population. They include students from diverse cultural backgrounds such as African Americans, Native Americans, Asian Americans, Hispanic/Latino Americans, and many others. Before we can begin to understand a child's behavior, we must first have at least a basic understanding of the child's cultural identity, including race and ethnicity. Otherwise, our behavioral expectations will be invalid, and we will be guilty of ethnocentrism and enculturation. We believe, however, that, in addition to the challenges, educators should consider the many educational opportunities of working with an increasingly diverse population of students. The first step, however, is for educators to learn about their students' cultures and the cultural influences on their behavior. A second, but just as important, step is for educators to have a clear sense of their own worldview and cultural identity.

African Americans are the largest minority group in the United States. They represent about 12.8% of the current U.S. population and, by the year 2050, will represent 14.4% of the population. Although their educational status has improved significantly, African Americans are still disproportionately represented in programs for students with special academic and behavioral needs. They are still more likely than white children to be behind a grade level in school and drop out of school. Nearly one of every two African American children lives in poverty, and they are less likely than white children to have the benefits of a college education.

The African American culture has many influences on the behavior of African American children. These behaviors have their foundation in the African American family and community. Unfortunately, African American parental attitudes and student behaviors are influenced by years of alienation. African American children frequently find themselves trying to juggle the relationship between the European American culture found within the school and their own culture taught within the African American community. African Americans are often treated as clients, not consumers, by school personnel. As with other parents, many African American parents feel that they lack the knowledge or confidence to confront school personnel regarding their needs. While many parents have developed a passive attitude—translated as a negative attitude by white school personnel—educators must recognize that all parents, regardless of color, want a good education for their children.

The Hispanic/Latino American population grew faster than any other racial or ethnic group from 1980 to 1998. Thirty million Hispanic/Latino Americans now comprise 11.9% of the U.S. population. Hispanic/Latino Americans include

Dominicans, Cubans, Puerto Ricans, Central and South Americans, and Mexican Americans. Mexican Americans account for the largest percentage of Hispanic/Latino Americans.

The primary influences on Hispanic/Latino behaviors include the Hispanic/Latino family, the Spanish language, and religion/spirituality. Family relationships and duties have an all-encompassing importance. Hispanics/Latinos are noted for their festivals and celebrations, usually centered around family, church, or community.

Touching and hugging are common during interactions, as are sharing and helping others within the community. Thus, Hispanic/Latino children are usually comfortable within cooperative learning environments and may perform less favorably in situations demanding individual competition. Establishing personal rapport with Hispanic/Latino students and their families is essential to effective teacher-student and teacher-parent relationships.

The Asian American population is one of the fastest growing ethnic groups in the United States. Asian Americans, 10 million strong, make up 4% of the U.S. population. Asian Americans include the Chinese, Filipinos, Japanese, Koreans and many other ethnic groups. While it is true that many Asian Americans are model students and almost 30% of Asians arrive in the United States with 4 years of college education, these facts often obscure the immense diversity within Asian American communities and the many existing challenges for Asian American students.

Asian Americans are also a very diverse group. For the Chinese, Japanese, and Koreans, however, Confucianism serves as the foundation for most social and cultural issues. According to Confucian society, the worth of a person is primarily determined by sex, age, and social status, not by the intrinsic value of life or self.

In many Asian cultures, boys and girls are grouped separately within educational settings. The lack of sexual segregation within the European American culture directly contradicts social mores of many Asian Americans. Other differences with regard to U.S. customs include the amount of sex education, dating behaviors, and methods of discipline.

The Native American population is a small but growing population. They make up 0.94% of the total U.S. population and about 1% of the public school population. The Native American population consists of approximately 400 different nations, languages, dialects, and customs. Many Native Americans do not share the same culture and certainly not the same behavioral traits. There are, however, some cultural influences on Native Americans of which educators should be aware.

Native Americans view respectful behavior, especially as demonstrated to their elders, as one of the most important social mores of Native American culture. Other behaviors frequently associated with Native Americans include the lack of eye contact when talking to others and nonaggressive sharing, observing, and listening behaviors. Many inaccurate myths and stereotypes continue to persist about Native Americans. These myths are frequently reinforced by the media, especially the visual media.

## DISCUSSION QUESTIONS

1. Discuss the concept of worldview and how it may contribute to better understanding of classroom behavior. Give examples for some of the ethnicities discussed in this chapter.

2. Frequently, the social skills learned by children within the home environment conflict with behavioral expectations within the school environment. Offer some examples of these conflicts and how they may be resolved in ways that are sensitive to cultural differences.

3. Discuss the most significant influences on Hispanic/Latino students' behavior (e.g., family, church). How may these influences be incorporated into the school environment to facilitate more effective interactions between the home and school?

4. What are some family influences for Asian American students that may have a positive effect on their academic performance?

5. What are some ways in which classroom teachers can better understand and clarify their own cultural identity and behavior?

6. What are some ways in which a classroom teacher can make the educational environment more inviting to students from different cultural backgrounds? How may these changes influence the behavior of some students and their relationship with others?

## REFERENCES

Altarriba, J., & Bauer, L. M. (1998). Counseling the Hispanic client: Cuban Americans, Mexican Americans, and Puerto Ricans. *Journal of Counseling & Development, 76,* 389–395.

Baizerman, M., & Hendricks, G. (1988). Refugee youth in the Twin Cities: Aspirations of the Hmong, Khmer, Lao and Vietnamese. *CURA Reporter, 18,* 1–7.

Banks, J. (1991). *Teaching strategies for ethnic studies.* Boston: Allyn & Bacon.

Banks, J. (1999). *An introduction to multicultural education.* Needham Heights, MA: Allyn & Bacon.

Banks, J., & Banks, C. M. (1989). *Multicultural education: Issues and perspectives.* Boston: Allyn & Bacon.

Berry, G. L., & Asamen, J. K. (1989). *Black students: Psychosocial issues and academic achievement.* New York: Sage.

Bruce, R. A. (1997). *Managing change in the coming millenium.* Louisville, KY: University of Louisville.

Bureau of Justice Statistics. (2001). Criminal Offenders Statistics Report. Washington, DC: Author.

City's schools lead U.S. in segregation. (2002, August 11). *Baltimore Sun,* p. 1.

Council for Exceptional Children. (2001). Where we are in special education today. *Today, 8*(3), 9.

Cushner, K., McClelland, A., & Safford, P. (2000). *Human diversity in education: An integrative approach.* New York: McGraw-Hill.

Derman-Sparks, L. (1990). Understanding diversity. *Scholastic Pre-K Today, 5,* 44–53.

Derman-Sparks, L., Gutierrez, M., & Phillips, C. B. (1993). *Teaching young children to resist bias: What parents can do.* Washington, DC: National Association for the Education of Young Children.

El Hispanic News. (1998). *Reaching Hispanics through print.* Portland, OR: Author.

Erickson, F. D. (1972). "F' get you Honky!": A new look at Black dialect and the school. In A. L. Smith (Ed.), *Language, communication, and rhetoric in Black America* (pp. 18–27). New York: Harper & Row.

Franklin, M. E. (1992). Culturally sensitive instructional practices for African-American learners with disabilities. *Exceptional Children, 59,* 115–122.

Garcia, E. (2002). *Student cultural diversity: Understanding and meeting the challenge.* Boston: Houghton Mifflin.

Gay, G. (2000). *Culturally responsive teaching: Theory, research, and practice.* New York: Teachers College Press.

Gladding, S. (2001). *The counseling dictionary.* Upper Saddle River, NJ: Merrill/Prentice Hall.

Gopaul-McNicol, S., & Thomas-Presswood, T. (1998). *Working with linguistically and culturally different children: Innovative clinical and educational approaches.* Needham Heights, MA: Allyn & Bacon.

Gorski, P. C. (2001). *Multicultural education and the Internet: Intersections and integrations.* New York. McGraw-Hill.

Grossman, H. (1995). *Special education in a diverse society.* Boston, MA: Allyn & Bacon.

Hale-Benson, J. (1987). Self-esteem of Black middle-class women who choose to work inside or outside the home. *Journal of Multicultural Counseling and Development, 15,* 71–80.

Heward, W. (1996). *Exceptional children: An introduction to special education.* Upper Saddle River, NJ: Merrill/Prentice Hall.

Hodgkinson, H. (2000/2001). Educational demographics: What teachers should know. *Educational Leadership, 58,* 6–11.

Huang, G. (1996). *Beyond culture: Communicating with Asian American children and families.* Washington, DC: Clearinghouse on Urban Education.

Ibrahim, F. A. (1991). Contribution of cultural worldview to generic counseling and development. *Journal of Counseling & Development, 70,* 13–19.

Ibrahim, F. A., & Kahn, H. (1984). *Scale to assess worldviews.* Unpublished manuscript, University of Connecticut at Storrs.

Improving reading skills. (2001, September 6). *USA Today,* p. 1.

Jones, S. (1985). *Parent partnerships and children at risk.* Topeka: University of Kansas, Education Service Division, Department of Education.

Kan, S. H., & Liu, W. T. (1986). Issues in Asian and Pacific American Education. In N. Tsuchida (Ed.), *The educational status of Asian-Americans: An update from the 1980 census* (pp. 153–164). Minneapolis, MN: Asian and Pacific Learning Resource Center.

Kluckhohn, C. (1951). Values and value otientations in the theory of action. In T. Parsons & F. A. Shields (Eds.), *Toward a general theory of action* (pp. 388–433). Cambridge, MA: Harvard University Press.

Ladson-Billings, G. (2000). Fighting for our lives: Preparing teachers to teach African American students. *Journal of Teacher Education, 51,* 206–214.

LaFromboise, T. (1982). *Assertion training with Native Americans: Cultural/behavioral issues for trainers.* ERIC Clearinghouse on Rural Education and Small Schools.

Lake, R. (1990, September). An Indian father's plea. *Teacher Magazine, 2,* 48–53.

Light, H., & Martin, R. (1985). Guidance of American-Indian baseline essays: Their heritage and some contemporary views. *Journal of American Indian Education, 25,* 42–46.

Losen, D. J., & Orfield, G. (2002). *Racial inequity in special education.* Boston: Harvard Press.

McCadden, B. M. (1998). Why is Michael always getting timed out? Race, class, and disciplining other people's children. In R. E. Butchart & B. McEwan (Eds.), *Classroom discipline in American schools: Problems and possibilities for democratic education* (pp. 109–134). Albany: State University of New York Press. (ED423584).

McEachern, A. G., & Kenny, M. C. (2002). A comparison of family environment characteristics among White (non-Hispanic), Hispanic, and African Caribbean groups. *Journal of Multicultural Counseling and Development, 30,* 40–58.

McInnis, K. M. (1990). *The Hmong in America: Providing ethnic-sensitive health, education, and human services.* New York: Kendall Hunt.

Morrow, R. (1987). Southeast Asian parental involvement: Can it be a reality? *Elementary School Guidance & Counseling, 23,* 289–297.

National Catholic Educational Association. (1987). *Integral education: A response to the Hispanic presence.* Washington, DC: Author.

National Center for Educational Statistics. (2000). *Mini digest of educational statistics.* Washington, DC: Author.

Nieto, S. (1996). *Affirming diversity: The sociopolitical context of multicultural education.* White Plains, NY: Longman.

Nieto, S. (2000). Placing equity front and center: Some thoughts on transforming teacher education for a new century. *Journal of Teacher Education, 51,* 180–187.

Okun, B. F., Fried, J., & Okun, M. L. (1999). *Understanding diversity: A learning-as-practice primer.* Pacific Grove, CA: Brooks/Cole.

Overbeck, C. (1984). A survival kit for teaching English to refugees. *Lifelong Learning, 8*(2), 29–30.

Pepper, F. (1986). *Cognitive, social and cultural effects on Indian learning style: Classroom implications.* Paper presented at the Mokakit Conference, Indian Education Research Association, Winnipeg, Manitoba, Canada.

Prendergast, N. (1985). *A Vietnamese refugee family in the United States from 1975–1985: A case study of education and culture.* Doctoral dissertation, Loyola University, Chicago. University Microfilms International, Ann Arbor, MI.

Priest, R. (1991). Racism and prejudice as negative impacts on African American clients in therapy. *Journal of Counseling & Development, 70,* 213–215.

Randall-David, E. (1989). *Strategies for working with culturally diverse communities and clients.* Rockville, MD: Association for the Care of Children's Health.

Rise seen in Hispanic education. (2002, December 5). *Baltimore Sun*, p. 1.

Rumbaut, R. G., & Kenji, I. (1988). *Adaptation of Southeast Asian refugee youth: A resettlement.* San Diego, CA: San Diego State University.

Schwartz, S. E., Conley, C. A., & Eaton, L. K. (1997). Diverse learners in the classroom. New York: McGraw-Hill.

Schwartz, W. (1996). A guide to communicating with Asian American families. New York: ERIC Clearinghouse on Urban Education.

Schwartz, W. (2001). School practices for equitable discipline of African American students. New York: ERIC Clearinghouse on Urban Education (ED455343).

Sleeter, C. E. (2001). Preparing teachers for culturally diverse schools: Research and the overwhelming presence of Whiteness. *Journal of Teacher Education, 52,* 94–106.

Spero, A. (1985). *In America and in need: Immigrant, refugee, and entrant women.* Washington, DC: American Association of Community and Junior Colleges.

Tatum, J., Moseley, S., Boyd-Franklin, N., & Herzog, E. P. (1995, February/March). A home-based, family systems approach to the treatment of African-American teenage parents and their families. *Zero to Three,* 18–25.

Tharp, R. G. (1989). Psychocultural variables and constants: Effects on teaching and learning in schools. *American Psychologist, 44,* 349–351.

Thornton, R. (1987). *American Indian holocaust and survival: A population history since 1942.* Norman: University of Oklahoma Press.

Tiedt, P. L., & Tiedt, I. M. (1999). *Multicultural teaching: A handbook of activities, information, and resources.* Needham Heights, MA: Allyn & Bacon.

Tollefson, J. W. (1986). Functional competencies in the U.S. refugee program: Theoretical and practical problems. *TESOL Quarterly, 20*(4), 649–664.

U.S. Census Bureau. (1993). *Current population reports.* Washington, DC: Author.

U.S. Census Bureau. (2001). *Current population reports.* Washington, DC: Author.

U.S. Department of Commerce. (1999) *Poverty in the U.S.* Washington, DC: Author.

U.S. Department of Education. (2001). *Digest of educational statistics.* Washington, DC: Author.

U.S. Department of Education. (2001). *Digest of Scholastic Assessment Test (SAT) score averages by race/ethnicity.* Washington, DC: Author.

Walker, W. D. (1987). *The other side of the Asian academic success myth: The Hmong story.* Qualifying paper, Harvard Graduate School of Education, Boston.

Zhang, S. Y., & Carrasquillo, A. L. (1995). Chinese parents' influence on academic performance. *New York State Association for Bilingual Education Journal, 10,* 46–53.

Zirpoli, T. J. (1995). *Understanding and affecting the behavior of young children.* Upper Saddle River, NJ: Merrill/Prentice Hall.

# NAME INDEX

# $\mathbf{S}$UBJECT INDEX